Long Way Out

A young woman's journey of
self-discovery and how she survived the
Navy's modern cruelty at sea scandal

Nicole Waybright
with Jim Bastian

SpeakPeace

The following story is true. Events in this book took place approximately eighteen to nineteen years ago at time of publishing. Real names have been changed, along with some identifying details, to protect the privacy of individuals. The events are retold to the best of the author's memory. Reconstructed conversations are based on the author's recollections as well as on interviews with actual officers and crew members from the USS *Curtis Wilbur*. Some dates are approximations. Occasionally, a character shown is a composite of actual personages that the author encountered while serving in the Navy. Everything that happened to the author while on active duty in the Navy is accurately reflected in this story through the eyes of the main character, Brenda Conner. The author has written this true account to depict events that occurred during the first wave of women to serve on combatant vessels in the U.S. Navy. It is intended to be part historical document and part literature, written as narrative nonfiction.

Copyright © 2017 Nicole Waybright and Jim Bastian

Printed in the United States of America

All rights reserved. No part of this publication may be reproduced, stored in or introduced into a retrieval system, scanned or distributed in any printed, audio, or electronic form without prior permission in writing from the authors.

First edition

ISBN-13: 978-0-9972161-0-3

Subjects include: self-discovery, journey of self-discovery, psychology memoir, psychology memoirs, women in the military, Navy, self-discovery books, women in the military books, military memoirs, military history, women military, military women, military history, military leadership, military memoir, military biographies and memoirs, true stories of military women

ACKNOWLEDGEMENTS

This project could not have proceeded without the support of the Navy veterans who provided proofreading and evaluation of the technical and historical aspects of the story, or were consulted on storyline elements, including but not limited to: Commander Kirk R. Benson, USN (Ret), and Commander Eric Lind, USN (Ret).

I would like to offer my sincere gratitude to those who provided expert assistance regarding both the technical and narrative aspects of the book: Steven Bule, PhD., Professor of Art and Architecture History, Utah Valley University, and Steve Rabson, PhD., Professor Emeritus, East Asian Studies, Brown University.

I would like to offer a special thank you to the following prepublication readers who provided invaluable proofreading, input, advice, and guidance throughout my writing journey: Pat Motta, Beverly Sweet, Lorraine Ouellette, and Mary Kirchmann.

I offer special gratitude to our publishing consultant for her stellar work in formatting, design, layout, and in general helping us across the finish line: Stephanie Blackman.

I would like to express my respect and admiration for my shipmates aboard USS *Curtis Wilbur* (DDG-54), as well as for all of the women and men with whom I served in the U.S. Navy during the years 1996-2001.

Finally, I would like to recognize Conner, Joe, Sparky, and all the rescue/shelter/foster dogs who taught me some of life's most important lessons, and who kept watch over me as I wrote these last eight years.

PREFACE

Author's introduction

Long Way Out is the narrative nonfiction account of my true life experience serving as a lieutenant in the U.S. Navy, during which time I survived a psychological crisis that upended everything I thought I knew and understood about myself. At twenty-three years old, when I was commissioned an officer in the U.S. Navy, I thought I had achieved my life's dream. At twenty-four, I found myself suffering from depression and mental torment. As my crisis unfolded, it became important to me to understand why I had chosen the particular life path and career of the military. That personal exploration, and the adventures and struggles I encountered and survived along the way, comprise the essence of this literary work. As a psychological journey, the story recounts my personal experience of self-exploration based on Jungian therapeutic principles, and details my search into many of my life choices, choices with which I had become disillusioned while serving in the military.

Long Way Out is intended partly as a woman's self-reflective journal and partly as military history. The narrative chronicles my psychological reflections at the time, as well as subsequent changes I underwent while isolated at sea and in ports thousands of miles away from my home in New England. Alongside the recounting of my psychological journey, this book provides a testimonial on the relationships between the men and women aboard one of the first mixed gender combatant ships, and in so doing, discloses the beginning of the tragic story of the first woman in U.S. history who commanded both an Aegis destroyer and cruiser. *Long Way Out* takes place during that commander's first tumultuous tenure as Executive Officer (XO) of USS *Curtis Wilbur* from 1997-1999, and it is well documented that she later became the first female commander to sit at Admirals Mast and be stripped of command for "cruelty and maltreatment" of her crew.

Intended for a wide variety of audiences

My story is a woman's psychological journey, a chronicle of my experience going through the process of individuation, a psychological process that was first named and defined by psychiatrist Carl Jung in the early twentieth century. I have made every effort to write in such a way that the psychological dynamics and storyline – which are often one and the same – will be understood universally, by all readers, regardless of their psychological background or experience. (A primer on Jungian Psychology resides in the Author's Note in the back of the book.) Although written from a woman's perspective, I believe *Long Way Out* will be of interest to both men and women who have experienced intensive therapy.

It is a woman's journey, but it also provides an honest look at a young person's experience in the military as I have not seen it portrayed before. I believe it will appeal to families of veterans and military families who long to understand what their loved ones have undergone in their day-to-day military lives. For veterans and military members, I feel there is much they can relate to and learn from. The portrayal is an atypical, raw look at life in the military, free of self-glorification or glorification of the service, which I believe will be important to veterans, military members, and their families.

As well, this book is written for those with an interest in psychology – in particular Jungian psychology and therapy-related issues centering on self-help and family dynamics.

An exposé of the surface warfare (SWO) Navy

Long Way Out presents an insider's unique look at the traditions and practices of the SWO (surface warfare) Navy. Those specifically interested in SWO naval history will be intrigued by the searingly honest portrayal of this longstanding officer community, with all its dangerous imperfections and its inglorious, self-destructive traditions. Many former surface warfare officers will readily relate to – and even see themselves in – the stories and episodes found in my book.

Who doesn't love a sea story

Long Way Out is at heart a sea tale. Over the years, I have found that people of all backgrounds – those with a connection to the military and surprisingly those without any connection to, or knowledge of, the military – are interested in the details of daily life aboard a Navy ship. I have spoken to a range of people, both men and women, from veterans and those who have an affinity for studying military life and culture, to those who never joined the military, and even to some who wished they had joined. Even in conversations with people who I least expected to show interest, I have found that most have wanted to hear about the "nitty-gritty" of military life at sea.

In attempting to write about ship life in a painstakingly authentic fashion, I aimed that readers could experience vicariously what it was like to wake up for an early bridge watch, live in a stateroom, watch flight ops, ride out storms at sea, or go on liberty in a Southeast Asian port. I also aimed for readers to be able to share in the day-to-day ups and downs of shipboard life, the tension of a young person entering the world of a Navy ship, the politics and decorum found in the officers' wardroom, the preparation for and standing of watches on the bridge, the complexity of the combat information center (CIC), and the technicalities of engineering, as well as in the struggle over the difficult philosophical questions that arise for many military personnel.

From its real-time warship bridge action scenes, to the self-reflective Jungian-based soul-searching of the main character, to the depictions of cruel conflict engaged in by the executive officer (XO), to the authentic portrayals of exploring Japan and Australia, I hope that *Long Way Out* will offer a glimpse into shipboard life as I experienced it as an average young person who joined the military.

A discussion on the narrative nonfiction genre

This book is my true life story. As a work of narrative nonfiction, it is told in third person through the main character, "Brenda." All names have been changed, but otherwise the story is an accurate representation, as I remember it, from my tour of duty as an officer in the U.S. Navy, from May 1996 to February 2001.

I found narrative nonfiction, and specifically third person, to be the best vehicle for telling my story in a literary format, and as well the best vehicle for telling a true story wherein the names are changed. The choice of relating the story in literary form was an artistic decision, made as my desire to write *Long Way Out* grew out of my graduate studies in literature. In keeping with the intention that *Long Way Out* is a literary work, I have changed my own name as well, creating the pseudonym of "Brenda."

The main character and her inner-journey (my inner journey!) are portrayed, explored, or otherwise revealed in a variety of fashions within the story: through nuanced self-reflection, in conversations with others around her, through feedback from other characters, and in her reactions to the situations and settings she encounters. The narrative focuses on Brenda's psychology and the way that her painful feelings and inner conflict lead to crisis that lead to self-exploration that lead to thinking about making changes. From early in the story, when she arrives in Sydney to meet her first ship, she begins her pursuit to find meaning in the events of her past, intuiting that these past events hold the keys to her understanding of the now-unwelcome choices she has made, choices which have resulted in finding herself as a gunnery officer onboard a guided missile destroyer.

A decade had passed before I began writing from memory, journals, correspondence from the period, and written and oral interviews with eyewitnesses. I have reconstructed events and conversations to reflect the essence of what occurred during those years and the spirit of the ways in which we, the officers and crew, tried to cope. Timeframes and order of specific events are approximate. All episodes in which Brenda finds herself are true stories…incredulous as some of them may seem. In some cases, I have altered and interchanged some aspects of events and personal histories of junior officers and enlisted personnel to disguise real persons. Since the story is told through the eyes of the main character, "Brenda," (based on my own observations), all events, conversations, feelings, and thoughts are related from her point of view.

In Navy culture, individuals are referred to by their naval positions (jobs or billets), e.g., position nicknames such as "GUNNO" for "gunnery officer" or "WEPS" for "weapons officer." This cultural style is used throughout my narrative.

In 2008, when I began work on *Long Way Out,* I started contacting my former shipmates who by this time had spread all over the country and the world. With one exception, all had retired or resigned from the Navy. When I told each person I contacted that I wanted to tell our collective stories by writing a book about our experiences aboard USS *Curtis Wilbur* from a humanistic and literary perspective, and asked if they would support my idea, the response was unanimously, yes. Through oral and written interviews, these former service members recounted their most painful and personal accounts, many complete with episodes of depression and mental breakdown, moments of feared insanity, descent into alcoholism, thoughts of suicide, and attempts at suicide. Some of these accounts, I was informed, were unshared even with those closest to them.

I believe time has provided adequate distance from the actual events to allow us all to open up about this period and discuss even those days onboard when we felt the most vulnerable and threatened. We now have over a decade and a half of personal growth through life experience and reflection behind us – the memories are no longer razor fresh, the post-traumatic sting has abated, and we are no longer in our twenties or early thirties.

Over the years, since resigning from the Navy (receiving an honorable discharge), I have found that there exists a bond between veterans that spans gender, generations, wars, and politics. The trust other veterans have placed in me, in sharing their stories, is forever sacred to me. Even though no one with whom I corresponded specifically asked that they or their stories be disguised, I personally thought it important to do so.

My intention is that this account can offer hope and healing, not only to those who are in (or have been in) the armed forces, but also to anyone who has undergone periods of crisis that triggered radical changes in their self-understanding.

***

Best Wishes to all who share in the journey of *Long Way Out*!

Nicole Waybright
June 2016 Rhode Island

* A glossary of naval terms is provided at the back of the book.

Chapter 1: The persona and its consequences

Waiting for a belated welcome aboard interview with the Captain

Brenda had been waiting outside the Captain's stateroom for fifteen minutes. She imagined that, to all outward appearances, she looked like the perfect, newly-assigned twenty-something ensign, dressed in her best khaki uniform, with every detail attended to. She wanted to walk away. Not because she was nervous about a generalized "welcome aboard" type interview with the Captain, but for reasons concerning integrity. She had only been in her new assignment for two months – an eternity – but she couldn't walk in and be honest with him regarding her thoughts and feelings about being onboard.

Despite the stress created by this pretense, she actually expected her meeting with the Captain to be the easiest part of her workday. In the past, she had turned these types of meetings into successes for herself, earning scholarships, internships, and entry into programs in college, ROTC, and at her CIA co-op. Over the last few years, she had become adept at relaying her plans for the future to those more senior to her. She had learned how to enthusiastically discuss the three major facets to her life so far: her love for science and engineering, how she looked forward to qualifying as a surface warfare officer (SWO), and how she was planning ahead for nuclear power school.

She felt confident that despite her reservations about what she should say to the Captain, all of her standard, impressive, and convincing interview lines of the past would flow out naturally, and she had no need to rehearse. Once she stepped inside the Captain's stateroom, she would sit with proper posture on the blue burlap couch across from his desk – shoulders slightly relaxed, her hands folded in her lap – ready to assume the role of the enthusiastic young junior officer, eager to earn her qualifications onboard.

Over time she had developed a repertoire of key phrases that had worked in her favor during interviews. "I'm actually looking forward to nuclear power school, sir," she pictured herself stating, while smiling and showing self-assuredness. "It'll give me the opportunity to apply my mechanical engineering degree, and all I've studied for." At one time she had believed those statements, she thought as she leaned against the bulkhead opposite his door. Now, however, she had gained an awareness that made them feel fraudulent, and increasingly she had begun to see herself as nothing but a pretender.

"Psst, it only gets better," Rob startled her from behind. "Remember that," he emphasized, as the more senior colleague junior officer continued past her down the passageway.

"Sure, Rob," she answered. But he had already passed through the door out of officers country and she could hear that he had reached the ladderwell to the bridge.

She actually viewed waiting, and her upcoming time in the Captain's stateroom, as a relief from bridge watch and her workday, normally loaded with performance anxiety and any number of firestorms. She had sought to be trustworthy in the performance of her duties. Above all, she had tried to go about her tasks and watches methodically, in a manner that was metered and thought-out. But onboard, she was tired all the time, suffering from sleep deprivation, and as the days at sea blurred into each other, she felt her emotional strength waning. On each day, some new and unforeseeable personal struggle managed to unfold as she took on real-time nerve-wracking bridge watches, new briefings to give on shipboard systems she didn't understand, and new tangles of technical issues involving the gunnery work of her division. With each task and with each watch she gave her every effort, but she often felt she was making little progress towards becoming an able bridge watchstander and manager of gunnery systems. She would tell herself, *okay, this watch is going to be different*, or, *today I'll start understanding the gun system*. But she tried and studied over and over, only to find on some other new day that those ambitions again hadn't materialized. As she went about battling her day-to-day tasks, facing them as best she could, she learned more about her nature. It was her own nature that was betraying, or possibly outgrowing, her past dreams and ideals, she had concluded. Rules she had lived by no longer seemed to apply, or now seemed unfathomable to her. Assumptions she had accepted throughout her life had turned upside down. But those rules and assumptions, regardless of the confusion they now elicited, were the ones that were familiar and on which she had relied to define herself; she experienced a certain amount of resistance towards letting go of them. There was security in staying with what one was used to, even if it did feel wrong.

She felt like she was at the edge of a cliff. She had learned so much about herself, and this inner process so infectious, that her foremost desire was to continue the exploration, accept with honesty whatever she found, and acknowledge her new sense of self publicly. But changing herself and her outlook, going forward with a life in which she could openly express her newly discovered feelings, felt like a daunting prospect in many ways. The sort of life change she was contemplating came with uncertain outcomes. But it also seemed to her that the process that had begun could not now be stopped at will.

    Her life had often been filled with role-playing, anxiety over trying to be something she wasn't, fear of discovery, and stress over trying to acquire skills she couldn't reach. Were she to leave her old values behind, the new path would be no less scary. In opening herself to honesty, she'd likely learn more things about herself, and about her past, that she wouldn't like. However, she decided that she would rather know herself and confront the things she had said and done. And from there she would do her best. Honesty seemed painful but healthier. She stared down at the deck, her arms crossed against her chest, still waiting, understanding that her thoughts would make her meeting with the Captain a challenge. She could hear CHENG (acronym title for the ship's chief engineer) inside the Captain's stateroom joking and laughing. She remembered the straight and pragmatic view of herself and the world that she had once held. She had never imagined the day would come when she would see herself as one of those people claiming to feel lost or helpless or wishing to "find themselves." Those who wallowed in such states deserved some sort of ridicule, she had thought at one time.

    The Captain opened his door just slightly. "I'll need about ten more minutes with CHENG, Miss Conner," he said.

    "Yes, sir," she answered.

    She remembered what she had looked like in the mirror, when she was readying herself for this meeting; she had noticed that the dark circles underneath her eyes had become more pronounced. After she had been onboard for about two days, she had stopped worrying about wearing makeup, and had decided to go natural.

    In preparation for this very belated welcome aboard interview, she had rushed on her spare clean-and-pressed khakis – ready to go with insignia and all – and a pair of shined boots, which she had stored at the far end of her closet for any last minute need. She wanted to make a "smart" impression.

But in spite of her most intensive efforts onboard, she usually found herself unsure if she ever accomplished any result that moved herself, the gunnery division, or the weapons department forward. She conferred with her chiefs and senior petty officers, and researched technical diagrams and manuals, but with little advancement in her understanding of the gunnery and missile systems. The one hundred ten percent she had given all of her life hadn't proved sufficient onboard for her to overcome her inherent limitations.

She was sure that she existed as nothing more than a placeholder in her position as gunnery officer. Feelings of uselessness accompanied her wherever she walked onboard. The gunners mates seemed to go on about their preventive maintenance and repairs whether she was there or not. Lately, an obsession had taken hold of her, in memorizing the path of a round of ammunition through the 5-inch/54-caliber gun. At any moment, she dreaded that anyone, including the Captain, might request of her to recite the sequence. On her stateroom desk, she kept the 5"/54 gun manual open to a line diagram depicting the operation (*manually insert projectile/powder case at lower loading station, lower hoist raises the projectile to load station ejector, round transferred to loader drum and indexes to transfer station, fuse setter sets fuse down, etc.*). Every time she walked into her stateroom, she compulsively pored over the page, trying to embed the illustration into her memory. On some days, she would stop cold in the passageway, and quiz herself. But she never could quite recall, by rote, all of the mechanical and electronic steps.

"Oh, it's GUNNO!" she suddenly heard, as CHENG exited the Captain's stateroom, laughing at a joke he had told.

"Hello, sir," she responded dryly, but politely.

"Hey there, GUNNO," the operations officer (OPS) greeted her enthusiastically from the direction of the wardroom as he approached the Captain's door.

"Hello, sir," she answered. Then she stepped aside so CHENG could pass and OPS could enter the Captain's stateroom. Once CHENG turned his back to leave, she watched the Captain remove the placating smile he had worn for CHENG's jokes.

"It'll just be a minute, Miss Conner," the Captain said, before closing his door with OPS inside.

"Yes, sir," she nodded, still not minding the extended wait. It was almost relaxing to be able to do nothing but wait and think, while she sort of paced in the passageway. She wished that she possessed the strength and guts to walk into the Captain's stateroom and be honest – to tell him she was ill-suited, and ask for a transfer out of the SWO community. But she knew that such a request was impossible, and she could only imagine the reaction from her department head, the XO (executive officer), and others. The Command and senior watch officer would likely increase her training substantially until she expressed a desire – real or not – to continue toward successful completion of her SWO qualification. She imagined "pep talks" and "special training" designed to motivate her. There would be peer pressure as others looked at her as a *dirtbag*, a SWO term used to describe someone perceived as lazy and who didn't care. At her stage, she was sure that it was impossible to voluntarily transfer out of the SWO community, unless she failed at multiple attempts to earn her SWO pin, her surface warfare officer qualification. Then she thought: Failing to earn a SWO pin – it just seemed too humiliating.

    She stared at the plaque mounted on the Captain's door, which was ornately adorned with the ship's seal and the gold leaf embellishments entitled to officers above the rank of O-5 (commander). Why didn't she have the fortitude and the confidence to speak honestly with the Captain, and to withstand the consequences of her questions? Why didn't she have the courage to ask him for his endorsement to serve out her time in another officer community? She wanted to tell him of her discovery that she was not – in the true sense – an engineer who was best suited to serve as his gunnery officer and representative on the bridge. And that for her sake, the sake of her peers, and for that of the Navy she wished to transfer. She would serve the Navy in a capacity where she could truly benefit the service; she would work hard as a supply or intelligence officer. She had always been methodical and she had patient attention to detail.

    She would have liked to express to the Captain that she was thankful for having served onboard this naval destroyer and, in doing so, she had been forced to face up to who she was; she had gained new self-understanding, and she wanted to move forward with her life, in a different direction, based on that understanding. She wanted to tell him that she had only chosen engineering because she had adhered to the conventional security she had been taught was so essential in life. And that, consequently, the credentials she had accrued in search of this security were a farce. *So did he understand?* she would have liked to have asked him.

But then she knew that her personal issues weren't his problem, and it wasn't his job to understand the ins and outs of her psychology. He was onboard to command and operate a warship.

In reality, she wondered if she would ever be able to give up her *persona* of an engineer and naval officer. Maybe she had worked and studied too hard at constructing those masks, and she would ultimately find herself unable to leave them behind. The money was good, and her position came with a certain amount of status. People thought that being an engineer and naval officer meant that one was doing well in life.

She scuffed the bottom of her steel-toe boots against the Captain's doormat, which read *"Commanding Officer"* above an inlay of the ship's seal. She wondered if investments, IRAs, job security, benefits, savings, and material success could compensate for inner emptiness. A liberal arts field may have been more nebulous than engineering, but who was to say where that pursuit might have taken her. If only she had aimed after her passion – languages and literature – and released herself to follow wherever that path led. Despite all of the ups and downs in life, she would have at least been left with something meaningful at her core.

She bent down and rubbed her khaki uniform pants against her shins. Walking the ship in steel-toe boots had given her shin splints; and she had banged her shins multiple times on the hatchways between shipboard spaces. As the ship steamed towards exotic Malaysia, she decided that she did have some value to bring into the Captain's office that afternoon. Throughout her days at sea, she had clung to scattered lights of positives. Administrative management of her division had come easily for the most part, and she enjoyed a good working relationship with the gunners mates. So, she recognized some skills within herself, allowing her to uphold a certain level of confidence.

"Miss Conner." Brenda watched as the Captain's door opened. "You can come in, please."

Chapter 2: Kids in the airport ... Symbols of the past

Sydney, Australia
Reporting Aboard USS CURTIS WILBUR (DDG-54)
The beginning

You're stepping off this plane into your dream, Brenda thought to herself, as she smiled at the flight attendant who was welcoming the passengers to Sydney, Australia. *You are a commissioned military officer...an ensign...a female naval officer assigned to a combat vessel...historic! All the result of the determined academic drive you've shown since you first set foot in school.* She walked down the narrow jetway and entered the airport, as she continued to privately congratulate herself. *This is an incredible and symbolic accomplishment. Women were billeted to the first combat ship just a few years ago...adventure!*

    Energized by these thoughts, Brenda walked through the international terminal in disbelief that she was actually in Australia. It seemed similar to the United States as she expected, yet the signs, the Australian names for things, the colors surrounding her, and the sizes and proportions still felt foreign at the same time. She wanted to soak up every nuance, read and see everything! She had new opportunities to embrace, ones earned through extreme dedication and hard work. Brenda followed the signs to immigration. *This is what you've always wanted*, she reassured herself, as she tried to shrug off a speck of apprehension.

    Brenda soon found herself sandwiched within a herd forming in front of passport control, as passengers from several international flights began merging in around her. Even as recently as a month ago, in officer training, she couldn't have imagined that she would be flying to Australia to start her first shipboard assignment. Living and working in exotic places, the chance to travel: that was what she hoped Navy life was going to be like.

    Reporting aboard a ship homeported out of Japan used to linger in her mind as some fuzzy goal out there for someday, but no longer; now she was on her way. Within a few hours, she might even find herself walking aboard. Most of her junior officer peers were driving to their first ships, to places like Norfolk, Mayport (Jacksonville), or

San Diego. Now, here she was, only eight months in, and the Navy was sending her out on her own, to a country that most in the United States never dreamed of experiencing. Brenda pulled her passport out of her purse and began to flip through each page, as a way to pass the time in line. She enjoyed studying the details of the ink stamps. They represented her past adventures. A few pages were already filled with stamps from her college study abroad in Spain, her trip to Venezuela over spring break, and from the extra trip to Spain she squeezed in between college graduation and commissioning into the Navy. She wanted to fill more pages!

Brenda shuffled along slowly with the part of the group moving towards the passport booths labeled, "Non-Australian Citizens." She found it remarkable to see so many people dressed for so many different climates and cultures in one space. Dress alone gave away at least part of the stories of these individuals. Herself, she was below the equator, but dressed from a northern climate, wearing sneakers and jeans; she imagined she appeared very American. No one could have guessed she was a naval officer. She looked more like a student, she decided, possibly a college exchange student. A group of kids around her age sitting on the floor in a circle caught her eye; she wondered what her college friends back home might be up to. She couldn't help but glance over at the group occasionally; and she found it increasingly harder to look away.

"You can join us if you'd like," one of the kids sprawled out on top of a few coats and backpacks called over to her, *like he had caught her!*

Brenda shot her glance back to the floor, feeling mortified. She hadn't meant for them to notice her attention. "I'm sorry," she reacted, smiling from embarrassment. "You remind me of some friends back home." *I'm headed into a very different type of environment now*, she wanted to explain; but she felt jetlag impeding her ability to express her thoughts clearly. Never in her life had she functioned well without sleep. "Excuse me," she placed her hands over her face and laughed. "I'm totally exhausted from the flights, as I'm sure you guys are, too."

"You can come and sit down with us," one of the girls invited her, backing her words up by waving Brenda over next to her. She seemed very sweet. Since the line had stalled anyway, Brenda approached the group of American kids, and converted her backpack into a seat cushion to join them on the airport floor. Normally, she kept to herself, having never been overly sociable, especially to anonymous people to whom she had little connection. However, she was attracted to this group.

"So what are you doing in Australia?" asked the first kid, who had called her over.

Brenda almost didn't want to answer him. She assumed by looking at this group that they were like her friends back home, who had no association or contact whatsoever with the military, and seemed immune from understanding it. In fact, her friends from high school and college never grasped how she could have joined the military. Eventually, after years of Brenda trying to justify her views, mostly in vain, she and her friends had all remained silent on the subject. Brenda studied engineering in college, but her friends' majors included film, theater, languages, voice, and other liberal arts. One of her closest friends graduated with a degree in archeology. After college, she went off to work a dig in Belize. Many of her other friends were living around Boston or in New York. "I'm actually in the Navy," Brenda finally answered. "I flew to Australia to meet my ship. It's out on a South Pacific deployment and it's scheduled for a port visit in Sydney." *There, I did it*, she thought, *I said it, even though they won't get it, just like my friends*.

"Wow, the Navy," one girl answered. "I could never do something like that."

Another asked, "So are you going to be like a sergeant or something?"

"No," Brenda smiled, feeling at home; that was the same type of question her friends used to ask. But she doubted that she could explain her rank in the Navy in a way that this group would understand. She never had found a way to successfully explain the rank structure within the military to her friends. Her friends were kids who volunteered for Greenpeace, gave money to PETA, and listened to alternative music. Liberals! To her friends, the military was practically a foreign concept, and existed far beyond the realm of their interests and political values. In her view, however, joining ROTC and the Navy had met some of her own particular needs to express nonconformity, and was much more exotic and adventurous than reporting into a regular engineering office job each morning.

Another girl from the group interrupted before Brenda could continue. "The Navy doesn't have sergeants. I know that much," she affirmed, while busily working on a spontaneous drawing in her sketch pad.

"I like your pencil sketches," Brenda complimented her,

fascinated by her work.

"It helps pass the time, like being stuck here," the girl replied. "See here," the girl showed Brenda, as she pulled out a finished sketch from her portfolio case. "If I like what I end up with, I combine the work I did into one of my projects."

Brenda nodded. She was amazed at people who took the time to work at art – something she considered to be a hobby, or side activity. In high school, she took a heavy science/math course load. And later in engineering school, it was all she could do to get her science/math coursework done on time, study, pass tests, participate in the engineering student co-op program, and complete the requirements for ROTC. She had no time for anything else in life, including hobbies, and besides, she had never considered herself very artistic. Instead, she had focused on the hard stuff, which to her mind, meant technical subjects that would lead to a solid career. Brenda smiled. She could hear a few of her mother's stock phrases repeating in her head. She had accepted them as true and had not thought much about the meaning behind them. "I'm not artistic. I have no artistic ability whatsoever," her mother used to repeat over and over while she was growing up. Her father had usually backed her mother's words up with his own style of humor, "I never got beyond stick figures," he would say, and then he would laugh. So Brenda assumed that she had no ability in the arts either, and growing up, the arts weren't valued as important areas of life to explore. The arts just weren't practical. Fine arts and liberal arts were something her friends were into, friends to whom her mom endearingly referred throughout the years as "free spirits."

"You're right about the sergeant thing," Brenda said, veering the conversation back to ranks and paygrades in the Navy. "It's complicated to explain, but I'm what's called an officer." She watched for the usual blank stares. "Enlisted ranks consist of soldiers and sailors who enlist through a recruiter after graduation from high school. They're the privates, sergeants, seamen, and petty officers. Officers train as midshipmen through ROTC in college or at the Naval Academy. They're the ensigns, lieutenants, captains, and colonels." Officers are commissioned by the president through congress, she was going to add, but her instinct told her to drop it. "What are you guys in Australia for?"

"We're part of an international art school exchange. We just spent two months in Florence, Italy. We'll be in Sydney for another two months before heading back to school in the States."

"Florence, that's awesome," Brenda responded, immediately captivated. "I've never been to Italy, but I studied abroad in Madrid for my Spanish minor. I loved it over there."

"It's so beautiful in Italy. I sold flowers on a bridge for extra spending money," one of the girls chimed in. "I don't know how it works in Australia yet, but I hope I can earn some extra money to travel around before the semester starts up again."

"Wow," Brenda answered, knowing she would never have tried to fulfill education and travel plans in such a spontaneous and unstable manner. In college, she strived for a sure thing, a practical major that would lead directly to a guaranteed job and career. What could one possibly do with an art degree? All that time and money spent. The conversation with these students reminded her of home, when she used to walk through the colonial-era neighborhoods of Providence's East Side, the streets filled with students from one of the most well-known art schools in the world. How could people major in these subjects? It was a question she tried to answer whenever she saw a student carrying art supplies or a portfolio, a common sight on those hilly streets. What would they do for jobs afterwards?

An immigration official began announcing instructions to the crowd, and Brenda drifted into her own thoughts. She had been through the mechanics of immigration lines many times before. *These art students*, she thought to herself, as she considered how majoring in Spanish literature would not have provided any more stability than majoring in art. Besides maybe to be a teacher, how could she have spent all that money on tuition for something with no clear job waiting at the end? "Liberal arts more or less trains you to be a bank teller," she could hear her father saying with clarity, regarding those types of degrees. Brenda feared that non-technical degrees, fluff majors, were going to land her friends right back at home, living in their parents' basements. She prided herself on her independence and certainly had no plans of moving back home after college. Being so intently career focused, she had already co-oped three semesters with the CIA in Washington D.C., while fully entrenched in ROTC and studying engineering. The salary at CIA was phenomenal for an engineering student, and it was the CIA! Now, the Navy provided a steady paycheck and a secure well-paying job. "If you can get in the government, you'll be all set," she could hear her mother saying, referring to the stability and benefits. Brenda banked on the Navy leading her to a powerful career on the outside, once she finished her five-year obligation. For now, she planned on combining her love for travel with her career in the Navy. She also hoped to find a way to use her Spanish studies; although being in Asia, she figured on shelving those hopes for a while.

"So, you have to go through immigration just like we do to join up with the Navy?" another asked.

"That's how it works," Brenda answered, finding the girl's question funny because the same thought had occurred to her. Flying across the world, going through immigration in a foreign country and using her personal passport, all to get to a U.S. Navy warship mid-deployment, did strike her as kind of weird. Everyone seemed to notice that the immigration line had started to move. As a momentary part of the group, Brenda gradually stood back up, and struggled to hang her backpack and bags all over herself, just as they were doing. "I enjoyed talking to you guys, if only for a few minutes," she said, wishing them farewell before facing forward in the line. "Sometimes Navy ships give public relations tours while in foreign ports," she added. But she didn't notice too much of a reaction from the group in regard to visiting a Navy ship. "Well, good luck to all of you," she said, trying to appear casual at leaving them. The group had become important to her during the few short moments she had spent with them. Brenda tended to view events symbolically, and this group symbolized her life prior to the Navy.

"Take care," she heard, and noticed a few waves as the group struggled with their multiple bags, all odd-shaped to carry their supplies. "Be careful!" she heard from the girl who had sold flowers on the bridge. "Please don't get killed," another followed. Brenda circled back for a quick wave, laughing to herself. Yes, those were the types of things she had typically heard from her friends in college, she thought. Countless times! So much so that she had habitually ignored those comments. What response was there for something so, just ridiculous! It was peacetime. Brenda grabbed one last glance back to form a picture of the group she was leaving behind; she used their image to remember how she had last seen her friends in the city. Then she scrambled around to ready her passport for the officials, as everyone in line appeared to be doing. She planted her feet behind the bold yellow line painted across the floor in front of the passport booth. Next, it would be her turn to cross the line and step through passport control.

"Here to visit?" the Australian immigration officer asked

Brenda, as she approached the glass booth and handed her passport to him through a small opening.

"Yes," she nodded, thinking her answer seemed harmless enough. She felt herself fading ever faster from extreme fatigue, and her response seemed easier than trying to explain everything. The officer handed her passport back to her. Relieved, she headed towards baggage claim, hurriedly flipping through the pages of her passport booklet to find her stamp from Australia. On page twelve, she found it: "IMMIGRATION AUSTRALIA, ARRIVED 26 MAR 1997, SYDNEY AIRPORT, 109F."

Chapter 3: Self-doubt is never far behind

You were selected into one of the Navy's most competitive and prestigious programs, Brenda again reassured herself, as she spotted her large green seabag moving towards her on the baggage conveyor. The commanding officer of her university Navy ROTC unit was a former nuclear submarine captain, so he had encouraged all strong science and engineering students – including Brenda – to apply to the highly selective Naval Nuclear Power School. Since the law only recently allowed women to serve on combat ships, she was slated to be one of the first women to attend the elite school. Nuclear powered submarines remained closed to females, but nuclear powered aircraft carriers were designated to begin receiving women into nuclear engineering positions soon. Brenda pulled her heavy seabag off the conveyor to the airport floor and stared at it for a few seconds, focusing on the stenciled block letters: ENSIGN CONNER. She still couldn't believe her name appeared in bold black after that rank.

Brenda exited the airport through the automatic doors, heavily slumped forward from the weight of her seabag over her shoulder. The hot humid air outside nearly suffocated her at first, being such a dramatic change from the air-conditioned airport and from where she had originated. She slowly stepped through the crowd on the sidewalk, feeling her jeans and wool winter sweater start to drench. "I should have changed my clothes inside the airport," she chastised herself under her breath, fighting irritation from jetlag. She felt disgusting suddenly; she wished that she could have brushed her teeth after such a long flight, but her toiletries were buried deep within her seabag. She approached the taxi area and dropped her bags to the ground. The walk beyond the airport doors had taken her less than fifty feet, but in the scorching heat her fatigue and nervousness about her ship intensified. She thought that she might become physically ill as she bent down on the sidewalk to open her backpack, to look for the papers containing her hotel information.

It would all begin at the hotel, she reminded herself. From that start, she would face the reality of reporting to her ship and carrying out the duties of a naval officer commissioned to a destroyer. There was no choice but to confront that reality. The opportunity to change her mind had passed in college, when she accepted a Navy ROTC scholarship along with the time obligation it entailed. Her acceptance into the nuclear power program, during senior year of college, added an additional year to her military obligation – she would serve five years instead of the normal four years, the extra year tacked on for nuclear power school. She would attend nuclear power school after serving onboard her first ship, a destroyer. Brenda remembered the letter of congratulations she received following her acceptance into the program, the blue three star admiral's flag embossed at the top of the stationary. *"Dear Midshipman Conner,"* the letter began. She had read it many times. *"I was very pleased to learn of your recent selection by Admiral Demars for entry into the Navy's nuclear propulsion program. You should be proud of this accomplishment which speaks well of your abilities and determination. I know you will find the training in which you are about to embark both challenging and rewarding. Your selection for the nuclear propulsion program is only the beginning of what should be a fruitful career. Congratulations and well done! Best regards, T. W. WRIGHT, Vice Admiral, U.S. Navy"*

Everything would work out once she got to her first ship, Brenda hoped. She had carried her nerves and doubts with her to the other side of the world. It's natural to be nervous, she told herself as she stood in line for the next cab; everyone's nervous when up against something new like this. She caught the faint aroma of eucalyptus in the breeze. "Eucalyptus trees," she exclaimed as she looked around, reminding herself of her exciting surroundings. She began to bury her doubts from a few moments ago. *She was in Australia!* This was what she had come for. And she had flown right back into the feel of summer!

"Miss, may I help you? Would you like a taxi into the city?" a man with a uniform shirt labeled "Taxi Rank Supervisor" interrupted her thoughts. He looked hurried, she noticed, when he finally caught her attention.

"Yes, yes, please, thank you," Brenda answered, still captivated by the eucalyptus. She barely finished her sentence before she and her bags were swept into the back of a van. Her overwhelming exhaustion made each oncoming event seem as though it was happening to her as she watched. She handed the driver her hotel reservations and they were off.

Heading out of the airport, Brenda sat in the back of the more compact Australian-sized minivan, fascinated by the feelings of a first glimpse at someplace new, trying to catch every sight as it passed. *Australia!* This travel was just the kind of thing she had hoped for right out of college. She had never expected the sight and smells of the eucalyptus forests, or the general look which resembled the United States. She relinquished herself to the entire scene and stopped trying so hard to catch every detail. After all, she felt she deserved a break; she was recovering from a twenty-one hour flight with layovers in Chicago and Los Angeles. The events in motion were all so much larger than her.

"So you look like you're in the military," commented the cab driver, in an attempt to start conversation.

"I look like I'm in the military, really?" Brenda answered him, amused that he was the first person ever to say that. *She loved that.* "How does that work?" she asked. "I usually get the opposite." In fact, Brenda relished people's surprised reactions whenever she revealed that she was a military officer, *in the Navy and onboard ships!* She delighted in the shock value of the choices she had made in her life and in the image she had poured herself into developing. Before being commissioned in the Navy, she had taken pleasure in telling people that she was an engineering major. Not only did majoring in engineering seem to go with some sort of guise that she must be smart, practical, and hardworking, but she also took pride in the fact that people could never believe it; and that motivated her. She consistently sensed that they didn't think she looked or seemed the type. As if there existed a type! Sometimes she felt like bursting out and saying, "See, women *are* in these fields!" However she never did; and she hoped that her mere presence would make some sort of contribution, even if it was small. Women were rare in engineering and in the military. She trusted that it would only be a matter of time before more women entered these fields.

"It's the green Army bag," the cab driver continued.

"Oh, you mean the green Navy seabag," Brenda teased back.

"Ah, Navy, sorry, sorry. I've driven many Yanks over the years headed to the U.S. military base in Alice Springs."

The traffic had begun to congest and stall. "What's going on here? I guess they have rush hours in Australia too," Brenda commented, regretting one more barrier imposed between her and sleep at the hotel.

"Rush hour for the morning commute," he answered as he slowed the cab to a stop.

"Did you happen to notice any U.S. Navy ships in port at the harbor in Sydney?" She was already trying to figure out a way to find her ship. Her voice trembled at the thought of receiving the answer, that the ship might actually be there.

"I assume then you're here to meet a ship."

"Yes, somewhere in Sydney. I have no idea if it's here, or if it will be arriving at all," she answered, trying to sound casual. The flight, the Sydney airport, the taxi – the next step leading to her ship was the hotel. Not too long ago, Brenda received a letter from her shipboard sponsor stating that his wife, along with a few other wives from the ship, were going to be staying at a specific hotel in Sydney when she was scheduled to arrive. He suggested in the letter that she meet the women at the hotel as a way to find the ship. Before leaving the U.S., Brenda made reservations at that same hotel through a travel agent in her hometown. "This hotel is going to be the starting point for my shipboard career," she added to the driver. *The adventure delighted her.* She was in Sydney, Australia by herself, without any information except for a hotel reservation; and she had no information regarding the ship's current schedule or where exactly she would meet it. She had to make it work all on her own. *For that, she couldn't wait!*

"I'm not sure if any Navy ships are currently in the harbor, but you should have a fairly good view of it from your hotel in King's Cross," the driver responded as they edged along at about ten mph.

"King's Cross, is that a section of Sydney? Is there a lot to do in the immediate area?"

"Oh, well, yeah, depending on what you're looking for. Well, there's quite a bit I would say. How did you come about staying there?" he asked. Brenda noted but brushed aside the subtle caginess in his answer.

"I'll be meeting some people there who're associated with the ship. I hope, anyway." Brenda set her hotel reservations down on the seat, and picked up the pages that had been underneath – her orders to report to the ship. She reread the words, "UNUSUALLY ARDUOUS SEA DUTY," written in Navy message format, all in caps. The authoritative and official nature of those words, which contained an element of challenge, sparked a feeling of awe and excitement within her every time she read them. She had signed on to the most historic and powerful of organizations. Soon, she would be an integral and working part of this forward deployed naval destroyer, homeported out of Japan. She expected the operations tempo (OPTEMPO) and the number of days at sea to be high, and she felt anxious about what that would really mean. "Then after the hotel," she continued, "who knows, Perth, New Zealand, Singapore, Thailand, Malaysia, Indonesia, Macau, Hong Kong!"

"Join the Navy, See the World!" the driver added as if singing a song.

"That's right. It's not just a job, it's an adventure!" Brenda repeated the widely-known Navy slogan, a bit sarcastically, but upbeat, forgetting her anxiety and enjoying a new moment. As the gridlocked traffic steadily broke up, Brenda sat fascinated by the similarity between Australian and Californian landscapes. And the people here lived in houses with small yards and streets culminating in rounded cul-de-sacs, just like in the suburbs of the United States. She had never seen that dynamic in any other foreign country, with the exception of Canada.

She gazed out the car window, back to trying not to miss one detail outside. "Do they call this style of house a ranch here?" But receiving no answer, Brenda assumed the driver couldn't hear her above the wind.

"So, what made you join up, if you don't mind me asking?"

Brenda closed the window to answer. "I had an ROTC scholarship in college. Plus, I majored in engineering. I've wanted to join the military ever since I can remember." Brenda remembered how, since junior high, she had been so drawn to the whole idea of going into the military and wearing the uniform. She had dedicated herself to believing in it, imagining she would have found a way to join even without an ROTC scholarship, even if it meant joining OCS or the reserves after college.

"And what type of engineering did you study?"

"Mechanical."

"It's rare for a lady, isn't it?" he asked.

Brenda sat up straighter so she could lean toward the front seat. This question she loved fielding, and in this case she felt the driver had posed it more out of curiosity than chauvinism. She imagined that each person she answered might begin to see the issue of women's careers differently, that women really did fit naturally into these professions. Anymore, the scope of women's opportunities had widened beyond teacher, nurse, or secretary, the choices her mother's generation had been given. Now women could choose those as well as any other path. She took pride in studying a non-traditional field in college, and in starting her career in a non-traditional job. "Well, my dad was a mechanical engineer," she began as she usually did, "and yes, women are rarer in the field; but it's becoming more common." She knew the second part of her answer was somewhat of an exaggeration. Only one other female besides herself studied mechanical engineering in her graduating class; but by the time she graduated, more had enrolled in the college of engineering as freshmen. Brenda had faith that the mere presence of women as competent colleagues would affect the most change. "I'm used to working and going to school in an all-male environment. The opposite would almost seem strange by now," she added.

The taxi reached the edge of the city. "We've passed so many golf courses," she commented to the driver.

"You a fan?"

"Not at all," she answered, hoping her hotel would turn out to be in the city. That's what she truly treasured, being in a city; she loved a bustling, gritty city, and the anonymity that went with it. She missed the location of her university and living right downtown. When she walked out of her on-campus apartment, every kind of food or store, anything she wanted, lay within a few blocks. She never brought a car to school; no one at her school did; everyone walked or took the "T."

Driving farther into the city reminded Brenda of the aspects of college she had enjoyed, like the Spanish literature classes she took as a respite from a draining course load of engineering classes. Literature studies came so naturally to her that they never really seemed like work. She took the literature classes, initially, to boost her GPA; but as time went on, she began to truly savor them. Once in a while, she would pause in a Spanish literature class to notice that often, not one male student filled a seat. Spanish classes encompassed the flip side of her life. She remembered especially flourishing in the upper level literature classes, even delving into a graduate level class where some mastery of Spanish language was prerequisite. And she had done quite well in it! Each semester, she applied for special permission from the college of engineering to enroll above the course credit limit, twenty-four credits as opposed to the normal sixteen, so she could take her Spanish classes. It was the only way she could indulge in what she truly loved to study, her true passion. By the time she graduated, she had accumulated enough credits to earn a minor in Spanish, just from acting on her personal attraction to it.

The arrival at the attractively situated hotel delighted Brenda.

Over the opposite edge of the street, appeared a panoramic view of Sydney Harbor beyond eucalyptus tree lined hills. "The view is phenomenal," she remarked to the driver, as she turned to dig her wallet out of her backpack. Always prepared, Brenda had specially ordered Australian currency from a bank in Providence before leaving the U.S. She anticipated that the long flights would render her virtually nonfunctional from fatigue; and she wanted to ensure that no loose ends were left untied in preparation for reporting aboard her ship. "Here you go. Thank you," she said to the driver, as she handed him the plastic AUD$50 bill. "I really like these plastic bills by the way, very cool!"

"They're unique to Australia. Good luck in the Navy!"

"Thank you! Right now, I just can't wait to check into the hotel and sleep."

Chapter 4: Hotel check-in ... The promise of a new adventure

The taxi pulled away from the curb, leaving Brenda alone on the sidewalk standing next to her seabag. She shared no connection to anyone or anything in Australia, but she didn't mind. She had experience traveling abroad, and she loved the newness and adventure of it. *The unknown of it!* She had studied in Spain and had toured much of the country on her own and with friends she had met in the study program; she had traveled to Greece with her best friend's family, where she had lived in the family's remote mountain village near the Albanian border; she had flown to Caracas, Venezuela during her last spring break to experience the city and briefly study language there. In each of those places, she had faced challenges with local customs, language, and in getting around; but she had demonstrated to herself in every instance that she could be resourceful in overcoming those challenges. She had full confidence in her ability to find her way in Australia. She loved those memories, which gave her the energy to pick up one end of her long seabag and drag it a few feet across the sidewalk to the hotel entrance.

She felt so independent and about the world! She had gained a level of financial independence early on. In high school, she had regular babysitting jobs on most weeknights, and she worked a variety of odd jobs in malls and in fast food on weekends. She deposited most of the money she earned directly into her savings account. In college, her Navy ROTC scholarship paid her tuition, and her engineering student co-ops at CIA provided a good student salary along with a cost-of-living stipend. Her savings, odd jobs, and engineering co-ops had given her independence and opportunities to travel and study abroad.

Before she entered the hotel, Brenda wanted to remain on the sidewalk just a moment longer to admire the Sydney skyline. *It represented the promise she felt!*

She had doubts about the hotel, however, as she opened the door. The entrance appeared unassuming from the street; and the art deco canopy hanging by chains above the single door looked in need of restoration. But she felt surprised and relieved when she opened the door and saw lush and colorful vegetation throughout the lobby.

Part of the lobby was enclosed in glass; straight across she could see an outdoor courtyard, and above she could see the sky. It looked and felt like a greenhouse inside, which, in her tired condition, was inviting. She thought for a moment that she might have a chance at fighting her jetlag quickly, even after having traveled halfway across the world, over the international date line and into the next day. Brenda closed the lobby door, eased her bags down, and relaxed while she enjoyed the mist and fragrances from the tropical gardens. She inhaled deeply to breathe in the scene, and exhaled while savoring the sensation of the rise and fall of her chest and the cool moisture on her skin.

"Hello, may I help you?" an employee interrupted her thoughts.

"Oh, my gosh, I'm sorry," Brenda responded, caught off guard. "I've had a long trip to get here. I'm just enjoying your beautiful gardens."

"No worries!" she replied, revealing a smile.

"I'm so tired, I'm walking around in a malaise," Brenda said, laughing slightly.

"Oh, no worries," the employee repeated. "Follow me to the office. You can leave your bags here for the moment."

Brenda nodded and smiled and left her heaviest bags behind, figuring she could get a luggage cart later. As she followed the woman over to the office, she started to gain a fresh outlook. The tropical atmosphere of the hotel and the woman's casual and friendly attitude made her feel welcome and at home. And she had already heard the disarming Australian expression "no worries" a few times since arriving in country.

"I have reservations," Brenda began, as they stepped inside the office. She placed her backpack on the counter and removed the fax confirmation of her hotel reservation. "My travel agent in the U.S. faxed my reservations and your hotel faxed this confirmation back," she said, handing it to the woman. "I'm also meeting a few other women here. They're associated with a U.S. Navy ship coming into Sydney," Brenda finished.

"Oh, a group of three American women?" the woman asked, as she typed at the computer. Brenda noticed from her nametag that she was the manager. "I was on last night when they called. Yeah, all three canceled yesterday evening."

"Well, did they leave any kind of message for me?"

"Umm, I'm afraid not. I'm sorry."

The news struck Brenda as a little dismaying. Why hadn't the women left a message regarding the reason for their cancelation? She speculated that the port visit to Sydney had been rescheduled, or removed from the deployment. "Is there something I might help you with to make things a bit easier?" the manager asked, sympathetically. Brenda wasn't sure how to interpret a cancellation with no message. Sure, the officers onboard and their families must have been busy during deployment, and a new ensign was probably not of much consequence... She felt slightly left out in the cold.

"Well, is it too early to check in?" Brenda asked, suddenly more uncomfortable in her heavy traveling clothes, and partially disoriented from straight-out exhaustion. "I guess I can worry about figuring out the rest later," she thought out loud. "I'd just like to get cleaned up, change my clothes, and rest a while."

"Your room's not quite ready yet, since it's very early morning. We still have to wait for guests to check out. But if you would like to freshen up, I can offer a fellow Navy woman a changing area and a shower back in the janitor's closet. It's something," the manager shrugged and smiled.

A fellow Navy woman! Brenda couldn't imagine the chances. In her travels, something always seemed to come together for her when she least expected it. And the manager's willingness to let her use the shower in the janitor's closet came as such a welcome relief, however unusual the concept may have seemed. A more laid back approach was ever present in Australia, and for now, it aided her in shedding a bit of the irritation that had mounted from fatigue. "Wow, you were in the Australian Navy? That's unbelievable!" Brenda remarked. Not liking how that sounded, she added, "I mean that, out of the blue, I ended up at a hotel managed by someone who served in the Australian Navy."

"I was in the Navy," the woman smiled. "I'd love to swap stories."

"That sounds good, after my shower. I'd like to take you up on your shower offer," Brenda replied, overwhelmed with thanks. She grabbed her backpack off the counter. "It just hit me. You must have noticed that my green seabag out in the lobby's stenciled ENSIGN."

"I did. And after you've freshened up, we can talk. While in the Navy I completed a short exchange on an American ship. Only a few weeks or so, but it was interesting enough."

"I would like to hear about it, and about your time in the Australian Navy," Brenda answered, as the manager motioned to follow her around back.

Chapter 5: A kindred spirit ... A woman's place is in the Navy

Brenda left the janitor's closet wearing shorts, sandals, and a summer top, feeling free after changing out of her winter clothes and showering. As she walked across the tropical courtyard, headed back to the lobby office, she imagined herself in an hour or so entering her hotel room, drawing the curtains closed, and climbing into a luscious bed in total darkness. She needed one last intermediary step to complete her journey to her ship: sleep.

Doing as the manager suggested, she left her seabag in back, near the shower, trusting it would be okay. It contained all of her uniforms, uniform accessories, clothes, books, notes, papers, and toiletries, everything she would need over the next four months of deployment. Having no experience to draw from, she hoped she'd packed correctly. She wanted to avoid the humiliation of missing any part of her uniform; and she wasn't sure how many females would be onboard to loan her anything she was missing, if necessary.

The manager looked up from her desk when Brenda reappeared through the door. "Feel better? We'll have your room made up soon. Your belongings will be fine in back."

"Great, thanks, I feel so much better. Still walking through a cloud, but refreshed."

"A shower always makes one feel better, no matter what's happened," the manager replied softly.

"Absolutely," Brenda agreed. She was still exhausted, even after freshening up, but the promise of a quiet hotel room all to herself gave her hope for recovering. She was familiar with all-out exhaustion; she had existed in a perpetual state of fatigue in engineering school: nauseous stomach, dizzy head, tightened throat, stinging eyes, and a constant feeling of panic that she would run out of time before she had to get to a class or exam, or turn in an assignment. Now, she worried about her jetlag, as well as finding her ship and getting there in a reasonable amount of time – *was it acceptable to rest at the hotel before checking aboard?*

During her first six months in the Navy, to her surprise, she continued living how she had lived in college, repeating her same treadmill lifestyle. As a newly commissioned ensign, designated as an officer in training for surface warfare officer (SWO) qualification, she began her first six months in the Navy at Surface Warfare Officers School (SWOS) in Newport, R.I. The school, all classroom work, was designed to prepare ensigns for shipboard life, work, and responsibility. Two weeks into the school, she began studying late into the night, every night, in order to pass the weekly Friday morning exams. The relief she felt after graduating from engineering school quickly faded once she started SWOS. She sustained a schedule of late night studying, with little sleep, until she graduated from the school. Her choices had a habit of trapping her in cycles where she craved sleep but never got enough, and where she constantly studied in a race to grasp the next milestone. But the milestones she reached never felt very satisfying or fulfilling.

She hoped that her lifestyle of jumping through hoops, with no rest, would come to an end once she reached her "real job" onboard a Navy ship. But after spending six weeks aboard a destroyer during midshipman summer cruise, between her junior and senior years of college, she had become skeptical.

"Have a seat if you'd like," the manager offered kindly. "I brewed some chamomile tea for relaxation."

"Oh, thanks," Brenda replied, as she pulled out a chair from underneath a small round table in the corner of the office. "Chamomile's my favorite, so calming."

"I assume then you're just starting out in the Navy," the manager began, as she served Brenda a cup of tea.

"I was just commissioned an O-1 ensign last May," Brenda answered, as she cupped the tea in her hands and took in the soothing aroma. She also liked listening to the manager's Australian English. "I graduated from Surface Warfare Officers School, SWOS, last month. I was depending on meeting up with those women."

"Relying on them to find your ship," the manager finished Brenda's thought, cupping her tea also, as she sat down on a stool behind the counter.

"Right, one was supposedly the wife of my shipboard sponsor. I don't know why they didn't leave a message."

"It could be an oversight on their part," the manager replied. "But sometimes the wives aren't so understanding or welcoming to Navy women, especially those aboard ships. You'll have to understand that," she added matter-of-factly, distracted momentarily by the computer screen.

"I do realize that," Brenda replied, feeling a mutual understanding. She imagined Paige must have been scarred by experience to be so forward with that opinion. She had heard stories of wives lobbying against opening ships to female service personnel, most recently, combatants. Being idealistically driven, she couldn't imagine women doing that to other women; but it was an unfortunate fact that the dynamic did exist, at least to some extent. "So now," Brenda continued, "I'm not sure where the ship is, or if it will be pulling into Sydney at all." She assumed an understanding listener in her Royal Australian Navy (RAN) acquaintance, always finding it easier to feel something in common with other people when far away from home. "I have a few phone numbers for the U.S. Navy base in Japan, and for the base in Newport, Rhode Island, where I started from. If I don't hook up with the ship here, at least I'll have the opportunity to experience a bit of Sydney before I move on to the next meeting point. Maybe Perth or Singapore, Thailand?"

"The Navy ships come into Sydney Harbor. You can easily take a taxi down there. It's not too far," the manager suggested warmly, as if she'd decided to take Brenda under her wing.

"I'll give it a try." Brenda started to stand up. "I don't want to take you from your work."

"No, no, it's okay. Please, it's a family-run business here," she answered, smiling over Brenda's concern for her work, and clearly wanting her to stay. "Please call me Paige, by the way."

"I'm Brenda," she introduced herself. "So did you like being in the Navy, Paige?"

"I did for the most part, but sometimes the women were impossibly harassed when I was in. The RAN had only just started implementing sexual harassment training about mid-way through my time in. People joke about the training, or talk about it like it's been a nuisance, but to me, the need was very real." Paige stared into her tea. "Men could check out of Australian society, go into the military, and freely act like pigs. Of course, where it was sanctioned, perfectly acceptable and encouraged, might I add."

Brenda nodded. "Some men seem to forget that military women are daughters, sisters, wives, and mothers. I've never understood that."

"But your age group will benefit from new awareness programs, I'm sure," Paige said, "and increasing acceptance of women in the military. I was too early."

"In the mid-90s it's easy to forget what it was like just a few years before," Brenda agreed. She understood that she was setting out on a military career at a better time for women. The U.S. military was starting to take sexual harassment seriously, as a valid issue. She couldn't imagine what life must have been like for women in the military before sexual harassment was defined legally and by policy, when sexual overtures and discrimination were considered normal and acceptable behavior – when women were considered annoying and a bother for even pointing out that there might be something wrong with the behavior. Her generation was going to be one of the first to benefit from decades of protests, marches, and court and legislative battles for equal rights and acceptance. She didn't view her gender as an issue or obstacle to her career. She had experienced wide acceptance of women in technical fields during engineering school, her co-op at CIA, in ROTC, and in her first year in the Navy. With the turn of a decade, new laws had been passed which opened opportunities to women and granted them rights against discrimination, exclusion, and harassment. Diversity and awareness education was becoming more prevalent. It really did seem as though the Navy, as well as society in general, was working to open attitudes and to advance the prevailing culture.

"The RAN opened ships to women in the mid-80s." Paige paused, "But it was hard. There were no high-ranking women for support, no role models. By the '90s, things were improving."

"In the U.S., we had the Tailhook scandal in '91. Tailhook changed everything," Brenda said. From her standpoint, the scandal had rocked naval culture to the core, changing the playing field dramatically for women. "You were an officer, right?" she asked Paige.

"I was a seaman officer, roughly equivalent to a surface warfare officer in the U.S. Navy."

"I'd like to ask some advice then," Brenda said, both sincerely and because she noticed a sadness in Paige's reminiscence. She wanted Paige to know that she considered her a mentor. "When I was still a midshipman in college, my mom and I visited the naval base in Norfolk, Virginia. The base had ships open for public tours, so we went aboard one. Very few ships were open to women at that time. I mentioned to our tour guide, a chief petty officer, that I would soon be commissioned an ensign, and my mom had asked him something about if he thought it would be especially difficult to be a woman aboard ship. He looked at me and said, 'See this door here,' he pointed. 'It's haze gray and it completely blends in with the rest of the ship. That is my clear advice. Blend in like this door; be just like this door.'"

For all Brenda's classwork, training, and influences, she had considered the chief's simple metaphor to be some of the most valuable advice she had ever received. She decided she would fit in as a naval officer, not as a female naval officer. She had set her sights on becoming an engineer, not a female engineer. She wanted to show, just by her actions, that women could do it and blend in like the gray doors with the rest of the gray ship. She hoped that by not distinguishing herself simply for her gender, she would further the overall cause of introducing women into technical fields. That was her personal means of contributing, her own decided style. "What do you think? Is that possible?"

"Absolutely, if you can manage it. If they'll let you," she answered, holding onto a far off look. "Things have changed since I was in. You'll have a better time of it. Don't forget who you are, or think that you have to dissolve yourself into being male. Women bring their own uniqueness to the military."

"Their own perspective and inherent instincts and talent," Brenda agreed.

"Absolutely, different organizational skills." Paige shifted gears. "So tell me what you will do aboard ship."

"I'm slated to be the communications officer. Not that I ever intended to be a surface warfare officer, or SWO, onboard ships, but that's another story. I originally wanted to be a pilot. Too many cool '80s fighter pilot movies," she laughed, attempting to hide how much that admission embarrassed her. "And my dad always watched those '80s Cold War defense industry documentaries on cable, shows about the stealth bomber, F-14s." She couldn't remember any of the other aircraft and missile systems. "Not to mention the Tom Clancy novels."

"I've read many of those."

"I like them," Brenda said, "but I find myself skipping through whole sections where he goes into too much technical detail. All the minutia is too much." She was becoming vaguely aware of the dichotomy within herself: an engineer not interested in technical aspects.

"Those are the parts I love," Paige replied.

Brenda smiled. "My dad worked in the defense industry." She had wanted to be like those men, those engineers who played important roles in the development of the ultra-cool high-tech

Long Way Out   29

defense systems. She wanted to be smart and accomplished in that same way. "I guess I was star-struck by flying, until the realities of the mental and physical training demands became closer and more real," she said to Paige.

"So why ships? Besides being in the Navy," Paige chuckled.

Brenda nodded in a way that showed she understood. The Navy included a variety of jobs, not all aboard ship. "After deciding against aviation, I still wanted to go into the Navy. But I set my sights on officer communities like Intelligence, Civil Engineer Corps, Supply Corps. You know, staff and restricted line, shore-based positions."

"Desk jobs. Serving in a more supportive role. Nothing wrong with that."

"I agree. I'm not sure if I'm such a real-time thinker, especially hands on," Brenda added, understanding that she was someone who needed to sit down, read, study, and think things through. "Unfortunately, the Navy took the staff and restricted line options off the table the year I graduated. You had to be non-physically qualified, NPQ'd, in order to go staff or restricted line."

"Not enough officers in warfare communities, or...?"

"Right, the Navy was suffering a major shortage of warfare officers." In Brenda's mind, that was how she had "ended up SWO," as many in the Navy put it. "I'm a hard worker, so I think SWO will turn out alright. You mentioned being a Seaman Officer?" Brenda asked, as Paige poured her another cup of chamomile from the kettle.

"Yes, and I specialized in navigation, which is very different in the RAN. In Australia, officers specialize more, and our training focuses on building a deep understanding of one chosen area."

"I would prefer that approach," Brenda answered. "In the U.S. Navy, officers receive a kind of generalized training and can then expect to rotate through many different jobs aboard ship. Can you imagine...I was sent to a three day school to prepare for my billet as communications officer! And officer tours are short in the U.S. Navy."

Talking to Paige overwhelmed Brenda's tired mind. She had so much in front of her to learn. As a first tour junior officer, she would be expected to divide her time between qualifying on the bridge and running the communications division. "You know I loved the feeling of standing watch on the bridge while steaming in formation with other ships," Paige continued. "I loved bridgemanship. Several warships would be out on station, in addition to other civilian merchant contacts. At one time a watchman had to be cognizant of all courses and speeds of all ships, their relative bearings."

Brenda started thinking about the bridge duties she feared: solving maneuvering board problems, calculating time to closest point of approach (CPA), calculating the 3-minute rule in her head, keeping track of relative bearings of multiple contacts, giving rudder orders, conning the ship to and from a pier, and divisional tactical maneuvering (DIVTACS)! *This ship bears 060 relative at ten knots; another ship bears 240 relative at fifteen knots. In five minutes, another ship will pass 6,000 yards off the port bow.* "It sure is an exercise in mental agility for anyone with a good head for numeracy, figures, and dimensions," Paige went on. Brenda nodded in agreement, but what Paige described were those real-time shipboard aspects that she dreaded. She had memorized the 3-minute rule for a test in SWOS – *a ship will travel a distance equal to her speed in knots times one hundred yards every three minutes* – but she had never been one to figure numbers in her head. It would all come together once she got to her ship, she was sure. "I had a real passion for driving ships," Paige said. "And I was quite adept at it, but..."

As Brenda listened to Paige's voice die, she leaned in towards her. "I bet you were great at it," Brenda said, and continued, "It's hard to be one of the first at anything. It takes a lot of courage to pave the way for others." People began to enter the hotel office to check out, and Brenda didn't want to remain a distraction. "I really enjoyed meeting you and hearing about your experiences, Paige. I'll remember them."

"No worries!" That made Brenda smile. "I've enjoyed the chance to speak with an American officer in the Navy. If you get back to Sydney, you'll have to stop in and let me know how everything's going. Make sure you take a card with our address."

"I would enjoy that very much, Paige, thank you. I'll go take a walk around the block. This neighborhood seems so avant-garde. It's calling out to me."

"Walk out the door to your right," Paige guided her. "You might even be able to see the ships from the top of the hill."

Fatigue barely allowed Brenda to process her conversation with Paige. For now, she refocused on being in Australia, and how this sort of travel enthralled her and embodied her spirit. So far, she had allowed nothing to hold her back, including family and personal relationships. This was her time and she was going to explore as much of the world as she could while she was single and without any commitments. Yes, she told herself, the farther away the better. Australia and Asia were fitting starts to her naval adventure.

Chapter 6: Ominous memories of midshipman cruise ... Brenda spots the American ships

Brenda repeated Paige's words to herself as she pushed the door open to exit the hotel: *See the ships from the top of the hill*; she could even hear Paige's Australian voice in her mind. She wasn't sure she wanted to be so lucky as to find her ship moored in the harbor. She was no longer a student arriving at school, or at a co-op/internship, where expectations mostly revolved around observation, learning, and performing small jobs and tasks for a mentor, under close supervision. The crossover from student to actual performer, in this case from a midshipman to an officer reporting aboard ship, was beginning to feel too threatening to grasp.

She remembered feeling relatively carefree when she reported aboard USS *Spruance* (DD-963) as a midshipman on summer cruise. Midshipman status, like student and co-op/intern status, included built-in leeway for lack of knowledge and experience, and included freedom to ask questions and to not know answers. She wondered what would be expected of her when she checked aboard her ship, the USS *Curtis Wilbur* (DDG-54), as a commissioned officer.

She couldn't shake the horrendous memories of the conditions onboard *Spruance* for its officers and crew. The leadership, or Command, onboard was cruel, and relied on a communication method comprised mostly of scattered rants and screaming. The second officer in command, the Executive Officer, or XO, was an incessant screamer with an edge that tore right through his officers. The crew was miserable. Her mentor on the *Spruance*, an ensign, worked 24/7 in port, and to what end or purpose, she couldn't discern; she had asked him several times why he needed to be onboard 24/7, and what his daily goals were, and he never could provide an answer. He had an apartment in Jacksonville, but he rarely left the ship. There seemed no resolution in sight for the issues onboard. The ship was aging; they were failing their equipment and readiness inspections by the day. She remembered the XO ranting in wardroom meetings, in his stateroom, in passageways, at officers call, everywhere. She observed how the junior officers onboard focused their time on avoiding getting in trouble with the XO, and circumventing "ass-chewings" and "flame-spraying," rather than engaging in any real management of their divisions. She felt badly for the officers and crew. But she took consolation in knowing that she was only a visitor on a six-week stint. Half of the junior officers, or JOs, insisted that not all ships were like the *Spruance*, and half insisted that *all* ships were like the *Spruance*.

Plus, she was seasick like she never could have imagined. Brenda shrugged off the seasickness memory as she stared down at the sidewalk. She had convinced herself that her seasickness was due only to the rare circumstance of a hurricane sortie. During her stay onboard *Spruance*, she had dedicated most of her days to writing observations in a journal. Later that fall, back in college, when the captain of her ROTC unit asked the senior class to write a weekly reflection about leadership, she relied on her cruise journal. She had pages of examples of negative leadership, instances of the XO chastising the crew in a demeaning and profane manner, and a pattern of life-threatening low morale and lack of motivation when the officers couldn't get the crew to take drills seriously. The attitudes all seemed to roll down from the XO at the top. Her journal entries and reflections had so impressed the captain, a former submarine commander, that he held them out as an example for the entire class and referred to her as one of his honor students. She felt a lot of pride, but at the same time, she also found her senior leadership journal frightening and foreboding. Not all ships were like that, the captain assured her.

Lost in her thoughts, Brenda hadn't stepped away from the hotel door. She looked around to find herself surrounded by the type of city neighborhood atmosphere she treasured. Even in her run-down condition, she managed a smile as she started up a steep, shaded, tree-lined street; her mind eased away from thoughts of midshipman cruise. She had one last reserve of energy that a combination of exotic travel and walking through a city could release in her. The worn but intricate and elegant architecture around her still retained its ability to relate the past history of this neighborhood. She imagined some sort of long past grandeur turned Bohemian. Colorful stately homes and historic brownstones from possibly the late 1800s or early 1900s filled each block. Tragically, she noticed the area had gone the way of many grand antique neighborhoods of the past. At some point in history people abandoned these homes, possibly to move to the suburbs. What was the catalyst in Australia's history, Brenda wondered, as she strolled farther uphill, concluding that Australia and the United States shared parallel histories in many ways. In Europe, people still lived city lives for the most part.

Suddenly, she realized she was walking within the heart of a red light district. The reason for the cabby's caginess regarding activities near the hotel, she gathered. What had happened here? She wanted to know. Brenda disregarded the X-rated advertisements and kept walking, recognizing the art-galleryesque neighborhood had much more than that to offer, in an architectural and artistic sense. When she reached the top of the hill, she discovered a cluster of naval ships. Australian ships or American ships, she couldn't tell from that distance. She pressed on towards the top of the hill until the silhouette of an American aircraft carrier became unmistakable, probably part of a battle group. *Incredible luck!* By chance, Brenda had found her destination. *Serendipity!* She stood with her hands over her chest, breathing in and out to calm her excitement. She had to hurry back to the hotel to tell Paige!

Brenda rushed through the lobby to find Paige, completely unable to distinguish among her emotions: relief, excitement, apprehension, and disappointment. "Your room's all set!" Paige called over from the office.

"Oh my God, I saw it! The aircraft carrier! It's American! I think my ship may be here!" She tugged on Paige's arm. "I'm trying to decide whether or not to change into my uniform and report right to the ship," she exclaimed, as Paige tried to hand Brenda her room key.

"I had your belongings brought up to your room. Listen to me, go and rest. At a later time, report refreshed, wearing a crisp uniform," Paige advised, leaning in towards Brenda, clasping each of her arms in empathy and with sincere hope in her voice.

"I'm afraid it could leave without me while I'm sleeping in my room! I don't know when it got here, or when it's leaving. But I'm unsure if I should report in this condition." How would she ever explain missing ship's movement? She could find herself facing dire consequences before she even reported in. Her arrival date to Sydney was well documented, she knew; and she was not sure how well her need to rest would be received as a valid excuse, especially since she had gathered from midshipman cruise and SWOS that the surface warfare officer community did not seem to value sleep. "You'll sleep when you die," she heard her midshipman cruise mentor repeat in her mind.

"Get some rest," Paige emphasized again. "They gave you a plane ticket and told you to make hotel reservations. Go it that way first."

"There's no choice. I have to do it. I have to report in. I can't chance the ship departing while I sleep, if it's even here."

Paige resigned. "Let me know if I can help you. I really wish you good luck, although I wish I could convince you to stay and rest," she smiled. "I can loan you a better iron for your uniform, if you need one."

"I do have one quick question. I was curious as to the history of this neighborhood. I mean, generally speaking." The question was important to Brenda; she was launching her shipboard career from here.

"My family's been here a few generations. There are many books on it. I'll give one to you. The history's closely tied to American and Australian servicemen."

"Tied to American servicemen looking for R&R?"

"Prior to the Second World War, it was a haven for thriving artists, theaters, cafes, intellectual and artistic activities of all kinds, avant-garde as you accurately deemed it. During World War II, the area was infiltrated by American servicemen, which sort of led towards the area's decline for a while."

"I'm not surprised such an inundation would have that effect," Brenda added regrettably.

"The influx of servicemen sparked an uptick in seedy nightclubs, strip clubs, the black market, rampant prostitution, you name it. A sort of 'Americanization' of the area, some call it. It recovered as an artistic center in the '50s, but a second wave of American servicemen on leave from Vietnam in the late '60s doomed the neighborhood into a stupor for quite a while. It's still trying to resurge. There have been a lot of efforts."

"The far reaching effects of wars, I guess. Thank you. I would like to read that book." The close of the conversation left Brenda to worry about more immediate matters, including weighing the consequences of resting, versus reporting to her ship in an all-out fatigued condition. Sleep deprived, she found it difficult to process a clear decision and map out her next move.

Chapter 7: Can't sleep now ... The wearing of the uniform

Brenda slid her room key into the lock and leaned her forehead against the door, savoring the sensation of resting her head against anything supportive, especially something cool. She rolled her head to the side to feel coolness on her cheek and temple. Gradually, she felt herself come back down from the high of spotting the U.S. aircraft carrier and battle group; and the impulse to report right in began to subside. Her eyes stung with pain. "I'm so tired," she repeated to herself as she breathed against the door, lightly gripping the doorknob. As her hand turned the knob, she regretted that she couldn't indulge her fantasy: drawing the curtains to darken the room before plunging into the hotel bed. Sleep would have to wait until after she checked aboard and returned to the hotel.

She opened the door to the hotel room and found it vintage small. Daylight seeped through partially closed curtains. And a desk lamp, left on for her she assumed, by whoever brought up her baggage, dully lit the back corner of the room. She judged that a few years had passed since the room was last renovated; but it was tidy and clean and retained a sense of the past. The room made her feel comfortable, she decided, as she walked towards the bed. It lacked the sterility of many modern hotel rooms.

She sat down on the bed, wishing she could lay down on it, wishing she had the courage to take Paige's advice and rest before reporting in. Maybe Paige possessed the kind of self-assurance that came from more experience in life. To Brenda, Paige seemed to reflect the kind of foundation a person developed after surviving success, failure, and loss, the kind of backing that enabled a person to communicate limits, explain decisions, and accept consequences. Instinctively, she knew she should rest, and report in when she was physically and mentally able. If the ship happened to leave that afternoon, she could calmly and professionally make a phone call, explain her actions, and coordinate alternate arrangements. However, she had no experience to go on; she feared her first impression; she feared getting in trouble and the consequences of veering off track. That, combined with all the eagerness of a person just starting out, left her with no other choice but to get dressed and report in.

She stood up from the bed and bent down next to her seabag; she carefully untied the cords at the top and started to lift it upright; but she had to grab onto the foot of the bed to right herself. Just bending down and attempting to stand back up made her dizzy. With her free hand she rummaged down through the tall narrow bag, knowing she had packed her white uniform somewhere near the top. At Surface Warfare Officers School, new ensigns were instructed to report to their first ships wearing whites. About a fourth of the way down her seabag, she felt polyester; she had found her white uniform. Everything on top of it, she threw to the floor in a pile.

Brenda carefully unfolded her Navy whites, laying them deliberately across the bed; she looked them over while rubbing her face to keep herself somewhat revived. She exhaled in relief when she saw the uniform had traveled well and retained a smart enough appearance for reporting in. She wasn't a fan of the look and feel of the 100% polyester material of the white uniform, but it had proved convenient under these circumstances; she had a virtually wrinkle free uniform after traveling across the world. She wondered if travel and convenience could actually have been the reason polyester material was used. Then she panicked that she might have forgotten to pack a uniform part. She nervously fished around for her white leather shoes, nylon white socks, white belt, brass belt buckle, undershirt, nametag, hard shoulder boards displaying her rank, and her cover (uniform hat), which she had all packed together in anticipation of reporting to the ship as soon as she arrived in Sydney.

Towards the bottom of her bag, she had packed other summer uniforms that she wouldn't need until later: an additional pair of summer whites, two pairs of summer khakis, and fifteen or so pairs of working khakis. All other winter uniforms she included as part of her separate household goods move to Japan. Unlike the Army, Air Force, and Marines, the Navy had multiple uniform varieties, which changed according to the context and the seasons. There were uniforms for office/shore environments, and different ones for shipboard environments. Dark navy blue uniforms were worn during the winter months, and khaki and white uniforms were worn during the summer months. Only working khakis were worn year round. Brenda hoped she had made the right decisions in packing, especially with the reversal of the seasons below the equator. The remainder of the deployment would be in tropical locales, so she figured she'd be okay.

After closing the top button on her blouse, she checked herself out in the mirror while she pinned her nametag over her right shirt pocket. She wore the uniform well in her judgment, even if she was tired. She nodded and congratulated herself. How in love she had been – since junior high school – with the whole idea of the military and being in the military! Now in real life, she saw herself the way she had dreamed, wearing the military uniform as an officer. A touch of something else resonated with her soul. Every time she wore the Navy uniform, she showed by example that women were also in the military defending their country. *And as officers no less!*

Brenda bent down and started sifting through the pile of clothes and books on the floor; she searched anxiously for her training notes and guidebooks; she wanted to review the protocol for reporting aboard her first ship one more time, so as not to miss an opportunity for a solid first impression. She picked up her *Watch Officer's Guide*, and opened it to the bookmarked chapter on "Honors and Ceremonies," which included a section describing the protocol for "coming onboard a ship." She reread the section, sitting cross-legged in her white uniform on the hotel floor. She remembered boarding and debarking protocol from midshipman cruise; and after reviewing the section, she felt reassured that she understood what to do.

Still sitting on the floor, she stared out the hotel window into an empty alleyway. The sight of the early 1900s brick masonry building opposite her window reminded her of the view out the window of her last apartment in Boston; her mind eased back to treasured walks through the streets of Boston during her study breaks. Walks through the city had always provided her with much needed solace before any stressful test or presentation. Scenes of past walks scrolled through her mind; she pictured the buildings, houses, people, sidewalks, and shade trees that she used to see. Allowing her mind to explore, it was on walks that her best ideas and dreams seemed to emerge. *I bet it's not even a half mile to the ships,* she concluded. *I'll walk.* Walking had always sorted things out for her.

Brenda removed her makeup from her toiletry bag, got up off the floor, and hurried to the mirror; she planned to cover up as much of her exhaustion as she could with makeup. She applied skin foundation, black eye liner, skin-toned eye shadow, and mascara. Then she tied her long brown hair back into a tight bun at the nape of her neck before leaving the room. Soon she found herself setting off, carrying her orders under her left arm in a black, professional looking folder, leaving her right hand open for saluting, according to custom. The shade of the mature trees in the neighborhood offered her peace and refuge as she walked. She focused on getting to her ship and fighting off uninvited nervous energy. This was everything she had worked for throughout her young life.

Chapter 8: The plight of the introvert ... ROTC warning signs ... Symbolic meanings along the way ... Brenda finds her ship

Brenda had not been aboard a Navy ship in almost two years, since stepping off the USS *Spruance* (DD-963) at Naval Station Mayport, Florida at the end of midshipman summer cruise. She headed up the sidewalk, thinking back to that summer, a time when she had been immersed in naval protocol, actually living it aboard ship. The masts of the American warships moored in Sydney Harbor began to peek into view as she walked uphill, but Brenda remained occupied by thoughts of summer cruise. For six weeks in Mayport, she boarded the ship, conducted herself in the wardroom, saluted the flag during colors, and interacted with all ranks onboard. She came a long way, militarily, during that time, she reminded herself. Her ability to conduct herself during midshipman cruise, aboard an active duty Navy ship, convinced her that she had what it took to embark on a successful five-year commission in the military (with the possibility of making it a career).

She needed that reassurance because in ROTC, she had encountered difficulty with many aspects of midshipman training. Learning and performing the nuances of drill and ceremony (D&C) had proved particularly challenging. She was embarrassingly awkward at drill, but she barely admitted it to herself. As a midshipman, she tried her best to blend into the marching formations, always nervous that she didn't maneuver herself within the formations quite right. After D&C sessions, her nerves were always shot. One semester, she volunteered for color guard with the hope that extra practice and instruction in drill would improve her marching skills. But at the start of the following semester, she decided not to rejoin color guard because the instructor and the midshipmen in charge never picked her for official color guard duties; and she had a sense that they did not want her back.

Each semester, she read and reread military drill manuals and rehearsed drill in her head; but she never could perform it as expected of a midshipman. She got by though, basically unnoticed, and she started skirting drill whenever she could. Drill was just one minor aspect of ROTC, she justified. And she told herself that once assigned to a ship in the "real Navy," she would never have to drill in any serious way, ever again.

So despite the difficulties she encountered in drill, and in other areas of the program, she pressed forward in ROTC. She continually reassured herself that hard work and studying would resolve her weaknesses. For four years, ROTC was a week by week, semester by semester struggle. Even though she recognized, at least on some level, that she was incompatible with most aspects of the program, she couldn't fully admit it to herself; such an admission would have meant letting go of her dream of serving in the military. So she trudged on in the program, through her freshman to senior years, ignoring her lack of ability as well as her lack of interest in the technical naval science courses, in military inspections, and in the extracurricular activities. She discounted the fact that she didn't fit in well with the other midshipmen. And, throughout, she remained utterly fascinated by the idea of the military.

She told herself that she had other more important attributes to offer the Navy. One in particular had for her trumped any doubts as to her fitness for the Navy. In ROTC, her strength had been academics, and Navy ROTC was academically focused. The program instructors touted an "Academics First" motto, which had resonated with her. The lieutenant advisors at the ROTC unit recognized her hard work and study in engineering, so they didn't bother her much about her midshipman military ranking. She ranked well academically, and poorly militarily, but she justified this too, arguing that engineering school required a tremendous amount of work and she had to put her schoolwork before ROTC activities. In her mind, the military ranking and evaluation as a midshipman were of little consequence; midshipman records went into the "circular file," the trash, after graduation. She remained focused on grades and achieving milestones on paper. Never once did she stop to consider the meaning behind her military ranking; she never felt warned that her low military ranking might have foreshadowed the future. She expected the active-duty Navy, the *real* Navy, to differ completely from the insignificant stuff she had to put up with in ROTC.

"Remember it's all just a game," her father used to say, referring to survival within the military. But that sentiment never sat quite right with her, and she never understood why she had difficulty responding to him whenever he repeated the phrase. She had some idea that she didn't want her career choice and chosen path in life to be minimized as a game. She aimed for a career that would make an impact and have larger meaning. She wanted to believe in what she worked at every day. There had to be more to life than task-oriented jobs, in which the tasks carried neither personal meaning, nor global meaning or purpose. Even when very young, she had begun to notice that actors, writers, musicians, and painters often continued their work well past the age of retirement. In contrast, many in other professions couldn't wait to retire.

Being an only child, she had spent her youth listening to adults – to her parents' friends, her grandparents' friends, cousins, etc. She never got bored listening to the adults while sitting around the house during gatherings with family and friends, at home or in others' homes, or in restaurants. She never asked to be excused early from the table to go play or to watch TV. In all of her listening, she heard a common theme: The adults found little or no meaning or fulfillment in the daily tasks of their jobs, or in the years of days they wished away until retirement. Brenda was searching for a way to be fully engaged, hoping to find as meaningful what she had undertaken and set out to accomplish. She chose to model her life and career around the Navy and engineering. She believed in the virtue of the military.

Brenda began to mentally rehearse the protocol for boarding a ship as she walked farther uphill. *"When reaching the...shipboard end of brow, face the national ensign, and render the salute...after which...salute the officer of the deck."* Okay, she thought as she continued up the sidewalk, recalling the exact verbiage from the *Watch Officer's Guide*. *"An officer coming onboard a ship to which he or she is not attached shall request permission to come onboard and shall state his or her business."* Okay, got it, I'll inform the inport officer of the deck (OOD) on the ship's quarterdeck that I am reporting aboard, and I'll show him or her my orders; salute the flag, salute the OOD, and request permission to come onboard, she repeated in her mind for her own sake.

Military protocols were often subtle, and personnel had to be on constant guard of every physical and spoken gesture within a given context. Military members also had to remain aware of where they went and in what uniform, who they passed by and where they could walk, both outdoors and indoors, according to rank and position. Blue floors, for example, were reserved for high ranking officers. She learned about blue floors from her Naval Academy classmates at SWOS when she tried to show them a quicker way out of the classroom building. "Follow me," she had declared, quite naively. "My leadership," she had joked. "If it's blue, it's not for you," one of the former Academy students had answered her, referring to blue floors as off limits to junior personnel. After a while and with experience, Brenda imagined that military protocol would come naturally to her and would no longer make her so nervous all the time. Around the base in Newport, she observed military personnel conducting themselves as if they'd been entrenched in this learned behavior since birth. Why should she be any different?

"Whoa, Ensign," a powerful male voice interrupted her thoughts. She stopped walking and looked up. In front of her on the sidewalk stood a tall lieutenant dressed in whites, his eyes obscured by aviator sunglasses. "Do you always blast past senior officers without saluting, Ensign? I ought to report this to your commanding officer," he declared indignantly.

Brenda had traveled so far inside of herself to rehearse checking aboard that it took her a moment to regain her surroundings. "I'm sorry, sir," she politely answered, gazing up at him. "I apologize for my mistake, sir," she repeated, as she calmly saluted him, squinting against the sun. He shook his head in disgust, jerked around, and continued walking, not bothering to return her salute. Was he even serious? Brenda asked herself. She glanced behind her down the sidewalk, and watched him as he disappeared into the hub of the red light district. Why would someone snub an apology for an obvious mistake, when no disrespect was intended? She felt as though she had experienced enough of naval culture to consider him out of line. Where was he headed in this neighborhood anyway? Here she was, trying to check onto her ship, half dead from exhaustion! She was the one trying to follow the rules and he was headed off, presumably, to an establishment in this neighborhood! How ironic, she rationalized. Then panic gripped her. *Oh my God*, she became deeply unsettled. Was he serious about reporting her? Was he on her ship? Had she ruined any chance for a solid first impression? She picked up her pace, rushing over the top of the hill, too tired to be rational, angry at the lieutenant for how he had treated her, and angry at herself for having allowed the situation to occur in the first place.

When she reached the bottom of the hill, she stood by herself for a while, facing the massive concrete piers, staring at the swarm of sailors in front of her. The piers were crowded with U.S. Navy personnel. There had to be thousands, Brenda observed, as she watched a steady stream of guys departing down the brows serving the aircraft carrier. Some were in uniform, but most wore military style civilian clothes. There was a certain look some of the military guys developed over time, she noticed. Besides the hair, it seemed to be the way they wore their jeans, belts, collared polo shirts, and shoes. Clean cut, but in some sort of military way that didn't convince her. A few blocks away, many of them would soon be sloppy drunk and entrenched in various bar scenes, ranging from the relatively benign to the nefarious. She wasn't any kind of moralist, by any means, but just a realist that clean cut didn't exactly mean anything.

She entered into the crowd, looking around for any sign of her ship, passing by various fast food and souvenir stands set up along the length of the pier. The entire carrier group appeared moored within Sydney Harbor. Some of the smaller ships, such as frigates and destroyers, were tied to the piers in nests, side by side. Brenda hoped someone on the pier would be able to tell her whether or not her ship was part of it all. Masts, antennas, and haze gray steel jutted out in every direction. She could barely stand her nerves, exhaustion, and Australia's summerlike heat in the white polyester uniform much longer.

Brenda approached one of the sentry stations along the pier. She returned the sentry's salute. "Hello," she greeted the young sailor, while overflowing with eagerness. "Do you know if the *Curtis Wilbur* is here, DDG-54?"

"No, ma'am, I'm sorry. I'm from the carrier, ma'am," he answered shyly, appearing shocked to be addressed. Seeing how uncomfortable she had made him, Brenda sympathized that she had taken him outside of his responsibility, which was to stand next to the podium in a sailors uniform and salute as required. Anything beyond that, no less involving officers, attached uncertainties with which he wasn't equipped to deal, she assumed. Besides, she nearly preferred that her question remain unanswered. That way she could sort of look forward to the possibility that her ship might not be there. Well no, she corrected herself, she wanted it to be there.

Brenda stood in front of the sailor, noticing his inability to make eye contact. Judging him to be about seventeen years old, she looked at him with empathy. "That's okay, Seaman," she said to him, as she spotted a binder sitting on top of his watch podium. "What about in your binder? Does it contain any info about what ships are here? Can I look at it?"

"Ma'am, it just contains the watch rotation. You can see here, ma'am," the seaman showed her, flinching a little as he edged the binder towards her.

Brenda closed her eyes for a second, feeling the adrenaline of fatigue and stress, resisting the temptation to slam the binder shut and walk off out of frustration. She reached back to massage a tight knot forming over her left shoulder blade, remembering what it was like a few minutes before to feel so low, powerless, and beneath another person. She didn't want to inflict the same stress and intimidation on the young seaman that the red light district lieutenant had just inflicted on her. If she did take out her anger on the seaman, it would only have been because, technically, her rank gave her the ability to get away with using another anonymous seaman, of which there were plenty, for the purpose of venting her own frustrations. During midshipman cruise, she witnessed the way in which the individuality and dignity of young sailors often got lost in the flow of the ship's work, and in the ambition of their superiors. Junior enlisted comprised the lowest of the low, especially if they had no rating, or occupational specialty. The youngest sailors were ripe pickings for officers, chiefs, and petty officers. Brenda relaxed her posture and tried to catch the seaman's eyes, "Good job, Seaman," she smiled. "You were helpful. Thank you." Most of the young enlisted sailors joined to escape home life, early influences, some isolated rural location, poverty, lack of education, or lack of direction. A vast majority enlisted from the South. She wondered how successful the Navy was in bringing out the potential in each individual. Did the military system work in that regard, in the majority of cases? In a Navy recruiting brochure, directed at parents, she had read, *"You gave them the values, we give them the opportunity."* Onboard her new ship, she expected to find out if there was any validity to that recruiting catchphrase.

"Thank you, ma'am," the seaman responded, as he pulled out another binder and looked through a few pages. She waited for him to finish with the second binder. "I appreciate you looking for me," she said, wanting the seaman to feel a sense of confidence that, at least in some small way, he had helped and contributed.

"No problem, ma'am. But I don't see a list of ships," he said.

"That's okay," she answered. "Have a good afternoon."

"Yes, ma'am," he replied, and went about his watch.

Already, between the lieutenant and the seaman, she felt many questions coming on. All that had happened since arriving in Sydney, and all that was said during her interactions with Paige, the red light district lieutenant, and the seaman, felt important and symbolic. Brenda had a natural tendency to internalize what she witnessed outside of herself. The nuances of people and events remained and stirred within her until she could adequately process the subjective meanings of them. Such was the orientation of the introvert versus the extravert...the inner-directed versus the outer-directed; searching for meaning through an inner process rather than concentrating interest solely on external objects and events. She understood that her introverted way of being – contentment in being by herself, analyzing and filtering events subjectively for meaning, and processing her feelings as a way of guiding her actions and conversations – resulted in an immanent and characteristic perspective that made others view her as "difficult," and sometimes aloof. She put people off at times without meaning to.

In contrast, her parents were more or less absorbed in the conventional, the mainstream, living lives that went along with the external events they felt subject to, often without question or challenge. In a clash of orientations, the unintended effects of Brenda's introversion made her mother roll her eyes and her father make some kind of judgmental "hmm" sound whenever she voiced her, often contrary, view of things. It was the extraverts who went to a party and enjoyed vacuous small talk, perfectly happy to glide the surface of events and relationships, seeking gratification from what was outside of the self. She had spent her life *trying* so hard to go along and to blend in as her parents did, forcing herself at times to say that she liked things that she didn't like, or to do things that she really didn't want to do. In her efforts to go along with things that subjugated her own wants – things that were incongruent with what she felt inside – she appeared awkward many times, because her *trying* tended to come across as forced and unnatural. She glanced over at the young seaman one more time before turning to walk away, hoping the best for him during his latter teenage years in the Navy.

She was surprised to learn that her presence, her rank in the Navy, had the power to intimidate other individuals, individuals who were young and much junior in rank. Couldn't the seaman see that she was only twenty-three years old? Through her own lens, the rank of ensign represented a nobody, someone young and green, starting out with no experience. In ROTC and SWOS, she had almost exclusively interacted with peers (other ensigns) and those senior to her. The few enlisted instructors at both places consisted of chiefs and senior petty officers who had long lost any sense of awe at officers. People made fun of ensigns! Ensigns goofed up! Practical jokes and tricks were played on ensigns! But that wasn't the way the seaman experienced an ensign, she realized. An officer's uniform with shoulder boards displaying a single gold bar had truly impacted this young sailor. In her young professional life, Brenda had never experienced an interaction where, by default, she was the higher-ranking person. She was more accustomed to feeling self-conscious as an ensign, like a little rookie kid who wanted to pass as just a bit older to measure up to those who had a few more years.

Everyone around us is our teacher in some way, she remembered a professor saying one afternoon in literature class; the young seaman and the red light district lieutenant as much as anyone else, she added for herself. The thought placed every individual on equal footing in her mind. Her status aboard ship was going to be something very new, and something she was sure she had done nothing to deserve. It was all too strange. At twenty-three and just out of college, she was going to be in charge of twenty or so experienced and specialized enlisted technicians, most of whom would probably be older than her. What other employer would put a recent college graduate – with no experience – in charge as a manager and leader?

Brenda shouldered her way through the crowd, looking for hull number DDG-54. Although she hadn't yet reported aboard her ship, she had an awakening sense that a painful path of discovery lay ahead – one which would include the intrapersonal as well as environmental spheres. As she walked, she returned the salutes of two female petty officers headed towards the pier gates. She was tired, but a moment later she realized that the women could have been from the *Curtis Wilbur*. She looked back to find them in the crowd; maybe they could have told her where the *Curtis Wilbur* was moored, but she saw that they were already out of earshot. So she continued forcing and plowing herself against the general flow of the crowd, which tended in the opposite direction through the pier gates to liberty.

As Brenda walked past the aircraft carrier, she noticed that the wings of the aircraft parked on deck were folded up to conserve deck space; she had never seen that except in photos. She made her way toward the edge of the pier to avoid the bulk of the crowd. The carrier and its aircraft barely held a second of her curiosity. Forget this thing about the seaman and the red light district lieutenant, she chastised herself. Where was she? In literature class analyzing characters in a novel? Why did she always have to search into everyone and every event in that way? She was supposed to be entering the real world! Living in and for literature was for people looking to "find themselves" or something maudlin like that…far outside the real world, she decided. That a connection existed between some theme from literature class and real life experience, well, there was just no way. Or that there was some practical purpose to literature! Those classes she enjoyed, but please, they revolved around abstractions for academia's sake. Good for professors sitting in a discussion salon with a group of students! Then what? "Wait until they get into the real world," she could hear her father saying with a sarcastic edge. Sometimes the pronoun "you" would replace "they" depending on the conversation. He or she's not living in the real world, her mother would piggyback. Being a kid, Brenda felt eager to agree with and to please her parents. She ignored her own instincts because she thought her parents were right in everything. If she sensed herself being seen as difficult, she immediately backed off and went with the flow. Maybe it was a child's survival. *The real world!* Brenda felt her shoulders tighten with nervous tension. How she hated that phrase! What comprised the real world and whose world was the one that was unreal? Mentally, there was nowhere for her to go to retreat from her father's sarcasm…recently her father had commented that the military wasn't the "real world" either.

Brenda took a few steps aside from one of the bollards on the pier, remembering from SWOS not to stand in the direct path of any mooring line that secured a ship to a pier, for safety reasons. She drifted over to one afternoon in Spain, in the setting of her Twentieth Century Spanish American Literature class. The students had just arranged the desks back into rows from a discussion circle. In her mind, she could see the professor's desk, and in front, a student desk on which sat a stack of corrected essays. The classroom building dated back to the seventeenth century, stereotypically beautiful in the way one would imagine Spain. As the students filed out of the classroom, they collected their corrected essays before disappearing out the door. No one had yet received an A that Brenda could see. She couldn't wait to retrieve her essay and see her grade and the professor's comments. Yes! She had gotten that A!, she saw, when she collected hers. She approached the professor, knowing he held an undergraduate degree in engineering from a university in Peru. "How could you have ever switched from engineering to studying literature?" she asked him. "Literature is so impractical. Nothing tangible emerges from it. You can't do anything with it. You can't get a job in it besides teaching college," she said to him.

Brenda stared straight into the aircraft carrier's gray hull, nearly losing all awareness of the pier and the sailors passing her by. She recalled the literature professor's answer, some kind of deep and meaningful BS about literature teaching him about himself and his life. He was Peruvian, but his father was a diplomat, so he had grown up all over the world and he was searching for his identity. "Busco mi identidad," he used to say. Whatever! Really! She had received an A on her essay analyzing the dentist in *Un día de estos*, a short story written by her most cherished author, Gabriel García Márquez. Her father was right, she determined – teaching college wasn't the "real world," and you had to become a "professional student" to get to that point.

*

In front of the aircraft carrier, Brenda cupped her hands and covered her face, so she could smile outwardly to match her thoughts: How she had loved studying Spanish and South American short stories, plays, and novels for her minor in college. The more abstract and obscure the characters, settings, and time/space relationship, the more she delved in, and with relative ease of understanding. She especially savored stories including elements of the fantastic, *lo fantástico*, set in some illusory world. Then she reminded herself why she had taken those classes. Those Spanish classes were so easy for her, and really helped to bring up her GPA from the engineering classes; and maybe Spanish would help her get a job someday.

Under the heavy sun, Brenda lifted her cover slightly above her head and pushed her bangs back underneath. She stood among thousands of people, or rather thousands of males. Her ship may have been the only one fitted for women in the entire battle group. The carrier had an all-male crew, she knew for sure. That thought made her want to be seen in her uniform. She pulled the polyester uniform from her sweaty skin in a few spots, and approached two second class petty officers wearing shore patrol badges. "Excuse me, Petty Officers, do you know if *Curtis Wilbur* DDG-54 is here?"

"Nope, sorry, ma'am," one of the petty officers responded after saluting her, but really he barely acknowledged her. He continued a few more steps before twirling back around. "Oh wait, ma'am, my good shipmate here says *Curtis Wilbur* is nested to the *John S.*

McCain, uh, DDG-56." *Serendipity strikes again!* "Thanks so much to you both!" Brenda exclaimed, feeling a lift from adrenaline.

Not much farther down the pier, she spotted "DDG-56" written across a banner hanging from the brow of a destroyer. *Eureka! Good job, Brenda!* she congratulated herself. In the past five hours she had landed in Sydney, Australia, found her hotel, met another Navy woman, and happened upon the American carrier group containing her ship.

Chapter 9: Boarding *Curtis Wilbur* ... Freedom suppressed ... A new boss, a new home, a new gunnery officer

Brenda tried to catch a glimpse of her new ship, the *Curtis Wilbur*, from where she stood, but the *John S. McCain* blocked her view. The *Curtis Wilbur* was nested outboard of the *John S. McCain* (moored directly to the *John S. McCain* rather than the pier); and since both ships were DDGs, or Arleigh Burke class guided missile destroyers, their silhouettes aligned. A group of male officers passed to the side of her. They were at enough of a distance that she didn't have to worry about saluting them, but she squinted against the sun to notice their ranks regardless. They were her peers, by rank, and they were too busy chatting amongst themselves to notice her or anyone else.

As she raised her hand to her forehead to shade her eyes and face, she noted for the first time, as she watched the male officers walk down the pier, that the male uniform cap (or *cover*, as she had learned to call it as a midshipman) was functional, unlike the female uniform cover. The male cover actually shaded their eyes and faces. She envied the male uniform. It flattered the male figure, and enhanced the notion of male military handsomeness. The male uniform had developed out of functionality and ceremony. But the design concept behind the female uniform seemed rather a mystery. The female uniform was some sort of unfeminine and unflattering bastardization of the male uniform, an impractical copy. The general design theme was "no curves," straight and dowdy, with pleated chest. The women's cover – an inverted bucket design with an artificial, non-functioning brim – didn't shade a woman's face or eyes. Where did the Navy come up with the inverted bucket idea? She doubted that particular design existed anywhere else in fashion, in any form, in any era, in any other part of the world. But the men's uniform and cover flattered them, she thought, as she watched the group of young officers stroll down the pier. They looked as though they were off to hit the town, reminiscent of some Hollywood WWII era film. Why did the women's uniform have to "de-flatter" and unfeminize?

Regardless of the style of their uniforms, military women put them on and wore them as they were taught to do at the Naval Academy, ROTC, OCS, or boot camp. Over time the uniforms came to seem normal. Brenda hadn't heard anyone comment too much about them. All Navy personnel – men and women, officer and enlisted – had to buy the prescribed uniforms at the Navy Exchange (NEX) uniform shop. The enlisted received an annual clothing allowance, and officers were responsible for buying their own uniforms. But with no choice in what to buy, and with over three hundred thousand of one's Navy peers dressed similarly, it all seemed normal.

It was time to board USS *John S. McCain* (DDG-56), cross over it, and report aboard USS *Curtis Wilbur* (DDG-54). Brenda took one last glance at downtown Sydney, and then she started up the *John S. McCain*'s steep brow. Three quarters of the way up, she stopped, faced aft, and saluted the *John S. McCain*'s ensign (the ship's American flag). Then she walked a few more steps to the top. At the top of the brow, she stood at attention, saluted the officer of the deck, and stated, "Request permission to come onboard."

The senior chief petty officer (E-8) standing the OOD watch barely acknowledged her. "Granted, ma'am," he answered as he returned her salute, and then he turned away. Brenda walked towards the podium on the quarterdeck, relieved that the senior chief had not given her a second thought or look. His casual reaction to her meant that she hadn't done anything wrong or out of place.

She set her folder down on the podium. "Senior Chief, I'm actually here to report aboard *Curtis Wilbur*," she began to inquire.

"Then keep walking, ma'am," he clipped, pointing to starboard towards her ship, before turning back to his previous conversation with another watchstander. *Well*, Brenda thought, as she walked starboard, between the *John S. McCain*'s gigantic exhaust stacks, a distinguishing feature of Arleigh Burke class destroyers, *this may be a moment the senior chief doesn't much care about, but to me it's huge.*

She then stepped off the decks of the *John S. McCain* and onto the brow of the *Curtis Wilbur. Her ship!* The brow, which bridged the ships at a slight incline, looked to be about ten feet across. Now, she told herself, she had to face the challenge of checking aboard and integrating herself into ship's company. As she walked farther across the brow of the *Curtis Wilbur*, the start of her professional career began to feel okay. But the stench from beneath her feet drew her attention down to the water sloshing below, between the two ships. Through the metal slats of the brow, she could see the ship's waterline, about twenty feet below her; the water was white, thick with jellyfish.

And there was that ship smell. That mix of diesel, oil, paint, and machinery that she remembered from midshipman cruise. Even pleasure cruise ships had that smell. *Ship sounds, ship smells.* Mixed with the smell was always the hum of machinery – auxiliary equipment and shipboard fans. The sounds of the *John S. McCain* and the *Curtis Wilbur* had overtaken the sounds of Sydney, of normal life and civilization. She could also hear the clanging of deckhands chipping paint.

In front of her, the *Curtis Wilbur*'s quarterdeck appeared professional and official. A first class petty officer (E-6), a third class petty officer (E-4), and a seaman (E-3), all dressed in whites, stood beneath a canopy, chatting away. The OOD, the first class petty officer, was leaning forward against the podium. The quarterdeck of a naval ship was the ship's showcase and gateway, serving both ceremonial and practical functions. Three quarters of the way across the brow, Brenda stopped and saluted the flag, and then she walked to the top of the brow. "I request permission to come onboard," she stated as she saluted. She stood at attention, and held her military ID card.

"Granted, ma'am," responded the first class petty officer, as he returned her salute.

Brenda stepped off the brow and onto her ship, understanding that this – her first step – symbolized the suppression of her personal freedom, and the end of any kind of shore-based life. The Navy, and all of its restrictions, was something she had chosen, she guessed...the culmination of all she had striven for in high school and college; *Of all of those nights and weekends studying engineering like mad!*

As she walked farther onto the quarterdeck, Brenda's initial excitement was being overtaken by feelings of hesitation. Momentarily, she began to see her goals in different terms; she could feel her perspective changing as her goals were now becoming reality. She began to wonder if her independent spirit had landed her in a place, and in circumstances, where that same spirit might not be tolerated. But no way, she thought. Her "against the grain" character and fiery young ambition were the very qualities that had enabled her to work against tradition and overcome gender restrictions to get here. She walked across the plastic mat covering the metal deck, which displayed the ship's official seal. Then she neared the podium and leaned in as she began her introduction, "Hello, I'm Ensign Conner. I'm reporting onboard. I have my orders right here." She opened her folder and removed her orders. She did it. She was reporting onboard.

"Welcome aboard, ma'am," the first class petty officer responded. And Brenda knew that her time on her first ship had started, officially. "Mr. Lineberry left a note in the OOD binder that a new ensign might check aboard this week in Sydney. You'll be the new gunnery officer, I believe, ma'am." Hearing that her arrival was loosely expected, Brenda understood that Paige had been right; she should have rested first.

But he said gunnery officer, not communications officer. "Oh no, no, that must be for someone else, a mistake. I'm slated to be the communications officer," she answered. Brenda smiled as she clasped her hands behind her back, waiting in anticipation for the petty officer to call her sponsor, Pete Lineberry. "Thanks so much for your help," she said to the watch team, jarred, but not too surprised to learn that she might end up in a completely different shipboard job. At this point, she guessed she had to prepare herself to take on whatever came her way.

"Lieutenant (j.g.) Lineberry is the gunnery officer?" Brenda asked, trying to appear casual.

"Yes, ma'am, and the strike officer," the first class petty officer answered. "Stand by, ma'am. I'll call him for you." Brenda nodded and smiled, wondering if her face gave away the wariness she felt inside. Her mother always told her that her face was a dead giveaway, and she assumed it was true. The petty officer stepped into a small closet behind a heavy oval shipboard door. Curious, Brenda peeked inside. She saw shelves overloaded with binders, stacks of plastic laminated sheets, and boxes of grease pencils. She would be standing this watch someday soon, she knew. OOD inport would probably be the first watch for which she would qualify. All of the binders and laminated checklists she saw represented shipboard procedures – divers over the side, personnel working aloft, etc. She thought of the understanding required of the OOD, and the strict coordination necessary between shipboard departments to ensure that procedures remained safe and did not conflict. The OOD watch was responsible for carrying out the ship's plan of the day (POD), and the coordination involved meant sailors' lives and maintenance of readiness.

Long Way Out

As Brenda waited for her shipboard sponsor, the friendly demeanor of the petty officers relieved some of her nerves. She related back to midshipman cruise, recalling how the crew had welcomed both her and the other female midshipman onboard the all-male USS *Spruance*. The petty officers always seemed willing to explain their jobs onboard and to help. She never experienced any disrespect first hand. Behind the scenes, who knew? She was sure the ranks were mixed with those who were for or against the presence of women. Society was changing, and sexual harassment and awareness training was prevalent everywhere.

In moments, Brenda was greeted by her sponsor. "Hello, I'm Pete. Welcome aboard!"

Brenda breathed a sigh of relief the moment Pete appeared on the quarterdeck. She immediately sensed a positive and welcoming nature in his manner and appearance; however, from her encounter with the red light district lieutenant, she felt hypersensitive about saluting. "I'm Brenda. It's nice to finally meet you in person," she answered, as she began to salute him. When in doubt, salute, she remembered learning in ROTC.

"No, no," Pete waved her off. "Please, you never have to salute me, or any other lieutenant (j.g.) onboard for that matter." He offered his hand to shake instead. He appeared tall and studious in a technical sort of way, very book smart. "I'm relieved you're finally here, good, good," he went on, his gestures underlining the goodwill behind his words.

"Yes, I'm here. I'm pretty exhausted, going on something like forty-five hours without sleep," Brenda spoke enthusiastically. In a split second, she decided against relating her arrival saga. They'd all probably been through something similar, and who really wanted to hear it? "It was a long drawn out thing, but I'm here now and looking forward to checking in," she said, sensing that Pete had somewhere to be. "Great! So will I be relieving you?" she asked, fishing for information based on the comments by the officer of the deck.

"Yes! You'll be relieving me. I'm very glad you're here," he emphasized with a quick nod.

"So you're the communications officer, right?" she asked, attempting humor to further break the ice. She realized that she was fast beginning to live the many stories she had heard in SWOS, about arriving to a ship anticipating one job, and being thrown into another.

"I bet that's what your orders said," Pete answered, taking a few seconds to get over his amusement. Then he pointed, "Did they send you to a follow-on school for COMMO?"

"Yes, I can see how that's funny," Brenda replied.

Pete began to gesture as if giving her the blessing of the Church. "Congratulations! Ensign Conner, you are hereby designated the gunnery officer."

"Great," Brenda responded, not sure what her new job as gunnery officer would entail – small arms, big guns, missiles? She glanced at the petty officers, who seemed to be enjoying the exchange.

"We're short on officers," Pete continued in his crisp speech. Brenda noticed that he had a habit of leaning forward and riding up onto his toes. "I'm currently running two divisions. CO division has fourteen gunners mates and two chiefs, and CM division has ten fire controlmen and two chiefs."

"So, I'll be taking over CO Division, the gunnery division, despite my orders," she replied. It was a disappointment because she had looked forward to her billet as the communications officer (COMMO). It had seemed like the one job onboard at which she might have done well. Missiles, guns, and small arms! She couldn't believe this was happening.

"Standby," Pete answered. "These sorts of changes occur all the time. Six months ago I was the deck officer, but I was originally slated to be COMMO."

"Sure, I understand," Brenda nodded, suddenly feeling skeptical about immersing herself in the surface warfare officer (SWO) career path. She imagined the constant job rotation left all SWO officers, both junior and midlevel, in a constant state of training throughout their careers. The system was designed to prepare *every* officer for command at sea, i.e., to captain their own ship after experiencing every shipboard job. But most junior officers (some 83%!) resigned their commissions after their four- or five-year scholarship commitment expired, years away from ever captaining their own ship. Likewise, few midlevel career officers ever advanced to commanding a ship. Brenda wondered how officers who stayed in the Navy as a career could strive beyond high-level amateurism when switching jobs so often, no matter how bright they might have been. Officers served as leaders, managers, and generalists, but she worried such a short time in one position would barely allow her feet to get wet. She longed to discover the thing she was good at, so she could embark on a lifelong focus, and build upon a solid foundation. The SWO career path impressed her as a jack-of-all-trades concept, where one never developed depth.

As a division officer, she hoped to grow her resourcefulness as a professional. Even though she was young, she hoped that she would intuitively understand how to utilize the knowledge of her chiefs and enlisted technicians to manage her division. She would be expected to learn her job as she went along from the highly trained and experienced enlisted technicians who worked for her. The Navy made a hard sell of the opportunity for young college graduates to develop leadership and management skills at such a young age, marketing that concept extremely well. But Brenda expected she would be leading and managing on shaky ground, due to her lack of experience. And learning she would become the ship's gunnery officer in a matter of days was a shock she hadn't expected.

"Officers are constantly transferred between billets, so you'll never know what job you'll be doing next," Pete added with a quick wave of his hand. "It's all a big surprise!"

"Sure, yes," Brenda responded cautiously. At the same time, she tried to look as if the gunnery officer news hadn't fazed her in the least.

"Why don't you follow me up to the wardroom for a meeting starting in about ten minutes, and I'll introduce you to everyone," Pete offered. *Incredible!* Events were already set into motion, and she could already sense the pace.

"Sounds good," Brenda consented. She looked at the petty officers and seaman manning the OOD watch. "Thank you both for your help in checking in."

"No problem, ma'am. Welcome aboard," they all answered. Brenda followed Pete as he headed towards an oval metal door leading inside the skin of the ship. As she entered a covered area on the port side confining a fog of cigarette smoke, Pete swung the outside handle of the gray door to the left to open it. Brenda stepped through the door, and swung the inside handle back to the right to firmly secure it. From midshipman cruise, she knew how to open and close the doors, and she remembered as well to lift her feet over the steel door frame to avoid black and blue shins.

"You'll be in charge of the 5-inch/54-caliber gun on the bow, the forward and aft Mark 41 missile VLS Vertical Launching System, the .50-caliber machine guns, all of the small arms, and the ammunition administration program," Pete explained as he walked. "Ammo admin is the fun part; it's a thing of high visibility for the

Command and will take up most of your time as a division officer." Brenda followed Pete up a ladder; her thoughts immediately focused on the two chiefs he had mentioned. How she hoped for strong chiefs to help run the gunnery division.

"How are the two chief gunners mates, the GMCs?" Brenda asked. Wrapped in a tired haze, she obliviously followed Pete through the fluorescent lit shipboard passageways. Sounds from mechanical equipment and from air shafts filled the spaces; the lighting made her eyes feel weird. She felt sure the outside world no longer existed for her; she had totally enclosed herself and cut herself off.

"You'll have Chief Dering, the GMG guns chief, and Chief Walden, the GMM missiles chief. They both have over twenty years in, and both are looking forward to retirement. They're frustrated, but remember, they still need to do their jobs."

"Frustrated with...?"

"Frustrated with the system overall and waiting to retire," Pete answered. "CASREPs were sent out on the VLS, CIWS, and the 5-inch/54-caliber gun over three months ago, which means all three weapons systems have been down, completely broken and inoperable. CASREP, by the way, is short for casualty report. If a system goes down, a casualty report is sent out over the Navy message system, so we say the broken system is CASREP'd."

"Okay," was all Brenda could come up with. Her experience during these first ten minutes or so onboard confirmed all of her perceptions from midshipman cruise, in addition to every sea story she'd heard during SWOS. Brenda took in a deep breath of ship's air, tasting paint, oil, and diesel fumes. All she knew was that she would soon be the gunnery officer, and she was the very one who had put herself there. A gunnery officer in charge of an array of broken weapons systems...it's going to be a challenge, Brenda thought. Pete impressed her as a very technical person, able to delve into the mechanical and electronic details. She had no idea yet how she would fare managing that process or the enlisted technicians.

"What's your degree in?" Pete asked, as he led her through a normal looking, non-watertight door displaying a brass plaque engraved *"Officers Country,"* an area of the ship off limits to the crew unless on official business.

"Mechanical engineering."

"Oh, then you'll have no problem getting up to speed with the mechanics of the gun and missile systems; you'll be all set," he said.

"Sure," she answered, trying to sound convincing. Pete had delivered his last statement with such casual and unquestioning surety; she hoped she wouldn't let everyone down. "Well, is it a matter of getting repair parts while deployed, or...?" she asked.

"Nope, we have no idea of the cause," Pete answered, opening the door to the wardroom. Inside, a large dining table occupied most of the room. A few vinyl couches, blue fabric armchairs, and end tables were positioned against the back wall. Brenda followed Pete across the room to take a seat; she noticed that the lamp on the end table next to her was bolted down for sea. Next to the lamp lay a few copies of *Proceedings*, a professional naval magazine dedicated to discussion of sea power. Paintings that depicted naval destroyers, dramatically steaming into harm's way with guns blazing in glory, dotted the wall behind her. Behind the Captain's chair hung a print of the *Curtis Wilbur* at full speed, leaving a ferocious white wake behind her. Above the print of the ship, a portrait of Curtis Wilbur the man overlooked the wardroom. His portrayal looked reminiscent of the 1930s-40s style portraits, idealizing the subject as bold and dignified. Brenda remembered reading in the ship's brochure that Curtis Wilbur was Secretary of the Navy under President Calvin Coolidge.

Pete introduced her to a few people sitting and standing around them while officers, chiefs, and a few first classes settled down for the meeting. As tired as she was, she knew she would never recall the details of those she met, but she felt reassured by the open friendliness with which she was received. "Ah, you're the new GUNNO, welcome aboard!" seemed to be the going response, and each time she agreed that she was the new GUNNO. One officer across the room even referred to her as Gunz as he waved. An anticipatory mood hung over the room as everyone laughed and chatted. Much of the laughter and chatter seemed overly animated yet cautious, a sign of people who were on edge, Brenda surmised. She tried to shrug off her senses, returning brief smiles and hellos in response to quick introductions.

Suddenly, everyone in the capacity wardroom rose to their feet. Brenda followed, not able to see over or between anyone. "At ease, at ease, folks," she heard, assuming it must have been the Captain speaking. When everyone sat back down, Brenda stared at his unusually short height, same as her, 5'3". As he spoke about the Australian port visit, she scanned the room. The Captain's humor prompted nervous chuckles and tight smiles. And Brenda realized that she too had her own gestures and reflections under strict control.

At the close of the meeting, Brenda followed Pete and the crowd out of the wardroom. "Psst...hey," she heard from behind. "Don't wear your cover inside the wardroom!" *Totally mortified! Shocked!* She felt her face blush bright red! "Excuse me," she responded, removing her cover. "I'm so exhausted from the trip here." I know better than that! she chastised herself. She was familiar with cover protocol in a wardroom from both ROTC and midshipman cruise. It was one of the few behaviors she assumed had been embedded into her movements and reactions.

"Don't give it a second thought," Pete turned back to reassure her.

"Ah...covers in the wardroom, you should buy us all dinner," she heard a lieutenant exclaim from across the room, the same one who had called her Gunz. Her sense of humiliation heightened, all over a custom with which she was already familiar. Outwardly, she smiled in an attempt to shrug off her negligence to her overtired condition. She bolstered herself that these types of protocols would soon be automatic. But for now she was left feeling on edge, knowing it was the seemingly unimportant subtle things that added up in people's minds.

"Let's go, I'll introduce you to our department head, the weapons officer," Pete offered, without showing any interest in the event involving her cover. She followed him out of the wardroom and into the passageway.

"XO coming through!" someone exclaimed. Everyone plastered themselves against the sides of the passageway bulkheads (walls) to make room for him to pass. "XO, XO," she heard various officers acknowledge him eagerly, propped up against the walls, as if grappling for every second of facetime they could muster. Brenda imagined it must have been something to have people prop themselves up against walls at your mere presence. It must happen all day and night wherever he walks on the ship, she thought. As soon as the XO passed, everyone went about their normal business. The experience left her feeling like a trespasser in some obscure subculture; she had to change herself to fit into this environment. Brenda followed Pete to their department head's stateroom. Just two quick left turns out of the wardroom, his stateroom was the first one on the left hand side of the passageway.

"WEPS, this is Brenda Conner, our new gunnery officer," Pete introduced her.

WEPS was sifting through a stack of papers. "Hello, Brenda, welcome aboard," he greeted her as he glanced up.

"Hello, sir, it's nice to meet you." Brenda purposefully looked her new boss in the eye and returned a firm handshake, surprised by her ability to recompose so quickly after the cover incident in the wardroom. Two racks filled the back three quarters of his narrow stateroom. The bottom rack was covered with strictly organized piles of manila folders. He used the top one for his bed.

"Well, GUNNO, we'll be in Sydney for five days," he started. *GUNNO! Oh my God! I'm speaking with my first real boss, the weapons officer!*

"Yes, sir," she answered, noting he was tall, rail-thin, and bookish looking, with gold wire-rimmed glasses that matched his sandy hair. His speech sounded wispy and uncommonly rapid.

"It would probably be best if you go out and enjoy Sydney." He stopped to look at her. "And get some sleep. Don't worry about duty, turnover, or getting up to speed on anything just yet. Have a good time and I'll see you when we get back underway."

Brenda couldn't believe it! The chance to explore Sydney on her own for five whole days! "Are you sure, sir? I can start turnover now or take care of any admin issues," she offered. Brenda looked around at the shipboard-like features of the stateroom, conscious of her overly-developed need to appear eager. The shelves were designed with lips at the ends to prevent items from falling during rough seas; hooks stuck up from the floor to chain loose furniture down. WEPS' collection of books was strapped down securely within his bookshelves. She wanted more than anything to show WEPS how hard she planned to work, and that she would dedicate herself to the department. She couldn't bear to let anyone down, including herself.

WEPS nodded, and closed his eyes for a brief second. "We'll get started when we get back underway, Brenda." And in his gesture, she saw that he acknowledged the sentiment behind her offer to start working. In that moment, she decided she liked WEPS. He continued, "I plan on taking a few days of leave while we're here. My wife lives in San Diego and I haven't seen her in months."

"Yes, sir," Brenda responded. Inside, she questioned if she really could enjoy her free time in Sydney, taking into account all of the uncertainty that lay ahead. Brenda imagined herself walking the city streets of Sydney, obsessing the hours until she had to report back to the ship.

"And Pete will be meeting his wife, too," WEPS continued. As Brenda listened to WEPS, she experienced her first taste of how people in the Navy lived. Their families flew in and out of exotic locales to see them; it all started to seem less exotic actually.

"It was nice to meet you, sir. Do you need me to check in with you at all this week?"

"No, just keep track of the ship's schedule; it's extremely fluid. Keep in touch with the command duty officer, the CDO, or the OOD on the quarterdeck."

"Absolutely, sir. I look forward to getting started when we get underway."

"Get here okay and everything?"

Brenda could tell he was preoccupied and merely asked out of courtesy, so she didn't elaborate. "Yes, sir."

"I look forward to working with you, Brenda. You look as though you haven't slept; you'll be a good SWO. And you don't have to call me sir all the time," he added with a split second smile.

"Okay, WEPS," Brenda responded using his title nickname, in an effort to remain compliant with his request and within the realm of acceptable protocol. She figured she was too new for anything else. Protocols impressed her as an edgy game, and she feared stepping outside of the rules.

"See you later," WEPS said, and then he looked back down and continued sifting through his stack of papers.

"Yes, thank you, WEPS," Brenda said, before following Pete out of his stateroom. They turned left and walked to the end of the passageway. "The last stateroom on the right in front of the women's head will be yours," Pete explained. "Most of the officers live in this passageway in little stateroom cabins." He stretched his arms out. "It's just like summer camp!" Pete's whimsical style of humor placed Brenda at ease. At least she could turn over (i.e., receive instruction and information on her new job, and in a week or so take over the job) with someone approachable, and for that she felt fortunate.

"I never liked summer camp," Brenda responded, half joking, half serious. By nature she was withdrawn and solitary. Anything like camp meant a controlled environment, which she hated. It also meant forced socialization. She never did well in groups or belonged to a particular clique in school, college, or anywhere. While still in high school, she purposefully selected a university weak in sports, fraternities, and sororities. She wasn't a joiner. She preferred to be on her own, doing her own thing.

"In the Navy you even get to sleep in bunks and have a roommate," Pete continued. I haven't had a roommate since freshman year, Brenda thought. Suitemates or apartment-mates were fine, just not sharing the same bedroom. "You'll share the stateroom with Julie, the first lieutenant in charge of deck division. She's another ensign who's been onboard for about three or four months." He pointed to the female head. "The female head is right here with a shower, toilet, and sink. There's one other female officer onboard, a lieutenant supply officer, which means she's a department head."

Pete gave Brenda's stateroom door three knocks. "No answer from Julie. Why don't you open the door, Brenda."

Brenda opened the door slowly, introduced to her new quarters for the first time. "Wow, this is huge," she exclaimed. The space far exceeded her expectations. It wasn't like the "JO jungle" staterooms of larger ships, in which six or more ensigns and lieutenant (j.g.)'s shared one stateroom. "Well, I see Julie's taken the bottom rack. I don't mind the top rack; that's where I slept on midshipman cruise." Brenda focused on some postcards taped to the wall cabinets on the right side. "I guess my side is the left side," Brenda said, "and the cabinet space, it's unbelievable," she added as Pete waited at the door.

Julie's tightly made rack and organization of her belongings appeared institutional. Brenda turned back to Pete, "Did Julie go to the Naval Academy? It looks very Naval Academy-like in here, not like a former college dorm dweller."

"Yes, she did," Pete answered. "And she played on the women's varsity basketball team."

"Yes, I can see that," Brenda answered, spotting a few team pictures taped inside Julie's cubbyhole desk. Other pictures showed a person made happy by the presence of family and friends.

"So, did your wife make it in?"

"She's arriving in Sydney today. She changed her reservations when we learned the ship was going to be delayed a few days."

"Are you staying at the hotel in King's Cross as originally planned?"

"No, we'll be staying in downtown Sydney."

Not in the red light district? Brenda held her tongue. "I like that hotel actually, and the surrounding neighborhood." She was no longer fazed that no one had left a message for her at the hotel desk;

she had last communicated with Pete by letter before graduating from SWOS. She had tried to call the ship several times before leaving Newport, but she had never gotten through. The ship was always underway, and phone lines were only available to ships when in port. Every time she dialed the ship's number from Newport, she had felt so nervous. The ship's non-availability due to being underway always came as a relief.

"Enjoy your time with your wife, Pete. I'll figure everything else out. There're enough people around if I need any help, and thank you. See you when we get underway."

"If you need anything, you know where to find me," Pete said. "The quarterdeck will have my hotel information." And with that, Pete left her alone in the stateroom.

Brenda scribbled a quick note to Julie and left it on her desk, *"Hi Julie, It's your new roommate Brenda. I just checked in this morning, and I'll probably see you sometime tomorrow. Look forward to meeting you! Brenda."*

The temptation of sleep lured Brenda; how she wanted to curl up into her new top rack, still wearing her whites. The ship's hum of machinery and fans was quiet and mesmerizing. But a quiet hotel room awaited her for the night and she knew, that once she lay down, it would be a long time before she would wake up. Now, she just needed to find her way off the ship and to a cab on the pier.

Chapter 10: Brenda comes undone ... SWO culture ... The cost of ignoring the warnings

Brenda arrived back at her hotel room and allowed herself to give in to her feelings of dread. After her glimpse of life and work aboard the ship, *she dreaded the next four years of her life!*

She stepped inside the room and closed the door behind her. In her wiped-out condition, she could barely control her anguish over what she had gotten herself into. *Pete telling her that she was going to be the gunnery officer! The uneasy and tension-filled meeting in the wardroom that reminded her of the meetings she had witnessed during midshipman cruise! Confining herself to life inside that high-tech metal destroyer!*

Beyond the uniforms, her patriotic ideas about joining the military, and her desire to serve in the military as a woman, she hadn't really thought through her decision to seek a naval commission. She hadn't added up what daily life in the Navy, living and working onboard a ship, would be like. Doubts about committing five years of her life to the Navy had first surfaced in SWOS, when she found herself up late on Thursday nights, well past midnight, trying to study and memorize details about seamanship, guns, missiles, computerized combat systems, engineering plants, damage control, and navigation for Friday morning exams. It was then that she started to admit to herself that she didn't have much aptitude for the baseline technical concepts necessary for her upcoming shipboard job. After initially resisting, she finally acknowledged that she lacked interest in those concepts as well. She remembered sitting on her bed, in the house she had rented in Newport with three other junior offices, exhausted, studying late into the night most weeknights, wanting to pull her hair out, because she knew that she had made a mistake in joining the Navy and that there was no way out of it.

Each week she studied and memorized and made herself pass the Friday morning exams. She passed all of them on the first try except for one, the infamous and feared MOBoard, or maneuvering board exam, which involved drawing geometrical diagrams to depict and calculate relative motion between ships at sea. She retook the exam and passed on the second try. And she had considered herself lucky because many who had retaken the exam had to try a few more times to pass; but despite passing, she still lacked even a basic grasp of MOBoard concepts. She just could not translate the visual geometric diagrams and mathematical calculations into an understanding, a visual picture of the relative movement between ships at sea.

She remembered how she had survived the bridge trainer at SWOS. It was literally a plywood mockup of a bridge, with computerized props to simulate the helm, lee helm, and the ship's course indicator. There was a chart table with navigation charts, a table to work out MOBoard problems, and some radio circuits. The students and instructors role-played. During the six-month school, her class had spent a half day in the "trainer"; but during that half day she had felt terrified by the thought of being selected to role-play the officer of the deck (OOD) or junior officer of the deck (JOOD) on the bridge. She especially did not want to play the conning officer, the watchstation responsible for giving course and speed orders to the helm and lee helm. The mathematical spatial understanding required to convert information from the nautical charts and MOBoard into conning orders of course and speed felt out of her grasp; especially since the conning officer was expected to process the information and calculations quickly, in order to maneuver a ship through a harbor, or in heavy shipping traffic, or in formations with other naval ships. She survived the trainer unnoticed by volunteering to play the radio talker. And after four hours, her class had finished with the plywood trainer.

For six months she worked through SWOS, refusing to allow herself to fail, trying to force her interest in the material. "Quitting" or "giving up," she had thought, wasn't a valid option. Now, faced with having to perform as a gunnery officer and bridge watchstander real-time onboard a warship, some part of her wished that the exam system at SWOS had worked and had washed her out into another officer community, such as supply. But she had also learned that washing out of SWOS was a near impossibility. The SWO community needed bodies, so the school made students repeat the courses until they passed.

As she stood just inside the door of her hotel room, her lack of natural ability – and interest – was what made the four years ahead of her feel so disconcerting. At SWOS, she noticed that some of the other ensigns already had an interest in naval science from books they had read, hobbies, building model airplanes and ships, airshows, sailing, etc. She had, at times, tried liking ships and aircraft as a hobby – she had even gone to a few airshows with her dad – but she had never stayed with it or taken to it. Nevertheless, she had continued to tell herself and others that she was fascinated by those subjects.

Through her teenage years, she had promised herself that she would never veer from her goal of joining the military, or lose sight of that dream by getting in trouble or going down the wrong track. And in reflecting back, she realized now that her parents weren't the type of people to ask questions that would have prompted her to dig beyond the surface of "*I want to apply for an ROTC scholarship, go into the military, and fly.*" They weren't the type of people who could help her look at who she was, or examine the motivations of her stated choices. It was never presented to her that it would be helpful to ask questions of herself, such as: What were her talents and interests? Did her desires and ambitions match her personality and abilities? How was she truly performing in math and science? Did she show natural ability and a real interest in learning the material? Such questions, vital for choosing a life direction, would have never occurred to her or to her parents. So, choices about career path were based on other matters.

Her father relentlessly insisted that she needed a technical background in order to get a job. And her mother was just generally excited to support her in engineering and the military because they led to stable jobs with a good salary and benefits; and she was proud that her daughter was smart in school, received good grades, and performed well in difficult classes. "I could never take those classes and do math like that," her mother used to say, as she would glance over Brenda's shoulder and get a quick look at the homework she was doing. She threw her support behind whatever Brenda chose to do, but she never suggested that Brenda explore her choices, or herself, in any way that penetrated beyond the surface; she had not lived her own life in that way and it would not have occurred to her to guide Brenda in self-reflection.

So Brenda glided the surface, and went around announcing that she wanted to join ROTC and go into the Navy; and any sense or indication that she might not have been a good fit was ignored by her, and not even considered by her parents.

Brenda sat down on the hotel bed and stared around the room, angry that she had chosen to start her life out of college in the Navy, locked up aboard a ship. She wanted to go back and undo the choices she had made. Her twenties were going to be spent waiting for her naval commitment to end, studying and working like mad to survive, enduring the various milestones that would be required of her in the Navy. She wished she had moved to the city to experience her twenties there, continue her Spanish studies, and try to make it as a writer. She got up and double-checked the lock on the hotel door. Safe within her room, she let go of her self-restraint, and she came undone. She tossed her cover onto the hotel room desk, and sat back down on the bed. When she looked in the mirror, she noticed that she looked rough. All that makeup, the skin foundation, eye liner, eye shadow, and mascara, meant to mask her exhaustion, had done nothing but reveal her insides. What was intended to create an attractive, professional first impression merely appeared as a caked-on mask! She stared down at the floor. The encounter with the red light district lieutenant, the incident with her cover in the wardroom, being assigned management of shipboard missile and gunnery systems, the mere thought of real-time watchstanding on the bridge of a warship! She went limp. Slowly, she slid from the bed onto the carpet. She crouched down on the floor and rested her forehead into her palms. *I hate this! The Navy! SWO! Oh my God! What have I done? I want out!* She would have quit right there if she could have, for her benefit and for that of the Navy.

Brenda rolled onto her side, her face wet with tears, her hair coming out of the bun. For the first time, she became consciously aware, and willing to admit, that she had disregarded every warning sign surrounding the Navy and SWO. All of the horrific sea stories she had heard in ROTC, and all she had observed on midshipman cruise! The underlying themes to most SWO sea stories were disturbing, and worst of all, consistent. Modern surface warfare tales didn't describe traditional military hardships, such as the horrors of combat or arduous shipboard or sea conditions; essentially, they were accounts of poor leadership, inadequate training, and of an officer promotion system based on self-service and self-preservation. Screaming XOs, department heads' shaking knees, the zero-defect mentality, and long sleepless periods! Some of her junior officer peers found those stories funny, but she never laughed. She felt beside herself as she lay on the hotel room floor. Her struggles with math/science and her insistence that she was great at those subjects! Her experience on midshipman cruise with the screaming and berating XO! Her ensign mentor who worked 24/7 and never left the ship! Her lack of aptitude for seamanship, navigation, and weapons systems! She should have known, but she had remained steadfast in her goals, ignoring every warning. This was the epitome – and "real world" consequence – of forcing herself to continue with things she didn't like.

Harsh, competitive treatment was steeped into SWO culture; or so she had been told by the junior officers onboard the USS *Spruance*. On her own, she had noted the satisfaction SWO officers took in surviving the treatment. And, sadly, it seemed that those who survived it, and stayed in the Navy, tended to perpetuate it. "*SWO eat their young*," and "*Stab, stab, look, stab,*" were common phrases/jokes heard around the SWO community. The phrases embodied a SWO cultural blend of pride and sarcasm. All SWOs, both the dedicated and the disenfranchised, loved to tell sea stories highlighting the harsh treatment of SWO officers, because they were proud to have survived it. And, a large portion of the dedicated lifers seemed quite willing to carry it on.

With the curtains drawn and the room dark, Brenda remained on the floor, knowing she could think, say, and do whatever she wanted within the safety of the hotel room without anyone knowing. Like most SWO junior officers, she was arriving to her first ship pre-instilled with knowledge of what was ahead. She would have to accept SWO culture and learn to thrive within it, at least to some degree, in order to survive. Onboard the ship, there would be significant peer pressure to accept SWO methods, join in, and think that the methods and lifestyle were acceptable and fitting. Then there was that nagging fear that as much as she studied and tried to learn on the job to become a competent gunnery officer and bridge watchstander, she just wouldn't be able to keep up with expectations, and match the learning curve of her peers. She couldn't imagine four more years of this life, especially when her experiences in ROTC and SWOS seemed to indicate that she would never fit in, no matter how hard she tried. She didn't want to face her future.

Chapter 11: Sleep at last ... The event cannot match the expectation

In her hotel room, Brenda awoke in the dark. She lifted her head slowly as she leaned up on her elbows to look at the clock radio on the nightstand. Hours had passed. She had slept through afternoon and evening on the hotel floor, dressed in her uniform. But she felt better after sleeping; her head was clearer. And the hotel room glowed with pink and light blue. Beyond the window, at the street edge of the alleyway, she remembered there was a neon sign – a vintage sign depicting a mermaid hugging a palm tree. *What a cliché.* She smiled, remembering that she had noticed what looked like a jazz lounge adjacent to the hotel.

On the floor, she began to undress, first unbuttoning her uniform blouse, then sliding her straight-legged pants off to reveal her feminine outline. She ran her hands along her curves, enjoying them, feeling they were nothing the military needed to hide. Being a woman was nothing that needed to be hidden. She pulled herself up onto the hotel bed, not wanting to wake up too much; she left her undershirt on – a men's size small white undershirt, a required component of the female uniform. Navy regulations required that the white neckline of the t-shirt show above the top button of the uniform shirt. She slid underneath the bed sheets, which felt cool against her skin. And being accustomed to the city, the outside bustle didn't bother her.

Over the next few days, as she would walk around Sydney, she knew that her thoughts would center on detangling the dynamics she witnessed during her first few minutes onboard the *Curtis Wilbur* – the physically short Captain who received an edgy, placating reaction from his officers...her sponsor, an obviously intelligent and dedicated officer but out of place and unsettled in that environment...her department head, smart, but very strained and on edge...the rest of the wardroom, a cluster of red and black eyes with forced smiles on young aged faces. She quoted a line from *Villette* to herself which, time and again, she had thought of since starting SWOS: *Life is so constructed, that the event does not, cannot, will not, match the expectation.*[1] Then she fell back asleep.

* * *

Brenda opened her eyes; she was relieved to see light shining through the edges of the hotel curtains. *She had slept through until morning!* She felt better, even mentally refreshed; she looked over at the clock radio on the nightstand; it was 7:03 a.m., early for her, a non-morning person, but she felt okay. She closed her eyes, wanting just a few more minutes of sleep, but then she remembered a warning from the lieutenant instructors at Surface Warfare Officers School, "After graduation, use all of your leave because you won't be able to use it once you get to your ship." She decided to use the free time afforded her to the fullest. She sat up slowly on the bed, and noticed her uniform lying on the floor where she had left it. She eased out of bed, lifted it off the floor, and hung it properly in the closet; she wanted to take care of her uniform.

A vibrant, independent spirit dwelled within her. She looked forward to exploring Sydney and spending her free time on her own. Later, she would have the opportunity to meet her fellow junior officers. Rest had revitalized her sense of self-preparedness; she felt ready to check out of the hotel, and move onboard the ship.

---

[1] Brontë, Charlotte. *Villette.* p. 415.

Chapter 12: Ever self-conscious ... To find that thing that is an expression of the self ... Moving in ... Meeting Julie

Brenda reached the top of the last ladder to officers country and congratulated herself: She had found her way through the ship without any wrong turns. She paused to rest, and allowed her seabag to slide off her shoulders. So many mazelike narrow passageways and ladders, how could an outsider distinguish? *And she had done it!* She had a private habit of congratulating herself for even the smallest of accomplishments. Since childhood, it had served as her own method of self-encouragement to keep going at whatever she was doing. She would soon be a pro, she thought, an insider and a naval officer onboard this ship. *The thought wowed her!*

Dressed in jeans and a comfortable summer top, she felt light and upbeat as she picked up her bags to continue on to her stateroom. She opened the door to officers country feeling that a sense of adventure had returned.

She found the officers' passageway empty and quiet except for the humming of fans and auxiliary machinery; she walked past the wardroom door, turned left, and continued on to the last stateroom on the right, just before the female head. The door was wide open. Brenda dropped her seabag to the floor and knocked three times on the open door.

"Come in," she heard.

"Julie, hi, it's great to meet you, I'm Brenda," she introduced herself, offering Julie her hand as she walked inside.

Julie stood up from her desk chair. "Hey," she welcomed Brenda, smiling as she returned her handshake. "We weren't sure when you would be getting here."

Brenda wasn't at all surprised to meet another female Naval Academy graduate who, right at first glance, appeared so serious and smart. But she felt tentative about having a roommate.

"I got here yesterday," Brenda began, as she used her leg to push her seabag over to the left side of the stateroom. "I'm not sure if you saw my note." She turned a latch to pull her fold-down desk out from the cabinets, remembering how to do it from midshipman cruise. Inside her desk, she saw a small locker for money and valuables, with some cubbyholes and small shelves above and to the side.

"I did. I noticed you at the meeting yesterday. You looked pretty wiped," Julie replied, laughing a little. "I'm glad you're finally here."

She felt ashamed that Julie had noticed her in the wardroom the day before, presumably with her cover on. Then she wondered if the red light district lieutenant had ever called the ship to report her.

"Wiped is an understatement," Brenda replied, but Julie had a look of her own going on. The area around her eyes was black from fatigue. If she hadn't known better, Brenda would have sworn Julie had been in a fight. She hoped shipboard life and duties were working out for Julie, but her worn look and tired eyes suggested otherwise. "So, Julie, Pete mentioned you've been onboard a few months," Brenda said, while opening her seabag to start putting a few things away.

"I got to the ship right before it left Japan. We first went to Sascbo to take part in anti-submarine exercises with the Japanese Navy. Then to Guam."

Brenda lit up. "Guam, that must have been so nice, so tropical! Beautiful white sand beaches, crystal clear water!"

"It was a working port," Julie answered casually. "We then weathered a tropical storm before Tandem Thrust, a joint exercise with the Australian Navy. The storm was rough, but the exercise was interesting, involving a lot of maneuvering on the bridge for ASW, air ops, and DIVTACS. That's my favorite part of all this," her face lit up.

"The fun parts, huh?" Brenda answered, reaching into a cabinet to remove some trash that had been left, realizing the Guam port visit was of no consequence to Julie. She had instead enjoyed the naval exercises, and apparently she hadn't minded enduring the heavy sea conditions.

Julie's face practically beamed. "Sure, standing bridge watches during the exercises and coordinating the deck work topside for the boatswains mates. All the cool stuff."

"Wow," was all Brenda could think of to say. Julie impressed her as the real deal, wholly engaged in her desire to become a surface warfare officer. And she had an unusual innocence about her, a first impression created by her smile; it was authentic, wide, and innocent, in a way most people lose as they accumulate experience in life. Yes, Julie seemed nice, and she seemed to offer her own unique way; but it was still hard for Brenda to shake her uneasy feelings about having a roommate.

She wondered how anyone could retain a sense of innocence about them after attending the Naval Academy. Academy stories were intensely disturbing, Brenda had found, more so than anything she had experienced or heard of in college: traditions, hazing, and sanctioned harassment built into everyday life, unofficial but sanctioned rituals, academic cheating scandals, parties at the homes of adult in-town sponsors involving alcohol abuse, bizarre activities and rituals considered as fun, sets of "real rules" one had to learn about, the unique language of "getting fried," "demerits," etc. The Academy removed college-age kids from society for four years, institutionalized them, and controlled every minute of their day. Liberty, Brenda perceived, was precious and scarce. Breaking the rules was a game to be mastered if one wanted any sense of self-determination, and liberty was the time to cram in everything forbidden. She wondered where Julie fit into all of those dynamics.

Brenda noticed the plastic hearing protection case hanging from Julie's belt loop. She was dressed in working khakis. "Were you working down in engineering? Do you have duty today?"

Julie held the plastic case up. "I'm not on duty, but I was working on my engineering quals before OPS called me off." She sat back into her chair.

Brenda continued unpacking some of the books and uniform articles she had crammed into the top of her seabag before she left the hotel. She wondered why Julie hadn't taken the opportunity to go on liberty in Sydney. She didn't have duty. Didn't she want to leave the ship ever, for a little break or free time? Then she remembered the lieutenant instructors at SWOS saying that junior officers were mostly left on their own to wade through the surface warfare officer qualification process. Often, that meant scraping for time afterhours inport and underway, in addition to fulfilling fulltime division officer responsibilities. Brenda wasn't put off by hard work, and she considered herself a self-starter, although she didn't want to work every night and weekend; but she found Julie's response unsettling – it implied a lack of support for her quals (qualifications) by her department head supervisor.

When Brenda removed her *Personnel Qualification Standards (PQS) for Surface Warfare Officers* book from her seabag, she felt a sense of panic; she began leafing through it. The book contained over three hundred pages of "line items" representing various

Long Way Out 75

fundamentals of shipboard operations and engineering. In order to qualify as a surface warfare officer, she would have to learn the information related to each line item, such as, *"list and discuss the tactical voice communications circuits used in SUW"*; and she would have to perform the functions required by other line items, such as, *"conn ship during a multiship tactical maneuvering exercise."* Each line item in the SWO PQS book was followed by a signature and date line underneath. Once a SWO candidate performed a function or explained a line item satisfactorily to a qualified surface warfare officer, that officer could "sign off" the line item for the candidate. Qualification as a surface warfare officer required qualification at the following shipboard watchstations: officer of the deck (OOD) underway (U/W), officer of the deck (OOD) inport, combat information center watch officer (CICWO), and small boat officer.

Brenda planned to start collecting line item signatures immediately. Her goal was to get all of her line items signed off within her first year onboard. Afterwards, she could request a SWO qualification oral board. If she passed the oral board, and the Captain, XO, and department heads were satisfied that she met the qualifications to be a surface warfare officer, she would be awarded the gold SWO pin to wear on her uniform, above her left shirt pocket. Because she was slated to become a nuclear surface warfare officer, (SWO N) or surface nuke, the SWOS instructors told her that she would have no trouble getting her SWO pin; her first ship would more or less push her through the SWO qualification process because the Navy was in desperate need of nukes. She hoped that was true.

In Brenda's view, the only reason she was onboard this first ship was to earn her SWO pin. Otherwise, the SWO pin carried little meaning for her, beyond representing a milestone on her way to nuclear power school, which would then enable her to move on to a nuclear aircraft carrier, followed by that technical job out there someday. She was scheduled to be onboard the *Curtis Wilbur* for eighteen months, but she planned on calling the nuke detailer to leave the ship earlier if she could get her hands on a SWO pin quickly enough.

"Does your department head normally allow you time, and support you in working on your quals?" Brenda asked Julie. She turned to a random page in her SWO PQS book entitled, *"COMBAT INFORMATION CENTER (CIC) PLOTTING PROCEDURES AND*

DISPLAYS FUNDAMENTALS"; she ran her eyes down the list of signature line items.

> *...Discuss proper plotting procedures on the DRT/DDRT for the following tactical situations:*
>
> *- Formation steaming*
> *- USW*
> *- Man overboard/aircraft in water*
> *- NUDET*
> *- Mine warfare*
>
> _____
> *(Signature and Date)*
>
> *Discuss the procedure for RADFO plotting and state the function of the plot.*
>
> _____
> *(Signature and Date)*
>
> *...*

At some point, she would understand the content of these pages, Brenda assured herself.

"It's hard finding time to work on quals," Julie answered. "On most ships you're on your own. But you should be alright working for WEPS, and turning over with Pete."

Brenda sat down on her desk chair to rest a moment. There was consolation in Julie's suggestion that WEPS may have been more amenable than Julie's department head, OPS, the operations officer, who apparently wasn't providing her with much support during her qualification process. Julie appeared tired and beat up, and Brenda hoped to avoid that same fate. Maybe Julie was too steeped in the ship, she wondered, too unwilling to take a break.

"Is your boss, the operations officer, good to work for?" Brenda asked. But then she regretted placing Julie in a situation where she would have to answer. She was too new onboard to ask such a question; she had just met Julie.

"We're on an Aegis ship, forward deployed to Japan with a high op tempo. OPS is under constant pressure," Julie said. She lounged back into her desk chair, letting her hands fall onto her lap, as if resigned. "He's good at ops planning at least. You're not going to get more operational than this ship, which is why I came to Japan. I love what I'm doing at least."

Brenda stood up from her chair and leaned back against the cabinets. She wanted to apologize for her question. "Have you been on liberty yet to enjoy Sydney, Julie?"

"No liberty since leaving for deployment."

Brenda nodded. Julie's response matched what she had heard about SWO life. "I never wanted SWO," Brenda started. "I wanted intel or supply. But, when the Navy forced our graduation class to choose a warfare community, I figured if I had to go SWO, I might as well go nuke. I thought I could at least specialize in nuclear power," and avoid the SWO jack-of-all trades career pipeline, she wanted to add; but she wasn't sure how far to go with Julie. Regardless, Brenda found the nuclear pipeline disconcerting as well. Even as a nuclear trained SWO officer, every few years she would still have to rotate through conventional SWO tours in operations, combat systems, etc. "Engineering is where I feel the strongest, more so than on the bridge..." Brenda started to say.

"I did," Julie interrupted with a sense of dedication and seriousness. "I've wanted to go SWO and serve onboard surface ships my whole life."

Brenda felt a jolt, a need to go back on her words to demonstrate to Julie that she really was onboard with everything SWO. But, then, in the next moment, she felt annoyed that Julie actually liked SWO. No one *liked* SWO, did they? In Navy culture, SWO was considered a dumping ground. The SWO community swallowed up every remaining body available after other warfare communities – submarines, nuclear surface, aviation, special forces – competed for the best and brightest of the officer candidates. That selection dynamic resulted in a mix of SWO officers, which included some like Julie who chose surface warfare, those who planned to use SWO as a stepping stone to another officer community (i.e., one not immediately available to officer candidates after graduation, such as supply, intelligence, public affairs, civil engineer corps, JAG, meteorology/oceanography, etc.), low to average performers denied by other officer communities, and high performing prior enlisted commissioned officers.

Brenda went back to unpacking her seabag. She would have preferred a roommate with whom she could have commiserated. The surface warfare community was fortunate that young officer candidates such as Julie still chose SWO, despite the community's reputation. Julie could have chosen another officer warfare community, such as nuclear or aviation. And, so far, the SWO community didn't seem to be treating her well; it didn't seem willing to reward Julie for her choice. Brenda turned to face Julie. "I'm sorry. I'm still tired," she said. "SWO wasn't my first choice, I admit, but I'm trying to make the best of it."

"My father's a retired Navy captain," Julie answered. "I grew up Navy, and sailing during summers and working on boats with my dad. I've sailed around the world. A few years ago, my dad and I designed and built a small wooden sailboat together. Working with tools, being out at sea, it's what I've known all my life. It's what I enjoy."

"And you want to build upon that," Brenda said.

"It's why I wanted the Naval Academy, and SWO. I loved the Academy."

"So serving onboard a surface ship as the deck officer suits you well then," Brenda smiled. It was the first time she had heard anyone say that they had loved the Academy. The people she knew claimed to hate it. Her friend Dana from midshipman cruise always swore up and down that she hated the Academy. She had learned that IHTFP (I Hate This Fucking Place) was a kind of secret code among Naval Academy midshipmen and graduates. All in all, however, Brenda liked Julie, and her down-to-earth style. Julie had joined the Navy for honest reasons. And Brenda enjoyed meeting people who had something in their lives that they delved into, as if that thing was an extension of themselves, or even an expression of the self. Her parents, too, seemed attracted to people who did unique things, or who were involved in a particular form of art, cause, or hobby. But her parents were drawn to those people and things in the same way that a tourist takes a bus tour through a few European countries, scanning the highlights; or, they were drawn to those people in the way that a person casually walks through a museum, admiring the exhibits, and brushing past them. They never got involved themselves. It was as if they were always at the zoo, admiring from the outside. Grounded in their pragmatics, they were instilled with an unconscious belief that things of the arts, causes, and other intangibles were nice to look at and admire, but were for other people; they were entirely content with concerns of their employment benefits and savings and insurance.

Brenda had repeated more than once that she needed a steady, predictable paycheck every week to feel secure; she couldn't deal with a life not premised, first and foremost, on a stable financial situation with savings and investments and IRAs. She had been taught to think that focusing solely on a stable financial picture, and doing so when young, was *the* start to a "good life."

However, she felt her feelings and sentiments toward what constituted a good life evolving away from a primary focus on finances and away from a life based upon security. She had a stable and high salary in the Navy. And at twenty-three, she had savings and investments and IRAs. But she had never felt as insecure and uneasy as she did now.

She wanted to do as Julie had described, find that *thing* that was an expression of the self. But, she had never considered looking outside of her upbringing – the ideas with which she had grown up. She had thought engineering and the military would be her *thing*, her expression of the self.

In relation to life onboard, Brenda wondered if she would find a peer mentor in Julie. During midshipman cruise, she followed her Academy friend Dana around, doing as she did. Brenda wondered if Julie would fit that same role for her – peer mentor; she already wished she could be the junior officer Julie seemed to be. "What was your major at the Academy, Julie?"

"Mechanical engineering."

"Cool, mine too," Brenda exclaimed, finally feeling like they shared something in common. "It's so important to have that technical background that will lead to a job. With a technical background, you can do anything," Brenda said, reciting two phrases commonly spoken by her father. As she uttered her last statement, Brenda started to feel pride again that she was on the right path, doing all the right things to set herself up for a career later. She was a young woman who had accepted what she had been taught, and went about the implementation methodically, as if there existed a formula to a successful life.

Brenda did feel strained in trying to keep her conversation with Julie going. "I hope you're able to take some liberty in Sydney, Julie," she added sympathetically.

"I plan to get away for some intramural basketball games with the ship's team. They're scheduled to play against a few other ships in the battle group." Talking about the basketball game brought back Julie's smile. So it was the Navy, sailboats, ships, and basketball for Julie, Brenda thought. Brenda didn't press her further. Events would unfold over time in such a way that she would soon understand life onboard a warship. Julie stood up from her desk chair as if to leave. She pushed the front of her short wavy brown hair down so she could put on her *Curtis Wilbur* ballcap. "Some of the other JOs are renting a van to go to Manly Beach just outside of Sydney. You could probably hook up with them for the day. I can introduce you," Julie offered. "They're all JGs," she added, referring to the rank of lieutenant (j.g.), or O-2.

"Sure," Brenda answered, as she pushed her seabag underneath her desk to store it. She wished Julie hadn't offered to introduce her to others just yet; she would have preferred to go into Sydney on her own; but how could she say no?

She followed Julie down the passageway to the guys' stateroom. Their door was open. Brenda remained in the doorway, standing behind Julie. She saw two guys about her age inside, one sitting at a desk chair, and the other lying on the bottom rack. "This is Brenda, my new roommate," Julie introduced her. The guy sitting at the desk chair glared at Julie, teasingly, but intensely, as if making fun of the situation. He had a sardonic, defiant, mocking look that made Brenda uncomfortable. Julie sort of giggled, and then laughed, "What?"

Replete in self-consciousness, Brenda never knew how to act in the Navy; and so she often found herself awkward, as if trying to prove she belonged and fit in with Navy knowledge and life. She remained in the doorway, expressionless.

The lieutenant (j.g.) lying on the rack got up, walked over to Brenda, and offered her his hand. "Hi, I'm Rich Windmiller, the damage control assistant, the DCA. Welcome aboard, Brenda. We met yesterday, but you probably don't remember."

"I'm sorry, I don't, Rich, but it's nice to meet you." Brenda returned his handshake, flinching inside from mention of her wardroom experience.

"I'm Jon Trey, the ship's navigator," the lieutenant (j.g.) seated in the desk chair said. "I remember you from yesterday, too," he smirked, and Brenda was certain he did remember.

Julie started, "I knew you guys were headed to the beach, so I thought I would introduce her." Jon looked at Julie while smiling and shaking his head.

"That's okay, Julie," Brenda stopped her. "I bet they're ready to go soon, and I'm not." She quickly inferred that Rich, Jon, and the other guy who had just walked into the stateroom, had formed somewhat of a clique. She wasn't interested in intruding upon their day. She was equally happy, or more so, to head into Sydney on her own.

"Hey, why don't you come along, Brenda. It'll be fun," Rich offered.

"I'm still tired. I was going to work on getting my half of the stateroom together, then maybe walk around Sydney a little."

"Come along, why not?" Rich insisted. But Brenda felt he was only being polite.

"The more the merrier," added the JO who just walked in.

"Sure," Brenda said, resigned. "When and where should I meet you guys?"

Chapter 13: At the beach ... Just SWO stories ... A persona to avoid

Brenda rushed back to her stateroom to collect her things for an early afternoon at an Australian beach – towels to rest on, sunscreen. When she arrived on the ship's quarterdeck a half hour later to meet the guys, she found them ready to go – sunglasses, Hawaiian shirts, beach gear. Rich had hired a car and driver for the morning.

When the guys saw her on the quarterdeck, they started across the brow. "The driver from the car service called the quarterdeck, he's waiting for us outside the pier gates," Rich called out to her. Brenda hurried to catch up to them, quickly going through the motions of stating to the OOD on the quarterdeck, "I have permission to go ashore," and standing briefly at attention while facing the flag, just as the guys were doing. They had all followed the correct protocol when leaving the ship in civilian clothes.

During the few short miles from Sydney to the beach, Brenda realized that her initial impression of the guys was correct. She was riding with a confident group who had formed a clique, with their own inside jokes, mostly sourced in sarcasm about SWO, the ship, and the Navy. Not wishing to interfere in their day off, she planned to spend a short time with them before taking a walk around the beach by herself.

"So I heard you're a SWO nuke," Rich offered, as the van bounced over potholes.

"I am. As soon as I get my SWO pin, I'm going to call the detailer so I can move on to nuke school."

"Here's the thing," Rich advised Brenda. "The coolest thing about Nuclear Power School is that people will be amazed and fall all over you just because you are there going through the school, and afterwards because you have graduated from it. The school's considered elite by everyone, the elite of the elite, so as much as you may hate being there or being in the program, the attention you get makes you feel so good…no…great, people fall all over you with admiration and thanks. They think you're a genius; that's really the best thing about it. Human nature sucks you right in," he finished while smiling, his head motioning up and down. "The whole nuke thing, being there really sucks though," Rich added, laughing while lounging on the seat in his bright, tropical shirt, shorts, and sunglasses.

"You're expressing that sentiment from personal experience?" Brenda asked. Naval Nuclear Power School was established in 1955 by Admiral Rickover, practically a cult figure in the Navy. Known as the "Father of the Nuclear Navy," he was famous for his unapologetic style of tyranny, holding a hard line on nuclear submarines, and throwing tantrums during candidate selection interviews. Admiral Rickover interview stories were numerous. Although Brenda's time followed his death, she had experienced the aftermath of his influence during her program selection interview at Naval Reactors in Crystal City, Virginia. From Admiral Rickover sprung the entire culture of the nuclear Navy. Nukes generally had a reputation for the kind of eccentricities that stereotypically went along with extreme technical intelligence. Membership to the nuclear community was gained after graduating from Naval Nuclear Power School, a six month classroom program consisting of grueling courses in nuclear physics, and Nuclear Prototype School, six months of follow-on prototype training, where students operated a live nuclear reactor under instruction (U/I). Upon completion of the one year instructional program, nuclear power school graduates were billeted to one of the nearly one hundred aircraft carrier/submarine nuclear propulsion plants operated by the Navy. Instructors at nuclear power school persistently reminded students they were the best and brightest, while the rest of the Navy slacked and paled in comparison. Brenda imagined that eventually the students started reminding each other of how they were the best and brightest, and on and on into their careers, creating the community's legendary cultish life-long exclusivity.

"I graduated from nuke school, but later washed out of the prototype follow-on training, back into SWO," Rich answered. "I'm glad to be back aboard ship. I don't mind going straight SWO." Rich's honesty surprised Brenda, both in regard to not graduating from the second half of nuclear power training and in admitting to the fact that the attention bestowed upon nukes played at least some part in his motivation. Even as a selectee, Brenda had already been the recipient of the type of attention Rich described. She knew it first hand and it did feel good. How could any human being honestly say it didn't?

Brenda casually pondered each junior officer in the van, deciding mainly to listen during the ride. Their conversation revolved around events and people on the ship, with each telling sea stories of recent experiences, many of which were humorous and often sarcastic about SWO life. Jon and Todd spoke little about their personal histories, with only vague mention of where they were from. Jon had mentioned in passing that he was from Kauai. And Todd didn't mention specifically where he was from, but she gathered somehow that he was from one of the Rocky Mountain states. A graduate of the Naval Academy, Rich was in the Navy by choice, or possibly by legacy, Brenda assumed, as he spoke in more detail about where he was from. As Rich described his home, she immediately recognized the neighborhood in which he grew up, in Southern California, along the Pacific Coast Highway. It was a gated community of multimillion dollar homes overlooking the California coastline. She had passed it many times while driving to the beach with her mother, during the few short years they had lived in California, when she was in grades three through seven. It made her think about how these three junior officers represented just a sampling of the economic and geographic diversity of the ship's company. The officers and crew of *Curtis Wilbur* must have drawn from everywhere imaginable with every kind of person onboard and integrated into the total sum.

The oncoming view of Manly Beach charmed Brenda as she sat up to look out the windshield. Arriving from over a hill in the van, a cove awaited them below, past brightly painted historical buildings. Beaches and shopping galore, the afternoon promised to unfold pleasantly. It looked like there was going to be plenty for her to do on her own so she would not be such a drag on the guys.

After the group settled on a spot in the sand, Brenda parted ways with them to enjoy wandering through this parallel universe; that was how she continually referred to Australia in her mind. If someone had dropped her off in Australia without telling her, and she had not heard anyone speak or had not seen any of the license plates, she would have sworn she was in California. How was it possible to travel across the world and land in a place so similar to the United States? In her few interactions so far with this ship crew – homeported in Japan – she could feel the energy the men and women had for Australia. Australia was medication for their homesickness.

*

"So, how's life onboard ship and SWO life in general?" Brenda cheerfully asked Jon, the navigator, during the van ride back to the ship.

"It sucks," he said, nonchalantly, and dryly, with a smirk and knowing eyes. In the guys' stateroom and at the beach, Brenda noticed that Jon kept this look on that worked to make others, or whoever he was conversing with, question themselves suddenly and feel self-conscious. Behind his look, he was extremely guarded. But his "look" was almost put-on and not completely serious. It was uncanny, and she couldn't describe it to herself. Was he joking, or was he serious?

Brenda looked at Jon and sort of laughed. "Great. That's just great!" she exclaimed in response, but he glared at her and his glare was unnerving, and then he laughed. So she stared back at him, mimicked his laugh, and turned away and stared out the passenger window. Then he laughed. She found herself shaking her head and smiling, a bit. Earlier, Jon mentioned his plans to submit his letter of resignation as soon as the Navy allowed – nine months to the day before his ROTC scholarship obligation ended.

As she sat across from him in the van, she glanced at Jon once more, and then turned to stare back out the window. His put-on, dry, mocking, half serious/half joking demeanor probably served as a good defense mechanism, a passive offense to survive onboard the ship, she decided. His persona, or protective facade, didn't invite questions, it intimidated, and it gave him the upper hand and a sense of control in a given interaction. She reminded herself, that Jon, like any second tour SWO junior officer, had no experience as a navigator before checking aboard *Curtis Wilbur*. He would have had to rely on the experience and knowledge of his lead quartermaster. She had never met anyone like Jon; he had his own style. She didn't think he was a bad person, necessarily, but she hoped to avoid him as much as possible.

Despite the prospect of returning from the beach to SWO life, Brenda and the guys arrived back at the ship feeling positive after a nice afternoon. On the quarterdeck Brenda parted company with the group and returned to her stateroom with the two new button-up summer blouses she had purchased from a sale bin at an Italian-style boutique, one white and one brown, neutral colors to go with everything. She knew from sea stories that collared shirts and closed-toed shoes were required apparel for some foreign port visits.

Julie wasn't in their stateroom, and Brenda hoped she was able to make her intramural basketball game. She must have been the only female in the game, Brenda thought. She was impressed by the junior officers she had met so far. Would she have a shot at keeping up with them?

Brenda stood staring at her seabag, not knowing where to start in organizing her things. She looked at Julie's side of the stateroom, knowing that the everything-in-its-exact-place look was never going to happen on her side. Neat organization of clothes and things was not her forte; but she supposed the inside of her cabinets and closets would remain private. She could shove everything inside, and at least give herself a shot at making the outward space appear military-like. Brenda was organized in the work she accomplished, but her desk and storage areas always remained a mess. However, as consolation, she reminded herself that she could find anything at any time.

As Brenda hung her uniforms, she remembered the seamstress at the uniform store on base in Newport wrapping measuring tape around her waist. "Let me take out the waist on a few pairs of uniform pants. I've been doing this many years; everyone gains weight on the ships, especially the women. This I know," the woman stated, in an Eastern European accent. During SWOS, Brenda had continued the strict regimen she had started during her last year of college: lifting weights Monday, Wednesday, Friday, and swimming laps Tuesday and Thursday evenings. She felt her weight perfect at 110 lbs. She understood that the diet onboard ship was designed for men, but she was going to try to exercise; she just had to stick to it.

"Fine, okay," Brenda recalled her response to the seamstress's insistence. "You can take out three pairs of uniform pants." Then she kidded with the woman, declaring, "That's not going to happen to me." But the seamstress ignored her. "Well, there's workout equipment on the ships and there'll be a pool on base," Brenda added.

Inside her stateroom, Brenda rolled the larger-sized uniforms into a ball and shoved them to the back of the closet.

Chapter 14: The trouble with Chief Smith ... The assertion of character ... Repressing the truth ... How one is supposed to feel ... The practical persona

Dressed in jeans, sandals, and one of the new summer blouses she had just purchased in Manly Beach, Brenda stepped off the brow of the *John S. McCain* onto the pier, excited that her quarterdeck protocol felt somewhat automatic, *just like during midshipman cruise!* And while performing the protocol, no one gave her a second look – not anyone passing by or either of the OODs onboard *Curtis Wilbur* or *John S. McCain*. She felt good all around. She was in Australia and her surroundings were beautiful. The sun was shining, the harbor water glimmered, she was embarking on a new career, she was young with no attachments, and she had everything going for her. She looked out across the piers at the rows of gray warships. She could see the duty sections of the various ships moving about the decks – officers in khakis and sailors in dungarees. Smells from the fast food stands set up along the piers filled the air, piquing her curiosity about Australian junk food. She figured experimenting a little with Australian junk food might provide a needed break from trying to organize her side of the stateroom.

Brenda made her way through the crowd of sailors on the pier and headed toward the food stands. Just something small and quick was all she intended on grabbing to take back aboard the ship. Traveling and being hit with so much newness had left her mentally and physically drained; she simply longed for some quiet time with a book in her rack. The bottom of her seabag was packed with Spanish and Latin American short stories and novels.

On the pier, Brenda welcomed the feel of the light harbor breeze and moist air, so different from the ship's desiccated air that dried out her skin. "Hey, hey ma'am," she heard from behind. Brenda turned around, but saw no one she knew. She had just gotten in line for a pretzel. "Hey, ma'am! That's you!" she felt a tap on her shoulder. She turned back around trying not to look bothered by the tap. "You must be the new ensign onboard," the person said. Word of her arrival must have traveled the ship more quickly than she had imagined.

"Yes. I'm Ensign Conner, new GUNNO. It's nice to meet you,"

she offered her hand.

"I'm Chief Smith onboard *Curtis Wilbur*. Where're you headed to?"

"I'm just grabbing something quick so I can head back to my stateroom and get things organized," Brenda answered firmly, showing an uncomfortable smile. She wanted to move on from him, and quickly. Something about this chief and his approach felt wrong, and she found herself reacting very strongly; if someone had asked her to explain why, she would not have been able to.

Brenda's mind spun. She left the line and rushed back towards the safety of the ship, the chief having so jolted her sense of security that she suddenly regarded the ship as her safe haven. Then she stopped abruptly at the bottom of the *John S. McCain*'s brow, wondering if she should have been more social, if innately she was too resistant to fitting in, too immersed in her own subjective take on people, situations, and issues. That way of being in the world was what made her father view her as difficult, as *the Queen* as he used to call her. Her natural inclination was often to go against the grain, do things her own way. In contrast, her father wanted to fit in with people, be liked, go out socially, and generally go along. It was vital to him to be liked by friends and acquaintances, to call them and go out often; and he concerned himself very much with what they thought. Brenda never cared about knowing too many people; she never concerned herself too much with what they thought; and for some reason, that outlook rubbed her father the wrong way. She doubted he was even aware of his reactions towards her. Until she had started facing the realities of calling herself an engineer and entering the Navy, she realized that she had never been conscious of the family dynamics that had been at play.

Gradually, she was starting to piece together how his sense of annoyance at her used to set in whenever she had asserted her character. His resentment was subtle and unintended, but it yielded a powerful influence over her, unconsciously. Now, in reflection, she wondered if that force had consequently impacted, or undermined, her judgment in everything she did, and in every choice she had made. Possibly, that was why she found herself with a degree in mechanical engineering onboard a high-tech destroyer. From her earliest memories of being challenged by him, she could remember that she had instinctively backed down in order to temper any underlying friction, so as not to create tension; she had developed a need to be seen as pleasing, and even to be like him.

Brenda nervously scanned the pier for the chief.

Regardless of her accomplishments – engineering school and ROTC – she still felt so displaced, even after the validation of being commissioned in the Navy. By virtue of working hard and sacrificing to reach her goals, she thought that she had deserved to have things go well and *feel right*. Things were supposed to be different. She was supposed to feel excited about her new job onboard ship; she was supposed to be able to learn navigation, seamanship, and the watchstations. She wasn't supposed to feel restless and further mired in confusion. Not after achieving what she had achieved! *She had worked so hard! She had done everything her parents had told her to do! So, why was she lost? She had been good and she had followed all of the rules and had satisfied everyone's expectations, never getting into trouble or causing conflict within her family! Kids were supposed to listen to their parents and be good and do what they were taught and she had done that!* And it had all landed her as an engineer and naval officer onboard a guided missile destroyer, and – even worse – destined her for nuclear power training.

Then she thought about how unstable she had felt – and must have seemed to others – throughout engineering school and ROTC. She had a sense that her instability had heightened during SWOS. She had acted inappropriately and immaturely without realizing it, and had sometimes interacted with friends and peers in a way that now embarrassed her. *She had been out of control in many ways!* She had tried on varying personas, one being a conservative military person who was technically competent and pragmatic in her approach to life, judgmental of those who didn't see life in practical terms. She had tried acting in certain ways that she thought might make her interesting or fit in with her engineering and ROTC peers; she was constantly trying to convince them that she was just like them, and as good as them. At times she had been socially over-animated, trying too hard. Reflecting back, she must have seemed *ugly*, wearing a metaphorical mask, gaudy and obnoxious, without any authentic substance underneath. She had ignored people's reactions to her and to many of the things she had said, because at the time, she wasn't sure how to interpret them, or process what they meant. She had been oblivious or dismissive of reactions to her and to her way of being in the world. She had existed as an unattractive package with no honest foundation.

She was sure that embarrassing and painful memories of things she had done and said in college and in SWOS would haunt her during her time onboard, and make her cringe when they surfaced at unexpected times during the day. Was it better to attempt to bury those thoughts and memories or to face them?

And it was disconcerting for her to realize that she would probably continue to act in inappropriate ways onboard the ship, while she tried to fit in and hold up a front. The shipboard environment would be one more place in a string of places, like engineering school and ROTC, where she would attempt to be someone she wasn't, in a fruitless search for a way to express herself and for a way to be. She would forge her best outer front to appear as an engineer and fit in in the military; but she would remain self-conscious underneath, while she repressed the truth of who she was. Onboard the ship, she felt she had no choice but to convince others of her validity as an engineer and naval officer, for mere survival.

But, if there was any truth to lessons from literature, from all of the life mishaps and struggles of the characters she had analyzed, she knew that repressing the inner self, or going about the world without awareness of the true self, was toxic to one's being. It was the repressions, the unnamed, undiscovered, and undealt with material, conflicts, feelings, and thoughts – which existed below the level of personal consciousness – that surfaced and expressed themselves *unconsciously*, in the form of acting out in ways one couldn't control and was unaware of.

Growing up, she had believed every word her father had said. Was he correct? Were there no real-world lessons in liberal arts? More times than she could count, he had repeated his story about psychology majors: A research study at the first college he had attended, according to him, concluded that people only majored in psychology to figure out their own problems – they were all mentally ill themselves. Was that true? He used to tell the story so sarcastically. She had first gained an awareness of baseline psychological concepts in an upper level Spanish literature class, in which the professor encouraged students to ground character analysis in psychology. Fascinated by the concepts and recommended reading, she read further and deeper into psychology in her spare time. *Modern Man in Search of a Soul* was her introduction to the works of C.G. Jung. On her own, she had only just begun to apply some of the concepts to her behavior and feelings.

She had no idea whether she was headed towards success,

survival, or disaster. She was locked into four more years in the military, legally. As she thought through the dynamics confronting her, while standing at the *John S. McCain*'s brow, she began to feel increasingly out of control. And those feelings intensified as she mentally listed what was immediately ahead for her: a restrictive military setting, a living-a-lie existence, an unfamiliar status as a leader and manager over weapons systems about which she knew nothing, and anxiety-producing shipboard bridge watches. To be employed directly out of college, under the best of circumstances, carried with it its own struggles and questioning, but to add to that a whole realm of psychological doubts made Brenda feel especially overwhelmed by the daunting list of responsibilities she faced.

"Hey, hey, ma'am!" She froze. "I know of a great place to eat in downtown Sydney. See that high rise tower. See it? Right on top of that tower, how about it? I go every time I have a port visit in Sydney. The staff all know me up there."

"Oh, it looks so cool," Brenda answered as she grabbed the handrail on the brow of the *John S. McCain*, practically shaking. "You enjoy yourself, Chief! Like I said, I'm really exhausted." She started up the brow, "See you back onboard!" she called out, realizing, also, that she lacked a firm grasp of fraternization rules, both written and unwritten. Her instinct was to avoid the chief further, for many reasons, if he would permit it. The nuances of fraternization rules among officers and enlisted personnel were fuzzy; and they were dependent on context and who was in charge. But, really, it wasn't out of concern for fraternization rules that kept her from the chief; it was a feeling she had about him. But, then, she told herself that it was nothing...just nothing, she told herself again. He certainly hadn't meant a date, she decided. His approach seemed cleverly ambiguous. Please just leave me alone, she begged in her mind.

But the chief ensued. "Hey, ma'am, now you look too new and too tired. I'm just trying to make you feel welcome and help out a new ensign. That's a chief's job. A chief makes an ensign an admiral, or else that ensign fails. Now, are you going to spend your liberty time in Sydney onboard the ship? Wait here. I need to grab something back onboard and I'll be right back."

Brenda let out a resigned "okay" as she stood frozen on the pier, clutching the *John S. McCain*'s brow, watching everyone pass her by. Was there anyone out there she knew? If she could all of a sudden recognize another officer from her ship, she would have a non-confrontational way out, but she recognized no one. Why couldn't pure luck come to her rescue? *Normally, I would speak my mind*, she thought. But she hesitated, being so brand new to this scene and culture. ROTC and SWOS constantly stressed the importance of a good relationship with the chiefs. Chiefs were the backbone of the Navy, invaluable! For sure, she didn't want her actions to damage her introduction to the chiefs mess. Why was this happening on her first night onboard? She resented being bullied by a chief seizing on an opportunity, pushing himself on her in the guise of help.

Hemmed in by sailors, Brenda stared back at a food stand selling kangaroo burgers, which she doubted she could ever enjoy.

"Come on, let's go, the cabs are at the end of the pier!" she heard the now familiar but unwelcome voice, crushing her hope that the situation would go away. She wondered if the chief had sought Julie out, the other brand new female ensign, in the same way. As Brenda turned around to address him, the chief shoved a sealed cardboard box into her arms, which she caught. He then headed down the pier carrying another box. By instinct of holding the box, Brenda felt compelled to follow after him; and she walked down to the end of the piers where she found him loading his box into a cab.

"Here, I'll take that," the chief said, standing in front of the open back door of the cab.

"What is it?" Brenda asked.

"Come on, get in, we'll get something better than what they're offering here on the pier."

The chief made himself comfortable in the front seat and chatted away with the driver, someone with whom he seemed to be on familiar terms. Brenda sat quietly in the backseat with the boxes, wondering what to do, not believing she was really there. Such a bizarre situation; why hadn't she put the box right down on the pier and left? She opened the back window to let the wind hit her face as she watched the pier and the ships fade off into the distance.

"So, are we headed downtown?" Brenda yelled over the sound of air blowing into the cab. She gripped the top of the front seat as they headed up a winding road, which could have led to the downtown, she figured; but it certainly wasn't the main road to downtown, which was clearly marked.

"Where are we going, Chief? What's in those boxes?" she asked.

"We just have one stop to make before we get downtown."

"What is in the boxes, Chief?"

"Just hats and other souvenirs from the ship I need to drop off first."

"For what?"

"I'm the Morale, Welfare and Recreation Officer onboard, you know the MWR officer, and there's some guys I promised some stuff to."

Disgusted, Brenda looked out the window to find herself in her original Sydney stomping grounds – the heart of the red light district, home away from home for some military. She took a moment she shouldn't have to admire the architecture of the neighborhood once again, as the cab wound through the streets. Eventually, the cab slowed down in front of a strip club where a man standing outside smiled upon sighting the chief. The man motioned the cab around to the back, below a tree. Excited, the chief rushed out of the car in his big clumsy manner, carrying one of the boxes. Brenda focused on a historical marker, knowing her inaction was putting her in danger. The marker mentioned the influx of American servicemen to the area during the wars. She couldn't figure out why she hadn't gotten out of the cab and passively walked out of the situation. That was what she knew she should do. It was still daylight, but she sat there; and she did not know why. She watched as the cab driver handed the chief the other smaller box through the driver's window.

The chief's statement, "Hold on, I'll be right back," did not even register with her. The scene was playing out too surrealistically to actually be happening. I'm not the first female to experience an encounter with this chief, she realized.

"What were you doing in there, Chief? Was that stuff taken from the ship's store?"

"Yeah, those are good guys in there, in the club. I promised them some stuff from the ship."

"At the strip club, are you kidding me?"

"Hey, what're you worried about? You're the kind, the kind of person who tries to follow all the rules, aren't you? The good girl! You remind me of Ensign Wettlaufer, your roomie. You know she's never drunk one drop of alcohol in her entire life? Don't think she's ever had a guy either, if you know what I mean. Anyways, we're heading to the tower now. I could eat; that's for sure; I could eat."

Brenda found herself still a passenger in a moving cab, her only consolation being the sight of the tower and her own visual verification that they were heading downtown towards it. Was she truly in a dangerous situation, or was she overreacting? It seemed funny to her how talk of bars, strip clubs, and fetishes had become normal since joining the Navy. Up front, the chief struggled to impress the driver, and the driver appeared increasingly amused by the chief's effort. She could only guess the chief knew him from a previous port visit in Sydney.

Was she or the other women onboard the targets of some design by the chief? She wondered if she'd ever know. The downtown high-rise hotel enjoyed an opulent character. An orange glow from the oncoming sunset shone through a glass enclosed vestibule. This otherwise would have been a gorgeous evening in the city, she regretted. Brenda stood off to a distance as the chief paid the driver; and she entered the hotel behind him. The chief set his sights on each hotel staff member, but his grandstanding and boisterous pandering defeated any possibility that they would see him as a frequent and distinguished guest, as he had hoped. For a second, Brenda saw a bit of the chief in herself. Hadn't she checked aboard the ship and trespassed where she hadn't belonged? In vain, the chief labored hard to gain the favor of everyone they had encountered – the strip club staff, the cab driver, and now the hotel employees. "Yeah they all know me there," she remembered him saying. No one knew him, maybe the cab driver, but no one else.

Brenda followed the chief to an escalator that led to an elevator landing. She leaned back against the rubber handrail, knowing she should go back down the opposite escalator and leave the hotel immediately. Or was she making something out of nothing? Suddenly, she turned to the chief. "I'll meet you up at the restaurant, Chief," she said, even surprising herself. "I need to go back down to the lobby. Get a table and I'll be right up." She stepped off the up-escalator and back onto the down-escalator.

"Okay, I'll get the best seat, I'll...," he started to say, but Brenda didn't wait for him to finish. I should leave now, she kept telling herself. The idea of taking a long elevator ride over fifty stories with the chief scared her to death, as did the consequences connected with both staying as well as leaving the hotel.

Brenda's thoughts turned to her reputation in the chiefs mess as she approached the front desk. "Hello, I can't seem to find my way to the tower restaurant. Is there a staff member who could escort me?" she inquired, hurried and shaking. Only a few people dotted the lobby. Brenda pressed her palms against the marble reception desk as she leaned in, waiting for an answer. The desk clerk signaled a bell person who soon appeared.

Inside the elevator, accompanied by the bell person, Brenda watched each passing floor light up. *This would have been the longest ride ever*, she repeated to herself. "Would you mind escorting me to the maître d'? Thank you," she said to the bell person.

The elevator door opened to a dim corridor of rooms leading to a restaurant at the far end. Brenda noticed the chief standing by an open hotel room door a little ways down the hall. The moment he spotted Brenda and the bell person, the chief began waving his hands to draw their attention. "Hey, I've got a room here right on this floor. See that? I just need to grab my bag and switch this bag for that one..."

"And I thought you were going to secure us the best seat in the house!" Brenda interrupted, as she and the bell person walked right past the chief and approached the restaurant. The chief followed behind, plodding from side to side as he walked. Brenda tipped the bell person and stood back to let the chief take the lead. The chief charged right in to shake hands with and greet each member of the staff stationed throughout the restaurant. Some reacted with good humor; others reacted awkwardly but complacently.

The chief started in on the maître d'. "Hey, now, we would like to sit right here at this table, the best view in the house, if you would be so kind." The maître d' obliged. "And I'll have a Mai Tai," he ordered from the maître d'.

"Why are you ordering from the maître d'?" Brenda leaned over to ask the chief.

A waiter immediately followed. "I'll have a Diet Coke, thank you," Brenda told him.

But the chief interrupted. "No, now, she doesn't want a Diet Coke. What do you want, a Blue Hawaii or a Scorpion, or how about a Pina Colada."

"*Piña* Colada, I had a Spanish minor in college," Brenda interjected, correcting his pronunciation, but instantly regretting offering any personal information. "No, a Diet Coke will be fine, thank you," she told the waiter. Then she turned to the chief, "In another situation, maybe I would've enjoyed a drink, Chief."

"Hey, let me tell you something, Ensign, or can I call you Brenda?"

Brenda adjusted her posture and looked at the chief before

surveying the room. The glow of Sydney's modern skyline nestled among the soft city lights aided in calming her. She loved the atmosphere of a city. It had been her main reason for choosing to attend college in the heart of Boston. In the tower, they were surrounded by the city's aura. Her first attempt to speak was interrupted by the onslaught of cold, conditioned air from the vent directly above. Brenda always felt so freezing indoors during good weather. She straightened her posture and crossed her arms to feel warmer. Then she lifted her head back up to address the chief.

"You know what, Chief, let's stick to Navy names. We're both Navy people; really that's probably best," Brenda told him in a style aimed at setting boundaries.

Brenda thought of all the sexual harassment training videos she had watched in both ROTC and SWOS, and she couldn't believe this. She wondered if a camera should have been on the two of them. Could any of the events that evening realistically have been classified as sexual harassment? There were no obvious overtures, nor any explicit lines that threatened her career or her ability to carry out her duties. Brenda thought about the way in which sexual harassment training was at once serious and fodder for many jokes. She remembered laughing at a few impromptu skits by JOs based on the Navy's "red light, yellow light, green light" training. This was a yellow light, she decided.

"Let me tell you something, Ensign. I've been in the Navy almost seventeen years. A chief will make an ensign an admiral, or will force an ensign out of the Navy. You understand me? The chiefs is everything. Officers depend on chiefs. Junior officers, like yourself, now, they have no use at first. It's the chiefs, you understand. Now here, what're your goals?"

It was another ambiguous statement. "Chief, I'm the first JO to acknowledge that chiefs and senior petty officers are the backbone of the Navy's everyday operations. I hold tremendous respect for chiefs and petty officers. As for my goals now, I would say to be a competent division officer, earn my SWO pin, and represent the best interests of my division."

"Well, let me tell you, the chiefs is where it's at. Stick with me, a chief will make you an admiral, or will cause you to get out of the Navy." Brenda finally reached the point where enough was enough, and she lacked understanding to describe any of it. She looked out to the city lights again, scanning the skyline, searching for the assurance and calm she needed for the response she was about to give.

Brenda placidly addressed the chief. "Chief, I am going to be straight with you. This whole thing, from when you approached me on the pier, to our conversation here tonight, your words, the setting, everything has made me extremely uncomfortable. Do you understand? I am very uncomfortable and I am leaving."

Brenda rapidly stood up and left an Australian ten dollar bill on the table to cover her drink. "What, I don't know what you're talking about, what are you saying..." she heard him exclaim as she rushed to exit the restaurant. Once at the elevator, she pressed the ↑↓ buttons repeatedly, attempting to force the elevator to arrive more quickly. Inside the elevator, she pressed the →← button, continuously, in a panic. She remained fully adrenalized during the entire ride down. She felt certain the chief would somehow be there waiting for her when the elevator door opened at the landing above the lobby. Physically shaking, she ran down the escalator, out of the lobby door, and hurried into a cab waiting outside the hotel.

"Take me to the ships please, to the piers, to where the big American Navy ships are, the big aircraft carrier with all the planes on deck, please, thank you."

Possibly sensing her mood, the feel of the situation, disinterest on his part, something, the cab driver did not engage her in conversation. She shook in total and utter fear as they drove to the harbor. She wondered what her next step would be, and what life would be like for her onboard after this.

Chapter 15: To report or not ... The cause of women ... A call to an ex

Brenda was a planner, rather than someone who acted on the spot. In an uninhabited area of the pier, she found a pile of rustic planks to rest on, where she could sit and think. She kept watch on the brow leading up to the *John S. McCain,* looking out for the chief, feeling chilled by nerves; if only she could get her thoughts together. Soft lights from the ships' masts created a warm ambience on the pier at night. Underneath the lights, a collective hum emanated from the crowd. Her decision on what to do about the chief, if anything, had to be made very soon, *immediately!* The chief would return to the ship shortly, and she wanted her actions to precede his.

But she felt guilty for even considering that she should tell anyone about her interaction with the chief, no less report him officially. What had really happened that she should complain about? Why should she complain? Why should she insert a question mark into someone's career, based on a few short-lived and ambiguous circumstances and conversations? She should deal with it, disregard it, wait and see if anything else happened with the chief. Right? She couldn't answer her own questions.

Who was she to report this chief with seventeen years in, when she had less than one year in? She wasn't grandiose in her thoughts, desiring to become some high profile star in the movement to advance military culture into accepting women. She had simply wanted to participate anonymously in the wave which sought to modernize the military and bring it up to the standards and thought of the late twentieth century – by earning a commission in the Navy, serving her country, and blending in as any male junior officer would. *Just by her presence and by doing her job!*

She looked to preceding generations and wanted to live up to the legacy of women – most of whom were anonymous and lost in history – who had fought for equality and rights in the military, in society, and in the civilian workplace. Women before her had faced nearly impenetrable societal barriers – blockades imposed by tradition, cultural norms, and generational attitudes and thought. Decades ago, most women must have considered the oppression and legal discrimination impossible to overcome. And even though antidiscrimination and sexual harassment laws and policies had become more commonplace in the 1970s and '80s, society at-large and the courts, as well as the military, still didn't seem willing to back women. In the '90s, things were progressing. *In previous times, women had little to no legal or protective recourse available,* she reminded herself. She had seen vintage photos of women who had been tortured in prison because they were lobbying for the right to vote. Idealistically, Brenda wanted to be worthy of the women who had come before her – all those now nameless and faceless women who had gathered at conventions, marches, parades, or who had dared to obtain an education or embark on a career. It was why she hoped with all her heart that she had talent enough to blend in and, as a naval officer, represent the cause of women positively.

After thinking of women's issues in global terms, she felt petty for making a big deal about her interaction with the chief. It was minor and inconsequential, *right?* Her incident could not even compare – or register on any scale – to what women of the past had suffered. She thought of Tailhook. Not more than five years ago, Lieutenant Paula Coughlin sacrificed her career as a naval aviator when she exposed behavior that became a national scandal.[2] It was

---

[2] Following the breaking news coverage of Tailhook in Las Vegas, the Navy took action to protect its aviator officers, specifically those who were the alleged perpetrators, because their behavior was in line with traditional and accepted naval aviator "warrior culture." Over eighty women, and seven men, were sexually assaulted at the convention of Navy and Marine Corps aviators. Until pressured by women's groups and public outcry, Navy brass had remained unconcerned to acknowledge that what had occurred in Las Vegas might have been wrong; they resisted advocating for officers (both male and female) who were victims of the unofficially sanctioned and tradition-based harassment. The Navy had initially tried to assign the scandal to the enlisted, and subsequent investigations had found no wrongdoing on the part of senior naval officers. Female officers who brought complaints up the chain of command were publicly branded as "sluts" and "hookers" by naval leadership, presumably in an effort to discredit the value of female naval aviators and minimize their accusations. Navy admiralship charged societal change as the culprit behind the "whole mess" and inasmuch condemned the very presence of female officers. This then became an official reprobation of female officers, who were seen as both diluting military effectiveness and weakening the military bravado which had been held as vital in the fabric of naval aviation. Evolving the Navy into an institution in which all Americans could serve their country was not a priority, and was considered counterproductive to the military mission. Even though the Navy's initial response to Tailhook was to protect its own against negative press and damage to the reputations of the offenders, society outside of the military was no longer willing to tolerate such harassment – and the Navy was forced to change. Lieutenant Coughlin suffered retaliation and later resigned her commission.

difficult, now, to imagine the culture that had prevailed in the Navy just a few years before. While still in high school, and into college, Brenda had followed news of the scandal from start to finish. She knew that she, and many other women in the Navy, were the direct beneficiaries of Lieutenant Coughlin's sacrifice.

She recalled *Top Gun* and the sexist and discriminatory comments the characters made about women. She couldn't believe she had been a fan of that movie, even joined the Navy, in part, because of it.

Then she thought about the possibility of repercussions against her, onboard *Curtis Wilbur*. For certain, she didn't want to be branded ship-wide as a troublemaker, by officer and enlisted, and male and female alike. If she reported the incident, would she be labeled a sensitive female, around which one had to be careful? Would people say, "the most minor inference causes her to scream harassment, so be cautious of working with her, always keep the door cracked with another female inside for a witness"? Or would she be marked as yet another reason to exclude women from combatant vessels? Brenda viewed the gradual integration of men and women in the military as a movement that would evolve into a cultural norm. Now that the Navy integrated both sexes starting on the first day of service (in boot camp and in officer training), serving alongside women was normal for the current generation of officers and sailors coming up. No longer were women dependent on men to defend their interests and their country. In the larger scheme, Brenda felt integration of women in the military was a promising way to eliminate the second class status of women in society at large. It was the pathway to equal rights under the law and in society, and the end of dependence.

Brenda wondered if the Command would conduct an investigation of her allegations against the chief, if she made them. How would her peers react? Would they shun her? They did not even know her – *one day onboard!* What if the chief's reputation and service record were impeccable, his credibility solid? In contrast, she had no credibility or reputation to offer, which potentially rendered her allegations meaningless.

A final and determining factor in the equation, Brenda was inherently too principled and headstrong for inaction. She had to report the incident, especially since the chief may have had a history of this type of behavior. She thought of his potential to intimidate and harass an eighteen year old female seaman, just out of high school and boot camp. Although Brenda saw herself as an inexperienced twenty-three year old, she had an obligation to the young women onboard to live up to her position as "ma'am" and as an officer. Chiefs possessed tremendous power over their subordinates, and she had to assume he'd taken this course before; and in the future, she didn't want him to take it with someone more vulnerable.

Brenda approached the row of telephone booths near the pier gates, feeling apprehensive. It was night in Australia, but around lunch time on the East Coast of the United States; and she needed to call someone who was just as steeped in Navy culture as she was, for one more opinion. All of her friends from SWOS were in transit and scattered all over the globe. She didn't have time to consider the possible fallout from a phone call to someone she had recently dated, and probably should not have been calling. The relationship hadn't ended well, but without other options for seeking this type of advice, she picked up the receiver and dialed. With the sound of the American ring tone, Brenda felt her stomach drop. "Hello," she heard.

"It's Brenda, I need to run something by you," she blurted, scanning the pier for the chief.

"Okay. No problem."

"How are you? Are you doing okay on your new ship?" she asked.

"Yes, everything's fine here."

"Do you like it?"

"Yes, so far I like it."

"Great, I need your reaction, and since your dad was a chief. I'm calling from Australia."

"Okay."

The more Brenda explained of her encounter with the chief, the more ready she felt to walk back onboard. "So what do you think? Was there anything inappropriate?" Brenda asked, picturing him on the other end of the phone line.

"Yes, this chief sounds like a dirtbag. It's a completely fucked story."

"So do you think I should report it?"

"Yes, definitely. I would."

"Was it sexual harassment, or at least an attempt?"

"Yes, for sure."

"Do you think I'll have problems with the chiefs mess

afterwards?"

"Probably not, if you're in the right. He probably has a reputation there."

"Okay, I'll do it then. Thanks for listening," she said.

"Take care. I've got to go. Bye," he said.

"Okay, good luck on your ship," but she heard the phone hang up. "Good bye," she said to an empty phone.

Wow, Brenda thought. She stared down at the metal shelf in the booth, wondering if she had elicited any concern, not sure how much she really cared. There wasn't even a "let me know how it turns out," nothing, only a person who wanted to free himself from her call as quickly as possible. But those thoughts were for another time.

Chapter 16: First night on board ... Early thoughts on the warship ... Julie helps out ... Reporting the incident

Brenda returned to the ship feeling nothing was real. It didn't seem possible that such a bizarre circumstance with a chief could have occurred on her first night onboard – *her first night!* How was that possible?

The ship felt cold inside and the passageways were empty. Brenda neared her stateroom shivering, her arms clutched around her chest. The interior of the ship seemed to be that of a gigantic metal organism, extremely complex, but also sterile, cold, and practical, far removed from things of the earth, Mother Nature, life and vitality...just gray steel, no warmth, no beauty, no aesthetics. Every object had a direct and pragmatic purpose – propulsion, management of food, sanitation, sleeping, offensively fighting the ship, defensively fighting fires. Living quarters appeared utilitarian with pipes, wires, and firefighting apparatuses hanging from the bulkheads. Nothing showed artistry or feeling. The ship and her job existed primarily for the purpose of the destruction of other human beings and their habitats. And then there was the collateral decimation of any living being – plant or animal – surrounding a ship's target. She could place symbolic protective "padding" – in the form of justification – between her job as gunnery officer and the business end of a ship's gun or missile; but the certain result of her job was to ensure that the gunnery and missile systems were mission-ready, which, in real unpadded terms, meant ready to kill – to kill for reasons decided by politicians, for causes she might never understand. By joining the military, she had agreed to participate in the killing of people she didn't know, because someone else told her to. And on Navy ships, the killing was stylistically far removed from the close-up street to street and hand-to-hand combat of the Army and Marines. The expanse of ocean and positions offshore spared Navy personnel from having to see and hear the human beings that were to become the ship's casualties. The horrors of war could thus seem far removed, and could be accomplished with the distant mere press of a button on a computer, like that of a video game. The realities of violence and killing were further masked with honors and ceremonies and officer decorum and political justification.

She tried to think more globally about the role of warships, justifying that Navy ships, in some instances, have performed humanitarian functions, bringing aid to war and catastrophe victims. But that wasn't the purpose for which these ships were built, and there have always existed other means with which aid could be transported.

Brenda knocked softly on her stateroom door before opening it gently. She put aside those unwelcome thoughts running wild through her mind. Instead, she imagined that most people were off the ship on liberty, or holed up in their staterooms, resting, reading, and enjoying time to themselves. She saw Julie seated at her desk, writing, and she hoped that she was able to leave the ship earlier to enjoy the basketball game.

"Hi, Julie," Brenda greeted her roommate, feeling subdued and nervous, as if she could feel the flow of blood through every vein in her head and neck. She feared, irrationally, that everyone onboard had already learned about her encounter with the chief.

"Hey," Julie answered, as she turned in her chair to face Brenda. She appeared happy, apparently eased of the stress that had burdened her earlier. But when she saw Brenda her expression changed to one of genuine concern. "How's it going?" she asked, more low-key.

Brenda pulled her chair out from under her desk and sat down, still undecided on whether or not she should mention her encounter with the chief, partly, now, because she didn't want to ruin what appeared to have been a good night for Julie, which was most likely rare. "I had a night I'm not sure about," Brenda answered. "Were you able to go to your intramural game?"

"It was a cool game. We won," Julie responded, deliberately holding back her excitement, probably, Brenda thought, because she didn't know how to react to her.

"I'm glad the game was good, and that you enjoyed it." Brenda paused. "Do you know Chief Smith well?"

"Yes, I stand a lot of bridge watches with him. He's standing U/I watches to qualify OOD underway. We have fun up there; we're a good watch team; he's a highly motivated chief."

"Wow, a chief standing under instruction watches on the bridge," Brenda responded. "That's extra motivated, unusual, like he wants to apply for an officer program."

"He's not actually a chief yet. He's a frocked E-6 signalman.

Did something happen?"

"I'm not sure," Brenda answered, feeling she could trust Julie; but she remained undecided on whether Julie would believe her, and be open to another take on the chief. "Something weird happened with him, and it made me uncomfortable. I'd like to run it by you."

"Go ahead. I'll help you if I can."

"It all started from a feeling I had the moment he approached me on the pier, in an effort, he said, to welcome a new ensign onboard..." Brenda loathed the story for its repercussions, serious allegations, and potential aftermath. Most of all, she didn't want to be this conspicuous female officer, getting involved in controversy on her first day. She wondered if her rendition of the story would end up evolving into different versions, as it passed from crew member to crew member and made its way around the wardroom...and she wondered who would be vilified in the retelling, herself or the chief.

"What do you think, Julie?"

"I'm completely surprised," she said flatly.

"What would you recommend?"

"I can't tell you what to do, but I would recommend reporting it. If you want, I'll help you."

"Have you seen WEPS onboard?"

"I'm not sure whether WEPS is onboard or not," Julie answered, taking a serious stance with Brenda, "but trust me, you'll want to report this to the command duty officer, the CDO." Brenda felt as if Julie had years on her. "The reason," Julie continued, looking straight at her, "is that Lieutenant Rooney is the CDO tonight. You're fortunate; there're some you wouldn't want to report this to. Lieutenant Rooney is sort of your boss, the combat systems officer, the CSO. He'll listen and act fairly. He's very approachable and easy to talk to. I'll go find him for you," she finished. Then she stood up and left the stateroom, maintaining a dry and professional manner to the end.

Left alone in the stateroom, waiting to report an ambiguous circumstance against a well-respected chief, to a senior department head she hadn't yet met, one that was "sort of" her boss;...she felt rattled, and nervous. She puzzled over what other situations awaited her over the next eighteen months, which would be similar in their power to create anxiety and uncertainty, ones like this that she could never expect or even imagine.

***

Brenda hadn't moved from her chair when she heard three knocks at the door. "It's CSO, Lieutenant Rooney, Brenda. Can I come in?"

"Yes, sir," Brenda responded. His voice and demeanor sounded disarming, but she continued to shake from nerves, and when he walked into the stateroom, she nearly lost her composure. Julie stood behind CSO in the doorway. From her chair, Brenda looked up at an extremely tall officer, with a large build, who towered over Julie, who herself was nearly six feet. A red badge stamped "CDO" was clipped to his right shirt pocket.

Her first night onboard could not have felt more humiliating. Why couldn't this frocked chief have just left her alone? Now, she, the chief, CSO, Julie, and probably the XO and Captain, were going to be left swimming in this gray area together. Her first night onboard, and she was going to accuse a chief of possible sexual harassment – humiliating.

"Hello, I'm Lieutenant Rooney," the CDO introduced himself. "I'm sorry this is our introduction, but Julie told me you needed to discuss an event that occurred this evening."

"Hello, sir. I'm Brenda Conner. It's nice to meet you. I'm sorry about the circumstances. I regret this is our first introduction," she began, barely holding back tears.

"It's okay, Brenda. Please tell me what happened."

"Sir, let me start off by saying that I never imagined something like this would ever occur on my first night onboard. *Something like this* is an accurate description because I'm not sure how to even classify the situation: as nothing, inappropriate behavior, sexual harassment..." Brenda lost track of how the room had rearranged, but somehow, she found herself standing in front of the doorway, facing the combat systems officer, who was seated in Julie's metal desk chair. Julie stood behind CSO.

A few more sentences into her story, Brenda could no longer restrain her tears. Her long flight, facing life onboard a ship in the Navy...every stressful event was piling onto the last one to create enormous pressure that she could no longer subdue.

As she ended her account, her emotions evolved into anger. She felt sure something similar or worse had happened to other women during the chief's time onboard, and during his time in the Navy in general. After all, hadn't she been on her own time, out on the pier minding her own business? She didn't ask for any interaction with the chief, or anyone. "And then he gave two boxes of MWR ship paraphernalia to an employee at a strip club. I assume the souvenirs were stolen from the ship's store," she finished.

CSO wrote notes as she spoke. "I'm sorry this happened to you," he said. "It surprises me, to be honest. He's not a chief quite yet. He's a frocked E-6, but he appears highly motivated, his credentials solid, with an impeccable service record as far as I know. His wife's in Japan with a fourth on the way." Brenda wanted to shake her head in disgust – the chief was married with a large family and was engaging in this behavior. But she withheld her reaction, having learned from Julie's professional and steady bearing earlier; she merely nodded at CSO as he spoke. "I'll relay everything you've told me to the XO. Try not to let this upset you too much. I know that's easier said than done," he said, showing empathy. He offered a smile for reassurance, and Brenda nodded, feeling slightly more at ease.

But she still questioned whether she had done anything wrong initially, according to fraternization rules, just by the very fact of going on liberty with the chief. "Sir," she asked. "Was I in the wrong to go out on liberty with a chief?"

"It's perfectly acceptable to be in a social situation with a chief and to go out on liberty together. You've done nothing wrong."

"Thank you, sir. I'll be okay," she replied. "I won't mention what happened to anyone." But she wondered why no one had noticed the chief's behavior before. And for those that had, why hadn't they reported him? The chief's character and behavior were obvious to her the moment she met him. Brenda sat down in her desk chair, wondering if Julie and CSO had any idea that something wasn't right about the chief.

"I'll be here all night if you need me," CSO said. "I'm on duty, so I'm not going anywhere."

"Thank you, sir."

"Okay, good night. Call me if you need anything." And he left the stateroom.

Julie sat down at her desk and returned to writing postcards. Brenda stepped up onto Julie's bottom rack rail to reach her own rack, and attempted to tuck in her sheets while holding onto the ladder between the bunks. Julie's bottom rack was perfectly made and pulled tight. In the movies, a drill sergeant could have bounced a quarter off her rack.

Within a minute or so Brenda gave up trying to make her rack like Julie's. She just didn't care about that kind of thing, making a tight bed, so she threw herself up onto her top rack, turned on her rack light above her pillow, and spread the sheets enough so she could sleep in them. She used the Navy issue sheets left by the wardroom attendants, but most officers brought their own linens aboard.

Before closing her rack curtains, she broke the silence between her and Julie. "I still can't believe all this happened on my first night," she said. "It's like it's not real."

"Neither can I. I'm really surprised," Julie answered, and continued to write.

"Julie, I appreciate your support and assistance tonight, especially since you don't know me at all."

"It's no problem. I'm glad you could report it to CSO."

"So am I, but I'm not glad there was a story to be told at all," she answered, and then she climbed down from her rack, deciding to change into her night clothes before she read. She specifically packed pajamas that could be worn in the passageway. Conveniently, only about a foot of passageway separated her stateroom from the female head. A small plastic sign stamped "female" was velcroed to the outside of the bathroom door.

When Brenda returned to the stateroom, she found that the overhead fluorescent lights had been turned off, and the reading light was on behind the curtain in Julie's rack. Brenda stepped on the rail of Julie's bottom rack, and pulled herself up to her top rack while struggling to hang onto the ladder. She'd get used to climbing up to her rack, she reassured herself, hoping she wouldn't at some point slip and fall onto the unforgiving hard epoxy stateroom floor. Instead of reading, she switched off the rack light above her head, rested her head on the Navy issue pillow, closed her rack curtain, and pulled her scratchy gray wool blanket up over her face. Sleep overcame her instantly.

Chapter 17: An anxious first morning ... The Kingdom of SWO ... Who she thought she should be ... A woman in engineering ... An emerging inner conflict

1MC Shipwide Announcement: *"Reveille. Reveille. Reveille. All hands heave out and trice up. Reveille."*

Five days of liberty in Sydney, Australia had come to an end for the officers and crew of the USS *Curtis Wilbur* (DDG-54). It was Monday morning, and the ship was scheduled to get underway, en route to Perth, Australia, on the west coast, on the opposite side of the Australian continent. While Brenda spent her liberty days exploring Sydney, she had started to realize that "liberty" didn't feel as free as one would like. Especially on the last day, she felt that nagging and stressful worry of having to get back to the ship on time...or else, or else she might miss ship's movement.

On Sunday night, when she had walked back onboard at seven p.m. – two hours before liberty was set to expire at 2100 – she had experienced the relief of, "okay, I'm back onboard, I've made it." The OOD on the quarterdeck told her that it was going to be a long underway, coming up. The ship was going to spend the next fifteen days supporting the aircraft carrier, USS *Independence* (CV-62), with flight ops before reaching the far away Australian coast on the Indian Ocean.

But despite the prospect of a prolonged underway period, *there was still some excitement in the air!* The ship was going to conduct operations with the Royal Australian Navy, the RAN; and in and around the passageways, she had heard the crew talk with enthusiasm about operating with the "Aussies." There was even talk of a possible exchange program.

"Reveille. Reveille. Reveille. All hands heave out and trice up. Reveille," she heard faintly, a second time, while still lying in her rack. The 1MC announcement over the ship's PA system had echoed into her stateroom from outside of officers country. Brenda opened her eyes to complete darkness. The stateroom had no windows, and she could barely see an outline of the two pipes that ran in parallel over the center of her rack, not quite an arm's length

above her head. She reached up and switched her overhead rack light on. It was to be her first official day onboard the ship, *her first official workday!* – showing up at officers call and quarters in uniform, working as a division officer, and standing bridge watch. Days of walking through the city streets of Sydney by herself, and touring the outlying areas, were over.

A second later, her watch alarm started beeping. *Those high pitched, piercing beeps!* She reached next to her pillow and silenced them. She knew that high pitched beeps from a watch alarm were going to be annoying sounds to wake up to every morning; but she had learned from midshipman cruise to bring an alarm that she could leave at the edge of her pillow and silence quickly, before her alarm woke her roommate, who might be on a different (and opposite) schedule.

Then, through her stateroom speaker, she heard the single word, "*Reveille,*" loudly and clearly. As she sat up in her rack she remembered that routine ship-wide announcements were generally withheld from officers country and from disturbing officers' staterooms. But depending on the ship's policy, the quarterdeck watch (when inport) or the bridge watch (when underway) sometimes broadcasted a single word of a routine announcement in officers country, to keep officers apprised of the ship's schedule. From what she could remember, *reveille*, meaning "to wake up," had origins in French, and *trice up*, taken from old nautical English, instructed those living in berthing to lift the bottom racks so the area underneath could be cleaned during "sweepers" and "berthing cleaners."

She was going to miss the city of Sydney. During her liberty time, she had taken two bus tours arranged by the USO and MWR (morale, welfare, and recreation) for U.S. Navy personnel – one to a national park and another to an animal refuge. With the number of U.S. warships in the harbor, there were thousands of sailors in Sydney; and to her relief, she had recognized no one on either bus tour. She had enjoyed the solitude of remaining anonymous, and of sitting on the bus by herself.

She began planning her morning. Before going to bed, she had slipped into the wardroom to look at the Plan of the Day (POD). For Monday, she read that "the uniform for getting underway" was whites, and that all personnel not on watch had to "man the rails." She saw that officers call would be held at 0700 on the ship's fantail. She hoped Julie could verify that this information applied to her; she couldn't imagine anything more humiliating than showing up in the wrong uniform, at the wrong place, at the wrong time.

Brenda could tell she was alone in the stateroom. She hadn't looked down to check whether or not Julie's rack curtains were closed, but she couldn't hear anything. Then she remembered Julie telling her, "I'm always up before reveille, at least by four a.m." Brenda wondered if she could survive on a schedule similar to Julie's, already awake and making rounds before the 0500 reveille announcement. How could Julie sustain that pace, and, if there was good management on the part of her department head, was it really necessary? It made Brenda uneasy to think about; Julie's schedule put into question whether life onboard the *Curtis Wilbur* would be a repeat of what she had seen on midshipman cruise. She had followed her mentor (or "running mate" as mentors were called in the Navy) around the passageways at all hours – midnight or five a.m. – begging within her mind for sleep. She observed that the officers looked and acted perpetually exhausted. The work schedule – if it could be called a schedule – seemed inhuman, driven by the SWO department heads' desire to maintain appearances for the XO's benefit, who wrote their officer career evaluations (FITREPs, or fitness reports). She knew that some of the department heads even stayed in their staterooms late into the evening inport, most evenings, doing busy work, just to ensure the XO wouldn't see them leaving the ship before he did. Such was SWO culture, she had learned. "Make sure the XO doesn't read the morning message traffic before you, no matter how early you might have to get up. You don't want to be caught by surprise, and receive an ass-chewing when the XO mentions something you don't already know about," the USS *Spruance* junior officers had advised her. One day she had asked, "But why doesn't the XO trust his officers to manage their work as necessary during normal hours?" The JOs, "schooling" Brenda on how things worked, had explained it all using sarcastic SWO humor, "This is the kingdom of SWO, *SWOdom*." She had witnessed firsthand, the way SWO dynamics left the officers in the wardroom guessing, and living on a constant, uncertain edge. The bullying leadership and management style, typical of the SWO community and practiced by many XOs and department heads, created what the community called "kneejerk management."

Brenda opened her rack curtains and sat so her legs dangled off the edge of her rack. She then placed her right foot on the second rung of the ladder between the racks, grabbed onto the ladder rails, and stepped down cautiously until she landed her left foot on the edge of Julie's rack. "I'm for sure useless," she whispered under her breath. If she could barely climb out of her rack, how was she supposed to climb up and down the side of the ship on a Jacob's ladder, or several decks down the infamously long ladder into the ship's shaft alley? She was certain Julie, being very athletic, had no problem doing those things. There was so much to learn onboard, not just academic knowledge and running the division, but the physicality of living aboard ship, a metal and artificial environment. Her memories from midshipman cruise, combined with subtle reminders of her own unsuitability, made her wary of what was ahead. She already wanted out of the Navy and out of the life she had chosen. Then she reminded herself that she *had* climbed down the long ladder, many decks down, to shaft alley (the spaces through which the ship's propeller shafts ran) behind her running mate during midshipman cruise – *she had made it through the six weeks of midshipman cruise, and with an evaluation of "outstanding"!* In fact, in her midshipman cruise evaluation, the XO onboard *Spruance* had written positively that she was "tireless," and "highly motivated" for naval service. Alternatively, she had also heard that as long as a midshipman showed up to cruise breathing and at least somewhat conscious, and the ship didn't have to do anything outlandish like bail the midshipman out of jail, well, then, the midshipman received an evaluation of "outstanding." The SWO community needed bodies.

  It was all so confusing. She wished she could curl back up behind her rack curtain, which offered comfort and a safe haven, a space in which to think. Before she got out of bed in the morning, she usually liked to meditate a few minutes and travel far inside of herself. Often, after she got up, she would jot ideas for short stories, derived from characters she had thought up in her mind, characters who lived alternate lives in contrasting settings, and who served as an escape and as compensation for the life she didn't live. The characters were as dear and as important to her existence as anyone real she encountered outside of her mind. If she could only find the opportunity to sit and write about them, as in a novel, or to submit a short story to a magazine, such as a women's or literary magazine. On that morning, she would have preferred to remain in her rack to experience those characters and the emotions they allowed her to explore, for just a few minutes; those characters suffered in parallel with her, and went about doing the things she wanted for herself but couldn't do. She knew that once she opened her stateroom door, the most powerful emotion she would experience would be anxiety. She would be forced to confront the now-regrettable reality of her dreams, goals, studies, and preparation.

She opened her closet and removed her white uniform shirt from its hanger. Onboard, she planned to tell everyone that she had a degree in mechanical engineering and that she had been selected for nuclear power; that way, they could assume she was smart. She was constantly afraid that others might not see her as she wanted to be seen, as a bright young engineer with leadership potential in the engineering field. Struggling for acceptance – this struggle to get people to accept her for who she wanted to be and for how she wanted to appear – seemed an unfulfilling and anxiety-ridden way of going about life.

She realized that she had formed an image of herself in the way that she had *thought* she should be, and in the way that she *thought* would satisfy or impress others. And her efforts to form herself in those ways, and her actions of conforming, backing down, and pacifying, had been up until now largely unconscious and unexamined. Almost every idea she had ever expressed, and even her entire path of study (save literature) had reflected her parents' ideas about life. The realization made her feel hopeless for her days ahead onboard the ship, in nuclear power school, and onboard a nuclear aircraft carrier. Would she find her own future sometime after her four years in the Navy? Would she make it that far? Life after her time in the Navy felt like a million years away.

"A woman in engineering! A woman in engineering!" her mother had exclaimed around the house over many years – *she couldn't get her mother's words out of her head!* Her mother had first started repeating that phrase when Brenda was in high school, when she had begun the process of applying to engineering schools and to ROTC. More recently, her mother had applied it to the likelihood that she could land a secure technical job in the military, and later in industry, due to a drive for women in those fields.

Brenda shook her head as she quickly grabbed a newly shined brass belt buckle off her desk. It had always bothered her that her mother hadn't repeated the phrase out of any deep-seated passion toward women's issues; she had repeated it out of pure pragmatics. It was as if she was saying: These diversity programs and gender quotas will give you "an in." Was her mother at all conscious of the fact that her "woman in engineering" idiom was reflective of the need, in Brenda's situation, to compensate for weaker grades in science and math, and low math SAT scores?

Brenda draped her white uniform shirt over the back of her desk chair so she could pin her nametag over the right pocket. Was her selection to the nuclear power program partially a farce due to affirmative action? She wasn't sure how well she had actually performed during her technical nuclear power interviews at Naval Reactors in Crystal City, Virginia. She did know that following the Tailhook scandal, the Navy was under tremendous pressure to recruit women, especially into technical fields such as nuclear power. Her SAT scores in math were average at best; her grades in engineering were good – she had made the dean's list every semester – but her scores and grades didn't seem to reflect the stellar scientific and mathematical aptitude that the naval nuclear program sought. If she had been a white male, would they have selected her into the program? "A woman in engineering!" she could hear her mother saying, as they had waited for the results of the selection board. Her mother had been excited for her to get into the program, and she did think that her daughter was especially smart, just like her father. Her mother had told everyone they knew about her candidacy.

She began to understand her own mixed feelings about her mother's commonly exclaimed phrase. Affirmative action programs were in existence to amend centuries of marginalization of minorities and women, and to protect qualified and able minority and female applicants from discrimination. The programs were not in existence to give someone like her – who didn't quite have the SAT scores and math grades – an edge.

But out of desperation to maintain the persona that she loved science and math, that she wanted to major in engineering, and that she was naturally suited to the military, she had – on some level – counted on diversity programs and gender quotas. She had been single-mindedly focused on her goals. Now, however, she couldn't help thinking that the compromises she made to stay on her path, the lies she told herself, her justifications, negatively affected her self-esteem.

If she wasn't female, would she have been awarded an ROTC scholarship? Would she have been accepted to her engineering school in Boston? She thought of those questions constantly, and they nagged at her self-confidence whenever she found herself in engineering and military settings. Sometimes, in college and in ROTC, she had looked around at her male peers and thought, wow, these guys must really be smart because they were actually accepted without any edge. Even the lieutenants at the ROTC unit where she had interviewed for her scholarship had made comments like, "You're female, you're majoring in mechanical engineering, you're in!"

She had spent her life trying to survive in programs that were based on what were truly her weakest areas – math and science. In high school, she had insisted to everyone – to all of her friends – that like all engineers, or at least like the stereotype she knew of, she was great in math and science but weaker in subjects like English. She had taken the most advanced math and science courses her high school had to offer, and had downgraded herself to college prep English; even though in reality, she had struggled with the math and science courses and had performed brilliantly in the humanities. She hadn't known to look at who she was. And, she had been in active denial without knowing it. She had existed unaware of her behavior: that she was trying to manipulate the outer perception of herself for others.

She had wanted to be seen by her friends as the one who was pragmatic, who understood what was "correct" to study in college, and who knew how to go about working towards a successful career. When she had discussed with her father that she wasn't interested in straight engineering design so much, he had suggested a career in engineering project management, technical sales, technical marketing, or technical writing. "You've always been good at writing," he used to say, "you should pursue technical writing of manuals." Since she did have a record of performing well in creative writing and in languages she decided along with her dad, over many conversations, that technical writing and technical marketing would make great career goals. She had never thought about the fact that one had to understand, conceptually, how an engineering system worked in order to write about it. So, in college, she didn't study engineering to actually design engineering systems or really to even understand engineering or to become an engineer, but to secure that technical background in the form of an engineering degree, solely for the purpose of acquiring the right job. Her father had *absolutely* convinced his teenage daughter that she *had* to study engineering to give herself any chance at finding a decent job after college. Whenever she had questioned him on that, he had gotten angry at her and had belittled her for her questions. Consequentially, she had stopped asking questions and she had made herself believe.

She picked her white uniform shirt up off the chair back. She found that reflecting back on memories, in a truthful way, was extremely painful. She remembered how she had tried – with presumptuous, even obnoxious, certainty – to impress the lessons she had learned from her father upon others. Armed with her father's ideas about the unquestionable necessity of a technical background, she had criticized her friends who were not going to major in a technical or science field. She had told them that they were going to end up working as bank tellers, living in their parents' basements!

It was curious to her that when she looked back on her Spanish studies and her study abroad, it was with complete fondness. She had felt confident in her Spanish classes, on solid ground. She had first signed up for Spanish I in college (even though she had had four years of advanced Spanish in high school), purely because she wanted to increase her GPA, to balance her lower grades in a few engineering courses. It felt shameful to her to admit her manipulative behavior. But, by chance, something fortunate had come of her attempt to "use" Spanish to increase her GPA: She had found that she loved the Spanish courses – *they had resonated with her!* She then applied to the university for acceptance into the "Minor in Spanish" program. She flourished in the high level Spanish literature classes she took, and even successfully completed the advanced graduate level Spanish linguistics course. The professor had been hesitant to let her into the graduate course at first, but she had proved herself, and she had done exceptionally well, with relative ease. She had felt passionate for the subject matter.

Onboard USS *Curtis Wilbur*, she knew that she would fall into the trap of compensating for any weaknesses on the bridge by saying that engineering was where it was at for her, versus being on the bridge. It would be a matter of survival.

She finished buttoning her white shirt. She was starting to dislike herself – tremendously. No, she was starting to *hate* herself. A mass of newly emerging, inner conflicting forces were at work.

Over the last five days, she had come across other officers, but she had never asked them any questions. She wasn't sure what she was expected to know, what was considered common knowledge, and what questions would make her look ill-prepared and/or ill-suited. She feared discovery and being unmasked, almost to the point of panic. The wrong question might expose her. She had forced herself into a career field that didn't match her talent, or align with her *self*, all to "get a job"; and it was causing her anxiety she wasn't sure she could withstand.

Julie entered the stateroom and headed straight towards her desk as if she had no time to spare. She appeared as though she had already completed a day's work. Looking at Julie, Brenda felt inadequate. "On my first day, I thought I'd go up to the bridge to observe getting underway," she said to Julie, as she watched her nervously.

"Have you seen the watchbill?" Julie asked. "You're the conning officer getting underway from the pier," she exclaimed. Then she rushed back out the door.

Brenda was left staring at the closed stateroom door. She would be the one, up on the bridge, front and center, giving rudder orders to the helm, engine orders to the lee helm, and line handling orders to the boatswains mates on the deck to get the ship underway from the *John S. McCain* and the pier. She stood frozen, immobilized in horror and disbelief.

Chapter 18: Getting underway ... Remember, this is fun ... SWO language

Brenda's stomach dropped. Her hands shook as she opened cabinets and pored through her books to find her *Watch Officer's Guide*. She had to find the chapter listing the standard commands for rudder orders to the helm, for engine orders to the lee helm, and for line handlers. She hoped she still had those commands memorized from SWOS. All she could find were novels written in Spanish and Portuguese, and lesson tapes on learning Cantonese! All stuff she planned to delve into during her spare time. She was finding everything but her Navy books.

"I'm back," Julie reentered the stateroom, looking like she was in the middle of a million events. "I wasn't going to leave you hanging," she said earnestly. "I need to change into whites for sea and anchor detail. OPS had me start rounds at 0230 this morning."

"Any advice?" Brenda asked as Julie undressed. "What I need to know or do, anything?" Brenda finally laid her hands on her *Watch Officer's Guide*. Thank you! she exclaimed in her head to no one in particular.

"Don't worry," Julie advised. Brenda noticed Julie's habit of going serious on her. "There'll be a harbor pilot onboard to get us underway from the pier and out of the harbor basin. Translate his maneuvering, course and speed recommendations into standard command format. Follow the Captain wherever he goes on the bridge. Courses, speeds, and the navigation track to exit the harbor have already been laid out by the quartermasters. Once the ship clears the harbor basin, the quartermaster of the watch will start recommending the next courses and speeds in advance using a stopwatch. The Captain will expect you to react immediately. The QMs will take fixes and point out navigational aids. We have a great QM1 onboard. You'll be fine."

"Okay," Brenda responded, aware she had no choice but to go along with events. She had to either remember the standard commands, or rememorize them very quickly. Exact verbiage had to be used by the conning officer, such as *Left full rudder, steady on course 030,* or, *All engines ahead two-thirds, indicate zero seven five revolutions for seven knots.* Maneuvering a large warship through the water with other ships (referred to as contacts) and navigational aids[3] in proximity was dangerous. The Navy didn't allow ambiguity between the conning officer and helm. Standard verbiage, the exact standard words, had to be used precisely and at all times when giving orders to the helm as the conning officer.

"Have fun up there. Remember, this is fun!" Julie exclaimed, appearing to mean what she said. "The navigation brief is given in the wardroom. You'll have to give part of it. Read it exactly as written on paper by the navigator and QMs. This Captain doesn't like any surprises or adlibbing. All briefings must be read verbatim as pre-approved by him." It was the best news Brenda had heard since arriving in Australia.

"Julie, you've put me more at ease. Thanks for your help."

"I've got to go. My checklist is a couple of pages, and that's no problem in itself," Julie answered, as she thumbed through it, "but OPS is on my back sweating every line item."

Brenda nodded but said nothing; she noted Julie's use of the word *sweating*. From her linguistics studies, she knew that the culture and plight of a group was reflected in their language – the group in this case being the surface warfare officer community. SWO language and vocabulary was telling. In the context of SWO, the word "*sweating*" had come to express the sweating of details or consequences, or to express concern over "getting flame-sprayed" or "receiving an ass-chewing" by a more senior SWO.

SWO language was symptomatic of its management and leadership culture: micro-management, zero-defect, and neurotically guarding one's career progress at all times. Officers were required to advance and promote – always. Failure to promote resulted in resignation from the Navy. The *"up or out" promotion system*, an official naval personnel policy, didn't allow officers to remain in one rank, position, or job for very long. Within this system, not only were officers required to constantly "move up," but they were also required to rotate through certain jobs and duty stations to check off specific career boxes, such as a tour at the pentagon. And they had to strategically avoid certain shore and shipboard tours considered to be career-enders. The promotion system placed SWO officers on constant alert in regard to their promotability, and it made them competitive against (and sometimes backstabbing toward) their peers. Onboard *Curtis Wilbur*, the four

---

[3] buoy, lighthouse, fog horn, etc.

SWO department heads were in competition for ranking – against each other – one, two, three, and four. The system instilled SWO officers with an unrelenting and nagging awareness that one misstep or mistake could result in a poor fitness report. And SWO department heads such as Julie's "rode the backs" of their division officers trying to ensure that no mistakes were made.

Reputation on the waterfront was key to SWO success as well. It took careful and cold study to master the complex web of the officer promotion system and to rise through the ranks. The fact that the SWO community attracted a specific type of ruthless careerist-mindset officer was a common point of discussion and the subject of SWO jokes. And for the most part, careerists occupied the ranks above lieutenant (O-3), ranks reached beyond the initial scholarship obligation from the Naval Academy or ROTC.

Julie finished changing uniforms and opened the door to leave their stateroom.

"I guess deck division carries much of the weight prior to getting underway, all the topside equipment, the lines, taking down the quarterdeck, etc.," Brenda said.

"Yep," Julie answered.

Brenda felt like the annoying little sister, and she didn't want to be, so she asked, just quickly, "Breakfast in the wardroom, is it formal or informal?"

"It's always informal. Just go in and sit down or take something out with you. I'll take you in if you want," Julie offered.

"No, you go ahead, Julie. But, do you at least have time to grab breakfast for yourself?"

"I haven't had a chance," she said.

"Okay," Brenda nodded. She wondered how much Julie's life onboard differed from the regimented and scheduled life at the Naval Academy. At the Academy, Julie had majored in mechanical engineering, played a varsity sport, and would have had to participate in the daily drill and exercises required throughout her Academy tenure. Brenda concluded that Naval Academy life for Julie must have been just as grueling and constant as life onboard a destroyer.

"Good luck on the bridge," Julie said, and she disappeared out the stateroom door. With no one looking on, alone in her stateroom, Brenda opened her *Watch Officer's Guide* to cram for conning the ship out of Sydney Harbor.

Chapter 19: A rude thought ... A technical background ... Impression management ... ROTC flashback

Dressed in Navy whites, Brenda peeked into the wardroom through the faux porthole in the door. If she did enter for breakfast, she wanted to be aware of what she would encounter. Was anyone inside? Would they ask her questions? Would they engage her in casual conversation? Would she seem to them like an ensign, who, in accordance with her rank, schooling, and experience, was ready to take on and learn watches and the responsibility of leading and managing a division? Would it show through her aspect and demeanor that she was trying to force the impression that she was a solid junior officer with command potential?

She was relieved to have found the wardroom empty; the table appeared as though everyone else had already been through breakfast. As she stepped back from the wardroom porthole, she made herself overtly admit – *to herself* – that after four years of engineering school, she had walked away with little conceptual understanding of the field she had studied. She wasn't *really* an engineer. A rude thought. But going further, she made herself admit that she was now in a situation where she needed to be able to apply a baseline technical knowledge, and, in the absence of that skill, was left teetering on unstable ground.

The admission that *in spirit* she wasn't *truly* an engineer and naval officer was painful; it took her breath away. *And it was her fault; it was the fault of the way she had approached her studies in college.* She hadn't gone to college to learn in the classical sense, but to get "that piece of paper" – as her mom often called it – for a job and whatever other accolades and distinctions it would bring. If she had approached college with the goal of *learning* and *developing herself*, she never would have continued to major in engineering. But instead, she had plugged, chugged, memorized endless materials, and passed tests by staying up all hours of the night for four years with barely a day's break. That phrase – *plug and chug!* It was everything she had disdained about her engineering degree. It was a popular engineering expression that described the act of mindlessly substituting numbers from an engineering word problem into an equation to come up with a numerical answer, regardless of conceptual understanding.

Even during spring breaks, she had taken all of her books home, studied, and had done homework the entire week. In disbelief that she had spent years repeating these cycles, she realized that she had wasted precious time. Reflecting back, she couldn't believe that she used to preach her dad's words to everyone: that they needed a technical background to get a job, and that it was the key to their futures. If only she had put her same intense drive and effort toward a field for which she had talent, and for which she had yearning. What she could have been doing, exploring, and accomplishing with that same hard work!

She opened the wardroom door, feeling she needed to have something for breakfast before going through a grueling morning which included attending her first officers call, meeting her division, and conning the ship away from the pier. She wondered if another officer would "pop in" for breakfast. It was a terrible feeling, being afraid of what might come at her in the next second, the next five minutes, in an hour, or on any following day. And she had put herself there. All she knew was that she despised being onboard a ship; it could not have been more wrong for her; *and she had put herself there! She felt trapped and out of control!*

She wondered if her unsuitability for the Navy and for shipboard life was that obvious at first glance. Would the pressure of "impression management" test her to the brink of her sanity? *Impression management* she had heard it called – unsettled obsessive fear-based planning; the constant framing of her responses and actions, keeping her true motivations hidden in an attempt to mold others' perceptions. She was undercutting her own honesty, when honesty might have been one of the most important qualities that human beings could hold onto in life.

She remembered reading about the danger of harboring a well-kept secret, that the unexposed secret slowly worked poison into the soul. Nothing was more damaging to the psyche than secrets, hiding and denying the truth. In literature, painful secrets destroyed characters, even though they thought the keeping of them was somehow helpful to themselves, to their families, to others around them, or to the society in which they lived. Secrets, lies, cover up, denial, going along, and a "company man" attitude seemed to result repeatedly in the destruction of characters and of those they tried to protect.

She walked over to a large silver coffee dispenser; next to it on a shelf was a stack of white paper cups, beside which were a few navy-issue fine china saucers and teacups, bearing the traditional nautical design of the blue fouled anchor. In ROTC, she had nervously anticipated every event, just like she was doing now. She recalled the mindset that had guided her just a year ago. She had participated in the ROTC program rather passively, being so pressed for time by her engineering classes. Most of the extra activities in ROTC hadn't interested her, and she had never seen the point in participating in them if they weren't going to lead directly to something, like a requirement for commissioning, or a bullet point she could list on an application. She did, on some level, recognize that no one in ROTC would have chosen *her* for any special position in the program or in an activity. But she had had plenty of self-justifications for dismissing that slight: ROTC activities didn't represent the real Navy, the midshipman leadership consisted of a bunch of militaristic and legalistic jerks, and, anyway, she didn't have time for extracurricular activities due to her engineering studies. Most of all, she had just wanted to get through ROTC the best she could. And she couldn't *not* get commissioned! And fail!

Onboard the ship, she foresaw that things would probably unfold in the same way that they had in engineering school and in ROTC. The commands of the conventional ships were under enormous pressure, from above, to award the SWO pin to nuclear candidates who would then begin nuclear power school. Brenda had just assumed the Command of the *Curtis Wilbur* would run her through the motions and quals of getting her SWO pin, followed by the Navy whisking her off to nuclear power school. The Navy needed nuclear power trained officers (nukes) badly. She wondered if she wanted to be "run through" and "whisked off"; but in reality she was counting on it, since based on merit alone, she might not make it. What kind of person did that make her? She wasn't sure, but she could not fail to get her SWO pin at any cost; she could not deal with that outer failure – a *Letter of Nonattainment of Surface Warfare Officer (SWO) Qualification.*

And in the back of her mind there was the presumption that "nonattainment" really wasn't an option. On midshipman cruise she had asked her running mate, "What if a JO doesn't qualify?" And he had answered, "No, no, the Command and senior watch officer will then train the hell out of you until you decide that the SWO community is paradise on earth...and you qualify." She understood that the pressure to achieve SWO qualification was not only on the Command, but also squarely on her. From talking to other JOs, she knew that there might have been a few captains out there that sometimes made it clear to a junior officer that he/she was never going to qualify aboard *his* ship. At all costs, she wanted to avoid the scenario in which the Command and senior watch officer took a specific interest in her qualification. As her running mate from midshipman cruise had warned, "Remember, the number of JOs a captain qualifies is part of his FITREP. Therefore, the XO will be on the senior watch officer's ass making sure you qualify."

After the insights she had made recently, regarding the hollow nature of many of her "accomplishments," she wanted to be able to earn her SWO pin sincerely. If she *was* awarded a SWO pin, she hoped it would truly be deserved.

She remembered the anger she had directed at some midshipmen in ROTC...those who had detected the truth about her. A few had perceived her incompatibility and had treated her accordingly. Worst of all, she understood that their manner towards her was for the most part deserved, which grated on her need to see herself as stable and competent. In her new shipboard assignment, she would have to try and change, or at least manage the impression she gave out. She had no choice, she concluded. But already she knew that Julie "saw" her, as did Jon, the navigator. Others probably had questions; she suspected it was that obvious.

Brenda remembered standing inside the kitchen of her friend Kevin's student brownstone in college. As he stirred his dinner on the stove, she complained incessantly about a series of disciplinary chits she had received from the ROTC midshipman battalion CO and XO, both other college students. Brenda despised both of them equally as much as they seemed to despise her, especially the girl billeted to midshipman battalion XO. They had given Brenda her first disciplinary chit that semester for carrying a non-regulation black purse around campus, while in uniform, in place of the horrid defeminizing Navy-issue black purse, which was manly, square, and blockish. The second chit she had received for failing to properly prepare for a uniform inspection after she had pulled an all-nighter for a fluid mechanics exam. Brenda could still clearly picture the uniform inspection, and the Marine-option midshipman who was conducting it, some liberal arts major. He stood in front of her as she stood at attention in the formation, and spatted out an exaggerated "UNSAT" at her face. What could she say? She had gotten an A on the fluid mechanics exam; it was worth it. The third time, the battalion XO wrote her up for giving an eight-minute speech to her platoon when the requirement was ten minutes. Brenda didn't understand; she thought she had covered the talking points more concisely.

She wrote a memo to the midshipman leadership, in her own defense, in an effort to explain her actions. In her memo – which she addressed to the midshipman battalion XO, a political science major – she had written of her engineering workload, how she worked on homework and studied night and day, literally, without a break, never going out or to a party, and how she often found herself barely able to get to ROTC functions or prepare for military inspections. But she received a memo in response that stated, "You are correct. There is no excuse. This is an example of a failure to pay attention to detail. As a platoon commander, it is your responsibility to set the example where board accountability is concerned."

That evening in her friend's apartment, Brenda lamented about this girl who was the midshipman battalion XO, about how she was a "flamer" and how she concerned herself with details of no consequence; and Kevin agreed. Then she asked for his honest opinion. Why had the midshipman leadership focused at all on writing her up? Half of those people partied, drank, and stepped outside the rules all the time! "Because they think you're clueless and you don't care," her friend cut her off, delivering the unvarnished honesty she had sought, as he continued stirring his dinner on the stove. Brenda shuddered at remembering the feel of such a hard truth, verbalized by a friend. She had no response for Kevin because she actually did care very much; and she knew she was inept.

Refocusing on what she needed to do, Brenda walked over to the dining table. A few place settings of fine china and silverware remained undisturbed on the blue linen tablecloth. Assorted donuts and pastries were arranged on an ornate silver tray beside a silver pitcher of milk. Brenda sat down where she could avoid the donuts and focus on the cereal. *Cool!* she noted as she picked up a box of Wheaties: metric, Australian-sized cereal boxes. As the ship resupplied at each port, she imagined she would encounter a variety of food products from various Pacific Rim nations over the course of the deployment. She was reminded of the odd-sized Diet Coke can that came out of the ship's vending machine the day before.

"Good morning, ma'am, would you like to order breakfast?" a

petty officer dressed in summer whites asked, as he rushed in to serve her. His arm patch signified that he was an electronics technician third class (ET3). She was driving herself crazy, finding herself at odds with *everything* onboard the ship, including all of the customs she was encountering. She found it difficult to accept the idea that junior petty officers from all enlisted ratings (engineering, combat systems, operations, administration, etc.) rotated to the wardroom to serve *her*, a supposed officer, in a formal dining setting, before they moved on to cleaning the floor and sink in her stateroom, not to mention the head. She wasn't sure how well she could accustom herself to being waited on as if she was royalty. Then, she asked herself: If wardroom decorum was an ingrained part of Navy tradition, why couldn't she just accept it as a normal part of living onboard the ship? For sure, being served felt nice; but she was merely an American kid who had done nothing special to deserve this sort of aristocratic treatment.

"I'm sorry I didn't get in here sooner, ma'am," the petty officer said. "I didn't know you had come in."

"Don't worry. I'm Ensign Conner. It's nice to meet you," she introduced herself.

"I know who you are, ma'am," the petty officer smiled. Everyone onboard seemed to know who she was before she ever had a chance to introduce herself. "I'm Petty Officer Hernandez. It's nice to meet you, too, ma'am. Welcome aboard."

"You don't have to worry about serving me. I'll take care of myself," she smiled. "I do have one quick question."

"Yes, ma'am."

"Is there any milk besides whole milk?"

"Sorry, ma'am. All we ever have is whole milk."

"Thank you, Petty Officer Hernandez. I'll be all set from here," she told him, not wanting to think of the potential damage drinking whole milk could have on her weight. *Whole milk*, Brenda thought. No woman would ever offer whole milk as the only available dietary option. She had heard stories of Naval Academy women who had developed eating disorders as they tried to keep their weight down while living on a diet designed for men. She hoped the military would someday recognize the added value women offered, and accept fully the unique qualities women had to contribute, rather than squeezing them into a male system. Military women were forced to operate inside a paradigm that went something like: *We are the men who have established rules and standards to fit our gender and you better live up to them.* Brenda always wondered what standards women would set, and if the men would be able to live up to those.

Brenda tried to rush her cereal down, but she could scarcely eat. "I'll get those dishes for you, ma'am," the petty officer rushed back over to her.

"That's okay, ET3. I'll at least put them up on the counter. Thanks for your help this morning." She wanted to return to her stateroom to give herself one last look-over before heading out to officers call.

Chapter 20: Introducing ... ROTC truths denied ... About technical ability ... Life's Little Instruction Book

It was 0630, and the time was coming for Brenda to introduce herself at officers call and at division quarters. After leaving the wardroom, she rushed back to her stateroom, walked directly to the mirror over the sink to check her hair and makeup one last time, and then she was off! She walked purposefully to the ladder near the entrance to the wardroom and climbed down one deck to reach the portside oval watertight door leading outside the skin of the ship. Just beyond the quarterdeck she stopped to allow her eyes to adjust to the dawn sunlight. After having been enclosed within the ship, with its dim passageways and compartments lit with fluorescent lighting, she could barely see well enough to walk safely on the decks, even with squinting.

As her eyes adjusted, she stood over the aft decks admiring the transition from dawn into a sunny morning in Sydney Harbor. She wasn't sure how she would fare at officers call and quarters, in the wardroom giving the navigation brief, or on the bridge when she conned the ship away from the pier and out into the seas. She only knew that she had no choice but to keep moving forward, facing each oncoming event of the morning as it came. Across the decks of the *Curtis Wilbur*, she saw enlisted sailors dressed in bright white uniforms, wearing traditional sailor hats (dixie cups), congregated by division at designated points around the ship. She saw the officers gathered near the aft VLS (vertical launching system), talking in groups of twos and threes.

She started walking aft towards the officers, uneasy about the level of formality she would encounter. She had attended OCall each morning on midshipman cruise and she knew not to expect a great deal of formality there, besides being called to attention and being put "at ease"; but she felt nervous about division quarters. On this morning, would she be required to drill her division in any way, or at least order them to attention or at ease? Would she have to perform any kind of inspection?

During her senior year of ROTC, she remembered dreading her billet as platoon commander, as it entailed leading the platoon in drill during the NROTC Annual Fall Drill Competition. She knew she wouldn't be able to do it, drilling the platoon, leading and performing military ceremony in front of an audience; and the thought of that event approaching had possessed her relentlessly during the summer prior to her senior year and during the first weeks of fall semester. But before practice sessions started, as luck and coincidence would have it, the midshipman battalion CO and XO fired her from her platoon commander billet, citing her three disciplinary chits (for the purse, the uniform inspection, and the eight-minute speech); they reduced her from platoon commander to squad leader. As Brenda continued to the aft VLS, she pictured her fellow college student, the midshipman battalion XO, calling her aside, very seriously, to inform her of the demotion. Brenda knew she had issues in ROTC, but so did this girl, so high and mighty as midshipman XO, simply another college student who had just as much to learn as she did. Brenda recalled the relief she felt once the girl had finished speaking; acting unconcerned, she asked if that was all, and she walked away.

Brenda closed her eyes at the memory, thinking about how she had discounted the episode and blamed her failure solely on the student battalion XO. She had continued on her military path, unabated by what was actually a telling piece of evidence.

Walking against the light harbor breeze, Brenda approached the VLS and sat down on the edge of the missile launcher, arms crossed over her chest, knowing that soon she would be responsible for its operation and maintenance. She wondered if she would ever be exposed: Would it come to light that she knew nothing about the VLS system or the missiles and torpedoes it fired? The thought of the first question anyone might ask her about the operation of the missile launcher scared her to death. Limited knowledge of the launcher, upfront, as a new ensign, might not have been alarming in itself; probably most junior officers fought a steep learning curve in their first jobs, she imagined. But she could no longer deny the reality that had started to close in on her in college and in SWOS: of all the talents naturally instilled in her character, innate technical ability was not turning out to be one of them. Nor did she even possess interest in science and math – the basis for understanding shipboard systems – no matter how much she tried. And that was never going to change for her, she was slowly realizing. Technical ability, an interest in science, math, and naval science, military bearing – all of those factors – were never going to suddenly come together for her at some future next place, such as aboard the *Curtis Wilbur*, at nuclear power school, or aboard a nuclear aircraft carrier. But, armed with an unflinching drive to never give up, she knew that she would have to hang onto the hope that if she worked at it hard enough, and really delved into her work, she could change.

She had spent her last night in Sydney in her stateroom, hovered over her notes from SWOS, trying to study the operation of the VLS, and the characteristics of the missiles and torpedoes the system stored and fired. But her attempt at memorizing the characteristics of Tomahawks, standard missiles, and ASROCs (vertical launch antisubmarine rockets), along with launch sequences, and principles of general VLS operation and maintenance, must have failed, she realized nervously, because as she sat on the ledge of the launcher that morning, she couldn't remember anything she had studied, only a few snippets here and there, basically how the forward Mk 41 VLS had twenty-nine missile cells and the aft VLS had sixty-one missile cells. Even a general grasp of the conceptual operation of the system – an alternative to memorization – seemed out of her range. "Hey, I need you for something," her new boss interrupted her thoughts, "and I need you to sweat this in the same way that I am." Brenda's heart skipped a beat.

She saluted him. "Good morning, sir."

WEPS returned her salute. "You've got two chiefs on the ROADs program. So you'll have to handle this yourself." She could tell he was agitated, but she understood that his agitation wasn't aimed at her. Before he could go on, someone else interrupted with a question. As she stood next to the aft VLS, looking up at WEPS, waiting for him to finish speaking with the other officer, she noticed the same unsettled manner in him that she had seen in the SWO department heads on midshipman cruise.

After finishing his other conversation, WEPS continued where he left off. "Working on this issue will be a good opportunity for you to get facetime with the XO," he said. She froze. *Facetime*, she thought...it was another one of those SWO words. Then, she remembered what Pete had told her. From him, she was to inherit two chiefs who were "Retired on Active Duty," as the joke went – *ROADs*. Before she could answer WEPS, a warrant officer across the way greeted her with a friendly, "Hey GUNNO!" and waved, and she returned his greeting.

She answered WEPS eagerly, while trying to keep her nerves calm. "Let me know what you need, sir. I'll get with Pete to take care of it."

"These days I'm relegated to Strike," Pete approached them and chimed in. "After this week I no longer plan on being GUNNO." Brenda smiled at Pete, as strike officer entailed seniority over the gunnery officer position. The strike officer was responsible for the close-in weapon system (CIWS - pronounced *sea-whiz*), and for the harpoon, SM-2, and Tomahawk missiles.

"Also, sir, to let you know, I'm on the watchbill to be the conning officer when we get underway," she told WEPS.

"Never mind that right now, GUNNO. You'll be fine," he answered, completely unfazed. "After OCall, follow Pete over to meet your division. A generator rental company in Arizona has written the ship three times regarding an unpaid bill on behalf of your leading petty officer's wife. XO's had it. Talk to Chief Dering and get this resolved. Write a response letter to the generator company for me to initial and for the XO to sign. Have it ready for when we secure from sea and anchor detail." She noticed that WEPS had a high w.p.m. (words per minute), and he annunciated every word with amazing swiftness.

She looked at WEPS, wondering if the unpaid generator bill was the crisis to which he had initially referred. "Isn't the unpaid bill solely the petty officer's responsibility, sir?" she asked. But from SWOS she knew it was the Navy's policy to intercede, at times, in the financial affairs of its personnel, not by actually paying the bills, but by acting as an intermediary with creditors, and by counseling petty officers and seamen on finances. In many ways, the Navy was like mom and dad. All of the "war stories" she had heard from the lieutenant instructors at SWOS about having to bail their sailors out of financial disasters came back. Especially those told by instructors who had served in Mayport, where apparently there weren't laws in place to protect consumers from buying cars and electronics at outrageous interest rates. A one hundred dollar per month car payment sounded great, right? From her influences growing up, she harbored no tolerance for that sort of financial irresponsibility. She had always been a natural saver, a trait in which she and her parents had taken special pride. Other kids' parents talked about how their teenagers spent their money on whatever. She had loved being different than that, and when she was practical and when she saved she felt such overwhelming approval from her parents; and she savored the approving smiles and surprise from other adults. In second grade, her mother took her to the bank to open her first savings account, into which she deposited her First Communion money. Brenda visualized the snapshot memory of herself and her mother sitting at the banker's desk. As a little girl, she couldn't understand why she had handed the woman money, only to receive a small booklet in return! But with time, she had watched the figures written inside the booklet grow, with money acquired from birthdays, holidays, babysitting and various jobs in fast food and at the mall. At twenty-two, immediately after graduating from college, she had started funding an IRA.

"Anything like this falls under the Navy's umbrella, unfortunately," WEPS answered. "You good to go?"

GTG, Brenda thought. "Yes, sir."

Then, WEPS turned to Pete. "And Pete, we received another fucking blast from the last ammo admin message. Get on top of this. I need a correction message by this afternoon to give to the XO before I have my ass handed to me."

1MC Shipwide Announcement: *"Officers call. All hands to quarters for muster, instruction, and inspection."*

The officers and chiefs, who had assembled around the aft VLS, climbed down a deck as a group to the fantail, and once there began to form into rows. In the background, she heard the officers' papers ruffling in the wind, and the murmur of the fans and motors of the ship. As the XO approached the formation, the group instinctively came to attention. "At ease," the XO responded casually. She looked around, trying to take everything in as she stood in one of the makeshift rows. She was nervous, but okay for the moment. The XO began reading down a list of announcements, which to Brenda sounded like mere abstractions. But only because she was so new, she reminded herself. Soon she would be a part of all this, and the announcements would apply to the tasks in which she was involved.

Just before the XO dismissed the formation, he briefly introduced her as the new gunnery officer. "Let's all welcome Miss Conner, our new gunnery officer. Let's make sure she's taken care of and has everything she needs to get started." In the few seconds after, she thanked her colleagues for their nods and hellos before the XO moved on to making the final announcements of the morning. She couldn't help but think that this XO appeared fair, approachable, and professional, not at all like the XO aboard *Spruance* or others she had heard of through SWO sea stories.

When officers call broke up and the formation splintered off into division quarters, Brenda migrated over to her division behind

Pete. At SWOS, she remembered, the instructors taught young junior officers to practice their introductions to their divisions beforehand, but she had decided to opt for a more honest and spontaneous approach. Outside of a general idea, she wanted her words to flow out naturally. As she approached CO and CM divisions with Pete – as he was in charge of both divisions – the leading petty officer (LPO) called the group to attention. "At ease," Pete responded. "Good morning, I would like everyone to meet our new gunnery officer, Ensign Conner," he began. "I'll be turning CO division over to her this week. As you know, CM division will stay with me and I'll be the strike officer. One of the first things we'll need to do to turn over CO division is to conduct an ammo count, so stand by for that. Ensign Conner, do you have anything you would like to say?"

She began speaking out of pure reaction. "I want to say hello and that I look forward to meeting and working with everyone soon." She had planned to go on, but she looked out at a division of blank uninterested faces. Maybe a few sort of smiled, she guessed; she wasn't sure. Momentarily, she caught the eye of the lone female of the two divisions, a third class fire controlman technician in CM division, who showed a slight smile, maybe, but Brenda decided to stop her introduction there. Plenty of time would soon be available to get to know the division on a more detailed level.

Before dismissing the two divisions, Pete opened *Life's Little Instruction Book.* "Learn three clean jokes," he quoted from the book. She wasn't so sure of the merit of that advice from the book, an interesting idea possibly; she had always found cutesy pop-culture coffee-table books like that to be annoying. "Watch a sunrise at least once a year," was the second quote he read from the book. "Learn to identify the music of Chopin, Mozart, and Beethoven," was the third. Chopin she loved, but that kind of book and its hollow quippishness wasn't her style. She looked down at her feet, hoping her face hadn't betrayed her thoughts. But then, she questioned her attitude toward the book; she would never have thought of something – possibly cool? – like reading a quote to the division each morning; and she wondered if something unusual like that might have been a good idea after all, serving to break up routine.

Pete turned to Brenda after instructing the leading petty officer, Petty Officer Brooks, to dismiss the division. "Follow me," he said, as the division scattered. "This is GMC Dering and GMC Walden," he introduced her to the two CO division chiefs, both E-7 chief gunners mates. Chief Dering barely returned her handshake. A quick and frustrated "Hello, ma'am" was all he seemed willing to offer. Chief Walden, however, appeared more open to her as he returned her handshake. From him, she received a more approachable, "Welcome aboard."

"I look forward to meeting you both and learning more about the division," she responded, attempting to show disregard at being discounted. Truth be told, she empathized with the chiefs. They had spent the last twenty years meeting new ensigns – countless young ensigns, who came and went every six months or a year or so, most likely without much consequence, leaving them behind to run the nuts and bolts of the division. Most ensigns were probably useless, she figured. And in the chiefs' position, she would have hated all of those stupid bratty ensigns, too.

"Okay, you know where to find me," Chief Dering answered, disinterested. "I'll be headed to the chiefs mess to have some coffee while we get underway." She noted he wasn't going to man the rails, as required of all non-watchstanders. But what could she realistically do?

Pete gestured as if to hold Chief Dering a moment longer.

Chief Walden smiled, "Are we all set then?"

"We're good, Chief. See you later," Pete answered, looking at Chief Walden.

"Welcome aboard," Chief Walden said to her, once more, before turning to walk away, wearing a half smile. She watched his half smile trail off within a few steps. She imagined he wasn't going to man the rails either.

"You need me, sir?" Chief Dering asked, seemingly impatient with Pete, her, and the entire system, Brenda deduced.

"Actually we do, Chief," Pete answered, standing straight up with his hands clasped behind his back. "GUNNO has something she needs to speak with you about." The letter from the generator rental company in Arizona had really been eating at her. All the letters and phone calls from businesses, creditors, spouses, ex-spouses, girlfriends, etc. that she'd heard about in SWOS! She had no tolerance for that kind of blatant irresponsibility and dependence on the Navy as mom and dad. However, she had planned on discussing the matter with the chief, so he could, in turn, discuss it with the leading petty officer. But before Brenda could start, Chief Dering grabbed the paper and waved the first class petty officer over with an exasperated, "Brooks, over here."

She stole one more glimpse of the city surrounding the harbor before turning back to the matter at hand. This was all happening in Sydney, Australia. She still couldn't believe it. "Petty Officer Brooks," Brenda began purposefully, "The ship received this notice with a letter addressed to the Captain. What's the situation? Because this kind of thing, unpaid bills, we can't have in the division. Do you plan on paying it?"

"I've taken care of that, ma'am," he answered. "I sent a check U.S. Mail last week from Guam. My wife's returned the generator. There's no electrical service available where my wife lives in Arizona with my stepson and stepdaughter."

"I'll write a letter from the XO that the bill's been paid," Brenda said. "Do you have a copy of a canceled check or money order for proof?"

"I'll get that to you, ma'am. Anything else?"

"No, thank you. That's all, but I don't want to get letters like this again coming to the ship. It's irresponsible. Everyone has to pay bills." And with that the petty officer turned to walk away, after simply answering, "yes, ma'am." Brenda turned to Chief Dering. "Chief, maybe we can meet in the gun mount later to discuss the status of the gun."

"Yes, ma'am, sure, whatever," the chief answered, balking at the notion. "WEPS already knows what's going on. You can have a copy of this." He handed her a brochure. "The Captain wants to protect the deck from the shells that fall when the gun shoots. Here're the specs for the best kind of matting to get." She stared at the brochure, wondering if the chiefs had been preconditioned to hate her after her episode with the frocked chief on her first night.

"Oh, and one more thing," Chief Dering said after Pete walked away.

"Yes, Chief."

"About that thing with *Life's Little Instruction Book* or whatever the hell it is. Mr. Lineberry reads it at quarters. Don't do that kind of shit. The guys hate it." And with that he left her standing there.

Chapter 21: The wardroom ... Barely controlled chaos ... SWO tour of duty ... Anything but this

1MC Shipwide Announcement: *"First call, first call to colors."*

All on deck scattered. Most escaped into the skin of the ship. Apparently no one wanted to be caught outside during colors.
One whistle blown over the 1MC.
The few hands left on deck halted to attention as the petty officer of the watch (POOW), aft on the ship's fantail, raised the flag to a recording of the national anthem. Brenda stood straight as an arrow at attention, staring out at the Sydney skyline, lamenting the loss of her freedom. Soon she would be out at sea, confined to the ship, surrounded by steel, her every hour regimented, her life marked by rigid discipline, even as all the people underneath the trees and buildings on shore – still visible to her – remained part of the world. All of her friends were living in Boston and New York in crowded apartments, dating, going out and trying on different jobs. Brenda closed her eyes and inhaled deeply. During colors, she recalled her final afternoon in Sydney, when she had rested, all by herself, lying in the grass beneath the umbrella of a large old tree, high upon a tranquil hill, possibly the highest point in Sydney. From her vantage on the hill, she could see the horizon, the city, the harbor, the famous harbor bridge, and the chic shops and restaurants below. Before her rest under the tree, she had visited the Sydney observatory. Then she remembered the refuge she had sought in the peaceful Chinese gardens downtown.
Three whistles blown over the 1MC.
All hands carried on as if nothing had happened.
1MC Shipwide Announcement: *"Set material condition yoke. Duty Damage Control Petty Officers make reports to DC Central."* Brenda quizzed herself. Material condition yoke was the intermediate degree of watertightness and protection, between x-ray and zebra. Condition yoke was maintained at sea, and inport when outside of normal working hours or when at war. All closures marked with an X, Y, circle X, or circle Y had to be secured, she recited inside her head.

***

1MC Shipwide Announcement: *"Navigation Brief, Wardroom."*

Brenda stood front and center in the wardroom, at the head of the dining table, feeling the eyes of every officer and enlisted sailor resting upon her. The room was crowded. She gripped the four page navigation brief in her hands, as if for dear life, remembering the valuable advice Julie had given her: *Read every word verbatim.*

The ship would get underway once she finished briefing – a powerful thought. On the bridge, she would have to give commands by relying on what she had memorized at SWOS, and on what she had been able to review quickly in her stateroom before breakfast. She hoped she would live up to the task of conning the ship from the pier and out of Sydney Harbor. She had no choice.

The wardroom was packed with white uniforms; all she saw in front of her was a sea of white – officer and enlisted. To her left, sat the enlisted quartermasters who kept the primary navigation chart on the bridge. Behind them, the operations specialists congregated, who she remembered kept a secondary navigation plot in the combat information center (CIC), located below decks. Other enlisted ratings such as boatswains mates, signalmen, and engineers also packed the room. Throughout her body, she felt the stress and tension of standing before this group; she reached back to massage that familiar tight knot forming over her left shoulder blade. She wasn't sure she could pull it off -- conning the ship for the first time from a pier within a busy harbor, especially when the ship was moored directly to another destroyer! She had planned on taking her first watch as conning officer when the ship was out in open ocean! Ship evolutions, such as entering or leaving port, seemed almost unmanageably complex. *Barely controlled chaos*, she remembered the SWOS instructors calling the complicated and intricate evolutions of entering and leaving port.

Without notice, the entire room suddenly stood up as the Captain entered and walked over to his designated chair. Once the Captain took his seat, he looked at her and waved his hand as if to say, begin!

She reacted, and began reading from the briefing papers as if unconscious, voicing every word on all four pages exactly as written in the most powerful voice she could muster. She briefed about hazards to navigation, maximum track deviation, safe speed, anticipated maritime traffic, traffic separation schemes, demarcation lines, navigation rules of the road, course and speed of each leg of the navigation track, weather, etc. When she finished reading, she looked up to find that the only person affected by the whole ordeal was her. For everyone else, the briefing was business as usual. *I did it*, she thought, relieved. *I stood in front of the wardroom and read the navigation brief on my first official morning aboard ship*, she congratulated herself. However, she was also aware that she had taken no part in the preparation of the brief, which required research, and a level of nautical understanding that was well beyond her grasp.

The Captain looked straight at her as she remained standing at the front of the wardroom. "Good job, Miss Conner," he said, and nodded. It was the acknowledgement she was looking for and needed to help her keep going with her morning.

"Thank you, sir," she responded, ensuring to remain metered, at least outwardly.

"Keep in mind, everyone," the Captain addressed the room. "Getting underway is a complex evolution. Don't concern yourself with the overall picture, that's my concern. Do your individual part effectively and the evolution will come together."

***

1MC Shipwide Announcement: *"All hands shift into the uniform for getting underway. The uniform for getting underway is summer whites. Station the special sea and anchor detail. Station the special sea and anchor detail."*

The wardroom erupted. Brenda remained standing at the head of the dining table, looking around as officers and enlisted sailors pressed to either side of her, pouring out the door to man their watchstations. One last quartermaster remained to gather up the charts. "I'll follow you up to the bridge, QM3, if that's okay," she said to him.

"Come on with me there, GUNNO." She turned around, caught off guard to see Julie's boss, the operations officer, sounding so willing to take her under his wing. For a moment, she delayed, not understanding, but then she went with him.

"Yes, sir, I'm coming," she answered.

"You're going to have to keep up though," he joked to her, endearingly even, as she followed him out of officers country to a ladder.

"Yes, sir."

"It can be tough at first to navigate a ship, over the raised doorways and up and down the ladderwells," he exclaimed as he started climbing, and she followed. "Everyone gets black and blue shins their first few weeks aboard ship, not to mention shin splints from the steel-toe shoes."

"Oh, I'm sure, sir," she said as they rushed up the first ladder to the bridge and onto the second. *Bang, bang, bang, bang!* The metal dirt-catch underneath the ladder crashed with each of their steps, so loud it sounded like thunder!

"Welcome to the bridge, GUNNO," OPS said as her head cleared the top rung of the second ladder. She tried to look beyond OPS to catch her first sight of the bridge, but against the sun shining through the windows, she could only focus on the outline of his red hair and glasses. "Stay with me and you'll be fine," he added, placing her somewhat at ease, which surprised her. She wasn't sure what to make of OPS. Maybe in those moments his willingness to mentor her was sincere. But in other moments, she had sensed something undesirable in him that was apparent, notwithstanding pleasantries in both his mannerisms and the way in which he spoke. Behind the surface of his assistance and his jokes, lay an underlying aspect that felt crass and insensitive, as if he carried the potential for mercilessness. Despite his seeming intentions of guiding her through her first watch, his speech sounded quick, short, suggestive that his normal bearing was one of being unfeeling.

She was already prejudiced against him; she had observed him speak to Julie a few times during liberty. Three mornings in a row, he had knocked on their stateroom door, after Julie had gotten dressed to go out into Sydney. "I need you to cancel your liberty today to take care of a few items so I can pass them up to the XO," he had said each time, handing her a list. Whenever she had tried to speak, he had cut off her words.

"This is make-work that I could have done on my duty day," Julie had commented to Brenda each time, once the stateroom door was shut.

"Has he left the ship at all since pulling into Sydney?" she asked Julie at one point.

"I don't think so," Julie responded, as she grudgingly lifted her khakis off the back of her chair to put them back on. For most of that week, Brenda watched Julie leave the stateroom in khakis, while she herself had left wearing a collared shirt, shorts, and sandals, or various other summer attire, for enjoying the day in Sydney.

OPS seemed to embody every rumor she had ever heard about the SWO community. He impressed her as that careerist officer who served his ambitions at the expense of others, and who callously grabbed for what he wanted. He had to have been those things, she thought as she took her first step onto the bridge from the ladder. According to the reputation of the SWO community, those traits would have enabled him to be noticed as a top performer within the promotion system and be selected for a coveted billet, such as operations officer onboard a forward deployed Aegis destroyer. Yes, OPS seemed a dedicated careerist. And she decided to keep away from him, if she could. "I'll be the OOD underway for leaving port," OPS said to her. "Rob over there will be the JOOD."

"Yes, sir. Sounds good," she answered and smiled. She did want to impress everyone on the ship that she was enthusiastic and motivated on her first day.

"And at all times on the bridge, be sure to wear a pair of binoculars around your neck," OPS guided her, handing her a pair. At first glance, the bridge had appeared calm and unexpectedly quiet. But as she followed OPS across the bridge and observed the way in which the officers and crew moved about and made preparations, she began to realize just how unsteady the calm was. So much tightness filled the energy of the evolution, as if at any moment it might snap and fall apart. No one appeared comfortable. Everyone appeared unconfident. She wondered if that uneasy sense stemmed from the system of constantly rotating officers, so that no one remained in one job for very long. When officers rotated back to sea, they returned rusty after a long shore tour. And their prior shipboard experience didn't necessarily help them, since they might have served in an altogether different billet (or job) on their previous ship. For example, they might have filled a position in engineering on their last ship, but a few years later, after a shore tour, they might find themselves in the operations department, and on a different class of ship! In the corporate world, the SWO career path was equivalent to working a year to eighteen months in logistics, then rotating to marketing for another tour, then rotating to engineering, then to facilities management, then to the IT department, where in each of those departments, the person rotating was the manager in charge.

But what was the solution? she wondered. Was the solution more in the model of other navies, such as in Australia, where officers specialized in navigation, engineering, or combat systems, and worked in those fields throughout their careers? Was it in longer sea tours? Enlisted tours onboard ships tended to last for a few years; but because of the way SWO officers were treated, in addition to the demanding nature of the officer jobs, it seemed as though no officer wanted to remain aboard a particular ship for longer than a short tour. From what she had heard, it seemed as though the officers constantly looked forward to moving on to their next tour. Turnover remained high and constant aboard ships, restricting officers to a state of perpetual training as if always new on the job. She looked around at all of the knobs, buttons, meters, dials, levers, scopes, and radio circuit plugins jutting out of every crevice and corner of the walls, floors, and ceiling of the bridge. While the bridge appeared intimidating, it also appeared as one big clash of centuries, mixing traditional nautical brass fixtures with modern radar, communications, steering, and navigational equipment.

Then she reminded herself that aboard ship, walls were bulkheads or partitions, floors were decks, ceilings were overheads, stairs were ladders, hallways were passageways, and rooms were spaces or compartments.

This was her second appearance on the bridge of a warship, only this time she wasn't holding onto any free pass, like that of being a midshipman. Now everything was real, and even though she may not have been expected to be an expert upfront, the Captain and other qualified junior officers would form an initial impression of her watchstanding potential. Most of all, she just dreaded being there, and she would have given anything to have been able to leave and go do something else. But her time on the ship and in the Navy was just beginning.

The JOOD approached her. "It only gets better," he teased, seemingly in an effort to make her relax and laugh. "You can quit following 'Oops' around for a while and stick with me," he said, jokingly referring to OPS as "oops."

"Hello, sir, I'm Brenda Conner." She noted the SWO pin above his left pocket and that he was a full lieutenant.

"You don't have to call me sir," he smiled. "I'm a division officer in your department, the fire control officer. Call me Rob or FCO."

She relaxed, overcome with relief to have met a full lieutenant who appeared easy going but still competent. Rob's demeanor differed from the anxiety-ridden, zero-defect, *the slightest mistake will mark the end of my career!* mindset she had experienced in many of the SWO department heads, including OPS and WEPS. "I'm here instead of a shore tour," Rob explained. "I loved my last ship and going to sea, so I volunteered to come back. I took another division officer tour instead of staying on shore."

He was onboard because he actually enjoyed ships and going to sea, she couldn't believe it. "Are you going to stay in the Navy afterwards?" she asked him, unable to restrain her curiosity.

"I'm going to see how it goes here. If I like it and I'm happy, I'll stay in for a while. I have to *feel* what I'm doing," Rob exaggerated his words, and she laughed. He had offered her a fresh outlook: She had met a lieutenant who was actually *serving* onboard this Aegis destroyer, rather than *using* it solely as an ultra-high-speed career marker. "Let's go over to the chart table so you'll understand the navigation track," Rob offered.

Brenda leaned over the chart table with Rob. "FIRST - !" she overheard OPS outside the bridge, on the bridge wing. His terse tone cut right through the wind outside. *First lieutenant, that's Julie, the title for deck officer*, Brenda thought. Hearing OPS start to tear Julie down over the walkie-talkie using such a harsh but hushed tone paralyzed her for a moment. She feared her impression of OPS had been correct, and when he didn't relent on the walkie-talkie, she and Rob could no longer concentrate on the navigational charts. She hesitantly glanced over at Rob, who rolled his eyes. Jon, the navigator, shot Rob a knowing look. They were all on Julie's side. Through the side bridge windows, she could see OPS' mouth pressed right up against his walkie-talkie, engaged in an all-out rant. Then she looked forward, out to the forecastle, where she spotted Julie directing line handling and deck preparations for getting underway with her senior chief and boatswains mates; she was dressed in whites and wore a life jacket and a hard hat. Every so often, Brenda saw Julie raise her walkie-talkie to her mouth to respond to OPS. She imagined that Julie must have been suffering with every blast that emanated from OPS' walkie-talkie. And surely, Julie was "screening" (or reinterpreting) OPS' rants for the boatswains mates, because despite the stress of the evolution, they appeared to respond positively to her.

"Is anything really wrong?" Brenda asked Rob.

"That's a familiar scene," he answered. "And the truth is, he'll treat us acceptably because we don't work directly for him." Being so new, she wasn't sure how to respond.

A second later, OPS stepped back into the pilothouse.

"Everything looks good," he smiled, and rubbed his palms together. "GUNNO, let's go over some of the things you can expect when we get underway from the pier." And he subsequently took her once again under his wing as if nothing had happened. "Don't worry about a thing," he said. "Rob and I are right here."

Chapter 22: Anchor's away ... Fear of discovery ... The floodgates to her past

1MC Shipwide Announcement: *"The Officer of the Deck is shifting his watch from the quarterdeck to the bridge."*

Brenda watched the boatswains mate of the watch (BMOW) hang up the 1MC microphone. She noted that the ship's public address circuit made the boatswains' and POOWs' voices sound so official.

"Captain's on the bridge!" announced the lead quartermaster.

"Attention in the pilothouse, this is Lieutenant Quinton. I have the deck," OPS announced to the bridge. The standardized announcement informed the bridge team that he had assumed responsibility as officer of the deck; Brenda watched as a QM2 (quartermaster second class) recorded the shift in the OOD watch in the ship's deck log, which was a legal document. The evolution progressed in rapid time all around her, and she could feel the nervous energy of it.

OPS bent down and addressed her covertly. "Say, attention in the pilothouse, this is Ensign Conner. I have the conn," he whispered. In the strongest voice she could muster, she repeated, *"Attention in the pilothouse, this is Ensign Conner. I have the conn."* Then, from various stations on the bridge, she began hearing several "aye, aye ma'am's." She looked around. The boatswains mate, the quartermaster, the helmsman, and other watchstanders had all responded to her announcement, which reinforced her realization that she really had become a part of everyday official shipboard business. The watchstanders had merely followed protocol, but she still found their responses to her, and the pace, difficult to fathom.

She continued to follow OPS around as he prepared the bridge for getting underway. Every once in a while, she watched him capitalize on a free moment to step out onto the bridge wing and berate Julie over the walkie-talkie, always in that cutting tone he had mastered. On the starboard side of the bridge, the Captain sat in his designated chair, which was off limits to all others. She saw that the Captain was speaking to the harbor pilot. Maritime pilots were experts on every feature of a given harbor, such as currents, depths, navigational aids, etc. As consultants, they boarded ships to aid them to safely get underway from the pier and navigate within a harbor.

"Follow the Captain, GUNNO. Do exactly as he says," OPS told her.

"Yes, sir." She followed the Captain and the pilot out onto the bridge wing, while eagerly trying not to miss one detail. *Translate the Captain's every command*, she kept reminding herself. If she missed one single word or action, the Captain might be forced to relieve her, on the spot, for the safety of the ship and of all others on the piers and in the harbor. It probably would mean her end as a naval officer. Never in her life had she personally played a part in such an intense operation with such dire consequences. In getting underway, the Captain and pilot had to account for wind, currents, tides and ship's forces, as well as for engine, rudder, and line handling commands. Further complicating the situation, the *Curtis Wilbur* was tied to the *John S. McCain* and not to the pier itself.

OPS rushed out onto the bridge wing and handed her a microphone. "Here, speak your commands into the microphone," he told her. "The helm, lee helm, and line handlers have to be able to hear you, as well as all of us."

"*Slack line 3*," she heard herself broadcast, repeating after the Captain. She could hardly keep up with what she was repeating. "*Take in all lines*," she echoed. The she heard the piercing boatswains' pipe for the first time since midshipman cruise.

1MC Shipwide Announcement: "*Underway shift colors.*"

"*Starboard engine ahead one-third*," she repeated. She then heard the lee helmsman reply, "*Starboard engine ahead one-third, aye, ma'am*," followed by his report, "*Engine room answers starboard engine ahead one-third, port engine stop, ma'am.*"

Mixed in were helm commands from the pilot, which were always followed by nods from the Captain that exclaimed, Go! Now! "*Right standard rudder*," she would repeat. "*Right standard rudder, aye, ma'am. My rudder is right standard, ma'am*," the helm would respond as quickly as she verbalized the commands.

Slowly, she watched how her parroted words carried the ship away from the *John S. McCain* and the piers. She stood leaning over the railing on the bridge wing, just as the Captain and pilot did, voicing their every command to the helm and lee helm. She gripped the microphone that OPS had handed her and spoke into it as if it might save her life. For a split second, as the warship made way into the harbor basin, she stepped back to gaze at the disappearing cityscape. She was really doing this. And hearing her commands broadcasted throughout the pilothouse jarred her. If she made a mistake or misspoke, everyone would hear. But she had no other choice than to let her fears flow and go on. From beginning to end, she remained steadily with the Captain and the pilot through each step, conning the ship from the pier and out of the harbor, forced to trust in herself that she could indeed perform real-time under pressure, at least at some level. Whenever she doubted herself, she looked to the Captain; she saw that he also felt the tension and the enormity of the evolution, and he continued regardless. If he could continue, then she could continue, she kept thinking. And she didn't have near his accountability and responsibility.

Once the ship reached the mouth of the basin, the pilot departed the ship by pilot boat, and the navigation track began. The first class quartermaster, wearing a stopwatch, aided the navigator in calling out recommended courses, speeds, and times. "The next leg is 500 yards, the nearest hazard to navigation is shoal water 600 yards off the starboard bow, nearest aid to navigation is a buoy off the port bow at 800 yards. Recommend course 110." As the navigator read out each recommended course and speed change, the Captain pointed his finger to prompt her to immediately give the corresponding standard command. In each instance, she had to translate the navigator's information into standard command format, and determine rudder direction. *"Left standard rudder, steady course 110,"* she announced in response to the navigator's latest recommendation. To her surprise, she managed to keep the pace and accomplish what was expected of her, all while standing front and center on stage. As the sea and anchor detail came to a close, she had a chance to catch her breath out on the bridge wing with the Captain and the operations officer.

"You did a good job today, Brenda. You're off to a good start here," the Captain congratulated her.

She felt guilty at receiving the compliment. She was cognizant that she had done nothing original besides parrot information and survive another dubious milestone. And the Captain impressed her as very politically correct. "Thank you, sir," she replied, still grateful.

"And good job, OPS," the Captain continued. "Everything went very well." OPS really did deserve the compliment, she thought.

"Yes, sir, Captain," OPS responded. "Request permission to secure the sea and anchor detail."

"Secure the sea and anchor detail," the Captain replied.

"Secure the sea and anchor detail, aye, Captain," OPS repeated before disappearing back into the pilot house. Repeat-backs were customary Navy protocol, in place to ensure orders were properly understood before execution.

Before leaving the bridge, the Captain nodded to Brenda once more, "I mean it. Good job, Miss Conner." She felt both exhilarated and exhausted. Maybe she could do it after all. It was the reassurance she wanted and needed to hear, as she looked out and noticed for the first time that she was surrounded by ocean. It was a lonely, cutoff feeling.

1MC Shipwide Announcement: *"Secure the special sea and anchor detail. On deck condition III, watch section II."*

Brenda was soon relieved as conning officer by the oncoming watch section.

***

Brenda left the bridge and sought the refuge of her stateroom. She had survived her first bridge watch, and conning, but the enormity of what would be expected of her on the bridge had started to sink in. She climbed down the bridge ladders, wary of her first *real* bridge watch, which was on the horizon for later in the day. She feared the bridge almost uncontrollably; she feared how long she could maintain her sanity under pressure to perform real-time. Someday up there, someone would ask her that question, or request of her to perform that task, of which she would be incapable. And she would be exposed and discovered.

She opened the door that separated the ladderwell from officers country, cognizant of how fortunate officers were to have a space of their own – their own staterooms. The enlisted lived in crowded berthing and slept in racks smaller than hers. From midshipman cruise, she knew that many of them sought refuge and relative privacy in their workspaces. She walked directly to her stateroom, opened the door, and found it empty. It was a liberating feeling to be in one's own space.

As she began changing uniforms, out of whites and into working khakis, it occurred to her that, having opened up the floodgates to her past, more and more episodes were rising to the surface, calling out for examination, each one offering some new lesson about herself. Rather than feeling tormented by them – many of which were now embarrassing to her – she agreed to herself to let them flow. She thought of a time when her high school physics teacher had given a few exams and labs that consisted mostly of conceptual questions, rather than questions that would have allowed her to pick numbers from a given problem and plug them into a memorized formula. Her grades on the conceptually-based exams and labs were in the D range, or nearly so! Even after relentless studying, reading, and memorization, she had still lacked the comprehension to answer the most basic high school physics questions.

"What am I going to do? I want to major in mechanical engineering. Conceptual physics is the foundation for mechanical engineering," she had asked her teacher. She only remembered the way he had looked at her, silent and without expression, possibly assuming that the answer to her question was obvious. But she hadn't understood the likely meaning of his silence until now. The person she was in high school had thought that all that mattered was a passing grade in physics for use in applying to engineering schools. Nevertheless, through her manipulation and determined drive, she had found a way out of receiving a poor grade in physics: She completed several extra credit projects and assignments to bring her grade up for her college application. Reflecting back, she thought it was too bad that her teacher had given her that break, and had awarded her a grade based primarily on her hard work and effort. But then, if he had given her a poor grade based on her exams and conceptual understanding, she probably would have blamed him for her low grade. The complexity of her rationalizations, and her drive to move forward in a direction that was contrary to a natural flow, now seemed incomprehensible to her.

Pausing, she looked in her stateroom mirror, wanting to ensure that her hair was still neatly tied up. She remembered a parallel episode in college, when she had discovered that her student number was highlighted in red on the physics professor's door, which meant that she was in danger of failing college physics for engineers. Once again, the professor's tests tended towards the theoretical. She recalled the times when she had sat in those college chair-desks in the physics building, panicking during his exams, not knowing if she could pull one single answer together or even write anything down. It didn't matter that she had spent several days and nights trying to study her notes and the textbook, scouring them for information and formulas she could memorize. Towards the end of the semester, she went to his office one afternoon, and begged him to pass her with a B- so she could keep her ROTC scholarship and apply to be a nuclear officer. Performance in math and science was considered vital by Navy ROTC.

She was ashamed of those instances. She had been taught that the reason to go to college was to get a job; and she had been led to believe that whether or not she liked engineering or had any interest in truly learning engineering was immaterial. Her parents had never mentioned a philosophy of choosing a course of study based on a sense of who one was as a person, or based on one's passions – the concept was alien to them, and it had never occurred to her. Her father used to say sarcastically that liberal arts was for kids "looking to find themselves." He had a way of minimizing, and unknowingly rejecting, the process of self-discovery.

She didn't doubt that her engineering background would open doors to jobs in technical sales or technical project management; but was that what she wanted? Her mother had constantly encouraged her to apply for an engineering job within the government – one from which "she could retire in twenty years." Throughout her childhood, her mother had talked about her father's cousin who had retired from the GAO and "had it made." Her mother's way of thinking had translated for her as *suffer your life away at a secure job you don't like, while waiting for retirement.* She had always been vaguely aware that this idea never felt exactly right to her.

But during her CIA co-op, she had learned how in the government, engineers and scientists started at a higher salary grade on the GS scale. Even as a co-op student, she had received a higher salary than the liberal arts co-op students. Heavily influenced by her parents' belief that salary was *the* deciding factor in choosing a college major, and key in appearing successful, she had allowed her co-op experience to reinforce their assertion that majoring in Spanish and languages would be an ill-conceived choice.

She had listened to her father who insisted that she would not be able to do anything with a liberal arts degree besides teach. And she hadn't wanted to teach. *"Underwater basket weaving!"* her father used to call non-engineering degrees. But after graduation, many of her friends who had majored in foreign language had found jobs in translation, interpreting, and in an array of fields of which she had never conceived. In view of her current plight, she now understood the hazards of overesteeming the monetary payoff, and the despair brought on by basing life choices on earning power. One of her friends was working for an environmental NGO in South America. Her letters were fascinating.

Faced with bridge watches and leading and managing the gunnery division, she realized that her playing field dynamics had changed since school, where she was able to move on from a class or from the subject matter once an exam was over; when, she could forget about, or dump, the material. Onboard the ship, the information she studied and memorized had to be applied and performed efficiently and competently.

Julie opened the stateroom door and rushed in. "Everything go okay up there?" she asked.

"I think so," Brenda answered. Julie began changing out of whites and into khakis. Then their stateroom IVCS phone rang. The IVCS ring tone had a computer generated sound. "This is Ensign Conner, sir," Brenda answered, which was a standard phone protocol she had learned as a midshipman. Julie looked at her, knowing it would be OPS.

"Hi GUNNO, is FIRST in there?" OPS questioned sharply.

"Yes, sir." Brenda handed the phone to Julie. She couldn't hear OPS' end of the conversation, but she was able to guess his tone from the look on Julie's face. Before hanging up the phone, Julie simply responded, "Yes, sir."

Brenda opened a bottle of pain reliever to subdue the stress headache she felt coming on. She wanted to say something encouraging to Julie. Julie was that technically competent female junior officer who could realistically aspire to be the first female captain of a combatant ship, who made a great representative and role model for all women seeking military careers. "I admired you out there on the forecastle this morning," Brenda began. "I saw you directing operations while wearing your hardhat and life preserver over your whites, all of the line handling and deck evolutions. You were impressive, and I saw the way the boatswains mates responded to you."

"Well, thanks" Julie answered, "but when OPS cuts in over the walkie-talkie, it makes it hard."

"Do you think you'll stick with SWO?" Brenda asked, but then she regretted her question. It was too soon and she knew that Julie wasn't ready to give up on the SWO Navy, her dream.

"I'm not sure what to think just yet. I love standing watch on the bridge," Julie answered. Then she bent her head down, raised her eyebrows, and massaged her forehead. "Rob is cool to stand watch with, isn't he?"

"He's like you, Julie. He's here for pure reasons. And he's very teddy-bearish!" Both girls giggled.

"Yes, he is!" Julie answered, and by then they were both laughing together.

"So, what did you do that one day when you were gone on liberty in Sydney?" Brenda asked, eyeing a brochure on Julie's desk.

"The Sydney Harbor bridge climb!"

"You mean you walked over the steel structure and catwalks, like five hundred feet in the air?"

"Yes, about that. It was awesome! I'm going to go extreme whitewater rafting when we get to Malaysia, if I can."

Brenda smiled. "That's not for me," she said, "even though I'm a good swimmer. I spent the last day in the park near the Sydney observatory, under a tree, sitting in the grass. I tried to take something from that place, some sort of peace or relaxation." Brenda started to feel the movement of the ship in her stomach.

"If you want to get chow in the wardroom, you can follow me in," Julie offered. Chow, Brenda thought. It was a Navy term but she hated the sound of it. "If the Captain is seated, request permission to join the mess," Julie instructed. "If he's not present, request permission to join the mess from the most senior officer at the table."

Boatswain pipe for lunch

Chapter 23: A strained wardroom ... Pitch and roll ... Singleness of purpose on the wrong path

Brenda followed Julie into the wardroom. When she stepped inside, she saw the Captain seated in his designated chair on the starboard side, midway down the length of the dining table. "Request permission to join the mess, sir," Julie addressed the Captain. The Captain nodded and gestured for her to sit down. "Request permission to join the mess, sir," Brenda followed. "Please," the Captain responded.

Julie sat down on the port side of the table, near the middle. Brenda scanned the table, quickly, and took the seat closest to where she was standing, on the end of the port side. About five officers were seated at either side of the table. The chief engineer, seated across from her, was fully engaged in storytelling. When Brenda sat down, he paused to acknowledge her, and then he continued, "...and that was at bar number ten or fifteen. The Australians love Americans, what can I say, they wanted to buy us drinks. How was I supposed to say no? I was sure wasted," he laughed. Brenda noticed that a few officers laughed with him, somewhat, while others merely smiled. The Captain smiled as if to placate.

The wardroom seemed a strained setting. She tried to blend in and remain unnoticed as she quietly ordered soup from the enlisted attendant. What she started to observe while seated and waiting made her aware of the touchy politics of sitting through a wardroom meal. From her cruise experience, she was already skeptical of interactions in the wardroom. Some junior officers claimed it was a place to joke and have fun with the CO, XO, and department heads, but she wasn't so sure. She felt cautious about joking around too much with seniors, and about letting one's guard down completely in professional circumstances. Senior officers were in authority and weren't on equal footing with juniors who, naively, tried to connect with them by telling jokes and engaging them in conversation. On cruise, she noticed that JOs tended to appear weak to seniors when they tried to seem interesting, or when they competed for attention. And within a few minutes, she started to confirm her theories. Conversation at the dining table, so far, had been awkward, and pauses were even more awkward. Every minute or so, an officer would initiate conversation, but always in a manner that vied for the attention and acknowledgement of the CO and XO. Sometimes the Captain would respond with polite tolerance, and other times his patience seemed to run thin.

Whenever her boss, the weapons officer, spoke, she cringed. And she noticed others around the table seemed uncomfortable as well. It was as if he suffered from a compulsion to please the Captain and XO, and to spark their interest in him by showing them through clever conversation how engaging and intelligent he was. She watched WEPS nervously over-animate his speech, and overact in his mannerisms; it made everyone ill-at-ease. She noted the Captain's annoyance. Earlier, Pete told her that their department head feared his career under this Captain. She tried to support her department head, who she liked so far, by smiling and listening as he spoke. But as he went on, he gave the impression of looking weak in character, and needy, before the Captain. She did find WEPS interesting, and possibly he was brilliant, but the ship and this social milieu seemed an awkward forum for him. She kept Pete's words in mind. Fear was a feeling with which she could empathize, fear that all one had worked for was slipping away. As WEPS spoke on about some nuance of Australian history, she glanced over at Jon the navigator. She found him looking impatient, yet sympathetic too, in a way.

Even though unwritten rules dictated that talk of official business was off limits during wardroom meals, there still existed a sense of constant grading and evaluation. Whenever the wardroom conversation went silent, the XO would cut in with a starter like, "Wasn't the golf great in Sydney?" The department heads would then chuckle and agree that it was, all with that nervous contention for approval. She had observed the same dynamic in other male-dominated work environments, recognizing it from lunches at her CIA co-op. She decided that she would remain unassuming and quiet during wardroom meals. And then maybe, she wondered, the Captain wouldn't view her as such a beggar, as he appeared to view some of the others. She was going to have to find her edge in those small ways.

Rock and roll! Suddenly the pitch and roll increased without warning and tossed the contents of the dining table. The officers shot up over the table, trying to grab dishes, serving platters, cups, and silverware. A pitcher of red punch slid right off the table, caught by the warrant officer just before hitting the floor. She never imagined this scene. During midshipman cruise, her ship had sortied for a hurricane off the coast of Florida, but she had remained racked-out in her stateroom the entire time, so seasick that she could not even move a finger or it would have prompted her to vomit and pass out.

She remained seated in her chair, gripping the armrests for stability, starting to feel – and look – sick, aware she might vomit or pass out at any second. The enlisted wardroom attendants rushed in to help bring the situation under control. Officers got out of their seats to chain their chairs to the floors. Someone, she wasn't sure who, she was so nauseous, chained her chair to the floor for her. A chain hung down from the bottom of each chair, and there were hooks spaced in the floor. "That's the course change," the Captain said. The IVCS phone attached to the arm of the right side of his chair rang.

"You look green, GUNNO! You'll need to get your sealegs!" the XO exclaimed.

"Yes, sir," Brenda answered, trying to smile.

"We all start out that way. It's okay," CSO added. Like WEPS, CSO seemed to differ from OPS, in that he appeared to show concern for the wellbeing of those subordinate to him.

"Ah, you'll be shipshape in no time," the warrant officer jabbed at her arm as he walked by. She hoped they would all turn out to be right. The other midshipman on cruise, her friend Dana from the Naval Academy, had given what Brenda was starting to think was good advice: "Have the corpsman document how sick you are, and get NPQ'd for seasickness. Mids do it all the time," Dana had advised, with "mids" referring to midshipmen. "People spend entire careers in the Navy without ever going to sea," Dana had told her. Brenda sat at the dining table, gripping the armrests, asking herself: *Why hadn't she taken Dana's advice?*

Brenda remembered how Dana, a member of the Naval Academy sailing team, had bounced all around the ship during the hurricane, completely unaffected by the seas. Dana had stood bridge watches while Brenda had remained imprisoned in her rack, incapacitated. But at the time, the process of applying for NPQ (non-physically qualified for sea) status had seemed nebulous to her; plus she wasn't prepared to document a history of seasickness; in fact, her onset of seasickness during midshipman cruise had come as a surprise. So, she ignored her seasickness then, and convinced herself that everything would be okay once she got to her ship someday.

She barely finished a few spoonfuls of her soup, which tasted like heavily salted corn syrup. She had ordered soup in an effort to watch her weight onboard, however, she realized the calorie count in this soup must have been off the charts. The other option was pizza. One by one, the officers began excusing themselves from the table. "Excuse me, Captain," each one stated, as they got up out of their chairs. The Captain always responded with a nod. She endured a few more comments about "getting her sealegs," to which she responded every time with her best "go along" smile. Then, she managed to lift herself out of her chair and excuse herself from the table.

She opened her stateroom door, and found her and Julie's personal belongings tossed all over the floor, absolutely everywhere. Their toiletries had mixed together and had fallen into the sink. The cabinet doors banged open and shut with each pitch and roll. Clothes were scattered about the floor. She braced herself in the door frame, as the seas worsened. She held onto her desk as she lifted her chair upright and chained it to the hook in the floor. She took two steps, holding onto her chained chair, and then she chained Julie's chair, which had fallen sideways. She picked Julie's uniforms up and draped them over her chair. The seas were getting too heavy to be able to stand up. She held her stomach and locked all of the cabinets closed. Her movements grew slower and more labored as nausea and dizziness overcame her. Her headache grew stronger from the rolling. *I need to get that letter written for WEPS about the generator*, she remembered. Then her Spanish, Portuguese, Latin, and Cantonese books fell out of her desk and all over the floor. She buried her head in her hands. It felt like a week had passed, not a few hours, since the ship had left the piers of Sydney, Australia that morning.

***

In the combat systems office, Brenda waited for a turn at one of the computers. She needed to type the letter to the generator rental company in Arizona for her LPO (leading petty officer), Petty Officer Brooks. The narrow computer space was crowded with petty officers, all waiting for a computer. She sat in the back corner, slightly hunched forward, holding her right forearm against her stomach; she pressed her left palm against her forehead to feel coolness and to counteract her dizziness. In the last half hour, she had learned that the entire combat systems/weapons department shared three computers. The computers and monitors were strapped down to a long metal table, positioned up against the wall. She watched the computers and monitors roll with the ship. It was mesmerizing.

"There're templates for letters to debt collectors on the shared drive," she heard WEPS, suddenly; and then she realized that she had passed out, possibly only for a few seconds. "Pete's on his way up to help you."

"Yes, sir," she tried to make herself come to. "I plan on working with Pete to turn over the division as soon as possible, sir," she answered, feeling herself regaining consciousness; she felt blood rising once again to her head. Then, she vaguely remembered a few people asking her if she was okay, maybe a few times over the last fifteen or twenty minutes; and of course, she had perked herself up to say yes, and to tell them not to worry. "Are you okay, ma'am, are you okay, ma'am?" she remembered hearing, more than once. She looked at WEPS, and then looked around, and realized that she must have been out longer than she had originally thought. The seats in front of the computers had cleared, and the last petty officers in the room had just left.

She was alone with WEPS, and she tried to compose herself. "WEPS," she asked.

"Yes."

"Did you ever hear about the incident with Chief Smith in Sydney, on my first night?"

"It's been taken care of," he answered, as if the incident was nothing, meaningless. "Don't worry about it. Forget about it and move on," he said. She suddenly felt embarrassed, and even foolish, for asking him about the chief and for bringing the situation up at all. She tried to appear casual, as if his response and the incident with the frocked chief hadn't fazed her. "It's being set up so that neither of you stand watch together on the bridge, nor relieve each other."

"Yes, sir," she nodded, not sure what to think. She had gotten a boost of adrenaline from bringing up the subject, because suddenly she felt a little better. She had a sense of WEPS' plight onboard. In the wardroom, she had witnessed the depth of his insecurity, his sense that at any moment the least event or interaction might sink his career, his several years invested in the SWO Navy, gone. She understood that he wasn't in a position to involve himself in any controversial issue, especially one that wasn't clear enough to seem worth advocating for. But she thought that her story had, at the very least, deserved a JAGMAN investigation. Without a doubt, other females had suffered similar experiences with the chief or more likely, worse ones. She was an officer, but what had he tried with an E-1 seaman or with an E-4 junior petty officer? It wasn't the first time the chief had acted out, she felt sure – someone like him couldn't help himself, couldn't combat his own behavioral patterns. She believed that at some point, the secrets would begin escaping from the walls of the ship. On midshipman cruise, she had learned that ships were incapable of containing secrets.

"Oh, and tell Chief Dering to keep that gun painted," WEPS changed the subject. "The Captain likes the gun looking painted and shiny for underway replenishments and for when we're close to the aircraft carrier. Tell him to do a oneover on the gun."

"But the gun's down, sir. Chief Dering said they've been working night and day on troubleshooting," she answered; but she was regressing back to scarcely being able to utter a word, with the feeling she would vomit at any moment starting to overtake her.

"The captain wants the gun looking good for the admiral on the carrier," WEPS answered in his brisk speech. "No rust. Painted. That's the Captain's priority, especially when we're tied to the pier. The Captain wants the gun to shine when the admiral walks down the pier."

She could tell WEPS didn't like what he was saying; he appeared nervous, frustrated, and agitated over it. So she answered, "Yes, sir." On her first morning, she had learned that a fresh paint job on the gun mattered more than if it worked, that appearances were the priority. "I'll get started with that ammo count this afternoon," she told him.

"If you need me, I'll be on TAO watch in CIC," WEPS said. But before he turned to leave, he said, "And make sure you take care of yourself. I'm here if you need me."

"Yes, sir, thank you," she answered. When WEPS left the space, she pulled a trashcan closer to her. Then, two petty officers walked in and sat down at two of the empty computers. She felt the temptation to give in to her seasickness. It was as if her seasickness was coaxing her to curl up onto the floor, and sleep. "Are you okay, ma'am?" one of the petty officers asked. "Don't worry, ma'am," the other petty officer said, "you should see how many guys are racked out in berthing, heaving their guts."

Brenda smiled. "I'm not the only one then," she said.

"No, ma'am, and you'll get your sealegs," they both assured her. She faced the computer screen and searched for this shared "d" drive that WEPS and Pete had been talking about, the one with all the letter templates. But she thought that she would pass out again at any minute. And then she reminded herself that she had an obligation to carry her weight, and to continue with her first official workday.

"Are you sure you don't want us to get doc, ma'am?" one of the petty officers asked.

"Not unless I actually pass out," she answered, and they all laughed.

She found her first job out of college miserable beyond anything she could have imagined. If only she could have had the option to serve the Navy in another capacity. But, she swore to herself that since she *was* there, she would give the ship everything she had. Then Pete walked into the room. "Let's get that letter done," he said cheerfully.

***

Brenda leaned against the computer table and balanced herself against the ship's rolls – port to starboard, port to starboard. Sometimes, she felt as though the waves were breaking over the bow, and that the water was holding the front of the ship under the surface of the wave for a second until the ship managed to right itself. The pitching, the bow to stern, wave to wave motion (as opposed to the port to starboard rolls), vibrated the ship in the most terrible manner; she felt as if all of the screws and fasteners that held the ship together might suddenly bust apart. While the ship plunged from wave to wave, she stood up slowly; she had to keep going with her workday.

She approached the XO's door, for the first time, holding the folder containing a printout of the letter to the generator rental company. The XO's door was tied open and the light was on. She found him seated at his desk, reviewing what looked like message traffic. She glanced down the passageway once more before she knocked on his door to enter. The passageways had emptied as the seas had intensified.

She gripped the XO's door frame and spread her feet up against it for balance while she knocked. "Excuse me, sir," she greeted him. She was only hand-routing the letter because WEPS had insisted that personally routing correspondence was always a good opportunity to "grab facetime" with the XO. Otherwise, she could have just placed the letter in the XO's inbox for signature. She felt at odds with her department head over the concept of fabricating circumstances to "grab some facetime." Instinctively, she felt it more beneficial to interact with the XO as opportunities arose naturally; forced situations always felt just that, forced and pleading to be noticed. But she wanted to work well with her new boss, and she realized that he was only trying to help her introduction to the wardroom.

"I'm routing a letter for your review, sir," she said.

"Very well, Miss Conner, come right in," the XO answered, as he reached for the folder she was carrying. And in that moment, she realized that she was handing the XO her first official naval correspondence for review, this letter to a debt collector. She watched the XO review the letter, eager to see if he would find any fault with it or mark any changes. She held onto his door, focusing her stamina on standing up straight, and on resisting the urge to hunch over, pass out, or vomit. *Vomiting in the XO's stateroom on her first official day, while routing her first official naval correspondence!* She couldn't imagine the humiliation; she would have never lived it down.

But the XO treated her with respect while she was in his stateroom. She was obviously sick; but he said nothing to taunt or tease her, even though the Navy had sent him a seasick naval officer. *A seasick naval officer!* She wasn't unfamiliar with humiliation in a military setting. Her self-consciousness for her seasickness reminded her of two-mile-runs with her ROTC unit, when she always came in last or nearly last. She was a good swimmer, and she wasn't adverse to other forms of exercise or to going to the gym, but running, she hated long distance running. And while she was in last place, winded, and struggling, they would always send another high-speed runner back, who had finished long before, to run alongside her. She stopped the memory; it was too painful.

"Don't worry," the XO interrupted her thoughts. He took a final glance over her letter, signed it, and lounged back in his chair. "Good letter. I have no doubt you'll get your sealegs and that you'll be fine going forward," he told her.

"Thank you, sir," she answered, and exited his stateroom.

A few steps out of his stateroom, there was a ladderwell. She grabbed onto the railing and sat down on a step. Her head felt as though it weighed a hundred pounds. *I have to keep going*, she told herself. She stood up while holding the railing, climbed down the remaining steps, and started down the lower passageway, carefully bracing herself against the bulkheads as she walked. Slam! The ship rose out of the water and crashed down flat. As an aftereffect, the ship vibrated for a few seconds, and she swore she could hear the water crashing up against the hull. She feared, irrationally, that the ship would capsize at any moment, leaving her trapped underneath a hatch in some windowless enclosed metal space.

She gripped a firehose reel to steady herself. Then, she thought to herself, how, in the past, she had taken pride in her stick-to-itiveness; she had thought there was merit and self-respect in applying a will-and-can spirit to overcome any obstacle, to keep working towards a goal no matter how difficult it seemed. And there *was* merit in that kind of perseverance, in many instances; but sometimes such determined drive could be blind and foolish, she had learned. As she faced each new situation in the Navy, as she lived with the consequences of her history and hard work, as she dissected the dynamics that led to where she was, piece by piece, she realized that she had focused all of her young determined drive in the wrong direction. The nights and days and weekends over years that she spent developing her weaker sides in math and science courses, in ROTC, and in the activities and sports she chose, had led to her to the wrong place – *for her* – down the wrong path. *What would have happened had she applied her same strong drive and work ethic to studying languages and literature, or history, areas in which she might have excelled? What if she had foregone the military? She could have delved into languages and literature and made those studies her life work, she could have been at the top of her field! She could have been working towards her PhD in languages!*

She pictured herself in some basement archive in Spain, passionately working to uncover a new medieval manuscript, or as her friend was doing, working as a linguist for environmental conservation in South America.

She remembered when she had shown up to her first two-mile-run with the ROTC unit as a freshman, newly arrived to college. She had spent the summer training to run one mile. In her ignorance, she had thought that one mile was a long way to run. Before ROTC, she had not had any exposure to running, through family, friends, or high school. She was sure that if she could manage running one mile, she would be set up and even ahead of her peers. No one she knew ran, *let alone a mile!* Although she had a desire to prepare herself by working out, she didn't know how. She was never taught to work out in gym class or even in high school sports. When she showed up to ROTC, she was shocked to learn – *immediately!* – that every kid there, except for maybe one or two others like her, could run two and five-mile segments like it was nothing. *Some could run ten miles like it was nothing!* She had never met people like that. In ROTC, she found herself surrounded by scholar-athlete valedictorians and salutatorians who had lettered and won state championships in track, cross-country, etc.

    She remembered herself running last and way behind the rest of the formation. Every run and PT session, throughout the four years, was humiliating. She should have taken her pathetic performance in running as a warning sign; but in her youth, she had thought that there was true accomplishment to hanging in there, to showing up time after time against the odds, and toughing things out no matter what. And regardless of signs that she didn't fit in and that she didn't like it, she continued to work at her goals of ROTC and engineering with singleness of purpose; she refused to waver, to be weak, or to quit. She sustained that determination for four years. Now she asked herself, why hadn't she accepted herself for who she was – accepted what were her strengths and weaknesses? Why had she insisted on working towards everything she was weak at? She had excelled in her language classes, and she had felt confident, at-ease, and content in them.

    She was lucky that she had been partially saved by her swimming. She was able to score an outstanding on the swim PRT (physical readiness test), which Navy personnel were allowed to substitute for the run. She also passed her first class Navy swim test on the first try.

    Still immobilized by her thoughts, standing by the fire reel, she reflected on how she had looked great on paper. Everything she did in high school and college was aimed at checking all the right boxes. When she applied for an ROTC scholarship, she had appeared like a dream come true: a female majoring in mechanical engineering with high grades! There was such a push for female technical majors going on in universities and in ROTC in the '90s. She regretted now that she had depended on that trend. And the high school activities behind her, including letters in two varsity sports, were mostly shams, she admitted to herself for the first time. Admitting those realities, even within her own mind, overwhelmed her with pain, regret, and embarrassment. In high school, she had joined the math team and played both varsity sports because she had wanted desperately to be good at those things, and to list them on her college application. At math team meets, she had competed in the lowest group, on the "E" team, never solving one problem. Regardless, she had stayed on the math team for all four years of high school and attended all practices and meets; she showed so she could list the math team on her college application. Her varsity letters in softball and tennis were pure flukes, too, since there simply weren't enough girls trying out during those particular years. In reality, she had accomplished little. She was a shell of milestones and accomplishments with no substance. She had existed to list grades and activities on applications. That was how she had lived her life and treated herself.

The feel of the pitch and roll decreased as she climbed farther down into the ship, and she started to feel slightly more functional. She wasn't actually sick, she had to remind herself. If she suddenly found herself on shore or in calm seas, she would be fine. "Need a tour guide, ma'am?" a petty officer asked. "With only a few days onboard, it's impossible to find your way in this maze of passageways."

"It is. Thank you," she straightened her stance and smiled. "I'm headed to the VLS." She was never lost in the ship for very long. Ever since she had checked onboard, petty officers had welcomed her and offered to guide her around the ship.

Chapter 24: The roughest seas in the world ... No secrets aboard ship ... Stand up for your people ... Ammo counts ... The flat hatter

The petty officer guided her aft and down one more ladder. "This is the door to the VLS space, ma'am," he said and stopped. "You'll be alright, ma'am?"

"I will," she smiled. "Thank you." The petty officer hesitated a moment before heading on his way, aft towards berthing.

She congratulated herself for at least having had the endurance to follow the petty officer down the ladder and through the passageways to get to the VLS. She placed her hand on her temple to have something cool over the throbbing pain she felt there. She wanted to drift into sleep and forget all of this.

Instead, she swung the door handle counterclockwise and pushed the door open. Sometimes the shipboard doors opened easily, and other times the ship's internal pressurization system made it a test of strength to move from one compartment to another. Arleigh Burke class guided missile destroyers (DDGs) were equipped with a collective protection system (CPS), designed to protect against chemical, biological, and radiological (CBR) agents. The system filtered supply air and over-pressurized certain areas of the ship.

She had no idea what she would find inside the VLS space once she opened the door. She only knew that of all the spaces her division "owned," the VLS compartment and the gun mount served as the primary work (and play) spaces for the gunners mates. Pete had given her an overview of the multiple computer and mechanical spaces owned by the gunnery division, as well as of the small arms and ammo lockers, vaults, and magazines. As the division officer, she was responsible for the maintenance, upkeep, and operation of the spaces and the equipment inside them. She secured the door behind her, realizing that this was the start of her first division officer "rounds." She looked at the rows of computer cabinets and racks before her, and stepped up onto the raised computer flooring. "Hey, it's GUNNO!" she heard. Heads turned and greetings came her way. "Welcome, ma'am! This isn't normal, ma'am! Roughest seas in the world, we're smack in the Great Australian Bight, ma'am!"

"Roughest seas in the world," she repeated as she looked around. "This is impressive," she said, commenting on the extensive entertainment system the gunners mates had put together. She saw videogame consoles, stereo equipment, TVs and VCRs. Ships were amazing, she thought, the way the guys hung out in these workspaces, making somewhat of a life within them. Anything happening on the bridge was a world away from this space.

"Don't worry, ma'am, half the guys on the ship are racked-out. You're not the only one seasick," one of the petty officers yelled back from watching a movie.

"You guys already knew?" she asked, as she walked farther into the space. "You're right," she admitted, feeling the importance of remaining honest with the division. "I've been very sick." She leaned against one of the computer racks, the "brains" of the VLS missile system, and gripped a metal handle. She had no choice but to be truthful with the division, otherwise, she knew they would see right through her, and possibly write her off. At twenty-three years old, she felt that she had to come of age as a division officer and young professional, *right now!* She had subordinates who depended on her. But, she had questions. How much of herself should she reveal and when, if ever? Where should she draw the line between revealing herself, versus acting as a leader and manager? She knew the division would probably appreciate honesty and authenticity more than any other character trait, but she had no experience in how to go about "leading."

"We know everything, ma'am. No secrets aboard ship!" a petty officer answered her.

"You guys watching *Platoon?*" she asked. She relaxed somewhat, feeling herself in familiar territory. In college, she had lived on the engineering floor in the dorm for two years. During freshman year, she had spent many hours hanging out, or trying to hang out, with the guys on her floor. One guy on the floor, in particular, was considered cool by all of the eighteen year old, first-year, male engineering students who populated the floor. His suite was considered *the suite* for hanging out, and he was interested in all things military. During freshman year, she had watched bits and pieces of *Platoon* and *Full Metal Jacket* more times than she could count, as well as many other popular "war porn" movies (war movies which gave the viewer a high from the depiction of military action and its horrors, the garish nature of military life, and graphic violence) of the '80s. Seeing young guys huddled around *Platoon* in the VLS reminded her of freshman year, and of the lessons she had learned. During freshman year, rather than keep to herself, and to her own friends, she had tried to fit in with those guys, be like them, act like she was interested in those movies, and really, take on another persona – that of an immature eighteen-year-old first-year male engineering major interested in all things military. Trying to be one of the guys, trying to show interest in what interested them, never did work, because for her, that way of being was inauthentic. She never did gain their favor, and she hadn't made them notice her more or include her much in their circle.

"Do you watch other movies?" she asked the guys.

"No, ma'am, we're trained killers."

"What about you, ma'am?"

"I've seen these movies over and over. They're well-acted and well done, and they're supposed to be antiwar, but…" She knew the gunners mates were smart, and that they would be watching her. She wasn't one of them and she shouldn't try to be.

"We've got *Apocalypse Now* on deck, ma'am."

"I love the smell of napalm in the morning," she answered, quoting Robert Duvall from the most famous scene in the movie, the best scene, in her consideration, the scene on the beach.

"See, GUNNO knows," one of the petty officers said.

"I know," she said. Then, she teased, "I knew the gunners mates weren't a division of antiwar peace protestors, flower children." She thought about conversations with her father growing up. In her family, there was no discussion of war on a philosophical level. Instead, there was a disposition of passively accepting and going along with war and the military; not liking it necessarily, or jumping onto any kind of patriotic bandwagon about it, but not diving into a movement or protest against it either. People who protested or questioned the status quo seemed annoying in her household. She had criticized protesters because "people fought and died so they could protest." She had picked up on her father's outlook; and around people who spoke and acted passionately against issues of war and conservatism, such as her friends, she usually found herself annoying them back with some kind of *"Oh, come on, whatever!"* response, usually accompanied by a sarcastically snide remark that she had learned from her father and repeated as a given.

"When are you going to take over for Mr. Lineberry, ma'am?"

"None of us can wait for you to take over, ma'am," she heard another in the background, but she ignored the comment.

"As soon as we count the ammo, we'll turn over," she responded.

"That's who you'll need to see for ammo, ma'am, Petty Officer Mimms," one of the gunners mates suggested, pointing toward the back. "But wait for Chief or for Petty Officer Brooks to see him," another said, in a lowered voice.

In the back corner of the space, she spotted Petty Officer Mimms sitting on a stool, alone, at the metal workspace desk, quietly working on some log books. She walked over to him. He was a large stocky figure with a shaved head.

"Hello, Petty Officer Mimms. I'm Ensign Conner."

"I know who you are, ma'am. Mr. Lineberry told me you would be down for the ammo count today. I log all ammo expenditures and draft the ammo admin messages," he said, and then turned to continue his work. She knew something of the ammo admin program from SWOS. The program was tedious, and carried high visibility for the Command. Ammo admin messages were drafted in code. Any mistake, one letter or digit off, generated a correction message called a "blast," which was copied by message traffic to everyone in the ship's chain of command – Commander, U.S. Pacific Fleet (CINCPACFLT), Commander, Naval Surface Force, U.S. Pacific Fleet (COMNAVSURFPAC), Commander, U.S. 7th Fleet (COMSEVENTHFLT), Destroyer Squadron 15 (DESRON15), etc. "Here's the manual. I suggest you read it, ma'am," Petty Officer Mimms said. "GMM1 Brooks will guide you through the count since he's the division LPO. He's two months senior to me."

She relaxed her posture. "What's wrong, Petty Officer Mimms?" she asked, really, out of sincere concern, dreading that interactions with him over the next year to eighteen months would go like walking a tightrope.

"You don't want to hear what I have to say, ma'am." He adjusted his ballcap and got up as if to leave. "Here, ma'am," he said. "I put together a custom-made spreadsheet for you. It'll facilitate your count." He handed her a clipboard with the spreadsheet.

"Thank you, Petty Officer Mimms. I appreciate your assistance. But I do actually," she paused, "want to hear what you have to say, even if I don't like it. If you'll be honest with me, I'll be honest with you in return."

She received an eye roll in response. Then, he said, "I don't think women should be in the Navy, ma'am, especially as officers." She nodded, stunned that he had actually said it. But he had given her the honesty she had asked for, which, surprisingly, made her feel good.

"I respect your opinion, Petty Officer Mimms. You can think what you want. You have that right. Isn't that what we're in the Navy for? I'm not going to try to dissuade you or convince you otherwise," she said, glancing at one of his logbooks. His work appeared meticulous and detailed, his block letters and numbers written neatly, and with care. "I can tell you that I like procedure, and work that is completed carefully and methodically. It's key for ammo admin. That's what the ship and the division require for this program." Petty Officer Mimms looked away, disinterested. "You're a gunners mate first class and I'm an ensign division officer. In terms of military protocol, that's the best I can offer." She could see she was losing him. "I hear you're an expert at what you do."

"Whatever, ma'am."

"Okay," she resigned. At least she knew where she stood with Petty Officer Mimms, and she didn't dislike him. She wasn't concerned, so much, if their relationship was strained, as long as he did his job well. According to Pete, he was the only petty officer onboard who knew how to run the ammo program, a program that had the potential to make or break the division in the eyes of the Command. His last duty station was at an ammo depot in the Midwest.

"Petty Officer Mimms, please take me to Petty Officer Brooks," she requested, "so I can get started with the count."

"Follow me to the small arms locker, ma'am."

***

Petty Officer Mimms opened the heavy, thick door to the ammo vault. "Here you are, ma'am. Anything else?" he asked. He secured the door open so the seas wouldn't swing it shut. They were so far below decks that the sound of the seas crashing against the hull was almost deafening. "Thank you, Petty Officer Mimms," she yelled back to him, competing with the overwhelming noise. "I'm good." The vibrations from the turbulent seas sounded eerie, being so deep within the ship. Farther below where they were, she could hear the metal of the ship stretching and creaking.

Petty Officer Brooks was already inside. "Come on in, ma'am," he waved her in. He was hunched over inside the cramped vault. She estimated he must have been at least 6' 4". "I can't stand up straight in any of the ship's passageways, ma'am," he said, as if he had read her face and thoughts. "My shoulders are always hunched over."

"Even I don't have too much overhead room to spare in this vault," she said. But she was at least able to walk in and stand up straight.

She looked around at the shelves of ammo and at the rifles in their lockers. "I've got everything prepared and laid out for you," he said. She was impressed by how he had organized the green metal ammo boxes into stacks, and by how he had labeled the stacks for the count. Each stack was strapped down and chained to the floor. From a quick scan, she could see that the order of the stacks matched Petty Officer Mimms' spreadsheet.

"This looks perfect, Petty Officer Brooks. Thank you," she smiled. She wondered if she had caught a break, if working with the division would be her refuge, the highlight of her time onboard. So far, the guys had seemed welcoming. If Petty Officer Mimms was her only holdout, then she counted herself fortunate. She realized her first official day wasn't all bad. In SWOS, the instructors spoke of the division officer's responsibility to *"fight for your people"* up the chain of command. *"Protect your people"* and *"stand up for your people,"* they had emphasized during the six month school. Those phrases, which everyone in the Navy used, rubbed her, and she wondered why she would need to protect "her people" from the Command; but such was the surface warfare officer community, she had found.

She regretted the reality that she probably would not be able to offer the gunners mates much guidance on technical matters; she would have to depend on the chiefs for that. But administratively, she hoped to represent the division fairly and honestly. She vowed to herself to give everything she had to providing the division and the individual gunners mates with the support they needed. After typing out the letter to the debt collector, Pete had told her, among other things, that the division generally performed their jobs well. But he had warned that the main impediment to progress was often the chiefs' long standing frustration and unwillingness to cooperate. "That kind of outlook and stance develops over years," she remembered responding to Pete, "and for a reason. It doesn't happen by accident and for no reason." She planned to respect the chiefs and to work with them as best as she could, keeping in mind that there would be nothing she could do to change them or the dynamics that had caused them to feel the way they did. She imagined the chiefs had grown tired of satisfying the often unreasonable whims of senior SWOs who grappled and competed within the promotion system. She was too junior to understand the entire web of dynamics that had shaped the chiefs. She only hoped to find a way to work with them.

"You can set your clipboard down on this shelf, ma'am," Petty Officer Brooks told her after organizing a few more boxes. "I'll bring each metal box to you. You'll only have to count, log, and sign each sheet," he said.

"I'm sorry, Petty Officer Brooks," she said, as she gripped one of the shelves as if her life depended on it. "I can't remain standing. I'm going to have to sit on the floor to count."

"A lot of us don't feel well, ma'am. I'm not at my absolute best either. We certainly can do this another day."

"I appreciate your offer," she said, "but let's see if we can at least get through this vault, as long as you're okay."

"I'm fine, ma'am."

"You're from the Midwest," she said.

"From Indiana," he smiled.

She sat down cross-legged on the floor. Being so sick, the cold steel floor helped to revive her. Petty Officer Brooks placed a green ammo box next to her and opened it. She began counting, bullet by bullet, keeping Petty Officer Mimms' custom spreadsheet on her lap to mark her progress. "I'll hold a flashlight for you, ma'am. This dank vault is pretty dimly lit."

"No, use it for yourself, please," she told him. "I can see okay." Petty Officer Brooks sat down next to her. "You don't have to sit on the floor with me, if you don't want," she smiled.

He waved her off like it was no problem. "I'm sure you're already aware of this, ma'am," he began, "but these are 9mm rounds. The Navy recently switched from 45s."

"I have a lot to learn about the division," she answered. Off and on throughout her life, she had gone target shooting with her father, and she was an okay enough shot; but she had never paid attention to the specifics and mechanics of the guns and rifles. Her father grew up on a farm, and during his short enlistment in the Army decades ago, he had served as a small arms repairman. Since he was so knowledgeable in handling pistols and rifles, she had relied on him to take care of the details during their shoots. Besides, every time he had shown her something about the mechanics of the guns, she had seemed to forget it minutes later.

"You didn't have a chance to attend the three day gunnery officer wonder course before you arrived, ma'am?" Petty Officer Brooks teased in good nature. "You were supposed to be the COMMO. Same thing happened to Mr. Lineberry and the officer we had before him."

"What can I say, it's crazy," she threw her hands up, realizing how information really did get around.

"That's the Navy, ma'am. Remember, a bitching sailor is a happy sailor," he replied.

"That's what they say," she said, having always found the saying unfortunate. "I'm open to anything you can show me. I'm very thankful. I've had some exposure to shooting growing up."

She rested her head in her hands, trying to stem the pounding in her temples. He hadn't responded to her last comment. She imagined he had heard it all before, from other new and green ensign division officers. Here she was, sitting next to her division leading petty officer (LPO), a gunners mate first class (GMM1) with ten years in the Navy. And she, the officer in charge, had no training in gunnery or missile specifics. And he worked for her! She could not believe that he actually worked for her – because she knew nothing! Who else, besides the Navy, placed a kid just out of college – in her early twenties – in charge of a division of twenty or more skilled technicians? Who else rotated a young person through completely different divisions every six months or a year or so, as the manager-in-charge of each one? How could anyone learn anything in that timeframe, or perform effectively? On top of running a division, junior officers also had to devote half of their time, or more, to qualifying as watchstanders on the bridge, in the combat information center, and in engineering. And many accepted this system! Many even defended it! Or, some complained but still stayed in the Navy, resigned to it. She had difficulty just accepting things and going along.

She envied officers who could show up – unfazed by the vast amount of information that they would be responsible for – and familiarize themselves with every knob, valve, and mechanical and electrical drawing in the span of a few weeks. But how could that have been the majority of junior officers? The instructors in SWOS taught that, "Officers are managers and leaders; they rely on their people for the details." But how could she evaluate the information "her people" reported to her when she had no knowledge or experience in their work?

At a time when surface warfare was growing increasingly complex, both tactically and technologically, it felt dismaying that she would never have the chance to focus on any one area – such as navigation, engineering, operations, combat systems, admin, etc. She had heard too often the saying, "Just when you've learned 30% of your job, it's time to move on." It was amazing that the modern surface Navy clung to a junior officer training and job rotation philosophy – and officer/enlisted management structure – that had been passed down from the wooden ships of the old British Navy: Every junior officer was to experience every shipboard job in preparation for command at sea – to become the captain of a warship.

Tens of thousands of junior officers rotated through various shipboard jobs during their four-year average time in. In the modern Navy, all of those jobs were technically complex. The system created generalists and jacks-of-all-trades aboard highly specialized ships. Just as an officer started to get comfortable in a billet, it was time to transfer to an altogether different one. That was why chiefs were considered the "backbone of the Navy": They spent their entire careers in the same field. An average of only 17% of junior SWOs stayed in after their initial four- or five-year scholarship commitment. The money spent on rotating JOs through various billets – before over 80% of them resigned their commissions! – was staggering. Most junior officers took the leadership and management skills they acquired at an early age in the Navy to the civilian market. If only she could have remained in one position for four years as a specialist, at least she could have learned something in depth and possibly made more of a contribution. As it stood, after a year or eighteen months, she would never manage gunnery or missile systems ever again.

As Brenda sat in the small arms vault, counting ammo she didn't know much about, she found the JO training system unbelievably outdated, not to mention embarrassing, as she glanced self-consciously at her LPO.

As she counted, she tried to recall any information she could from SWOS concerning guns and small arms. Recalling anything would have helped her morale. But as hard as she tried, she couldn't remember the details of any of the naval guns and ammo she had studied. The introductory school had covered such a broad sweep of the entire seagoing Navy, that the subject of guns and ammo had barely been touched upon. She remembered one fact she had memorized: "A small arm is a weapon with a bore diameter of 0.6 inches or less." And that was about all she knew.

Her LPO broke the silence between them as the clamorous seas crashed against the hull. "The sound's more intense being well below decks and right at the edge of the hull, isn't it, ma'am," Petty Officer Brooks said.

"It gives me the creeps actually," she answered. If she was destined to drown while trapped in an ammo vault, several decks below the surface, she guessed there was not much she could do about it. She hoped that whoever was standing OOD on the bridge knew what they were doing.

"Ma'am," he lowered his voice. "I wouldn't recommend being alone in any space with Mimms. He's psycho, I mean crazy. He has an arsenal of knives in his berthing locker. We're *all* scared of him. And he doesn't like women in the military. He'll hate you. None of us go near him."

She felt for Petty Officer Mimms. He was an outsider. "Well," she sighed. "I guess he can hate me as long as he does his job. But I understand what you're telling me. And I very much appreciate it."

Petty Officer Brooks leaned in, "He's a devil worshiper. I'm only warning you for your own safety."

"Okay," she exhaled her response. "Thank you," she emphasized, wanting to express that she appreciated his candor. She wanted to develop an open relationship with her chiefs and LPO (leading petty officer). "I have something for you, too, Petty Officer Brooks," she said. "I owe you an apology. You're the division leading petty officer and I should have afforded you more respect at quarters. How I handled the issue of the generator was a rookie mistake, and uncalled for. I'm sorry."

"Honestly, ma'am, I didn't like you very much at first over that."

"You had every right, believe me. The ship will send the letter. Otherwise, I trust you to handle it from there. All I ask is to let me know if anything changes."

"It's a difficult situation with my wife. She's twelve years older than me. Her teenage kids, my step-kids, are on drugs, drinking, everything. They're all after my paycheck. I want a divorce, but with her living in the Arizona desert, and me on a forward deployed ship out of Japan, it's nearly impossible."

In her few days onboard, she had learned that forward deployment created problems and hardships a person couldn't imagine in their most disturbing dreams. Being single with no attachments, she had simply never considered the hardship. "I'm sorry," she said sympathetically, not knowing how far to go. "I can get you in touch with the right contacts at the JAG office, or with the family counseling center in Yokosuka. Let me know of anything you need, or if you simply need to talk."

"I will, ma'am, thank you."

Another gunners mate surprised them both. "Hey, ma'am, I brought you a hat!"

"Well, thank you!"

"I'm Petty Officer Finn, your repair parts petty officer, your RPPO. I felt it my duty to bring you a ship's ballcap so you can stop wearing the khaki banana hat. It's embroidered, *GUNNO*, on the back." He showed her, and she took it and put it on.

"No, you have to bend the brim first," he exclaimed.

"I like the brim flat," she answered.

"No, you can't wear it that way, ma'am," he insisted. They were both laughing.

Seeing she had amused him, she sat up straight and answered, defiantly, "I like it." And Petty Officer Finn left the space singing down the passageway: "GUNNO, she's the flat hatter!" She didn't mind. If the guys had a few harmless laughs at her expense, she figured it good for morale.

Petty Officer Brooks turned to her. "Finn followed you and Mimms down here, you know, ma'am, none of us trust Mimms."

"Oh, gosh," she wasn't sure what to say. "Thank you, Petty Officer Brooks," she said. She didn't want the gunners mates to feel that they had to protect her, *their officer!* And then, possibly he had read her thoughts again because he added, "It wouldn't have mattered with a male or female GUNNO, ma'am. We kept him from Mr. Lineberry at first, as well."

She nodded and smiled. Many dynamics were at play.

Chapter 25: A dot in the ocean ... To seek self-awareness ... Insignificant events have instructive value ... The inner world of feelings ... The creation of a persona

Start of Day 2 onboard
Time 0300, First bridge watch 0400 - 0800 (4 a.m. - 8 a.m.)

Brenda awoke to her first early morning at sea, after having settled into her rack sometime after midnight. Three a.m. had arrived so suddenly. She reached to the side of her pillow and silenced her watch alarm, hoping the beeps hadn't disturbed Julie in her rack below. The ship rocked and rolled and pitched with the seas. She could hear the metal of the ship stretching and creaking, and she remembered that before, she had only heard that sound when she was far below decks. She felt worse than she ever had, even worse than she had felt in school when she had forced herself out of bed, weighed down with the flu or a cold. She turned her pillow over and pressed her face against it. Her head felt sluggish from seasickness, and her eyes throbbed with shooting pain from exhaustion, but the coolness she felt from her pillow gave her a moment's relief.

Less than three hours of sleep before her first watch! But three hours of sleep a night was the norm aboard surface ships, and you were lucky to get that, people had told her. She forced her eyes to stay open. In one hour, at 0400, she would have to show for her first bridge watch in the regular rotation. She now grasped the type of strain and pressure that lay ahead, how it was going to feel and how it was going to affect her. There would be four more years of predawn and midnight watches, four more years of wishing like anything for rest, and four more years of disrupting her body's normal cycle – for a way of life she had learned she did not want.

She eased her head up from her pillow. She had to get dressed and get going. *In her life, she had made all the wrong choices, been wrong about everything!* Outside the hull, she imagined the seas churning the ship, beating against the destroyer and tossing it, heeling it to port and then to starboard, pitching it forward and then aft. The shock and vibration was loud; she could feel the vibrations in her body and in the sides of her metal rack when she touched them.

She pushed her gray wool blanket aside; she could hear the engines droning, and feel them tremor as if they were operating on the deck just below her stateroom. The sound of the engines propelling the ship against the force of the seas followed a rhythmic pattern as the ship climbed each oncoming wave, pitched over the crest, and slammed flat into the trough. After the shock waves dampened, a stillness persisted for a second before the engine drone picked back up, and the stateroom walls began to shudder again, along with the entire contents of the room. The metal chairs, desks, sink, cabinets, and rack frames vibrated at different frequencies.

The destroyer was a mere dot in the ocean, and powerless against these seas. Julie told her that the storm wasn't going to let up for another day or so. She got nervous that she hadn't yet gotten out of her rack. *She couldn't be late for her first watch!* She would have to make herself accept this life; she had made herself accept her lifestyle in engineering school, why not this? This was only the start of her second day onboard, underway.

She realized that overnight, the air in the stateroom had turned stuffy and humid. Her skin felt clammy and her nightclothes had a slight dampness to them. Then, above the background noise, she heard the ventilation system kick on, and she began to feel a draft of cold air flowing over her rack curtain. She pitted her will against the seas and sat up slowly. She had committed herself to a role in which her peers and shipmates depended on her to take her bridge watch. It had been her alone, who had obligated herself to performing these shipboard duties. As she sat up in her rack, it came over her that she had once again landed herself in a setting where listening to her body and to her feelings was forfeited. She would have to continue to brush her feelings aside, fight them, and ignore them, in order to function at all.

She wanted to let her body have its way, and allow her head to sink back into her pillow. She had learned that there were consequences to not heeding her physical and emotional needs. She had made choices that had led her to engineering and the Navy because she had disregarded her feelings over her young lifetime, existing disconnected from them, and in ignorance of who she was. She hadn't wanted to know who she was because it would have disrupted her plans. Her presence onboard the ship as an engineer and naval officer was no accident, she reminded herself. Since junior high school and through college, she had planned her life carefully, going about her own self-designed chain of future milestones for her education, career, and personal choices like an unstoppable steam train. Nothing happened by pure chance or accident, there was always a complex, sometimes indiscernible, chain of choices, dynamics, and influences leading to an event.

Her mind wandered over the history that had led to this point. She turned around slowly, balanced her right knee on the edge of her rack, and labored down the ladder, rung by rung, as the ship pitched and rolled; she thought about how she had failed herself in almost every decision she had ever made. She realized that her decisions and choices had merely been symptoms of her denial and of her efforts to build a persona. Before she eased herself down to the stateroom floor, she stepped carefully onto the edge of Julie's rack. She didn't want to disturb her roommate while she was finally able to sleep.

Through her thin socks, she felt the coolness of the stateroom floor against the bottoms of her feet. She kept hold of her rack ladder, trying to keep steady against the seas.

Why had she never acquired an awareness of her feelings? Why hadn't she known to seek self-awareness and awareness of her environment? She had taken as gospel her parents' attitudes, values, and concepts of how to live, and she had – without realizing it – asserted and defended those out in the world, judging others, trying to influence others to live in the same way. *She had thought she knew how to go about life; that she was right.* And she would have never considered another take on life, at least not before she had landed herself onboard this destroyer and attempted to perform a role unquestionably wrong for her. It was a realization that made her want to meet with every one of her friends, and anyone else she may have tried to influence, and apologize.

"But you're not going to be able to find a job! You can read about art history in your spare time as a hobby," she remembered pleading with her friend May, as they walked the city streets of their college campus one afternoon. "You'll have to go back to school to get a masters in computer programming or an MBA in business, or something else real, after wasting all of your tuition money," she had pointed out, hoping to change her friend's mind about her major. The conversation had taken place on one of those beautiful New England spring days in the city, when the breeze across the streets and sidewalks offered a faint hope of warmth. They had just crossed the subway tracks that ran along the center of the main thoroughfare through the campus, when she had finished her sentence.

"Fine, then I'll do that," her friend barely answered, her words short.

"But, what are you going to do for a job?" Brenda persisted. "I mean, maybe a curator in a museum, but those jobs are few and far between. I was so relieved when Kathleen switched from film to biology, and Danielle from journalism to teaching."

Brenda let go of her rack ladder, astonished by her own words and behavior. For four years she had persistently goaded her friends about jobs, where they would live, and how they would pay their bills. *Had they started saving?* she would ask. She used to joke that her goal was to marry a nice, boring engineer who brought home a steady paycheck (like her own), and who prided himself on investing and saving money.

When she was a child, it had appeared to her that her parents had treated her well, and that they were all close; she had never fought with her parents and she had thought that she had lived a good life with them – that she had had a great childhood as far as a conventional family setting was concerned. But what would have happened if she had tried to be herself, gone her own way, and not repressed who she was to satisfy her parents? When she talked about her own ideas, her own views and interests, and what she wanted to study, she had met with resistance, even hostility, and lack of understanding. Her parents were always sort of amused by her ideas, as if she was "cute." They looked upon anyone who was passionate for a subject, idea, or cause as "cute." So, she had always backed down immediately. They all seemed to get along okay, as long as she didn't rock the boat with her ideas, questions, and interests.

And she had learned, without being conscious of it, to say things and to take stances that she knew her parents would agree with. She had convinced herself that she agreed with and believed in those things.

After remembering her conversation with May, she wondered why any of her friends still kept in touch with her. She had spoken that way to May and to her friends relentlessly, as if she had had all the answers. But there were a few times when friends had rejected her, and when they had decided to step away from her, sick of her harping. Standing by the sink as the ship tossed from side to side, she had to hold her head in her hands to stem the pain and to keep from vomiting; and she realized that she had never been – and would never be – in a position to tell anyone else how to live.

Her flashback of that warm spring day in the city, walking the streets of her college campus with May, led her to remember her study abroad in Madrid. She had filled the summer before her senior year with the Spanish sun, her pursuit of the literature classes she loved, and with riding the trains all over Spain on the weekends with other students in the program. She had applied for the shortened, six-week study abroad program, not nearly enough time to seriously improve or work on her spoken Spanish, but at least it was something. Her ROTC unit had originally denied her request for a semester-long study abroad; they had said that she needed the leadership training she would receive from her upcoming billet as platoon commander. But grudgingly, her lieutenant advisor had allowed her to schedule her midshipman cruise around a shorter summer study abroad. "Miss Conner, I'm going to turn on the TV someday to watch the news, and I'll see you shuttling off to the moon, or some other thing you've finagled," he had said. "Yes, sir," she had answered, excited to go to Spain. She now realized that because she wasn't particularly passionate about ROTC, she had been trying to "finagle-in" the things about which she was passionate – things which didn't fit within the parameters of ROTC and engineering.

In her time so far in the Navy, she had begun to take note of how seemingly insignificant past events, certain key ones, were accumulating in her mind, and that she had previously failed to understand the instructive value within these. And every once in a while, when she felt herself all-out distressed and cursing herself for having joined the Navy, one of those events would surface to consciousness; and each time, she would progressively learn something more of its significance.

During her study abroad in Spain, she had taken four classes. One of them was an art history class, taught in Spanish, that met every morning for six weeks in the Prado museum. The class was led by an American woman, an adjunct professor living in Spain. The professor was memorable for Brenda because she was the first person in her life who had taught her how to look at a painting, notice its detail, and interpret and appreciate its characters, images, themes, and styles. For the class, the students were required to write a midterm paper and prepare a final oral presentation about two different paintings and/or sculptures in the museum.

On the day the professor returned the midterm papers, Brenda unexpectedly gained a lesson about herself, and about the way she had gone about her life. The professor didn't hand her midterm paper back with those of the rest of class. While the other students in the class sorted through the stack of graded papers, the professor asked her aside, privately, in the entranceway of the museum, and told her that she would refrain from grading her paper. "Oh my God," was all Brenda could remember of her response. She wanted to crawl into a hole, embarrassed. She remembered reacting defensively at first, feeling angry as well as surprised that her analysis of her chosen painting was not worthy of a grade at all, *any grade!* Then, she started to listen to what the professor was saying, initially only because she wanted to know how she could improve her grade, or at least get one. She remembered standing in the museum in a hall of successive white arches, feeling herself breathe as the professor described how she had misinterpreted the theme of the painting, in its entirety, and how research was required to discuss the history, period, and analysis. Then, gradually, she came to realize that her teacher was speaking to her with empathy, and that she wanted her to learn. Brenda recalled the feeling of letting her guard down, and of disarming. And subsequently, she allowed herself to receive what the professor was trying to tell her.

She lifted a newly pressed khaki uniform from her stateroom desk chair, remembering how she had felt at a loss upon exiting the museum. Despite listening to the professor, she had remained skeptical that the content of her paper could have been so far off. She walked directly to a park bench just outside the museum doors, and sat down to review what she had written. As she read through her paper with newer eyes, she found the tone superior, mocking, sarcastic, and disrespectful of the work she had tried to analyze, and even of the study of art history in general. In her writing, she had minimized the symbolism in the painting by making up her own interpretations of it based on no research. *Research and serious study behind art? Wasn't art class in junior high and high school the blow-off class?* She hadn't considered that there was any underlying research and study to art.

After reading only three pages, she rose from the bench and began the long walk across the city back to her host mother's apartment. She passed the metro entrance near the museum, and a block farther the bus stop, opting to walk and to think. Why had she signed up for an art history class to begin with? she kept asking herself, as she navigated the streets and plazas of downtown Madrid. She remembered thumbing through the study abroad catalog in her student apartment in Boston, thinking that the course description – *Historia del arte de España, enseñada en el Museo del Prado* – sounded interesting enough, something different. She assumed the course would be easy, a no-brainer. By the time she crossed the bridge over the Manzanares River to her host mother's building, she still wondered fundamentally, how she could have failed at writing a paper on *art history!* The chance that she wouldn't be able to pull the class off made her nervous. Who failed a summer study abroad class? *Much less one in the arts!*

Later that afternoon, she sat down to lunch with her host mother. "You're the twenty-third student I've hosted," she told her in Spanish. "And you're the most serious. Most study at the discotheques. Go to the university library. Take this book I'll lend to you," she said as she got up from the table to retrieve it. "Look to the history, the era, the setting of the painting, the artist, the symbolism, the style, open yourself to taking it seriously – open your heart as well as your intellect. You're in your room reading and studying more than I've seen from any of the other ones, but you don't respect. You'll get it, I know."

Brenda thanked her, grabbed her backpack, and rode the metro back across the city to the university library in Madrid. From the shelves, she pulled nearly every reference book she could find on her chosen painting and its era, and stacked them high in her carrel. Over a few nights, she stayed late until closing, reading text after text from varying authors. Gradually, she began to open herself to the analytic method taught in class, and developed an approach to researching and writing her paper.

The reading introduced her to a world of expression and symbolism mediated through art, beyond the only world which she had ever known – the tangible, practical, and task-oriented. As she rewrote her paper from scratch, having found none of the original salvageable, she realized that the content of her first paper represented a reflection of herself – of her own outlook and behavior in life. She had thrown her first paper together flippantly, with an underlying attitude that lacked respect toward the assignment and the painting, as her host mother had pointed out. The study of art history – and the arts in general – had impressed her as nothing more than a hobby…the easy…the fluff…of lesser importance than the practical…the caliber of "underwater basket weaving."

Her new understanding of the painting left her with the severe realization that she had lived cut off from – or had at least minimized

– an important aspect of herself...a realm of life that dealt with the heart, the symbolic, the expressive, the intangible, the inner world of feelings and passion. But even this major self-discovery was not enough to thwart her effort to get into the military. It was all too foreign from what she had lived, and from what she had been taught, and she hadn't known herself or trusted herself well enough to act on her new discoveries. At the time, she had felt more apt to disregard them, write them off. But a seed had been planted.

Having become more open to a new avenue in life, the next week she turned in her rewritten paper and received an A+. The professor noted that she had analyzed the painting effectively and with depth and research, and that she had detected talent in her analysis of the art.

Brenda picked her khaki uniform up by the collar and pinned her ensign insignia to it. Since that summer in Spain, she had felt grateful that the professor had handed her initial paper back to her, rather than passing it through. Her conversations with the professor and with her host mother had led her to open her eyes to an entire part of life that she had dismissed as inconsequential and nonessential: the arts, and the fulfillment one can gain in life through expression through the arts, through creating something, through using the arts as a medium for self-expression. As Brenda clasped her bra and reached for her white undershirt, she now understood why she had packed two art history books inside her seabag...two of the very books she had used to rewrite her paper. The decision to include those books must have been unconscious; they were a reminder of how she had previously discounted an entire vital layer of human experience.

Standing in front of the mirror, she pulled her hair back tight. She found her past utilitarian and businesslike approach to life cold and unsatisfying. She imagined that her rigid and stern qualities had made her appear unattractive. The thematic lessons she had resisted from her literature classes, those that she had ridiculed, she now found more relevant than any of her learning from her science and math classes. She found it hard to reflect back. It felt alarming, even threatening. No heart or depth of feeling had been behind her choices to become an engineer and join the Navy, because she had lacked entrance to those qualities within herself. For some, engineering *was* truly an art, but for her it had been merely a pragmatic decision. She had lived completely out of balance, leaning towards the rational and intellectual, while trivializing, or existing oblivious of, the spiritual and feeling components of her life.

Brenda buttoned her khaki shirt, leaving the top button open where the neck of her undershirt showed, as prescribed by uniform regulations. Studying with the aims of a secure job, saving money, and investing early for retirement had once seemed like such vital goals. She could hear her best friend and roommate in college speaking as clearly as if she had been standing inside her stateroom. "Nate was just saying to me on the phone in his British accent," Kathleen told her one afternoon, as they folded clothes in the basement of their student brownstone, "Brenda's a very practical girl." She remembered laughing, feeling proud to have been thought of in such a way. That was exactly how she had wanted people to see her – living smartly and taking care of things pragmatically. Convinced of the "rightness" of that lifestyle, she had had a strong need to convert everyone else to the primacy of those values.

Brenda held her hand to her forehead, trying to stem her headache. She could barely process the thought of heading up to the bridge. She realized that her comment to May – warning of the dangers of majoring in art history – had been directly quoted from her mother. As a child, whenever Brenda had asked about studying art, or even archeology at one time, her mother had said that the only job available would be as a curator at a museum, and that those jobs were hard to get. Brenda imagined that she had spouted engrained statements like that from her parents thousands of times without ever having questioned them. Such statements she had heard over and again during her childhood, when she had talked about various subjects that she had loved and that were of interest to her, subjects that she had wanted to study and pursue.

Her father had insisted that subjects like history and literature were okay as hobbies, but not as a major. She had accepted everything her parents said and did without question. She thought – or assumed since early on – that they knew the best way to live. She had loved bragging to her friends about her parents' plans to travel, and about their knowledge of how to invest and look towards retirement. It shocked her sense of security and her foundation to bring to light that their way of life may not have applied to everyone, including her.

Brenda clasped the button on her khaki pants, and used her towel to wipe at some of the tarnish on her brass belt buckle. She had sleepwalked through her life, imitating what she had lived and seen at home as a child, never thinking to question what had been repeated at her while growing up. Coming to the understanding that she had followed their model, as if on autopilot, surprised her, because she had thought that she was her own person, engaged in her own life. In actuality, she had planned her life herself, but in accordance with her parents' concepts of life.

And that was both her fault and the result of unintended consequences on the part of her parents. Her parents were nice people who loved her and would do anything for her. They just weren't the type of people who could look into, or understand in depth, who a person was, or comprehend the complex psychological and environmental factors that shaped a person and their feelings, behaviors, and dreams. So they had never looked into her, or provided her with a space where she would be allowed to be different from them, and at the same time, she hadn't known to look into herself; and she had grafted exactly who her parents were onto herself. It happened that their way of being wasn't wrong necessarily, but that it didn't work for her. She was a different person entirely, an introvert, with completely different needs...versus the extraverts her parents were. But all of those dynamics, on her part and on the part of her parents, had been unknown.

While she was growing up, her father's outlook had mirrored the times which prevailed during the Reagan-era '80s. He was a moderate, but slightly to the right – a business conservative but not a social conservative – compliant with the mood of the status quo and of authority, without questioning much or getting emotionally involved. Her parents lived in a safe zone, without risk, and without bucking any system in any way. They worked in careers considered secure, with guaranteed stable incomes, benefits, and retirement savings. The same outlook had been pressed onto her, and she had taken it in as her own. From there, she had gone about the world, operating from the point of view of those values and concepts.

She was reminded of her *Oh, come on!* response to friends or anyone else who sought an artistic, less traditional, or anti-establishment approach to life. Those who didn't aim their college studies at a guaranteed job she saw as wishy-washy. Those who fussed over the environment or the whales, seals, peace or other causes she mocked as melodramatic. She had assumed her father's stance unquestionably, having been made to believe in his way in order to avoid friction within her family setting, and to avoid the annoyed brushoffs that any of her natural expressions seemed to bring on; she didn't want to hear the comments that "she was a pain" or "in a mood" when she expressed what came from within herself. Her parents had a habit of joking about times when they had perceived her as difficult, so she became accustomed to righting herself along their lines to conform and to please. They had called her *the Queen* when she expressed herself. But she had retained some of her spirit, she remembered, and smiled; she had been spouting off about issues, mostly in regard to women's rights, since she had learned to utter her first words.

But it was tragic, she realized, as she thought back. She had taken on this guise of a politically conservative young woman, poised to join the military as an officer; but that existence had been a shell. Quite clearly she remembered arguing in favor of sides that she felt went along with the persona she had created. She had even taken the Navy's side against the environmental nightmare of Vieques.[4]

Since joining the Navy, many long-forgotten and disregarded conversations had surfaced into her consciousness, reminding her that there had been moments when her more authentic feelings *had* found their way out.

On the night of the republican convention, she had lain on the couch across from the TV, strung-out in pain from having had all four impacted wisdom teeth extracted. She had felt outraged by the ultraconservative speakers, and their views on women, race, the environment, and the role America should play in the world. Despite her pain and the effect of her prescribed painkillers, she had still managed to make her comments known from the couch. Entertained, her then-boyfriend had shrugged off her rants. Even though there had been occasional moments such as this when she spoke from a more genuine inner voice, she now thought to herself, she had never searched out or integrated that truer self into her outward stance or even into her voting; she had voted her persona, who she had convinced herself she was.

She remembered vaguely thinking during her study abroad, that she and her teacher had graduated from the same university, and "despite" majoring in art history, her teacher had found a way to

---

[4] The environmental and health disasters which were created by decades of U.S. Navy ship to shore bombing exercises off the coast of Puerto Rico, which have resulted in birth defects, cancer, heavy metal contaminants in the coral and eco systems, and islanders' exposure to chemical agents.

make a career of her life's work and study. She taught an art history study abroad class, but her main work involved consulting on procurement and restoration projects for the museum. And May was living and working in New York City at an auction house that specialized in fine art. They had both found jobs in their chosen fields.

Brenda pulled up on the black laces of her steel-toe boots. People used to compliment her that "she had her head on straight." She should have thought to ask them exactly what they had meant by that expression. Her hard-earned, sensible goals were edging her towards despair; her commitment to the military was going to trap her in struggling from one unwanted milestone to the next as she had always done – SWO pin, nuclear power school, job in a technical field someday (possibly technical writing, as her dad had always encouraged) – in an unending and exhausting chain that was not going to lead her to anyplace she genuinely wanted to be. Then, there was that nagging question: What might she have accomplished had she applied her work, ambition, and drive toward a path in a field that had suited her character? *How she would have been on fire to study languages, pouring herself into literature and history!* She had really loved Spain, its language, history, culture, and geography.

She rested her head against her stateroom door, underneath a yellow sign posted on it that read, "WARNING: Air conditioned area. Keep this door closed." Sleep had always been a central issue, and throughout her life she had needed an inordinate amount of it just to function. As an infant and young child, her mother would put her down at seven p.m. and she would sleep straight through to seven a.m. the next morning. In adulthood, she needed at least seven to eight hours; and she always felt like her truly deep sleep came in those essential early morning hours, which historically made school and normal work schedules difficult for her. But she had always forced herself into conforming, even though she was naturally a night person who performed her best work after dark.

Maybe I am acting ridiculously, she suddenly thought. Hundreds of thousands currently served in the military, and countless millions were veterans who had suffered far worse physical and psychological conditions. Maybe she was pathetic in lamenting that she couldn't handle five years in the military during peacetime, or that she hadn't been listened to in exactly the right way as a child. She *was* pathetic, she concluded; she needed to get herself into gear and tough it out. WEPS had set her straight on the issue of sleep. Embarrassingly so! She cowered against her stateroom door in self-consciousness for having even mentioned sleep to her boss. She hoped that she hadn't irreparably damaged her relationship with him; she feared she'd have to put in even more energy so he would be sure to see what a dedicated worker she was and that she believed no sacrifice of time or hard work was too big. She walked back to the mirror over her stateroom sink to check her insignia once more before she left. *Why had she mentioned anything at all to him about sleep?*

*

Earlier that night (actually only five hours earlier!) at around ten p.m., she had gotten ready to go to sleep in her rack. She had thought nothing of it, wanting to get at least five hours in before her upcoming bridge watch – before she had to get up at three a.m. So she climbed the short ladder to her rack, a task she now more easily accomplished, and crawled right in. After fighting against seasickness and nerves throughout her first day, she wanted to curl up in her cool sheets and sleep. She had even congratulated herself on learning how to better climb into her rack. Every shipboard adaptation had encouraged her a little further.

Then, around ten-thirty p.m., the IVCS phone rang. She sat up in her rack, reached over the sink, and picked up the receiver thinking it would be OPS. Even in port, he had habitually called the stateroom at all hours of the day and night for Julie, waking them at random. If Julie happened to be sleeping – as it was, she only seemed to catch two to three hours most nights – he wanted her awakened, even for the most trivial of issues. Julie had appeared more exhausted with each day that had passed, and she looked weary, absolutely forlorn. It was a common sight onboard. She noticed that many onboard appeared tired, rough, and aged. Those with years of sea time behind them – ten, fifteen, or twenty years in the Navy – tended to appear much older than their actual age. When she reviewed Chief Dering's service record, left on her stateroom desk by Pete as part of division officer turnover, she was shocked to read his birth date; he was only forty-one. The chief appeared in his late fifties, at least.

"This is Ensign Conner, sir," Brenda remembered answering the stateroom phone.

"Are you in bed already?" WEPS asked, his voice cracking with strain and stress.

"Yes, sir. I have the 0400 to 0800 rev watch on the bridge," she replied.

"I need you to come down to CIC. I'm on watch until 0200. The rotation differs from that of the bridge."

"Sir, I was hoping to get some sleep before watch, at least five hours. Could I check in with you in the morning?"

"I stand midwatches, too, Brenda," he replied calmly. "This can't wait. It's urgent, straight from the Captain." His voice was on edge and agitated. *Straight from the Captain!* Brenda thought, taking on his same jitters.

"Yes, sir. I'll be right down," she responded. She hung up the IVCS phone and managed to rush her khakis back on. She didn't feel well, but she was as charged up and as nervous as WEPS was about this issue from the Captain. Despite her body's resistance, she pulled her boots on and threw her hair into a bun. Then she opened her stateroom door to the dark passageway, illuminated in red for darken ship. The dark, red passageway calmed her. She loved the feel of the shipboard passageways at night, having remembered it from cruise. The only people moving about the ship were watchstanders, and as she walked she savored the subdued red glow, the quiet emptiness, and the prevalent ship hum.

From officers country, she climbed a few decks down and entered into the utter blackness of the combat information center, where WEPS was standing watch. She stopped to take in the atmosphere of the space. All action emanated from CIC, and no longer from the bridge as in the vintage days of World War II. She spotted WEPS seated up front at the tactical action officer (TAO) console, surrounded by enlisted watchstanders manning consoles, radar scopes, and plot tables. Blue fluorescent lighting, watchstation consoles, and screens displaying ship and aircraft contacts lit the space enough so she could make her way around. The ceiling, walls, and doors were painted black. The space looked just like in the movies, and in recruiting commercials, where they showed watchstanders engaging in adrenaline surging action at various consoles in a dark space.

She approached WEPS. "If you go to sleep by midnight you'll be fine," he began as he removed his headset. "That'll give you three hours of sleep before watch which is plenty. You shouldn't need more than three to four hours a night. You won't have time."

"Yes, sir," she replied, in total disbelief at herself for having ever thought otherwise. She immediately regretted what she had said earlier on the phone about sleep. Everyone else in the SWO community worked on this schedule, and after hearing everyone talk about it like it was normal, she guessed it was normal after all. She remembered the instructors at SWOS talking about the 2000 to 2400 (8 p.m. to midnight) bridge watch as if it was a reprieve. It allowed JOs to catch up on a few days of lost sleep. With the watch ending at midnight, one could get five to six hours of sleep in before division officer (DIVO) rounds the next morning. The 0000 to 0400 (midnight to 4 a.m.) midwatch was the worst, they had said, because on most ships, officers still had to report to OCall and quarters at 0600 or 0700, and a full workday followed.

But deep down, she still felt something wasn't quite right about it, so she asked, "But don't the CO's standing orders state that watchstanders should have at least four hours of sleep before taking the watch?" WEPS turned to look at her and said, "C'mon." He almost laughed, and then he shook his head in disbelief.

"Okay, sir," she resigned herself. She took a seat in the metal swivel chair next to him, in front of the CO's console. The chair was bolted to the deck and had seatbelts.

"As the TAO you have weapons release authority, right, sir?" she asked. She tried to imagine the scene in CIC during an all-out naval battle as in WWII, every seat filled with watchstanders providing reports to the TAO, the ship shaking and vibrating with the firing of guns, missiles, and torpedoes. She wondered what other naval enemy in the current world actually had the ability to fight an aircraft carrier based battle like that.

"That's right, depending."

"Is the issue concerning the gun and VLS both being down, sir?"

"The Captain's concerned about the non-skid paint on the deck surrounding the gun near the red danger circle." His speech sped up. "The gun ejects shells as it fires. They hit the deck and form what we call 'smilies,' nicks in the non-skid paint in the shape of a smile. We have about $20k in the budget for protective padding. The Captain has made this a top priority." She dug her nails into the green vinyl cushioning on her seat. "Without the padding, the gunners mates have to patch up the non-skid after each gun shoot. Now you may ask, why is this a big deal when the gun's inoperable?" She continued looking at him. "It's a big deal because the Captain says it's a big deal. Get with Chief Dering. He may give you a hard time but you've got to get on top of this. Sweat it out."

Word came over the radio that the aircraft carrier was

commencing flight ops, and radio chatter filled the room. "Have Chief take you into the gun mount to gain an overview of the troubleshooting. The issue's a source of poor morale for the gunners mates. If we can perform a gunnery exercise soon, it'll boost their morale." WEPS put his headsets back on and got on the radio with the aircraft carrier. The carrier group had changed course and the seas had calmed some.

*

She let go of the flashback and began to ease the stateroom door open carefully as to not wake Julie. *She had to get to her 0400 bridge watch on time!* But before she could open the door, the IVCS phone rang. She rushed across the stateroom to pick up the receiver, knowing it would be OPS. He was calling, she guessed, because during his TAO watch, which would have started at 0200, he had probably thought up tasking for Julie. She didn't think WEPS would call the stateroom at three a.m. unless it was dire. "This is Ensign Conner, sir," she answered the phone, in as much of a professional voice as she could muster just after three a.m., and being sick. She glanced over at Julie's rack curtain, thinking that she deserved to have it remain closed.

"Hey, GUNNO, this is OPS. Is Julie there or is she on watch?" It was that friendly upbeat voice, that in reality, was snide and snippy.

"No, she's here, sir, sleeping." Julie slowly opened her rack curtain, and Brenda handed her the receiver. Then she stood and waited for Julie to finish. After this phone call, she imagined that Julie would probably have to whisk her uniform on and report to OPS. Onboard ship there was no going home at night after the workday. The workday was 24/7; and both of their bosses lived directly across the passageway. Unlike her recent college graduate peers, she lived at her job. Military life blurred the line between the personal and private. Worst of all, there was no option to leave if you didn't like it or weren't suited for it for whatever reason. All who entered the military were legally bound to stay.

"Aye, sir. I'll get that done first thing before OCall this morning," she heard Julie say. Then Julie handed her back the phone.

"Why the freak is he calling you at three in the morning when OCall is at 0700?" Brenda asked.

"I don't know. He gets bored on watch," Julie answered. Then she lay back down in her rack and closed the curtains.

"It's freaking ridiculous," Brenda commented, as she stuck one last bobby pin in her bun and left the room to make rounds for watch.

Chapter 26: First bridge watch ... Haunting memories provide enlightenment ... Estranged from the authentic self ... A persona in her father's likeness

Time 0330 Brenda tried to psych herself up for her first bridge watch in the regular rotation as she made her way through the early morning passageways of the ship. At that hour, however, and with all she had experienced over the past few days, she found it difficult to make herself feel anything positive, let alone excitement, for her new role. So much had been thrown at her in such a short time, more than she ever could have imagined. At three-thirty a.m. she found comfort, and even motivation, in the thought that she had withstood and survived her introduction onboard, so far. She felt certain enough that she could depend on her inner strength, which had never let her down, to continue to get up, keep going, and make it through her time onboard. Brenda continued walking, reminded of the resolve she had shown throughout engineering school. Four years of stressful nights and weekends packed with unrelenting hard work! And no matter how tired or stressed she had ever become over a class or exam, she had remained unwilling to back down. Many late nights she had spent studying at her desk, vowing not to give in to exhaustion. Surely, she could continue her previous pace and resolution for another four years in the Navy. That hope helped numb her fear and anxiety toward whatever lay ahead, all the trials and events she would never be able to foresee.

Brenda carried those thoughts with her as she descended deeper into the ship, headed down to CIC to start her pre-watch rounds. Maybe those thoughts were something from which to draw inspiration, she wondered. She remembered back to other new places and jobs, how after not being there for very long, she would stop, take a moment, and realize that she had become accustomed to her surroundings as if she had always been there. She could find consolation in familiarity, despite her sense of the job, or her interest in the work. So, she set her mind on viewing her new environment in much the same way, and decided to will herself into a sentiment of belonging. As Brenda stepped through each shipboard compartment, she tried to seize on a new sensation, of looking forward to being onboard. And she went about preparing for her watch with a renewed outlook, that she just might be on her way to becoming a pro.

Mostly the ship appeared vacant at that hour, which left her with the sense that she might have been traversing a ghost ship. Brenda stopped for a moment and leaned against an emergency stretcher strapped to the bulkhead. Staring into the lengths of long empty gray passageways ahead intensified her loneliness. Only the raw sounds of vibrating steel and fan motors over the drone of engines reminded her that pockets of watchstanders were alive and well throughout the ship. Since leaving her stateroom she had passed two petty officers who had acknowledged her as ma'am. As if she actually deserved that level of recognition! But she understood it wasn't personal; it was just protocol.

She carried a folder containing a pad and a few index cards that she had prepared from her SWOS notes. The instructors at SWOS had emphasized the importance of gaining an overview of the ship's schedule and of the tactical and navigational picture prior to watch. She approached the door to CIC, but then she stopped to glance at the cards once more before she entered. *"Information to gather before relieving the watch,"* she read. *"Course, speed, ship's contacts, navigation track, operations in play, current evolutions, events scheduled, aircraft under ship's control, who the ship is in communications with, weather, combat systems sensors in operation, status of weapons systems."*

"Okay," she said to herself. Then she opened the door to CIC. Across the space, she saw OPS seated at the TAO console. She focused on the large flat screens above his head which displayed the ship's position relative to the carrier battle group. For a junior officer like Julie, she imagined the watches weren't burdensome to grasp. Julie probably didn't need to fear questions on the bridge nor performing as a new junior officer of the deck or conning officer. Her skill level was most likely consistent with that of a competent young ensign, engaged in learning and training. Brenda noticed how the other officers responded to Julie, demonstrating fondness, and confidence in her as a colleague.

Brenda walked across the dark space, in and around the consoles, scopes, and plot tables, and approached OPS. "What's up there, GUNNO?" he turned around in the TAO chair.

"I'm headed up to watch on the bridge, sir," she answered, cautious of him.

"Very good," OPS exclaimed. "You're holding onto some

Long Way Out

notes there, GUNNO?"

"Yes, sir, index cards for watch turnover. I've always been a studier and researcher beforehand," she said awkwardly, and then she abruptly stopped herself, not wanting to sound too eager and overzealous.

"It takes time to get into the groove of what you need to ask," he answered and smiled. "New people come and go all the time. You'll get up to speed."

"Yes, sir," she replied, realizing OPS may have just normalized her experience for her. What he said, "It takes time," and, "You'll get up to speed," came so rapidly and off the cuff, as if she belonged onboard like everyone else. She felt encouraged, as if she might actually fit in.

"The carrier commenced flight ops earlier in the night once the seas calmed," OPS began. "She's been maneuvering quite a bit to maintain good winds. We're assigned as planeguard, meaning we're standing by to recover a downed aviator or man overboard in the event of a crash or mishap. A few rules to understand: never come within 6,000 yards ahead, 4,000 yards abeam, or 2,000 yards astern of the carrier; never turn towards the carrier; remain off her quarter, never going forward of her beam. Our station is 170 degrees relative, 3,000 yards astern. You'll be responsible for maintaining station on the bridge within 300 to 500 yards." She flipped the pages of her notepad, trying to write down his every word. She couldn't ask him to slow down or to stop, no matter how much she wanted to, as she feared giving herself away. "Here in CIC, we provide radar, plot, navigation, and MOBoard support to the bridge," OPS continued. "Don't rely on the carrier's reported course and speed over the radio. It almost never matches her actual course and speed. The carrier often reports one course and speed, but then maneuvers for flight winds as she needs. You'll need to judge her course and speed changes according to the alignment of her white and blue stern lights. Our current course and speed is 040 at eight knots. We are off the carrier's starboard quarter. If she turns to port, follow around in her wake. If the carrier turns to starboard, order left standard rudder and come about 45 degrees left of original course. You'll see us cross through her wake and then you can follow back around to starboard. As for contacts, there's one merchant ship about five miles off the starboard bow heading away from us, southeast." She continued writing after he finished. "Any questions?" he asked.

She looked at OPS, unable to form a single question. "No, sir," she simply replied, realizing she wasn't going to have the fortune of easing into her first bridge watch in the normal rotation while the ship "steamed" solo out in the open ocean, as she had hoped. And she hadn't considered that flight ops would ever be performed in this high sea state.

"Have fun up there, GUNNO." OPS smiled and got back on the radio with the carrier.

***

Brenda remained standing behind OPS a moment, staring up at the high-tech flat screens that spanned the front of CIC. The ship was operating in such dangerous proximity to the massive carrier that OPS had already moved on from her. She listened as he radioed back and forth with the TAO onboard the carrier. She imagined the constant and rapid pace onboard this forward deployed destroyer would never let up during her time onboard. Forward deployed ships out of Japan had the highest op tempos in the world.

She turned around and made her way past the radar scopes, computer consoles, and plot tables. As she neared the exit, she reminded herself that she had gotten exactly what she had wanted. It was a thought that pained her to the point that she could no longer stand to think about it. She wished she could stop time, leap backwards, and discontinue the chain of events that had led her to the Navy and to a warship, and now, to a bridge watch. *Engineering and the military*, she repeated to herself, fine for Julie and others like her, but not for her.

She closed the oval watertight door to CIC behind her. If she could piece through her past, and understand *how* she had come to place herself aboard a destroyer, and *why* her direction in life had seemed to spiral beyond her control... *Why* had she stayed dead set on goals that would have never delivered for her? *Why* had she wasted time being so sure she was living right?

She was unsure exactly how it came to be that she now found herself even asking those questions, because she had taken the path taught and encouraged by her parents, in whom she had entrusted her unquestioned faith. In fact, she had thought herself ahead of – and better off than – her friends and peers. In her view, those kids were directionless, aimlessly living about in crowded urban apartments, while employed at odd jobs, or as interns, trying to find consolation within go-nowhere humanities pursuits. "The problem with colleges these days," her father had repeated on numerous occasions, "is that they're encouraging kids to study liberal arts, which trains you for nothing; it's a degree which isn't worth the paper it's written on and you can't do anything with." Sometimes, he would sort of sneer and laugh, and add, "so kids can go out and find themselves or something." He had always seemed so bitterly exasperated over the idea of "finding oneself"; and she had assumed, in the absolute, his same attitude.

Having adopted his words and sentiments as her own, she now felt alone to pretend her way through a setting in which she had no business, onboard an engineering marvel of a naval warship, where her lack of understanding might even be dangerous. She was able to admit to herself, with a sense of shame, that she had been grandiose, with a mistaken vision of herself. While growing up, she had been convinced that others were looking at her in awe of her straight-up way of being, her independence, and her maturity for demonstrating such togetherness and practicality at such a young age. But who, besides her parents, as she tried to remember, had really been impressed by her plans, and by her way about the world? A few relatives, maybe, who didn't know her very well. But mostly, she had been performing for an imagined audience, consisting of friends, parents, and family, who she thought, viewed her as strong in engineering and ROTC. Their viewing her in that way had been important to her; she had kept going for them. But as she remembered comments and reactions from friends and family in a new light, she concluded that most, besides her parents, were probably indifferent either way to her specific plans.

Unlike her, they might not have viewed engineering and ROTC as the only and most sensible and solid option in life, the only one worth aspiring to. And they might not have seen her as she had wanted them to. She remembered her best friend Kristin teasing her a few times before freshman year of ROTC: "I'm coming, I'm coming..." her friend had gasped, impersonating her, pretending to be out of breath and running far behind the formation. At the time, she had been surprised that someone would think of her in that way – *not physically fit to keep up, out-of-place and out-of-step in the military?* "What, why would you think that?" she remembered reacting to Kristin.

Her ROTC squad leader had once called her to inform her that he was going to rank her at the bottom of the squad militarily. She remembered the alarm she had felt, upset that he didn't view her as a capable midshipman, troubled that despite her herculean efforts to the contrary, most in the ROTC unit still didn't view her as up to par. When she had asked him to pinpoint what exactly was wrong with her performance, he had evasively only answered that it was hard to explain. She had thus disregarded him since he hadn't named specific reasons. As she had done on a number of like occasions, she dismissed the evaluation as having been completed by a student in ROTC who she saw as rather incompetent. Her justification was bolstered by her boyfriend who had said of the squad leader's evaluation, "He should talk." But the episode had stayed with her.

As an engineering major, she had a few classroom friends with whom she regularly worked on group projects. As she remembered, she tended to work on the project write-up, while the others did the core of the engineering work. They would be crowded around a computer in the lab, laying out designs on AutoCAD and performing calculations, while she watched from the sidelines. No one in the group had ignored her, but then again, no one had felt drawn to consult with her on detailed design issues either. She passed the mess decks, and glanced at the mess specialist petty officers and seamen preparing breakfast. She hadn't fooled anyone, she thought; only her parents were believers, and even then, sometimes she wasn't so sure about her dad.

Her mother had always bragged about her maturity and independence. But, as she was beginning to realize, only someone immature like herself, and cut off from emotional life, would have needed to remain so safely on a straight track, avoiding risk, taking no chances, pretending she was someone she wasn't, refusing to look into herself.

Her memories both haunted and enlightened her. In some respects, her inborn motivation and ambition – traits that she had always liked about herself because they had made her want to strike out into the world and make a positive difference – had let her down; they had led her to keep going in engineering and ROTC. She had misused and misdirected those traits.

She passed through the double doors of an airlock, part of the system designed to defend the ship against chemical, biological, and nuclear warfare, and continued down the passageway; she pressed the weight of her body against the outside of the second door to secure it behind her, against the fan pressure. She couldn't imagine herself on the bridge in a few minutes, looking out into the darkness at the aircraft carrier's lights, responsible for every move of the destroyer on which she stood, and on which a few hundred slept.

She had always felt passionately for causes and ideals. The military had satisfied her need to engage in a cause, and it fell safely within the boundaries of what she had been taught and what would have been tolerated in her house. She had tried her own ideas a few times, with consequences that slammed down on her to the point that she swore she would never try them again. Bucking her parents, or resisting, would have meant conflict and disapproval.

Her approach to life had been well-thought out and sensible! One of the reasons she had focused on engineering, was because it was more difficult to obtain an ROTC scholarship as a non-engineer. Military branches actively recruited engineering and science majors. For that fact alone, she never would have wavered from her course of study. After five years in the Navy, she planned to join the league of former military officers who were highly sought-after in private industry for their leadership and management skills.

She thought she could pursue her dream of the military, and at the same time, be an active participant in the movement to open opportunities for women! She wanted women to be able to obtain an education, go to college, and study and pursue whatever they wanted – fulfill their life's dreams without obstacles created by discrimination.

She would never have considered majoring in women's studies in college, as her friend Jennifer had done. What would she do for a job? And she had no desire to be like her friends, and frolic around with some liberal do-gooder group (as her dad called it) as a volunteer, or for little money, as part of some peace or environmental thing. Or in relation to Spanish, she was unwilling to live as some poor graduate student, bumming around Spain for a few years while she studied Spanish, languages, and literature. Many of her peers had chosen to start their lives out in those ways, but an uncertain frivolous life, even right out of college, had seemed far too nebulous and unrealistic to her. She had grown up listening to constant conversations about saving, investing for retirement, IRAs, and Blue Cross.

She now felt as though her choices were alien to her authentic self, and she felt estranged from them. She stopped to scan the depths of the second ladderwell leading to the bridge, hoping no one was close by. The air she breathed felt heavy with salty wetness, paint, and oil. She barely kept her breath *because it hurt her to think that she had existed at the mercy of a compulsion – of nearly pathological levels – to cast a persona in her father's likeness!* She had emulated his thoughts, interests, and talents as if they were her own, convinced that they were indeed her own. Her actions had partly been conscious, but mostly unconscious. She imagined varying tiers of conscious awareness existed within oneself. An irreversible curiosity was born, to dig deeper.

It had never occurred to her that emulating her father might have run contrary to who she was, and that doing so was causing incongruity within herself, and between herself and the world; she had brought disaster onto herself, and she had negatively impacted those around her. In her decision-making processes, the only viable options in life consisted of those which *he* was good at, and the goals *he* thought worthwhile. She began to climb again, her distress increasing, knowing she would soon encounter the white and blue stern lights of the massive carrier out the bridge windows.

Everyone in her family, including her mother, had considered her father as the one who was intelligent and knowledgeable. On matters of politics, history, etc., she and her mother had deferred to her father. She remembered trying to encourage her mother, telling her, "mom, you're also smart." But to Brenda's dismay, her mother had always answered that she wasn't as smart as her father, or as her. "I don't have a mind to retain things like you and your father do," her mother would say. So as a child, Brenda set out to be smart like her father, enjoying her own natural love for school and learning, and a real curiosity for further education. In that moment aboard the ship, she felt comfort in reminiscing; she used to sit on the floor of the TV room as a child, and sift through her parent's books, mainly ones about archeology, or ones including maps of countries with explanations of the people and their languages.

In mapping out her own life, she had persisted in modeling herself after her father through her teenage years, and into her early twenties, she now realized. She craved to understand *why* she had pushed so hard towards his extreme. She continued her ascent to the bridge, glancing left into the soft red glow emanating from the quartermasters' chartroom. She remembered wanting anything but to emulate the pattern her mother had followed. Like many women of her generation, her mother had decided not to finish college, and had dropped out at about the time she married her father. Brenda grew up watching her work the type of office jobs that had traditionally been allotted to women. And she guessed she had reacted to, and rejected, her mother's choices. She had always felt a desire to break free from the traditional cycles which had governed and controlled women's possibilities for centuries.

She pictured her mother chuckling, facetiously referring to Brenda as the "women's libbah." The sounds of the bridge came into range, and she tried to remember how she had responded whenever her mother had said that. She supposed she had always felt, deep down, as if her mother's teasing trivialized her feelings and passions for the issue.

So many memories flooded her mind. Her mother had never seemed that passionate about any particular cause herself. And when Brenda had spoken passionately for a political issue, her mother had always looked uncomfortable if it was anything in contrast to what her father said. Her mother was loyal to him. To her mother, he was so much smarter than herself. Her mother used to call her father and a close friend of theirs "the encyclopedia volumes I and II." Brenda had wanted to be smart like the "encyclopedias I and II," and at some point she had stopped asserting her own opinions if they were contrary to those of her father because she hadn't wanted to be minimized. She wanted to be seen as bright and like him.

In one sense, she was now experiencing the challenges and opportunities she had dreamed of. She had accomplished her goals of becoming an engineer and an officer. But she was learning that her dreams had never really been hers. They were the result of what had been pressed upon her. Now, these same challenges and opportunities felt nightmarish. Bridge watches and managing and leading as a division officer in charge of weapons and missile systems – she still couldn't believe it. She wanted out. A do-over.

Chapter 27: Total blackness ... The bridge at night ... No role models for female officers ... Convincing others who she is ... A downed plane

Brenda stepped onto the bridge from the ladder. The space appeared almost pitch dark except for a few lights on the helm console. As she searched the dark, she started to see a slight green glow from the ARPA radar at the center of the bridge and a few reflective gages and indicators; but she couldn't make out the figures of any of the watchstanders. She could hear the wind whistling against the bridge windows and the drone of the ship's engines, but otherwise the bridge was silent. The smell of brewed coffee mingled with the stench of paint, oil, grease, and sea salt.

She took a step from the ladder and braced herself against what she thought was the door to the head. The seas were still heavy enough that she needed to hold onto something to stabilize herself. Until her eyes adjusted and she could get her bearings, she had no choice but to wait.

Soon, the lights on the helm console began to come more into focus, and she started to inch her way forward. By now she could see the outline of the helmsman, who appeared fixated on the rudder angle indicator to maintain the ship's course in the higher sea state. She then took a step toward the chart table and noticed someone turn a red lamp on over the table at the front of the bridge on the starboard side, below the bridge windows, next to the ARPA radar. On the table, under the light, she spotted a pad of maneuvering board (MOBoard) paper and a set of parallel rulers. She inhaled deeply and tried to keep calm. Slowly, she started to look towards the port windows, dreading the sight of the carrier's white and blue stern lights. But then she suddenly felt calmer when she saw how soft and vague – and agreeably distant! – the carrier's lights actually appeared. She couldn't see the carrier, only her lights.

Through the bridge windows it looked as though the ship was headed into total blackness. The ocean was indistinguishable from the sky. She turned towards the hushed voices she started to hear, and she assumed the voices were of oncoming and offgoing watchstanders turning over the watch. She had no choice but to take her watch as conning officer as well, and trust that everything would go okay and that she would get through the next four hours.

She knew that it was nearing a quarter to four. In SWOS, the instructors had taught the students to relieve the watch at fifteen minutes before the hour. As she stood at the chart table, holding onto it, waiting for her eyes to further adjust to the darkness, she saw a figure approaching her who she guessed was the officer she was scheduled to relieve. She hoped she would remember the protocol for relieving the watch; if she failed to recite the correct lines or go through the proper motions, she might give herself away. But then she reminded herself that she had gotten through her first watch as conning officer on the morning before when the ship had pulled out of port, and she had even been complimented on her performance. But her ability to survive so far hadn't relieved her nagging and constant question: What level of knowledge did they expect from her and how quickly was she expected to learn? She did want to learn and to develop herself as a competent officer and, specifically, officer of the deck. She just questioned whether or not that aspiration was realistic.

"The bridge is dark and quiet at night," the approaching figure said. "Remember me? I'm Brad."

"I do," she said, feeling more at ease. He seemed calm, down-to-earth. Brad was another ensign who had been onboard for a few months. He was the COMMO, the ship's communications officer; he held the billet that was supposed to have been hers. She had met him briefly while the ship was still inport and he had seemed friendly and easygoing enough. If she couldn't remember the exact turnover procedure or precisely what to ask before watch, she imagined that with Brad, someone who was also so junior, it wouldn't be such an issue.

She glanced out at the aircraft carrier's white and blue stern lights again, the lights that would serve as her guides as she conned the ship to remain on station off the carrier's starboard quarter, positioned to possibly rescue a downed aviator. Three hundred people lived onboard *Curtis Wilbur*, she reminded herself; most of them were sleeping. Some five thousand lived aboard the aircraft carrier. They were all dependent on the bridge watches on both ships to safely navigate and avoid a collision while operating in such close proximity. She raised her right hand to salute Brad, and quietly stated, "I'm ready to relieve you."

"I'm ready to be relieved," Brad replied, returning her salute. She smiled, pleased with herself for having completed her first line naturally, as if it was nothing.

"Psst, you're late," Rob whispered, leaning in towards Brenda and Brad.

"Oh my God, I'm sorry," she cupped her palms over her mouth. "But, it's quarter of," she answered. "I thought the watch turned over at 0400 and that I needed to be here fifteen minutes beforehand."

"Don't worry, I was teasing you," Rob reassured her, looking amused. "There would have been no way for you to know. Just remember, JOODs and conning officers relieve on the half hour, OODs on the hour."

"I will. Thank you," she replied, nervously hoping to convey that she did care and that she wanted to do things right.

"It's okay, you'll be fine," Rob emphasized. She nodded, appreciating any offer of understanding.

"Just for tonight, though," Brad added kiddingly.

"I know. It won't happen again. I'm sorry, you're missing sleep now," she apologized again, realizing she was becoming accustomed to humility at every turn.

"Once your eyes adjust, I wouldn't look at my face," Brad warned. "I got the bends on our last day of liberty, scuba diving off the Australian coast. It was the most painful sensation of my life; I thought I was going to die on my way up through the water."

"I can see a little now," she answered, noticing how the veins in his eyes and face had burst; pools of blood had blotched beneath his skin, and two red golf balls had encircled each eye. "It does look so painful."

Suddenly the combination of the ship's movement, fatigue, and the sight of Brad's bloodied eyes started to make her feel lightheaded. She grabbed onto the helm console to steady herself.

"Are you going to be okay?" he asked.

"I'll be alright. Let's turn over," she suggested, fighting mild faintness and the feeling that she might throw up, "so you can get back down to your rack and sleep."

She followed Brad through the bridge as he familiarized her with the Captain's Night Order Book, the navigation chart, the ARPA surface radar picture, lighting measures on the *Curtis Wilbur* and on the carrier, tactical voice nets, comms authentication, and finally the ship's course, speed, and propulsion plant lineup. There was more; but hearing much of this information for the first time, in this context, and feeling bombarded by terms and acronyms of which she had never heard, she tried to focus on the main picture:

course, speed, and the fact that her ship was designated as the planeguard rescue destroyer. She just hoped to get through and survive these bridge watches for the next year or so; then she could escape to nuclear power school, where hopefully things would somehow come together.

*

Time 0400 "Attention in the pilothouse, this is Lieutenant Trenton. Lieutenant (j.g.) Styron has the deck." Her nerves tightened at hearing Rob's announcement; it interrupted the dark and quiet calm. So she stopped to catch her breath.

"*This is LTJG Styron. I have the deck,*" the oncoming OOD followed.

"*Aye, aye, sir,*" the helmsman's announcements came next. "*Steady course zero-four-zero, checking zero-four-nine,*" he shouted. "*Engine room answers all engines ahead one-third, indicating zero-eight-five turns and three-six percent pitch for eight knots...*" continued the long string. Behind the helmsman's report, she could hear "*aye, aye, sirs*" coming from all around her, as watchstanders throughout the bridge acknowledged the change in OOD.

"Brenda," Brad guided her, "approach Todd, the OOD, and request permission to relieve the watch. I'll be standing right next to you."

"What do I say?" she whispered to Brad. Then she immediately proposed an answer to her own question: "Just something like, 'I request permission to relieve the watch, sir,' or maybe, 'to relieve the conn?'"

"Either one sounds good," he encouraged her.

She looked at Brad, resigned to the inevitable; she knew she had to go forward and execute these protocols, even though she felt shaky about them. She nodded at him and began her approach to the OOD. Within seconds she faced Todd, raised her right hand to salute, and stated, "I request permission to relieve the watch, sir." She remembered Todd as one of the guys from her daytrip to Manly Beach in Sydney. Outside the bridge windows, aircraft landed and took off in a constant rhythm from the carrier's flight deck. Brad remained with his eyes on the movement of the aircraft carrier, while Pete, the junior officer of the deck, stood over him.

"Did you conduct a walk-through before coming up to the bridge?" Todd asked.

"Yes, sir," she answered.

"What engines are online?" Her mind blanked; she had finally been confronted with that on-the-spot questioning she feared, despite realizing it was a style most likely necessary for running the watch and for training. She took some comfort in Todd's manner however, which didn't impress her as confrontational so much as intended for her learning. He continued, "Did you stop by CCS in engineering to talk to the EOOW, the engineering officer of the watch?"

"No, I only knew to go to CIC to talk with the TAO," she replied.

"It's okay. Next time, be sure to stop by engineering. You'll need to be aware of the plant lineup, including electrical generators online, maintenance issues, drills, etc., and how those configurations affect speed, reliability, and maneuvering."

"Yes, sir," she answered, and continued, "because of planeguard, I would guess we're in a full power lineup, both engines on both shafts."

"Brad must have told you."

"He did," she remembered just then, "and I'll be sure to walk through engineering next time," she added, trying to communicate her eagerness.

"Do you know what close-in planeguard means?"

"That we're standing by to recover a downed aviator or man overboard, if necessary," she replied, fearing every next question.

"What's our station relative to the carrier?"

"One-seven-zero degrees relative at 3,000 yards."

"Did you initial the Captain's Night Orders?"

"Yes, sir."

"What lights do you see out there?"

"The carrier's white and blue stern lights and runway deck lighting." Her heart pounded.

"Very well," Todd answered. "Turn over the conn."

"Turn over the conn, aye, sir," she answered, and walked back over to steady herself on the helm console. She almost couldn't tell if her nausea was from seasickness or nervousness.

***

Time 0405 Brenda caught a brief reflection of herself in one of the bridge windows. She saw a young woman wearing a ship's ballcap, beneath which dangled a few wisps of stray hairs. Truly she *was* a real part of this ship, she realized; and she occupied a billet in an official capacity, a reality she still couldn't believe. She wondered what sort of role the bridge might play in her life over the next couple of years. She glanced around. Her surroundings appeared like a set out of a World War II movie; it seemed like an occupational setting for other people, maybe even for other men, specifically. Movies, documentaries, and history books all showed men standing upon the bridges of warships; and therefore men populated the images that surfaced in her mind when she pictured the Navy. The men in the movies and documentaries never seemed to waver, and knew precisely what to do and how to act under the most harrowing of circumstances. They gave daring and brave commands and made life and death decisions; they accomplished extraordinary feats. No role models existed for young female junior officers, she began to think. Who had ever heard of a young twenty-three year old girl directing the operations of a warship, while authoritatively giving orders in a female voice? And wearing a modified men's khaki uniform, with a hair bun sticking out below the back of her ballcap? What forerunners could she and her young female colleagues look up to? Young women had only themselves to look to, she guessed. They had to go about their days and careers fitting in as if women had been onboard these ships for the past hundred years. Acting in direct contrast to traditional patterns definitely added a level of uneasiness and struggle, Brenda decided. But no, she corrected herself. Her thoughts may have had credence, but they weren't the source of her difficulties. Her challenges were more personal.

Brenda saluted Brad, "I relieve you."

"I stand relieved," Brad saluted in return. "Ready?" he then asked.

"Sure," Brenda nodded, managing a smile.

"*Attention in the pilothouse, this is Ensign Hanson. Ensign Conner has the conn,*" Brad announced as he handed Brenda his pair of binoculars.

"*Attention in the pilothouse, this is Ensign Conner. I have the conn,*" Brenda followed, overcome by the seriousness of what she was undertaking. She couldn't help reminding herself that she wasn't on a ride at Disneyland; and she prayed her voice hadn't sounded shaky.

"*Aye, aye, ma'am,*" announced the helm. "*Steady course zero-four-zero, checking zero-four-nine, engine room answers all engines ahead one-third, indicating zero-eight-five turns and three-*

six percent pitch for eight knots..." This time, behind the helmsman's report, she heard *"aye, aye, ma'ams"* all around her.

"*Very well*," Brenda answered as she stared straight ahead at the carrier's lights, fascinated at the way they barely made the ocean visible in the darkness. Such blackness, dotted by the gracefully moving carrier and her glowing lights, struck her as tranquilly alluring. Fire flashed from the afterburners of the jets as they were catapulted off the flight deck. Everything she now saw in person had once seemed so exciting in the movies; and she thought about how at one time she had fallen in love with the idea of it all.

Brad leaned in towards her. "See, you did everything right," he said; then he smiled and disappeared down the ladder.

"Brenda, over here," Todd called. "Pete's close to qualifying OOD. He'll be running the watch, so do as he says unless I direct you otherwise."

Pete turned to Brenda. "Ignore the pink eye," he told her. She stepped away from him. "See the gradual shift in the white and blue stern lights on the carrier?" Pete asked. "She's turning to starboard; order left standard rudder," he said calmly.

"*Left standard rudder*," she repeated.

"*Left standard rudder, aye, ma'am*," the helmsman answered, and reported, "*My rudder is left standard, ma'am. No new course given.*"

"*Very well*," Brenda replied to the helm.

"Watch the needle on the ship's course indicator," Pete instructed, pointing. She shifted her weight into the slight heel of the turn, having never imagined such an unnerving sensation as feeling her own words move this 8,000-ton destroyer. All she could do was place her trust in Todd and Pete's hands, and hope that she could make it through the watch.

"*Passing zero-three-zero to the left, passing zero-two-zero to the left, passing zero-one-zero to the left...*" the helmsman reported.

"Belay your passing heads," Pete whispered to Brenda.

"*Belay your passing heads*," she repeated.

"*Belay my passing heads, aye, ma'am.*"

"Do you see us crossing through the carrier's wake?" Pete asked.

"Yes."

"When you see that we've crossed her wake, come back around to starboard," Pete instructed.

"When we're about 45 degrees left of course?" she asked, so

nervous she could scarcely utter her question; she was looking for an exact formula to memorize and follow.

"Just about," Todd said, holding the IVCS phone to one ear, "use her wake as a guide as Pete instructed you."

"By ordering...rudder amidships, followed by right standard rudder?" she asked.

"That'll be fine," Pete answered. "See how we're just outside and above the carrier's wake? Follow her through the turn," he added.

"*Rudder amidships,*" Brenda ordered, feeling both Todd and Pete directly over her shoulders. Watching out the bridge windows, she felt as though the ship was turning a hundred miles per hour.

"*Rudder amidships, aye, ma'am. My rudder is amidships, ma'am. No new course given,*" answered the helmsman.

"*Right standard rudder,*" she jumped to the next command, seeing everything happening so fast.

"*Right standard rudder, aye, ma'am,*" the helmsman repeated, and reported, "*My rudder is right standard, ma'am. No new course given.*" Every turn seemed to accompany an increase in the ship's vibration. She placed her hand over her chest and looked to Todd and Pete for reassurance that everything was okay; but she received no reaction. To them, she imagined, all of this was normal.

"Steady course one-one-zero," Pete instructed. As Pete guided her through conning the ship, Todd had remained on the IVCS phone with OPS in CIC. The watch in CIC was in direct communication with the carrier, obtaining course, speed, and maneuvering intentions.

"*Steady course one-one-zero,*" she ordered.

"*Steady course one-one-zero, aye, ma'am,*" the helmsman answered. "*My rudder is right standard, coming to new course one-one-zero, ma'am.*"

"*Very well,*" Brenda acknowledged.

"*Steady course one-one-zero, checking one-one-nine, ma'am.*"

"*Very well,*" Brenda replied to the helm, trying to take in that she had hung on through the maneuver; the ship was coming into station off the starboard quarter of the carrier. As she glanced over at Pete, she noticed this nervous habit he had of tapping the center of his chest with his right forefinger. And she realized she wasn't alone, at least, in feeling the intensity of these maneuvers; it was an awareness that helped humanize her experience.

"Bridge, combat," she heard OPS' voice coming over the IVCS

speaker from CIC.

Pete moved in around her. "Excuse me," he said hurriedly. "Sure, sure," Brenda replied, stepping back and out of the way. "Bridge, aye," he answered the IVCS call.

Then, another comms circuit lit up. "VICTOR-FIFE-FOXTROT, THIS IS GOLF-NINER-HOTEL, OVER." She recognized the broadcast as a tactical signal. Todd reached in front of her to grab the red phone above the MOBoard table.

"Are you up to answering the carrier over the tactical circuit?" he asked her, handing her the phone. Hold the handset key and say, "This is Victor-Fife-Foxtrot, Roger, Over," Todd instructed.

"THIS IS VICTOR-FIFE-FOXTROT, ROGER, OVER," she repeated over the circuit, looking at Todd for any sign that she was correct, wrong, anything.

"VICTOR-FIFE-FOXTROT, THIS IS GOLF-NINER-HOTEL, MIKE SPEED TEN, OVER," the carrier radioed.

"THIS IS VICTOR-FIFE-FOXTROT, ROGER, OUT," Brenda answered, knowing that the order "MIKE SPEED TEN" indicated the carrier's speed and was not to be repeated by her in this context. She watched as Todd logged, "V5F DE G9H M SPD 10 K," in the tactical signal logbook.

"Increase speed to ten knots," Pete instructed. "Look at the engine chart," he showed her, pointing to ten knots on the chart, "that would be ahead 2/3."

"All engines ahead 2/3, indicate pitch and turns for ten knots," she ordered, and looked to Pete for approval.

"All engines ahead 2/3, indicate pitch and turns for ten knots, aye, ma'am," responded the helmsman. *"Engine room answers all engines ahead 2/3, indicating pitch and turns for ten knots, ma'am."*

"Very well," she acknowledged.

"Good job," Todd encouraged her. Then, she watched Todd sort of laugh to himself as he continued, "Apparently, the carrier has someone new on the tactical circuit, too."

For a while, the watch remained quiet as the ship steamed behind the carrier. Brenda kept to herself on the port side of the bridge; she had her guard up against any questions that might give her away. Most of all, she tried to remain at a safe distance from Todd and Pete, as she listened to them discussing optimal winds and maneuvers for flight ops. Whenever she noticed either one sketch at the MOBoard paper, manipulate the wind wheel, or calculate mathematical problems (out loud or in their heads), her adrenaline surged and a painful pounding in her head followed. She had expended indefatigable effort in convincing others, and herself, of her love of gadgets, mechanics, computers, and anything military or technical. Only the impressions and thoughts of other people mattered, right? Did it really matter what you lived through every day, so long as the milestones others expected of you had been achieved? All of the plans she had spoken about for her future had once seemed like the coolest thing...

*

Time 0530 "The coolest thing," she repeated, as she cupped a mug of warm coffee. Then she watched, in horror, as another reality unfolded out the port bridge windows...

Brenda turned and looked to Todd. "All engines stop," he instructed her.

"*All engines stop,*" she repeated.

"Boats, Captain to the bridge," Todd ordered the boatswains mate of the watch.

"*All engines stop, aye, ma'am.*"

"*Engine room answers all engines stop, ma'am.*"

"Rudder amidships?" she asked Todd.

"Rudder amidships," he nodded.

"*Rudder amidships,*" she ordered the helm.

"*Rudder amidships, aye, ma'am. My rudder is amidships, ma'am. No new course given,*" answered the helmsman.

"*Belay your passing heads,*" she voiced, taking a leap. By this time, Pete was engaged over IVCS with OPS; and Todd was communicating over bridge-to-bridge radio with the carrier's OOD, while simultaneously instructing the lifeboat crew on the walkie-talkie.

"*Belay my passing heads, aye, ma'am,*" the helmsman acknowledged. Then, the 1MC shipwide announcement, "***Captain to the bridge,***" came over the PA system from the boatswains mate of the watch.

From around the bridge, she started to hear bits of radio chatter out of various circuits. She assumed someone would take the conn from her, but so far, that hadn't happened. So instead she remained where she stood, keyed up from the most sobering and bloodcurdling scene of her life. All she could do was wait for instruction, while she wondered if she had witnessed the death of a pilot. She no longer felt detached from the nighttime takeoffs and landings she had been watching. Standing on the bridge of the *Curtis*

Wilbur for the last hour and a half she had experienced flight operations like a live show, where she remained safely in the audience, uninvolved in the actual danger or risk. From her vantage point, she had merely watched successions of two white circular lights of engine fire lifting off the carrier. Each set of engines preceded the next, and on and on. But, that one last time, she watched the twin engine lights lift off, only to drop. Then, in the next second, she remembered feeling promise. Possibly, the pilot had kicked on the afterburners, because she saw the engines flame bright orange and red as the plane struggled to climb. In hope, her eyes followed the engine lights up and above the carrier, but in the next instant there was nothing more to see. And a portending chill rushed through her.

"Captain's on the bridge!" the boatswains mate of the watch exclaimed. The CO had arrived from his at-sea cabin, situated just aft of the bridge. Brenda stepped aside, fearing when he or someone else might turn to her with tasking. Looking around though, she observed tense energy in everyone's movements and voices. All of the watchstanders had landed in this situation together, she realized. And they had all reacted with calm, so she decided she needed to do the same.

"Ensure the lifeboat crew is ready to get in the water at any moment," the Captain said to Todd, as he made his way to the front of the bridge. Brenda watched as Todd leaned over the chart table with the Captain to discuss status. Todd's level of interaction with the Captain as officer of the deck, and his presence on the bridge, would forever remain beyond her grasp, Brenda acknowledged. No amount of studying and memorizing would raise her to his level. She stared back out at the lights of the carrier, trying to quell tears and the pain and embarrassment of facing herself and her reality. Over and again, since checking onboard, she felt made to suffer jabs from the truth, ones she would have rather ignored and denied. The price of any self-awareness seemed to consist of abandoning everything for which she had worked and dreamed. Her thoughts and realizations left her apprehensive about the future. What would she do for a job? Did any talent lie within her, and would she discover a way, at least in some small part, to contribute something positive of herself in the world?

"We'll remain astern of the carrier until further instruction, while the carrier's helo performs recovery operations," she heard the Captain say to Todd, as he walked towards his chair.

"ALL UNITS IN GOLF-NINER-HOTEL, THIS IS GOLF-NINER-HOTEL. EXECUTE TO FOLLOW, SCREEN ZULU ZULU CALL SIGN GOLF-NINER-HOTEL, 1116-0415 CALL SIGN VICTOR-FIFE-FOXTROT, 0509-0415 CALL SIGN WHISKEY-SEVEN-TANGO, BREAK, BRAVO CORPEN 000, ALPHA SPEED 10, WHISKEY SPEED 20, OVER."

Brenda hesitated. She started to reach for the red phone to answer the tactical signal, but Todd cut in. "The carrier's giving us a box to steam within," Pete commented, as he began plotting the ship's assigned screen sector on the MOBoard. "An imaginary pie slice in the ocean," he added, finishing the calculation and placing the plotting tools down on the table. At the same time, CIC called up with their recommended course and speed to station at the center of the box. The MOBoard so confused Brenda that she swore her brain turned to mush and blocked her thoughts whenever she attempted to process numbers and do geometry on it. She looked down at the MOBoard paper and tried to understand the diagram Pete had created. There was bearing relative to the carrier and true bearing of the screen sector boundaries, plus calculation of time and recommended course and speed to station using the nomogram at the bottom. For the moment, however, Brenda felt relieved for having survived this one instance of not having to perform a MOBoard calculation. She had escaped exposure again, by pure chance.

She glanced around the dark bridge, as if scanning a potential audience from onstage. She saw the quartermaster of the watch (QMOW), the boatswains mate of the watch (BMOW), the helmsman, the signalman, Todd, Pete, and the Captain. As of yet, none of the watchstanders had paid any special attention to her; she simply existed as part of the mechanics of the watch, another in a long endless line of new ensigns. More than anything, she desired to develop and maintain a dynamic of arriving to her watches as a competent member of the bridge team. She didn't want to become a sideshow or joke where she might draw unwanted attention. "Oh no, it's Miss Conner on watch," she could picture the guys snickering amongst themselves in the back of the bridge. So, with those thoughts in mind she planned to survive each successive moment. Currently, the ship was on standby, awaiting further orders from the carrier. Any second now, the carrier would transmit another tactical signal to execute the screen sector. And as the conning officer, she would be expected to order the course and speed to arrive on station.

She peered down at Pete's calculated course and speed. Todd

had since had her place the ship in bare steerageway, meaning the ship had just enough forward movement that it could still be steered. Current course was 285, and she would need to steer course 096. Looking down at the MOBoard circle, graduated in degrees from 0 to 360...right rudder was what she needed.

"ALL UNITS IN GOLF-NINER-HOTEL, THIS IS GOLF-NINER-HOTEL. SCREEN ZULU ZULU, STANDBY... EXECUTE, OVER."

Todd reached for the red phone. "THIS IS VICTOR-FIFE-FOXTROT, ROGER, OUT," he answered the carrier and logged the tactical signal.

"Execute the screen using standard rudder," Pete nudged her. And so she announced the course and speed orders to the helmsman, using Pete's MOBoard calculation. In the back of her mind she was partially comforted by the idea that she would never be alone on the bridge, left to carry out MOBoard calculations on her own. She knew, as well, that there was something terribly wrong with viewing her situation in those terms. She wondered how long she could survive on the bridge in the way she just had, relying on the skill of others and hiding her own lack of skill, in an effort to remain undiscovered.

Chapter 28: The stress of a put-on persona ... Survival through memorization ... Searching her past for clues ... Unconscious dynamics with her father come to light

Time 0645 Over an hour had gone by since the crash. The bridge team stood at their various stations around the bridge silently, looking tired, just waiting for their watches to end while the ship steamed within the screen sector assigned by the carrier. Time went slowly, and Brenda's thoughts turned dark. But she found comfort in her despair and in allowing her dark and depressed feelings to flow.

This stretch of her life was never going to end, she imagined, as morning brought light onto the bridge. *Would she continue to work harder and harder into forever, trying to grasp milestones that gave her little personal satisfaction, except that they were over?* The milestones she had ahead were ones on this ship, at nuclear power school, at the nuclear engineering plant onboard an aircraft carrier, at a technical position in a private company. Her job at the technical company would be based on the background she gained in the Navy; her cycle would never end. At that future company, she would have to plan and hide her true self and lack of engineering aptitude, while ensuring that people saw her as a technically smart, savvy engineer. Her heart would race in anxiety over every technical question. She would continue to boast of her love for math and science; she would marry an engineer who worked a few cubicles down from hers; she would hope her husband and children could patch her voids in fulfillment and self-expression. She would even have to remain concealed from her husband; she would need him to see her in the way she had worked so hard to establish. As a couple, their combined salaries would get them a nice house and life in a suburb, and they would appear very successful and happy. She gazed out at the seas, which still hadn't let up. She had her right forearm pressed into her stomach to stem her nausea. The perpetual stress and strain of hiding, of wearing a mask, a put-on persona, seemed an exhausting, long haul.

"The Great Australian Bight," Todd commented, slightly laughing to himself, "the roughest seas in the world." Brenda looked over at him. On and off, throughout the early morning hours, she had listened to him joke about the absurdities of the SWO Navy. She could barely stand to listen to him, because as much as he joked about everything he thought was funny and even mindboggling about the Navy, he still seemed happy and willing to remain a part of it. He was joking sarcastically about how the ship had deployed with an almost completely new and inexperienced crew, which was normal, and that more than half of the wardroom (officers) on the ship had turned over during the past year. He had laughed about the continuous training and retraining onboard ship, and that Navy ships were, what he called, "school ships." As a new person thrown in as the gunnery officer and conning officer, she hadn't found the situation funny. Everyone knew and joked about these decades-long issues in the Navy. But she imagined that trying to change the deep-running mechanics and culture of the SWO Navy would be like moving a mountain – "the machine" was in place. She wondered how Todd could reconcile remaining part of an organization for which he held such paradoxical feelings. Not her, she thought. She planned on getting out of the Navy as soon as she could.

But, she couldn't totally blame Todd for leaning towards staying in. He was finishing his second shipboard tour, and he seemed to have mastered bridge watchstanding and the multiple associated tasks. As the auxiliaries officer, responsible for EE and EA divisions which maintained engineering systems other than the main propulsion equipment, he sounded versed enough in the engineering plant. He had even qualified engineering officer of the watch (EOOW) on his first ship, an unusual accomplishment. She wished she had his talent to learn it all so quickly, or even just to learn it.

Being after sunrise, she could see the deck equipment on the ship's forecastle. Except for the anchor chain, she couldn't identify any of the gear she saw, which should have been basic seamanship knowledge. In SWOS, she had memorized the definitions and functions of deck equipment like pelican hooks, hawse pipes, bitts, capstans, and wildcats for tests. But by now, she could barely remember any of that information.

Thinking about her lack of understanding of the very basics increased her anxiety. She watched the way Todd stood OOD. He didn't mindlessly run through the motions of written and memorized procedures during the watch or during the crisis of the crash, as she would have done. He used understanding, information from reports given to him, and the framework of procedures to make decisions and to determine what courses of action needed to be taken. He applied situational awareness. She feared that if she qualified officer of the deck someday, she would be completely dependent on her verbatim memory of volumes of procedures, definitions, and manuals, which, due to her lack of conceptual understanding, she would have to apply nearly blindly – *she couldn't think of anything more dangerous or unsettling!* As an OOD, she would have to anxiously pray that not one event would take place that would veer off any written (and *memorized*) procedure.

Her entire approach to engineering was to memorize and follow formulas without thinking about what was occurring conceptually. In her life, she was used to following the rules as they were written, staying safely within the lines, and never diverging from given formulas and paths. That mindset had governed her approach to every facet of her life – ranging from day to day details to broader decisions.

"Follow the formula," her father used to tell her. "For each problem, write down the numbers and turn the pages through the chapter in the textbook until you find the formula. Then, substitute the numbers into the formula." She had spent many school nights, through high school, seated at the kitchen table with her father while he tutored her in math and science homework. He had dedicated himself to sitting down with her, helping her as she needed, through honors math and science homework. She had barely cleared the hurdle of adapting from regular math to algebra in eighth grade. Then, she had battled her way uphill through advanced classes in geometry, trigonometry, and physics with the help of her father. "Following the formula" was probably an acceptable approach for him because he inherently understood, conceptually, what was going on. But when she reached twelfth grade calculus, she hit a wall and found herself faced with the choice of either dropping down a level or failing. She dropped down a level and blamed the calculus teacher, who had a reputation for being difficult and for not being a very good teacher. The oncoming summer, she audited a calculus class at a local college to prepare herself for the upcoming four semesters of advanced calculus required in engineering school. Her mother had seen the "community education" class advertised in a brochure. In college, she became adept at manipulating calculus equations, a skill which was necessary to work the formulas in her engineering classes. Her life had been all about doing whatever was necessary to pass tests and courses to get to engineering school, and to keep progressing forward. She had sustained that plug, chug, memorize, and play-it-safe approach right through to graduating *cum laude* with a Bachelor of Science in Mechanical Engineering. She couldn't explain how her car worked or how to use one tool, but she had that mechanical engineering degree for her career ahead.

She stared out at the desolate ocean, thinking about how her parents had fully supported her in what she had set out to do. Her father had even helped her out once in a while in college with a few difficult projects. Her parents had moved her in and out of countless dorms and apartments, and had assisted her in setting them up; her mom listened through her relationship breakups; they were completely there for whatever she needed, always willing to help her with anything she needed. They would go to any lengths for her.

People around them always liked her parents, probably because they were nice people, honest, dependable, supportive, and within the lines. Her parents worked conventional jobs, talked about benefits and investing their money, bought houses in planned suburbs with neighborhood covenants, and looked forward to traveling in an RV out west during retirement. They constantly cleaned and organized the house, worked in the yard, and spent time searching out stores that had a certain product on sale.

Somewhere inside, she had always sensed her own personal inclinations running contrary to the safe and practical life her parents led. She preferred to feel her way through her decisions, and to attempt more creative solutions even though they might have unknown and unclear ends. At times, when she had delved into writing, or into literary analysis projects, she had felt a surge of confidence and contentment. *Even a thrill!* She enjoyed the subtle nuances in a story, and immersing herself in studying the development of the characters. Deep within, she derived a profound sense of purpose from studying literature, as if she had been born to probe every complex, dark literary theme and character that crossed her path.

During her week of liberty in Sydney, she had taken a night to remain in her stateroom. Fall was coming on in Australia, and the nights were turning cool. She had planned on organizing her belongings, in an attempt to make her side of the stateroom appear as orderly as Julie's. After a few minutes of looking around, and not knowing where to start, she found the folders containing her Spanish literature papers. That evening, she sat on the floor of her stateroom, going through the papers she had written, searching for clues and insight into the person who had written them. That person, who only dated back to about a year ago, had decided that engineering and Navy ROTC were goals that deserved any amount of sacrifice; and she wanted to get into that person's mind.

Many of her literature papers seemed immature to her, she was surprised to discover. And as she continued to read them over, she felt increasingly embarrassed. Her running themes seemed to revolve around making fun of the psychological elements of the plot. She treated characters who searched within themselves – or who set out on a path of self-development or self-discovery – with sarcasm and resentment. Several of her papers ridiculed characters for "wallowing in attempts to search out their pasts," i.e., "find themselves." Often, she had mocked authors' themes as impractical. In one paper, she had argued that the author should not have wasted so much time on pointless artistic pursuits, and that producing tangible results would have been more worthwhile in furthering his political cause and the cause of his country. In an unconscious manner, she had studied literary characters through the lens of her dynamic with her father, in an imbalanced approach that favored the rational over the emotional.

Now, everything she had taken for granted and accepted as reality seemed so disarranged, and even vexing. She remembered being a star pupil early on in reading, writing, history, and language arts, but her parents never fully embraced those subjects or encouraged her in them. They acknowledged her talent in those areas, but then related it to engineering. Possibly, her father was so technically gifted, he had never thought to consider that her nature might have differed from his, and that she didn't have a conceptual grasp in math and science. Why hadn't either of her parents ever pointed out that math and science might not have been right for her? Or, that she would look ridiculously awkward employed onboard a ship? *After living together all those years, hadn't they known her at all?*

She wondered if parents existed who applied a sense of discovery in getting to know their children. Were some parents eager to recognize and support their children's particular interests and talents and give their children a safe space where it was accepted to be themselves and explore? Human nature and tradition tended more towards forcing one's values on children and creating mirror images of oneself, rather than allowing children a space where they might become unique individuals, she imagined. On the bridge at seven a.m., the idea of breaking free of her parents' mindset provided her with a feeling of promise for the future. She was tired of pleasing others in her role as the good girl, "behaving" and going about doing what she thought everyone wanted her to do.

She decided that she really admired Todd's style of bridge watchstanding, which seemed to stem from study, natural understanding, and some experience. She guessed he approached bridge watchstanding, or bridgemanship as Paige had referred to it, as an art. Over the watch, she carefully observed the way Todd received information, sorted through it, and developed each course of action. He acted with a sense of surety. It didn't matter if he was exactly right at every moment because his decisions were based on a stable foundation. Todd seemed to have found the thing he was good at – being a naval officer. She imagined there must have been a level of personal reward in pursuing one's talent. For the next four years, at least, she would have no option to pursue her own talent. "The only thing you can do with those things is teach," her father used to say about her interests in languages and writing. She had started not to believe him.

"The gunners mates already told me yesterday," she said to Todd and Pete, "that the Great Australian Bight has the roughest seas in the world." She was acutely aware of its effect on her.

"Stare out at the horizon, ma'am," the lead quartermaster recommended, as he leaned against the chart table. "The horizon line is stable, and helps with seasickness. It's the best remedy."

"Thank you, QM1," she turned and said to him. "Everyone's been telling me that, but I've had trouble keeping my concentration on the line." She guessed that her efforts to conceal the degree of her seasickness were for naught. She appreciated the quartermaster's help and concern, but she was embarrassed. In self-consciousness, she wondered how much amusement she was providing for Todd, the quartermaster, and others. If she did become some sort of joke for them, she would have to just ignore it. Her credibility was in being a nuclear candidate. She would try to make everyone think that qualifying on the bridge was simply a required step to get to where she really wanted to go – nuke school. As she stared out at the seas and tried to focus on the horizon, she was left with a feeling of anxiety, anticipating that she wouldn't be able to control the perceptions of others.

She looked at the carrier just below the horizon, a gigantic ship reduced to a distant gray blur underneath the clouds of another imminent storm. "I wonder what happened to the pilot," she commented, as if to everyone. "Do you think we'll ever know?"

"Not sure," Pete answered. "The carrier's been engaged in recovery ops all this time."

She tried to fix her concentration on the horizon, as the QM1 had instructed. But, she struggled to maintain her focus on it for even a minute. She saw the horizon closing in as the storm neared. No one else on the bridge seemed affected by the seas, which she found unbelievable. The watchstanders just stared out into the sunrise, waiting and waiting for eight a.m. and the end of the watch. Every so often, one of them shifted around. The quartermaster would take a fix or the boatswains mate would polish brass. And depending on the winds, fragments of conversation between the lookouts on the bridge wings would drift into hearing range.

"I have Starbucks coffee, ma'am. I reserve it for my favorite ensigns," the lead QM approached her. She turned to answer him, just as a wave crashed over the bow. The wave held the bow of the ship down into the water, delaying it from rising for what seemed to her like an eternity. Todd and Pete grasped onto the wire rope that spanned the bridge overhead. She reached for the wire rope, but she wasn't tall enough. She barely had the chance to grab onto the radar console in time to prevent herself from falling and sliding across the smooth epoxy floor of the bridge.

"Whooh!" the watch team exclaimed collectively; many laughed anxiously. QM1 was holding onto the chart table.

"I felt my internal organs rise independently of the rest of my body, and slowly drop," Brenda remarked to the quartermaster, clutching her stomach. She feared the mere smell of coffee might undermine her efforts to keep from vomiting.

"We could see ten to fifteen-foot seas shortly, Miss Conner, according to the weather report," he advised her.

"I can handle ten to fifteen-foot seas as long as I've reached status as one of your favorite ensigns," she teased the QM1.

"You and the first lieutenant," he replied, referring to Julie.

"So, you don't like Navy supply system coffee, the kind with the stock number stenciled across a nondescript brown bag?" she asked.

"I'm from Seattle. I drink Starbucks, ma'am."

"I could have stereotyped you from Seattle, QM1," she joked. "The whole grunge thing."

"It's the funky rimmed glasses," he smiled.

"On my last ship, I survived on black coffee alone for a month," Todd remarked. Brenda believed him. The sunrise revealed a ghostly thin figure, and more, she could see that his khaki uniform hadn't been washed in ages; it appeared greasy and dirty. He continued, while laughing, "CHENG survives on black coffee, cheese puffs, and spray-can cheese." She rolled her eyes, remembering CHENG and his obnoxious drunk story from her first lunch in the wardroom.

"Where are you from, Todd?" Brenda asked.

"Nowhere. Colorado, sort of. I went to University of Colorado."

"No family either," he elaborated. "You'll need to learn to identify the seas, Brenda, in addition to Group 1, 2, and 3 merchant ships."

"Sea state 6, right now," she offered, following Todd's lead to shift the conversation back to work. "Very rough," she added, having memorized the chart at SWOS.

"Good, Brenda, sounds about right," Todd encouraged her. He then referred to Pete, "Is your OOD oral board still on for this afternoon?"

"As long as the Captain doesn't delay it again," Pete answered.

"This Captain hates qualifying junior officers. Too much liability," Todd answered, smiling at what he had said.

Pete appeared unamused. "I predict that after my OOD board, the Captain will give me my final oral board for my SWO pin on the day I leave the ship," he replied.

Todd snickered, his sarcastic laugh becoming louder. His laugh wasn't directed at Pete, but it was consistent with the way in which she had experienced him all during watch, grinning as if at the entire Navy. "No gun or CIWS shoots either. Too much risk," Todd remarked.

"The Captain's interested in turning over a sparkly, shiny ship to the next CO," Pete commented, and continued, "That'll provide him with an outstanding officer fitness report and a Meritorious Service Medal."

"Another thing," Todd turned to Brenda. "The Captain hates your boss, WEPS; he thinks he's a geek."

"Great, we're back in high school," she retorted.

"WEPS is very nervous," Pete explained. "He's fallen into the micromanagement/zero defect mentality."

"And this Captain's a screamer," Todd said, chuckling in irony.

"Like most surface warfare COs and XOs, he's made a sport of it."

"Less so with CHENG and OPS," Pete interjected.

"Screaming, sounds childish," Brenda said, miserably. "I've never heard that term so much, 'a screamer', until I went into the Navy."

"SWO department heads fear that any mistake made by them, or one of their junior officers, will kill their career instantly, and undo five to ten years invested in the Navy," Pete explained. "So micromanagement is the preferred mode of self-protection. It's the poorest leadership and management you can find." Then he paused, "A separate contributing factor to micromanagement…constant and high turnover, which perpetually leaves department heads with junior officers who lack training and experience. And the situation is made worse by the department heads being new themselves."

"All this to look forward to," Brenda replied.

Todd leaned his head back and laughed. "Everything you've heard is true," he said to her.

"Two more years and counting," Pete stated.

"Thanks for starting me off with the right attitude, guys," Brenda sighed, as she barely hung on from seasickness and exhaustion, waiting for seven-thirty a.m. to arrive, and her first at-sea workday to start.

Chapter 29: Seasickness mounts ... CHENG has a laugh ... Alone in her rack ... Flooded stateroom ... Initiation comes to an end

The ship thrashed. Brenda thought only of getting to her ginger tablets. Before leaving for Australia, she had researched that ginger settled the stomach and remedied seasickness. Since she had planned on arriving to her first ship prepared, she went to a local health store and purchased a large bottle of ginger tablets. In reality, she doubted a spice would be any match for these seas, but she needed to try. Fighting tears, and hunched over at her stateroom closet, she tried to will herself not to be sick for one more moment until she could get to those tablets. She pushed her mess of clothes and books aside to get to where she remembered storing the bottles.

Slam! The rolling of the ship finally slammed her stateroom door shut for good, to her relief. She had felt too sick to walk the few steps across the room to close it, or to care. She hoped no one had been around to hear or see that she had left the door ajar, to open and close with the seas, port to starboard and back. Julie was gone, and she had the room to herself for the moment. As she remained crouched down by her closet, unable to move for fear she would vomit, she reminded herself of how hysterics and crying would not mend her situation or get her off the ship. She would have to stay calm, and outlast every minute of each day, persisting and finding strength to keep herself together.

Behind her, she had less than three hours of sleep coming off the 0400-0800 bridge watch. Ahead, she was looking at a full workday in rough seas. She began to slowly walk across her stateroom, clutching her oversized bottle of ginger tablets into her abdomen, and repeating to herself that everything would turn out fine. She needed to get herself to the wardroom, where she could get a cup of bottled water. The taste of the water from the ship's tap – she wasn't sure if she could stomach. She exited her stateroom and labored down the passageway towards the wardroom, feeling extremely unsteady. When she neared the door to the wardroom, she leaned against it for support. Then she reached for the velcro band on the seasickness bracelet she was wearing on her left wrist, and tightened it severely. The bracelet had a sewn-in bead, intended to apply pressure to the P6 acupuncture point on the inside of her wrist. If her research panned out, she hoped it would aid her against these seas.

"What're you holding, GUNNO? A big bottle of pills?" CHENG laughed. "Already?"

She ignored him, and followed his lead through the wardroom door. Once inside, she inched her way towards the water dispenser, keeping one hand pressed against her forehead, and the other holding the bottle of ginger tablets into her stomach. Out of the corner of her eye, she couldn't avoid seeing CHENG in the back of the wardroom, exaggerating his movements for her sake as he fell into a deliberate lounging position across one of the couches.

"Will those pills help you grow sealegs, GUNNO? What's that on your arm, a bracelet?" he called out to her from the couch, razzing her.

"Maybe, sir, to the first question," she expressed weakly, "and yes to the second," she continued, feeling surprised that she still had the energy to disdain both his obnoxiousness and the fact that he wasn't the least bit affected by the seas. "And they're not pills, they're ginger tablets. After the hurricane sortie on midshipman cruise...," she started to explain, but lacked the will to bother finishing with him.

"Aren't you supposed to take seasickness pills twenty-four hours beforehand?" he asked.

"That's what the label says," she answered.

"You carried the whole bottle in with you!" CHENG exclaimed, finding even more humor in his observation.

"Leave her alone, CHENG," the XO cut in, as he entered the wardroom followed by CSO. "She'll have her sealegs soon enough," the XO added in support.

"I'm confident of that, don't worry," CSO said, as he walked in behind the XO. She thought of the incident with the chief on her first night in Sydney, and she hoped CSO wouldn't hold that against her.

She decided her circumstances were disgraceful and unresolvable. She lifted her head gradually, in an effort to keep her nausea in check, and forced herself into swallowing her seventh ginger tablet, as instructed on the label. Since others were in the room, she placed her hand over her neck to fight her retching, hoping to salvage at least some dignity from the situation. Then she rested her head against the coolness of the metal water dispenser, desperate for relief. She was unsure if the support shown by the XO and CSO made her feel better or worse. In the wardroom that morning, in the company of the XO, CSO, and CHENG, she came to terms with the inevitable: She would soon be racked-out in her stateroom. And before she knew it, the water in her styrofoam cup had sloshed all over her with the seas.

"Brenda," CSO approached her, "go lie down in your stateroom for a while. Pete's got officers call and quarters for you. It's okay, you guys haven't turned over yet."

"Is it possible to get used to these seas, sir?" Brenda asked.

"Definitely," he answered. "I have no doubts," he added with encouragement.

She was averse to sloughing her work onto others, forcing her colleagues to pick up her slack. CSO walked over to a large bowl of saltines strapped down to the wardroom galley counter. "I'll help you back to your stateroom. And we'll bring this bowl of saltines," he told her.

***

Time 1130 Brenda lay in her rack, defeated by the ship and the seas, left with no choice but to listen to her body, which told her not move one inch, not an arm, leg, or finger. So she remained motionless, still dressed in her khaki uniform, drifting in and out of sleep. Every so often, she came to enough to wonder how much time had passed since she had left the wardroom with CSO and the bowl full of saltines. Six hours or one hour might have elapsed; she had no idea. For all she cared, she could have died.

"Brenda," she heard CSO knocking on her stateroom door. "Doc, HM1 Aquino, will be up to see you," he cracked the door open. She wanted to answer and let him know to come in; but she felt too ill to speak. "Let me get you some water," he offered, "and I'll help you get some saltines down," she heard him say before her door closed again.

Sometime later, the corpsman, HM1 Aquino, entered with CSO. "Can you sip some water or take a bite of cracker, ma'am?" the corpsman asked. She felt herself fading in and out of time and consciousness. "CSO brought you some," he added.

"Thank you, sir," she replied, referring to CSO.

"I'll try," she muttered, wanting to show her deep appreciation for their assistance. A bit of understanding may have been all that kept her going; but the idea of food made her gag, and she couldn't take it in.

"CSO is going to leave the room, and I'm going to help you turn onto your side," the corpsman advised her. "I then need you to pull down your pants and underpants, ma'am, so I can administer a shot to your buttocks. It will help you, for sure. Have you taken anything else, ma'am?"

"Ginger," she said softly.

"And you have the bracelet. I like those alternatives," he told her. With tremendous and sluggish effort, she unzipped her pants and pulled them down as the corpsman had instructed. She was too sick for modesty, and the corpsman's approach was professional and matter-of-fact. "They work," he said as he gave her the shot. "But you have to take them far enough ahead of time, ma'am," he finished. In a second, the shot was over.

"You can pull your pants back up, ma'am. CSO left some more saltines here for you. I'll put them next to your pillow. We'll both check in on you periodically."

"Thank you, HM1," she managed.

"The best thing is to sleep until the seas calm. Pick up the IVCS phone and dial sickbay if you need anything, ma'am."

"Thank you, HM1," she tried to say again, getting some energy from adrenaline, but he had left.

***

Time 1230 Brenda already missed the company of HM1 and CSO – of anyone. She was miserable lying alone in her rack, sick, without any concept of time, and uncertain of what the next few hours or days might bring her. *Would she ever recover from the seas? What if the storm persisted over the entire week, all the way to Perth?* Would she remain racked-out for several more days, gross and un-showered, lying incapacitated in an oily and disgusting khaki uniform? The ship had a long way to go to get to Perth, situated on the opposite end of Australia. *And with the way Navy ships traveled, not taking the shortest distance to their destination but traveling in a thousand circles to conduct training exercises on the way!* She hated the feeling of abandoning, or not even starting, her duties as division officer, and she hated placing other officers in a position to have to stand *her* bridge watches.

She was fed up with lying curled up in her rack, and she needed to know the time. So, she took a chance and moved her hand towards her rack curtain, disregarding what she knew to be true, that she shouldn't move. She thought that if she could just glimpse through the curtain at the clock over the stateroom door. But as she began to reach, sickness so overcame her, that she felt the burn of all seven ginger tablets flame up through her chest and throat, in a most violent and painful manner. She heaved a mess of ginger, saltines, and whatever else she had eaten, over the side of her rack and onto the stateroom floor, over and again, unable to stop the tide.

Maybe it was hours or a few minutes later that she woke up again, to a sound which she thought might be water sloshing back and forth across her stateroom floor. She slowly rolled onto her side, in disbelief that any of this could be happening; she breathed carefully, so as not to move too suddenly. From her top rack, she looked down at the floor and saw that her stateroom was flooding from beneath the door. Suddenly, her head felt clearer and she was able to move, but she couldn't tell if the water was coming from the pipe near the doorframe or from the passageway outside. The stench of ginger and sickness, mixing in with water, filled the room, creating the most foul and rank air she had ever breathed. After the corpsman had injected her, she initially felt worse. But the deep sleep that followed seemed to help. On midshipman cruise, she remembered a corpsman had given her those mysterious pink seasickness pills that everyone in the Navy talked about. Those had made her more dizzy and faint than the seas. The corpsmen were lifesavers and highly skilled, but she was skeptical of the meds the Navy dispensed, especially since the military used non-FDA approved drugs. She curled back into the fetal position. The stress of watching the putrid mess on the floor below, sloshing back and forth, increased her anxiety because she knew she needed to clean it up before Julie returned. But then she fell unconscious again to the sound of the fluid sloshing port and then starboard, port and then starboard, with the rolls of the ship.

"Ma'am," she heard a female voice. A seaman cracked the door open. "Are you okay, ma'am?" she asked softly. "A pipe burst in the empty stateroom across the p-way."

Brenda turned onto her side, and saw that the seaman had a mop and bucket with her.

"I'll clean it up. Thank you," Brenda told her, appreciative of human contact.

"I'm assigned as a wardroom attendant, ma'am," the seaman said, smiling shyly.

"I know. If you can leave the mop and bucket. I don't want you doing it. Maybe check back in twenty minutes to make sure I'm up and cleaning." Brenda returned the seaman's smile. She drew hope and encouragement from her ability to speak.

The seas had calmed somewhat, and with every foot the seas died down she felt herself easing back to life. She remembered recovering rapidly on midshipman cruise after the seas had decreased. After all, she didn't have some virus or disease, she only needed the stability of land or a flat ocean. She climbed down her rack ladder, stepped into the fluid mixture, and picked up her flip-flops, which were floating in the mess. Then she began mopping, while standing in the ankle-high mixture, dressed in sweat-ridden khakis. The seasickness phase of her initiation, she hoped, was ending.

Afterwards, she took the most challenging shower of her life. All of the little things she had never thought of before...bracing her hands against the wet shower walls to stand up, the water on the shower floor splashing with the rolls, the seas throwing her shampoo, soap, and conditioner off the shelves in the shower...

Chapter 30: Don't you realize I'm dangerous? ... The First Lady of Aegis ... A milestone for women

Two Months Later

Brenda stood outside the wardroom door. It was Sunday night, and she didn't want to go inside and see that OPS had posted the ship's plan of the week (POW), which listed upcoming operations and exercises; she wanted no part of performing them on the bridge. How long, she asked herself, could she stall off conning during critical bridge evolutions, such as underway replenishments (UNREPs) or formation steaming in close company with other ships (DIVTACS)? All of those evolutions required real-time helm and lee helm orders along with accurate and fast maneuvering board (MOBoard) calculations. All that on a tense bridge where she was expected to perform center stage!

Recently, she had focused on qualifying for out-of-the-way watchstations such as aft steering. Qualifying aft steering and helm safety felt akin to buying insurance against conning during the intricate evolutions. How long could she persist? The other day, the senior watch officer, CSO, had spoken enthusiastically about giving her more "watch opportunities" on the bridge. *But don't you realize I'm dangerous, she had wanted to say.* She remembered smiling at him in response, as if she had appreciated his offer. "Great!" she had said. And resisting the hesitation she felt inside, she thanked him. He was a good person and a good senior officer, and she had lied to him.

Brenda cracked open the door to the wardroom. "Come hang with us, Brenda," the warrant officer waved her over from one of the couches in the back as she entered. The warrant officer, and Pete, Neil, and Rob from her department, all of whom she considered her shipboard friends, a group she found compassionate, mentoring, and accepting, were inside. She wondered if something was up because it was rare to see people hanging out in the wardroom.

She hesitated, but then smiled and nodded in agreement. She had wanted to slip into the wardroom unobserved, where she could have opened the fridge, scooped some leftovers onto a plate, and hurried back to the solitude of her stateroom. Since checking onboard, avoiding the wardroom had felt like a natural tendency.

Her perception of a shipboard wardroom had formed during midshipman cruise, where the command climate (morale) had descended to such a low that the junior officers avoided the wardroom at all cost, only venturing in for required meetings and meals.

Onboard *Curtis Wilbur*, wardroom life wasn't entirely different. So far, the Captain had treated her well, but most of the officers *despised* the Captain. And to add to the stressful atmosphere, OPS' treatment of his JOs had grown increasingly depraved and ruthless. All of the officers knew what was going on but no one knew what to do about it. Those dynamics and others had caused wardroom morale – the morale of the officers – to plummet.

"Join the conversation!" Bill invited her again. She set her reluctance aside for Bill, and took a seat on a lone sofa chair to the side of a semicircle of couches. Despite many years at sea, Bill retained a patient and nonjudgmental manner with junior ensigns like herself, and he seemed to genuinely enjoy mentoring. Those personal qualities had endeared her to him. He had risen through the enlisted ranks to E-8 senior chief, and had made chief warrant officer a few years before. All ranks onboard consulted with him, including the Captain. If Bill had suddenly left the ship, taking his years of sea time with him, she feared it might sink. A similar dynamic rang true for the other warrant officer onboard, as well as for the Limited Duty Officer (LDO) who ran the combat information center.

"I came in here to stealthily sneak leftovers out of the fridge before watch," she teased Bill, speaking across the coffee table. Her head pounded from fatigue from strings of midwatches and reveille watches. But a bit of redemption was in her immediate future, she reminded herself. Her upcoming 2000-2400 bridge watch promised sleep afterwards, almost six hours from midnight to six a.m.

"Have you heard about the First Lady of Aegis?" Bill asked her enthusiastically.

Brenda stiffened and looked at him. "I'm not sure," she paused and remained still.

Bill sat up. "She'll be the First Lady of the Navy's most modern combat systems capable platform," he elaborated as if relaying good news.

"Our new XO coming aboard in Hong Kong," Neil clarified for her.

Brenda shrunk into herself, and felt her stomach drop. She sat back into her sofa chair, and breathed. Then, she surveyed the room, confirming that everyone appeared upbeat about the news. She had heard rumors of a new female executive officer, mostly from the gunners mates. Brad had also mentioned something about a female lieutenant commander SWO, who was currently assigned to the destroyer squadron (DESRON) and awaiting orders to the *Curtis Wilbur*. She had remembered the exact moment when he had told her about the woman's impending assignment to the ship. They had gone shopping together in Singapore, and she had been rummaging through a sale rack of bathing suits in a mall sportswear store. She had dismissed both sources – the gunners mates and Brad – hoping and believing there could not be any truth to talk of a female XO.

She edged forward on her chair and leaned to address Neil. "The new XO is that woman at the DESRON, the lieutenant commander?" she asked.

"The Navy assigned her to the DESRON to earn her TAO qualification," he explained. "News of her assignment as XO just came down through official channels."

"I had heard something," Brenda answered. She had to react well, she knew, but she actually found the news disconcerting, more upsetting than any of the other unknowns she had feared encountering in the wardroom. However, she was observant that her colleagues in the room – all male – viewed the news as positive, and seemingly of no consequence, as if the development was a normal course. She inwardly appreciated their response, and the notable absence of prejudice, clearly a sign of societal progress regarding women's roles. Apart from the incident with the chief on her first night onboard, the mixed male/female crew seemed to exist as if ships had been integrated forever.

Brenda smiled to herself while she sat in her chair, because she thought she may have landed in an opposite world. The men celebrated, or at least accepted with no visible reservation, this new milestone for women in the military, and she did not. Neil especially, was a proponent of women in the Navy. His fiancé was the lieutenant navigator aboard USS *Blue Ridge*, the Seventh Fleet flag ship; he often spoke of her career, and of the success she had achieved.

Brenda tried to appear unfazed by the revelation. "I'm often the last one in on this kind of news," she eventually said.

"Then come hang with us more," Bill replied. She smiled, and feigned interest in the AFRTS (Armed Forces Radio and Television

Service) broadcast blaring from the wardroom TV. On screen, a Navy petty officer and an Air Force airman alternated in reporting.

She remained outwardly calm, but the news of the next XO had actually shaken her. Since first hearing the rumors from the gunners mates, and then from Brad, all she had thought was ...*Not now! It was too soon!* Women had recently joined the crews of combat ships in 1994. Since then, integration had been slow and very limited. In the Seventh Fleet, the *Curtis Wilbur* was surrounded by all-male ships. In all of Yokosuka, the *Curtis Wilbur* was the only integrated combatant ship. Brenda wanted to scream, even as she stayed seated in her sofa chair. Or, better yet, she wanted to get up on a soapbox. The cause of women in the military was near and dear to her heart, a cause that ever-smoldered within her. *At present, any woman would automatically be unqualified for assignment as executive officer of an Aegis destroyer!* That was the argument she wanted to lecture on, but she kept herself in check. She doubted that anyone – male or female – without proper experience could arrive onboard and ably serve as the executive officer on the most technically capable warship in the Navy.

She shifted her gaze from the television to readdress Neil. She trusted his opinion; he was prior enlisted (he had been enlisted before becoming an officer) and a colleague of hers in the weapons department. She enjoyed the sanity he offered when sharing her observations of SWO life with him, and she had come to view him as a mentor within the department. "I just can't imagine," she started cautiously, "that any woman could have enough combat systems, weapons, or operational experience to serve as XO of a ship like this. By law, she would have been restricted to oilers, tenders, salvage and other noncombatant ships throughout her career."

"She has some weapons systems experience from serving as combat systems officer at the DESRON," Neil replied.

"That's a staff position, not operational," she countered out of genuine concern. She wasn't sure how well a majority male crew would accept a female XO, who had spent her career serving on noncombatants, and who held a makeshift TAO qualification. She wondered how a woman, who seemingly lacked in experience and knowledge, could achieve success as second in command of a guided missile Aegis destroyer and pave a solid start for the advancement of women. Such a woman would have to be a resourceful leader, one who wouldn't fear the gaps in her knowledge and experience, but rather, who would artfully compensate for them.

She would need to possess the capacity to engage in research, and positively exploit the counsel of her subordinates. Would she do the latter, a large pool of experienced advisors would be at her disposal: like Bill and Neil who were prior enlisted, the department heads, the other warrant officers and LDO, sharp JOs like Todd and Rob, and the invaluable chiefs.

"I'm not disagreeing with you that her assignment is somewhat political," Neil offered her in support, "but it may turn out just fine."

"Only time will tell how her inexperience might play out," Pete commented.

Brenda got up and walked aft to the water cooler. "Don't you feel the imbalance?" she asked the guys. "The Navy would never have promoted a male surface warfare officer, who had spent his entire career serving onboard noncombatants, to executive officer of an Aegis ship." She pulled a cone shaped cup from the bottom of the dispenser, feeling the irony for the side of the argument she was on...*she was undercutting a female senior officer based on little fact, before the woman had even had a chance to check onboard!* But promotion of a woman to a high level command at sea position at this early stage, sounded hurried and out of turn to her. She knew that, after Tailhook, the Navy was under tremendous pressure to promote women into command positions; but she also thought that the Navy should have let the process occur naturally, allowing women to rise up the ranks as they accumulated knowledge and experience.

"She didn't have the opportunity to earn the TAO qualification as she progressed up the SWO pipeline," Neil said.

"There's no way she *wouldn't* know, that she was assigned this command due to her gender, and to the Navy's desire to keep up with the times," Brenda asserted as she filled her cup. *She'll be insecure; she'll be dangerous*, she wanted to add, but she didn't want to press too far.

"She'll get up to speed," Bill encouraged. "She'll learn the Aegis weapons systems when she gets here."

"As XO?" Brenda asked. "That's not the way to introduce women; she'll have to be a real crackerjack." *She'll have to survive the steep learning curve required for mastery of integrated anti-air, anti-surface and anti-submarine shipboard systems and technical strategy.*

"She has all of us; we'll help her make history," Bill assured her. Brenda gave in to Bill. He always spoke to the junior officers as equals and fellow officers, which she wasn't sure she would have been able to do in his same position. Warrant officers held a unique place in the military, being junior in rank to the newest ensign, but highly specialized in their knowledge and experience – experience earned through years of living and surviving these shipboard environments. "Something new and interesting in my career," Bill added. "She'll be the first female XO of an Aegis destroyer."

"I just wish the Navy would've waited for female officers to acquire a reasonable amount of legitimate experience, before moving them into command positions."

"There's a lot of excitement about her. Danielle met her briefly aboard *Blue Ridge*," Neil said. "She's become sort of a heroine to women in the SWO community."

"That's encouraging," Brenda replied, and decided that all she could do was hope for the best.

Chapter 31: A belated welcome aboard interview with the Captain ... Resistance setting in ... Forced to misrepresent ... Bridge flashback

"Miss Conner." Brenda watched as the Captain's door opened. "You can come in, please."

Brenda interpreted the Captain's bearing as welcoming but remote, in line with the demeanor she expected in a commanding officer. She entered his stateroom, searching herself for support, hoping to surface her own creation of a character to complement his, that of the promising and interested junior officer actively weighing the potential of a military career. To shore herself up, she recalled examples of successes from her past interviews, when she had excelled in formally discussing her future with mentors and reporting seniors, back when she had striven to become a junior officer and could discuss those plans free of any inner conflict. She was, at least physically, that same person who had walked into offices at ROTC, Naval Reactors, and CIA, poised to discuss her future ambitions and educational background. Now, however, she felt resistant, and nearly unwilling, to dive back into the shell of a person she had been when she had first joined the Navy.

"Have a seat, please, Miss Conner," the Captain said as she stepped inside. The silence was interrupted by the ringing of his phone. She smiled tentatively as she seated herself across from him and watched him lift the IVCS phone receiver to answer the call, presumably from the bridge. As she sat waiting, she visualized herself on the morning of her nuclear power interviews, during fall of her senior year of college, entering the enormous glass corporate-looking buildings of Naval Reactors in Crystal City, Virginia. The atmosphere was overwhelming, and the secretive nature of the program had added to the intrigue of her experience. There, she had faced a full day of unknowns, and had expected the type of aggressive interviews that had become legendary in the Navy. She knew she would be subjected to two types of interviews – informational (consisting of general job interview questions) and technical (oral boards consisting of math/science problems). She understood her strength would be in the informational interviews and that she would need to rely on those to compensate for any weaknesses that surfaced during her technical interviews.

On that day, when she had walked into each nontechnical interview setting within that intimidating campus, which served as the brain of the nuclear power program, she had fortified her courage by thinking of how vital her interview performance would be to her future. Fueling her was self-satisfaction and an eagerness to discuss her resolve, excitement, and ideas for her future. She remembered navigating the challenging and adversarial style of questioning well during the nontechnical interviews, even when sitting across from Admiral DeMars himself, the then-Director of Naval Nuclear Propulsion. She had learned to sell herself, and her acquired credentials.

Four more years of naval service lay ahead. She saw no other choice but to force from within herself a reignited drive for an engineering and military career. She remembered her CIA co-op and how starry-eyed and on-fire she had been to serve at the heart of the Agency, where the cool spy stuff happened. At CIA, she had made her way to becoming one of the first student co-ops to serve in the Directorate of Operations (DO), even though the student placement office had originally informed her that the DO didn't accept co-ops. In her persistence, she had taken the student office's pronouncement as a challenge, and proved them wrong, just by making cold calls to branch directors in the DO as she read through the CIA internal phone book. She called the directors, introduced herself and her credentials, and offered her services as a student. Three directors offered her interviews, and all offered her a position. Each had specially complimented her on giving an excellent interview, and for having presented herself well. Ultimately, further security clearances had barred her from one position, but she did serve one semester in the DO. She excelled there, assisting an analyst who was tracking the finances of Osama Bin Laden, and who wanted to compile a "Bin Laden encyclopedia" of the early '90s. She remembered her supervisor complimenting her, saying that he never thought he would be giving a student co-op a $500 Exceptional Performance Award (EPA). She had demonstrated capability in research, and in aiding her mentor in managing projects. She was able to sort through piles of message traffic from varying sources, and instinctively prioritize what information was important.

She had been romanced by the notion of being at CIA, and walking through their fascinating headquarters building. But now, she wondered if working for such an organization had ever suited her.

The need to misrepresent herself to the Captain tore at her conscience. She was reminded of *"la apariencia"* from Spanish literature, and stories of financially destitute aristocrats who adorned themselves in the finest cloaks, but were naked underneath. She wore a newly pressed khaki uniform and shined boots to meet with the Captain, but the content of what she planned to discuss no longer appealed to her – lies that felt empty. No longer did she want to float through life, unreflectively, doing what had been engrained in her, while smartly providing pat answers. In the military she had no choice for the next four years. It was, in a sense, a mental prison.

She began to conceive a simple twofold strategy for surviving the interview. She thought of Rich Windmiller and what he had said during the ride to Manly Beach in Sydney; she would latch onto the eccentric genius reputation that nukes enjoyed; she would also discuss the theme she had written of in her college admission essay, when she wrote of her passion for engineering vs. pure mathematics: She wanted to become an engineer, since engineering was a practical application of mathematics; she had a passion for tangible, workable, and usable results. A major in pure mathematics, she had written in her essay, was too theoretical. Life had to progress and remain focused on that which yields functional results and work accomplished!

As she waited for the Captain to finish on the IVCS phone, she reminded herself that neither the Captain nor SWO – nor the ship nor the other officers – were to blame for her presence onboard. Her current situation stemmed from her decisions alone.

She clenched the arms of her chair, watching the Captain as he hung up the phone. She waited for him to utter the first word, reminding herself repeatedly of her stellar on-paper credentials, and that she would be speaking to a senior officer who lacked the perspective of having worked with her directly. A sit-down with a colleague junior officer, such as Rob, Todd or Jon the navigator, would have warranted an entirely contrasting approach. She stood bridge watches with them. Those guys knew her for who she was, and to them, she would have had to appear humble and apologetic, convincing them that she was learning and trying. Her few encounters with the Captain had gone well, however, and he had seemed complimentary enough.

"I wanted to formally welcome you aboard," the Captain began. "I apologize for the few delays in our meeting. From where I sit, you appear to be doing very well, on track as a junior officer. How's everything from where you're sitting?"

"I feel well acclimated onboard, sir," she started. "I'm looking forward to working through my SWO qualifications, while leading the division, in preparation for nuclear power school." Trite as she judged her answer, she hoped it had sounded politically correct and noncommittal enough to please this Captain. His reputation onboard, and her impression of him, was of being very politic.

"Very good," he looked at her. "You did a great job during the sea and anchor detail out of Sydney. Keep focused on your qualifications. I'll be leaving the ship before you qualify. But from what I've seen, you're off to a great start."

"Yes, sir, thank you," she replied.

He raised his index finger and motioned as if she should wait. "Excuse me, please," he said, and he proceeded to call the bridge again. She remained still, wondering if his comments had been substantive, or if they had stemmed from his nearly flawless political correctness. Had his words been hollow, as hers were that afternoon? She understood how this Captain had the luxury of encouraging her without consequence, since his reputation would never be linked to her obtaining a SWO pin. His change of command ceremony was scheduled for soon after the ship's return to Japan, so he would be long departed before she ever qualified. She remembered receiving his compliments following the sea and anchor detail in Sydney, knowing she had merely accomplished taking direction from others. Since then, she had watched Julie conn during the entire evolution of getting underway from the pier. Julie had given line handling commands and helm and lee helm orders, while the Captain stood behind her, *not prompting her very much, if at all!*

So far she had survived her few interactions with the Captain while on bridge watch. Whenever he came up to the bridge, she placed herself at a distance, sort of unavailable for immediate questions. But sometimes as conning officer she had to call him with a standard report from the bridge; and in those times, she made sure to adhere to the preplanned script. As she sat in the Captain's office, she stiffened her posture and metered her breathing. Bridge watches, just thinking of them stressed her...it seemed incomprehensible that she had countless more to come. She felt "bridge panic," as she had personally named it, was now so ingrained in her psyche that years would pass before she would be able to free herself of it. In fact, so great was her present on-going psychological trauma, she imagined she would dream about the bridge for years to come.

As she sat on the Captain's blue burlap couch, just waiting, she could almost hear the background noise from last night's midwatch, when she had to call him from the bridge to make a contact report. A drunken mariner from a nearby merchant ship had been singing in an unidentifiable language over bridge-to-bridge VHF radio; it was a background sound not uncommon on midwatches. The sound was monotonous and relentless over the radio. "Blah, blah, la dee da...Blah, blah, la dee da..."

She visualized Todd, who had turned to her quizzing, "GUNNO, what do the CO's standing orders state regarding contact reports?"

"The Captain's standing orders state to report contacts with CPAs of less than 10,000 yards," she remembered cautiously answering Todd while leaning back against the ARPA radar and clutching her binoculars defensively.

"When the contact abaft our port beam looks at us right now, what does he see?" Todd continued. Brenda, feeling herself under the gun to understand these geometric relationships of vessels in sight of one another, searched her memory of the Navigational Rules of the Road.

"Here," Pete grabbed a piece of maneuvering board paper. "Visualize the spacing of the two ships and their relative motion," he guided her as he sketched the circumstances. The question was so easy, and her embarrassment at not answering unaided so great, that her self-consciousness had welled into sweat and blush. She was glad that it was dark.

"He sees our stern light," she said.

"Why?" Todd asked.

"Because he's more than 22.5 degrees abaft our beam," she answered, almost verbatim out of the book.

"Which of our side lights does he see?"

"None," Brenda shook.

"So, what is he doing according to the Rules of the Road?"

"He's overtaking us."

"Is he?" Todd probed.

"Yes," she answered.

"So if you're the OOD, what do you need to do?"

"Instruct the conning officer to make a contact report to the Captain, if the ship's CPA will be 10,000 yards or less."

"What if the Captain's fast asleep?"

"It's both required and perfectly acceptable to wake the Captain at any time, as many times as necessary, according to his standing orders," she spat out from somewhere. She continued, "I would open up the white binder to the page containing the contact report outline, and fill it out with a grease pencil."

Pete grabbed the white binder, opened it up and handed it to her.

"Show me what you've filled in before you call the Captain," Todd requested.

Captain, this is <u>Ensign Conner</u>, the <u>Conning Officer</u>. I have a <u>contact</u> off the <u>port quarter</u> with a target angle of <u>065</u>. The vessel has <u>right</u> bearing drift and has a CPA off the <u>port beam</u> at a range of 4000 yards. This is an <u>overtaking</u> situation. Curtis Wilbur is the <u>stand on</u> vessel. My intentions are to <u>maintain course and speed</u>.

She remembered calling the Captain in the dead of night. "This is the Captain," he had answered over his stateroom IVCS phone. She read the form verbatim, her heart pounding out of her chest for fear he might ask her a follow-on question, based on her contact report. "Okay, thank you," he replied before ending the call. And she had made it through the call safely, with no further questions.

"Would you contact the merchant ship over bridge-to-bridge," Todd asked after she hung up the IVCS receiver.

"No, because everyone's acting according to the Rules of the Road and intentions are clear."

"Right," Todd said. "Because the CO's standing orders state not to communicate maneuvering intentions with other vessels on bridge-to-bridge radio, unless the intentions of the other vessel are unclear or unknown. Say you were going to communicate with a merchant ship over bridge-to-bridge, what would you say?"

"This is United States Navy Warship 54. My course is 000. My speed is twelve knots. I intend to maintain course and speed," she replied.

"Most of the time the merchants won't respond. Time is money to them, and they rarely change course and speed, unlike us."

*

As Brenda's flashback ended, so did the Captain's IVCS phone conversation. He hung up the phone and turned to her. "Nukes are some of the smartest people I've ever met in my life," he started again, "and are some of the best officers I've known. You shouldn't have any problems qualifying. I'll support you in any way I can. The strides women have made in the military have been incredible. Onboard we promote equal opportunity, no less is tolerated, and I welcome all female officers and sailors. I'm proud to have commanded one of the first integrated warships. I truly mean that. Keep studying and standing watches."

"Yes, sir, thank you," she replied nearly silent.

"Okay, good afternoon, Miss Conner," the Captain stated, as if to send her off. "Keep up the good work."

"Good afternoon, sir, thank you. I will," she answered and exited quietly. She had survived another instance.

Chapter 32: Sleepless SWO life ... WEPS has a heart ... Chief Smith in trouble

Brenda opened the door to her stateroom, removed her small spiral notebook from her back pocket, and tossed it onto her stateroom desk. It was 0800, and she had just come off the rev (reveille) watch (0400-0800) on the bridge. She was surprised to see Julie's rack curtains closed, and her khaki uniform hanging over her desk chair; so she closed the stateroom door gently behind her, as not to make a sound. Julie almost never slept or took a nap after officers call, which had been held at 0700 that morning.

The stateroom was dark, except for the light left on over the sink. Brenda had grown to appreciate her roommate, and the mutual understandings that had emerged between them. They left the sink light on, always. They were both struggling to cope with unpredictable schedules; and by day, they aided each other in their own subtle ways.

As she tiptoed around the stateroom, she began undressing. She hurried because she wanted to manage one hour of sleep before getting ready for small boat training, scheduled on the POD for 1000. It had become vital for her to squeeze every minute of rest she could out of a day, here and there. She had started to take the advice of other JOs who spoke frequently about their strategies for grabbing catnaps and "nooners" (referring to a nap in one's stateroom during lunch). But her catnaps never proved to be enough to help, and sometimes they seemed to intensify her drowsiness.

She could never release herself of the feeling that SWO life and culture was nothing short of crazy and ridiculous. But there was tremendous pressure to think that it was "normal" and "okay." The culture pressured new arrivals into thinking that, really, they had always lived this way...it was normal for everyone, even on the outside...*and what's wrong with you for thinking this way of life is abnormal?!* Two to three hours of sleep per night...she believed there had to have been another way. She couldn't help thinking that much of the kneejerk chaos and lack of sleep was more the result of poor leadership and management than the watch schedule.

She set her watch alarm for 0845, laid it down next to her pillow, hugged her gray wool blanket, and closed her eyes; but the darkness brought her no calm. After coming off the reveille watch, she should have been up and involved in ship's work, she thought; she should have been making rounds through her division's spaces. She dreaded that WEPS might call the stateroom at any second. And if she didn't answer her IVCS phone, he might then come knocking on her stateroom door, asking, "Are you sleeping in there?" She imagined hearing his voice cracking under his stress, between his frantic knocks.

She hoped that WEPS was on watch in CIC, which would prevent him from learning of her workday morning catnap. *If he was sitting TAO watch, he wouldn't be able to come knocking on her stateroom door!* Just so she could pull off this hour of sleep, she had planned ahead, delegating any follow-up from officers call and quarters to Chief Dering for the morning. Sharing those types of responsibilities between chiefs and division officers was common underway, due to varying watch schedules.

For rest, she had reduced herself to hiding to find sleep, hoping never to be found "racked-out." During her initial weeks aboard the ship, she had tried napping in her rack in short stints, but Jon the navigator had quickly accused her of having rack lines on her face one day after a "nooner" she had taken in place of lunch. Then, she had tried stealing fifteen minutes here and there by putting her head down on her stateroom desk; but she found herself equally discovered when she sprang her head up whenever anyone knocked at the door. The last time she had tried napping at her desk, it was the navigator who had knocked on the door looking for Julie.

"You have rack lines," he had said, dryly and void of emotion.

"I wasn't in my rack."

"Yeah, but you were sleeping."

"So I was," she answered.

"So you were. Where's Julie?" he had asked. She could still see the smirk on his face, although she swore that there might have been a trace of sympathy in his expression. He claimed to take naps all the time, but he was defiant about it.

Incessant absence of sleep, combined with confinement to a ship, and being surrounded by ocean for days and weeks at a time in a regimented environment, had gradually crushed down on her sanity. Pathetically, she had once locked herself inside the VLS missile canister space, just to catch an hour of sleep. But even then, she hadn't fallen asleep for fear the gunners mates might find her. They slept there all the time, *but she was supposed to be the officer!*

SWO culture demanded the lifestyle. The Captain put pressure on the XO, who put pressure on the department heads, who relentlessly pressured down on the division officers. SWO department head life was the fiercest of all shipboard management tiers. The officer FITREP system of ranking department heads one, two, three, and four against each other heightened the zero-defect *winner-takes-all* SWO management philosophy.

She eased herself into sitting up in her rack, realizing that sleep was never going to happen during this one hour time period. She thought of WEPS, and how part of her felt for him; his eyes were sorely bloodshot and surrounded by red circles. She felt that she shared a common bond with him: They were both struggling for survival in their separate ways – a kinship in subsisting on the edge. She wondered how WEPS maintained functioning on watch at the TAO console in CIC, on only two to three hours of sleep per night.

Unlike OPS, however, WEPS allowed his division officers leeway. WEPS was empathetic; he had heart. Over the past few weeks, she had started to conduct her morning walkthrough of her division's spaces *just prior* to officers call and quarters, since the gunners mates had proved reliable in ensuring sweepers and cleaners got done beforehand. OPS would never have tolerated knowing that any of his division officers were not up at least two hours before officers call began at 0700, ensuring sweepers got done before the XO walked through, and that message traffic had been read. SWO mentality went something like: There might be some item that the XO mentions at the morning department head meeting that you don't know about, or that you're not already on top of, and...PANIC. Each morning, OPS stormed through his department's spaces, as if with whip in hand, flaming at his division officers. Or, depending on who was around, she had seen him quietly belittling his DIVOs off in a corner, without mercy. WEPS was aware, Brenda knew, that each morning she set her alarm to the last possible minute before officers call; but he never said anything. She could only guess it was because her division's work got done, and she had never heard of any complaints about the division's everyday work.

With both of them being so tired, she had had her spats with WEPS; but they still basically got along and they never seemed to hold anything against each other afterwards. The day before, she had been particularly exhausted and she had shot back defensively at WEPS. "Why are you flame spraying me?" she asked while out of breath and running on the treadmill. The destroyer had a small workout area, carved out of a wide space in a passageway, consisting of three treadmills and a limited lifting area. She thought she was doing a good thing by working out. The semiannual Navy PRT (physical readiness test) was fast approaching.

"What the fuck are you doing?" WEPS had asked her, his wispy voice cracking into a high pitch. "It must be nice to have all this time to work out."

"It's after knockoff of ship's work," she exclaimed between breaths. "The PRT is coming up. I have to do the run test, since there probably won't be an Olympic-sized pool at the next port for the swim option; and I'm about to bulge into the fat uniforms I shoved into the back of my stateroom closet!"

"Just get off the fucking treadmill, and make sure there's no rust visible on the gun before we're alongside the replenishment ship tomorrow afternoon."

"Take the guys off troubleshooting the gun repairs?" she had asked. "They've been working day and night with that tech chief who came onboard in Singapore from SIMA. We'll only have him for a few days, we're shorthanded, and I didn't see any rust."

"Get with Chief Dering and Chief Walden, and tell them to get the guys back outside sanding and painting. The Captain wants the ship looking... We don't have time to fucking work out. What are you... I can't believe you..." he had yelled at her. But then he had sighed, closing his eyes for an extended second, before smiling a little, in the way he had come to show his frustration with her. Then he retracted his earlier sentiment, "when you're done working out," he added. And he walked off shaking his head.

"Thank you, sir...I'll look at the gun with Chief, don't worry..." she had called to him down the passageway. And after her workout, she had made sure to take care of any rust for WEPS. As of late, she and WEPS had developed these types of interactions, which seemed to leave them both "humored" and at a loss, accepting the inevitability of defeat within an impossible system.

*

"Brenda, what are you doing up there?" Julie asked from her rack below.

"I was remembering something. I was sitting cross-legged in my rack. I didn't realize I was rocking back and forth. I hope I didn't wake you," Brenda answered. "I've never come off the reveille watch to find you in your rack, though. I was worried if you were okay."

"It's difficult to keep working after only two hours of sleep," Julie answered, "which is what I managed before going on midwatch." Brenda suddenly sat still. For so long, she had waited for any hint, of any form of complaint from Julie, a flow of honesty and recognition from her about the sick SWO culture. But, in what she had just heard, she felt no satisfaction. Julie's comment about sleep was indicative of loss of heart, a hint that she might have started to cave within the system. *It couldn't be, not Julie!* Brenda thought. *Not Julie!* "After you relieved me off the midwatch at 0330," Julie continued, "OPS called the stateroom, so I couldn't get to sleep before OCall this morning at 0700."

"I wish I'd been in our stateroom to answer the phone. I would've told him you weren't here," she interrupted Julie. "Although, I've started sleeping through my watch alarm, and in my life I've never before slept through alarms," she added. She had begun to follow the protocol of other JOs, in asking the person she was going to relieve on the bridge to give her a series of wakeup calls before her night watches. But then she had also started to sleep through the rings of the IVCS phone, which she would have never thought possible. She took some comfort in knowing she wasn't the only JO who had started sleeping through alarms and wakeup calls. The situation was resolved by sending a messenger down for JOs who, deep into the deployment, were starting to sleep through alarms and calls.

"No, it's okay," Julie resigned. "After OCall, I came here to grab a half hour power nap before I'm scheduled to lead small boat training at 1000."

"Power nap is BS SWO cultural justification," Brenda offered, aiming at the system and not at her roommate. "OPS with his geeky voice, bad breath, and dandruff," Brenda lashed. "What, of such importance, does he have for you at 0330 in the morning?"

"I leave every conversation with OPS with ten new items on my to-do list, all of which are the number one priority for the day."

"That's so typical SWO," Brenda interjected.

"Yes, it's inspection preparation, writing and routing messages, topside preservation issues like sanding and painting, all at the same time," Julie finished.

"OPS doesn't care if he leaves the ship ever, goes on liberty or visits any ports," Brenda asserted, having never seen Julie resort to power-napping.

She heard Julie lean back against the bulkhead in her rack. "He treats his JOs the same way he was treated as a junior officer," Julie responded. "He's under a lot of pressure, and lacks sensitivity in his relations with people."

"It's that SWO *take no prisoners* thing," Brenda nearly interrupted her.

Then, she heard Julie's rack curtains open. "That's not what I wanted to tell you, though," she said. "Something involving Chief Smith."

Brenda pushed her curtains aside so she could see Julie. "You know I'm outside all the gossip circles," she said.

"It got out to the crew about you with Chief Smith in Sydney," Julie advised. "And now, the Captain has taken him off the bridge watchbill."

"The navigator told you."

"Yes. Chief Meyer somehow got wind of what happened to you, and came forward with allegations of attempted rape in a Sydney hotel room. That's possibly why his face was so bruised after liberty. She fought him off."

"She's a damage control chief, a DCC, a firefighter; she's physically strong," Brenda commented.

"He was already unpopular in the chiefs mess, and intensely so now. The chiefs are united behind Chief Meyer." Julie held up her palm to keep Brenda from speaking. "Chief Meyer said that initially she took care of the situation within the chiefs mess."

"What does that mean?"

"I'm not sure," Julie said. "I guess Chief Meyer just said that she had handled it and didn't think to report it, until she heard what happened with you. Then another incident surfaced with TM2 Dobbs. So the Captain has assigned CSO and SUPPO to conduct a JAGMAN investigation. And now, almost every female onboard has come forward, in a chain reaction, each with some sort of inappropriate interaction with Chief Smith, some more serious than others. You did the right thing. There'll be a Captain's Mast soon; he'll probably be busted down to E-5."

"From frocked chief to second class petty officer," Brenda interjected, hardly able to internalize the news. It was as if all of these secrets really had escaped from the walls of the ship. Even Chief Dering had mentioned to her offhandedly that, "Chief Smith was a dirtbag," and he had wanted to let her know that "he wasn't really a chief but a frocked chief."

"The Captain wants to fly him off the ship to the carrier ASAP, and then to Singapore. Chief Smith claims all the women onboard are in a conspiracy against him, so standby. He's unofficially restricted to the chiefs mess right now."

"That must be great for Chief Meyer," Brenda retorted sarcastically. But she took the news as an overall positive, since removing the chief from circulation was the only good news possible that early in the morning. Brenda and Julie climbed out of their racks to ready themselves for small boat training.

Chapter 33: Small boat training ... Thoughts of New England ... Chief Darrow has a plan ... A rough ride

1MC Shipwide Announcement: *"Assemble all non-qualified junior officers on the fantail for small boat training at 1000."*

Brenda leaned over the ship's railing, chilled by the dampness of the Northern Pacific Ocean. She stared off into the horizon at endless gray, as she waited for Julie to start the small boat training. As the non-SWO qualified junior officers gathered amidships, she watched Julie interact with her senior chief. She admired Julie for her fluency in deck operations and for her ability to tackle and keep pace with the steep learning curve required of junior officers. She had started to accept that certain facets of being a division officer were going to remain out of her reach.

The boatswains mates had one of the ship's RHIBs (rigid hull inflatable boat) set up and hanging from the boat davit, ready to be lowered down the side of the destroyer and into the sea. From what she saw, and from the bits and pieces she could hear of Julie's conversation with her senior chief (E-8) boatswains mate, it seemed as though they worked well together, and that he took the time to explain things to her. Brenda felt that she was developing that kind of working relationship with Chief Walden, the chief gunners mate in charge of the VLS, but not with Chief Dering, the chief gunners mate in charge of the 5"/54 gun and small arms. On the VLS side, with Chief Walden willing to work with her, she was starting to gain some project management skills, a methodology. She had learned the importance of listening, really listening in detail to her chief and to the gunners mates; she had learned to compile their reports and information, sort through it, and ensure the necessary information got to WEPS.

She turned around and looked back over the ship's railing. Being from New England, she had shared a relationship with the ocean her entire life. She had always loved looking out at the expanse of the ocean and at the hues that were mirrored in the water at different times of the day by the sun and clouds and by the beaches and islands of the northeast; especially in evening, when the coastal waters appeared glassy and reflected reds and light blues and pinks and oranges. The ocean had always been accessible to her, within a few miles of where she had lived growing up. She clutched her arms across her chest to safeguard as much warmth as possible in defense against the raw winds blowing amidships across the deck of the ship, from port to starboard. In her past on the Northeast Coast, whenever she had looked out at the ocean, she had never felt daunted by the cold and gray, or by the damp or by the harsh weather conditions that came and went according to the seasons.

She missed driving to the beach, parking her car in some sandy and windblown parking lot, and walking the wooden boardwalks over sand dunes and through scrubby brush and sea grass to access the beach. The seashore represented feelings of freedom and calm; and she loved breathing in the moist salt air and listening to the seagulls. She hoped that along the way in her life, she would always have access to the ocean, and that she would be able to visit it regularly.

Onboard the ship, she longed to gaze out from the deck into the ocean and feel the same sense of calm, healing, and peace that she had felt when she had looked out at the ocean from the coast back home. She wished this ocean inspired the same feelings within her as the ocean off of the sandy, grassy, and desolate dunes of Cape Cod and Rhode Island, and the rocky, sparse, and romantic inlets of coastal Maine. But all she felt was the cold and unfeeling mechanics of the ship's engines below her feet; and all she heard were waves crashing against the metal hull, and all she saw were mounts to hold .50-caliber machine guns, antennas used to hone in on and kill enemies, and the covers of canisters that held deadly and destructive long-range missiles.

The wind was strengthening so she removed her ship's ballcap and secured it underneath her khaki belt against her hip. Then she gripped the ship's steel cable railing and peered down over the side. She saw the seas destabilizing beneath her, increasing in choppiness and in height. Above, she noticed the gray cloud cover thickening. Even in the forlorn winter skies over the New England ocean, she had still derived comfort. But in the skies surrounding the ship, she sensed dread and despair and the hopelessness of her life onboard.

Julie had just started the training. She was explaining that she was going to talk everyone through the process of lowering a small boat into the water and how to board; she would outline a junior officer's responsibilities as boat officer and the responsibilities of each crew member. "...A small boat crew consists of a coxswain, engineer, bowhook, and sternhook," she had started to explain. She spoke with confidence and understanding, and Brenda noticed, she wasn't reading off notes.

She was determined to follow every word Julie uttered, really take in and absorb what she was hearing, and keep up with each step as performed by the boatswains mates. Then she would be versed in raising and lowering small boats, *or so she wished!* Even as the wind increased, and the skies grew darker and grayer, Julie remained undeterred. She simply spoke louder and more confidently. At one point, Julie's senior chief handed her a rain slicker, and while she donned it against the battering wind and rain, she continued the training uninterrupted.

"Never bend the sea painter to the stern of the boat, or to the side of the bow, away from the ship," her roommate explained, pointing to a line used during boat launch. As Brenda listened and took notes, she feared she'd walk away from Julie's training with nothing more than a signature in her SWO PQS book.

"The lower block of the forward fall is slacked down to the bowhook first," Julie continued. At one time, Brenda reminded herself, she would have considered obtaining a signature in her SWO PQS book to be a viable goal in itself; it would have made sense to her to stand at the training, listen, collect notes, get another line item signed off, and afterwards, continue hunting down signatures until her SWO PQS book was filled. With the book signed off and full of signatures, she could then cram for her SWO qualification oral board. She wouldn't have necessarily cared about the information she crammed; she would have just tried to get through the oral board so she could "successfully pass," forget about the information, and move on to the next milestone.

"...The cranes that hoist and lower the RHIB boats over the side are referred to as slewing arm boat davits..." As Julie spoke, the RHIB boat swayed as it hung from the crane and jerked down towards the seas. In the center of the RHIB stood the coxswain and another boatswain crew member, probably the bowhook or the sternhook. She feared for the boatswains mates, as they performed such a dangerous procedure in the face of a rising sea state, while fighting strong winds and oncoming rain. She looked back out at the ocean, having grown tired in her life of trying to convince herself and others that she was suited for this sort of real-time arduous activity, and for the Navy and for engineering.

"Feel free to ask me any questions," Julie announced, wrapping up her training. Brenda glanced down the side of the ship. She saw the remaining boatswains mate crew and the engineman climbing down the Jacob's ladder to board the RHIB, while the seas violently struck the hull. "It's going to be a bit of a rough ride. Who wants to go first?" Julie asked the group of junior officers. "I wish I could," she added, "but I'm already qual'd; and unfortunately, the weather won't allow me the time."

"It's not too rough to be doing this? Isn't the weather deteriorating?" Brenda heard herself asking out load. Her willingness to voice her question to the group surprised even herself.

"No, ma'am," the senior chief boatswains mate answered. "We wouldn't put anyone in unnecessary danger for training."

Brenda's nerves tugged at her, urging her to volunteer first and to raise her hand to rid herself of the experience as soon as possible. But while she hesitated to step forward, Brad volunteered with enthusiasm, which rescued her at least momentarily.

"You dropped your memo pad on the deck, ma'am," Chief Darrow said to her.

"Thank you, Chief," Brenda smiled in return. As she took the memo pad from the chief's hand, she turned to catch a glimpse of the RHIB boat. She spotted it bouncing up and over the crests of the windswept waves, speeding away from the destroyer and disappearing for long seconds into the troughs of the waves. "Why are you at small boat training for JOs, Chief?" Brenda asked her, curious as to why a chief electronics technician (ETC) had attended junior officer small boat training. Chief Darrow was one of four female chiefs onboard. As an E-7 electronics technician, she served in an enlisted rating with few females. Her division officer – a warrant officer – and all of her subordinate petty officers, were male.

"Getting a jump on my SWO qual. I'll be commissioned an ensign when we get back to Yokosuka," the chief answered.

"You're going SWO," Brenda replied, disappointed, as she continued to follow the RHIB with her eyes.

"Not SWO," the chief corrected her. "I'm not putting up with that bullshit. I've been accepted into the Limited Duty Officer program. I'll be an LDO," the chief said, referring to a commissioning program open only to warrant officers and E-6 and above with a minimum of eight years of service. LDOs served only in their specific fields of expertise, and unlike most commissioning programs, a bachelor's degree was not required. In the chief's case, she would manage a division of electronics technicians as the division officer and technical expert.

Brenda nodded and said nothing. Whenever the RHIB rode over the top of a wave, she was able to spot Brad seated in the rear of the boat, wearing a fluorescent orange lifejacket over his khakis. The chief's news of becoming an LDO had increased her uneasiness; but regardless of her own feelings, she understood that becoming a commissioned officer would have been the next logical step for someone as dedicated to the Navy as Chief Darrow was. Brenda offered her hand to the chief and congratulated her. Maybe the chief's news was good. In most cases, she had experienced officers who were prior enlisted as more capable and knowledgeable. They possessed the backing of maturity, combined with experience from their enlisted service, and deservingly, they commanded greater respect from peers and subordinates in general. "What made you want to leave the chiefs mess?" Brenda asked.

"A major milestone, becoming an officer," the chief replied. "My father passed away from alcohol-related causes when I was a young teenager, leaving my mother and I extremely poor and living in Memphis. We both worked so she could purchase a house, an incredible accomplishment for a widow with a teenage child – two women. We're both very proud."

"Soon you'll be Ensign Darrow," Brenda encouraged her and smiled. But she feared the chief misunderstood the realities she would face as part of the wardroom. As an LDO, on a ship such as a destroyer, she would be working as a division officer for a SWO department head. Brenda could tell that Chief Darrow subscribed to the popular misconception that status as an LDO would make her immune to, and place her above, putting up with all the SWO "bullshit," as she had called it. She seemed to assume that she would have special status that would give her more leeway to speak her mind, to stand up to the SWO department heads, and to "tell it like it was"...a kind of special license unattainable to an officer without "old salt" enlisted experience behind him/her. Some of that was true, but there were limits.

Brenda searched the ocean again for the RHIB, feeling uneasy. The chief's news reminded her of the plight of the one LDO they had onboard – Ensign Jason Arnett. Working directly under OPS, he despised being part of the SWO wardroom. She remembered Jason's anger when he told her how, inport, he had worked day and night without end and had seldom been able to go on liberty to see his family, adding, "I'd do anything to give up my LDO officer commission, and go back to being an E-8 senior chief, leaving the SWO wardroom behind forever."

"I won't have to put up with the SWO shit," Chief Darrow repeated, "because I'll be an LDO, with similar status to the warrant officers onboard. I don't mind telling these SWO lieutenant and lieutenant commander department heads what needs to be done."

Brenda merely nodded. She wanted to comment that the warrants had a separate and unique standing onboard; and she wished she could have warned the chief that she might have been overestimating what she could expect to get away with once she became subject to the written and unwritten hierarchy and decorum of the wardroom. LDO or not, she would still be an ensign. But Brenda also understood that it wasn't her place to advise the chief on her plans for her career. "Thank you for picking up my memo pad, Chief. They barely fit into the back pockets of female uniforms," she smiled.

"Men's uniform design evolved out of utility," the chief replied.

"Women's uniforms are reverse designed, bad copies," Brenda stated, watching the RHIB boat coming in towards the ship. She thought about how she could never perform the job of the boatswains mates; they didn't deserve jokes that implied they weren't as "smart" as other more academically-oriented, or technically-oriented, enlisted ratings.

"Who's next?" Julie turned to the crowd. "Who's never been out on a RHIB?"

"Me, I'll do it," Brenda said raising her hand.

"Ensign Conner says she'll go next," Chief Darrow stated forcefully, above the crowd. "Go ahead, ma'am," the chief said, encouraging her, as Brenda paused.

Julie handed Brenda a lifejacket and practically started to dress her. "Put this on," she instructed, "and I'll make sure you've tied and secured it correctly." Brenda looked down at her chest to match the ties, zippers, and clasps; and before she had even put one together, Julie took over, tying all the ties for her and zipping her up. "It's rough out there," Julie said. "You could bounce out of the boat; the water's cold; there're holes on the side of each seat for your hands; hold them tightly. BM1 is a safe and experienced driver; he's the best coxswain onboard; don't worry and trust his ability; climb down the ladder slowly and safely; hold on to the side ropes, and not onto the plastic rungs. Take as much time as you need to climb down. Hold on no matter how rough it gets. The last three rungs land you inside the RHIB."

"Thank you, Julie," Brenda answered her, understanding her clearly. As Julie finished securing her lifejacket, Brad's head began to appear above the edge of the deck, as he finished ascending the ladder. Brenda wondered about the exact distance she would have to climb down, against the gray metal hull, before she would reach the RHIB. She guessed it was maybe twenty feet down to the water.

"That was a great ride!" Brad said, as he stepped off the ladder and onto the deck of the destroyer, his uniform soaked through.

Brenda approached the side of the ship. When she looked down, she saw the rope ladder pounding against the steel hull, in rhythm with the impacting winds and waves. "I'm going to hold onto you until I feel you have good footing on the ladder, and you're holding on," the senior chief boatswains mate told her. Brenda couldn't remember any of this extra help for Brad, but she trusted the boatswain chief to judge what she needed. "The hardest part is the first step over the side, ma'am," the senior chief continued. "Then just ease down rung by rung, holding onto the sides of the rope ladder. Once you place your first foot over, you'll be good to go. No matter how hard the winds and seas slam you against the side of the metal hull, don't let go. I know you're a good swimmer, ma'am, but these waters are rough and cold."

Brenda gripped the metal posts on the deck, to which the ropes of each side of the ladder were tied, and felt for the first rung by dangling her boot, before planting it. "Don't look down, ma'am, just stare straight ahead at the gray hull as you climb down," the senior chief guided her. She then placed her opposite foot on the rung, leaving the safety of the deck of the destroyer; she grabbed onto one side of the rope ladder with one hand, finding it wet and slick, before transferring the second hand. "Good job, ma'am, you've got it," she heard the senior chief again. Her uniform was already soaked through, just from having stepped over the side. The water was freezing, and she was glad at least that she was a strong and confident swimmer, although she didn't know if she was a match against the forceful seas that were crashing against the hull. She eased down a few rungs, one hand at a time, one foot at a time. The rope ladder gave with every step, and the wind forced her and the ladder to bang up against the gray metal hull a few times. Brenda paused where she was, now more than midway down the side of the destroyer. "Perfect, you're almost here, ma'am," she heard from the boatswain crew below.

She took another step down from where she was; and not recognizing that she had stepped onto one of the last three rungs, she felt the arms of one of the boatswains mates grab her and lift her onto a seat. "We've got to go, ma'am, it's too difficult to remain alongside in these seas," the coxswain told her; and with a force that threw her back into her seat, they were off. The coxswain hit the throttle to head out into the seas, and Brenda realized she was the de facto boat officer. She held tightly onto the holes in the seat, stunned by the actual enormity of two to four-foot seas. She was used to looking down on these waves from the bridge; but from the RHIB, she couldn't see over or in front of them. The coxswain revved the boat straight up the inside of the waves, before they dropped over the other side of each crest. The repetitive pattern slammed them all down against their seats, over and over, endlessly. Time moved slower than Brenda had ever thought it could, as the movement thrust her painfully onto her wooden seat each time. The seas were freezing cold, and she kept thinking that she wasn't onboard a ride at Disney. If the coxswain flipped the boat, their survival would be precarious. Brenda had confidence in her swimming, but she still wanted the experience to end as soon as possible.

"It's getting too rough out here, ma'am. With your permission, I'd like to head back in," the coxswain called back to her.

With her permission, he had said. Addressed to her, the question sounded ridiculous, she thought. "Return to the ship, BM1," she answered him.

"Return to the ship, aye, aye, ma'am," he answered, and turned back. The destroyer looked alarmingly far away, and she couldn't wait to get back to the stability it offered. She held on, bouncing out of her seat and slamming back down onto the wood, soaked with freezing seawater, looking forward to her climb back up the Jacob's ladder to the safety of the destroyer.

Chapter 34: Calmer seas ... Progress for women ... Women in combat means equality ... Chief Smith airlifted away

On the bridge, Brad saluted Brenda. "I relieve you," he stated.

"I stand relieved," she saluted in return. *"Attention in the pilothouse, this is Ensign Conner. Ensign Hanson has the conn,"* she announced.

"Attention in the pilothouse, this is Ensign Hanson. I have the conn," Brad followed.

"All set then?" Brenda asked, looking at Brad and Rob. They were standing on the starboard side of the bridge, next to the Captain's chair. "I'll see you guys later," she said. "I'm going out on the bridge wing for a while."

She turned to leave, but Rob interrupted her by nudging her shoulder. "Don't look so glum. Hey, remember," he said. "It only gets better. It *does*," he emphasized.

"Thank you, Rob," she answered. "But I'm not so sure."

From the chart table, Brenda walked over to the side door leading out to the bridge wing. She gripped the handle on the oval door and swung it counterclockwise. Before she pushed the door open, she turned to give a last wave to Brad and Rob, but they were both standing at the center of the bridge, behind the ARPA radar screen, looking through binoculars at a distant contact off the port bow. So she leaned her weight against the door and forced it open against the wind. The wind, she thought as she secured the door behind her after stepping outside, it never seemed to let up out on the bridge wing, no matter how calm the weather, or how slowly the ship made way through the ocean.

She leaned over the railing, facing the ship's bow, and inhaled deeply. She had finally made it out to the bridge wing. Over the course of her four-hour bridge watch, she had glanced out to the bridge wing now and then. She had felt drawn to venture out there, as if, while standing on the outdoor nook, high up on the ship, looking out into the ocean, she might discover some solution that would rescue her from her situation. Mostly, however, she wanted to find a place where she could rest and be alone with her own thoughts.

She noticed the calming weather and seas had brought a milder, warmer wind. If she could have untied her hair, letting it lose and free, she would have. She had become accustomed to the formalities of assuming and relieving the bridge watch. But although she had grown less wary of the protocols, she still knew that the formalized procedures would never feel quite natural. It was as if someone else routinely slipped inside of her skin to perform those protocols and recite the proper lines. On most days, she felt miscast wearing her uniform, as if dressed for a costume party.

"Nice day to be out here," she heard WEPS voice, accompanied by the sound of the door to the bridge wing opening. She turned around. WEPS had just stepped down from the threshold, and he was followed by Pete.

"Yes, sir, it is," she said as she slid over against the railing to make room for them.

"Nice to finally be outside," Pete nodded and agreed, as he leaned over the railing next to WEPS. "*Sea-whiz*," he then said, referring to the close-in weapons system (CIWS), which his division operated and maintained. "It's a multimillion-dollar six-barrel anti-ship missile defense gun with a Navy-wide reputation for being both unreliable and a maintenance challenge," he rattled off as if repeating a tagline he had committed to memory.

"Don't we know it," WEPS commented casually.

"Although we have FC2 Lorian in our back pocket," Pete said, in a more serious light, speaking over the wind. "She's very smart and an excellent CIWS technician; and she understands how timing in the delivery of information up the chain of command is key. I plan on bringing her to sit in on the status meeting tomorrow."

From the bridge wing, Brenda could see FC2 Lorian at work with the team of CIWS technicians. She was high up on the ship's superstructure, strapped in fall protection gear, working between various dismantled sections of the CIWS, giving some sort of direction to the others around her.

Brenda had been vaguely aware that FC2 Lorian had recently risen in status as the lead in the CIWS troubleshooting effort, out of the ten or so CIWS fire controlmen onboard. The chief in CM division was brand new to CIWS, having recently transferred to the fire controlman rating from another enlisted rating that had been phased-out.

As Brenda listened to WEPS and Pete discuss changes to the CIWS plan of action and milestones (POA&M) document, she started to realize, more than anything else, that both men were unfazed by the idea of women serving aboard ships or by serving alongside women. In earlier decades, she imagined that a female would never have been considered as a lead for any mechanical troubleshooting effort. If one had, it would have been noted as a remarkable event.

Brenda felt the warmth of the sun upon her, and unzipped her dark navy blue foul weather jacket. She leaned her back against the metal bulkhead, beside the door to the bridge, and placed her hands comfortably into her pockets. In her mind, she ran through the roster of female petty officers onboard. In the engineering department, a female gas turbine mechanic second class (GSM2) worked as a hands-on mechanic and served as a watchstander in both the engineering central control station (CCS) and in the main engine rooms (MERs). Within the main propulsion (MP) division, the petty officer had earned the trust of the GSM senior chief and of her colleagues. Brenda knew from general conversations with the warrant officer in charge of MP division that GSM2 Rees had become one of the primary go-to petty officers for maintenance and repairs. In the operations department, a female operations specialist first class (OS1) stood watch in CIC, as one of the main air traffic controllers when *Curtis Wilbur* was assigned "alfa-whisky" (AW - air warfare commander) duties by the carrier. Air traffic control responsibilities had stepped up on the *Curtis Wilbur* since a series of CASREPs ("casualty reports," sent by Navy message indicating a system was inoperable) had rendered the battle group cruiser unavailable for AW duty. There were so many female petty officers onboard now, Brenda realized. Since she had arrived to the ship, a few more had checked onboard who were trained in fields that had been closed to women as recently as a year ago. The number of female enlisted sailors now neared twenty, out of a crew of over two hundred eighty.

She viewed the influx of female petty officers and seamen, and the success many had achieved onboard, as an indication of progress in the history of women – a history that had remained nearly unchanged deep into the twentieth century. But she also knew to guard her enthusiasm, because in history, expanding roles and choices for women seemed forever vulnerable to setbacks. She thought of a documentary she had seen about Eleanor Roosevelt, which had introduced her to the idea of remaining cautious in perceiving progress. According to the film, Eleanor Roosevelt had felt discouraged during the post-World War II years, when society (or, the dominant male voice of society) decided that working women, who had supported the war effort, needed to retreat home. They were no longer needed in the workplace since the men were returning from war.

She had often tried to place herself in the minds of the women of the postwar era. She wondered what dreams some of them may have had for their lives. And she imagined that the country had probably suffered, in some way that could never be known, from having lost the feminine perspective in military and business during the decades that followed the war. The presence of women might have – undoubtedly would have! – influenced the course of events during those decades in a different direction.

She hoped that the floodgates were now open for good. She had read of statistics taken at the end of World War II, which indicated many women had not wanted to leave their jobs. They had gained a taste of independence, but employers had forced them out. The postwar government (a largely male voice) had launched an active propaganda campaign through news, posters, movies and other media to secure public sentiment – that women should regress home to a single, traditional role, without choice. The pressure to conform was high. In the 1990s, Brenda hoped the pressure to conform would act conversely, guiding the military (one of the last major holdouts for restricting women) into gradual and permanent change, in pace with outside society.

She had heard all of the prevailing reasons for excluding women from combat: women crack under pressure, they get pregnant, they aren't physically strong enough, they become promiscuous, there's not enough space onboard, they need special head and berthing arrangements (like the men didn't!), it's better if the top brass remains male for the sake of tradition, etc. And those very arguments still kept women off submarines. In 1994, congress repealed the law that had excluded women from serving on combatant ships (with the exception of submarines). That same year, USS *Dwight D. Eisenhower* (CVN-69) was the first combatant ship to deploy with women as part of ship's company; however, a majority of ships were still all male.

Already Brenda had sat face-to-face with junior officer peers, her own age, who questioned allowing women to serve onboard submarines (by law women were still banned from submarines), or in other naval combatant roles. Such experiences with her peers always left her with her mouth hanging open, in disbelief. If it was necessary to have a military and to go to war, then she hoped that the opportunity to defend one's nation would be available to all Americans, negating the need for women to be protected and to be defended.

She abhorred the idea of a draft; but for the sake of equality, she felt that if there was to be a draft, both women and men should be subject to it. How could women expect legal and social equality, and at the same time, acquiesce to a draft system that excluded women? The system was in place for the protection of women, thereby creating inequality. Additionally, it upheld that women couldn't quite serve with the same efficacy as men. What was the message? ...See, women really *are* inferior.

She saw that the team of CIWS technicians had disassembled the radar dome – the system's distinguishing characteristic – famous for its resemblance of R2D2 in *Star Wars*. Beside her, WEPS and Pete still discussed CIWS; her attention drifted in and out of their conversation.

"It must be nice for you being male," Brenda remembered her sarcasm, when she had responded to a student colleague from SWOS, while she was still stationed in Newport. She had tried to convince him of her views on equal rights for women in the military. By the end of their conversation, she had found herself sounding bitter, but she hadn't wanted to come across in that way. "I'm sorry," she had apologized. "I've experienced so many similar conversations lately, and they've all taken me by surprise." This had taken place inside a bar, at a table far off to a corner, where she had been seated with three other ensigns from her class section at SWOS. They were part of a larger group that was scattered about the bar; some were mingling, some were dancing, some were at tables. In frustration, she had discontinued her argument; she had sat back in her chair in silence. The scene in the bar was the usual – the smoke, the noise, the people screaming over the crowd and blaring music, trying to be heard. She always dreaded crowded bar and club scenes, finding the experience boring and repetitive. But somehow military culture seemed prone to those scenes (everyone was away from their friends, family, and home, and lacked roots where they were), and she found herself a part of the bar setting more often then she would have preferred. The inside of this bar was different at least; it was in the basement of an old stone building in downtown Newport. However, like most bars, the lighting inside was low, and the crowd looked the same – put-on, insecure, needy, various stages of drunk. The background volume blurred into a single white noise so that she felt like she could have rested her head into her palms and slept comfortably, right at the table. After having taken exams all morning at SWOS, and having sat through a full afternoon of classwork, she was tired.

"I'll buy you a beer," one of the guys offered.

"No, no thanks, maybe some coffee," she told him.

"Coffee then," he said. "You're not a beer drinker?"

"No, but not because of any moral objection," she clarified, holding up her palm. She had never been a drinker. And it wasn't out of religious reasons. "Well, maybe a Kahlua and cream," she gave in, and sunk her face into her hands.

"I'll get you the coffee, since that was what you wanted," her classmate offered. He stood up and disappeared into the crowd, headed for the bar.

She was at the bar that evening because she enjoyed socializing with her classmates once in a while. Earlier that afternoon in the SWOS building, after class had let out at 1600, the guys in the desks surrounding hers had started tossing out places to meet for the evening. "You never come with us!" one of them had called over to her, as she stood up from her desk to leave. In response she nodded, and agreed to join them. She then accompanied the group in walking out to the parking lot; all of them were dressed in the winter working blue uniform. She got into her car, drove home to the house she rented with three other ensigns, showered, and changed to go out for the night.

When her one classmate returned to the table with coffee from the bar, she thanked him, and tried to present her argument again. "About the submarine community," she began. "All I'm saying, is that you guys can say that women shouldn't be allowed on subs and there is no consequence to you personally. No one is ever going tell you that you can't pursue your chosen career because of your gender. That's all." She remembered trying to list the submarine community as one of her career choices in ROTC. Her lieutenant advisor had handed her back her "service selection sheet" for her to redo. She argued that she didn't understand, she was going through the same ROTC training as the guys, and all midshipmen were unproven at that point. "It's the law," her advisor had answered, "no women on subs."

"Why would women even want to go into the military?" the guy seated next to her, on her right, asked.

"Some women do, some don't. Just like some men do and some don't," the ensign who had gotten her the coffee cut in. He was seated directly across from her.

"Yes, and some women are suited to the military and some aren't. The same goes for men, some men are suited, some aren't. The choice of whether or not to go into the military isn't your choice to make for someone else," Brenda stressed. "Barring service by law restricts women's choice."

"I support women in the military," the ensign to Brenda's left answered. For a moment, she began to relax her posture, feeling encouraged that she had more support at the table than she had originally assumed. "I'm just stating in practical terms," he then continued, "that there's not enough room, for instance, on submarines. It's close quarters. Where are women going to sleep? How are men and women going to pass each other in the passageways?"

Brenda had participated in many of these casual discussions about the role of women in the military, where she found that responses were often vague and it was unclear exactly where her male colleagues stood on these issues. She had found that they didn't always seem to know where they stood. She had heard repeated arguments/statements from male peers who claimed they were in support of women on submarines, but then placed conditions on it, or expressed doubts about its feasibility.

Let down, Brenda simply asserted, "Those issues work themselves out. They've worked out on ships, even on small ships like Coast Guard cutters that go out to sea for extended periods."

"What submarine have you served on?" the coffee ensign directed his question toward the "there's not enough room" statement. Brenda cautiously listened as he motioned to speak again. He went on. "Before I became an officer, I served on two different boats. Submarine life is cramped, but accommodations can be retrofitted."

"It's just reality," the ensign to her right answered. Brenda felt surrounded. "Differences in physical strength. Would a woman be able to turn all of the steam valves?"

"What about in the buttercup firefighter trainer last week?" Brenda asked him, referring to the mock "USS Buttercup" damage control trainer at SWOS. "You shored up a bulkhead with a female partner, patched a pipe, and started a submersible pump surrounded by four feet of water. And they have steam valves on nuclear surface ships, too, by the way, which are currently open to women."

"I couldn't turn all of the steam valves onboard my subs," the coffee ensign answered. Brenda hadn't realized he was prior enlisted. He was the first ex-submariner she had heard argue in favor of women. She had mostly experienced the opposite. "Procedures on ships and subs are accomplished through team effort," he emphasized, "utilizing known strengths and weaknesses of each member."

"Women bring a feminine perspective, something that has been missing in the workplace and in the military for too long," Brenda stressed, trying to get the last word in when she noticed the server arriving with their appetizers. "Women may not always bring the same physical strength to a unit," she tried to slip in quickly, "but they bring other organizational, planning, and decision-making skills unique to them, that a group of all men would lack. In field units, they can liaison with local people, who would see a group of men arriving to a village solely as a threat, for example."

"When congress loosens the restrictions, I'll support it," the ensign to her left said.

"It's inevitable, you know, the progression," Brenda said.

"I'd like as many women on ships as possible," he responded, laughing at his oncoming joke. "In fact, I'd love to be one of the only guys on a mostly female ship; I'd be the first to volunteer for that ship."

"A chick ship," Brenda conceded.

The server arranged the dishes on the table, but the arrival of the food hadn't stopped the conversation. "It would feel weird to me," the ensign to her right said, who had originally started the conversation, "to be out in the field in an infantry unit, for example, and have a woman next to me."

"If the person was there with specific training, you'd see her as a colleague," Brenda answered.

"I think most women could do the job once trained," the ensign to her left granted. "But then I go back to thinking of the issue in terms of my wife. Should it really be her job to go into combat? I think it's my responsibility to ensure my wife and children are safe."

Brenda sat back. She had had this same conversation with differing names and faces many times before. The dialog had always gone the same, and by the end, she had always felt left where she had started. She had had it pointed out to her that the notion of men protecting women was a drive that was imbedded in human nature; and she even accepted that it might have been engrained in human DNA. But in life, no matter the setting, whether in families or in communities, she had learned that men could not always be counted on to protect; sometimes they couldn't be depended on to follow through in supporting their families. How many countless women had suffered in abusive situations from leaving themselves financially and/or situationally dependent on a man? Complete dependence with no other options available, endangered women. She felt it was one of the reasons why women had to pursue equal rights under the law; the military seemed one of the last traditional holdouts. "The instinct to protect also resides in women," Brenda said to the guys, "although I agree that the instinct may exist in differing forms. I wish society could progress beyond restricting women based on the assertion that men *have* to protect women, that women aren't capable of doing it themselves. Or women will never be able to gain equality." Women *are* capable of protecting themselves, she wanted to add. She had much more to say, but instead she resigned. "Let's eat and talk about something else," she finished, tired. And they all moved on from the subject.

1MC Shipwide Announcement: *"Flight quarters, flight quarters. All hands man your flight quarters stations. All hands not involved in flight quarters stand clear."*

On the bridge wing, standing next to WEPS and Pete, Brenda turned and peered back at the flight deck. She saw the rotation of the helo's rotors and soon felt the steel deck vibrating beneath her feet. "There he goes," WEPS said, referring to Chief Smith. "Good," Pete added, and then stepped inside the bridge.

"It's amazing there're still guys like him around," Pete commented as he followed WEPS inside.

"There're plenty," Brenda said, as she secured the door behind the three of them. She imagined Chief Smith strapped inside the helo, as it lifted him off the ship and over to the aircraft carrier. She hadn't yet heard the results of the frocked chief's Captain's Mast. She wondered if any substance would come of the allegations put forth by the females onboard.

Chapter 35: Liberty boat to Hong Kong ... Her fantasy has to wait ... Wives, girlfriends, and women onboard ... Brenda meets the new XO ... The Captain's speech

From the *Curtis Wilbur*'s quarterdeck, Brenda looked out across the bay at Hong Kong. She wanted to believe that the new female XO coming onboard was going to make history, as the warrant officer had predicted a month or so ago when they were hanging out in the wardroom discussing her impending arrival. Around her, she felt the chaos of Victoria Harbour, one of the busiest harbors in the world. Large merchant ships, small fishing boats (referred to as *junks*), speed boats, pleasure craft, and ferries headed in all directions – out to sea and among the islands comprising Hong Kong. Beyond the harbor, she saw a modern city skyline, crouched within a valley, underneath the backdrop of a mountain range. She longed to get to that city. The crew had been absolutely energized by the promise of modern Hong Kong, and she had taken some of that excitement in for herself. The gunners mates had informed her of how the city was one large shopping mall, and she had read in the *Servicemen's Guide* that shopping was the national pastime of the people in Hong Kong. And how she also yearned for the quiet and solace offered by the temples and gardens of which she had read; amongst the crowdedness and commercialism, these offered traces of peace, and could be found scattered within the city.

Evening had set in, and Brenda watched as the city lit up, skyscraper by skyscraper, in pace with the sunset. She hadn't known what to expect of Hong Kong, but from the ship, the cityscape appeared bright and spectacular. Hong Kong seemed to her, to be the type of place that offered endless possibilities just by being there. Leaving the ship, however, meant embarking on a forty-five minute ride across the bay by ferry. The ship was anchored far out into the bay, as pier space in Hong Kong was scarce and expensive. In the Navy, the crews referred to the ferries that transported them from ship to shore as "liberty boats." She found the term fitting, as she stood at the top of a set of metal stairs leading down to a makeshift dock, which had been assembled by the boatswains mates at the ship's waterline. She watched as a small ferry, tied to the floating dock, rocked back and forth in the choppy harbor water, while passengers from the ship loaded onboard, seeking liberty.

Brenda felt tempted to walk down the accommodation ladder to board the liberty boat. So far, she had spent her first day of shore leave in Hong Kong on the ship, waiting for OPS to release Julie and Brad. She glanced back at the quarterdeck, hoping they would appear. But not seeing them, she took one step down the ladder. Liberty had commenced at 0800 that morning, and since then, the ferry had been departing according to an unpredictable schedule – approximately every two or three hours. She felt for Julie and Brad, but she craved not to miss an evening in Hong Kong, nor an opportunity to witness the introduction of the first female XO of an Aegis destroyer, which would take place on shore.

"Three gongs just sounded over the 1MC, ma'am. That means you've got ten minutes," Petty Officer Brooks warned her, as he brushed by. He had duty and was standing petty officer of the watch at the quarterdeck.

"I know. I heard the quarterdeck sound them," she smiled, hoping Julie and Brad would emerge from the skin of the ship. She watched as everyone streamed down the steps and onto the liberty boat, except for the junior officers who worked for OPS. Throughout the day, OPS had continually promised Julie and Brad that after they reported to him on the next item, he would allow them to depart the ship. "Certainly, OPS wants his division officers to attend the Hail & Farewell party for the new XO," Brad had insisted to her earlier that morning. With each passing hour, Brenda had witnessed Brad's anger intensify. He had refused to change into his khakis, and had remained dressed in civilian clothes all day as he ran about the ship at OPS' will.

Brenda hesitated but decided to take a few more steps down. On this, her first naval deployment, she felt she had wasted too many liberty days onboard the ship, waiting for OPS to release Brad. Not wasted, she thought, as she delayed going down any farther. She had always waited onboard for Brad because she had wanted to, because they had started to spend most of their time off the ship together. Meeting up with him on liberty had provided her with purpose, something to which she could look forward during the unending strings of days onboard. She glanced back up at the quarterdeck and then continued down the remainder of the steps. As she approached the floating dock, two gongs sounded over the 1MC, signaling that the liberty boat would depart in five minutes.

"Ma'am, are you going ashore to meet the new XO?" Petty Officer Brooks approached her, as he assisted with coordination of the liberty boat.

"You guys know everything," she answered, eying the quarterdeck for Julie and Brad.

"We've heard she's a force, that she's not even qualified, ma'am. And that they just sent her to the DESRON as staff to get her SWO pin before coming aboard to take charge as XO."

"Not to get her SWO pin, that's wrong," Brenda replied. "It was to get her TAO letter. You have to trust the Navy and naval leadership," she said, before stepping onto the liberty boat. "Be careful in Hong Kong," she teased, changing the subject. "I've read about the hostess bars in the *Servicemen's Guide*. I don't want any incidents cutting into my liberty. Follow up my speech at quarters, and talk to the guys again about protecting themselves with condoms," she said. "I'm serious," she finished. A few weeks ago, after their port visit to Thailand, she had knocked on the door to the chiefs mess looking for Chief Dering. One of the chiefs had laughed and told her that he had a cold, but later she had learned that he had contracted gonorrhea of the mouth – the clap. A few days later, chief had mentioned to her that while on deployment, he and his wife both did as they pleased. She was his third wife, and he was her fifth American serviceman husband, he had told her. He had gone on to mention that his wife was from Asia, although he didn't say from where specifically. Brenda had merely responded, "Okay, Chief." Nothing she heard surprised her any more.

"I know you're serious, ma'am," Petty Officer Brooks said, shaking his head and waving to her as he started back up the steps. "Don't you have too much fun, either, ma'am," he called to her.

She made her way towards a section of the boat that appeared fairly void of people, and sat down in one of the hard plastic seats; she relaxed her head back against a porthole.

Then Brad startled her as he sat down in the next seat over. "Every time I tried to check out with OPS, he added ten more things to my list, all of it make-work," he exclaimed, out of breath.

Brenda opened her eyes, and spotted Julie shuffling towards them through the crowd. "I tried to check out with OPS earlier than usual," she said, as she sat down next to Brad, "to give myself some buffer, but he wouldn't let me. Then he'd add a bunch more things to my list, all of them the number one priority, as always."

"I thought we would miss Hong Kong," Brenda responded,

"and the new XO."

"I think she's woefully unprepared to be XO of a DDG," Julie sighed, as she sat back in her seat, "but the Navy has put her in that position." Brenda nodded, disheartened by Julie's growing disenchantment with the Navy, because it was a dynamic that should not have been occurring. OPS should have been grateful to have an enthusiastic and smart junior officer like Julie working for him; he should have mentored her, supported her, and guided her; he should have groomed her to become a stellar department head. Instead he cruelly mistreated her, along with all of the other junior officers in his department. He was concerned only with obtaining a zero-defect record and the right catchphrases for his officer fitness report (FITREP). His JOs were simply tools for his use, at his discretion, for his own career advancement. OPS was a product of SWO culture. As a division officer and department head, OPS had consistently ranked number one. He was perfectly poised to screen for XO, and later for CO of his own ship – not an oiler, tender, or outdated frigate, but a shiny, new, advanced and high-profile destroyer or cruiser.

"We all figured out that Rob and Jon, third and second tour division officers, have more sea time than the new XO does," Brad added, as one boat gong sounded, indicating the liberty boat would leave in one minute.

"OPS isn't going to the Hail & Farewell? That's strange," Brenda commented.

"Hey guys!" OPS sat down in the row of seats across from them, friendly and enthusiastic. His breath was awful.

Brenda gripped onto the pole in front of her seat as the boat departed. The choppy harbor water bounced the boat from side to side. The three junior officers sat in silence for the next forty-five minutes. Truly, no means existed to get away, Brenda lamented.

***

At the new XO's Hail & Farewell party in Hong Kong, Brenda looked at her reflection in a mirror that ran lengthwise along the wall of the restaurant. She wondered how anyone would be able to tell whether she was one of the officers from the *Curtis Wilbur* wardroom, or whether she was a wife or girlfriend of one of the officers, or whether she was there from an American women's volunteer organization that offered support services for U.S. military personnel and other American citizens in Hong Kong.

She made her way towards the buffet table which featured an array of Chinese dishes. The atmosphere of the party was subdued. The restaurant was a musty vintage and the lighting, dim. She kept to herself and within her own thoughts as she sampled a few items from the buffet. The familiarity of the foods – the sights, tastes, and smells – reminded her of home, surprisingly, since she recognized most of the dishes from Chinese restaurants in the United States. This particular restaurant had catered to American sailors for nearly a century. The food and the decor of the restaurant reminded her so much of home that she fantasized about walking out the door of the restaurant, directly onto a street in the U.S. She visualized herself walking from the restaurant and down the street until she reached an apartment she might live in, any nondescript apartment, such as the type that twenty-somethings rented. She imagined herself living in that apartment and holding an entry-level position where she could start at the bottom and learn, or where she would be in graduate school; she would begin making her life decisions all over again. She would take her lessons from the Navy with her and go about her new life.

But that fantasy would have to wait four years. She remained to the outside of the crowd. Off to a corner, she spotted a lone table underneath a television. Holding a plate full of food and a cup of soup, she dodged rows of red and gold lanterns and tassels hanging from the ceiling to reach a table that promised her some space to herself. She planned to mix with the officers and guests again after she sat down and enjoyed her food and a moment of peace. Most of the women she saw around the restaurant, she assumed, were visiting wives and girlfriends. Brenda cupped her hands around the warmth of her soup. She hoped the women at the party knew, and that society knew, that women were also serving in the military.

Looking around the party, she thought about the societal life of officers, and how it had changed – specifically, how the role of women had progressed beyond holding social soirees for husband officers and climbing the social ladder within the wives club. It amazed her to think that the social involvement of an officer's wife used to weigh heavily into his career and officer FITREP. That part of Navy societal milieu had faded, thankfully. Nowadays, most of the officers' wives she had met were officers themselves, or they had college degrees and their own careers and lives. Women now had their own independent importance and their own contributions to make. They could strive towards goals that weren't dependent on their husband's career and status, choosing their own path.

On the TV mounted on the wall, she immediately noticed that the broadcast on the American news channel was slanted towards a traditional view of U.S. military life. The channel had focused solely on showing images of young women, some of them still teenagers or barely into their twenties, waiting on the piers for men, holding babies and toddlers.

Her thoughts turned to the women onboard, and the new, complicated dynamics they faced. The women of the *Curtis Wilbur*, a combatant ship, had no prior role models to whom they could look for guidance. If Brenda could have, she would have changed the channel. On the TV, they were showing image after image of women greeting their men; they were showing one side of military life. The news never seemed to air military women and their sacrifices, and the way they, along with their families, experienced both progress and setbacks. With the number of women at sea and deployed all over the world in the armed services, she wondered why the news cameras hadn't yet captured the increasingly common plight of men waiting for their service member wives and girlfriends who were stationed abroad, or fathers whose children awaited their mothers, or the subsequent effects of this.

She stared out the window next to her table into a narrow alleyway filled with neon Chinese characters, lit up and blinking among mazes of drooping power lines. She had enjoyed the walk through the Wan Chai district of Hong Kong to the restaurant. She loved the feel of an old city. By luck, they had lost OPS on the liberty boat pier when he suddenly dropped them to get into a cab with the Captain and the current XO. Brad had angrily commented, "And all the fretting I did on the boat thinking he would walk with us all the way to the restaurant!" Brenda had only looked at Brad and nodded; she had felt the same intensity of dread all during the choppy ride across the harbor, when they all sat in silence. On her own liberty time, she wanted anything but to walk with OPS to the restaurant and have their spirits weighted down by his presence.

Instead, Bill, the warrant officer (CWO), had joined up with the three lost JOs – her, Brad, and Julie – along the way as they walked, offering to guide and accompany them through the antique streets and alleyways of the Wan Chai district of Hong Kong. He told them he had spotted the three of them with their maps open, pointing in various directions, and they looked like they needed the help of an "old salt." Bill was a veteran of the Wan Chai neighborhood, he explained to them, having been to Hong Kong at least ten times before. "This is history," he said. "We're on liberty in Hong Kong right before it will turn over to China." Brenda remembered soaking up the busy atmosphere of the streets, and gazing at the Chinese characters. She wished she could find the opportunity to study them. The art, look, and mechanics of language resonated with her. She was always on the lookout for language; she wanted to absorb every aspect of foreign language she could. Too bad she hadn't traveled to Hong Kong for a study abroad, or to teach, or for a language internship, she kept telling herself. So many of her friends from language classes were in Spain and other countries, teaching English, studying as graduate students, and developing their foreign language skills.

"We're walking through naval history," Bill repeated during the walk. "The restaurant hosting our Hail & Farewell has served as an outpost for American sailors for a century." The warrant's history lesson was apparent, because as soon as she had stepped off the liberty boat, she was surprised to discover that the Navy had established its own corner of Americana in Hong Kong, and that an entire volunteer network existed to support Navy personnel. The Fenwick Pier/Fleet Arcade hosted American stores, restaurants, lounges, recreation areas, a library, and a U.S. bank and post office. "And more history," Bill said. "We're getting our fourth female officer besides Brenda, Julie, and the supply officer," he exclaimed. "The new XO will bring the total to four."

"In perspective, that's quite a lot," Brenda added, as she followed happily down the street behind Bill, Julie, and Brad.

"Watch your head with those drooping power lines," she warned Bill, as he opened a rusted metal door that showed its age through several layers of exposed paint and ornate vintage hardware. She stopped on the sidewalk a moment to take in the scene of the neighborhood and city streets before following Bill, Julie, and Brad up a dark staircase leading to the second floor. It took a second for her eyes to adjust to the dimly lit interior of the staircase and the restaurant, but she could hear the noise of the crowd. It looked and sounded like most of the *Curtis Wilbur* officers and guests had arrived. She saw a number of people she didn't recognize. She and Julie stayed together. "Who are all of these women?" she asked Julie.

"Visiting wives and girlfriends?" Julie answered, as they mingled into the crowd towards the hors d'oeuvres table. "Everyone wants to come to Hong Kong for the shopping. But, I'm not sure who they are," Julie added. Brenda really had no interest in meeting or being involved with the wives and she wasn't sure why. Maybe she felt superior because she was *breaking through tradition with her presence onboard the ship.* But WEPS' wife was a neurosurgeon in San Diego, a fact of which he was very proud. Pete's wife had majored in computer science at MIT and worked as a programmer in Tokyo. In a short time, his wife had become proficient in Japanese. Still, many wives seemed to be living out the traditional "Navy wife" role. Whenever she saw what she judged as a housewife living the Navy-housing/Navy-Exchange-and-Commissary-shopping/I-have-four-kids-hanging-off-of-me life, her thoughts usually turned critical.

The traditional Navy wife role entailed a woman following her husband to duty station after duty station, uprooting her children, often not being able to stake out a life of her own. She had heard nothing but complaints about the constant moving and the harm the lifestyle did to marriage and children. The divorce rate among military marriages was high, especially since every aspect of family life had to revolve around the military member's duty. Volumes had been written about the dysfunction and special problems associated with military marriages and children. But then, she stopped mid-thought, and asked herself: Who was *she* to tell others how to live, considering her own performance onboard ship and the decisions *she* had made in her past? No, she was in no position to judge or to tell others how to live.

As Brenda and Julie stood around the hors d'oeuvres table, a woman approached them. "Hello," the woman said, and nothing else.

"Hello...ma'am," Julie responded, clearly caught off-guard by not knowing who the woman was or how to address her.

"Hello," Brenda followed, wondering whether she should refer to the woman before her as ma'am. But curiously the woman didn't respond right away; she stared at them, coldly and intensely. Unnerved, Brenda felt compelled to break the silence, "I'm sorry, I don't know you," she said awkwardly. "Are you a family member, one of the wives or volunteers maybe?" But immediately after she had uttered her inelegant statement, intended to fill an uncomfortable space, she felt her heart jump into her throat. She knew right then that the unknown woman had to be the new XO.

"I'm the reporting Executive Officer, Lieutenant Commander

Heather Gates," the woman returned sharply. Brenda could feel the woman's deep blue eyes piercing her like daggers. "I'm sorry, ma'am, I..."

"How could you know," the new XO interrupted her, but with a style that subtly demeaned the person who had asked the question.

There would be no way, Brenda had thought. "I'm Ensign Conner, ma'am," she introduced herself. She had done exactly what she had hated; she had identified this senior naval officer as a wife or girlfriend, specifically one not in the Navy.

"I'm Ensign Wettlaufer, ma'am," Julie followed. The new XO nodded at them and moved on into the crowd, unfeelingly. Then Brenda and Julie retreated together to an ornately carved wooden bench off to the side, not saying a word to each other.

*

The memory of her introduction to the first female executive officer of an Aegis combatant in history made Brenda shrink inside herself with regret. Still sitting at her table, off to a lone corner, underneath the blaring TV, she looked up to find Julie, Brad, Pete, and Neil heading towards her.

"Trying to get away from everybody?" Brad joked.

"From myself," Brenda answered, and they all joined her at the table.

"You did a great job organizing this event as part of your Bull Ensign duties, Neil," Brenda complimented him, and smiled. According to naval tradition, the most senior ensign, referred to as the Bull Ensign, wore oversized rank insignia on each collar and was responsible for coordinating wardroom social activities. Designating an officer as a Bull Ensign was, by definition, a form of hazing. Brenda had smiled while making her comment to Neil because she knew that he shared her distaste for naval hazing traditions, which were meant to build camaraderie. It seemed as though the biggest fans of those traditions were the Academy graduates, and old-guard conservatives, who seemed to feel that without those traditions the Navy would somehow fall apart. To the latter group, it seemed changes in tradition were threatening.

"Okay, everyone gather around. Let's get the festivities started," the Captain called over the crowd.

"Listen," Pete said. "The Captain's going to say something entirely inappropriate about the departing XO being Filipino, and the oncoming XO being female," he whispered.

"I'm not sure he means anything by it," Brenda answered.

"He's just PC; he goes overboard. I think he does believe it. He believes whatever he's supposed to believe, at least outwardly." She was reminded of a picture that the Captain submitted for the cruise yearbook. In it, in his typical politically correct fashion, he was jointly cutting a cake with three African-American sailors for Black History Month. Was this contrived, real, was he just trying too hard, or...?

"Let's get started, folks," the Captain announced again, and the room quieted immediately. "I'll take the liberty to speak for all of us when I say this night is bittersweet. Because we have to say goodbye to a very well-respected XO, with whom we have been proud to serve. But we also eagerly and graciously welcome a new XO to the *Curtis Wilbur* wardroom. And I'm sure she'll be no less than stellar, and succeed proudly as your XO."

Brenda glanced over at the new XO. She was seated one table away from the Captain, staring at him without expression, her small blue eyes intense. The Captain continued, "You folks have done an amazing job during deployment. I am proud to have served with all of you. You're some of the finest officers our fleet has to offer. Our ship's reputation is second to none in the Seventh Fleet. The rear admiral regards *Curtis Wilbur* as one of the finest ships in the Navy. And our finest hour just might have been when the ship absolutely shone those many times when we were alongside the aircraft carrier."

"I guess he doesn't care that the gun and missile systems are down," Brenda whispered.

"We look shiny," Brad said.

Neil smiled, and Julie remained focused on the Captain, as he continued, "This Hail & Farewell marks history, and we should all feel the pride that comes with playing a true part in an historical event. As we are all aware, it was not too long ago that Filipinos by law served as stewards onboard Navy ships."

Brenda looked over at Pete. "Totally inappropriate," he said as he was shaking his head.

"We've come a long way in the military as evidenced by our festivities tonight. The fact that we have a Filipino XO is a credit to the Navy." The Captain extended his arm towards the incumbent XO, Lieutenant Commander Navarro, who nodded, as if on cue. Brenda noticed Pete looking exasperated, and she smiled. The Captain continued, "A Filipino XO is being relieved by the first female XO of a U.S. Navy Aegis destroyer, Lieutenant Commander

Heather Gates. We all share the privilege of witnessing this event. So, to Lieutenant Commander Navarro, I say thank you for your outstanding service as XO of *Curtis Wilbur*, one of the finest DDGs in the fleet today, and to Lieutenant Commander Gates, welcome to one of the finest DDGs in the fleet today." The Captain extended his hand to Lieutenant Commander Gates, and she smiled complacently, showing little emotion.

"Inappropriate, amazing," Pete repeated.

"I'm not sure how much criticism he deserves," Brenda said quietly. "He is open to diversity. He's what the SWO community creates; he's an all-around phony and careerist, trying to speak about breaking down barriers for minorities and women with no heart behind his words. He's probably close to the best you can expect." Brenda paused for a reaction from Pete. "I'm not defending him, necessarily," she continued when she saw little agreement in his face, "but within the context of SWO, I think he meant well."

"I disagree," Pete said.

Chapter 36: The XO next door ... Maybe something good can come of this ... Girl power ... With or without a role model

Brenda had begun to hear sounds of cruelty from across the passageway. She feared cruelty, feeling the infliction of it was the worst of human evils because it was intentional. She entered her stateroom and gently closed her door, so as not to alert anyone to her presence. She was conscious of the way sound and movement echoed throughout the metal ship. *"What the fuck are you doing, CSO?"* she heard the new XO scream, in the stateroom across the passageway. She stood silent behind her stateroom door, dressed in Navy whites, her ear an inch or so away from the door, her hand gripping the knob. She wanted to listen to this woman; she longed to learn about her; she wanted to hear her voice, her intonation, how she chose to speak to those subordinate to her authority and leadership, how she phrased her questions, if she possessed the capacity to feel.

She knew she was eavesdropping, but she justified that her desire to listen was fair. For the next year of her life, she would be subject to the power afforded this woman by her position as XO. In the Navy, assignment as the ship's executive officer gave one authority over every operational, managerial, and administrative detail onboard. Caught in those details were the officers and sailors who performed the work. There were no set work schedules onboard Navy ships, per se. Under the umbrella of the Captain, the XO decided when individual officers and sailors could go on liberty, on leave (vacation), or if they would even be allowed to leave the ship on a given night – all based upon shipboard demands. Inadvertently, XOs decided how often the residents of Navy ships could see their families, or if they could try for a personal life.

She wished she could have just dismissed what she had heard, or even decided that she had overreacted to what she had heard, but the new XO really had screamed so vilely *"What the fuck are you doing, CSO?"* at the ship's most senior department head. Late last night, the new XO had moved into the empty stateroom across the passageway; she was to reside there until the current XO departed in Okinawa.

Brenda remembered when she had first realized that the new XO would be temporarily living across the passageway from her. It was before duty section muster in the morning. She had just taken a shower and had stepped out of the women's head wearing a bathrobe, when at the far end of the passageway, she had spotted the new XO walking toward her. "Good morning, ma'am," she had greeted her, hugging her towel, shampoo, and conditioner to her chest. But for a few seconds, she heard no reply from the new XO. Not knowing what to do, she waited as the new XO continued towards her, up the passageway. Just before the new XO reached the door to the empty stateroom, she acknowledged her. "Hello, Ensign. I'll be your neighbor for a while," she said, before disappearing inside.

"Yes, ma'am, welcome," Brenda replied before the new XO's door was completely shut. Then, she escaped back into her stateroom feeling jolted and embarrassed over the interaction. Why did she have to run into the new XO just after exiting the shower? Was it appropriate for an ensign to "welcome" an oncoming XO? Then, she started to understand that, for the time being, while the XO lived across the passageway, her stateroom would cease to be her place of refuge and solace where she could think and be herself. She and Julie had been fortunate to live at the end of a dead end passageway, next to the female head. For so long, no one besides the supply officer ever ventured down their way. Each day in the Navy somehow became worse than the one before, she thought. She would now feel on edge, nervous and afraid, even in her stateroom.

At SWOS, the instructors regularly gave advice on handling SWO XOs who were "screamers": They said to listen, remain calm and quiet, and answer, "Yes, sir," once the screaming XO was finished. But a few hours after duty section muster, at around midmorning, she had learned that the new XO was going to reach beyond the conventional and stereotyped SWO XO screamer. She had learned this at the expense of her department head, WEPS.

At around ten a.m., she had freed up some time to study. She sat down at her stateroom desk, holding a cup of hot jasmine tea, ready to memorize some of the more common engineering casualty control (EOCC) procedures, which she hoped would allow her to answer more of Todd's engineering questions on the bridge. But after about ten minutes of studying, she heard the new XO start to scream at WEPS in her stateroom across the passageway. She knew it was WEPS in there because she had heard him knock on the XO's door and greet her when he had walked in. While sitting at her desk, she had listened and waited while the crassness and the yelling ran its course. She had remained immobile in her chair, cupping her tea, knowing she was powerless to help WEPS in any way. When the new XO had finished, when she had heard WEPS reply "yes, ma'am" before closing the door and exiting, she had collapsed her head into her palms, trying to rub the headache out of her forehead.

In the span of one morning – the new XO's first morning onboard – Brenda had confirmed her original suspicions, and her initial impression, that Lieutenant Commander Gates was cold and probably cruel. It was heartbreaking to realize that there *was* truth to the rumors that Lieutenant Commander Heather Gates was an angry tyrant. So why had the Navy selected Gates as the service's rising female star?

Before the ship pulled into Hong Kong, she had hoped against hope that the chatter circulating about Lieutenant Commander Gates would turn out to be false. However, even then, she feared that the rumors might be valid because she had overheard WEPS and CSO speaking privately. CSO remembered Heather Gates from the Naval Academy, where as an upperclassman, she had mercilessly screamed at the plebes; she had used her position of authority to harass and torment those subordinate to her.

Brenda knew that she needed to start her midday duty section rounds soon, but she remained just inside her stateroom door, listening as CSO briefed the new XO on the shipboard system for rotating JOs through various watchstations and monitoring their progress towards SWO qualification. Realizing that she would soon be subject to the new XO's rants as well, she tried to stay calm. She thought of Rob, and how he regularly told her that things would only get better; she trusted Rob, but she feared that he would turn out to be wrong.

Before Brenda had returned to her stateroom to grab a quick snack before duty section rounds, she had felt uplifted. After breakfast, the Captain had signed off on her qualification for her first real watch, one she knew she could handle: officer of the deck (OOD) inport on the quarterdeck. After spending most of the deployment standing the watch under instruction, she felt prepared to take her first watch as the actual OOD inport during the afternoon. Some responsibility would finally rest upon *her*. Now, however, with the new XO onboard, she dreaded to ever venture out of her stateroom again.

"That's not what I wanted to know," she heard the new XO scream at CSO. *"I want to know why I'm on the fucking watchbill to conn the ship out of Hong Kong, CSO?"* She could picture the new XO glaring at CSO, with her small deep-set blue eyes. *"Aren't you the fucking senior watch officer,"* she raised her voice, *"in charge of writing the watchbill? I'm going to be the XO of this ship! Don't you ever put me on the goddamned fucking watchbill again unless I order you to do so!"* Brenda heard an object hit the door, something thrown, possibly a water bottle or another type of plastic container.

"Yes, ma'am," CSO answered.

"Why did you put me on the watchbill in the first place?" the new XO challenged. Brenda could feel the defensiveness and insecurity behind the new XO's question. It was a fact that Lieutenant Commander Gates did not possess the amount of experience that was usually required in order to serve as the XO of an Arleigh Burke guided missile destroyer; but Brenda now wondered *if she lacked ability in basic shiphandling as well!* She questioned how that could have been. Lieutenant Commander Gates had at least served aboard non-combatant ships. Women had been serving as surface warfare officers aboard non-combatant ships (albeit not in large numbers), such as oilers and tenders, since the late '70s. She should have had basic shiphandling and seamanship down. Her lack of experience would then have only been in weapons, operations, and combat systems.

But Julie had commented on the liberty boat ride to Hong Kong that someone had figured out that both Rob and Jon the navigator, as division officers, had more sea time than the new XO. Brad had said that he had heard that she hadn't even served a normal department head tour. Her career path was a mystery, and as far as anyone could tell, unpublished. It was strange because SWOs usually loved to boast about their career paths.

She thought of the awkward moment between the new XO, herself, and Julie in the Chinese restaurant on the night before, when the new XO acted so strangely during their short introductory interaction. The new XO had approached them and immediately stared straight at them, expressionless. Her blue eyes had penetrated into them, without breaking the stare, belittling them into submission until they felt so uneasy that they said something awkward to break the silence; the new XO had made them feel small. Brenda was reminded of an animal that might stare down another one, not breaking eye contact, as a way of establishing dominance…it gave the feeling of a predator sizing up its prey. Certainly, the aggressive stare had made Brenda feel unimportant, submissive. Just thinking about it made her ill-at-ease, and she wondered if she could have responded in some other way…one that hadn't subjected her to a position of feeling awkward and inconsequential.

In contrast, the new XO could have walked up to them and introduced herself as a professional officer should have, instead of standing directly in front of them and contentiously staring into their eyes for too many intimidating seconds. The encounter had felt weird, bizarre, socially awkward. Brenda didn't want to excuse her own responsibility; she had responded compulsively out of age-old prejudices (innocently enough) by asking if Gates was a family member, officer's wife, or volunteer.

Then she heard CSO answer the new XO's question as to why he had put her on the watchbill to conn out of Hong Kong. "At the request of the Captain, ma'am," he responded. "Symbolically, newly arriving officers usually conn the ship out of port, and departing officers conn the ship in. It's one of the Captain's traditions."

"*I'll speak to the Captain. Remove me from the watchbill and replace me with an ensign in need of training. Now, get the fuck out of my stateroom,*" she finished, her voice hushed and coarse. Her rantings struck Brenda as those of an unstable person. Brenda listened for CSO to leave. After giving him a moment to clear the passageway, she slipped out her stateroom door.

Outside the skin of the ship, the sun glimmered over the green mountains that framed the Hong Kong skyline. Brenda stood back from the quarterdeck for a moment to allow her eyes to adjust to the daylight from the dim lighting inside the ship. But she felt ready to take her first official OOD inport watch.

"Ma'am, this is the women's quarterdeck watch coming up," Seaman Chapman called to her as she approached the podium. "I'll be your MOOW."

"Perfect, I need a good messenger of the watch, Seaman," Brenda replied, as she walked over to speak with the offgoing OOD. She had stood watch regularly with Seaman Chapman, both on the bridge and on the quarterdeck. The seaman had related her personal story to her – enlisting in the Navy from an inner-city Chicago high school, her readiness to find a new life. The recruiter had promised her enlisted journalism school right out of boot camp, but she served instead as a nonrated deck seaman. She spent her days engaged in work such as hanging from the side of the ship, seated on a wooden board eased down by ropes, as she painted and scraped at the haze gray hull. It was important work, but a far different scenario from what the recruiter had promised her. The seaman had confided to Brenda that she cried every day, especially during the hard labor of day-to-day deck work. Her dislike for those jobs had grown intense enough that she feared how many more days she could survive working on the decks until she was able to take the journalist rating (JO) entrance exam.

Lately, Brenda had found herself emotionally invested in the seaman's success; she felt angry towards the recruiter in Chicago for luring Seaman Chapman into the Navy, when he would have known from her test scores that she wouldn't be sent directly to enlisted "A" school for journalism. After boot camp, right after high school, some recruits were sent to enlisted "A" school, where they directly learned a skillset, or rating (similar to a "trade" in the civilian world). Graduation from enlisted "A" school enabled a young seaman to start his or her time in the Navy within a rating; for example, a gunners mate seaman (GMSN) after graduating from "A" school, would immediately start their time in the Navy in a gunnery division. But not all new recruits had the benefit of a good high school, and/or good test scores, and some landed in the Navy as nonrated deck seamen, without the immediate benefit of going to "A" school to acquire a rating. Nonrated deck seaman was considered the lowest of the lowest positions in the Navy. And it was challenging to work one's way up from a deck seaman. The recruiter in Chicago would have known Seaman Chapman's immediate plight from her test scores.

Brenda couldn't remember exactly when she had become interested in the seaman's welfare. It had happened gradually as she noticed how bright the seaman was, how much potential she had, and how far into despair she had fallen. The seaman simply hadn't had the benefit of a good high school. Julie was Seaman Chapman's division officer; but as bright and as technically competent as Julie was, she seemed somewhat oblivious to the personal career paths of the seamen in her division. Since help with studying and writing was something Brenda could offer the seaman, she had started to mentor Seaman Chapman for the journalism exam. *"Maybe something good can come of my days onboard..."* Brenda had pled, as if with God – if only she could help her division and Seaman Chapman and others like her. A few weeks ago, she had asked Julie if she minded if she helped Seaman Chapman, and Julie had offhandedly commented that it was fine with her.

"And TM2 Dobbs is the petty officer of the watch, ma'am," the seaman added when Brenda had finished turning over with the offgoing OOD.

"Girl power," TM2 winked as she took the 9mm pistol holster from the offgoing POOW.

"I liked Hong Kong," Seaman Chapman said. "And I'm actually here," she exclaimed. "I can't believe it sometimes."

"Request permission to sound three gongs for the liberty boat, ma'am," TM2 Dobbs asked Brenda.

"Very well, sound three gongs for the liberty boat," Brenda replied. "Petty Officer Dobbs," she added. "The passdown log states to sound the gongs in officers country today as well, since it's the last day of liberty. The offgoing OOD backed that up."

"Yes, ma'am," Petty Officer Dobbs replied; she sounded three gongs throughout the ship.

"Ma'am, it's exciting about the new XO," Seaman Chapman started. "It's inspiring. It makes me think I can set goals and accomplish them in my life. She's a role model for me, for all of us."

"She certainly is a new development," Brenda answered the seaman, "in our society and in the Navy. Remember that you're smart and capable with or without a role model. You stand a vigilant watch on the bridge; you're studying for the journalism exam. You have a lot ahead."

"True, ma'am. She still seems amazing," the seaman reaffirmed.

Brenda nodded, and then the new XO appeared out of the skin of the ship. Lieutenant Commander Gates approached the quarterdeck, dressed in civilian clothes – shorts, sandals, and a sleeveless blouse – her long blond hair tied back into a ponytail. The quarterdeck watch saluted her. She walked up to Brenda, stood in front of her and stared. Brenda's heart pounded out of her chest.

"How can we help you, ma'am?" she asked.

"I don't need your help, Ensign," she glared.

"Yes, ma'am," Brenda responded.

Still standing in front of her, the new XO looked over at TM2 Dobbs for a moment; then she turned and faced Brenda again. "Tell your petty officer of the watch over there," the new XO began, right in front of TM2, "never to sound a nonemergency announcement in officers country again. Got it?"

Brenda looked at the new XO, wondering why she hadn't admonished her in private, as the Navy taught – to praise in public and criticize in private. It was her first watch as OOD inport, and the new XO had undermined it. More importantly, however, Brenda wondered if the new XO realized that she had just established her reputation in the eyes of the crew. She had shown extreme disrespect towards TM2, standing two steps away from her, and talking about her as if she wasn't there. TM2, who was a respected and tough senior petty officer, would for sure set the story loose around the ship.

"Yes, ma'am," Brenda simply replied, sorry for herself, the seaman, and the torpedoman second class (TM2), that this woman had somehow been selected as the Navy's chosen representative for women's progress.

The new XO continued. "When we pull into Okinawa, no one will leave for liberty wearing open-toe shoes, or a sleeveless or collarless shirt."

"Yes, ma'am," Brenda answered, surprised because Lieutenant Commander Gates was wearing open-toe shoes and a sleeveless shirt. The interaction had grown strange. She couldn't imagine why the new XO had decided to relay dress code policy information to *her*, which should have been promulgated administratively down the chain of command. Brenda turned to address Petty Officer Dobbs. "TM2, sound two gongs to indicate the liberty boat will depart in five minutes. Don't sound the gongs in officers country."

"Yes, ma'am," TM2 Dobbs responded, and disappeared into the quarterdeck shack, displaying a defiant and confident acquiescence, sourced from ten years in the Navy.

Brenda watched as the new XO left the quarterdeck, and headed down the steps to board the liberty boat. CSO, who was also on duty that day standing command duty officer, passed by the quarterdeck to drop off the sea and anchor watchbill. "Good news," he said to Brenda. "You'll be conning out of Hong Kong tomorrow morning," he smiled. "This will help you get ahead on your SWO PQS. *Conn the ship through an anchoring evolution*," he quoted from the PQS book, before disappearing aft towards the fantail. Then, Brenda saw WEPS scurry past her to catch up with the new XO. Brenda hurried down the steps, wanting to ask WEPS why he would go anywhere with the new XO. "Brenda," he said, out of earshot of the POOW and MOOW, "I almost missed the liberty boat because you didn't sound the gongs in officers country." And then he stepped onto the boat.

The liberty boat departed the ship, and the three women – officer, petty officer, and seaman – remained silent for the remainder of the four-hour watch.

Chapter 37: Brenda the administrator ... Survival acceptance of the inevitable ... A flat hatter ... A growing awareness ... The "B" team

Brenda sat in front of one of the common-use computers in the combat systems maintenance central (CSMC) office, approving repair parts orders in the shipboard non-tactical ADP program, the Navy's computerized supply network, also known as SNAP. GMM2 Finn, the division repair parts petty officer (RPPO), initiated all supply orders for the division in the SNAP system, from rags to 5"/54 gun and VLS parts; those orders were then sent for approval through the system to the chiefs; and from there, she usually received an urgent call to her stateroom, or anywhere Petty Officer Finn could find her on the ship, pleading with her, "Ma'am, please get down to CSMC and approve the orders in your SNAP queue, please!"

She always complied immediately; she wanted to support the division in any way she could. To ensure the orders were legitimate and necessary, she depended on the chiefs. At first, she had asked them about each and every order, but after a while she had come to trust them, and she had learned a little more about which details to delve into and which ones to let flow. Chief Walden generally responded to her questions with patience and understanding, but Chief Dering responded to most of her questions with eye rolls and exasperated sighs, and always with coffee mug in hand, stained black inside. Knowing almost nothing about the gun and missile systems, she felt self-conscious around Chief Dering, who seemed endlessly frustrated and tired of explaining everything to her, someone he knew would soon rotate to a different job – and she worried – someone who he thought didn't have the aptitude for the concepts.

She approved the last order, and started to get up out of her chair when she noticed Petty Officer Mimms come through the door.

"Hello, ma'am," he greeted her dryly, as if saying hello to her had tried his last nerve.

"Hello, Petty Officer Mimms," she answered, as he approached her chair.

"Here's the ammo admin message for the upcoming SM-2 and

harpoon missile onload, ma'am," he said, handing her the printout of the Navy message, along with a floppy disc to route to radio.

"Thank you, Petty Officer Mimms," she said. "You do an incredible job at this."

"Verify the coding yourself, ma'am," he said.

"I'll see all the coding is correct, Petty Officer," she said patiently, as she reached for the manual from him.

"Here's the coding from the manual, ma'am," he said. She searched through the coding requirements on the pages he had marked off in the manual and compared them against the message. She wasn't surprised to find a perfectly coded ammunition administration message, which was no small feat since the manual for the program was a three hundred page soup of letters and numbers in strings of codes.

"Thank you for the perfect message, Petty Officer Mimms. I'll route it to the Captain."

"Yes, ma'am," she heard him say, as he dogged down (fastened) the door leading out of combat systems maintenance central (CSMC) and left her. Ah, whatever, she smiled to herself. His response had improved from his standard, "Whatever, ma'am," which had usually accompanied more blatant mannerisms of belligerence and disapproval. She could count on him for honesty.

She had cautiously sensed progress in relating to Petty Officer Mimms. She had talked to Chief Walden about giving him more responsibility, in line with a first class petty officer. Petty Officer Brooks was two months senior to Petty Officer Mimms, so most of the leading petty officer responsibilities fell on him. But GMM1 Mimms also needed the experience. She thought he had earned and deserved the right to be assigned more leadership and management tasks. The division had written off Mimms for his eccentricity, but she believed he had talent to offer. She accepted his ways up to a point. At times she cut him off sharply, but she never raised her voice and she always remained respectful. "One could say you're Petty Officer Mimms' number one advocate," WEPS had said to her once in his stateroom while she was routing an ammo admin message.

"Yes, you could, sir," she answered.

"It's your choice, be careful," he warned.

"It's my choice, sir," she had replied, before leaving to route the message to the XO.

Relentlessly, she countered Petty Officer Mimms' pushbacks,

stressing the importance of his job to him, asserting to him that his work was the most professional she had seen onboard. Ironically, she could depend on him to do his job correctly every time, with a higher percentage of follow-through than she had seen from anyone else in the division. Sometimes she felt in the middle of a game with Petty Officer Mimms – who would give in first? His job was vital. She needed him to keep doing it. He was the only one onboard who understood the ammo program. And maybe she could get through to him.

It was afternoon and she felt in good spirits for a change. Before lunch, she had survived "conning the ship underway from an anchorage," as CSO had quoted from the line item in the SWO PQS book. She left the CSMC space and carried her positive feelings and energy with her through the haze gray passageways, on her way to meet Chief Walden in the VLS. Her workday was planned. After checking in with Chief Walden regarding the missile onload, she would route the ammo admin message up the chain of command.

But an incessant undercurrent always pulled at her, reminding her of reality. That morning, following her reading of the navigation brief to a crowded wardroom filled with sea and anchor watchstanders, she had climbed the dual ladders to the towering bridge, not knowing what to expect: She had no idea how to conn an 8,000-ton warship out of anchorage and she hadn't seen it done before. Recently, she had ascended beyond nervousness and fear over her shipboard watches, and into a state she could best describe as sort of a 'survival acceptance of the inevitable,' of whatever might happen, and an equal acceptance of the condition that she was powerless over changing her life while in the Navy.

She had gotten another major line item in her SWO PQS book signed off, but she didn't feel she could righteously be considered adept at carrying out an anchoring evolution. *She had performed it once!* She had accepted the signature because the months were ticking by and she had to earn her SWO qualification prior to the eighteen month mark. Secretly, she even hoped that enough other JOs would need training that she wouldn't have to conn through an anchoring evolution ever again. She didn't feel too proud of herself.

She saw Petty Officer Finn approaching her in the passageway. "I approved those orders in SNAP, Petty Officer Finn," she assured him.

"Thanks, ma'am," he said. "But stop, I've got to fix your hat. I can't let my division officer walk around the ship with a flat hat brim. The other guys will make fun of me. My DIVO can't be a flat hatter. You do it on purpose, ma'am."

"Fix it, please, and then I've got to meet Chief in the VLS," she laughed.

She let Petty Officer Finn bend the rim of her ballcap before she swung the door to the VLS open. Chief Walden had already reassured her that all of the checklists and equipment were in order for the upcoming missile onload, and that the GMMs – the gunners mates (missiles) – were prepared. "We'll take care of everything," he had repeated to her over and again. She had no choice but to trust him in his work – work that involved use of a shipboard VLS crane to lower a 15-foot guided missile, weighing over 1500 pounds, equipped with a 130-pound warhead, designed to travel over a speed of Mach 3.5, into a narrow missile canister on the aft deck.

She made her way through the rows and columns of missile canisters, relieved that Chief Walden's personality and character differed entirely from that of Chief Dering's. Unlike Chief Dering, Chief Walden generally kept her informed. She knew that he told her what she wanted to hear, and fed her a minimal amount of information. But he seemed to understand just how much information kept the chain of command out of the division's business. In SWOS, the instructors regularly gave the following advice: If you have a SWO XO or department head who's a micromanager, keep him busy with enough "other" information so he won't constantly be prying and micromanaging your division to death in a zero-defect way. She had found the concept outrageous, but SWO JOs seemed to talk about it all the time as if it was acceptable management practice. She didn't do that; she told her boss everything.

Chief Walden had effectively managed the troubleshooting effort to clear the VLS CASREPs, so the system had become fully operational again. And she had decided that she couldn't ask for much more.

She entered the main VLS space and saw that Chief Walden and GMM2 Marcello had organized a series of checklists and schematics across a bulletin board. The sight shot waves of shame through her for being a gunnery officer who had never grasped the technical reasons underlying why the VLS had ever been CASREP'd.

Onboard, recalling her memories had become painful because she had developed an awareness of what those memories meant, and of the truth behind them. Standing in the VLS looking at the schematics, she was shaken. She imagined herself back in Visual Thinking class, a class she had taken second semester freshman year of engineering school. She had hated the class because it was unstructured and designed to encourage engineering creativity: There were no tests or specific problem set assignments. Over the course of the semester, the students had to create a portfolio of engineering design concepts. She had only succeeded in the engineering classes in which she could memorize equations and find the right numbers to substitute into those equations.

In the Visual Thinking class, the students' primary project consisted of designing and building a small remote control car, which they had to race at the end of the semester. Her classmates were unanimously excited about the upcoming competition and chance to show off their engineering prowess; but she couldn't think of anything she would rather have done less. She partnered with her friend Kevin who understood exactly how to go about the project. One day she approached him with a schematic showing some wires, a battery, a motor, and other components. Kevin looked at her with a quizzical expression, and asked if she had gotten it from her dad. She had; and she knew what it meant to tell him she had. Using her dad's schematic, Kevin single-handedly built a formidable car that did well in the races. She did the write-up. They got an A.

"Don't worry. You don't have to know all of this. That's not your job," Chief Walden began. "But I do want to explain some basics," he said. Chief Walden had a soft manner of speech. "This way you can learn for yourself, and be able to explain if anyone up the chain asks."

Symbolically, Brenda imagined there to be a knowledge line, that junior officers, chiefs, and enlisted technicians could be found on, at various points; and she had never been sure where she, as an ensign, was supposed to be on that line. Thinking of her own lack of knowledge, she wondered, how much did Pete, Rob, Neil, and Julie really understand with regard to the various billets they held? She knew they lacked the detail of their enlisted technicians. But how much did they know? "I appreciate your time, Chief," Brenda answered.

"It'll keep them off our backs," the chief added. She understood exactly to whom "*them*" referred. The chief lived a paradoxical existence, antiestablishment by nature but existing within and under the ultimate establishment of the military. He was an enlisted chief, but also an enigma; he wasn't the average "blue collar" chief in appearance or manner. He came across as more of a creative, free spirit. Outside his military duties as a lead gunners mate technician, he engaged in the study of arts and literature. To Brenda, he clearly seemed an artistic introvert, out of place in the military. She didn't understand what he was doing in the Navy; he was hiding onboard the ship from the world, possibly. Why not get out?

"Here," he handed her a typewritten paper. His tone always sounded unassuming. "I've jotted some notes for you to study and carry around." She spent the next half hour listening about computer checks, loading sequence electronics, and much more that she couldn't name. She wished she could have thanked him for the lesson by understanding more of what he was trying to teach her. But as much as she wanted to learn, another part of her also wondered how much of herself she needed to invest in this information. After a few months, she would be moving on. In her career path as a surface warfare officer, especially as a surface nuclear officer, she might never again work with the VLS.

When Chief Walden had pointed to the last schematic in the row on the bulletin board, she spotted some college text books on the VLS desk. "Whose are these?" she asked, opening the cover of one.

"Some are mine; some are Petty Officer Marcello's," the chief answered.

"Correspondence classes?"

"My PhD. Marcello's working on his associates degree."

"For use outside the Navy?" Brenda asked.

Chief Walden went silent. Petty Officer Marcello spoke up. "I've thought about applying for an ROTC scholarship in engineering to become a nuke. But...I don't care too much for the Navy at times," he laughed, "so I'll probably get out and use the GI Bill to go to college and get a real job. I might need a letter of recommendation from you, ma'am."

"I'll help you in any way to apply to those programs. You would do well in ROTC, or better yet, on the outside." She and Petty Officer Marcello had sometimes laughed because they had discovered that she was two months younger than him. It was a dynamic that amused both of them, being in their early twenties. And in this case, she could write him a formal letter of recommendation, signed by his "supervising division officer." As a division officer, she was constantly instructed by the Navy that it was her job to encourage bright petty officers to stay in the Navy. She had found that concept to create an ethical dilemma. As a human being, she felt it was wrong for her to use her position to persuade anyone to stay in this Navy life. So she had tried to remain neutral, advising the petty officers and seamen to follow what they felt was their own path. Only they could determine whether staying in was right for them or not.

"What about your PhD., Chief?" she asked.

"I'm studying philosophy."

"I'm unsurprised," she smiled. Every facet of society lived onboard the ship.

The chief reached into his back pocket for his wallet. "Some pictures of my family," he showed her.

"Thanks for showing me, Chief," she managed, trying to show interest. She considered the chief's family a personal matter but since she liked and felt grateful for Chief Walden, she looked at the pictures. "They look like nice kids," she said. And they really did, she thought. But the family looked large, and to take care of so many children, especially under conditions of prolonged absence on a forward deployed ship, and on a chief's salary. "I'm sure the separation must pain you, Chief," she said. She resented the way the military consumed family life.

"I've spent my career stationed in Asia. My wife's from the Philippines. We plan to retire there. I never plan to live stateside again. She never has and I've never fit in in the States. I prefer the lifestyle in the Philippines, the community living. In my wife's village, the kids play together, families live together, help one another."

"I used to meet a lot of Filipina women in Subic Bay," the chief continued. Brenda hardened. She had heard of American servicemen treating Asian women as if they were trash and marrying them as if they were objects. And she had heard of Asian women marrying these men for economics, using them, and praying on their homesickness, all to escape their own circumstances of poverty. Chief Walden was losing her. "I wrote a bunch of them," he continued. "Something about this one was different, her letters." He had referred to Asian women as "them" and as "one," as if they were merely a pool of potential wives or objects of sexual fulfillment for men. She had heard the guys talk about how Asian wives and girlfriends were "submissive," which she doubted was actually true. She wondered about the *true* feelings of these "submissive" women.

"We've been married many years. We're very happy," he finished, seeming sincere.

"She looks like a nice woman who loves her family," Brenda replied, looking at the photo.

"I'd like to introduce you to her," he said.

Brenda couldn't imagine what she might have in common with a housewife with four children, but she had also learned that she had a lot to learn. "Thank you, Chief," she replied, deciding his offer to meet his wife was a compliment. Chief Walden was a lost soul in the world, and she did like him. "I'd like to meet her," she added, after a pause.

Then she turned the conversation from the personal. "You're the only chief onboard with a coffee mug that's clean and white inside. Chief Dering's is stained black, black."

Chief Walden smiled, and turned to address her before exiting the space, "Because I'm on the 'B Team', like you are."

She stood, stunned, and just breathed. Petty Officer Marcello laughed. "It's alright, ma'am," he said. "You wouldn't want to be on the 'A team', would you?"

She said nothing for a moment before she joined him in laughing. "Maybe it's okay... that it's true what you guys are saying," she shook her head. They were right, she realized. She wouldn't want to be on the "A team," as some kind of "company man." She just hoped she could one day get out of all of this – the ship and the military – clean, never to look back.

Chapter 38: Messages ... ROTC flashback: cornered in an attic ... Screening flak

Brenda secured the door to CIC behind her. Then she made her way around the maze of consoles and computer equipment directly to where WEPS was seated at the TAO chair, facing the overhead large screen displays that showed the navigational and tactical picture for the battle group.

"What do you have for me, Brenda?" WEPS asked quietly, as he continued looking forward at the displays.

"The ammo admin message for the SM-2 and harpoon missile onload, sir. For your signature," she smiled, as she handed him the folder containing the message.

"And you're sure it's right," he stated casually. His words sounded as calm as the atmosphere in the space. No multi-ship exercises were in progress and the watch appeared fairly relaxed. She took in a breath, in preparation to answer. "Ah, ah," he said, raising his palm, smiling as he waved her off. He placed his hand back down to hold the folder in place while he initialed the message. "I don't want any blasts," he said honestly. "You know what I mean, not with this new XO."

Hand routing messages up the chain filled the majority of division officer workdays. It was not uncommon for DIVOs to spend an entire day running back and forth over changes made here and there in a message. Navy messages were subject to high visibility by other ships in the squadron and by higher-ups such as the squadron and fleet commanders. Over the last few months, she and Petty Officer Mimms had achieved a 100% rate of accuracy on their ammo admin messages. Brenda gave herself some of the credit. She had come to understand the program fairly well, and she had caught and corrected a few glitches in his messages before routing them up the chain.

"From what I can tell from the manual, it's correct, sir," Brenda started. "I'm confident in it, but sometimes I feel like these messages are somewhat of a gamble every time they go out." After she finished her last word, a call came in from the carrier to which WEPS had to respond. She looked around CIC while she waited for him to finish the call. She always tried to be as honest with WEPS as she could about her feelings, how she really felt about what was going on and about what they were doing. To her he seemed reasonable and realistic, and tolerant of (if not humored at times by) her particular bent on the Navy. She envisioned that many other department heads would not have accepted much of what she had to say, and especially not her last statement admitting the uncertainty of the ammo messages. In her head she could hear some imaginary, nondescript SWO department head snapping back, "That's not want I want to hear, Ensign. Is it correct or not?" The truth was that she couldn't guarantee error-free coding, so how could she say otherwise? She had only just started learning about the ammo program a few months ago.

Onboard, she had learned about taking risk and about trudging forward even if the outcome was uncertain. She had gained a willingness to accept the consequences of going forward based on trial and error, and to work through new circumstances as they arose, whether they were comfortable or uncomfortable for her.

In her mind, she could still hear the stern reprimand she had received from one of the lieutenant instructors at her ROTC unit just after she had been commissioned. His reprimand and treatment of her had served as her first glaring and undeniable sign that she had made a catastrophic and irreversible mistake in committing herself to the Navy. The reprimand had been traumatic because afterwards, she could no longer deny that she was out of place in the military; she would always be out of place, and that condition would never change as she had originally thought it would, as if by magic or through some other mysterious means. She had survived her time in ROTC based on one underlying assumption: Once she graduated and got commissioned, the contrariety she had experienced in ROTC would disappear – she would suddenly and instinctually understand all things technical, along with seamanship and shipboard engineering, and she would fit into the Navy, and develop the ability to get along fine within its rules, regulations, outlook, and culture.

The sound of background radio chatter began to intensify in CIC. The group of operations specialists (OSs) who were seated in front of their respective consoles, all wearing headphones, were preparing for an air intercept control exercise. In the midst of the increasing activity in CIC, she thought back to the first day she had reported for official duty in the Navy as an ensign, when the reprimand had occurred. After she was commissioned (following

Long Way Out 295

graduation from college), she had some lag time before SWOS started in Newport, so she had to report for temporary duty at her ROTC unit in Boston in the meantime. On a beautiful and warm summer morning in the city, she had entered the brownstone that housed the NROTC unit for her first day of official duty, no longer as a college student midshipman but as a commissioned ensign. After closing the vintage glass-paneled front doors behind her, she walked into the mahogany-lined foyer, and noticed the building was summer empty – she was at the ROTC unit when none of the students were there. She stood immobile, just breathing. The reality had suddenly hit her that, unlike her student days, her military career no longer existed in some far out future. It was going to begin that morning. As she started up the winding staircase in the back corner of the foyer, on her way to find the other ensigns that had been "stashed" at the unit, awaiting their various Navy intro schools to start (SWOS, flight school, submarine school, etc.), she felt the weighted certainty that not much would go well for her from that point on. Nothing felt right. She remembered how dark the staircase was, lit only by a few rays of sun that passed through the curtains over the entrance doors.

"You're an engineer, you can find a way to get all of these old computers and printers running," the aviator lieutenant instructor had approached her later that afternoon. She was seated at a desk, eating her lunch alone in the office which had been temporarily assigned to the small group of "stashed" ensigns.

The manner in which the lieutenant entered the room and spoke to her was unnerving. She looked around the cramped and musty office. She was trapped in a converted attic, segregated on its own floor from the other offices of the four story brownstone. "Do you want this as your project, Miss Conner?" he asked, almost accusingly.

"Yes, sir," she answered, knowing she had no other choice. She remembered fearing him in those moments. On that afternoon, he appeared angry and aggressive, and she knew he could get away with conducting himself as he pleased.

"How long will it take you, Miss Conner, to hook up all this equipment?" he asked, pointing to a stack of dilapidated boxes filled with disheveled computer equipment. She remembered her nervousness. As a new ensign, she wanted to make a good impression and she wanted to please.

"Sir," she started as she looked around, not wanting to

disappoint him. "I'm not sure if everything's here. I'll start by surveying what we have, to find out if the right programs are included, if they can be installed, if the necessary equipment is here, if it can all be hooked up, or if it still even works. I'll talk to the other ensigns. As soon as I open these boxes, I'll give you an estimate, sir. When do you need it for?"

The lieutenant cornered her in the cramped-in room, underneath a low slanted gable. "When your department head on your ship asks you for an estimate," he chastised her, "he'll want an exact timeframe." She backed up against the wall, not knowing what to say to him; she wasn't sure whether the project would take her two hours, two days, two weeks, or whether she'd be able to get the '80s-looking equipment running at all.

"I'll need two days, sir," she said, hoping to cover herself. "But if you can tell me when you need the project completed?"

"That's an unacceptable response, Miss Conner. Your department head on your ship is not going to accept that kind of answer," he admonished her. When he turned to leave, the SWO lieutenant instructor, who she had known as an unreasonable and slightly cruel instructor, stepped into the room and interjected threateningly, "That's right, Miss Conner. When your department head on your ship asks for an answer, he'll want a definitive one." She couldn't tell, but it seemed as though they gave each other a knowing look, meant to serve as a laugh between them.

Once the two lieutenants exited the small attic room, she closed the door, stepped inside a closet, and locked the door. She cried her eyes out, knowing right then that she had made the biggest mistake of her life in joining the Navy and obligating herself to something she had no way of getting out of. She wished that she could have stated to both of them, "I quit," as she headed down the winding stairs of the brownstone, leaving the Navy behind forever. From that afternoon on, she understood that her time in the military would be bleak and miserable, clouded with obfuscation and the feeling of being trapped.

Over the next few weeks, she and another TAD (temporary assigned duty) ensign worked at setting up the antiquated computer systems. They tracked down and cannibalized parts. Brenda even used her own money to buy a few missing components at an oddball secondhand computer store she had found in Boston. They had actually gotten a few of the systems up and running. On one morning, she related her story about the aviation lieutenant to her ensign colleague, explaining how he had approached her in the attic office. "It's no big deal," her colleague had commented nonchalantly. "He pinned me against the wall that week because I didn't make enough photocopies," he laughed, in the same way she had seen others laugh off this type of behavior at times.

"So you think that was okay?" she asked. The other ensign shrugged his shoulders as if he had no answer for her and didn't care about discussing the issue further. She was left with mixed feelings. She was angry at herself for her inability go along, and, adversely, angry at the other ensign for his ability to go along.

Then one day, the same aviator lieutenant walked into their office. "Don't worry," he said. "We don't need the computers hooked up after all; they're too obsolete; pack them all up." The symbolism of the computer episode was not lost on her. She saw the aviator lieutenant as a representation of the kind of unappealing command relationships she might be facing for the next five years; and her feelings of being cornered in an attic summed up her realization that she would be unable to express a choice and leave. The entire episode became a new symbol of the choices she had made in high school and college, giving her a painful sense of powerlessness.

Inside CIC, Brenda rested against the swivel chair next to WEPS. From the vantage point of standing onboard ship next to her department head, her initial time at the ROTC unit as a "stashed" ensign seemed like years ago. She looked at WEPS and contemplated leaving with the ammo message; he had already initialed it, and he was busy on the radio and she needed to get to the XO's office so he could sign it off.

"Just do your best, Brenda. I'll take care of the rest," WEPS said as he finished his conversation with the TAO onboard the carrier. He pushed his right earphone back from his ear. "Thanks," he added before she motioned to leave.

"Yes, sir," she answered quietly. She understood – in terms of SWO culture – the meanings behind her department head's comments: "Just do your best" and "I'll take care of the rest." It was why she didn't mind working for him. His first comment acknowledged, indirectly, the reality that neither of them had experience with the ins and outs of the ammo program. For experience with ammo messages, they both relied on Petty Officer Mimms to a large degree, who had been stationed at an ammo depot somewhere in the Midwest before transferring to the ship. She thought of WEPS' second comment – "I'll take care of the rest" – as she secured the door to CIC behind her. She was aware that he meant if a message blast came back from the depot, copied throughout the Seventh Fleet, he would screen the flak (or blowback) from the Command. At Surface Warfare Officer School, and in her conversations with peer SWOs, she had learned that *"screening flak"* from the top of the chain was considered central to the job of department heads and division officers. Not only was screening flak a culturally accepted management strategy, but it was also meant as a measure of goodwill, of endearment almost, to protect subordinates from the harsh irrationality of many SWO commanders. "Screening is the primary job of division officers and department heads," she had heard many surface warfare officers repeat. But really, she had always thought, there shouldn't have existed such a need to "screen." And she didn't necessarily want to be screened; she would rather have known the truth behind what was going on. If the Command was upset with what they were doing, she figured that she was better off knowing. But she appreciated her department head, and his care towards the wellbeing of his division officers.

Chapter 39: XO to XO...Who needs sleep ... Once a veteran ... Just a little weight gain

At the Coke machine right outside of CIC, Brenda stopped and removed seventy-five cents from her pocket. While deployed at sea, the supply department kept the ship's soda machine stocked with soft drinks from around the world as they resupplied at each port. She looked at the *Coca-Cola Light* can she retrieved from the slot at the bottom of the machine, and saw that the words on the opposite side of the can were printed in Thai.

As she continued down the passageway, she thought of the SM-2 and harpoon missile onload, hoping it would go safely and methodically, especially with the arrival of the new XO. She felt a great deal of loyalty towards her division and her department head. First, she wanted no one to get hurt. But aside from that baseline wish, she wanted the gunners mates to perform well so they could take pride in their work, and she wanted the department to look good overall for WEPS' sake.

She climbed the ladder to the XO's stateroom holding the folder (containing the ammo message for the missile onload) and her can of *Coca-Cola Light*. She had always felt comfortable enough routing messages and briefs to Lieutenant Commander Navarro for signature. He rarely asked questions; his nature was serious, but approachable and fair. She planned to be in and out of his stateroom; then she could grab dinner leftovers in the wardroom, put her head down on her desk for a few minutes, or read, and get ready for bridge watch later that night.

1MC Shipwide Announcement: *"Knock off all ship's work."*

She noticed the passageways were empty. Sometimes underway, there were down periods when the ship appeared uninhabited. On some evenings, the ship would go to "darken ship" at sunset for training purposes, and the passageways would feel especially eerie. When darken ship was announced over the 1MC, all lights except for those with red lenses were turned off, making the warship nearly invisible at sea to the human eye.

This was going to be one of those quiet nights at sea, Brenda thought to herself. Besides those who were manning watches on the bridge, in CIC, and in engineering, the rest of the crew seemed nowhere to be found. She imagined some may have been hanging out on the mess decks or in berthing. Most were probably hidden away in their workspaces, sprawled among instrument panels, pipes, valves, tanks and other equipment, listening to music, watching movies, playing video games, cards or musical instruments, reading, painting, etc.

She approached the XO's door, but instead of knocking she stood silent. She could hear Lieutenant Commander Navarro and Lieutenant Commander Gates inside. Her first instinct was to turn and walk away. The ammo message could go out the next day, with no harm done. And that way she could route it through Lieutenant Commander Navarro when he was alone. But then she couldn't believe what she was hearing, so she remained outside the XO's door. How could it have been the third time in two days that she would find herself eavesdropping on the new XO? First with WEPS when she was studying in her stateroom, then with CSO before her first OOD inport watch, and now. Ships offered no privacy, and she guessed such a privilege could not be expected. It made her wonder what other JOs had heard and come across over the course of the first day underway with the new XO.

"Waiting for the XO to route a message?" Neil asked. His approach startled her. She was standing close to the door and Neil had approached her from behind.

"Yes, or I was," she answered, adding, "Listen, a second."

"I've heard already, everyone has; everyone's talking about it," Neil sighed. "I dread writing Danielle about what's been going on," he said, referring to his fiancé who currently served aboard USS *Blue Ridge* as the ship's navigator.

"With everyone calling her the First Lady of Aegis, it's heartbreaking," Brenda said.

"Danielle will be disappointed. No," he paused, "disappointed won't begin to describe how she'll feel. She, or we, both thought that Gates' promotion to XO of a DDG was indicative of some sort of breakthrough in the Navy for women."

"It is, or sort of, or it was supposed to be," Brenda answered, confused about what the promotion of Lieutenant Commander Gates meant for women in the Navy.

"I almost think it's a setback," Neil said. "Danielle had imagined her as a heroine to women in the Navy, a role model. But this is pitiful," he said, and then paused. "Well anyway, I've got to route this ASWEX message for WEPS tonight. Maybe I'll come back another time."

"I'm not coming back another time," Brenda said.

"Have you knocked?" Neil asked.

"No."

"I'll knock," he said.

"Okay," Brenda agreed. "I feel bad for the department heads," she said while Neil knocked. "WEPS and CSO are going to get the brunt of her at department head meetings, PB4T, and everywhere else. It'll be worse for them than it will be for us."

"It'll be miserable for all of us," Neil replied.

Brenda and Neil listened to the conversation between the current XO and Lieutenant Commander Gates while they waited outside the door. Lieutenant Commander Navarro wanted to leave the ship as soon as they pulled into Okinawa, the ship's next port visit, where the missile onload would take place. He wanted to go on leave so he could spend time with his wife and family before reporting to his next duty station. *But Lieutenant Commander Gates could not empathize.* She wanted him to stay onboard until the end of deployment when the ship reached Yokosuka. He talked about his personal status as a geographic bachelor (married but geographically separated), a status common to most of the married officers and crew. *She did not care.* "Understand that the ship was originally homeported out of San Diego. My wife and family live in San Diego. I haven't seen them in several months," he calmly explained. "Work to be done onboard the ship is more important," she yelled.

Brenda rested her feet by leaning her back flat against the bulkhead opposite the XO's door. The new XO started to scream at her peer; the current XO answered her with a mix of patience and disbelief.

"Un-fucking-believable," Neil muttered under his breath.

Easing her feet had brought Brenda comfort, so she rested her head back against the bulkhead as well. The bridge had shifted to six-hour watch rotations and she was fatigued beyond what she ever could have imagined. She was still working hard to try to make herself believe in the SWO cultural mentality that sleep was unnecessary. Two or three or four hours of sleep a night was normal, she had tried to convince herself. Sometimes, she couldn't believe that the Navy insisted that a person who only received two to three hours of sleep per night was fully prepared to manage the ship's equipment, stand watch over complicated systems in engineering and in CIC, and conn a destroyer safely through the ocean. But it was the pressure to accept that mentality that kept the system going and cycling, forcing newcomers to conform.

The system affected the enlisted as well. She remembered overhearing the gunners mates in the VLS. They were joking around and Petty Officer Marcello was describing his "favorite duty nights inport." "You know," he said, "those nights when after getting off midwatch, you have to muster with the duty section at 0330 for sweepers or some nonsense. Then after an hour or two of muster, you're lucky if you can get an hour or half hour of sleep in before reveille. Then, the best part is that after about one or two hours of sleep, we're expected to perform 'safe and effective maintenance' on the ship's computer and electronic systems during the workday. That makes sense," he had said.

Brenda clung to the knowledge that she would not have to stay in this lifestyle forever. And when she got out, she wasn't going to refer back to her military service as if she had been a hero who had made some kind of special sacrifice. She'd be a veteran by a technicality because it was true that she had volunteered to go into the Navy, and she was going to stay in through her obligation; but to look back on her service with any sense of grandeur, nostalgia, or pride would be a lie about the past. She had drive and education behind her. Once discharged, she planned to move on with her life and confront whatever challenges were ahead, far from the memories and confines of anything military. And she resolved to do her best to remember the truth of what her time in the military had been like, and to avoid recounting her military experience to others in a way that glorified the military itself or her own performance within it.

She looked at the XO's inbox, and then at her folder containing the ammo message. "You know, Neil," she said. "We could both drop our messages in the XO's inbox for him to review, sign, and return to WEPS tomorrow morning at the department head meeting. I'm tempted. Then I could go to my stateroom and rest before watch. But then, this message contains coding for onloading an SM-2 and harpoon."

"I've got to discuss a few details of the anti-submarine exercise with the XO," Neil said.

"And, of course," Brenda teased. "WEPS unceasingly reminds us that we need to manufacture every opportunity to steal facetime with the Captain and XO."

Neil shook his head. "WEPS is a fucking idiot sometimes. He does say that kind of thing often."

"It's SWO culture," she replied.

Neil smiled. "It is that," he nodded. "When I was enlisted I loved the Navy. Now, especially now, I'm liking it less and less."

"Those forced interactions like 'stealing factime' lead WEPS to trouble more often than not. I've learned good and bad from him."

"You have a good bit of compassion for WEPS," Neil said.

"He's one of the better department heads to work for. And I think it's true across the board that entire division officer workdays are spent in line, waiting to hand-route paperwork up the chain."

"It can take hours," Neil replied.

"Division officer life," Brenda smiled.

Then she heard the new XO scold the current XO. *She didn't want to be left alone on the ship for the upcoming SM-2 and harpoon missile onload and live missile firing exercise! She wanted Lieutenant Commander Navarro to stay onboard until the ship returned to Yokosuka!*

But he argued again that he'd miss almost three weeks with his family; he suggested she needed to trust the combat systems and weapons department heads and that weapons onloads and firings were standard. In response, *the new XO became inflamed.*

Brenda stared straight into the bulkhead. Lieutenant Commander Gates sounded at once menacing and afraid. These experiences – weapons onloads, gun and missile firings, bridgemanship – should have been stacked solidly behind her. *"You think your fucking family is more important than our work here!"* she berated Lieutenant Commander Navarro.

Brenda stood up straight from leaning against the bulkhead. She started to place the ammo message in the XO's inbox. But then she froze. She suddenly realized that the new XO wasn't going to trail blaze history for women. She wasn't going to learn from and use the knowledge of those around her as a path to being effective; she was going to attack when she felt insecure and incompetent. She wasn't going to recognize others' strengths, and apply them; she was going to instead feel threatened and tear others down.

The XO's door opened and Brenda stepped aside, otherwise Lieutenant Commander Gates would have plowed right into her.

"You were here first, but if you want, I'll go in," Neil offered to Brenda, as they watched the new XO storm down the passageway.

"I'll go," Brenda said. "Yours is going to take a while."

Brenda paused a moment to allow the situation to settle before entering the XO's office. "I'd like to route this ammo admin message to you, sir," she said to the XO, as she walked in.

"No problem, Miss Conner," the XO replied, composed. "As part of our XO turnover, go ahead and route your message through Lieutenant Commander Gates first. You'll probably find her in her stateroom. And then I'll sign it off for you. You'll find me later on the bridge."

"Yes, sir, thank you," Brenda answered.

*

After leaving Lieutenant Commander Navarro's stateroom, Brenda took a detour down to the VLS to grab a few more ammo manuals before heading up to the new XO's stateroom. She wanted to enter prepared. When she reached the bottom of the first ladderwell, she rummaged a tissue from her front pants pocket. Her nose constantly bled from breathing the ship's desiccated air. As she neared the ship's library, she stopped in the passageway to rest a moment and rub her face; she felt so tired. In her stateroom mirror that morning, she had looked haggard and strung-out.

She glanced forward and aft to ensure no one was around, and then looked down at her figure. She pulled her right pant leg tight around her thigh and tried to judge whether or not it still looked thin enough. Three weeks ago, she had removed uniform pants from the back of her closet that she had once considered forbidden – the three pairs the seamstress at the Navy Exchange (NEX) in Newport had made bigger in the waist. Back then, she had sworn to herself that despite what she encountered aboard ship, she would take care of herself by eating right and exercising. But since then, she had started losing her battle against physical and emotional exhaustion. She focused her stamina on just getting through each day – officers call, quarters, daily division work, studying, and watches.

And to worsen matters, the wardroom diet was designed for active males in their twenties, and was heavily based in corn-starched soups, meats, white rice and breads. That diet, along with the growing number of meals she had replaced with junk food from the ship's store and vending machine, had caused her to increase from a size two to an eight. She had recently acquired the habit of snacking on junk food like blueberry Pop Tarts and Pokémon sticks instead of eating right. She dreaded the strained small talk and tense atmosphere of lunches and dinners in the wardroom; thus she avoided them. And often, she looked to snacking to mollify her during the tediousness and boredom that isolation at sea seemed to bring on. Mistakenly, she had relied on the hope that her sources of exercise – walking the passageways and climbing the shipboard ladders to route messages, check division spaces, and go on watch – would prove sufficient to maintain her previous weight.

"Ma'am, we've got our books! We're headed to the ship's library to study!" Seamen Chapman and Kitson called to her from the mess decks.

"I'll meet you in the library tomorrow like we talked about, Seaman Chapman. Good job," Brenda encouraged her. Unlike Seaman Chapman, who was a nonrated deck seaman, Seaman Kitson already had a rating. She was a seaman operations specialist (OSSN) studying to make third class petty officer (OS3). Brenda found inspiration in seeing the two young women studying together, supporting one another. She pulled herself together and continued toward the VLS where she could review the ammo message once more before her first encounter alone with the new XO.

Chapter 40: You make me laugh ... Gates' insurmountable barrier ... Have a great Navy day ... Okinawa, almost paradise

Approaching the stateroom across the passageway from hers – the new XO's temporary stateroom – Brenda found unnerving. Having no other choice, she walked up to the new XO's door and knocked.

"Come in," she heard.

"Excuse me, ma'am. I'm routing an ammo admin message," she began tentatively, as she opened the door. In her arms, she held the stack of manuals she had retrieved; she thought of the stack as "going in armed."

"Thank you, GUNNO," Lieutenant Commander Gates replied, while she motioned for her to enter. "I was like you as an ensign," she greeted her, "the gunnery officer. You remind me of myself."

Brenda looked at her, put the stack of manuals down on the floor, and handed her the folder containing the message. "Yes, ma'am," she answered, showing no emotion.

"You make me laugh, Ensign," Lieutenant Commander Gates said, amused. "I've never had someone come to me carrying so many manuals."

"Yes, ma'am," Brenda managed a smile.

"I was in charge of the ammo program when I was a division officer," she added.

"Yes, ma'am," Brenda replied. Then, wondering if Lieutenant Commander Gates was trying to relate to her as her supervisor, she decided to offer more of a response. "Oh, well, that's interesting, ma'am," Brenda said, but she felt she had only sounded awkward.

Lieutenant Commander Gates gave no indication of a response as she began to review the ammo message. Brenda scanned the plaques Lieutenant Commander Gates had on display in her temporary stateroom. Like most of the officers and crew, she wondered who was responsible for the presence of Lieutenant Commander Gates onboard *Curtis Wilbur* as second in command. All the plaques in the world could not hide her inexperience. She predicted that the aura of accomplishment that Lieutenant Commander Gates was trying to render through her plaques would fall meaningless on the officers and crew. Her behavior since checking onboard had been far more telling and revealing. In the minds of those who lived and worked onboard *Curtis Wilbur*, Lieutenant Commander Gates had presented herself as a tyrant – untrustworthy, unpredictable, unfeeling, and unprepared to serve as second in command of a warship.

News of Lieutenant Commander Gates' violent reaction to having been placed on the watchbill to conn out of Hong Kong – when she had thrown an object at the senior watch officer (CSO) as she screamed at him – had traveled quickly around the ship. Rumor had it that Lieutenant Commander Gates feared the bridge, and that she was an incompetent shiphandler. Talk of her aggressive behavior on the quarterdeck in front of Petty Officer Dobbs and Seaman Chapman, and in the current XO's stateroom over the missile onload, had also spread. Already, there were so many examples of her erratic and abusive behavior flying around the ship that Brenda couldn't recall all of them.

She wanted to remind Lieutenant Commander Gates that there were no private or sacrosanct spaces onboard. On the other side of the forward bulkhead of the XO's stateroom was the admin office where the yeomen (YNs) worked. In the staterooms in officers country, the wardroom attendants were always present, and the JOs and department heads who lived there could hear what was going on in the other staterooms.

She suspected that Lieutenant Commander Gates was largely unaware of her behavior, which seemed to stem from insecurity. A good leader with strong instincts and the willingness to learn might have been able to overcome inexperience, and turn a bad start around. But it had seemed that Lieutenant Commander Gates was fighting an insurmountable barrier – herself. She had given the officers and crew reason to believe that her mental stability, leadership ability, and technical acumen were all in question, as well as her readiness and willingness to learn. She appeared overly controlling and aggressive as a way to compensate for the things she lacked. She was biting, cruel, duplicitous, and petty in her interactions with subordinates. The display in her stateroom of honors and awards – whatever they were – would most likely never override the conclusions that had already been made about her.

Brenda tried to imagine what it must have been like for Lieutenant Commander Gates to walk onboard the *Curtis Wilbur* for the first time, rife with inexperience, knowing that everyone knew it. Or was she even thinking of such dynamics? Her bio, which most

SWO officers would be flaunting by now, could not be located by anyone so far. It would have taken a woman with unusual courage and self-awareness, Brenda thought, to recognize that she was unqualified for the billet of XO, both personally and professionally, and to turn it down, in the best interest of the officers and crew of the *Curtis Wilbur*, the Navy, and the future of military women.

And she wondered, if Lieutenant Commander Gates had no talent for the Navy (she was seemingly afraid to conn the ship out of Hong Kong), why did she stay in?

As a female surface warfare officer, she should have had plenty of experience on the bridge after spending her career on auxiliary ships.

She watched as Lieutenant Commander Gates continued to look at the ammo message. Based on her own history of having forced herself through engineering and ROTC, and trying to conceal her lack of ability and aptitude, Brenda felt some sympathy for Lieutenant Commander Gates. But she wanted to understand what had made Lieutenant Commander Gates persevere within the Navy for over a decade, when she seemed to fear its most basic tasks. Most dedicated SWOs would have relished the opportunity to mark the start of their sea tour by conning the ship out of port. Why remain in denial, blind to one's incompetence and unsuitability? Why manipulate impossible circumstances, positioning oneself as XO of a guided missile destroyer, with the aspiration of becoming CO of a warship? The answers to those questions ran deeply, Brenda imagined. She doubted if Lieutenant Commander Gates even acknowledged such questions, let alone provide answers. Familial expectations, an inability to comprehend another way of life, too much time invested in the Navy to leave, an ego that depended on success as a naval officer, or a fixed delusion that she really was a competent leader and qualified for Command – all of those dynamics and many more might have been in play. If only a different, more capable woman had been selected for this historic role, Brenda lamented as she looked at her.

"Verify the coding for me," Lieutenant Commander Gates requested.

"Yes, ma'am," Brenda answered as she reached down and picked up the manual on top of the pile. She opened it, placed it on the lieutenant commander's stateroom desk, and started to compare the codes listed in the manual against those typed on the message. She couldn't distinguish between her disdain and her sympathy for

Lieutenant Commander Gates. As Julie had said earlier onboard the liberty boat to Hong Kong, the Navy had put Gates in this position. And through no fault of her own, her career path had been limited by gender restrictions. A rumor had been going around that she had served as a division officer onboard a destroyer tender, an auxiliary ship which provided maintenance support for destroyers, and an FFT, an outdated frigate used to train reserve units. Many had said that she hadn't served a SWO department head tour, with the exception of the few months she spent in a staff position (on land) at a destroyer squadron.

"It looks like you understand the program well," the new XO complimented her.

Brenda glanced at the golden SWO pin clasped above Lieutenant Commander Gates' left shirt pocket, which should have symbolized achievement of full status as a surface warfare officer. Yet unlike her male colleagues, she had been barred from the majority of the Navy's ships. The restrictions imposed on women had been unfair, Brenda thought. Restrictions on women – right or wrong – had left Lieutenant Commander Gates inexperienced, but that wasn't the crux of her problems onboard, she concluded.

Brenda's emotions swayed back and forth. "Thank you, ma'am," she responded after a pause. "I've had a good teacher in Petty Officer Mimms, one of the first class gunners mates in the division."

"Have a great Navy day," the new XO replied, as she handed the ammo message back to her, initialed. Brenda almost winced. She hated that expression, and that kind of sendoff seemed annoying, and just wrong for evening, especially after everything that had happened since she had checked onboard.

"Thank you, ma'am," Brenda answered politely, as per protocol; and she exited Lieutenant Commander Gates' temporary stateroom, completely confused.

As Brenda opened the door to her own stateroom, she thought about the earlier defensive posturing and aggressive behavior she had witnessed in Lieutenant Commander Gates. She remembered when she had walked into her graduate level Spanish linguistics class as an undergraduate. On the first day of class, the professor and the other graduate students had looked at her as if she didn't belong and should not have registered for the class. But Brenda remembered not caring what they thought because despite her undergraduate status, she knew that she had the ability that justified her being there. That semester, she sat down at her desk, participated in class, and subsequently wrote her papers without difficulty. She received an A in the class. If Lieutenant Commander Gates truly possessed the talent to serve as executive officer of a guided missile destroyer, despite her lack of experience, she would have been able to conquer the steep learning curve inherent in serving as second in command of an Arleigh Burke destroyer.

Across the passageway, she heard Neil knock at Lieutenant Commander Gates' door. After a few seconds, he greeted her. As Brenda sat at her desk, she thought about how the new XO was going to set a poor example onboard, and make everyone's lives a living nightmare.

*

On her way up to the bridge to find Lieutenant Commander Navarro, Brenda paused on the landing between the two ladders to check the ammo message one more time. She didn't want to think about how the new XO would react to a blast. Negative leadership may have worked to some degree, she thought, but it motivated people for the wrong reasons; the resulting work, accomplished out of fear, couldn't have been as good – as well-crafted with quality, with care, and with the right energy.

Out the bridge windows she could see the sun setting. The bridge was already dark. She walked directly past the silhouettes of the watchstanders and bridge equipment and approached the current XO. He was seated in the XO's designated bridge chair, gazing out the front windows, his feet rested upon the mantle.

"Excuse me, sir," Brenda interrupted his stare, and his thoughts, she regretted. "I have the ammo message for the onload for your review. It's been initialed by Lieutenant Commander Gates, sir."

He took the message from her, opened the folder, and initialed it. "These are sad days for me," he said, pensively. "I love driving ships. I look forward to conning the ship one last time into Okinawa."

"Yes, sir," Brenda answered, feeling empathy for him, since to do what he really loved meant endless separation at sea from his family. When he handed her back the message, she took it from him, and headed back down the bridge ladders towards sleep.

*

Okinawa seemed a beautiful tropical island with white sand beaches and crystal-clear turquoise waters – *simply paradise*. Brenda exited the oval watertight door to the quarterdeck into warmth, and breathtaking views of endless uninhabited beach less than a hundred feet from the pier. When she reached the forecastle, she made her way to the edge of the ship and found rest in sitting on a chock. Once seated, she removed her ballcap so she could feel the healing of the sun on her face. She looked out onto the island, wanting to take something for herself from its beauty, possibly wellbeing and a sense of peace. For the destroyer, she wished that a resplendent setting like this could mend the plight of its shipboard inhabitants. If only the serene beauty of an island could remedy the dark mood within the ship, which had been created by the instability of having a new and volatile XO.

The officers and crew were learning that random attacks were the norm under this unpredictable XO. No one knew how she might come down on someone in the next second, hour, or day, nor would they know what might spark her next outburst. There was a heightened state of anxiety and vigilance on the ship…obsessing over what would set her off, or when.

Due to the strict hierarchy of the chain of command, subordinates were nearly powerless to stop the forces moving downward against them. Brenda now understood clearly, that the chain of command and naval leadership meant nothing without a competent and steady leader at the top who subordinates could follow and trust. The top leadership set the entire tone, morale, and level of workmanship. All onboard (with the exception of the Captain) had obligation by military law to obey the new XO. They were, in absolute, in her hands. Since following this particular leader and honoring the chain of command was potentially dangerous, Brenda wondered about the roll and obligation of the officers…especially if the new XO's actions fell just short of the line of gross impropriety, but never actually crossed that line in a clear black and white sense. A sensation of foreboding was soaring through the passageways of the ship; it had become evident in the faces, walk, and speech of most of the officers, and all of the crew.

Adding more tension to matters, Okinawa was a working port, which allowed the officers and crew only slight respite. When a port visit was designated as a "working port" visit, everyone still worked a full day before liberty was granted, usually at 1600 or 1700. Last evening for R&R, Brenda accompanied Neil and Rob to a Mexican restaurant on base. Both on and off the ship, she enjoyed their company and the working friendships she had formed with them. She remembered the guys hipping her to the new XO's initials: *H-*

A-G, Rob had spelled out to her while laughing and eating a burrito – *Lieutenant Commander Heather A. Gates.*

"No!" she had protested, "it can't be true, everyone will have a field day with those initials!" For a while that night, the group of junior officers had let themselves be free – at dinner indulging in burritos, tacos, chips and salsa, and in the taxi laughing about the ship and just generally having a good time.

As Brenda glanced over at the ammo barges tied to an adjacent pier, while sitting on the forecastle, she remembered riding in the cab that evening with the guys. Through chain-link and barbwire fencing, she had caught a few glimpses of the buildings and architecture directly off base on the Okinawan civilian side. She saw no Okinawan architecture or traditional villages, as she had expected. Natural palm trees and tropical vegetation were scattered among the marks of decades of American naval and marine corps presence – drab military architecture dating back to WWII that extended off base, depressing-looking U.S. military housing, and "establishments" off base that catered to lonely young men with time on their hands.

Most American warships pulled into Okinawa for the sole reason of onloading weapons. Recent in the psyche of the Okinawan public was a well-publicized atrocity by American servicemen against an elementary age schoolgirl – brutal and violent rape. Before pulling into port at Okinawa, *Curtis Wilbur* officers and sailors were ordered: YOU ARE NOT ALLOWED TO TRAVEL OFF BASE FOR ANY REASON. The order restricting R&R to the base had come from echelons of naval command high above *Curtis Wilbur*.

The *Curtis Wilbur* was tied to an enormously long weapons onload pier. The R&R taxicabs dropped their passengers off right below the ship's brow leading to the quarterdeck. Brenda remembered being the last to step out of the cab that evening, behind Neil and Rob, when she heard a 1MC announcement, *"Assemble all officers on the quarterdeck."*

She had looked up the ship's brow and had seen Julie standing quarterdeck watch as the inport OOD. Two "side boys" (petty officers in ceremonial dress) stood across from each other to form a passageway to the first step of the brow. Behind the ship, the sun appeared as a perfect half circle above a yellowed horizon. "We'd better get up there so we can get in line," Neil had said. Brenda remembered following the guys up the brow and standing with them during the brief ritual. *Gong, gong,* the petty officer of the watch sounded the quarterdeck bell. "*Lieutenant Commander, United States Navy, departing,*" the announcement followed. Lieutenant Commander Navarro made his way down the line of officers, shaking their hands and wishing each one well before passing through the side boys and departing down the brow. The ship's former executive officer – Lieutenant Commander Navarro – had departed the ship four hours after entering port, Brenda remembered thinking. She lamented a ship without his protection and fairness.

After Lieutenant Commander Navarro had officially been gonged off the ship – an honor according to old Navy custom – his taxi drove down the pier out of Brenda's view. Then she left the ship also, to take a lone walk on a warm dark tropical beach. The half sun had disappeared below the horizon. The ship had officially been handed to the mercy of a new XO, Lieutenant Commander Heather Astrid Gates.

Chapter 41: The XO's three-hour inspection ... Missile onload can wait ... A noble GUNNO

Brenda resented having been forced to attend the new XO's messing and berthing inspection on the morning of the missile onload. Resented? No, she was furious, or more like in disbelief! Just before the ammo barge was about to come alongside the ship to begin the long, tedious, and dangerous process of onloading the missiles, the XO had demanded that she, WEPS, and CSO, along with two of the most senior gunners mates responsible for conducting the onload, had to report to combat systems berthing to continue with "berthing cleaners."

"Female on deck!" Brenda called out before she swung the handle to open the door to combat systems berthing. "Female on deck!...Female on deck!" she announced a few more times as she opened the door.

"Everyone hears you, GUNNO," the XO turning around, chastised her. She was holding a flashlight and wore a white glove on her right hand. Her face was a portrait of intense anger.

"Ma'am, I wanted..." but the XO cut her off with a wave of her hand.

Brenda scanned the berthing space. Designated berthing cleaners sprayed, wiped, and scrubbed around racks stacked three and four high that were narrower and shorter than her own. She wanted to know – when had the morning gone awry? All missile onload messages had been routed and sent out, checklists had been signed off and reviewed, and she had read the safety brief prepared by Chief Walden in front of a packed wardroom.

Earlier, she had enjoyed perfectly brilliant skies and warm comfortable temperatures amidst island beauty, as she stood next to Chief Walden on the aft VLS, while he supervised the lifting of the VLS crane from within one of the missile canisters. She remembered looking out at the view, thinking about how the preparations for the onload were progressing like clockwork. Feeling confident that all things were working together for the successful completion of this evolution, she was amazed by Chief Walden's zen-like direction as he managed multiple events in parallel; she noticed how his calm and in-control vibe seemed to resonate down, through the actions of the gunners mates.

Brenda had remained with Chief Walden most of the morning, acting as more of an observer than anything else. "Just waiting for the barge to come alongside," Chief Walden had said to her.

"Aye, aye, Chief," she had smiled, and he had chuckled in response.

1MC Shipwide Announcement: *"Standby for XO's inspection of messing and berthing spaces."*

"Don't worry," Chief Walden said. "Chief Dering and I had Brooks swap out the berthing cleaners to free up the gunners mates."

Since checking onboard, she had never involved herself much with "berthing cleaners" because she had never needed to. Even on a normal workday, she rarely attended messing and berthing inspections, only once in a while when the gunners mates were in charge. But mostly she delegated berthing concerns to the first class petty officers in the division, supervised by the chiefs. There had never been any problems. Not having to attend berthing cleaners was a relief in a number of ways. Not only was it one less item she had to worry about on her workday schedule, between watches and division work, but when Pete showed her around combat systems berthing during her first days onboard, she decided that as an officer she would stay clear of berthing unless there was a problem. An officer's presence in berthing (with the exception of the XO's daily inspection for safety, health, and sanitation), she decided, was practically an invasion. The enlisted had no place private to themselves onboard, only a sort of coffin-sized privacy behind their rack curtains, and some storage within a footlocker.

She viewed her absence from berthing as a matter of respect and trust, which she believed, had to run down the chain of command as well as up. In the division, she strove to establish a sense of self-worth, self-respect, and self-development on the part of all individuals. She wanted each gunners mate to focus on the work for which they showed talent and interest. Along those lines, she and Chief Walden shared the same management philosophy, and as long as the work in the division was completed properly and on time, she hoped they could continue with that approach.

Prior to Lieutenant Commander Gates' arrival, berthing cleaners had been routine and effectively done – important, but not the focus of the workday onboard. Brenda watched as an entire work crew of boatswains mates, gunners mates, and fire controlmen, under the direction of the command duty officer, accepted the ammo barge alongside. Chief Dering appeared on the VLS deck and motioned for her and Chief Walden to speak with him in private.

"XO's mad," Chief Dering said, his hands on his hips as he looked down at the deck in defiance. "WEPS is down in berthing; CSO's on his way down. XO says the gunners mates originally on the berthing cleaners bill need to clean. She doesn't want substitutes. That's final."

"She's dangerous," Brenda said, and then caught herself.

"What about the Captain?" Chief Walden asked.

"XO's running the show," he answered. "Says the ammo barge will have to wait until berthing is acceptable."

Chief Walden was angry but said nothing. He just stared at the deck and shook his head. Then he finally said, "A missile onload can't be conducted in this frame of mind; it's unsafe."

WEPS approached them from behind. "Brenda," he said. "Go down to berthing. CSO is headed down there. I just sent Brooks and Gaines down there. Chief Walden and I will handle the barge for now."

"What about..." Brenda started to exclaim.

But WEPS cut her off and simply said, "Go, please, Brenda, please." And she did what he said. She saw WEPS' eyes were red from stress and exhaustion.

Brenda wanted to scream, cry, run off the ship, exclaim, "I quit!" and fly home. But she entered combat systems berthing instead. Males lived in berthing according to the department in which they worked – combat systems, operations, etc. The females onboard lived together in a separate berthing. Since there were no female gunners mates, Brenda had no idea how female berthing was handled, or who supervised it; but she had never heard of any problems. Inside, GMM2 Gaines and GMM1 Brooks – VLS crane operator and loading supervisor respectively – were spraying disinfectant into the showers. They had just arrived and the XO had directed them to start cleaning the showers, a job that normally would have been delegated to a seaman, or at most, a third class petty officer.

"I kicked WEPS out of berthing," the XO started, in front of an array of weapons department sailors.

"Yes, ma'am," Brenda answered. "What can I do for you, ma'am?"

"This messing and berthing inspection is going on three hours, and that's unacceptable," the XO snapped.

Long Way Out 317

"Yes, ma'am," Brenda answered. She wanted to ask her if she was interested in the ammo barge coming alongside, and in observing the SM-2 and telemetry harpoon missile onload. She wanted to ask her if she was interested in the safety of lowering a 15-foot long guided missile, equipped with a 130-pound warhead, designed to travel over a speed of Mach 3.5, into a narrow missile canister on the aft deck. And was she interested in either the safety or schedule of the ammo depot personnel onboard the barge?

Living conditions for enlisted were institutionalized to the extreme to maintain health and sanitation in spaces inhabited by twenty, forty, sixty, eighty or more men or women – all who used the same head and shower facilities. There seemed no other method of housing the dense population of a warship. If health and sanitation were truly at risk at that moment, the issue needed to be addressed, but at a safer time.

As she stood in combat systems berthing, far down into the ship, she regretted that the new XO had already broken the trust necessary for her to become an effective leader onboard as second in command. Respect and individual worth, Brenda feared, would be disregarded as a rule under this XO.

She remembered WEPS instructing her that SWO officer evaluations were written every second of the day, which was fine, because she wanted out. "Ma'am," Brenda started quietly. But all of the combat systems petty officers and seamen inside could hear. "I was wrong not to pass the berthing cleaners substitutions up the chain of command," she stated, as if her fingers were crossed behind her back. "That will be corrected in the future. Can Petty Officers Brooks and Gaines be released for the onload?"

"Noble, GUNNO," the XO answered and then ignored her. When CSO appeared in berthing, the XO grabbed him by the upper part of his sleeve and pulled him around to the side. Berthing went silent. There would be consequences, Brenda thought. Because the combat systems crew was loyal to CSO.

Brenda heard an insistent tone in CSO's voice when he spoke to the XO, but she couldn't make out his words. After a moment, CSO walked over to Brenda and took her aside. "Tell Petty Officers Brooks and Gaines to get cleaned up and go back topside to the VLS onload."

"Yes, sir," Brenda nodded, quietly. Then, she walked over to the showers and kneeled down to speak to the petty officers. "Go back topside," she said. "Quietly, just do it. Chief Walden and

WEPS are up there."
"Yes, ma'am," they both whispered.

Chapter 42: A rocket into space ... A path of destruction ... An irrelevant leader ... Whales and sea life

On a cool spring afternoon at sea, off the coast of mainland Japan in the northern Pacific, Brenda joined a few of her junior officer colleagues out on the bridge wing to observe the live missile firing exercise. An SM-2 and a harpoon – both million-dollar-plus missiles – would be launched. As she looked around, she saw that everyone who had a reasonable excuse for being on or near the bridge had come up, hoping to catch a glimpse of the missiles just as they were launched from the ship. She decided that most of the officers and sailors around her exuded the sense of excitement and anticipation that she had tried to muster within herself, but couldn't. Over the past few days, she had walked about the ship making every effort to appear enthusiastic about the live firing: *Isn't it exciting? This is what we've all trained for, what we're all onboard for. This is the mission of the ship!*

Brenda walked to the railing to look out at the seas, wishing to soothe her intense unhappiness. But the seas appeared more akin to a prison, acting as a physical boundary that trapped her onboard. Gradually, she realized, she was shedding her longing to be someone she wasn't, someone technical who enjoyed a natural curiosity for engineering, specifically the military science of ships, missiles, and planes. It embarrassed her to remember that during her freshman year, she had plastered her dorm room walls with posters of navy and air force aircraft, including a calendar with such pictures. In reality, except for the stealth bomber, she couldn't identify any of the planes. One afternoon, her college friend Kevin had spontaneously walked around her dorm room pointing to each aircraft and naming them for her.

With regard to the missile launch, she only cared that the department and the gunners mates were successful in their work at making both launches occur safely and successfully. She had finally admitted to herself that she really didn't care much about military aircraft or whether she watched the missiles launch or not; and she really didn't care about witnessing the fire power or the explosion out of the launcher.

"Don't forget," Rob said as he leaned over next to her to scan the horizon with his binoculars, "It only gets better." He was assigned as officer of the deck during the shoot, and he had stepped out onto the bridge wing to ensure the port horizon remained visually free of ships. Despite all of the advanced radar tracking systems and air support, there still existed a degree of risk, as well as the urgent need to take every possible precaution to ensure the firing range was completely safe and void of other ships and aircraft. The ship was underway in a quadrant of a U.S. Navy OPAREA (operating area) designated for live missile firing. For training, weapons systems testing, and exercises of all types (surface, subsurface, air-to-surface and surface-to-air exercises), the Navy gridded areas of the world's oceans and shores for use as OPAREAs. "Remember, you're livin' the dream," Rob chuckled, before heading back into the bridge. Brenda let out a purposefully contrived laugh, appreciating his attempt to console her with humor, however sarcastic.

As she continued to wait, she thought about how the gunners mates had told her that seeing a missile launch from the VLS was like watching NASA launch a rocket into space. The display of fire, power, sound, and vibration was a sight, GMM1 Brooks had forewarned her. He had told her to prepare herself by donning double hearing protection, and to hold on, because when the missiles fired, the ship would list and she would feel the shock waves vibrate right through her body. "If we're lucky," he had said, "we'll be able to see the missile detonate on the horizon."

"Well, maybe we will," she remembered answering him. But she couldn't cast out of her mind her concern for the seascape and any birds and sea life, from the smallest crustaceans to dolphins and whales, that might have been unfortunately living in or passing through the area of detonation. No one seemed to consider or mention the impact on marine life or environment, or the destruction of the underwater formations and the ecosystems in the crevices and open water. Why explode *live* missiles for exercises versus simulation dummies? She pictured the missile exploding in the ocean, and all of the life there dying and frantically trying to escape the annihilation and forces of the crushing pressure waves, all for a training test.

There was pressure to accept that this was a sacrifice that needed to be made.

Brenda looked into the bridge to see if the XO had come up to observe the firings. She didn't see her, but she predicted that she would observe both launches from the bridge. Observing a high profile exercise from CIC, she thought, would feel threatening to Lieutenant Commander Gates, since her lack of knowledge and inexperience would lay open to exposure. She was second in command of the ship, the secondary warfighter onboard after the Captain, but she had no experience in interpreting the information displayed across the widescreen displays and scopes in CIC; she would not understand the actions of the watchstanders, the meaning of the radio chatter, or the sequence of fast-paced decisions that controlled the protocols for the Aegis Combat System (ACS), the SPY-1D radar, the Command & Decision System (C&D), and the Weapons Control System (WCS).

She wondered what the next few months would hold for the officers and sailors onboard *Curtis Wilbur*. The XO's menacing presence continued to produce stories that all shared pettiness or the infliction of humiliation as their punch lines. "It's like she takes sadistic pleasure in how she treats people," she remembered Neil saying.

"Among both male and female crewmembers..." Brenda had answered, "No one likes her." No one likes incompetence, especially combined with a lack of humanity and humility, she had thought to herself. "And that no one likes her has nothing to do with her being a woman," she had also said to Neil. But she was afraid that people off the ship would think that the officers and crew of the *Curtis Wilbur* had rejected Lieutenant Commander Heather A. Gates solely because she was a woman.

The XO seemed to use any opportunity – or was it every opportunity – no matter how trivial, to tear down and degrade a subordinate. Did the woman have any control over herself at all?

Brenda walked back over to her spot against the bridge wing railing. Besides the JOs who had come topside to witness the exercise, a group of enlisted sailors had congregated off to the side, away from the officers, hoping to observe the shoot as part of their ESWS (enlisted surface warfare specialist) qualification.

"*This is the Captain speaking,*" Brenda heard over the 1MC. "*My time is winding down on Curtis Wilbur, and I can't stress enough how proud I am to have served with each and every one of you. I am especially proud to congratulate the combat systems and weapons departments on a safe and flawless missile onload. Bravo Zulu. It's moments such as those that make me proud to be in the*

Navy. I'm proud of every Curtis Wilbur sailor. Looking out and watching Petty Officer Gaines expertly and safely operate the crane to lower the SM-2 into the VLS, assisted by GMM1 Brooks, GMM2 Marcello, and GMM2 Finn was especially inspiring to me as your commanding officer. It's with a heavy heart that I'll be leaving this great ship soon after we reach our homeport in Yokosuka, Japan. It remains an honor to be your commanding officer. Whether it's anti-submarine warfare, close-in plane guard, air ops, SEAMERLION, COBRA GOLD, TANDEM THRUST or fulfilling alpha-whisky duties for USS Independence, Curtis Wilbur sailors have hit a home run every time. Now this is no time to let down. Although we're nearing the conclusion of our deployment, we look forward to a safe and on-target live firing coming up in minutes. I am confident that Curtis Wilbur's performance will be no less than stellar. So keep up the good work and be proud of your ship and what you have accomplished together as shipmates. That is all."

Brenda continued looking out to sea, trying to remain detached and unfazed by the Captain's remarks, which struck her as delusory and disingenuous. They were to be expected, and mostly she found herself unsurprised. The remarks were in perfect keeping with the Captain's character and nature; and it was as she had figured: This phony, company man, careerist Captain would ride out his last month or so as CO, and not touch the volatile issue of Lieutenant Commander Gates – Lieutenant Commander Gates, who had nearly thrown the missile onload into chaos over manufactured concern for the berthing inspection.

But she also knew that she had her own issues to sort out, regarding her role as gunnery officer. In the days leading up to the exercise, she had questioned herself relentlessly as to what her role should have been during the VLS missile system workups, pre-fire preparation, final checks, and launch. She had worried that the planning and the gunners mates' work was happening around her and without her, and that as the division officer, she should have been more hands-on in the management and day-to-day operations. And now, during the exercise, she felt as though she should have been participating actively in some way that was meaningful and that contributed to the outcome. She kept picturing the guys during World War II and the gunnery scenes she had seen in movies. Were those junior officers, who were billeted as gunnery officers, actively calculating trajectories, supervising the mechanics, announcing salvos?

In modern times, the TAO handled those responsibilities in CIC by sitting in front of what amounted to a computer console.

She had asked Chief Walden repeatedly about what she should have been doing as gunnery officer to prepare for the missile firing; was she doing enough? "There's nothing more you need do," he had told her many times, in his soft way. "During the exercise go topside to observe the firing for your SWO qualification." Between bridge watches, she had floated around to CIC and the various VLS watchstations, inquiring about the status of the equipment and checklists. She had tried to learn what she could. She had observed a few of the checks as they were being performed, but how could she really know what had been accomplished well, what had been rushed through, how many (if any) corners had been cut...those unknowns made her ill-at-ease.

If she had only known more about the missile systems, she could have actively supervised the progress of the gunners mates, she thought. Awaiting the launch, she felt that all she had accomplished was to route completed checklists and VLS reports up the chain of command to obtain signatures, hoping at each point, that no one would ask her any detailed technical questions about the system.

On the bridge wing there was a slight wind, so Brenda left the railing and walked over towards Pete. "You've brought up quite a few camera lenses," she said to him, as he was setting up a tripod on the bridge wing. She noted that leading up to the exercise, he was spending his time testing for the exact combination of lenses and angle that would enable him to capture the millisecond when the missile would clear the launcher.

"I'd like a good picture for the fire controlmen to have," he said. He seemed very matter-of-fact about his task, and unlike herself, unworried about his role as the strike officer during the harpoon portion of the shoot. If she had been billeted as the strike officer, she knew that she would have obsessed over where to station herself and how she was supervising the preparations.

"So you feel good that your division is prepared for the firing?" she asked.

"Yes," he stood up and addressed her. "They've done their work. They're on standby. It's now in the hands of the operations department. The best thing you can do is witness the shoot, or go down to CIC," he said. "There's nothing more for you to do right now."

Brenda wished that Pete's comment could have relieved her self-consciousness and feelings of inadequacy. During the firings the gunners mates acted in a support role, manning the local consoles in the missile launchers, prepared to operate the panels on an as-needed or standby basis during an emergency. It was the team in the combat information center, under the direction of the officer standing the TAO watch, that performed the actual firing remotely, as they advanced through the detect-to-engage sequence. On a daily basis, the gunners mates worked in the background, conducting preventive and on-the-spot mechanical and electrical maintenance. Their work was so advanced that Brenda wondered if she would ever have a chance to even scratch the surface of what they did during her short time onboard.

"*STRIKE!*" the XO approached Pete, referring to him by his title as strike officer. "Get them out of here," she whispered, with "them" referring to the group of enlisted sailors standing off to a distance on the bridge wing, who were there to observe the firings for their ESWS qualification. "I want *them* out of here," she emphasized. The XO had shown herself to possess a special antipathy – tempered by arrogance – for enlisted personnel.

"Yes, ma'am," Pete answered her. "But I believe they're up here to study for their ESWS qualification. Lieutenant Trenton is the officer of the deck, ma'am," he said, referring to Rob. "It would be best to address the situation with him." Lieutenant Commander Gates stared in outrage at Pete, as if she actually wanted to kill him in that moment, before she walked away. Brenda then forgot the problems that pulled at her personally and peered into the bridge. The XO had Rob off to a corner. As the OOD, he held the overall responsibility for the operation of the ship and for the management of the bridge. Less than a minute later, the Captain appeared on the bridge wing. He approached the group of enlisted sailors and made a spectacle out of shaking each petty officer and seaman's hand; he walked down the line of sailors while he congratulated each on an outstanding effort in coming to the bridge to observe the missile shoot. He reminded Brenda of a politician. She would never know for sure if the Captain had performed this maneuver completely by accident, or was it intentionally staged, to allow the sailors to remain on the bridge, defusing another volatile XO scene? In a matter of days, Brenda thought to herself, the XO was making herself irrelevant as a leader; and people, including the Captain, were starting to work around her.

"Here, put these on, Brenda," Pete handed her a pair of binoculars.

"Do you ever think about the whales, the seascape, and the sea life where the missile detonates?"

"I do," Pete answered.

"I never would have before; and there was a day when I would have rolled my eyes at the notion," she said.

As the countdown to the missile firing neared, Brenda felt the excitement building around her. "*All hands topside don hearing protection*," she heard the boatswains mate of the watch announce over the 1MC.

Then she heard radio chatter, blasting loudly over the 1MC, broadcasted from CIC for effect. "*...holding an unknown, commencing engagement on track one-zero-two-five, SM-two, salvo size one.*"

"*Commencing engagement on track one-zero-two-five, SM-two, salvo size one,*" came the repeat back from a watchstander.

"*Commencing engagement on track one-zero-two-five, SM-two, salvo size one,*" the TAO repeated.

Brenda imagined the operational scene in CIC, knowing that it must have been exciting for the watchstanders to actively engage in a live exercise, in which they actually fired a salvo. Suddenly, she felt herself thrown back as the ship listed, and then righted itself. In milliseconds, she heard the fiery explosion of the missile leaving the VLS canister; she listened as it screamed into the sky.

"There it is! There it is!" she heard someone call out. "It's tracking the drone," another exclaimed. A collective cheer emanated from the crowd.

"Got it," Pete said. "I'll know for sure when I get these developed."

"Follow it in the sky to the horizon, ma'am," one of the petty officers showed her, pointing.

"I see it; I see it," she smiled, answering the petty officer.

The whole ship burst out cheering when the missile detonated on the horizon.

Brenda looked over at Pete, who also appeared unmoved by the events in progress. "I'm going down to the VLS to congratulate the gunners mates," she said. "Then, I'll probably go to CIC to observe the harpoon firing." She turned around and headed below decks.

Chapter 43: What is patriotism ... Lessons learned onboard

Brenda rotated the wheel on the hatch to the 5-inch/54-caliber gun mount. She tugged and pulled at the wheel to turn it, clenching her hands around the spokes. In the movies, she thought, the officers and crews aboard ships, subs, and aircraft, especially in crisis, always seemed adept at maneuvering around equipment and through spaces, reacting in real time, opening and closing hatches, climbing up and down ladders, and dismantling and jury-rigging mechanical and electrical equipment on the fly. Onboard, she had noticed that some of the officers and crewmembers appeared naturally suited to life at sea, while others struggled. Some days, to her, it seemed unnatural that human beings should live within a gargantuan metal enclosure, climbing around tanks, valves, pumps, and other mechanical and electrical equipment, with gages protruding everywhere, in an artificial and human-made environment. The constant physical work entailed in getting through an average day at sea wore at most officers and sailors. Basic tasks such as using the heads, sleeping in a shipboard rack, passing through airlocks and watertight doors to walk from one end of the ship to the other, port and starboard (twelve hour) watch cycles, and subsisting during strings of twenty-four hour work cycles, took a toll on those living aboard. The gamut of reactions to Navy life could be read on the faces of any group in any given section of a passageway or workspace, and it ranged from depression, despair, signs of early aging, chronic fatigue, all the way to acceptance, pride in one's work, enjoyment, and even fulfillment in the life at sea. Brenda wished she could have fallen into the latter category; some of the guys regularly told her that they loved going to sea.

But every move she made onboard felt foreign, and she was sure that she appeared awkward and out of place to her shipmates. However, she had going for her that she genuinely cared about her division. Despite her shortcomings, she tried to create a work environment in which those in her division felt safe to express themselves as professionals, put forward ideas, and learn to be confident in the work they performed. Outside of that, she understood that her ability to contribute was limited, but despite being tired most of the time she continued to try. She was at least relieved that the daily work of the division was going well, and so far, she had enjoyed a positive relationship with the gunners mates.

With both hands clenching the wheel, she pulled the hatch open. The door to the gun mount was several inches thick, heavy enough to withstand an explosion in the magazine. She reminded herself that after her freshman year of NROTC, she had planned on applying for a support role within the military. If she had just graduated one year earlier, she thought, she could have opted for supply, intelligence, or some other restricted line (non-warfare) community within the Navy. Had that plan materialized, she might have enjoyed a level of success during her naval service. As an officer in one of those communities, she could have worked hard and achieved results that would have allowed her to look back on her naval service and feel that she had contributed in some positive manner, or at the very least, that she had understood her job and performed it well.

But during her senior year of college, the Navy changed its policy: All physically qualified midshipmen had to choose a warfare (referred to as unrestricted line) community. The restricted line officer communities such as supply, intelligence, cryptography, etc. became closed to midshipmen who were physically qualified for line duty.

By her sophomore year, she had given up on her childhood dream of aviation, without any regret or remorse, understanding even then that she had lacked the sort of physicality required for flying, and especially for the training. The thought of parachuting out of a plane felt frightening, and she could never get the training scene out of her head from *An Officer and a Gentleman*, where the main character underwent an underwater egress training in which he had to sit in a cab that ran down rails, flipped him, and trapped him underwater – seat belted and disoriented – at the bottom of a swimming pool.

What she hadn't given up on in college, she realized, was her awe at serving in the military, an awe that had kept her locked into ROTC. She wished that she had matured beyond her youthful notion of patriotism while in college – *I love my country so I am going to express that by joining the military!* Then, she might have progressed earlier on towards the understanding she held now, that patriotism and pride in country came in varied forms, many of them abstract, and that supporting militarism or serving in the military didn't necessarily equate to patriotism. Or at least, the military wasn't the only vehicle available to show or to express one's patriotism.

All of the war movies and documentaries she had watched with her father, the work he was doing in the defense industry, his voting tendencies and his positive regard for the Reagan era, their proximity to a Marine Corps base during the short time they had lived in California, and her friend's father who was a lieutenant colonel in the Air Force, had all made a strong impression on her psyche while she was growing up.

Crouched in front of the gun hatch, she asked herself: Why had it taken an experience of this magnitude to open herself to the viability of other paths in life, ones she wished she had considered, ones that would have been more appropriate for her? She now esteemed in a new way the values of some of the friends she had known in college, especially her suitemate, who had taken a low paying job for an environmental organization after volunteering there during summers, and her other friend who had joined the Peace Corps. Working for land preservation and environmental causes domestically, and for the education of those around the world, they were probably doing more to protect and further American interests than she was. They were just as engaged in work for their country as she was, and at the same time, for humanity and for the environment, and even in a larger global sense.

In contrast, she had put herself in a position where she could be used indiscriminately for war and for the destruction of another place and people, a different culture she might not have understood, for a cause she might not have understood, at the behest of a few politicians who might decide her fate, and the fate of thousands like her...for, what were their motives? For some philosophical or ideological vision they had of how the world needed to be ordered? Her friends were trying to protect at-risk human life, animal life, and even plant life from destruction, and were working for their country by peaceful means, while she was training to wreak death and destruction.

She had never before considered the wide breadth of what it meant to be patriotic, or to reach and think beyond popular, canned, ready-made, and conservative concepts of patriotism. She regretted many of the things she had said to her friends. She had felt superior to them in choosing the "right and sensible" technical career path, and for volunteering to go into the Navy. But she now realized that they were working to promote a culture of peace, and that working for peace, through non-violent means, could be just as patriotic as anything she was doing, and very likely much more meaningful. Why not promote a culture of peace as being a patriotic virtue, versus a culture of war? she had started to question.

Brenda lifted herself through the gun hatch, wondering whether the lessons she was learning onboard about herself were worth the utter misery and anger she felt, now that she was trapped within the ship, performing in an incompatible job. Were the lessons she was learning worth sacrificing her twenties, living in a restricted environment, her individuality completely restrained, spending weeks isolated at sea, stopping for a few days or hours here and there in Asian ports? She had wanted to travel and see the world, but at most of the ports she felt so sick from exhaustion that she walked the streets and sidewalks nauseous, unable to function well from fatigue, with such pain in her eyes from lack of sleep that it was a struggle to enjoy and experience the many exotic and historic cities she was able to visit.

The combination of her Navy crisis, reflecting on her friends' career choices, rejecting some of her parents' values, starting to accept her own individual feelings, rejecting the need for a technical background…these were all coming together to force her to consider searching for a life path that had meaning…meaning without the need for patriotism expressed through a war culture. She had started to broaden her thinking about the significance of the work that needed to be done in the world…in a different scope than she had originally considered. What would her new path entail, and where would it lead her?

Brenda walked into the main space in the gun mount, regretting that she had chosen to immerse herself in a world of metal, coldness, guns, and missiles. She was starting to rethink her participation in all of the U.S. military forward-presence missions the ship embarked on, the supposed purpose being to secure peace in the world. In *The Naval Officer's Guide*, she had noticed an isolated, non-contextualized quote above chapter thirteen that read, "The deterrence of war is the primary objective of the armed forces." But the more she read similar language in books recommended by the Navy as "suggested reading," the less it resonated with her as truly being peaceful language; it read as language crafted by stern military strategists who accepted war culture, support of the military and militarism, and the need of a large military as a means to "peace."

She had started to wonder. And as the towering gray warships of the battle group pulled up and moored adjacent to the humble cities and towns of the countries they visited, the American presence felt more to her like "peace" through intimidation, force, and dominance. The ship's forward presence deployments were the manifestation of a conservative world view, a theory of world order in which the U.S. – seeing itself as exceptional – was to act as the world's super-power; this was interpreted as its destiny. In this line of thought, as an inherently benevolent super-power, the U.S. required a large military (domination of the seas and control of strategic points on land) to enforce this world order for the good of all and to protect U.S. interests. If a country or power stepped out of the bounds of the U.S. world vision or violated U.S. interests, as a world policeman, the U.S. would intervene with its colossal military – thus, many of the elective wars were sold to the public as "protecting our freedom."

She had started doubting the belief system she had developed through discussions with her father, who held to the prevailing old-guard conservative superpower views of the '80s. She remembered that during her student co-op at CIA, she had accepted – without a thought or question – that the CIA operated throughout the world. In her Navy classes, she had learned of peacekeeping forces, power projection, sea control, and the importance of American domination of the seas. She had seen bumper stickers on cars around base that read, "The United States Navy - the sea is ours." It was in *Forward...from the Sea*, the document describing the Navy's post-Cold War "operational concept," that she had first read of the Navy's shift in mission, and was introduced to new terms such as *strategic deterrence of war*, *power projection to preserve peace*, and *peacetime forward-presence operations*. Such language didn't seem to embody the right energy, at heart, to bring peace, she now thought.

While living and working onboard the destroyer, she had become aware of the staggering resources and energy it took to operate and maintain even one destroyer – the fuel and time in training alone! If only those same resources, the resources it took to maintain even one destroyer, were put to domestic use in just one area of America in need, to address poverty, education, conservation, joblessness, a crumbling infrastructure, then maybe the U.S., and the world, if it followed such an example, might be a different place.

She decided she wanted to serve her country in a different capacity, not in the military, as popular rhetoric had guided her to do. The military may have been needed in some form, but did it need to act so largely and so heavy-handedly in the world? And did it need her especially?

Brenda climbed farther into the gun mount. "It's me. I'm here for the division officer maintenance spot check," she called out to the gunners mates.

"We're up here, ma'am, hold on a sec," she heard one of the guys call down.

Brenda sat down on the deck cross-legged, next to the local control console (LCC) for the gun, and looked around the space. It was clean, orderly, and well-maintained. The daily magazine temperature report for the space was up-to-date, meticulously filled in and ready to be filed. The weekly test of the magazine sprinkler systems had been conducted and logged as satisfactory on the magazine temperature record, displayed on the bulkhead in a transparent frame. As she scanned the space, she couldn't help but question if she would have learned as much about herself if she had gone into the supply corps, for example, and had had a manageable time of it in the Navy. If she hadn't been confronted with her own failures and limitations, would she have discovered her need to change, grow, explore, even to become a more authentic person?

"I'm going to schedule a division meeting this afternoon in the VLS to pass down a few policy issues," she called up to the guys. But she feared they had already heard about the XO's newly promulgated policies during quarters with Chief Dering. Her concern stemmed from the way he curtly voiced unwelcome news, injecting it with his own abrasive and demoralizing attitude.

Earlier, in the combat systems office, Neil and Rob had told her that the XO had barely mentioned the successful missile firing at officers call that morning, neglecting the opportunity to capitalize and build on the high morale that had resulted from it. She had instead announced a highly restrictive protocol for all future port visits. "No one, and I mean no one," she had said, "shall leave the ship without signing out in a liberty log, and signing in and out with the same liberty buddy, no exceptions. Everyone must return to the ship accompanied by the same person he or she left with. Liberty will expire every night at 2200, so there will be no more staying in hotel rooms on liberty or staying out late. No one will wear open-toe shoes such as sandals, or sleeveless shirts, or short-sleeve shirts without a collar."

"But there haven't been any incidents to warrant restricting liberty," Brenda had exclaimed in response. "She's treating us like children!" But Rob had stopped her before she could comment further, stating that the news only got worse. "As soon as we reach our homeport of Yokosuka," the XO had announced, "first class petty officers will no longer be allowed to stand quarterdeck watch as the OOD, no exceptions. They shall be relegated to standing petty officer of the watch only. Qualified chiefs will no longer stand OOD watch on the bridge. Any questions or complaints, don't bring them to me because I don't want to hear them."

That morning Brenda had typed up a chit to the Captain requesting permission to conduct a gunnery field day before the ship's scheduled return to Yokosuka; she planned on organizing the event herself if the Command would let her. Each first and second class gunners mate would be assigned to a firing station – 9mm, .50 cal, M14, 12 gauge shotgun – where they would train their shipmates in safe use of the weapons, and then supervise the trainees while they shot the weapons off the side of the deck. The field day would allow the gunners mates to engage in their specialty, demonstrate their rating to their shipmates, and satisfy Navy-mandated training requirements. She also saw it as a great morale and confidence building exercise for the division, and potentially, for other crewmembers who participated. It had bothered her that during inport duty and quarterdeck watch, non-gunners mate watchstanders and members of the duty security alert teams were required to carry small arms (specifically a 9mm in the case of the quarterdeck watch), but they received little (if any) training in the firing and handling of those weapons. She had remembered the idea of a gunnery field day from SWOS, when she had rotated through a one day gunnery officer course taught by a chief gunners mate. On her chit, she had compiled a list of ways in which the gunnery field day could benefit the ship overall; she planned to submit her chit up the chain of command to the Captain.

*

Sitting on the deck in the gun mount, Brenda waited for the guys to finish their work up in the gun. The leading petty officer on the GMG (gunners mate - guns) side of the division, who had recently made first class petty officer, had the guys inspecting the seals around the pistons and operating shafts for hydraulic fluid leaks. Petty Officer Falk was diligent, quiet, and methodical, the type of person who only spoke when he felt there was something important enough to say. She was relieved that he had made rate (meaning he had been promoted to E-6 first class petty officer), not only because he deserved the promotion, but also because she had gained another solid first class petty officer for the division, one focused on the gun. Petty Officers Brooks and Mimms were reliable and knowledgeable, but they were GMMs, focused on the VLS and missiles.

As she continued to wait for the guys to finish, she kept reminding herself that following the return to homeport in Yokosuka, lay the promise of a month long post-deployment stand-down. Lieutenant Commander Gates' "leadership" felt maddening to her. She didn't understand her new liberty and quarterdeck watch policies or her timing in promulgating them. Immediately following the success of the missile exercise, Brenda had felt the crew's energy transform from a dark mood of uncertainty and instability to one of accomplishment. She had witnessed the crew walk about the ship with a sense of pride. The tone of their speech had lightened; they greeted each other in the passageways with a feeling of elation. During her rounds before bridge watch on the night after the missile firing, she had heard people celebrating throughout the ship. The crew had organized a celebratory poker tournament on the mess decks. Before her evening dog watch[5] on the bridge (1600-1800), it had been her turn to sample the crew's mess. (Per Navy regulation, an officer had to sample the crew's mess every day, and rate the quality and quantity of the food, the cleanliness of the plates and utensils, and the cleanliness of the servers.) As she sat on the mess decks, filling out the form given to her by the chief mess specialist (MSC), she had even noticed the mess specialists (MS) celebrating the success of the missile firing while they cooked in the galley. Everyone onboard seemed to feel that they had played a role in the live missile firing exercise; a multifaceted crew had come together. Morale had peaked at an all-time high. Over the 1MC, the Captain had congratulated the crew because the admiral on the aircraft carrier was proud of them. They could have ridden on high spirits back into their homeport of Yokosuka.

"Did you guys enjoy the holiday routine set by the Captain yesterday as a reward for the missile firing?" she asked the GMs,

---

[5] Dog watch: A method of shifting the watch cycle so that one particular watch team does not consistently stand the midwatch. First dog watch (1600-1800), second dog watch (1800-2000).

raising her voice enough so they could hear her up the ladder, deep into the gun. "It was certainly well deserved. You guys did an incredible job on the missile shoot. And I have an idea about possibly scheduling a gunnery field day. We'll talk during the meeting in the VLS." As of late, she had turned herself into a cheerleader of sorts. She had tried to encourage the guys to study for the enlisted surface warfare specialist qualification (ESWS) pin, and she had submitted their accomplishments (for example, repairing the VLS) for awards – anything for morale. She found herself increasingly in the middle, straddling between the division and interpreting the positions taken by the Command. She had started to give up on her frantic quest to snatch her SWO pin and steal away to nuclear power school; she had found a level of fulfillment in the administration of the division – one area in which she had a chance at making a difference for others.

"We did enjoy it, ma'am," Petty Officer Finn answered as he climbed down the ladder. "How's my favorite GUNNO?" he asked.

"Well, I have no competition," she joked. "What's a GMM doing hanging out in the gun mount with GMGs," she asked GMM2 Finn, while still seated on the deck.

"I like it here," he answered. "Can I fix your hat, GUNNO? You can't walk around the ship with your brim flat."

"Sure," she gave in.

"Otherwise they're gonna make fun of you, ma'am," he insisted.

"Good," she smiled.

"Are we good or what, ma'am?" GMG2 Taylor addressed her as he skipped the last few rungs of the ladder.

"You are. The missile firing was great the other day," she said. "Everything went off without a hitch."

"Ma'am, the ammo message for the firing," Petty Officer Mimms popped in.

"Thank you, Petty Officer Mimms."

"Yes, ma'am," he stated dryly and a bit exasperated. He then left.

Petty Officer Finn shook his head. "Mimms," he exclaimed.

"Don't worry about Petty Officer Mimms; he'll be alright," Brenda smiled.

"Later, GUNNO, later, everyone," GMM2 Finn said before disappearing out the hatch.

"I already told them about the XO's policy changes," Chief

Dering said to her, off to the side, as he climbed through the gun hatch. "So you don't need any meeting in the VLS."

"Okay, Chief," she nodded, somewhat frustrated. "But I would also like to talk to them about the changes because they're going to affect morale. I'd like to set up a meeting for fifteen hundred in the VLS."

"Fine, no biggie, ma'am," he answered curtly, while looking away.

"Okay, Chief," she said again, but calmly, restraining herself. She had come to abhor his response of "no biggie" whenever she asked anything of him. Not only was that response dismissive, but it left her never quite sure if he would follow through with what she asked for. A few weeks ago, she had gone to WEPS for advice; she told him that she wished she could somehow dig in and work with Chief Dering, and that she hated that she had to beg information from him.

"I know," WEPS had acknowledged, obviously aware of the challenge of Chief Dering. "He's close to retirement and bitter," he said, and then he had closed his eyes for a second. "I'm sure we can't get any more out of him. Do your best," he had advised.

And so she went to Pete for advice because Chief Dering had been Pete's chief when he was gunnery officer. "My guess is he hasn't changed in years," Pete had offered.

In truth, she empathized with Chief that he worked for her, a young and inexperienced ensign with little to no understanding of the systems in her charge, systems that he had spent a lifetime mastering. But on the other hand, the Navy had assigned them on the ship together as officer and chief petty officer. Chief was onboard to serve as the hands-on technical expert, while she was assigned to provide oversight, mainly administrative. Most of the lieutenant instructors at SWOS had acknowledged personal experience with her same issue, but none had ever offered any clear or usable advice; they simply said it was the division officer's responsibility to motivate the chief. At twenty-three years old, Brenda wondered how such a feat could realistically be accomplished. But she was fortunate that Chief Dering ensured the division ran well, and she now had three great leading first class petty officers who took care of daily operations. She had developed a trusting relationship with Petty Officer Brooks; GMG1 Falk was new but solid; and Petty Officer Mimms was reluctantly coming along.

"Chief, I heard that the CASREPs have possibly been completely cleared on the gun?" she changed the subject.

"Yup, already talked to WEPS about it."

"Okay, yes, Chief," she answered. She watched as Chief leaned into one of his exasperated postures. His response was what she expected. Whenever she approached him, whether in the chiefs mess or in the gun mount, she could see him start to jut his hip out to one side, while he rested his opposite hand against a bulkhead; his free hand always held his chief's coffee mug in front of his chest with a firm overstated grip. When he answered her, he always looked off to the side or at the deck, and bounced his hip in frustration.

"I have an idea, Chief," she said, gaining some enthusiasm.

"What's that, ma'am?" he said, nearly drained of his patience.

"Assuming the gun is repaired and the PAC fire test is successful, let's have a gunnery field day. The gunners mates missiles had their day with the missile firing. Let's balance it off for the GMGs. I'll organize the whole event."

"Never happen," he said.

"What do you mean?"

"It'll never happen with this Captain. You'll never get that."

"I'm putting in a chit to the Captain. Why not?"

"Good luck, ma'am," he said as he began to walk away.

"Wait, Chief, listen," she crawled out of the gun hatch and went after him, ignoring his attitude. "If I can get the field day scheduled before we get back to Yoko, will you support it? I would need your help to plan the 5"/54 exercise, and for you to supervise the guys while they instruct and shoot during the field day."

"If you get it scheduled," he said, and he finally walked away from her.

"Remember our meeting in the gun mount and later in the VLS, Chief," Brenda called out to him as she crawled back into the hatch to supervise the division officer spot check. She felt like some progress had been made: It was positive news that Chief and the GMGs had made progress on – or possibly repaired – the gun after so long, rendering it operational once again.

Chapter 44: An outrageous twilight zone

It was daybreak when CSO came up to the bridge to let Brenda know that she would be giving a training brief that afternoon on antisubmarine warfare (ASW). She remembered seeing the top of the sun peering over the early dawn horizon through the bridge windows, as she had poised to protest her assignment to him. "But I don't have any time to prepare, sir!" she had wanted to blurt out before he had finished speaking. However, she refrained from reacting. "I'll prepare something, sir," she had answered instead. Last minute schedule changes, which were the norm on surface ships, had increased in frequency since Lieutenant Commander Gates' arrival. The XO kept the department heads in a constant kneejerk mode of management, inciting them to run around the ship frantically jumping through hoops for her. The schedule changes were not the fault of CSO, Brenda understood. And of all the department heads onboard, CSO remained the most even, the most metered, absorbing and screening flak and hostility from the XO, ensuring those in his department had the support they needed to fulfill their duties. That was why she held back from complaining out loud when he had assigned her the briefing at dawn. And, she knew that she was capable of going down to her stateroom after bridge watch, sitting at her desk, and researching some aspect of antisubmarine warfare to put a brief together.

Brenda stared up at the rudder angle indicator. During the entire four-hour watch, they had changed course once. The helmsman, a hefty boatswains mate third class from Brooklyn, New York, colorfully tattooed from head to foot, had silently kept the ship steady on course, as they headed for an operational grid in the northern Pacific, near Japan. "Make sure ma'am has the coffee she wants, whatever she needs up here," the BM3 had broken the watch team's silence, speaking in his heavy regional accent – to which he added his own style of slow drawl. Brenda turned to BM3, nodded, and thanked him, as she was the only "ma'am" on watch. His comment was directed at QM1 Westgear (the quartermaster of the watch [QMOW] and the ship's lead quartermaster) who regularly kept a pot of Starbucks brewed on his watches. "But don't give me the frou-frou shit," BM3 reminded QM1. "Make a pot of the Navy supply stuff for me." Everyone onboard liked BM3 Callahan. They took him for who he was, as there seemed to be no other choice with him. Brenda enjoyed listening to his stories during quiet watches, when he stood boatswains mate of the watch instead of helmsman. He liked to talk about "being Irish in Brooklyn." "I should bring a tape recorder, BM3," she used to tell him. "You can do what you want, ma'am. Don't matter to me," he would say. Todd, the OOD, would always laugh, finding humor in her interactions with the BM3.

QM1 left the chart table to brew some coffee – both kinds at once – on the other side of the bridge. He had a soft spot for Petty Officer Callahan as well, as all of them did. QM1 had over fifteen years in the Navy and was a superior quartermaster. He told Brenda many times that he never wanted to make chief; he wanted to retire as an E-6 first class petty officer. He didn't want the politics of the chiefs mess or that higher level of management. He enjoyed being a quartermaster, and the everyday tasks of maintaining the ship's charts and tracking the weather. The enlisted had the option to stay in the Navy without the requirement of having to advance in rate. In contrast, officers were required to advance in rank on schedule, otherwise they had to resign their commissions or retire.

She often thought that Jon, the navigator, was lucky to have a solid first class petty officer such as QM1 to do the navigation work for him.

While two kinds of coffee brewed on the port side of the bridge, aft where the BMOW hung out during watch, Brenda walked starboard over to Neil, who had been leaning over the chart table updating the OOD log. "I filled in for WEPS at eight o'clocks last night," he told her quietly, referring to nightly eight o'clock reports, a type of status meeting (ship's readiness, security, damage control, admin updates) customarily given in the XO's stateroom onboard naval ships. Brenda leaned over the chart table beside him and rested her elbows on the charts. Todd was standing behind them, scanning the horizon for contacts through his binoculars. All during the morning watch, the radar had remained clear. "The XO had the department heads lined up," Neil continued, "bitching up a storm, screaming over schedule changes, enlisted evaluations, topside painting, and admin issues. After dismissing the other department heads, she asked me to stay behind."

Todd let out a laugh. "What a privilege to be one of the senior division officers in the department," he commented.

"You get to sub for WEPS at eights while he's on watch," Brenda said.

"I dread walking into her stateroom," Neil sighed, as he set his pencil down. "It's miserable. She screamed and bitched at me that the E-6 and below enlisted evals weren't on her desk, that the weapons department evals weren't done."

"Was it true?" Brenda asked.

"She pushed the due date back at the last minute. There wasn't time enough to comply. It's like she takes sadistic pleasure in making demands you can't possibly meet. While I stood there, she called WEPS in CIC and reamed him out. She loves to pick up the IVCS headset in her stateroom and call WEPS and CSO while they're on watch in CIC and scream into the phone. After she bitches them out, she slams her headset down, breaks it, and calls the ICman (interior communications electrician) to fix it. Lately, IC2 has started to automatically come up to her stateroom after eight o'clocks to put the phone back together." Brenda said nothing, and Todd looked amused in the particular way he had when he found the Navy amusing. "Danielle majored in psychology; her guess is that she's bipolar," Neil finished.

"Everyone's saying that but I don't know, except that she does seem to suffer from some mental illness," Brenda said, noticing that none of them seemed to understand how to describe Lieutenant Commander Gates' behavior.

"Bipolar, I wouldn't be surprised," Todd sort of laughed, as he lowered his binoculars, letting them hang from his neck.

Brenda shook her head and looked over at Todd. After standing watch after watch with him, she wanted to hear him acknowledge straightforwardly that the XO's behavior was outlandish and incomprehensible, that she abused her power and that she was incompetent, demeaning, and even dangerous – that they were living in some outrageous twilight zone situation and that something needed to be done! She almost commented to him that she was tired of his cynical style of humor that fell just short of overtly stating his feelings regarding the Navy and SWO, but she refrained. She had noticed that some officers seemed willing to state their thoughts about the Navy, SWO, and most recently the XO, outright. But others seemed reluctant about verbalizing and expressing their thoughts, even though they saw what was going on. They were cautious, or they just simply wouldn't admit what was going on. Or, she wondered, they felt it was their professional duty to keep silent and work as best as they could within the situation. In SWO culture, officers were accustomed to maltreatment, and the pressure was on to "suck it up and tough it out."

Among her peers, and to her department head, Brenda had tried to let her thoughts and feelings be known. She hoped that if the junior officers discussed the issue of the XO honestly, then maybe they could take some kind of action within the chain of command.

Brenda stared up at the clock and watched a few more seconds of her bridge watch tick by, knowing that when she climbed down from the bridge at seven-thirty a.m., she would have to scrape a brief together on a topic about which she knew very little – antisubmarine warfare – and prepare for officers call and quarters.

As well, she had a list of messages that she needed to write, route up the chain, and send out through radio for some upcoming gunnery exercises. She thought about her department head and how career surface warfare officers needed a perfect record for promotion within the Navy's up-or-out personnel system, which meant if an officer didn't promote on schedule, he/she had to resign or retire, whichever was applicable. The desire and competition for that perfect record, and getting the "right tickets punched" when selecting billets – whether at the pentagon or for sea duty – formed the basis of surface warfare officer culture. An officer couldn't stay in the Navy for very long, or enjoy a career, without becoming adept at this intricate, bureaucratic personnel system. It informed how SWOs managed their shipboard departments on a daily basis, how they micromanaged, and how they reacted to adversity and crisis and to each other. It informed what type of officer would be attracted to making the Navy a career. She felt as though every move they made as a department could be traced to WEPS' perception of how his officer FITREP would be affected. Her department head fretted every detail and mistake as if each one might end his career.

"WEPS must have been frantic after the XO called him on watch in CIC," Brenda said to Neil. "I can picture him jittery, frenzied over his career and FITREP."

"I went down to CIC afterwards," Neil said, shaking his head. "He was all spun up. He won't stand up to her, no one will, not with careers and FITREPs on the line."

"The XO's wrong about WEPS," Brenda stated to Neil, after a pause. "He's a brilliant person. Instead of tormenting him, she should recognize his talent and use him as a resource, as a good leader should."

"She's too threatened," Neil responded, but added nothing else in defense of their department head. He picked up his pencil and began studying the last two fixes on the navigation chart. Brenda understood Neil's mixed feelings. WEPS' constant fear that every action they took onboard might sink his career grated on her as well. But she had come to admire her department head's ability to understand highly technical and abstract concepts at first glance; she had watched him turn around newly acquired knowledge in an instant, and apply it pragmatically and successfully – especially on watch as TAO, directing air and surface exercises over the radio. "It's too bad," she said. "WEPS was the top bridge watchstander on his first two ships, ranked as the number one junior officer on both tours. He's one of the smartest people I've ever met."

"It's unusual in modern day to meet someone versed in discussing the classics," Neil replied. "But he can also be his own worst enemy."

"Tension starts to fill any space the XO enters," Brenda said. "The air tightens, everyone tightens, until she leaves and everyone is granted relief."

"She still won't dial the correct phone down in CIC," Neil said, "even after yesterday." He walked over to study the ARPA radar picture, and Brenda followed him. "The department heads have repeatedly asked her to dial the IVCS phone at the TAO console. That way, while they're sitting TAO watch, they don't have to get up and leave the watchstation to answer the phone. She won't do it," he emphasized, keeping his voice down. "The XO continues to dial the phone on the adjacent steel column a few feet away from the watchstation, so that they have to stand up from the TAO chair and leave the watchstation to answer the phone when she calls, every time."

"I was in CIC for yesterday's scene," Brenda answered.

"It's already a part of ship's lore," Neil said.

"I just wanted to go down there to work on quals," Brenda replied. She had been sitting at a console next to the CIC officer, Jason Arnett, the limited duty officer (LDO), when the phone on the column a few steps away from the TAO console rang. "The XO's the only one who calls that phone," Jason had commented to her in frustration, "and she has a knack for calling at the most intense points during an exercise, a total lack of awareness and safety."

"I know," Brenda had answered him, knowing Jason was angry and there was nothing she could say. She looked over at CSO, who was sitting TAO watch, engaged in an air exercise with the carrier; he was signaling to an OS (an enlisted operations specialist) to answer the phone for him.

The next thing she knew, OS2 Watkins was holding the phone receiver in disbelief. "The XO hung up on me, sir," he said to CSO.

Minutes later, the XO stormed into CIC, enraged. While the operations specialists were controlling aircraft in flight, the full enlisted watch team stationed at their consoles, she gripped the back of CSO's khaki collar, and held it while she threateningly told him to next time answer the goddamn mother fucking phone himself, no matter what he was engaged in. She then stared into him, and picked up a set of headphones off the seatback of the next console and wacked him in the back of the head with them. She wanted a written outline for the ship's website, she demanded of CSO, and she wanted it now. Brenda, dumbfounded, remained in her chair, her training stopped, while Jason, the CIC officer, walked past and observed each of the CIC watchstanders to ensure they remained focused on their air traffic control duties. The XO had cared nothing about the air exercise nor the safety of the pilots in the air. "I can't help you now," Jason had told her quickly. "We'll have to resume your training another time." So Brenda tried to hang around CIC and absorb as much as she could on her own.

*

For a few minutes, Brenda, Todd, and Neil had been standing on the bridge, gazing out at the horizon in front of them in complete silence. "So much for praise in public, criticize in private," Todd commented, referring to a common Navy leadership mantra.

"It's unbelievable," Neil stated.

"The explanation's in Thailand," Brenda said.

"The XO's TAO qualification," Todd laughed.

Brenda stared over the ship's forecastle into the undulating seas, picturing the Thai hotel-restaurant, where she, along with Rob, Neil, Pete, and Bill had learned the story behind their XO's TAO qualification. The restaurant was adorned with luscious flowers and tropical green leafy bushes, stereotypical for Thailand. Brenda remembered walking the hundred-plus degree streets of Pattaya Beach, a resort town, on shore patrol with Bill, holding a walkie-talkie and constantly peeling her drenched polyester white uniform off her skin. To find relief from the Thai summer heat, Bill had walked over to the hotel bar to buy bottled water for the two of them, while Brenda sat down by the pool with Rob, Neil, Pete, and a few other junior officers from various ships within the battle group. "We heard HAG, I mean, Lieutenant Commander Heather A. Gates, is your XO onboard *Curtis Wilbur*," one of the JOs exclaimed when she took a seat at the table, in the shade.

"You know about her?" Brenda reacted.

"Her reputation precedes her," the JO responded. "She's well-known across the waterfront. I've been telling your shipmates how I witnessed her TAO qualification."

"You'll want to hear this," Neil said. "It seems much of our speculation was correct."

"Her TAO qualification is a sham, a joke," the JO said. "She's spent the past few years getting multiple master's degrees on the Navy's time and money. She's never served a regular SWO department head tour."

When Bill took a seat, Brenda handed him a hundred Thai baht for the water, and the JO related his story: In a race to qualify Heather Gates for command, the Navy assigned her TAD (temporary assigned duty) to his prior ship, a destroyer, for a few months. "She was handed her TAO qualification," he had said. After Lieutenant Commander Gates sat TAO watch six or seven times, often parroting a qualified TAO, the ship was pressured to qualify her; it had become apparent that the Navy had chosen her as the face of its high profile program to integrate women into command positions ASAP, and her TAO qualification was urgent. While onboard the destroyer, Lieutenant Commander Gates – officially billeted as part of embarked DESRON (destroyer squadron) staff – behaved in a hostile manner toward the department heads who tried to train her. She had routinely snapped, "got it," followed by a penetrant stare, for which she had become famous; she pretended that she already knew or already understood what they were trying to teach her. Over the radio, during the few exercises in which she had participated, she had spewed chatter that made no sense, at critical times when she was supposed to be in control; she was weak and lost in CSI (combat systems integration).

The JO explained that he had wanted to feel sympathy for her, but she was dangerous, grossly lacking in situational and tactical awareness; she was always right, and she treated the enlisted watchstanders harshly, like dirt, affording them no respect. She simply viewed the enlisted and other junior officers as existing to serve her interests in checking off her TAO qualification, to which she seemed to feel entitled.

Brenda remembered wishing that the Navy had chosen a woman such as Julie, who would have risen to the challenge, who would have respected those who taught her, who would have understood the information thoroughly. During her freshman year of ROTC, the SWO lieutenant instructor was a female surface warfare officer. She seemed to be a fair and competent officer. Women had served in the Navy as surface warfare officers since the late '70s on non-combatant ships. So, why was Heather A. Gates chosen for such high profile duty? Julie, or a woman like the senior lieutenant instructor at her ROTC unit, would have been great candidates to serve as the Navy's first historic female captain of a destroyer or cruiser. Now, one of the first female captains of a destroyer or cruiser was – disgracefully – going to be Heather A. Gates.

Another JO at the table, who had never met Heather Gates, shrugged off the accounts as typical SWO. "She's what the SWO community breeds," he had jeered. "SWO eat their young, micromanagement, flame-spraying screamers, frantic inspection preps, backstabbing..."

"She's worse than typical SWO," Brenda had interrupted him. "The difference between Lieutenant Commander Gates and other career SWOs – what sends her over the top – is her outrageous behavior combined with incompetence as a shiphandler and tactician, not to mention her lack of experience," she asserted.

*

On the bridge, Neil raised his binoculars and looked out toward the port bow to see if a merchant contact, which the ship was slowly overtaking, had come into view. "I heard CSO a few minutes ago, by the way, about the ASW training briefs this afternoon," he interrupted her thoughts. "If you want, I'll lend you an ASW manual with a good introductory section you can use as a reference for your briefing."

"I'll take you up on that, thanks, Neil," Brenda replied. She had become accustomed to preparing quick briefs on a variety of topics about which she knew nothing. Assigning junior officers to give training on topics with which they were unfamiliar was a common training tool in the Navy, the idea being that the junior officer would research the topic and learn by teaching. For each briefing assignment, she had written her entire brief out word for word on her notecards, and had memorized the delivery. She didn't know what else could be done when assigned a brief to be given in front of colleagues and senior officers in the wardroom, on a topic about which she knew nothing. For her at least, in that situation, a freestyle presentation given from bulleted ideas was out of the question; only memorization seemed viable. Actual learning became subordinate; she just aimed to "get through" without embarrassment. She only hoped that the audiences would learn from her presentations.

"Go ahead and grab the manual off my stateroom desk after watch," Neil offered. Then he paused, and braced his palms against the chart table. "I'd rather be working at the fucking McDonalds on base than onboard this ship," he confided.

"So would I," she agreed. She massaged her eyes and face, tired from having gone to her rack at midnight before rising again at two-thirty a.m. for watch. "Although I'd rather the McDonalds be in Boston than on base," she said.

"There's not many of us onboard from New England," Neil smiled.

"I miss home," Brenda said. "It seems like everyone's either from the South, Texas, or the Midwest."

"People trying to escape their circumstances, get an education, better their lives," he said. "My same reasons for enlisting."

"I hadn't realized that you were originally a deck seaman starting out," she said.

"I used to love the Navy," Neil replied. "That's why after I was enlisted, I went ROTC at UMass and came back in as an officer."

"I know," she said, adding, "I appreciate you loaning me the manual."

QM1 approached Brenda and handed her a paper cup filled with black Starbucks coffee. "Fresh from Seattle, ma'am, with a packet of Navy powdered creamer."

"You're kind to the watch team, QM1, thank you," she said. "I only wish it had been brewed in Seattle."

Chapter 45: The antisubmarine (ASW) briefing ... It's tough around here

1MC Shipwide Announcement: *"Assemble all officers in the wardroom for training."*

Brenda looked up at the loudspeaker from her seat at the wardroom table. Then she scanned the plaques and framed prints on the walls, aware that they were meant to inspire a sentiment in all those who entered the wardroom that naval service was indeed noble and glorious, an endeavor of honor. She held her ASW briefing notecards in her hands, concealing them in her lap while still trying to commit them to memory, wishing that her disposition would allow her to view the wardroom, and everything it represented, from the idealized perspective portrayed in the prints. In the framed prints, wooden ships and vintage destroyers made way through fierce and heavy seas while battling the enemy and sinking him. Onboard the ships, the guns and canons were blazing, producing fire and smoke in vivid and powerful colors that elicited a sense of reverence for unswayable power and admiration of indomitable spirit. Deep oranges and blues, highlighted by soft yellows and greens, were effectively used by the artists in creating lifelike textures of fire, water, smoke, and steel, which, together, left the viewer with a sense of veneration for heroic naval battle.

The eighteenth, nineteenth, and early twentieth century naval portrayals she saw dotting the wardroom walls were elegant examples of stately nautical art, which in their era, had served as the public face and historical record of military battles and exploits; they were interpretations that idealized and romanticized war, and showed military feats as noble, triumphant, and having "just cause." The vintage portrayals differed little, in a thematic sense, from the modern portrayals of military service that had moved her to serve, she realized.

In her era, she had been fascinated by the idea of the high-tech military of the Cold War '80s. Cable documentaries about modern air and spacecraft, Tom Clancy novels and movies, and recruitment-minded films such as *Top Gun* had at one time seemed so alluring to her. On weekend afternoons, her father often watched those '80s cold war defense systems documentaries that were prevalent on cable channels at the time. So as a kid, she had soaked in the Reagan era; she had been this Reagan-era kid, wanting to go to air shows to see the Blue Angels, making up spy games based on the premise of the evil empire versus America. Spy movies and novels about the military and the CIA had captivated her. Ronald Reagan was the president during her elementary school years, through junior high, and into high school. Her father seemed to think he was a great president, and she hadn't realized there was anyone out there who had thought otherwise.

As she served and lived onboard the *Curtis Wilbur*, the remembrance that she had once been romanced by depictions of military service seemed almost mortifying. Her past sentiments toward the military now seemed foreign, and even inconceivable to her. All things military, especially the wearing of the uniform, had once held tremendous appeal, and had stirred great pride within her, leading her to actually join the military.

She rose to attention with the other officers around her. The Captain had entered the space. When the Captain took his seat, he cued Neil to begin his brief. "Let's go," he said, and nodded. Brenda began splitting her concentration between taking notes on Neil's brief, and queuing her briefing notecards in her head. Once in a while, she thumbed through her cards to check herself, while making sure her actions weren't noticed. She closely followed the numbers on the bottom right-hand corner of each of Neil's PowerPoint slides. Each successive slide meant progression toward her brief.

"Hydrophones are essentially underwater microphones, detecting the acoustic energy emitted from a target," Neil explained. "In passive systems, the azimuth of a signal can be determined but not range." Brenda wrote as fast as she could, especially ensuring she copied down any sample problems, word for word, number for number. At times, she struggled to keep her interest focused on the subject matter. She thought about how the background of Neil's title slide had showed a photo of a ballistic missile submarine (SSBN) surfacing, surging through the ocean, creating a powerful wake in its path. She thought about Neil's journey toward becoming an officer, how being an officer had its privileges but carried a different set of issues than what the enlisted faced. She thought about how at slide 2, the XO had tried sliding in through the wardroom door, hoping to remain unnoticed, opening it only as far as necessary to slip inside. Brenda had never remembered seeing the former XO late for anything.

Brenda began copying down another sample problem from Neil's next slide, number 23 of 25. *"Towed array contact 040/320R, ship's course 050T,"* she wrote, *"ship steers new course 150T..."* She saw that the supply officer had not taken her designated seat on the starboard side of the wardroom table, in the chair to the left of the Captain. Onboard *Curtis Wilbur*, the Captain, XO, and supply officer had assigned wardroom seating – the XO sat to the right of the Captain, and the supply officer sat to his left. Brenda instead saw SUPPO, Lieutenant Susan Farrell, seated by herself on one of the couches in the back of the room, holding a clipboard in her lap, subtly reading through paperwork.

Brenda shifted her glance to refocus on the sample problem displayed on the projector screen. She wondered if anyone else, besides her, knew of the XO's threat to fire Lieutenant Farrell. Last week, Brenda had learned about the threat by accident, when she had exited the shower stall in the women's head one evening to find the supply officer standing in front of the mirror above the metal sink, scrubbing at her face so hard and repeatedly that in a few areas of her face, it appeared that she had scrubbed her skin raw. Brenda set her notecards down on the table, and pressed her palm into her stomach, remembering how she had felt ill as she had witnessed the supply officer injuring her face.

"Contact regained 070/290R," Brenda jotted in her spiral notebook. She looked quickly over at SUPPO, hoping that the XO's threat had been an empty, pitiful attempt at negative leadership, applied from the vintage mindset of using cruelty and threats to control subordinates rather than exercising leadership by example. Brenda remembered when she had closed the shower stall door behind her in the women's head, and stood in place, shocked because she had walked into a scene that she couldn't square with the reserved, together, dedicated career officer that she had known since checking onboard. She wished that she had been able to help SUPPO on that evening, but instead she had felt useless and at a total loss.

"Solve for true bearing to actual contact," Brenda wrote as she remembered looking for any evidence of tears as SUPPO had stood in front of the sink scrubbing her face, but she could see none. SUPPO had appeared detached and mechanical, which had alarmed her more than if she had found her crying. She had wanted to ask SUPPO if she was okay, or if she could help, but she felt those

questions minimized the depth of the anguish she was experiencing, anguish which was a result of the horrifying circumstances onboard. Those questions were incapable of reaching into the core of the sick dynamics onboard that were undermining peoples' lives and careers. She was a young ensign, standing in the women's head, her hair soaked, her toiletries bundled in her arms; sideways, she was leaning them against the stall door so she wouldn't drop any of them. She didn't know how she could begin to aid SUPPO in her distress over shipboard dynamics that were out of their power to influence or change. While looking at SUPPO's reflection, and hers behind SUPPO's, Brenda had wanted to break down herself. She had wanted to tell SUPPO they were all smart, hardworking people, who, in any other similar employment situation, would simply leave. But of course that option was unavailable here. On some days, it seemed as though Lieutenant Commander Gates was bent on playing with the minds of her officers for cruelty's sake, driving them to the point of mental breakdown, for some reason which Brenda could not understand.

After standing behind SUPPO for at least a minute, looking at both of their reflections in the mirror, SUPPO had acknowledged her. "I'm nearly the most incompetent supply department head in the fleet," she had said, breaking the silence between them. "The XO's assured me of that."

Brenda almost took a step towards SUPPO, but the sense of emotional detachedness in the supply officer's speech made her pause. "You just came from the XO's stateroom," she responded, instead of approaching her just yet.

SUPPO remained in front of the mirror continuing to scrub. "She's threatened to fire me."

"She's out of control," Brenda answered. She took a step towards SUPPO and placed her toiletries on the counter. She had an idea as to what had sparked the XO's threat, and if her assumption was correct, she knew that the basis of the threat was arbitrary and meritless. Earlier that day, Brenda had been at her GQ (general quarters) station on the bridge when the XO had stormed up the ladder, screaming, "Where is the goddamn supply officer! Where is the goddamn supply officer!" She remembered how the bridge had gone silent, while Rob, the OOD, had rushed over towards the XO, trying to stem a scene in front of the enlisted watch team. The ship had been heavily engaged in a battle group wide general quarters – *all hands man your battle stations!* – exercise with the aircraft carrier for four hours. During the extended GQ, the supply department had served milk, water, and crackers. And the XO was livid about the milk.

Brenda placed her palm on SUPPO's shoulder. "She's completely irrational," she said.

"I did everything by the book during the extended GQ, just as the XO had asked. Do you remember the milk?"

"I do, Susan," Brenda answered, hoping to reach SUPPO as a person. She had never before called SUPPO by her first name, but when she had first checked onboard, SUPPO had asked her not to call her ma'am. "You don't have to call me ma'am, or SUPPO, all the time," she had requested. But regardless, Brenda had called her SUPPO as per Navy custom. Susan was a department head, and she wanted to give her the respect corresponding to her position.

"She tore me apart for serving milk," Susan said, "just like for everything I do." Brenda wondered if she should get help, but onboard there was no one to go to; and telling another officer about this incident – Susan's private expression of her anguish – wasn't her decision to make. There was no neutral third party onboard to go to, such as a chaplain or ombudsman. "I went to the Naval Academy," Susan continued. "I've had a good career; I was going to stay in the Navy for a full career. In two weeks, I'm submitting my letter of resignation."

"The next tour will be better, lieutenant," Brenda said. "I know you were a top rated department head on your last ship."

Susan remained scrubbing. "I will never put myself in another situation where I can't leave," Susan eventually said, "where I'm trapped and can't walk away, where I'll have to sustain this abuse and keep coming back for more."

"I understand that, it's what I've learned here as well," Brenda answered. "It's why I would never stay in the military. I don't want to be controlled, or live in a controlled environment." Then Brenda remembered cupping her hands over her face because she couldn't continue to watch Susan scrubbing at her skin. "Please stop scrubbing, Susan," she finally said. "Let me get you some aloe for your face. I have some nice fresh aloe from Thailand."

Brenda finished copying down the remainder of Neil's sample problem. "Are there any questions on the material I've covered?" he asked the capacity wardroom. When no one responded, Neil brought up his last slide: a short, one question quiz. Brenda immediately recognized the tactical maneuvering problem as one of the exact ones Neil had gone over in his brief. She had copied down the sample problem statement and solution in full. She began writing down the quiz problem statement, *"Ship's course 090, hydrophone effect 200..."*

"Sketch maneuvers, where to drop acoustic devices, discuss measures..." Brenda continued to write. She copied the solution verbatim from her notes, walked to the front of the wardroom, and handed Neil her paper. "I'd like to give my brief next, if possible," she said to him.

When he nodded in agreement, Brenda remained at the front of the dining table, holding her notecards, hoping that she had prepared enough to brief on autopilot during the next five or so minutes. While she waited, she couldn't take her eyes off the vintage nautical art, and the elegant silverware and place settings in the wardroom chest. Together, an atmosphere was created, left over from when officers hailed from aristocratic classes. Now, a college degree, along with the Naval Academy, ROTC, or OCS separated officers from the enlisted. But the college divide wasn't always completely clear. Some prior enlisted officers, for example, didn't hold degrees. And many enlisted personnel earned bachelor's degrees during their service through correspondence or night school, or in rare cases, they had earned a two or four-year degree prior to service.

When the last person handed their answer sheet to Neil, the Captain cued her to start with a nod, followed by, "Go ahead, Miss Conner."

"SONAR," she began in reaction, "sound, navigation, and ranging." She could feel her right calf shaking. Her hands trembled as well, and she hoped that her nervousness was not visible to the audience. "In this briefing," she continued. "I'll review basic acoustic theory and onboard ASW sonar systems..." As she went on to discuss basic definitions for terms such as sound intensity, source level, spreading, and radiated power, she remained on auto pilot, not trusting herself to form one coherent sentence if it be spontaneous. She felt as though she had memorized syllables of a foreign language, only to regurgitate them before an audience who was supposed to learn from what she said.

Towards the end, she dreaded asking if there were any questions because someone might have one. "Are there any questions?" she asked. Brenda looked out at her audience, at her colleague officers; she saw SWO pins, and tired, darkened, and disinterested eyes. She wondered if one person had paid attention.

When Josh, the disbursing officer (DISBO, assistant supply officer), started his brief next, Brenda's mind drifted off. She was sure that Josh would give the same type of pat brief from an introductory section of a manual that she had given. She attempted to understand the bridge between her '80s-era influences while growing up, and the underlying themes behind the vintage portrayals. She had believed in the time-honored concept of the military shown in the prints. In high school, military recruiters had visited wearing full dress, sharp and starched uniforms. They had shown a video featuring crisp, fast-moving and adrenalin-surging cinematography. The narration had begun with something like, "You must become something great, to become part of something even greater...you can fight for what you believe because it's worth believing in...become something greater than yourself..." The background music periodically thundered a passion-inspiring "call to arms," featuring the bold, resounding blend of trumpets, low brass, and parade-style percussion.

She found it difficult to acknowledge that military recruiting methods, such as commercials and poster images, and hype in news media, movies and books, could have worked on her; she had thought she was smarter than that, above that, unsusceptible to the influences of advertisements. Looking at the vintage images around the wardroom, she decided that she had been seduced by modernized portrayals of age-old themes. She realized that young people like her perpetually joined up as generation after generation of elders, government leaders, and recruiters portrayed war and military service as enticing, heroic, honorable, and worthwhile for the next generation. Brenda wondered if she would ever find herself encouraging the next generation to join as she had joined.

When Josh flipped to his last notecard and asked if anyone had any questions, no one responded. "Good briefs, everyone," the Captain interrupted, and proceeded to leave, followed by the XO. Neil motioned to Brenda to look at a paper he was holding. "Look at this," he showed her. "The XO got a fucking zero on the ASW evasion quiz."

"I guess if something happens to the Captain, and she's in command while we're being hunted by a sub, we're sunk."

"Our lives, and the lives of the sailors are in her hands," Neil said.

Brenda paused, and then added, "But my quiz should be a zero, too, Neil, really it should be..." She was starting to feel prepared to admit to others that she was not adept at working through technical problems. In the case of this ASW problem, the solution required a conceptual understanding of the physics of sound. The admission to Neil about her quiz was the first of its kind for her; it was like a trial to see how such an outward admission would feel.

But Neil had remained focused on the XO's quiz. "Un-fucking-believable," he interrupted her, disgusted. "Most every officer on this ship got a zero," he added as he shuffled through the solutions, "even those who stand OOD on a regular basis. This stuff should be basic for a qualified OOD."

"It looks like WEPS and CSO got it," Brenda said as she looked, "Julie," she added. But Neil still appeared fed up and angered by the results of the quiz. "I can see why many of the officers failed," Brenda said, trying to console him. "The U.S. Navy has all this high-end technology, the most advanced in the world, but the officers constantly rotate through so many different jobs, they never develop experience in any one of them. It's no Tom Clancy movie," she joked. "If Tom Clancy had been able to go into the military himself he may have had a different view of it; he probably wouldn't have crafted such an idealized portrayal."

"It's true," he acknowledged, and laughed a little. "You always have a reality check waiting. Your reality checks are a welcome break," he said.

Brenda then noticed WEPS approach SUPPO. "Why weren't you at the table, sitting next to the Captain?" he asked her, appearing at wits end.

"The XO asked me for these budget stats five minutes before the briefings started," SUPPO answered, matter-of-factly. "I had no choice. She told me to have them to her as soon as this meeting's over. So excuse me," she said. She then walked past WEPS and left the wardroom. Under HAG, Brenda noticed that working relationships among the officers had started to break down.

"The XO makes impossible demands," Brenda heard Pete comment to Rob, "then she gets upset when you can't meet them."

The XO opened the door just enough to lean her head in. "Where's the weapons officer?" she demanded, in front of all ranks congregated within the wardroom. Brenda watched Lieutenant Commander Gates' eyes search him out and finally spot him. "I want those leave chits, WEPS," she declared across the room, and slammed the door behind her.

"I hate this," Brenda said to Neil. "I'm never going to commit myself again to a job that I can't walk away from," she added, thinking of what SUPPO had said to her.

"It's fucked," Neil answered, as he shut down his laptop. "I still haven't gotten my leave chit back for my wedding," he said. "It's been sitting in the XO's inbox for two months. Danielle and I specifically set a date during the Christmas stand-down so we could both get leave, and not have it get screwed up."

"Forty-eight hour turnaround," Brenda commented sarcastically, referring to the ship's written leave policy. According to ship's policy, all requests for leave had to be approved or disapproved within forty-eight hours of when they were first submitted up the chain of command. The XO had the authority to approve leave chits, but only the Captain could disapprove them.

"Danielle submitted her leave chit back in April when we got engaged," Neil said, "and she received it back from her CO within two hours with a huge note of congratulations. Danielle's a first generation naval officer. Her father is a retired master chief. She has a large Filipino family back in San Diego trying to plan our wedding."

"You might not be able to show at your own wedding," Brenda said.

"Whenever WEPS or CSO ask her about my wedding chit, she flies off the handle."

"What about going to the Captain?" Brenda asked.

"CSO told me he'll go to the Captain if necessary, but we're not quite there yet. The department heads are still trying to work with her. They're hesitant just yet to go around her and violate the chain of command."

"I doubt this Captain would cross her anyway," Brenda said. "He's biding his time until the change of command when we get into Yokosuka. The bottom line is that no senior officer, Captain and above, will make any waves about this XO because she's female. If the XO was male, and word got out of this behavior to the destroyer squadron commander, the Captain might have had more leeway to do something; the XO might be fired."

"A new Captain will be onboard soon," he said. "Although I'm not optimistic about much improvement. I think she's a favorite of someone high up in the brass. I've started asking Jon to check with the XO on the status of my wedding chit, since she no longer seems to allow the department heads to ask her about it."

"The navigator seems to have a special way with her," Brenda responded. "The XO seems to bend to anything he says." Brenda didn't know how she viewed Jon's unique and calculated manner of surviving SWO life and politics. In some inexplicable way, he had charmed the XO with his cynical, contemptuous, and pessimistic stance toward SWO life. She seemed entranced by his sardonic humor, his attitude, and the put-on confidence he projected. She laughed at everything he said. The XO found him hilarious, and that kept Jon from receiving the daily dose of abuse to which most everyone else seemed susceptible. He had the XO wrapped around his finger, and the irony was that he couldn't stand her. Just like all of the other officers, he absolutely could not stand her! It was amazing that she couldn't see what Jon was really doing, making a fool of her. During bridge watch, Jon had confided to her and Julie that he was only trying to survive until he could resign his commission; he was simply waiting out the end of this tour until his ROTC scholarship obligation expired.

"Jon uses his good relationship with the XO to his advantage," Neil agreed, "which is why I ask him, almost daily, to check on the status of my chit."

"Maybe Jon can use his influence to allow you to get married," she joked.

Neil smiled. "I don't know," he said. "The other day, in a rare snap at Jon, she told him that she would sign my chit when she was goddamn good and ready."

A moment later, WEPS approached them. "I need all the rest of your leave chits from the gunners mates, torpedomen, and sonar techs," he said to Neil and Brenda, in nervous, rapid speech.

"I gave them to you, sir," Brenda replied, impatiently. "What about the gunnery field day before we get back to Yoko? Did you have a chance to ask her about that?"

"You can have a field day for combat systems personnel only," WEPS replied. "The Captain doesn't want that kind of liability, especially right before the change of command."

"I thought this was supposed to be the military," Brenda responded. Then she felt badly for the attitude she had given her department head, who was under enough strain. "I'm sorry, sir," she said.

"I know, Brenda," he answered, closing his eyes for a moment. "I understand your frustration."

"It's just that we need ship-wide small arms training, and not just for combat systems personnel. All second and third class petty officers onboard go to the target range once, qualify, and then stand watch on the quarterdeck holding a loaded 9mm. Could you ask her again, sir? Or I could submit my chit to the Captain?" she suggested.

"I'll see what I can do, please, Brenda," he answered.

"Have you heard any news on my leave chit for my wedding?" Neil asked him. "I see it continues to sit in the XO's inbox."

"I'll ask her again," WEPS answered. "It sits in her inbox, unsigned. By some miracle, your chit always stays at the top of the stack where we can all see it, no matter how much paperwork people put in there throughout the day."

But it was afternoon, and Brenda knew that the XO had already settled into her daily grudge against WEPS. She had tried routing a message earlier, but the XO had screamed, "I'm mad at your department head right now," before slamming the door. On any given day, if the XO decided she was angry at a particular department head, she would refuse to see him or her or any of their division officers for the rest of the day, or to discuss any more business related to that department. Since most shipboard work had to be routed and/or approved through the XO, she simply became a roadblock to progress.

"It's nearly impossible to get messages chopped and released lately," Neil said. "The XO just sits on them. I got the flying water bottle the other day. I tried to discuss the content of the ASW 'lessons learned' message with her, but she got defensive, swore at me, threw me out of her stateroom, and almost hit me with her water bottle. Then she threatened my surface warfare qualification, screaming that I'll never get a SWO pin onboard her fucking ship – all in front of my chief."

"She can't refuse *you* a SWO board," Brenda exclaimed.

"I don't need a SWO pin from her," Neil answered, almost casually, "or from this Captain. I have my silver ESWS and coxswain pin[6] from my enlisted time. If she blocks my SWO qualification, I'm not going to fight her. I'll just get out of the Navy."

"It's the XO's job to ensure JOs qualify and department heads are trained to be future XOs," Brenda replied, upset at the possibility of the XO denying Neil his SWO pin. She couldn't think of anyone more deserving. "XOs are supposed to provide leadership and guidance," she said. But Neil's perspective on earning his SWO pin

---

[6] Enlisted qualified coxswain

didn't surprise her. She had never witnessed him cave to the pressures of taking on a careerist mindset, or fretting over FITREPs. He was simply an aboveboard, competent junior officer. Why the XO had taken a special dislike to Neil, she wasn't sure.

"I'll make sure you get a SWO board," WEPS said, and then he and Neil resumed their conversation about the wedding leave chit.

As Brenda listened to their conversation, she thought about Lieutenant Commander Gates, second in command of the guided missile destroyer upon which she stood. Lieutenant Commander Gates knew little more about antisubmarine warfare, or any other type of naval warfare, than she did. She looked at the photo of Gates, which hung on the wall beside a photo of the Captain and a plaque of the ship's seal. Both commanders wore the formal service dress blue uniform, and proudly sat before the American flag. Lieutenant Commander Gates would most likely never have to answer for the danger she posed to the ship, or for her destruction of lives and careers, Brenda thought. Navy leadership had already failed its sailors by promoting her through the years to the rank of Lieutenant Commander; now they had promoted her to the position of XO of an advanced guided missile destroyer. And she guessed that because Gates was female, senior naval leadership would be afraid to act against her. They would continue to promote her to positions of increasing responsibility, Brenda predicted.

Every few seconds the wardroom vibrated in rhythm with the drone of the ship's engines. Somehow, Brenda found the ship's never ending low and dull monotonous hum soothing, and in her most nervous times, she often turned to it. WEPS shook his head, and glanced around the wardroom. "All of this that's going on," he said; and then he refrained from finishing his thought. "I've applied to leave the SWO community and laterally transfer into foreign affairs," he announced to them. "My undergraduate degree is in physics, but my master's is from your alma mater, Brenda, in international relations."

"From SWO to Foreign Area Officer, designator 1710," Pete stated, as he approached the dining table. "Congratulations, that will be good for you, WEPS," he said.

"I thought you wanted to screen for XO," Brenda reacted, "and later for CO of a ship?"

"You think SWO is how I want to spend my life?" WEPS nearly snapped.

"I hope your selection is successful, WEPS," Neil said, offering his hand.

"I think you'll be brilliant at foreign affairs, sir," Brenda said to him, regretting her earlier outburst.

Neil looked at all of them. "It's tough around here," he said, as he packed his laptop into its carrying case. Then, all four officers, WEPS, Neil, Pete, and Brenda, picked up their daytimers and materials, and left the wardroom.

Chapter 46: Man overboard ... Everybody dance now ... Zombie

1MC Announcement: *"Assemble all junior officers on the bridge for man overboard training."*

Brenda didn't mind seeing man overboard training listed on the ship's plan of the week (POW). She had conned during man overboard drills a few times with relative success, maneuvering the ship around full circle – 360 degrees – to an acceptable distance from which to recover "the man" from the water. Man overboard drills were conducted during slow periods in the ship's schedule, and when no other ships were close by, when one could look out and see absolute open ocean.

While standing out on the bridge wing, Brenda removed her heavy all-weather coat, and then she adjusted her ballcap to fit tighter around her head. Petty Officer Finn seemed so proud of the ballcaps he had ordered for her, with the label of *"GUNNO"* sewn in gold cursive on the back above the plastic adjustment band. She didn't want the wind to blow her ballcap overboard, especially not one the gunners mates had ordered – out of affection – for her.

She felt some promise for the afternoon. The breeze off the seas felt warmer than she had expected, and the sun was coming out. Following the training, a "steel beach" picnic was scheduled, during which the crew could dress in civilian clothes for a short time, blast music on the fantail (aft deck), lay out on beach towels, grill hotdogs and hamburgers, and drink "near beer" and canned sodas.

It was Sunday, and on Sundays the ship followed a "holiday routine," which meant that the crew was allowed to sleep in a half hour (or sometimes an hour) later, and the workday was shorter and lighter. Along with that relaxed atmosphere, there was a feeling in the air of relief and anticipation – the ship's long southeast Asian deployment would soon be coming to an end.

As Brenda glanced around the bridge, she noticed that nearly the entire wardroom had showed for the man overboard training. It was an excuse to come topside. It was as if the officers had decided to take a chance and venture out from their respective miserable dark states of hibernation, brought on by the arrival of the XO. The day was bright and sun-filled. As she looked out to sea, she couldn't see even a wisp of one cloud in the sky. The break in the weather, combined with excitement that the last few days of the deployment had finally come, seemed to give the officers hope.

In an attempt to make the man overboard training "fun" – to convert the training into some sort of freewheeling morale booster – the XO had requested that each officer bring a CD to the bridge. The song of each conning officer's choice would be played over the loudspeaker while he/she conned to rescue "the man in the water." When Brenda first heard of the XO's request to bring a CD to the training, she had been speechless – *Did she really want to blast a JO's choice of rock music while the ship trained to recover a person in peril, a person whose life depended on skilled and timely action by the conning officer and other departments throughout the ship?* Incredulous, she had thought that the XO's morale boosting idea sounded at the least inappropriate, and possibly even grossly negligent.

She wasn't sure how man overboard training was conducted aboard other Navy ships, but she knew how the training had been carried out by the former XO, Lieutenant Commander Navarro. The former XO had worn a stopwatch around his neck during the drills. He had emphasized that each second of action taken by the officers and crew brought them closer to saving the life of a shipmate. The drills were conducted in a positive but serious manner that motivated all personnel to excel, and to act with a sense of urgency and intensity. "A shipmate's life is at stake and dependent upon every second of YOUR action," he used to say.

He gave all shipboard departments a maximum of twelve minutes to work in conjunction to rescue the person in the water. Factors such as water temperature, visibility, wave height, currents, ability to locate the person overboard, swimming capability of "the man," possible injuries sustained, and nearby shipping traffic, meant that the chance of survival was not always high. Recovery was often made more challenging by sonar equipment towed astern or by close formation "steaming" with other ships.

During man overboard training, Brenda had learned that it was surprisingly difficult to maneuver a gigantic destroyer back around in a circle, close to where the person had fallen overboard. The operation required deliberate and careful shiphandling on the part of the conning officer.

Given all that was at stake, Brenda had difficulty viewing a man overboard drill as the setting for a "fun" morale boosting activity. To her, it seemed Lieutenant Commander Gates acted inappropriately at every turn. The former XO had made it clear that it was his goal during man overboard drills to ensure the crew was well-trained to act quickly and safely, automatically knowing what actions to take – *to save lives!* She wasn't quite sure what Lieutenant Commander Gates' goals were during this "training."

While Brenda leaned over the side, she reviewed in her mind the standard maneuvering procedures for recovering a man overboard. The steps were clear, she thought, as she silently recited them. When hearing the 1MC announcement, "*Man overboard, port (or starboard) side,*" order full rudder towards the side from which the person had fallen, order all engines ahead full...about two-thirds of the way around, start backing the engines, possibly the inboard one first, continuously easing the engines and the rudder from there to bring the ship alongside the person, as close as possible.

It was the Captain's preference to maneuver the ship "ahead full" around in the tightest circle possible to bring the ship alongside "the man." It had always sounded strange to her that the guiding principle in rescuing a man overboard was to maneuver the ship as if aiming to hit the person in the water; but it was this method of conning that brought the ship closest to "the man," accounting for set and drift. There were three primary recovery methods to choose from – the Anderson turn, the Williamson turn, or the racetrack turn. Each turn differed in advantage according to type of ship (size, maneuverability, single or twin propeller, power), time of day, sea state, visibility, speed, winds, and position of the person overboard (if known). The Captain preferred a variation that combined these methods. But the most important immediate action was to order full rudder to the side from which the person had fallen to shift the stern (and propellers) away from the person.

She continued visualizing the drill and rehearsing it in her head. She wanted to be ready if they called her name to conn. She surprised herself in that she actually didn't mind if they called her. She stood watch as conning officer twice a day and she needed the practice and experience of conning during a man overboard emergency. But she couldn't help thinking that it would also be fine if they didn't call her to conn. She feared fouling up the exercise in front of all of the officers and crew, and she already had her SWO PQS line items signed off for man overboard drills.

She glanced to her side and saw CSO leaning over the rail, a few feet away, when all of a sudden she began to hear over the loudspeaker a bluesy rasping voice that wailed, *"There is a house in New Orleans, they call the Rising Sun..."* followed by the 1MC announcement, *"Man overboard, port side, man overboard, port side!"*

"Left full rudder, all engines ahead full," Bill the warrant officer ordered over the loudspeaker, as the conning officer for the drill.

"Left full rudder, all engines ahead full, aye, sir. My rudder is left full, sir. All engines ahead full, sir," the helmsman repeated. At the same time, the boatswains mate of the watch sounded six short blasts of the ship's whistle, a lookout threw a dummy (named "Oscar") attached to a life ring over the side, another lookout threw a smoke float over the side, and the signalman hoisted the signal flag OSCAR (a red and yellow international nautical flag symbolizing man overboard). All personnel not on watch or involved in the recovery had to complete a face-to-face muster with their divisions. On the lower decks, Brenda could see deck division (the boatswains mates) preparing for the recovery of the man. The SAR (search and rescue) swimmer had arrived on station. And from observing past drills, she knew that CIC would have adjusted the scale of the dead-reckoning tracer to 200 yards per inch to track "the man" in the water.

While personnel throughout the ship reacted to the drill, and while the BMOW announced, *"Report to your mustering station. Traffic to mustering station is up and forward, starboard. Down and aft, port,"* and *"the man has been in the water one minute,"* Brenda glanced over at the XO to find her laughing and enjoying Bill's conning song. She wasn't monitoring the drill or paying the least attention to it; she had no stopwatch. And the drill seemed a chaotic mess, made so by the disorienting music blaring in the background.

"Okay, everyone," the XO shouted above the music to the officers. "I want everyone to talk and enjoy themselves and listen to the music."

Yet, none of the officers seemed to know how to react to what she said, so they all kind of murmured "yes, ma'am" and stood around on the bridge wing and in the bridge, watching Bill conn. It was normal during man overboard training for officers not directly involved in other aspects of the drill to wait for a turn to practice conning. And there was – supposedly – a serious drill in play…but those waiting for a turn to conn stood awkwardly, feeling the incongruity of the scene, with blaring rock music and an XO who was ignorant to those elements of the drill that should have been considered the most vital.

"*House of the Rising Sun*," Brenda commented to CSO, who was leaning over the side next to her, "that could only be Bill's selection," she shook her head, amused.

"Did you bring up a song?" CSO asked.

"I brought a song up she hates, sir," Brenda answered dryly, referring to the XO. A second later she couldn't believe what she had just said. "I'm sorry, sir," she started to say.

CSO looked surprised, but laughed a little. "Sounds passive aggressive," he answered, sort of chuckling to himself.

"*Oh, mother, tell your children, not to do what I have done*," the song pounded in the background, as deck division prepared amidships for a shipboard recovery of the man. CIC had started to pass bearings and ranges to the bridge, which could barely be heard over the music. The XO continued to pay no attention to the actions of the crew during the drill. She simply seemed to get a kick out of watching Bill conn and listening to his song.

"Chief Smith, he's gone. I can't believe it," CSO said, changing the subject, as they both looked out to sea while the ship circled at full speed.

"I'm sorry about that, sir," Brenda answered, leaning into the ship's list to port.

"Don't be sorry," CSO answered. "Initially, though, the former XO and I were in disbelief. That night," CSO explained, "I thought that what you were telling me was so out of character for him. The XO felt the same way. I remember the XO leaning back into his chair and saying, *no way, I don't believe it*. However, we couldn't ignore your claim. You were in tears; obviously something had happened. I think the XO could have been more proactive in his actions, but at least he didn't ignore it, first separating you guys on the bridge."

"So, how did the story leak, sir?" Brenda asked. "I never said anything to anyone."

"Rumors started going around the ship, and afterwards, Chief Meyer told us of her encounter with him, the attempted rape. She said she had handled it, and didn't think to report it, until she heard what happened with you. Then, another incident surfaced with TM2 Dobbs. That's when we started the investigation. SUPPO and I interviewed every woman onboard. We discovered that the SMC had approached almost every female, in some way, perhaps testing the waters to see how far he could go."

"What's going to happen to him?" Brenda asked, still questioning the meaning behind the events of that night, which now seemed so far off, as if a decade had passed since then. SUPPO had told her that Chief Smith's Captain's Mast had lasted a full day. He virtually had no defense, and had showed no understanding that what he had done was wrong. The Captain gave him a maximum penalty: He busted him from frocked E-7 to E-5, reduced his E-5 pay in half, kicked him out of the chiefs mess, threw him off the ship, gave him ninety days restriction, and recommended a general court martial. She imagined that the frocked chief had probably gotten away with his behavior for years.

"He'll be processed out of the Navy, probably an administrative discharge, or under Other Than Honorable conditions, or a General Discharge, unless he appeals," CSO answered.

Brenda nodded, still looking over the side at Bill's recovery of "the man." He had conned the ship fairly close in. *"Well, there is, a house, in New Orleans, ...they call the Rising Sun, and it's been the ruin of many a poor boy, and God, I know, I'm one,"* the song ended, and everyone clapped for Bill.

Julie was next, and Brenda started to hear a country-rock ballad from the Reba McEntire CD Julie often played in their stateroom. *"She said here's your one chance, Fancy don't let me down, here's your one chance, Fancy don't let me down,"* recounted the heavy-hearted voice in its mid-south twang. Brenda wasn't a fan of country music, but she had grown to like the song. At the start of the first strummed chords, the XO had, rather out of character, complimented Julie that she liked Reba, too. But no bond could ever come from one compliment, when hundreds of previous insults lay in its path.

The Captain appeared impressed by Julie's maneuvering of the ship – by her engine and helm commands, and by her use of the wind. "Good maneuvers, Miss Wettlaufer," Brenda heard the Captain compliment Julie. "I like your approach, very well executed," he followed. "Good use of the rudder and twin screws."

But just as the Captain complimented Julie, Brenda glanced over at the XO and saw that her face had suddenly fallen cold. She started glaring at Julie as she conned.

"Did you see that?" CWO2 Caruso (another warrant officer in the combat systems department) asked as he leaned over next to

Brenda and CSO. "The look the XO shot her after the Captain complimented her."

"I saw it," Bill answered, approaching them.

In the background, Reba was still belting out, "*She said here's your one chance, Fancy don't let me down. Here's your one chance Fancy don't let me down. Lord, forgive me for what I do, but if you want out, well it's up to you.*"

Then, a moment later the XO walked up to the four of them and asked, "You guys all enjoying yourselves?"

"Yes, ma'am," Bill tried to answer for them, as they all feigned smiles. The XO then disappeared inside the bridge. Brenda walked away and started watching the boatswains mates below, as they secured from the drill. They were packing up the dummy, Oscar, who had been rescued from the water. But she continued to listen to the conversation between the two seasoned warrant officers and CSO, as they spoke candidly, without her in their immediate presence, someone who was so junior. "She can be like Jekyll and Hyde," she heard CSO saying, referring to the XO. "I remember her vaguely from the Academy – she was two years ahead of me – and my strongest recollection is of her frequently screaming at someone. She was in PXO class when I was at department head school in Newport, and my wife and I invited her over for dinner. She was as nice as she could be. At first, I was pretty optimistic about working for her, despite the rumors I had heard. But I was proven wrong within hours of her stepping aboard the ship, when she wasn't even XO yet."

Rob had started his turn at the man overboard drill, to the background of the Rolling Stones, *Paint it Black*. "*I see a red door and I want it painted black*," she heard. "*No colors anymore I want them to turn black.*" She thought about how they had all become such cynics, and they had all started out with such idealism.

"They say a bitching sailor is a happy sailor," Neil said, as he leaned over next to her.

"Officers and sailors deserve better than that saying," she answered.

"It's a saying that reflects our plight under the XO," Pete said, in a hushed tone. "We can all revel in bitching and complaining about her, but I'm not sure much else can be done."

As they all looked out over the side, Rob brought the ship up alongside the life ring that had been thrown into the water, and then made a few jokes about Oscar the dummy. Everyone laughed, and his humor made for a nice respite for a few minutes. The boatswains mates below were making a spectacle of rescuing the life ring. And Brenda wondered about this mix of "fun" and lifesaving training.

She only knew that for the length of Heather Gates' eighteen month tour as executive officer of USS *Curtis Wilbur*, life was going to remain hellish, bizarre, and confusing for most onboard, especially for the officers. The officers did their best to screen most of the flak from the crew, but the crew knew what was going on. Her pathetic attempt at allotting the officers "some fun time" by allowing them to play music as they conned was never going to make up for the fact that she had zero respect for her officers and crew. Command climate (morale) aboard the ship had reached rock-bottom under Lieutenant Commander Gates.

Brenda remembered a few other fragments from the military recruiting video she had watched in high school: *"strength of character, strength of purpose, strength of moral power, strength of camaraderie, strength to do good today, strength to command, strength to obey."* She wanted to know what these military messages and themes meant for her, Neil, Pete, WEPS, CSO, and the other members of the *Curtis Wilbur* wardroom, as naval officers, in the face of this catastrophe. What should be done? What ethical and legal courses of action were available?

As the "bitching sailor" adage implied, grumbling within officer and enlisted ranks was a culturally accepted part of Navy life. But outside of unofficial chatter within ranks, a firewall of intimidation, both cultural and legal, existed for officers and sailors to remain silent and subordinate about issues. ROTC and introductory Navy classes taught that officers and sailors had a right to raise issues through their chain of command, which was lauded as the primary recourse for military members. However, raising the issue of Lieutenant Commander Gates through the chain of command involved appealing directly to her, and then to the Captain, or circumventing the XO and approaching the Captain without the XO's knowledge. The only other option available, if a satisfactory response was not obtained from the Captain, was to bypass him and address concerns regarding the XO to the destroyer squadron commander – the commodore. Culturally and logistically, it just wasn't feasible.

Julie approached them, laughing. "Boats played the wrong track on my Reba CD," she said, referring to the boatswains mate of the watch. "I can't believe it."

"No one was listening to the words," Brenda tried to console her. "The XO even exclaimed that she likes Reba. I like the CD, too. It's all good."

Julie turned dark for a moment. "She didn't like the Captain complimenting me on my ship maneuvers."

"No, she didn't," Greg answered.

"Who's next," Brenda heard the XO call out.

"I am, ma'am," Brenda held up her hand.

Brenda handed her CD to the BMOW. "Here's my CD, any track, or start it from the beginning, BM2," she instructed him.

"Man overboard, port side, man overboard, port side!" the BM2 announced over the 1MC, to the background of Brenda's CD.

"Left full rudder," Brenda ordered over the loudspeaker. *"All engines ahead full."*

The ship turned sharply at full speed, heeling severely, pressing Brenda against the railing. As the ship swung around in the seas, bounding towards the man in the water, she could hear the XO laughing almost uncontrollably in the background. As Brenda held the microphone to her mouth to start backing the engines, the XO exclaimed, "Yanni! I can't believe you, GUNNO. Yanni and man overboard recoveries will be etched in my book of sea stories, forever, GUNNO."

Brenda's mood turned dark. Her attempt to express veiled resentment and hostility toward the XO – passive aggressiveness, as CSO had called it – had failed. She had checked the Yanni CD out from the ship's library, having heard the XO mention that she didn't like Yanni.

After finishing her drill well enough (having brought the ship to an acceptable distance from the man), and *"Secure from man overboard drills,"* had been passed over the 1MC, Brenda rushed down to her stateroom to change into jeans and a t-shirt to attend the steel beach picnic. On the aft decks, music was blaring, the grill smoked the entire fantail, and the crew was laughing and having a great time. Some were even dancing. After having a hot dog, hamburger, some potato salad, and a soda, she went back to her stateroom, climbed up to her rack, and put a Cranberries CD in her walkman. The Cranberries represented her generation: Generation X.

But it was her nagging self-reprobation that crowded her thoughts. She was disgusted by her passive-aggressive, feeble behavior during the drill: selecting a CD for the sole reason that the

XO might hate it. She felt embarrassed for her behavior – *What was wrong with her, and why was she acting out in those ways?*

If she could just take a quick nap, before reporting to bridge watch again...

By the time the song "*Zombie*" came on, she had fallen asleep with her headphones still over her head, her walkman still playing, her back propped up against the bulkhead in her rack. "*It's the same old theme since nineteen-sixteen. In your head, in your head, they're still fighting, with their tanks and their bombs, and their bombs and their guns. In your head, in your head, they are dying...*"

Chapter 47: Who cares about morale ... Indiscriminate shooting into the ocean ... The Junior Officer Protection Association (JOPA) ... A modern woman in search of a soul

> 1MC Announcement: *"Muster all combat systems and weapons department personnel not on watch, on the fantail for training."*

It was the afternoon of the gunnery field day. Brenda walked over to one of the .50-caliber mounts, amidships, and surveyed the small arms stations forward and aft along the decks of the ship. The gunners mates had worked hard all morning to set up the training stations – 9mm, 12 gage shotgun, M14, and .50 cal. – and she wanted the afternoon to go well. Chief Dering brushed past her. He was in his element directing the GMs and handling the small arms. Chief Dering, originally cynical and uninterested, thinking that the event would never be approved, had stepped up and done most of the planning for the field day. And it seemed, he was unable to pass up an opportunity to swagger about the decks as the small arms hot shot.

The Captain had denied her request for an all-crew small arms shoot. Instead, he had granted a field day limited to "combat systems and weapons department personnel only." Brenda wasn't sure why the Captain had limited her request. Word around the ship was that he was such a stickler on appearance that he never wanted the ship to look bad in any way – possibly the shells could nick the paint, some said. Others said that he feared someone getting hurt "on his watch," that he was "big on safety" but only for the sake of his own skin, i.e., he was worried about liability. She guessed that the non-combat systems petty officers – the yeoman, operations specialists, quartermasters, etc. – all who wore a 9mm on quarterdeck watch inport would have to wait awhile for any kind of small arms training.

It wasn't long before Chief Dering commenced the exercise. All hands topside had been issued hearing protection and Brenda had donned hers. The exercise was deafening with pistol, shotgun, and machine gun fire spraying the ocean over the side of the ship. The ship was DIW (dead in the water), and the gunners mates had thrown fifty-five gallon drums over the side for use as targets. She started making rounds through the training stations, making sure everyone got a turn and that the event was flowing smoothly. Chief Dering's exercise plan was straightforward: After the groups spent a given amount of time at a station, where each individual was allowed to take a turn, he would call a cease fire and rotate the groups. From what she observed, the gunners mates were doing a good job running the firing stations and providing instruction. She was glad that the event was going well. The crew needed a break, they needed something, and she wanted the gunners mates to end the deployment with somewhat of a positive feeling about their work.

"If I can help in any way, let me know," Neil approached her. "I'm still surprised WEPS and CSO got these shoots through."

"It wasn't without a lot of unnecessary grief from the XO," she answered. "I was standing outside the XO's stateroom during CSO's last attempt to get her to approve the CIWS and 5"/54 firing exercises. Their biggest obstacle was getting past her to reach the Captain." A few feet away, she watched as one of the second class gunners mates instructed a seaman gunners mate on proper mounting of the .50-cal machine gun. She hadn't realized how colossal the .50 cals were, and subsequently why they required steel mounts bolted to the deck of the ship. She was the gunnery officer, but she hadn't before seen the .50 cals outside of their storage lockers.

"I've heard all about the XO's rant over CIWS," Neil said.

Brenda nodded and held the clipboard and notes she was carrying against her chest. "You have to live these stories to believe them," she replied. And then she started to think about the pain the XO had inflicted on the department heads while they had sought approval for the CIWS and 5"/54 shoots – routine gunnery exercises aboard a destroyer. Last week, she had gotten in line outside of the XO's office behind the LDO, Jason Arnett, and a few petty officers who were routing routine reports. When suddenly, within earshot of those in line, the XO started screaming at CSO, *"Are you an idiot? Are you the worst fucking naval officer in history? I should fire you. I promise you I'm going to end your career!"*

"Two major pieces of equipment have been repaired by our sailors, ma'am," CSO had explained in response, referring to the 5"/54 gun and CIWS. "We need to test them to definitively clear the casualty reports."

"I don't want to test them because it's a pain in the ass to do

that!" she screamed, gaining an audience outside of her stateroom, composed of enlisted personnel who had started to slow down while walking by her stateroom. The LDO, Jason Arnett, had tried to move some of the eavesdroppers on. He had even asked the petty officers who were standing in line to come back at another time. Brenda later realized that she should have done the same – move people on, although she didn't agree with asking the petty officers to leave the line. She had felt that everyone was hearing the truth of what was going on.

She had grown tired of the common SWO "wisdom" that JOs should act as filters for the Command. In this mindset, JOs were expected to screen flak (ridiculous orders/admonishments) that came down from the Command, in an effort to shield subordinates. At the same time, the JOs – being in the middle – tried to make subordinates believe that orders (specifically the bad ones) were originating from themselves...all to protect the Command. She had heard of this "leadership" tactic time and again from colleague JOs and department heads, but she believed it to be a dishonest leadership style, fraught with a sense of "covering up."

And, such an expectation placed upon the shoulders of JOs was a de facto cultural admission that senior SWO leadership failed more often than not. Sailors easily deciphered the origin of orders, whether they originated from division officers, department heads, and/or from the Command, no matter what they were told. She felt that Navy leaders, including Lieutenant Commander Gates as the executive officer of the ship, should take responsibility for their conduct, words, and orders. Naval leaders were supposed to set the example and lead by example; not establish and rely on a system wherein JOs were expected to clean up after them, and in this case, shoo petty officers away from the truth.

While Brenda and Neil stood amidships, surrounded by endless Northern Pacific Ocean, Brenda started sifting through her notes on the gunnery event. "If you've heard the story," she said to Neil, "then I'm sure you've heard the most damning part. CSO tried to convince her to approve the firing exercises for many reasons: mainly, to test the guns before pulling into port, to clear the CASREPs, and to satisfy required exercise periodicity. But he had also argued that the shoots would be great for the morale of the sailors who had just fixed the equipment. That's when she interrupted him, and screamed at the top of her lungs, '*I don't give a fuck about their morale!*'"

"Un-fucking-believable," Neil swore in anger. "A naval leader who thinks the crew's morale is insignificant. We're lucky we're not at war."

"So, in response, CSO answered her quietly," Brenda continued. "He said, 'I'm letting you know, ma'am, that I'm forwarding this request to the Captain.' And she screamed, '*Get the fuck out of my stateroom, CSO!*' She threw him out and that was the end of their conversation. So, apparently, the Captain signed off on the CIWS and 5"/54 shoots, and then CSO and WEPS were able to tack on this small arms field day," she finished.

Neil said nothing at first. Brenda stood looking at him.

"She takes sadistic pleasure in reaming out her department heads and DIVOs. Daily life working for her isn't just unpleasant, it's fucking ridiculous," he said.

"She's certainly made the department heads' efforts to schedule these shoots very public," Brenda said. "And with only a short time to go, the Captain doesn't seem willing to do anything about her or to rein her in. Not with her apparently being favored by naval leadership as some sort of poster child for women in command level positions in the Navy."

"Our criticism has mostly been targeted at the XO," Neil said, "but it should be targeted at the Captain for letting this go on. In the standard CO/XO model, the Captain plays the good cop while the XO is in charge of administration and discipline. But we have an extreme situation."

"CSO keeps telling me that not all ships are like this, but after midshipman cruise, and all the sea stories I've heard, I really wonder," Brenda said.

The ship rocked gently with the seas as sailors fired machine guns, shotguns, and pistols nonstop off the sides of the decks. She continued to think of the XO. Lately, during midafternoons, a line formed outside of the XO's stateroom that stretched down the full length of the passageway, past the admin office and around to starboard towards CSMC (combat systems maintenance central). Lieutenant Commander Gates had recently stepped up XOI (Executive Officer's Inquiry), a form of nonjudicial punishment (NJP) unique to naval service. Brenda usually saw Julie in the XOI line, waiting with her sailors from deck division, mostly nonrated seamen. The XO had started targeting nonrated deck seamen for the slightest of disciplinary infractions. It had turned into a disgrace. The young seamen were easy targets, and they were the most powerless to protect themselves. One afternoon, Brenda had approached Julie while she was standing in line to ask her what was going on, but Julie had simply warned her, "Don't ask." Brenda had never been to XOI. The gunners mate rating required advanced study and schooling, which elevated the sailors in her division out of the running as easy targets. Under the former XO, the XOI line had never been long. With HAG, it grew in length daily.

Just then Pete approached the group. "I just got off watch," he said. "I'll stay out here for a while and help where I can."

"We were sort of having a JOPA meeting," Brenda smiled, referring to the term *Junior Officer Protection Association*. It was an informal but widely known term used to describe the need for junior officers to band together to "protect themselves" against career-minded senior officers. "I guess the XO's been chosen as the Navy's rising female star, and that's that," she said, feeling the need to sum up the previous conversation.

Brenda turned to Pete. "Aren't you going to shoot, ex-gunnery officer?" she asked him. She herself had planned on shooting.

"Something about shooting indiscriminately off the side...," Pete said, and smiled. "I'll stick around and help supervise the stations."

When Pete walked away, she lost some of the feeling of accomplishment she had derived from scheduling and setting up the field day. She hadn't before considered the effects of bullets shooting through the water at high velocity. Without thinking, she had gone along with the accepted practice of shooting over the side for training and to expend ammo. The ocean was one big catchall, right? But where did the bullets end up? Did they hit anything? What lay in the path of all of those bullets? Fish, sea mammals, what? She had never once considered the impact of shooting into the ocean – "shooting up fish," as GMM2 Marcello had jokingly referred to the exercise during morning quarters. They would never shoot into the woods like that, *indiscriminately*, would they? Navy ships fired ammo and missiles into the ocean for training all the time. Her job was to see to this type of training, and advocate for it. She now wished that she had waited to get back to Yokosuka to schedule the small arms shoot at the range. Why had she had to kill and torture unknown sea life to learn her lessons?

She remembered an event she had previously disregarded as nothing. In the L.A. airport, while traveling to Australia, someone had handed her a brochure about stopping the Navy from deploying bombs and sonar off the coastline of California. Apparently, Navy active sonar training and research exercises were maiming whales, dolphins, porpoises, seals, otters, etc., causing them to bleed to death, in some cases. The piercing sound induced tissue hemorrhaging and rupturing around the brain, ears, lungs, swim bladder, and often perforated their ear drums. These injuries destroyed the mammals' ability to navigate and search for food, which many times culminated in a painful and slow death. An aversion to naval sound regularly resulted in extreme "avoidance" behaviors in marine mammals, with the result that they would often try to escape towards shore, sometimes culminating in mass strandings on beaches. Other technologies, such as satellite, were now available the group claimed, but "moneyed interests" and being heavily steeped in older methods had kept the Navy stuck in outdated sonar technology. The brochure suggested additional alternatives such as ramping up sonar exercises in a gradual way that allowed the mammals to first leave the area. Brenda remembered that she had thrown the information away by the time she had reached the gate of her next flight. But now she wondered. And as the gunners mates continued on with the field day, she restlessly tried to push aside what she had read in the brochure while riding the airport shuttle between terminals. The ship had completed multiple antisubmarine exercises with sonar, and was now engaged in gunnery exercises, and there was nothing she could do about it.

 Meanwhile, Chief Dering had started gathering the enlisted combat systems and weapons department personnel on the aft decks (on the helo landing pad) to debrief them on the exercise. In an hour, the ship would begin the CIWS and 5"/54 maneuvering firing exercises. There was excitement in the air. Under the former XO, while the CIWS and 5"/54 were under repair, the ship had conducted a few PAC fires (pre-action calibration firing) – simple exercises involving shooting two salvos of three rounds of 5"/54, and three salvos of CIWS for testing. Some PAC fires were successful, while others weren't. Testing of the guns had come to a grinding halt under Lieutenant Commander Gates.

 Brenda walked around while the gunners mates secured the small arms equipment. Lingering on her mind was the nervousness and humiliation she had felt in the wardroom that morning, over her response – or lack of one – to the navigator's question following her briefing for the 5"/54 gunnery exercise. She had done so much prep work that she had thought that she would be safe from questions during and after her brief. A few days before the brief, she had made sure to personally distribute a copy to everyone involved in the evolution – all ranks and watchstanders. She had even asked each participant to please contact her beforehand if they had any questions prior to the exercise. She never heard from anyone.

There was one sentence from the official firing exercise instruction that had played over and over in her mind as she had routed her brief up the chain, and as she had stood in front of the crowded wardroom giving her briefing: *Make sure that you thoroughly think through each step of the exercise and get a good mental picture of the exercise.* She knew that if someone asked a question following her brief, the idea expressed in that sentence was going to be her Achilles heel. Between watches and routing messages, she had studied and researched various publications, instructions, and directives about the firing exercise, but even still, she had lacked a good understanding of the exercise diagram (the movement of the ship around the target), and the courses, speeds, and track for the OOD. She had never seen this type of exercise, and she couldn't picture it, or understand it well enough to really think it through. She only knew from seeing a diagram that the ship would make a racetrack turn around the target (a "killer tomato," a large orange inflatable balloon). She hoped the plan, along with a photocopy of the diagram, would suffice for everyone else's understanding. The exercise would be controlled from the watch in CIC, both tactically and operationally, with the TAO (scheduled to be WEPS) and watch team providing courses and speeds. So far, no one in the chain had asked any questions. Each of the key exercise participants had signed off on all of the paperwork and had their own copies.

Standing at the front of the wardroom dining table, she had read all five pages of the brief – bore reports, standard gunnery commands, safety pre-cautions, checksight observer responsibilities, misfire/hang fire procedures, and on and on.

When she concluded her brief, it looked like no one was going to ask any questions, as was normal. But then she saw Jon the navigator lean back in his seat and stretch his arm up. "GUNNO," he said, "I didn't get a chance to ask my question earlier." Her heart stopped.

"Yes, NAV," she said. The room was so full of officers and enlisted personnel that she couldn't see any of the wardroom chairs, sofas, or tables.

"I'll be the OOD during this exercise," the navigator began, "and I was looking at the diagram for maneuvering in a racetrack turn around the killer tomato target, and..." and she heard nothing. She had blanked until she heard him end with, "I'll be the one on the bridge, and I need to understand how to maneuver the ship." She looked at Jon and he looked at her. She felt busted, self-conscious, but she knew Jon's request was valid. He had a way of cutting into her during every interaction they shared, exposing her cover up, her dishonesty, and her attempts at creating the impression that she was on top of everything and knew what she was doing. With unclear motivations for these assailments, he had never done anything to make her change her mind, that he was someone to keep at arm's length.

In reaction, she held up the exercise diagram. She looked at WEPS and at Chief Dering, and started, "There're two runs around the track. The ship starts out on a course of 000," she began, looking at Jon, when WEPS suddenly interrupted her, and nervously tried to explain the concept, using an overabundance of words mixed with non-lexical utterances...uh...uhm... It almost seemed as though he was trying to give himself space for thinking through the maneuver, even as he tried to explain it. Chief Dering assisted here and there, anxiously clarifying a few points about the exercise. She kept thinking of another paragraph from the firing exercise instruction: *The best plans for firing exercises are futile, if not presented properly at the designated pre-fire brief. In order to field questions, every aspect of the exercise must be considered. Remember, you'll be expected to become an overnight expert. People will expect to be able to ask detailed questions and get a knowledgeable, concise answer.*

When WEPS finished, Jon said, "Thank you. My question is answered." Brenda looked at Jon, resenting him for asking a question he knew she couldn't answer, when he could have waited until after the brief.

"Does anyone have any more questions?" she asked.

"Very good," the Captain spoke up, ending things. "Good brief, GUNNO." She didn't know how he could have given her a compliment.

"Let's make sure that all of our heads are in the game," the Captain said as he stood up. "This is one of our last major exercises before pulling into Yokosuka. Let's make it a success. If everyone does his or her part, the whole will come together." When he exited the wardroom, people gathered their things and followed. Brenda, left standing at the head of the dining table, gathered her notes while she tried to recompose herself.

"Odd description of the firing run, Brenda," Jon approached her. "I know you've never seen or been involved in a gunnery exercise before, more than a simple PAC fire, but some advice..."

"Yes, Jon."

"Don't rely on your department head to bail you out during a pre-exercise brief, or your chief, for that matter. Your chief isn't an OOD, and WEPS hasn't stood bridge watch in years. Remember, he's just spent over four years away from ships on shore tour, department head school, and grad school."

"What can I say, Jon. You keep me honest," she answered him, showing no emotion, and left the wardroom with her things. In a strange way, she was indebted to him for holding a mirror to her, regardless of what motivated him to do so.

She had to acknowledge, although grudgingly, that he was right about her. She was nothing more than a sham onboard the ship, an inauthentic person, a hollow persona. She couldn't wait until the day when she could get out of the Navy and start her own life. She felt ready to steep herself in the individuation process described in *Modern Man in Search of a Soul*, and in the introduction of the book *Psyche and Symbol*. As she had learned from her reading and reflection, she had unconsciously created a persona in order to satisfy the demands and expectations of her parents. She felt ready to search inward and to focus on developing *the self* (the whole person, integrating the conscious and unconscious realms), rather than simply creating an outside persona *ego*, designed to satisfy how she had wanted others to view her. As she gained insight into *the self*, her true center, she could journey towards establishing a path in life based on self-knowledge, and live her own existence. She could find a sense of fulfillment in life and in her chosen field or career as she continued her lifelong quest to gain knowledge of *the self*. She would cease sole focus on evolving her mask (persona), at the expense of her true inner self. Naming this process had given her a sense of hope that she could live her life free of the confusing and incongruent duality she had been experiencing so keenly onboard.

Since checking onboard, she had unwittingly embarked on this painful – and at first unwelcome – search inward, working to bring to light actions, thoughts, and behaviors which had been unconsciously motivated. She felt ready to strip away her multiple layers of persona. Up to now, her mask of an engineer and naval officer had been her life's focus, the focus of her conscious life, and a painfully poor and forced fit.

She would have to halt her heretofore unconscious repetition of her parents' way of life and views. She would have to continue to courageously reflect on and own the ways in which various influences in her life had guided her into becoming the person she was right then. Previously, her decisions had been made unconsciously, the influence of a deeply rooted parental "should" and "ought" which led her down wrong paths disguised as secure ones. She would have to find the courage to step out on her own, and listen to her newly emerging inner voice.

Her wish was to be an authentic person. But authenticity was risky, and frightening, because it meant showing the world who she really was, and not who she thought others wanted her to be. She would have to admit that she wasn't truly an engineer, for example. And she would have to admit the truth behind her military service.

Chapter 48: The killer tomato ... I am what I am

On the bridge, Brenda felt relieved that the first half of the exercise was over. The small arms field day was a success and the 5"/54 firing was due to start in minutes. After months of tedium at sea and focusing on repairs day after day, the gunners mates had finally been given a chance to perform the "action" aspect of their jobs. Even Petty Officer Mimms had saluted her happily as he had passed by her on the decks. She could tell that he had been in his heyday during the small arms exercise, suited up in the black helmet and vest worn by the VBSS (visit, board, search, and seizure) team.

Brenda had never asked about joining the VBSS team, headed by CSO and Chief Dering. The purpose of the team was to board other ships and search out contraband (which happened rarely in the Pacific). Since the team had enough members, she hadn't been faced with the decision on whether or not to try to join as part of her capacity as gunnery officer.

And finally, she had gotten to see what a killer tomato looked like. Petty Officer Marcello had brought her over to see it before the GMs put it in the water. "Here it is, ma'am," GMM2 Marcello had said to her, laughing. "You've been wanting to see it. A large inflated orange balloon."

"Do you think the 5-inch/54 will hit it?"

"Oh, for sure, ma'am," GMM2 Finn had answered.

"Then afterwards it'll stay in the ocean for a million years, ma'am," Petty Officer Marcello had laughed.

Brenda had elected to observe the 5"/54 gun exercise from the bridge; her main goal being to understand how the ship maneuvered to track and fire at the "killer tomato" target. She wanted to be able to picture the tracking runs when she coordinated future gunnery exercises. She resolved not to be caught off guard during her next gunnery briefing.

She watched the sun reflect off the seas as she waited on the bridge for the start of the exercise. "I'm on the bridge to watch and learn," she said to Jon, the navigator, who was standing OOD. "I know you are, GUNNO," he nodded, as if he approved.

Scratchy radio chatter began sputtering up from CIC over various circuits. As the ship started making practice turns around an imaginary "racetrack" in the sea, and CIC was running through the Aegis detect-to-engage sequence to zero-in on the killer tomato target, Brenda took as many notes as she could. She braced herself against the door to the bridge wing as the ship listed severely while Brad, the conning officer, turned the ship at full rudder at full speed.

Then momentarily, the JAG officer, a lieutenant, distracted her from taking notes. He was riding the ship for a few days, onboard temporarily from the base in Yokosuka to handle legal matters for the crew – divorce, child support, legal and financial issues, etc. He approached her, all keyed up for the gunnery exercise, exclaiming, "*God, I love this stuff. It's so much fun, and you get to do it every day. I envy you. It's all so cool. I would never have gotten to see stuff like this had I gone to a law firm!*"

"No, I guess not," she answered him, trying to smile and not seem rude. She was running on her usual max of four hours of sleep. And she wanted to tell him that she wasn't up on the bridge "for fun," and that she was trying to keep up with taking notes on the exercise...and that he was distracting her! She often felt annoyed by shore-based personnel who rode and visited the ship as if it was an amusement park, star-struck by ship evolutions, bridge watch, CIC, the weapons systems, the culture, eating in the wardroom, and everything else onboard that she despised. This JAG had so far approached his temporary (and short) stint aboard a destroyer as if he had gone to Disney World. Lawyers, doctors, and chaplains were commissioned as lieutenants (skipping over ensign and lieutenant junior grade) after graduating from a special shortened OCS (officer candidate school) designed for those professions.

Jon the navigator did little to hide his annoyance at the JAG lieutenant. As the JAG walked around the bridge saying things like, "I love shipboard life. This is so cool. I should have gone SWO," Jon started walking to whatever side of the bridge was opposite to that of the JAG.

Suddenly, she heard WEPS' voice over the net, "Salvo 1, fire..." And the 5-inch/54-caliber gun boomed, listing the ship, even as the ship raced through the water at full speed, firing successive salvos. *The gun had gone off with no issues; she was so relieved!* Now, the gunnery division could pull into port knowing the gun was fully operational.

After the shoot, Brenda headed straight out to the forecastle to congratulate the gunners mates. They looked pleased with themselves. She saw them smiling and kidding with each other.

They were finally freed of the burden they had carried for nearly the entire deployment – that of a nonoperational gun.

She was also eager to check on the performance of the matting they had ordered to protect the deck from "smilies," those annoying nicks that formed when the 5"/54 shells hit the deck after each round was fired.

The padding had protected the deck somewhat, they noticed, but there still were a few smilies formed in the non-skid paint on the deck where the spent shells had cut right through the padding.

"Twenty thousand dollars for this, and we've got to sand and paint the smilies as we did before," Petty Officer Brooks commented.

"Well, it helped some," Brenda said, as the guys left to go and get their sanding and painting gear, before another ship or shore installation might notice the smilies in the paint, which would upset the Captain. "Well, we can at least celebrate the success of the gun repairs!" she called out to them.

***

The deployment was coming to an end. By late afternoon, the ship would be moored, inport, Yokosuka, Japan. Brenda had mixed feelings about pulling into port. She was excited to see her new home; but the families, the balloons, the celebrations – she didn't want to be part of the fanfare on the pier or even see it. After what she had experienced during her time onboard, celebrating this deployment – in any way – seemed a farce. She understood that everyone would be celebrating the return of loved ones, but even so, she couldn't bring herself to participate in the festivities. Besides, she had no one waiting for her, and she didn't have a place to live on shore. Right now, her home was in her stateroom onboard the ship.

She had requested to CSO, the senior watch officer, to be assigned to the aft steering watch during the sea and anchor detail, and thankfully, he had granted her request. Aft steering, located deep within the ship, felt like a safe and secluded space in which to stand watch while the ship pulled into port. She could avoid even peripheral involvement in the activities on the pier, and remain out of the way of everyone. She wouldn't have to smile and pretend she was excited and ready to join in on the "fun." After the ship moored in Yokosuka, she planned to walk directly up to her rack in her stateroom and sleep there. She didn't even know if she would bother to remove her khaki uniform.

Brenda turned her eyes away from the aft steering rudder angle indicator. She had been staring at the indicator – and often blankly through it – on and off for the last two hours of the watch. The engineman (EN), electricians mate (EM), machinists mate (MM), and master helmsman – her watch team – had struck up a few conversations, but mostly, in the wake of this upcoming and monumental shift in everyone's life, the watchstanders had remained silent.

She looked around the aft steering space, grateful for a quiet watch so far. Every piece of equipment in the space, along with the solid metal grate flooring and bulkheads, was painted a deep rust red. She had never been to Japan, nor had she ever laid eyes on her new hometown of Yokosuka, she kept thinking. Over the past few weeks, Japan had existed for her as a series of mountain ridges that were sometimes visible on the horizon, depending on how far off the coast the ship was operating. From the bridge, she had tried to catch a glimpse of life in Japan through her binoculars. During slow watches, she would lean over the bridge wing railing, and try to view the villages, houses, and apartment buildings that dotted the coastline. She had enjoyed a similar "hobby" off the coasts of more forbidden and mysterious regions, such as Vietnam, the Philippines, and islands off the coast of China. During early morning reveille watches, she would look forward to sunrise, when she could start to see the fishing boats from those countries. When her watch started at 0330, the clusters of fishing boats were but green points on the radar scope, or faint lights in the night, their lanterns barely detectable to a large warship. But at sunrise, she could actually see the tiny fishing boats with their high bows, which curled up into a point, barely seaworthy, bobbing up and down with the waves, encased in early morning fog. She couldn't believe how far out to sea people ventured in those small fishing boats.

She thought about how the upcoming arrival to Japan meant finding a place to rent in town, learning to live on the Japanese economy, buying a car with the steering wheel on the opposite side, obtaining an Armed Forces Driver's License, adjusting to ship life inport, leaving on short underways lasting two to four days each week, and a myriad of other factors she hadn't yet considered. What was it going to be like to live in Japan?

She was twenty-four years old and free from any personal commitments. She looked forward to having plenty of time ahead to reevaluate her mid-twenties. She was reminded that they were all so young onboard. The average age aboard the ship was twenty or twenty-one, she guessed. The department heads were in their late twenties to early thirties. The XO was around thirty-five. The Captain was thirty-nine or forty. It was the young and life-inexperienced on which military recruitment preyed. The young were vulnerable, impressionable, and needy to show their worth; the military had to grab up such as these if it was to remain in existence. She couldn't imagine herself falling for military hype and rhetoric in her later years, or standing for the treatment.

The young needed to prove themselves, and most, like her, lacked the confidence gained from life experience to say: *This isn't for me and that's okay; there are other and more positive ways that I can make contributions to the world.* Her inner desire to prove herself...the idea she could do it...her unwillingness to explain to others that the Navy wasn't for her and that she was failing miserably...had all prevented her from walking away. Why couldn't she declare herself honestly to the chain of command, request a letter of nonattainment of surface warfare qualification, and seek a transfer to another officer community (if possible)? An inability to accept fully and admit publicly her shortcomings – and to bear the consequences of this – remained a barrier. She still, wrongly, equated quitting with failure. She predicted that she would accept a SWO pin, if she managed qualification.

She had read that, "The need not to look foolish is one of youth's many burdens; as we get older we are exempted from more and more, and float upward in our heedlessness, singing Gratia Dei sum quod sum (Thanks be to God that I am what I am)."[7]

---

[7] Updike, John. *Self-Consciousness: Memoirs.* p. 250.

Chapter 49: Home in Japan

1MC announcement: *"Secure the special sea and anchor detail. Set inport watches. On deck condition III, watch section I."*

"Request permission to secure the watch, ma'am," the electricians mate asked, interrupting her thoughts. They were finally there, she thought, moored in Yokosuka, Japan – home. She noticed that the machinery in the engineering spaces had suddenly gone quiet, down to the low, inport hum of generators and equipment meant only to keep the ship going for maintenance and for inport working and living: no propulsion. Still seated, her legs stretched out over the hump of a tank, she turned to face the watchstanders. "Yes," she smiled. "Secure the watch! Go see your families, or whoever, or go home or on liberty, whatever you're doing!"

"We all live onboard, ma'am. Ain't nothing here," one of the guys answered, as the watch team exited through the hatch.

"Well, enjoy, anyway," she managed to answer.

She remained in aft steering, deep within the ship, as far astern as one could venture. She drifted into her old familiar habit, living the separate lives of those fictional characters who resided far within her mind. She was relying on this process of coping and meditation ever more as her crisis evolved. She was permitting them greater entrance, these characters that she had held as personal for as long as she could remember. The characters were vital to her wellbeing, were objects of meditation, and enabled her to experience meaning in times of chaos and confusion. She often reverted to living inside her own head, which allowed her to tolerate her part in the world around her, especially now, as she lived onboard this ship. The characters lived more of the life that she would have preferred, and in more desirable places. In contrast to the mask she struggled with, they had traits she would have chosen for herself. The characters and their life situations evoked feelings within her, and she was able to emote through them. They atoned for the shortfalls of her reality and choices; they provided a means through which she could accomplish goals more fitting to her core. Through them, she could live the life of spontaneity and authenticity for which she so longed.

Through her characters, she could smile to herself or feel

happiness during the worst of days. They served as mechanisms for her to grieve and process. As she underwent each daily confrontation with herself, facing one personal crisis after the next, the characters usually followed in some parallel way that aided her to cope. She was learning the lessons that life was offering her, one day at a time, in her own way, a style of journey that corresponded to who she was as an individual.

The Belgian surrealist, Magritte, wrote, "Inspiration is the moment when one knows what is happening. In general, we do not know what is happening." Since checking onboard, she had felt herself on her way to that abstract point described by the artist; she was becoming cognizant of what was happening, and of what had happened in her earlier life. She realized that although she struggled with how to fulfill her military obligation versus how to be honest regarding her role as a naval officer and engineer, she was now aware of herself and of her surroundings in a way that she had never been.

She had opened her mind anew, feeling as though previously undiscovered channels into her senses had opened and cleared. Her experiences onboard had led her to understand her past in a new light; she had uncovered the significance in them. She concluded that her presence onboard the ship was the result of a variety of specific forces at work. It was the result of the way her parents had interacted with her...the way she was cut off from her emotional life...the way her psychology had unfolded at the hands of parents who never viewed her as an individual living her own journey...the way the Navy just happened to need SWO officers at that moment in time...the way she had been steered into a technical field and taught to minimize the humanities...the way she had gone about her goals with unabashed singleness of purpose.

But she did wonder if her father would resent her once she started to go her own way and discuss her life in her own terms, according to her own values, and not in accordance with his. She had become cognizant of the uneasy reactions and uncomfortable laughs she had usually managed in response to many of his remarks that had minimized aspects of life which she had found meaningful. She felt angry at herself for the way she had shrugged off his comments as funny, and as part of his sense of humor, in the past. She decided she would push on despite his possible rejection.

Brenda got up off the tank, climbed over to the hatch, and turned the wheel to open it. Then she began her ascent from the engineering spaces to officers country. On her way to her stateroom, she noticed that WEPS had an angry and nearly rant-like sign affixed to the outside of his stateroom door that read, "SLEEPING, DO NOT DISTURB!! DO NOT KNOCK!!" He must have posted it seconds after the ship had secured from the sea and anchor detail, she thought. And then she walked directly to her rack.

***

One month of post deployment stand-down had officially begun, and Brenda was relieved not to be on duty. During stand-down there were no official workdays. Only duty section officers and crewmembers had to report to the ship, and she didn't have duty for the next day and a half. The stateroom was dark, with only the sink light on. The absence of windows allowed her to get lost in time in that room. She had been lying in her rack thinking about how one could live onboard the ship and have all physical needs met with no reason to venture outside. The darkness of night or the light of day held little importance inside the skin of the ship.

Before she could get too comfortable in her rack, the IVCS phone rang. She sat up, but then ignored it and let it ring, refusing to lean down over the stateroom sink to pick up the receiver. No one would know whether or not she had been in her stateroom to answer the phone. It wasn't so much an act of defiance; she wanted only to sleep the afternoon and night away. *No one would know*, she thought, wondering how her daily life had come down to what she could get away with and what wouldn't get her in trouble. Authoritarian rule hung over her head every minute of the day and night now, in her new chosen life and career. She lay down and rested her head against her pillow once again. She was too tired to care about those phone calls from WEPS, which often began with, *Are you in your rack?*, or *What the fuck are you doing in your rack?*, or *Were you sleeping?*

She contemplated answering the phone, but then she heard a knock at the door. "It's me, Brad, open up!" she heard. "If you're in there, let's go into Yokosuka. Let's go get Yakitori. Neil recommended a place."

"You can open the door, Brad," Brenda answered, exasperated. She would never get sleep! she realized. And right now, she had nothing to fear from sleeping. Post deployment stand-down had officially begun, and she was not on duty!

She opened the curtains to her rack. She had changed into her sweats and t-shirt.

"Oh, come on, let's go out," Brad said, standing in the doorway.

"I was going to sleep," she answered.

"Aren't you excited that we're finally in Japan?" he asked. "I haven't been here since my study abroad in Tokyo. That's why I want to get out there."

Brenda sat up in her rack, not knowing how to answer him. Brad had minored in Japanese, like she had minored in Spanish. If they had pulled into port in Spain, despite her exhaustion, she might have felt just as eager as Brad did to get out there. "I'll get dressed and meet you on the quarterdeck," she resigned. "Give me a few minutes."

Chapter 50: Just say no

Brenda finished buttoning her shirt. She then opened her stateroom door in response to a series of rapid, frenzied knocks. In the passageway, WEPS stood in front of her looking incensed and frantic.

"From the sign on your stateroom door, sir, I thought you'd be sleeping," she said.

"This is something both of our careers could depend on," he answered.

"What?"

"Why don't you join the XO and I for dinner in Yokosuka."

"Tell her *no*, sir, that you're tired," Brenda said.

"I'll be joining her and you should come, too," WEPS said.

"No one else could make it?" Brenda asked.

"I'm asking you to please join me with her."

"You know she can sustain being nice for short durations, when she wants something, sir," Brenda said. She felt sorry for WEPS. She didn't have the heart to ask: *All of the other department heads say no to her, why can't you?*

"We're leaving in twenty minutes. I need to know, now," he stressed. "Come on, finish getting ready, and let's go."

"Why not say no to her?" Brenda asked. "I would only go so you wouldn't have to be alone with her, but I can't do it. The way she treats people," Brenda looked around the stateroom. "The way she treats Julie," she emphasized. *The way she treats you, sir*, she wanted to say.

WEPS appeared almost out of control and manic, his eyes bloodshot red from exhaustion.

"I can't go to dinner, act nice, and pretend everything's okay," she added, and then paused before saying, "It's dishonest. I'm sorry, sir."

And with that WEPS slammed her stateroom door shut and left. *"Oh, I hate the Navy!"* she screamed, exhausted. She guessed it had been WEPS calling her IVCS phone, after all, and not Brad.

Chapter 51: Adventure!

Brenda exited the familiar setting of the US Navy base abruptly when she passed through a set of revolving gates into Yokosuka, Japan. *She had literally switched worlds within a few steps!* The streets suddenly grew narrower and busier, signs bearing Japanese characters in all colors and fonts protruded out over the sidewalks, many of them flashing in neon. Colors on the signage were different shades than she was used to seeing in the States.

She had traveled the world, but this was the first time she felt as if she was in a place where she was illiterate. It gave her a strange and lost feeling. She couldn't read, or even reason out, one sign. As she walked down the sidewalk, she couldn't distinguish between stores, restaurants, or other businesses from the outside. Throughout the rest of Asia, names and phrases on many street signs had been spelled out in Latin script, or even in English, underneath the various foreign writing systems, such as Thai and Chinese.

But she loved the adventure of what she was seeing! She looked at Brad as they walked. He looked so casual and at home in his loose summer civilian clothing. During the last few port visits, she had spent nearly all of her liberty time with him. She had found a companion in searching out historical and tourist sites with him, in discussing the languages they encountered, and in attempting Mandarin and Cantonese. When she shared her passion for languages and literature with him, it gave her respite from the misery of her life onboard, with all of its confusion and anxiety that wore at her.

"What is Yakitori, anyway?" she asked as they walked.

"It's like Japanese shish kabob – beef, chicken, and vegetables on a skewer, grilled in sauces. It's great!"

"Can't wait!" Brenda said.

"Japanese characters are called *Kanji*," Brad explained, as they passed an entrance to what was obviously a large department store. Brenda spotted rows of makeup counters inside, characteristic of the ground floor of any department store. "They're borrowed from Chinese; there're thousands of them. Foreign words are spelled out in a different alphabet," he pointed to a sign as they walked, "called *Katakana*, representing syllables and moras, syllabic. *Hiragana* is the other alphabet used for Japanese words," he pointed to another sign. "For westerners, they also sometimes use Roman letters they call *Romaji*."

Brenda nodded and smiled as they passed a 7-Eleven. The streets were lined with a conglomerate of house-like structures, apartments, and stores. Wires wound every which way, and alleys led in all directions. Everything was clean. The streets were clean; there was no trash to be found off to the sides. And it was all so modern looking. She loved the adventure of her new home! The streets of Japan held the potential to intimidate unadventurous foreigners, to intrigue adventurous foreigners, and to hopelessly confuse those in both categories. Although tired to begin with, she felt exhilarated from all the unfamiliar flair!

She loved looking at the art of characters, letters, and words of foreign language. She was fascinated by studying the way in which a foreign culture used language to express itself, within its own society and to the outside world. Spanish literature had provided her with a ticket into a foreign writer's stream of consciousness, the chance to journey through epochs ranging from medieval society to modern society. She loved the developmental history of language, and studying the structure, origin, rhythm, and usage of language. Her study had enriched her understanding of her own English.

That was why she had taken a chance during her senior year, and had enrolled in the graduate level Latin class taught in Spanish, which detailed the evolution of Spanish from Latin. The class had altered the manner in which she viewed every written word in Romance languages. History could be interpreted just from the words and letters in language, she had learned. It dictated trends, such as why Portuguese language retained more Latin verb tenses and vowel sounds than Spanish, and why Spanish had strayed further from Latin and had been watered down, in some respects, over the centuries. She had planned to use her knowledge from her graduate class as a basis for studying Portuguese onboard the ship. But she now understood that she would never have that chance.

"You'll get used to the Kanji in no time," Brad said, "using the trains, driving around. You'll have at least fifty characters memorized sooner than you think so you can get around."

"I think I will," she answered, as Brad looked at the map Neil had drawn out for him to get to the Yakitori restaurant. "I'm following you," Brenda said, "and you can do the talking in the restaurant."

Her fascination and excitement for Japan had been marred slightly, by what she had seen on the quarterdeck before leaving the ship. A first class petty officer who had regularly stood OOD inport during deployment was standing petty officer of the watch as part of the XO's new policy. "First class petty officers will no longer stand OOD inport; they will be demoted to POOW," the XO had reminded the officers before the deployment ended.

Brenda felt the XO had betrayed the first class petty officers. So when Brad bent down to slide the magnets on the quarterdeck officer status board, next to both their names, from the *aboard* column to the *ashore* column, Brenda had snapped, "I don't participate in that. Leave my magnet in the sort of unlabeled column." She was on her own time, and she hated being tracked.

"I'm sorry about the magnet thing on the quarterdeck," Brenda apologized to Brad, as she followed him down a narrow alleyway.

"RM1 standing POOW is some of the XO's handy work," Brad responded.

"I know," she said, grateful that Brad had understood her reaction on the quarterdeck.

"The XO hates me; she thinks I'm worthless," he stated, with animosity. And Brenda noticed that Brad, normally a lighthearted, laid-back person, appeared awkward at expressing anger. It was as if being in surroundings that were constantly hostile – where he was always on the defensive and fearful of being undermined – was new to him. He was now the object of abuse, as the XO had started to target him.

"I would give anything to be back home in New Hampshire, teaching history at a local school."

"I know," Brenda nodded.

"I know you think history is a fluff major," Brad said.

"No, I don't think that anymore," she answered him. "It's a long story…"

"What about the Naval Academy?" she asked Brad, after a pause.

"I hated the Naval Academy," he replied. "I've never admitted that. In high school, all I wanted to do was go to the Naval Academy. When I got accepted, I thought it would be the greatest thing in the world. I wanted to go SWO. *I chose it*," he emphasized. "Now, I can't believe it."

"Japan was my number one preference for a duty station," Brenda said. "If I was going to do this, I wanted to do it big."

They turned into another alleyway barely wide enough to allow pedestrians to walk in single file. The sun was going down, and with all of the signs and hanging paper lanterns overhead, Brenda could scarcely see the sky. Traces of light escaped through the tiny windows of houses on either side of them. Brenda wished that she could have seen inside those windows. The neighborhood was old, and she wanted to know what the old Japanese homes looked like inside, how the people lived. A few blocks ago, they had walked through a modern world of flashing lights and the new construction of malls, convenience stores, and fast food restaurants. Now, she walked through vintage alleyways, dimly lit by hanging paper lanterns, which alternated red, blue.

"The Spanish refer to this time of the day, twilight, as the crepuscule, *el crepúsculo*," she commented.

Brad stopped in front of a doorway blocked by curtains, and hanging beads that glowed from the light of the inside. She loved the way the paper lanterns lit up the environs in twilight.

"This is it," he said.

"I would have never known there was a restaurant here," she said.

"You'll learn to match the Kanji on signs with the Kanji on your map. You'll have to learn to get around that way, especially on the buses and trains."

They stepped through the hanging strands of beads into the aroma of grilled yakitori. Brad spoke fairly confidently with the host at the door, Brenda noted. Many people, even after years of studying a foreign language, still remained intimidated to use it when immersed in an environment of native speakers, often afraid of making a mistake, or of sounding clumsy or uneducated. But, she had learned in Spain that she had to risk all of that and just go for it, at times. Americans weren't accustomed to speaking foreign languages, but in Spain she had found that people appreciated her knowledge of Spanish, even if she did sound like a foreigner.

Brenda had never experienced anything like the layout of the Japanese restaurant. The restaurant tables were on raised platforms with woven straw-like surfaces. The patrons sat on large square cushions in front of low lying tables, instead of on chairs. Brenda followed Brad onto one of the raised platforms, but before she lifted herself up, the host stopped her and pointed to her shoes. "Remove your shoes to step up to the platform and sit down on the tatami mat to eat," Brad guided her.

Brenda turned to the host. "I'm sorry," she said. And the man nodded.

"Put these plastic slippers on over your socks," Brad showed her. "You're going to find the portions in the restaurants here very small," he said. When they ordered several plates of Yakitori, the waiter looked confused and questioned Brad, who assured him it was okay. "He keeps asking me if I'm sure I want to order that much," Brad laughed.

They enjoyed a nice, quiet dinner, and they left the restaurant full. On the walk back to the ship, they veered into an enormous mall, with five floors built in the style of any hometown American mall – a bit tacky with stores full of gadgets and expensive clothes. "I used to collect Hello Kitty stuff when I was in elementary school," Brenda commented.

"So, do you want to rent a place out in town with my friend, Matt, from the Academy? He minored in Japanese as well," Brad said. "He's onboard one of the cruisers, *Mobile Bay*."

Before Brenda could answer, she spotted the XO and WEPS walking toward them, eating ice cream cones. "She hates me," Brad said, when he saw her.

"Don't worry, she'll be nice," Brenda said, as the XO began to approach them.

"I dread every morning I wake up on that ship," Brad said, while the XO was still far enough away.

"It has nothing to do with you…she's psycho," Brenda assured him. "And she's learned she can get away with more and more."

"Once the CMS Custodian inspection begins, she'll never let me leave the ship. Last night, I got her *'Get the fuck out of my stateroom, COMMO!'* routine." Brenda felt the awkwardness as Brad animated his anger. "She would have thrown her chair at me," Brad continued, "but it was chained to the floor, secured for sea."

"She can really sink her teeth into admin inspections," Brenda acknowledged, right before the XO's approach.

"GUNNO, COMMO, it's great to see you both out in town enjoying yourselves." WEPS stood behind her smiling, eating his ice cream cone.

"Oh, yes, ma'am," Brenda replied, wanting to cringe at any social interaction with HAG. After a few seconds of pause, when no one seemed to find anything to say, the XO walked off.

"I know what you're thinking," WEPS whispered to Brenda in passing. "But, Heather and I are becoming good friends."

"She's not capable of that," Brenda said. *And she's your boss. She'll come down on you just as hard when you return to the ship because she has no respect for you,* she wanted to say. She wanted to remind him that to the XO, people were either career stepping stones or they were no one. But instead she said, "Good night, sir." And that was the extent of the interaction, before they all parted ways.

"Let's get back to the ship," she suggested to Brad. "I'm tired. My eyes hurt."

"I dread every morning I wake up on that ship," Brad repeated.

Chapter 52: The Captain's change of command

The weather was perfect for what Brenda had coined: *the Captain's wedding*. She sat among the change of command guests, scanning the audience in attendance for the ceremony. How crisp and clean everyone and everything appeared. American and Japanese dignitaries were seated in places of honor, side boys were stationed in two lines on the quarterdeck, rows of folded chairs were arranged in perfect rectangles and adorned with white linen seat covers, a podium was positioned beneath a white canopy to shield speakers from sun and rain, and officers and chief petty officers were dressed in service dress whites.

The Captain – who actually had never been married – had spent the entire post-deployment stand-down fretting over the details of the ceremony, in the mode of a young bride. In fact, his change of command ceremony had cost more money, and had entailed more planning than many weddings. As Brenda witnessed the ceremony, she hoped for two things: that the change of command directional signs had aided guests to find the ship, and that the Marines would fire the ceremonial cannons properly and on cue.

The supply officer was given a budget of twenty thousand dollars to spend on the change of command, and the incoming captain had earmarked another fifteen thousand for renovations to his stateroom. It was a brand new ship, practically, and Brenda had asked SUPPO what needed to be done to the CO's stateroom that cost fifteen thousand dollars – an amount of money that could have sent a kid to college – and SUPPO had thrown up her hands. Brenda had spent her entire stand-down period working on two agenda items: finding a way to have wooden change of command directional signs made in town, which would then be placed along the roads on base leading to the ship, and coordinating with the Marines to provide ceremonial cannons.

"The directional signs can't be fuckin' laminated paperboard, they have to be fucking wood!" WEPS' voice rang in her head, preventing her from paying attention to the ceremony, as she sat in the audience among the junior officers, dressed in service dress whites. "Where the fuck are those change of command signs, Brenda?" he had asked every day. He was under enormous pressure from the XO. As a foreigner new to the country, figuring out how to have wooden signs made in Japan had seemed nearly impossible. The hardware stores were completely different, and the price of wood was astronomical. She didn't know where to start. Not knowing the language or how to read, how would she find someone in Japan to custom make wooden signs, stenciled, and in English?

So, Brenda had called the chief in charge of the print shop onboard the aircraft carrier, who referred her to the MWR (morale, welfare, and recreation) hobby shop on base, where they supposedly had some wood, along with printing and painting capabilities. The hobby shop director had suggested laminated paperboard, "I don't know about wood," he had said, "but I can print you up some nice professional paperboard signs," he had offered. She had then written a memo up the chain of command outlining the hobby shop director's suggestion: professional, printed, laminated paperboard signs bearing, "*Change of Command, USS Curtis Wilbur DDG-54*" with printed directional arrows. But that was not acceptable, according to WEPS. "Cardboard or paperboard signs? Are you kidding me?" his voice had cracked, screeching at an abnormally high pitch. "The XO wants wood!"

Such was life aboard *Curtis Wilbur*, under the executive leadership of Lieutenant Commander Gates. Every detail onboard, even a simple task such as having signs made – which could have been efficiently and professionally printed on laminated paperboard – had become a matter of frantic and disproportional urgency. Brenda found it increasingly difficult to work and concentrate under these conditions of constant chaos and heavy-handed abuse, which seemed to have no purpose. It had started to affect her. Being berated every day over finding a way to produce wooden signs – a seemingly impossible task in Japan – had peaked her stress. It seemed many officers onboard were starting to come undone. The chain of command, and the leadership and management structure onboard, had started to unravel.

But the gunners mates had saved her in this instance. During the stand-down, on one fortunate day, Petty Officers Brooks, Falk, Marcello, and Finn approached her. "Give us a couple of days, ma'am," they had said. "We don't have much to do right now." She couldn't help thinking to herself, were we in wartime, we wouldn't have time to do any of this.

"I can't bring you guys into this," she had told them.

"Leave it to us," Petty Officer Finn had assured her.

And then one afternoon, a few days later, Chief Walden had approached her, in his unassuming way, nudging her to follow him below decks. Laid out across the passageway, outside the VLS space, were seven painted and stenciled wooden signs. "I've done a bit of woodworking in my day, ma'am," Petty Officer Brooks told her. "We got the division together, rented time in the wood shop, and got it done for you, even Mimms. We're mostly all single or geo-bachelors[8], living aboard, so we didn't have anything else to do."

Brenda remembered standing in the passageway, in front of the row of signs, with her hand over her mouth, wanting to cry – over wooden signs no less – because she felt such deep gratitude for the gunners mates. "Thank you, thank you," she had managed to say.

At dawn, the division drove the ship's van around base, hanging the signs for her. "Never let them see you sweat, ma'am!" Petty Officer Marcello had called out to her, as he slid the door to the van shut.

And then there was the issue of the ceremonial cannons. According to the Captain, or the XO, she wasn't sure which, they couldn't be fired from the pier, which the Marines had told her was standard for ceremonies. So, she had to arrange for a crane to lift the cannons onto the ship, which also meant arranging for a barge to come alongside – a barge with a crane. It had been another nearly impossible, unnecessary, and money-wasting task that had caused her and WEPS to "jump through hoops" for no good reason. From the moment they were assigned the task, HAG had hunted them down almost hourly throughout each day, screaming at them, until it was all arranged. The Marine captain (O-3) Brenda had spoken with for the arrangements had told her that he was in disbelief over the request to lift the cannons aboard ship. "This is ludicrous!" he had exclaimed. Brenda remembered not giving him much of a response. "I just need it done, sir," she had told him.

*

The sound system echoed the voice of an admiral. Brenda sat among the officers, having long lost track of what the admiral was saying, something about congratulating the ship and the Captain for winning the "Battle E" (Battle Efficiency) award. The officers and crew would all get "Battle E" ribbons to pin above their left uniform pockets. The award was given to a select number of ships for

---

[8] Geographic bachelor: service member geographically separated from his/her spouse and/or family.

maintaining a "high state of battle readiness," and for "command excellence" and "superior performance" in such areas as operations, engineering, and logistics. Brenda wasn't too into awards, as they so often seemed political more than anything else. And in this case, the recognition felt hollow. She wanted to work for a cause, make something better, but not for the sake of recognition.

She wasn't sure how much hope to hold out for the new Captain. Fifteen thousand dollars to renovate a stateroom on a ship only a few years old? People had already begun talking. People said he was self-conscious about being one of the few COs that had graduated from ROTC and not from the Naval Academy. Someone told Brenda that his wife had stormed off the ship in anger, and the story was they were initiating divorce proceedings. The new Captain would be living onboard the ship as the last Captain had – no residence out in town. Aside from what she knew about the renovations, Brenda wondered if any of the rumors were true. And would the new Captain apply any leadership over Lieutenant Commander Heather A. Gates?

Chapter 53: Painting in the rain

The ship was underway again. On another rainy and haze gray afternoon at sea, Brenda, along with her colleague division officers, the department heads, and chiefs, stood about the aft decks, supervising petty officers and seamen while they painted in the rain. There was an underway replenishment (UNREP) scheduled for later that afternoon, and despite the rain, the XO demanded that combat systems and weapons department topside areas be repainted. The XO had noticed a few spots of rust, or so she had claimed to WEPS and CSO.

Brenda had noted that it seemed highly important to SWO captains – or at least to the former captain and the new captain – that their ships "looked perfect" while alongside the replenishment ships. It was a mystery to her, why it was so important to them to impress the mostly civilian crews of the non-commissioned oiler ships. *Did they have some sort of special pipeline to the admiral or something?* she had always wanted to ask. She recognized that it was important to keep the ship as rust-free as possible, but under the former XO, the divisions had taken care of painting as part of the normal work routine. These frenzied *stop everything and start painting in the rain!* sessions – mostly before UNREPs – had started after Lieutenant Commander Gates had taken over.

Prior to leaving port, Brenda had learned that the new Captain was probably going to do nothing to improve life onboard, or to rein in Lieutenant Commander Gates. The enlisted were already calling him "ostrich," the gunners mates had informed her, according to the myth that the birds buried their heads in the sand. In response, she had kept silent. It was difficult to defend the new Captain after the scene that had gone down just prior to knock off of ship's work on their last weekday inport. It had rained relentlessly on that Friday afternoon, when the guys had looked forward to some release, or at least to go home to their families or to the lives they had scraped out in Japan.

After lunch on that Friday, she thought it would be a good time to hide away in the ship's library to study. At 1530, she had gone topside to check on the weather, but found Chief Walden and the gunners mates wearing rain slickers, painting the division's topside spaces. She then noticed that the entire department was topside. According to Neil, another "painting in the rain session" had begun after the XO had stormed into the combat systems office, and flame sprayed WEPS over rust she had found.

When Brenda first approached the gunners mates out on the fantail, she noticed that they were applying paint over paint, a slipshod – and temporary – remedy at best. They hadn't sanded the initial layers of paint off, nor sanded any rust that might have been there. She had almost said something to Chief Walden, but when she looked at him, he stated, "There's nothing more to be done than just slap the paint on so we can eventually go home." And she had nodded in response, remaining silent, because she essentially agreed with him. "I never thought I'd have to stoop this low," the chief had added.

Brenda remembered standing amidships, looking at her watch on that Friday, seeing 1700, noticing that the other ships on the waterfront had let their crews go. She could see down the line of cruisers, destroyers, and frigates moored to the piers; she saw only remnants of duty sections. *"Knock off all ship's work"* over the 1MCs of the other ships had echoed across the waterfront between 1600 and 1630.

"A little wet out here?" Neil had approached her and Chief Walden. Rain dripped from their ballcaps. Their khaki uniforms were drenched.

"So much for *'haul over all hatch hoods and gun covers'* over the 1MC," Brenda answered, referring simply to the routine of closing all openings topside prior to rain, and taking cover inside.

"Oh, we did all that," Chief Walden said. "But, then she sent us back out to paint. You can't paint in rain," he emphasized.

"Every afternoon when it rains, she sends us out here to paint in it," Neil stated.

"I had a Captain like this awhile back," Chief Walden said, gesturing towards the new Captain, who was also standing amidships, but high up on the superstructure, wearing a rain slicker, watching an entire department, and a few boatswains mates from Julie's division, painting during the downpour.

"The XO's getting worse under this Captain," Brenda said.

"We can only hope that the Captain will prevent this situation from occurring in the future," Neil said.

The entire combat systems and weapons departments were held hostage that afternoon, slapping paint on rust, fighting the torrential rain, until 1800.

*

Two days later, on Sunday morning, she had experienced a sense of the new Captain's demeanor that had left her with a feeling of foreboding. She had found his bearing was reserved, straightforward, restrained, which might have been promising. But there was also something detached about him.

Saturday into Sunday, she had stood duty combat systems officer. And due to schedule changes, she had found herself with few duty enlisted personnel available. For Saturday evening sweepers, she had to beg, borrow, and steal seamen from other departments to aid with sweepers in the combat systems spaces. Prior to the Sunday morning 1MC announcement, *"Sweepers, sweepers, man your brooms, give the ship a clean sweep down fore and aft, sweep down all lower decks, ladderwells and passageways, take all trash to the receptacles provided on the pier. Now, sweepers,"* she had arranged to borrow a few seamen from the operations department, but that still hadn't been enough help. So, as she had done Saturday evening, she assigned the borrowed seamen to the most obvious places, grabbed a bucket of cleaning supplies and a broom from the gunners mates' spaces for herself, and headed down to the more obscure spaces. Successful sweepers, and messing and berthing inspection, were the keys to any given duty section being released from duty on time.

In an obscure space, far below decks, she swept and cleaned, ensuring the hatches were closed and no one could see her, when a door opened. When she looked up, she saw the new Captain standing in the doorway, looking surprised, and then enraged. She froze, terrified, while he told her calmly, and coldly, "Miss Conner, I'm only going to tell you this once. I don't ever want to see one of my officers with a broom in his or her hand, ever again. Do you understand me?"

Brenda's hand shook as she placed the broom aside, against the bulkhead. "Yes, sir," she managed. He left and closed the hatch behind him. She stood in the empty space, far below the waterline, wanting to break into tears. She had only wanted her duty section to be released on time, and so she had gambled that she wouldn't be seen with a broom in hand...but instead she had earned herself an introductory berating by the Captain.

Nothing mattered, not how hard she worked, nor how many hours she spent onboard the ship trying to make things right, nor how much she tried to study. She tried to tell herself that anything that happened with a broom had to be insignificant, that her reaction was disproportionate. But she knew that what had happened wasn't insignificant. Her nerves would remain on edge, every minute she was onboard. Every day, something unpredictable would happen, and she would always suffer the consequences for it.

And at that moment, she decided that she would tell Brad, yes, that she would rent a place out in town with him and his friend from the Naval Academy, who had also minored in Japanese, and who served onboard USS *Mobile Bay* (CG-53).

Her morning had turned worse when she appeared for duty section turnover. While the enlisted duty section watchstanders mustered and got into formation, CHENG, who was standing CDO, took her aside, furious. "You're combat systems passageways look like shit, Brenda!" he exclaimed. "Now tell me how we are going to turn over the duty section?"

"Combat systems spaces are swept, sir! I was shorthanded and we started early. The combat systems spaces are spotless. The borrowed petty officers and seamen worked like crazy."

"*Get a fuckin' clue, GUNNO!*" he spat in her face, and she swore she could taste and smell alcohol on his saliva. She knew that on his last ship out of Pearl Harbor, he had been convicted of a DUI. Rumor had it that he would never make XO or CO because of it.

Neil, the oncoming duty combat systems officer, approached her when CHENG walked away. "I was going to compliment you on how good everything looked, considering how shorthanded you were. I'll take the duty from you. And I'll deal with CHENG," he said.

Ten minutes later, after speaking with Neil, CHENG let the duty section go on time.

She rushed to her stateroom and she couldn't get her khakis off fast enough to leave the ship. After walking down the brow, she planned on exploring the area around the base, taking trains at random, and walking through some of the ancient and medieval Japanese towns that surrounded Yokosuka; she longed to enjoy the aged temples and gardens. Maybe Brad would later be interested in Yakitori, if the XO would let him leave the ship. The thought sounded remarkably inviting to her.

Maybe she would even take a book with her, such as, *Los funerales de la mamá grande*, she thought. Her time onboard had strengthened her belief that literature shaped the entirety of life, and opened subjects, worlds, and people, which otherwise, in normal life, were inaccessible. She enjoyed forming dreams and fantasies from books, dramas, and movies. And she harbored a natural affinity towards analyzing and discussing themes introduced in fiction. Literature sparked insight into self and society, with the ability to teach a lesson absent a stern (or formal) process of teaching that lesson. She had learned the most in life through delving herself into characters – seeing, hearing, experiencing, and sharing a character's insights, or empathizing with a character's lack of insight. Human nature never changed, and literary characters had already encountered everything out there, in some form. She had brought many characters and lessons into her life through books.

The events of those preceding days inport haunted Brenda as she watched the rain drop onto the ocean, as petty officers and seamen painted in the rain, while the ship made way through the ocean.

Chapter 54: The XO on the bridge

When Brenda took her bridge watch as conning officer at 1130, one of the carrier's helicopters had just landed on the aft deck to pick up the Captain. He was about to fly off the ship to attend a meeting on the aircraft carrier, and tensions onboard had started running high. With the Captain off the ship for the afternoon and evening, the XO would be in charge.

As the weather deteriorated, Brenda stepped out onto the bridge wing, on Todd's orders, to update him on the whereabouts of the Captain. She saw the Captain hurrying across the aft deck to the helo wearing flight gear.

The pilots had been given an "amber deck," and the helo's rotors were engaged. Brenda, as the conning officer, stood by to take direction from Todd. With the rapidly shifting weather, he was concerned that they risked losing acceptable winds to give the helo a "green deck" to launch. In order to launch or recover a helo, the ship had to maneuver to within strict wind and pitch/roll envelopes for safety.

While Brenda scanned the horizon for contacts and looked at the ARPA radar, Todd stood next to her at the center of the bridge, updating the helo pilots on wind direction and speed over the comms circuit. After verifying conditions for launch with OPS, the TAO in CIC, he then turned to Lieutenant Commander Gates, who was sitting in the XO's chair on the port side of the bridge. "Request permission to set green deck, XO," he requested.

She sort of nodded, not clearly acknowledging him, while she stared forward out the bridge windows. Todd walked across the bridge purposely to her chair, "Request permission to set green deck, ma'am," he stated, with urgency.

All attention on the bridge turned to the XO. "Green deck," she stated, barely, looking so nervous she could hardly speak.

"Green deck, aye, ma'am," Todd repeated. "QM1, log green deck," he directed the quartermaster, while he got back on the comms circuit to notify CIC and the helicopter pilots that take off was authorized. The timing was vital in this swiftly changing weather, while the ship was still within optimal wind, pitch, and roll conditions.

Over the 1MC, the BMOW rang four bells and then announced, "*Curtis Wilbur, departing,*" the standard announcement given when the commanding officer departs a ship. Suddenly, the ship started to vibrate as the helo lifted off the aft deck, and the BMOW rang one bell (called the stinger). The noise of the rotors was deafening for a moment as the helo flew past the bridge.

When the pilots reported "all operations normal," Todd approached the XO again. "Request permission to set red deck and to secure from flight quarters, ma'am." She simply nodded again. So Todd answered, "Set red deck and secure from flight quarters, aye, ma'am."

"Secure from flight quarters, boats," Todd ordered the boatswains mate of the watch.

"Secure from flight quarters, aye, sir," the BMOW answered. And over the 1MC he announced, "*Secure from flight quarters.*" And all went quiet. No contacts were visible by sight or by radar.

Then Brenda looked to the back of the bridge, and saw WEPS stepping off the ladder. Since he stood TAO watch in CIC, she rarely saw him come to the bridge.

"I love being up on the bridge," WEPS commented to Brenda, as he approached.

"I know you do, sir," she said.

The XO got up out of her chair and walked towards them. "During the last few weeks, the Captain and I have found ourselves the only ones in attendance at wardroom meals," she said, slightly shaken. "From now on, all department heads are required to attend all wardroom meals except if on watch. Understand?" she asked, directing her question to WEPS.

"Yes, ma'am," WEPS answered.

When the XO walked off and disappeared down the bridge ladder, Brenda checked that the XO had cleared both ladders to the bridge, then she joked with WEPS, "No more sneaking rice and soy sauce from the wardroom galley for you, sir."

WEPS smiled and shook his head. There were key moments when WEPS had been honest with Brenda, and this had ensured her loyalty. Wardroom meals had become a "joke" among the officers. When the XO had figured out that officers were covertly lifting leftovers from the wardroom galley fridge on off-hours, she had ordered SUPPO to keep the wardroom galley locked: off limits to all officers. *No officer was to be allowed leftovers from the fridge!* the XO had screamed at SUPPO. But SUPPO had started to leave the galley key on her desk, in an available way, to the officers.

"When they make her CO of a ship someday," Brenda said to WEPS, referring to Lieutenant Commander Gates, "what is she going to do? The Captain handles all shiphandling on the bridge with the OOD and conning officer."

"She'll have her XO do it," WEPS answered.

"That's going to appear highly irregular to her officers and crew," Brenda said. And Todd started laughing.

A moment later, CSO appeared on the bridge, which was also rare.

Then Todd started laughing again and said, "Did you notice the XO's knuckles during flight ops, while she gripped the arms of her chair; they were white."

They all sort of smiled and shook their heads. Then Brenda asked Neil, the JOOD, aside. She had watched him manipulate the wind wheel nomogram with ease during flight ops. "Will you go over the wind wheel and wind MOBoard with me again?" she asked Neil.

"No problem," he answered. "It'll be a slow watch from here on in."

She didn't want to be like Lieutenant Commander Gates, who she had just watched gamble with the lives of the pilots and the Captain when she gave a "green deck" without any understanding of wind and pitch/roll envelopes, and how and why the ship had maneuvered to its current course and speed. During helo ops, Brenda had felt relieved when Todd had assigned Neil, and not her, to perform wind calculations and to determine the flight course for optimal winds to launch the helo. *And that made her disgusted with herself!* She wanted to continue to try to learn.

Chapter 55: Helm safety

Brenda had conned during the last two underway replenishments (UNREPs), but on this afternoon, she was slated to stand the helm safety watch. The ship was ramping up for its rendezvous, as it was called, with an oiler to refuel. The bridge had turned into a busy and chaotic sight as additional/replacement watchstanders arrived for the special evolution, and took the watch from the existing bridge team. Brenda had had the conn as part of the normal watch rotation, and Brad had just relieved her of the conn for the UNREP. They had quickly gone through the motions of watch turnover, *I relieve you, I stand relieved, Attention in the pilothouse, this is Ensign Conner. Ensign Hanson has the conn*, and *Attention in the pilothouse, this is Ensign Hanson. I have the conn*. There were no contacts and nothing of interest to report besides the standard information involved in watch turnover. All aspects regarding the UNREP had been briefed earlier, in the wardroom.

As soon as Brad freed her of the conn, Brenda grabbed a headset and took station behind the helmsman assigned for the UNREP; he was a qualified master helmsman on whom the ship relied for most special evolutions.

The bridge was jam-packed with watchstanders. Rob had relieved Todd as OOD, and had already called out, "*Attention in the pilothouse, this is Lieutenant Trenton. I have the deck*," and the helmsman and lee helmsman had responded with their reports of course, speed, and engine status. While the Captain and conning officer focused on the actual approach alongside the oiler, the OOD, while remaining involved and cognizant of those aspects, also managed the entire watch team, including the boatswains mates, navigation team, coordination with CIC, and topside activities.

Brenda raised the mouthpiece on her headset to her chin, ready for when Brad would move out onto the bridge wing with the Captain, and begin voicing conning orders over the loudspeaker. She looked around. The bridge was crowded; the atmosphere was tense. The ship had taken position astern of the oiler, awaiting the moment when the replenishment ship would fly her *Romeo* flag close up, signaling that she was ready for *Curtis Wilbur* to come alongside. Various bridge watchstanders were walking about the bridge, talking into a multitude of comms circuits to CIC and to different UNREP stations. Radio chatter, wind noise, and the vibration of the engines filled the space. As usual, the comms circuit was scratchy, and at times sporadic, Brenda noticed through her headset. But the comms circuit between the bridge wing and the bridge was often like that, and though it made her nervous, she had thought that she had gotten used to deciphering commands over the static and crackling in the circuit. Everyone else seemed to survive with it, and hear okay. By this point, she had stood the helm safety watch at least seven times, *and successfully!*

Before she knew it, the oiler appeared closer and closer into view through the side bridge windows, and Brad had followed the Captain out onto the bridge wing. Commands to the helm and lee helm began coming in over the circuit in fast succession, and she had started repeating the commands back while supervising the helm and lee helm. *"Come right, steer course 219,"* Brenda heard through her headphones.

"Come right, steer course 219, aye, sir," she repeated back over the comms circuit, as she watched the helm. *"Steady course, checking course 224 magnetic, sir."*

"All engines ahead full, indicate pitch and turns for twenty knots," she heard.

"All engines ahead full, indicate pitch and turns for twenty knots, aye, sir," she responded, watching the lee helmsman. *"Engine room answers all engines ahead full, indicating pitch and turns for twenty knots, sir."*

The conning officer's course and speed orders not only came in through the comms circuit into Brenda's headsets at the helm, but they were also broadcasted throughout the bridge and bridge wing, as were Brenda's repeat-backs. Everything was going well for a smooth and well executed approach to the oiler. The navigator was calling out bearing and ranges to the oiler. The *Curtis Wilbur* had sped up to about six knots over the replenishment speed, approaching the oiler at an angle. Brenda saw out the bridge windows that they were just about alongside the oiler, paralleling her *Romeo corpen*, or replenishment course.

Once alongside, the conning officer slowed the ship to replenishment speed, and the two ships "steamed" in parallel, with about 220 feet between the two ships. During an UNREP, once the fuel lines were connected, both ships hauled down their respective *Romeo* flags, and hoisted their *Bravo* flags, indicating transfer of fuel. Keeping proper distance between ships, and maintaining speed around twelve to fourteen knots was vital; speeds greater than sixteen or seventeen knots required greater separation between ships to prevent them from being pulled together by the forces of the Venturi effect (a funnel effect that induced seawater to flow between the ships at high velocity).

Course and speed changes were minimal during UNREP, while the two ships were connected by fuel lines, mostly limited to a degree on the helm or an rpm turn on the engines. Commands such as, *"Indicate one one two revolutions,"* would come over the comms circuit to the lee helm, and Brenda would repeat, *"Indicate one one two revolutions, aye, sir. Engine room answers one one two revolutions for two revolutions over thirteen knots, sir,"* as she supervised the lee helmsman's actions.

As the evolution progressed, the comms circuit became increasingly static; as well the wind blowing into the microphone on the bridge wing made it more difficult to hear. *"Come right, steer course 225,"* she heard. She could picture the conning officer and the Captain gaging the ship's distance to the oiler by the flags on the phone and distance (P&D) line, strung between the ship and the oiler, which marked every twenty feet. By eyeing a marked fixed point on the multicolored pennant flag, the conning officer and captain ordered courses and speeds to keep the point midway between the two ships to maintain station in parallel with the oiler.

"Come right, steer course 225, aye, sir," she repeated. *"Steady course, checking course 232 magnetic, sir."* The helmsman was doing a perfect job. She had stood behind this second class boatswains mate at the helm a handful of times now; and he was calm and professional under the most stressful of circumstances. She admired him for his composure.

"Come left, steer course 224."

"Come left, steer course 224, aye, sir," she repeated. *"Steady course, checking course 231 magnetic, sir."*

The ship had settled into the evolution, and orders of course and speed increments had gone on like that for over a half hour. But clarity over the circuit was worsening; she could barely hear over the crackling.

"Come left, steer course 223."

"Come *right*, steer course 223, aye, sir," she repeated. The helmsman gave her a split second glance, and she immediately corrected, "Come *left*, steer course 223, aye, sir. Steady course, checking course 230 magnetic, sir." As she gave her repeat-back she heard the Captain angrily yelling "LEFT!" from the bridge wing.

She didn't understand why she had repeated the command in error, and she swore she *had* heard *right*, barely, in the circuit; she knew the ship was on course 224, and that the change was *supposed* to be *left*.

But even though she had corrected herself a split second later, she knew that her mistake was unforgivable. She had repeated a command to the helm back incorrectly!

Course and speed orders continued over the circuit from the conning officer, and Brenda expected that she would be relieved – or fired – at any second. The XO stormed to the front of the helm, faced her, and glared straight into her eyes. Brenda knew that CSO, as the senior watch officer, would follow any second. She had recovered herself, somewhat; and in the few seconds, or minute or so, since her erroneous repeat-back, she had prepared herself for any consequence. But the XO glaring at her, the XO's penetrating eyes staring straight into hers as she stood directly in front of her, was causing her to lose nerve while she had to listen for continued orders to the helm and lee helm, check them, and respond. Brenda felt herself sweating, unable to breathe normally. She feared she had been sweating so much she had drenched her khakis. She had stood helm safety watch quite a bit, and she couldn't believe herself, the mistake she had made, and what she had done!

Brenda stood behind the helm console, facing the XO's direct glare for what seemed like an eternity (but was probably a minute or so), while the oiler was feet away from the side of the destroyer, both ships "steaming" at high speed. She kept thinking of how all onboard the destroyer and oiler depended on her to listen for the next command from the conning officer, repeat it back over the microphone, and verify that the helmsman steered the correct course. But the XO's glare, with her sharp blue eyes, landed so intensely on her psyche…her glare was so penetrating that she nearly broke down and called out to CSO, as the senior watch officer, to take the watch from her.

CSO approached her from behind. He had hurried in from the bridge wing, or from some far point on the bridge. "I'll be right behind you," he said, as he put on a set of headsets for himself. "You've got the watch."

For a second, Brenda couldn't answer him. Fortunately, no course or speed orders had come through.

"Yes, sir," Brenda said, trying to recover herself. And she kept going with the watch, repeating commands to the helm and to the engine order telegraph. With CSO behind her – someone who must have believed she could pull through – she found the stamina to continue.

But, through most of her remaining watch, the XO continued to stand directly in front of her, and glare straight into her eyes. "Don't fuck up again, GUNNO," she eventually said, after about fifteen minutes of staring straight at her over the helm console. Brenda had tried to look directly at the console to avoid the distraction of the XO's unnerving stare. "Next time she stands this watch," the XO said to CSO, as Brenda repeated back another conning order, "I want either you or Neil stationed behind her, the entire time," she said, and then she walked away. Brenda noted that the XO must have known that Neil had been a qualified master helmsman in his enlisted days.

By the end of the underway replenishment, when the ship had started to "break away" from the oiler, gradually increasing speed by about four to eight knots, "steaming" at an angle to leave the oiler behind in the open ocean, Brenda was shaken and had a migraine in full swing. She could hear the celebratory "break away music" blaring over the 1MC, which sounded like a song she had played in high school marching band. She experienced some relief that she had survived her watch, and that she had kept with it, and had repeated the remaining commands back correctly. As she removed her headset to leave the helm console, once the UNREP had secured, and the oiler was safely far away, the XO came and stood directly behind her for a minute or so. She could feel Lieutenant Commander Gates' breath against the back of her neck; she stood frozen, afraid to move. Eventually, the XO whispered, "Don't fuck up again, GUNNO, I mean it."

When the XO went down below decks, Brenda stood at the back of the bridge, near the head, replaying the scene of the missed command in her mind, wondering how she could have said *right* instead of *left*, when – despite the static – she knew it *should* have been *left*! She just kept picturing herself standing behind the helmsman, headset on, microphone in her hand, listening for the next command from the conning officer on the bridge wing, repeating it back over the comms/speaker system, verifying the helmsman's actions, over and over, wishing the replay in her mind could have changed the reality of the past.

CSO motioned for her to follow him into the chart room, a half deck below the bridge. Once inside, he closed the hatch. "Are you okay?" he asked.

"What's going to happen to me, sir?" she answered.

"I have confidence in you," he said. "Your choice, I'll put you back on during the next UNREP, or you can take a break on the next one, and I'll assign you somewhere else."

"Put me back on, sir," she answered, nearly emotional. "I know you have to assign Neil as well," she added, "to stand behind me."

CSO nodded. "By the next watch, you'll be back on your feet," he said. And then he swung the handle on the door to exit the chartroom.

***

Brenda left the bridge knowing there would be consequences from the new Captain over her performance at helm safety, and that her SWO pin was in jeopardy, and rightly so. In her mind, she had formed an image of everyone's panic out on the bridge wing, when she had erroneously repeated back the rudder command to the helm, *right* versus *left* rudder direction; she could picture the momentarily suspended looks on everyone's faces – the Captain's, the conning officer's, the OOD's – until her correction came through and the ship was safe.

She had more than ever begun to fear criticism. Craving favorable reception by her peers, she despaired over being thought of as inadequate, even incompetent, or as an untrustworthy watchstander. Every comment about her performance on watch she took seriously, to an extreme. She had a desire to succeed but she wasn't sure how; she longed for a favorable officer fitness report.

Before she had gone down below decks, after the UNREP, the Captain had brushed past her, and she had found herself unable to look at him. She was ashamed, and she needed to be able to earn her SWO qualification; she needed his approval. She doubted she would ever get it. She had a sense about the Captain, that he was possibly unforgiving. But why should he have been forgiving, she asked herself, as she approached the passageway to her stateroom. His responsibility for all of the lives onboard and for this massive destroyer (paid for by American taxpayers at a price of over one billion dollars) was overwhelming.

She feared that helm safety would be the last straw for her, as far as the Captain was concerned. A day or so earlier, when the ship had gotten underway from Yokosuka, she had been assigned as the conning officer. Once out to sea, but while they were still out on the bridge wing, the Captain had asked, "So, Miss Conner, how did you feel about conning out of port this morning?"

Brenda remembered looking at him as he squinted, the sun's glare gleaming off the corner of his wire rimmed glasses. She searched herself for an honest answer. "I was a bit nervous," she admitted, "but I think it went well."

He turned cold, staring back at her icily. "That's not good, Miss Conner. I don't need conning officers who are nervous. You should want to be doing this." And she remembered herself spinning into an emotional panic. How could she have said that! She felt embarrassed and foolish and she had known better.

*

"Don't be so hard on yourself, Brenda," she heard Brad's voice from behind. She wasn't sure how long she had been standing in front of her stateroom door. "It could have happened to any of us," he said, referring to the right/left error on the bridge.

The broom incident, conning out of Yokosuka, and now the captain's helm safety judgment, she thought. It all added up to failure. "I know," she nodded, her hand on the door knob. But she felt the incident went much deeper than "it could have happened to anyone." She didn't belong onboard a warship, performing these types of activities; the explanation behind her error at the helm console reached far into her history, and into her psychology, and into her reasons for having pursued engineering and the Navy.

"You don't seem any different from any other junior officer," Brad said.

"It seems strange to me," she answered, "to call myself a gunnery officer, an officer of the deck, a conning officer, or someone who prepares gunnery exercises, with little idea of what I'm doing."

"You *are* the gunnery officer," Brad answered. She shook her head, because the officers onboard held titles such as the DCA (damage control assistant), the communications officer (COMMO), the strike officer (STRIKE), the fire control officer (FCO), etc., but they had only been in those jobs a handful of months. Their job titles were the result of random assignments. Even so, she felt she couldn't match up to her peers with regard to tackling the learning curve required to gain even a baseline knowledge of her job and the watches. If she would have had at least some natural talent to grasp the fundamentals of the watchstations and military life, she might have had an easier time onboard despite the misery of SWO culture and the XO.

"Thanks, Brad, I'll see you later," she said. She opened her stateroom door and saw glass shattered throughout the stateroom, everywhere; the tiniest shards covered the floor, as well as their chairs, desks, and sink. She then noticed two fist-sized dents in the cabinets above Julie's desk. Brenda closed the door behind her and stood there, silent and emotional. The punches that had caused the dents had been strong and powerful, she thought, as she walked toward the cabinets and ran her fingers across the indentations. She then pulled out her desk chair, sat down among the glass, and rested her head on her desk. She understood the rage and frustration that had caused those dents, the products of all-out despair; and it further affected her emotions to learn that Julie had been driven to act out physically, to the point where she had injured herself. Brenda acknowledged that she didn't belong there, that she was biding her time, but Julie was different, a great junior officer, someone with promise for naval service, who, despite conditions onboard, still retained a macroscopic view of naval service: She still believed in the Navy! How could someone do this to Julie, drive her to this point?

Brenda knew that she had a major advantage over Julie – that of being the gunnery officer vs. the first lieutenant (or deck officer). Julie's division dealt with topside issues visible to anyone on the pier or to ships passing at sea. And in the SWO world, the ship's appearance mattered more than the functionality of systems and equipment. OPS and the XO were relentless and constantly at her, and Julie's dedication to the Navy forbade her from giving in. Julie's case seemed one in which knowledge and hard work never improved her lot onboard. Over several months, Brenda had watched Julie's eyes blacken, and her disposition grow increasingly expressive of feeling disheartened and dejected. It was an unnecessary development, and one she hated to witness.

She blamed Lieutenant Commander Gates, as well as OPS. The climate aboard *Curtis Wilbur* was unjustified. The solution to Lieutenant Commander Gates' plight seemed so simple: If she respected the officers, and the efforts of her crew, she would, in return, receive their respect, and productivity and morale would increase. Brenda knew that the gunners mates were aware of her own lack of technical savvy when it came to the gun and VLS. But they worked well for her because it was her human side they saw and responded to. But Lieutenant Commander Gates targeted and set out to destroy her best officers.

Brenda lifted her head off her desk and glanced around the stateroom. The glass and dents she saw evoked turbulent and insurgent thoughts. If she could have left the Navy legally, without being labeled a deserter or U/A (unexcused absence), without going to jail, she would have. Maybe some might have labeled such a desire to be that of a quitter, but she didn't consider it so. She didn't consider walking away from an abusive situation wrong or quitting.

Inport Yokosuka, Brenda vied for every day off she could get. Most workweeks were seven days, or six at a minimum. She was sure to leave the ship on non-workdays and when she didn't have duty. Finding days off was a constant chess game. But Julie stayed onboard and worked her heart out, even on weekends, even when she didn't have duty. She was strong and committed. And OPS and the XO constantly targeted her, as they did Brad and other JOs.

Several nights earlier, when Brenda had stood combat systems duty officer, Julie was drafting an eighth revision of a message. As Brenda was ready to climb into her rack for the night, Julie had returned to their stateroom, holding a stack of printouts.

"Can I look at the stack of revisions?" Brenda had requested to her roommate. As Julie handed her the stack, Brenda noticed that Julie's ankle was taped. She had pleaded with Julie to go to medical, as the ankle had dislocated a few times, but Julie was still walking on it and playing basketball with the ship's team. Were it not for playing basketball, she would have never left the ship.

"It's the XO," Julie said, "HAG," she added, as Brenda began to sift through the stack.

"Each draft is the same," Brenda said, "a few different punctuation marks here and there." Some of the marks had been changed back in later drafts. "Busy work for no reason," Brenda concluded. The surface warfare community had a reputation for dragging department heads and JOs into work on off hours and weekends, calling officers out for minor mistakes, making them revise messages over and again, but Lieutenant Commander Gates had gone above and beyond the call of normal SWO. It was a hostile work environment, the type that could drive some to commit suicide.

"Is this new Captain going to do anything?" Brenda asked.

"No," Julie shook her head. "And he's not so new anymore. He's been onboard awhile now."

She had heard that some of the department heads had approached the Captain about the XO. Rob had told her, and Neil as well, that each complaint, mainly about trying to get messages chopped (routed and edited) and released, and general treatment, had been quashed by the CO. CSO, Neil said, had tried to raise the Captain's awareness about the XO more than once, but the CO had answered, "I'm sure she has her reasons and I support the XO." He had made it clear, Neil had said, that the subject was closed.

"She's female and a rising star," Brenda had answered, repeating a comment she had often made during these now regular conversations, "the CO doesn't want to make waves."

*

The glass could be swept, Brenda thought, as she remained seated at her desk, surrounded by shards, but she wondered if anyone would ever fix the dents in the cabinets or if they would remain as a permanent record of what had once occurred onboard *Curtis Wilbur* under the leadership of Lieutenant Commander Gates. Three knocks at the door interrupted her thoughts. She knew they were from Chief Walden. She opened the stateroom door as shards cracked under her feet.

"Are you alright?" he asked.

"Yes, Chief," she answered. "How can I help you?"

"My wife and I are having a BBQ after my daughter's christening this Saturday," he said, glancing inside, "if you would like to come, 1 p.m., you're welcome. It'll give you a break."

"Thanks, Chief. I'll stop by," she said.

"In the VLS this morning," he went on, "you mentioned that the Captain has ordered us to turn on VLS anti-icing...in midsummer," he said.

"Yes, in midsummer," she answered, "anti-icing."

"A Navy tech note came out last week in the message traffic," he said, showing her a copy, "that the anti-icing feature still has some bugs in it and should be disabled unless you're operating in a sub-freezing climate. I've spoken to other GMCs around the waterfront; the other ships have all disabled their anti-icing systems. Everyone knows the VLS anti-icing system is faulty; it's not news. Turning it on in this heat could fry the system, irreversibly. That's millions of dollars."

"The Captain says we have to turn it on," she answered.

A moment of silence passed between them.

"I spoke to WEPS about it," the chief continued. "It's ninety degrees outside right now. I explained to WEPS that, with the turn of a screwdriver, the VLS anti-icing light on the CSMC panel can be lit but the system remain off. The panel shows the system is 'on'. The Captain can check the light."

"If WEPS says the light's on, then it's on," Brenda answered. "I'll talk to you later, Chief," she said. He answered okay, and she closed her stateroom door. She was beyond caring what games were played, or by who.

Chapter 56: Complainers, whiners, and bad apples

When Chief Walden left her stateroom, Brenda went down below to find Bill: He would know how to help Julie. Bill and Greg, the two combat systems warrant officers, acted as surrogate Navy dads, in many ways. Lately, Greg had been particularly outspoken regarding what he perceived as the XO's intensified cruelty against Julie, ever since the former Captain had complimented Julie's shiphandling maneuvers during the man overboard exercises.

Brenda knocked on Bill's door. "Come in, Brenda."

"I know why you're here," he said. "I wrapped Julie's hand myself."

"So, she's okay," Brenda said. "She was called out for minor points during the UNREP, wasn't she, while she was directing operations out on the decks. I can picture OPS holding that stupid walkie-talkie at his mouth, cutting Julie in that harsh, hushed tone he's mastered."

"You know the drill," he answered. "Stay away from your stateroom for a while, if you can," he suggested. "I'm going to help her clean the glass. She won't let me do it alone."

"Can you take her to medical, or should she speak to someone?"

"Navy psychiatrists are interested in whether or not you're fit for duty, not in treating you," he said. "I might know someone. We'll take good care of her. And, we'll be getting a new OPS in a week," he added with optimism. "There might be some hope there."

"I trust you and Greg," Brenda answered, and she closed his door and left.

As Brenda exited aft officers country, down below, she wasn't sure how to judge the impending arrival of a new SWO department head – a replacement for the current OPS. Most SWO officers she had met above the rank of lieutenant, who stayed in the Navy beyond their scholarship obligations, seemed to be those who adhered to the prevailing careerist and SWO mindset.

She knew that the XO was going to miss the recently promoted Lieutenant Commander Quinton (OPS). He was departing the ship ranked as the number one department head, his officer fitness report filled with all the right buzzwords. He had screened for XO, and was on the fast track to captain an Aegis destroyer or cruiser. Within the

SWO community, Lieutenant Commander Quinton was on the move.

She had started to develop the idea that those officers who were truly loyal to the Navy were those who questioned, stood up, and submitted or offered constructive criticism of the service. But it seemed the Navy wanted the opposite. Reformers and thinkers were forced out via the promotion system. She saw it happening onboard *Curtis Wilbur*, as the Command hammered down on CSO, who treated subordinates humanely, and who tried to stand up for their equipment, training programs, and morale. For every strike of the hammer on CSO, OPS was elevated.

A few steps out of aft officers country, Brenda spotted WEPS down the passageway. She was tempted to veer down a different passageway to avoid him. Her plan had been to leave the ship at 1700 for dinner. The situation reminded her of the popular SWO junior officer term: *JO escape*, which referred to a JO's effort to leave the ship in evening undetected by his/her department head. "Evasion" routes leading off the ship were referred to as *JO escape routes*.

Brenda felt grateful that WEPS allowed his division officers to simply go home at the end of the workday. It was common SWO practice to make division officers "check out" with their department heads – to go over "tickler items" – before they could leave the ship. This often led to extended time onboard, late into evening, as DIVOs ran around taking care of this and that detail. It was why OPS often kept Julie and Brad onboard until nine, ten, eleven o'clock. The department heads had to undergo the same checkout process with the XO before leaving at the end of the day. To Brenda, this system of begging to leave seemed childish, humiliating, and degrading. *Couldn't officers be trusted as professionals to judge when it was appropriate to go home at night, after working hours?*

"Chief Walden spent a fucking hour and a half in the Captain's stateroom yesterday afternoon," WEPS complained to her, as he approached her in the passageway.

"It's his right, sir," she answered, dryly. "It was his appointment to discuss his chief semiannual evaluation, and he took the opportunity to discuss his concerns onboard."

"Fucking Chief Walden," WEPS paused. "The Captain's pissed," he said, angrily. "I had to hear all about it."

"What would you like me to do about it, sir? Let's see, why would something like that happen? If the Captain didn't want to listen, he should have stopped him," she shrugged, and then they walked away from each other.

Brenda unlocked the padlock to the VLS missile canister space. She walked past a stack of stereo and video game equipment. The gunners mates had moved all of their off-time entertainment to a remote corner of the canister area, as the XO had ordered all personal equipment to be removed from division spaces, throughout the ship. The new policy had completely eroded morale. In most cases, there wasn't much personal equipment in the spaces, just a little entertainment for long, often tediously boring underways. Under the former XO, the division chiefs had done a good job policing division spaces, ensuring no obstructions or safety violations existed. The XO's policy had only resulted in "more creative hiding." In the gunnery division, both chiefs, and all of the petty officers, swore to her that the equipment in the corner of the missile canister space did not obstruct the VLS mission or safety. Since the space was padlocked, and only the gunnery division, and WEPS, had a key, she accepted.

Brenda sat down on the cold floor, her back against a missile canister, just for a few minutes of rest. She thought about Chief Walden's meeting with the Captain, and the futility of his efforts to make the Captain aware of the climate onboard. In SWO, those who raised issues and didn't okay the status quo were branded as disgruntled complainers, whiners, and bad apples: Those who couldn't hack it.

Chapter 57: Balanced reactions

As the summer weeks drifted by, the ship's schedule remained unpredictable – a few days underway, a few days inport; or every once in a while, the ship would go underway for a week and a half or two weeks at a time. Being single with no attachments and living in a foreign country, Brenda didn't care. But for forward deployed officers and sailors with families, life was harsh and unstable. CSO had confided to her, one afternoon while they were standing on the fantail, that following the last deployment, he had knocked on the door to his apartment, where his family lived in a nearby Japanese town, and his small son had refused to answer the door. "He didn't know who I was," CSO had said.

"Your wife and family didn't greet you on the pier?" she then asked.

"No," he simply answered, and moments later she chastised herself for asking such an inappropriate question, one that was none of her business.

Brenda remembered CSO's wife telling her that she hated living in Japan. She felt trapped, lonely, and isolated, and she wanted to leave.

Despite her struggles onboard, Brenda still remained focused on earning her SWO pin early. She kept in touch with the nuclear SWO community detailer by phone. He had promised her orders to nuclear power school as soon as she got her SWO pin. Therefore, if she got her SWO pin ahead of schedule, she could leave the ship early. Officer recruiting numbers were down, he had lamented, especially in the nuclear surface community. Nuclear power school, thousands of miles away in Orlando, seemed a sanctuary, a haven awaiting her, following her time aboard *Curtis Wilbur*. In reality, she knew the school was demanding, the most intense, stressful, and extreme engineering school in the Navy. But any shore-based duty station, away from the *Curtis Wilbur*, held promise. As long as she didn't have to go to sea, especially under the command of the Captain and Lieutenant Commander Gates, she knew she could survive.

Brenda had learned that in the military, one's life ran according to blocks of time at a particular duty station. She needed only to survive the weeks and months until she was freed from her current duty station, in this case, the *Curtis Wilbur*. And then she could wish her time away at a different duty station.

She thought of the entries she had made in her senior-year ROTC leadership journal. The Captain of the ROTC unit, a former submarine commander, who taught the senior-year naval science class, had complimented her on her "balanced reactions" to difficulties she had faced in ROTC. "Very mature and balanced reaction," he had written underneath a few of her journal reflections. "Excellent entries and reflections, great leadership and followship examples, observations, and discussions, exactly what I was hoping for in these journal assignments. I am very impressed with your entries," he had written throughout the pages of her journal.

As Brenda stood OOD watch on the quarterdeck of the *Curtis Wilbur*, inport Okinawa, she hoped she could maintain her "balanced reactions." She hoped she could keep her sanity. "Keep this spirit, Miss Conner, you are very bright," she pictured his writing beneath one particular reflection. At some point, she reminded herself, one way or another, her time onboard would come to an end.

She realized that her journal of reflections showed signs of the only positive feedback she had ever received from a military source. And it was feedback based on her writing, interpretations, and reporting, rather than on any actual performance. She wished that she had taken note of that fact before.

The third class operations specialist (OS3) standing petty officer of the watch, addressed her, "I'll be returning to the States during Christmas stand-down to have the breast reduction operation I was telling you about, ma'am," she confided. "But, please don't tell anyone, ma'am. Only a few people onboard know. It's too painful for me to exercise, or to do most regular activities. I'll be using a civilian doctor back home with the money I've saved in the Navy."

Brenda looked at her and nodded supportively. "It's your decision," she answered, hoping the right words would come to her. "It's very serious as well. Be sure to discuss it in depth with your doctor, or a counselor, or someone you trust." She scrambled for the "right" words in these situations. She was an emotional mess, and still, many on the ship regularly approached her, wishing to talk and to confide an array of personal and professional issues. There was her leading petty officer's divorce from an estranged and older wife living deep in the desert of Arizona. And then there was an eighteen year old seaman who had spent one night with a new Japanese girlfriend, his first sexual experience, and ended up married with a baby months later. The teenage seaman cried during many of his helm midwatches.

"It was right before the deployment," he cried regularly, his young face red, tears streaming. "I didn't even want to, and she's much older than me." All Brenda had to offer the E-1 seaman was nodding and listening. She had once seen the seaman in the Navy Exchange (NEX), shopping with his "wife" and baby. The woman looked like his mother. If she didn't know the seaman was eighteen, she would have guessed he was fifteen. He was naive and he had become a father in a foreign country, tied to a woman he didn't know, who was part of a starkly different culture.

Then, there was Seaman Chapman's utter despair as a deck seaman; she was still studying to make the enlisted journalism rating. And added to the list was the postal clerk second class (PC2) who didn't fit in onboard, but liked talking to her. And her recently promoted third class gunners mate, who had lived a common urban legend when he had met a Russian prostitute in Tokyo in a bar, only to wake in a hotel bathtub, naked and robbed, with the floor flooded and owing $6,000 in property damage. She lent an ear to whoever needed to talk, but as she listened, she knew that she was just as lost as they were, or more so.

Brenda leaned against the quarterdeck podium, dressed in Navy whites, paging through the green, cloth-covered, OOD logbook. About two hours had passed since Jon the navigator, the current CDO in charge of the inport duty section, had taken her aside and berated her. "As soon as CSO gets back onboard," he threatened, "I'm going to talk to him and ensure that your OOD inport qual is yanked. You should have told me about this." She remembered not being able to breathe until he had finished speaking. She felt her belief in herself plummeting, and her surface warfare qualification slipping away. Her SWO pin meant everything – it meant leaving the ship early to go to nuclear power school. Without the pin, she would be stuck onboard for an extra year, which seemed...she couldn't bear the thought.

"I apologize, Jon," she remembered answering the navigator. "I never could have predicted that an unsubstantiated rumor that someone had urinated on the mess decks was that important." When she had taken the OOD watch from a chief, he had told her of the rumor; but he had also told her that he could find no evidence or truth in it. After taking the OOD watch, she had sent her messenger of the watch (MOOW) down to the mess decks to check out the situation, and to speak to the chief mess specialist in charge of the galley. She had even called the MSC; he had checked around, and assured her there was nothing to worry about. She had then decided to disregard the rumor, but Jon was incensed that he had heard it from someone else, and she hadn't told him. Now she stood to lose her qualification to stand the one watch she actually didn't mind standing, even though no urine had ever been discovered!

Fifteen minutes after Jon had threatened her OOD qual, CHENG and Rich Windmiller, had returned to the ship so drunk that the two could not walk or keep food down. CHENG had vomited all over the quarterdeck and they both had to be carried to their staterooms. She had called Jon to inform him of that incident, but because she had logged the incident in the OOD book, his anger had increased. It was a cultural norm that "incidents" involving officers weren't logged. And Rich Windmiller was Jon's stateroom mate.

CHENG and Rich had done this before, and had received quiet, gentlemen's talks in private, with no consequences, as was customary for naval officers. Rich had once been put "in hack" for a day (unofficial punishment for officers, restricting them to the ship) following a second incident, but during that day, he was still allowed to leave the ship to play with the ship's softball team because he was an invaluable homerun hitter. After the game, his "in hack" period had ended. Month after month, Brenda had watched enlisted – under identical circumstances – receive Captain's Mast. At mast they were usually busted in pay and rank, and restricted to the ship, officially.

Jon the navigator had her on edge. She feared losing her inport OOD qual and her chance at a SWO pin, almost to the point of irrationality. She had recently spoken to a JO onboard another ship, who had told her that the captain of his ship had sat him down, and explained to him that he wasn't going to qualify him. "I really don't care," the JO had said. "I'll do my time on this ship and then get out of the Navy."

"I hate my ship," Brenda had answered. "We all want off of it." And still, part of her couldn't imagine the kind of acceptance (and confidence) exhibited by the JO. Brenda was trying to pull out every last stop to qualify. The last Captain had awarded Pete his SWO pin fifteen minutes before Pete left the ship. She had thought that if Pete had managed to squeak his pin out at the end, then maybe she could – maybe she could earn her pin early and get orders from the nuclear detailer to detach from the ship. She just couldn't give up, nor cope with the prospect of extra time onboard.

She thought about the nerve-wracking lengths she had to go to in trying to get justice for Petty Officer Wheeler, a gunners mate second class (GMG2). The XO had denied his leave chit for a short, three day underway coming up. "When the ship's underway, the crew's underway," the XO had stated to her, flatly and devoid of emotion, when she had gone to her stateroom to appeal the petty officer's case.

"His wife is due to have a baby during our underway period," Brenda had argued in support of his leave chit. "She's living by herself in the Navy lodge, in a two star hotel, alone, ready to give birth at any second. Nothing during this underway involves the gunners mates."

She remembered the XO turning to face her, staring into her eyes, "People have babies every day, GUNNO. It's no big deal," she insisted.

"It's a big deal for Petty Officer Wheeler, ma'am. This is their first child." She had already explained that CSO, WEPS, and Chief Dering had approved the special circumstances of the leave chit.

"The answer is no. No one is allowed leave while the ship is underway. *And, I don't care about the life of a goddamned third class petty officer!*" she screamed.

"I'll have to take the chit to the Captain, ma'am," Brenda had informed her before leaving. She hadn't bothered to correct the XO, that the gunners mate was a second class, and not a third class petty officer – for she wouldn't have cared.

The next day, Brenda found the returned leave chit sitting in her inbox, unsigned by the Captain, with an "X" across it, in his pen. She felt that she needed to *do something* for this petty officer. Upon receiving the chit, she climbed the ladder to officers country and knocked on the Captain's door. She was told to enter; the captain was writing at his desk and obviously unhappy to see her. "Sir, please reconsider the Petty Officer Wheeler leave chit," she started. "His wife is alone in the Navy Lodge, due to give birth at any moment. The situation could turn life threatening for her and the baby, with no one to help her in a foreign country on an unfamiliar naval base. I'm asking you, sir, to reconsider and please sign," she held the chit, shaking and feeling as if she was throwing her SWO pin away. By some miracle, he took the chit from her, signed it, and handed it back to her; he then continued to work at his desk, as if she had never come in.

She couldn't believe that she had stood up to HAG, and won a victory for one of the gunners mates.

She ran to WEPS' stateroom, then to CSO's, and then to the chiefs mess to find Chief Dering. "Give Wheeler his signed leave chit and tell him not to show for the underway. No one needs to know," she said, and left the mess. When the ship got underway, GMG2 Wheeler wasn't onboard, and no one talked about it. The gunners mates knew not to talk about the absence of their shipmate.

Chapter 58: A missed opportunity ... Truth sanitized

On the last day of the ship's underway back to Yokosuka, Brenda had, unbeknownst to her, missed a chance to inform the destroyer squadron of her experiences with HAG. She had heard that the XO had come down with a fever and was locked in her stateroom sick, so she had gone to the wardroom just after lunch to grab some leftover spaghetti and salad. She had never expected to find an unknown SWO lieutenant commander sitting at the wardroom table, going through paperwork. "Getting something to eat? Grab a seat why don't you," he invited her, while motioning for her to sit down next to him. She had no idea who he was. She had never seen him before, and she could only conclude that he had come off the helicopter that had landed on the ship earlier in the afternoon.

"Yes, sir," she had answered, cautiously.

"So how's life onboard?" he began asking her. "How do you like the Navy, surface warfare? Think you'll stay in? SWO for life?"

All of these questions, and she didn't know who he was. "Fine, sir," she answered, tentatively, after a pause.

"Think you'll stay SWO?" he asked.

"I'm not sure, sir," she replied as she held her plate and began to stand up. "I have to get back to my stateroom to prepare for watch, sir," she said. "Please excuse me, sir."

During her watch, the helicopter flew off the ship; in it was the lieutenant commander. She was standing watch with Jon the navigator as OOD, and Julie, as JOOD. She was the conning officer. "You look sleepy, GUNNO, go get *SET*," Jon had said to her, in his feigned, serious manner.

"Get *SET*?" she had asked. Julie giggled with her hand over her mouth. Julie regularly stood watch with NAV. He liked her as a watchstander. Along with Bill and Greg, he respected Julie's ability, and if they could have done something to defend her against the XO, they would have.

"*SET*," Jon answered, "*Siberian Exposure Temperature*. Go out to the bridge wing, put the wind to your face, and wake up," he said. "Go, go."

"No matter how tired I am," she answered, "I've never once fallen asleep on watch, but I'll go," she said.

"I have to get *SET* all the time," Julie said, still laughing. Possibly because Julie had gone to the Naval Academy, she seemed to love hazing-type activities and to find them fun, and funny. Many of the Academy grads seemed to get so excited over group "spirit and camaraderie building" activities. When the officers of the *Curtis Wilbur* wardroom appointed Julie as the George Ensign (a "fun and morale-building" designation as the most junior ensign, opposite the Bull Ensign), she had reveled in the unofficial duties of her new "position."

As SWO officers, Brenda questioned, why weren't they allowed to function as a unit of serious professionals? Why inject these childish and sophomoric antics? she wanted to know.

As Brenda swung the handle on the door to the bridge wing, she noticed Jon climb up to the XO's bridge chair and sit down – defiantly. Onboard Navy ships, it was ABSOLUTELY PROHIBITED for anyone to sit in the Captain's or XO's bridge chairs. Just seeing Jon climb up there made her nervous. She looked at Julie, who threw her hands up and said, "Don't look at me, he does it all the time." Then she ignored Jon and went outside.

She was surprised to find Neil on the bridge wing. "Having fun yet?" he asked.

Brenda rolled her eyes. "If the CO or XO ever caught Jon in one of their bridge chairs," she said.

Neil shook his head. "It would be serious," he agreed.

"Who was that lieutenant commander onboard?" she asked.

"He's the mystery man. He gave me the third degree. My guess is he's from the DESRON, and that they've gotten wind of what's going on with the XO. That's just a guess."

"Then, I missed my chance!" she reacted. "But when I saw him in the wardroom, how was I supposed to know who he was? And even if I had known he was from the DESRON, talking to him would have violated the chain of command, bypassing the Captain and XO."

"He asked questions and I answered them," Neil said. "But he never did say where he was from. Don't get too upset." He paused. "No one else spoke to him because they didn't know who he was either. In the highest brass somewhere is her advocate and protector anyway," he said. "She's hand-selected as someone's golden child."

"I missed my chance," Brenda repeated. "And I didn't even know it."

She had fantasies about going to the press. The *Navy Times* often published stories of scandals in the Navy. The situation with Lieutenant Commander Gates had to be the stuff of scandals and headlines, she thought: the cruel and depraved leadership of one of the first female line officers chosen to serve as executive officer of a combatant ship, her danger to the ship and crew, her liability to the cause of women in the Navy, the failure of naval leadership in placing her in that position, their unwillingness to acknowledge their misstep or to do anything about it. The Navy had felt so politically pressured to assign a woman to a command position aboard an Aegis warship, that they immediately promoted a woman with no experience. And once the Navy promoted her to this position, they seemed afraid to remove her or to discipline her because she was a woman. An amazing story!

Articles had begun to appear with greater regularity in the *Navy Times*, covering incidents of rape, sexual harassment, hazing, blood-pinning (pinning an officer's warfare pin, such as aviator wings or a SWO pin, directly through the skin and onto a person's chest), the Naval Academy cheating scandals, and accidents at sea. But most of the news reports had exhibited the same subtly minimizing tone.

The investigations conducted by the Navy were weak and political, and seemed to report little beyond the official statements penned by Navy public affairs officers (PAOs). Were the incidents even taken seriously?

Navy personnel were forbidden to speak openly to the press. "The good of the service," or "in the interest of national security," she had heard repeatedly. She had learned the political meaning of those phrases: Some issues were best kept under wraps from the public. Protecting the service's reputation and public image seemed to reign paramount over righting wrongs. Hiding behind these catchphrases allowed flawed, inefficient, and costly modes of operating to continue unchecked (with careers spared), while a misinformed public went on funding the organization through their tax dollars.

On midshipman cruise, she had experienced firsthand how the Navy dealt with press. When a few reporters were scheduled to come onboard USS *Spruance* (DD-963) and tour the ship for a human interest piece about Navy life at sea aboard a "tin can" destroyer, the Command, along with a public affairs officer (PAO) from the Pentagon, maintained control of the environment. They hand-selected the officers and sailors that would be stationed along the tour route and be "visible" in and around the ship, staged as if they were "going about ship's business." On the day before the press visit, more Navy PAOs arrived from the pentagon to brief selectees on appropriate answers, questions, and statements. All non-selected shipboard personnel, including non-selected officers, were instructed to remain below decks, in berthing or in their staterooms, out-of-sight. The result: There was no reporting of the ship's rock bottom morale, failed inspections, or weak and unaware command leadership – widespread problems that plagued the SWO Navy. A chief onboard had told her that press interviews, and visits by politicians to ships and bases, never reflected reality because entire "audiences" and "crowds" were preselected. Navy PAOs were "omniscient and omnipresent," he had said. But he wasn't sure the public was cognizant of the extensive staging behind the scenes when they watched reports and documentaries on TV about military life, or when they read the resulting articles. "Military aficionados out there, and young kids eager to join, eat the stuff right up," the chief had said.

While on active duty, speaking to the press entailed tremendous risk, and for any officer considering a naval career, speaking to the press candidly, and truthfully, was often a career-ender, if what one had to say did not reflect the official Navy line. It was also a breach of the chain of command.

The officers onboard *Curtis Wilbur* didn't talk much about options to address the issue of HAG. They were all busy trying to survive daily life under her. They uniformly assumed the Navy would continue to promote her, and that nothing could be done. Many wanted to take action but felt an obligation to adhere to the chain-of-command concept, which prevented them from attempting to breach it.

Chapter 59: A beautiful house in Japan

Brenda held her breath as she entered the smoke break, the small covered area amidships on the port side, where the crew was allowed to smoke. They had pulled into port during late morning, and she had duty that day and night, which she was standing for Neil. She felt relieved that her OOD inport qual hadn't been "yanked," as NAV had put it, over the alleged "urination on the mess desks" episode. After the quarterdeck watch, when NAV had threatened to pull her qual, she had gone straight to WEPS to inform him of what had happened. "Forget him," WEPS had said. "He's a jerk, nothing's going to happen. I'll talk to CSO."

Her work was done for the day and she wanted to walk out to the forecastle to rest a moment and look out at the water. She was thankful that she worked for WEPS, who supported his subordinates and always did his best to shield them from the mayhem of the Command. She could rely on him to listen and act fairly. But Julie's life had grown worse under the new operations officer who recently checked onboard. At first, Brenda had been surprised by the new OPS. He seemed more humane than the former OPS, Lieutenant Commander Quinton, and smart enough. But after a few weeks, his disposition began to change. The XO despised the new OPS. He didn't quite have the ruthlessness of Lieutenant Commander Quinton. According to word around the ship, he was on the verge of being fired.

Julie had confided that life had been much better onboard under Lieutenant Commander Quinton, she now realized, because he was very good at operations, and therefore, could keep the XO out of most of their business. During a recent one week "quality of life" stand-down, Julie had taken a few days of leave. Her parents had flown to Japan to visit her. On her second day of leave, the new OPS called her back into the ship to start a routine JAGMAN investigation that wasn't due until three weeks after her leave was due to end. "I know that calling me in was directly driven by the XO," Julie had told her. "And I hadn't seen my parents in a year and a half."

*

Brenda looked forward to going "home" to the house she had

rented out in town with Brad and his Naval Academy friend, Matt. She had to admit that it was a beautiful house, very large, with a tatami (straw mat) room separated by a rice paper slider off the living room. They each had their own bedroom with one to spare. The house had an upstairs and downstairs bathroom with Japanese heated toilet seats and a shower that spoke to them in Japanese. Most housing accommodations in Japan were small, but three single JOs combining their housing allowances and COLA (cost of living allowance) left them with more money than they could spend. So they lived in this ritzy neighborhood. Next door to them was another house full of single junior officers. Her bedroom had a balcony and she loved the view of the green misty Yokosuka mountains and shoreline.

Working with the base housing office, and a few different Japanese real estate agents had been an interesting experience. Brad and Matt had both studied abroad in Japan during their time at the Naval Academy, and had studied and experienced Japanese culture while living with a Japanese family in Tokyo. Brenda had unwittingly ended up feeling she was the culturally unaware, obnoxious American in moments, while searching for a house.

She gazed across the Yokosuka waterfront from the ship's forecastle. Gray warship after gray warship of all different shape and size – cruisers, destroyers, an amphibious ship, a minesweeper, were tied to a line of concrete piers as far as one could see. The cacophony of 1MC announcements from these ships echoed down the waterfront.

The housing office on base had aided them with signing the Japanese language lease, and with all of the legal issues involved in renting on the Japanese economy. The office staff was bilingual. "How do you speak such flawless Japanese, and read it?" she had asked the housing counselor assigned to them.

He laughed. "In this office, we all grew up on the Yokosuka naval base, and we all still live here. Most of our mothers were Japanese and our fathers were Navy. We've lived on base or a few miles from it all of our lives." She had later learned that he was married to one of the other housing counselors, who had also grown up on the Yokosuka naval base, and spoke native Japanese because her mother was Japanese as well. They lived a few blocks outside of the base. It was a fascinating enclave subculture.

"You're very fortunate to be thoroughly bilingual," she had said to him. "There's so much opportunity knowing a second language, especially one such as Japanese."

She had also heard of many American couples, stationed in Yokosuka, who opted to send their kids to the Japanese schools, rather than to the DoD schools on base, which according to rumor, were marginal. A chief had told her, "When my wife and I came here from the States, we enrolled our son in the Japanese schools."

"Did he know one word of Japanese," she had asked.

"No, but he started in the first grade and picked it up instantly. The schools are great here. He's learning far more than he would in the States," the chief had said. He had seemed very pleased with the education his son was receiving in Japan.

She had one reservation about life in Japan: "Be prepared," the housing counselor had told her. "Winters in Japan are cold, and Japanese houses don't have central heating. Buy yourself a good kerosene heater. You'll be wearing your winter coat to the bathroom in the morning," he laughed.

At least she could go "home" in evenings, to this beautiful house she had rented in the town of Nobi, with Brad and Matt. From Yokosuka, the house was a half-hour train ride, where she then picked up a bus to her neighborhood from the Nobi station. She enjoyed Japanese culture, and how the people lived. Everyone was kind and helpful, despite her awkwardness as a foreigner. She attempted Japanese whenever she could, and no one had scowled or laughed at her or made her feel like a second class citizen. It was safe in Japan. Crime was almost nonexistent, and she never felt she had to look over her shoulder at night, as she constantly did in the U.S.

Matt was never home; he seemed to have an opposite underway schedule. The house was furnished with boxes for tables, and they sat on Japanese cushion pillows from the Navy Exchange. Their refrigerator was empty, with the exception of sushi that Brad and Matt sometimes bought at a local store. When Matt was home, he usually had a Japanese girlfriend with him, a different woman each time. He regularly went up to the club district of Tokyo, *Roppongi*, "to meet another Japanese girlfriend," he often said. He claimed that Japanese women thought it was cool – a status symbol – to have a western boyfriend, and that they liked to show him off to their friends. "Maybe I'll marry one before I leave," he had said to her a while back, and Brenda had bitten her tongue at his use of the pronoun *one*. But, the women had all seemed nice. Most had seemed embarrassed, and surprised, to meet her in the morning. After she had met any one of Matt's girlfriends, she knew she'd never see her again.

Brenda decided to go back inside the skin of the ship. She looked forward to the end of her duty day tomorrow. Twenty-four hours from now, in late afternoon, she would be able to leave the ship. She enjoyed riding the Japanese train and bus home. She had memorized the *Kanji* symbols for her stops, and learned they weren't as intimidating to decipher as she had once assumed. She and Brad had split the cost of buying a used Toyota Corona from a petty officer who was returning to the States. They shared a great car for $600, but she almost never drove it. Brad needed it to drive home from the ship at ten or eleven p.m., after OPS would finally let him leave. She still needed to get used to driving on the left side of the road.

But every night leaving the naval base and experiencing Japan was a treat, Brenda thought as she neared her stateroom, hoping for twenty-four hours to pass so she could go home. Not everything was so bad.

Chapter 60: Promotable

In forty-five minutes, Brenda had an appointment with the Captain to discuss her first ensign FITREP – her first real evaluation as an officer. She feared what she might face, such as seeing her failures listed out on paper by her senior officers, if that was what was in store for her. She foresaw that in the Captain's office, she would have to answer for all of her shortcomings.

She thought of the idea of another person putting their personal thoughts about her to paper. At twenty-four years old, just starting out, she predicted she might face a massive backlash for her choices, in the form of reading on paper, all the ways in which she didn't belong as an engineer in the Navy aboard a warship.

But she also craved guidance, counseling, advice, and assistance from those more senior to her. She wanted to know how she could improve her performance in this role. She hoped that she had demonstrated her work ethic to her superiors, along with her earnest attempts at keeping on top of the hard work, not to mention her studying. She was on the brink of not being able to withstand much more failure. Confronting her failures, almost on a daily basis, wore at her, despite the secondary gain of learning about herself. She only hoped that her performance as a division officer would temper some of the low scores she anticipated.

It seemed especially frightening – and invasive – that this particular Captain and XO would be the ones evaluating her. How much credence could she give to *their* evaluations of her? But she realized it didn't matter how they evaluated her because she knew the truth.

To kill time before her meeting, she had filled her morning with errands and diversions. Before lunch she had gone down to the ship's barbershop for a quick trim, a straight line cut across her bangs and in the back, just below her shoulders. The SH3 (ships serviceman third class) in the barbershop had nervously told Brenda that he had never cut an officer's hair before; and probably, she assumed, he had never cut a female's hair before. She hadn't meant to cause added anxiety for another person. Her bangs had started to hang down past her eyebrows, and the auburn coloring she had used since college had started to form a two-toned line halfway down her hair. She had viewed the ship's barbershop as a quick solution.

When Brenda entered the Captain's stateroom, dressed in a crisp, newly pressed khaki uniform, shoes and belt buckle shined, he was sitting at his desk. He appeared guarded and noncommittal as he invited her to take a seat.

"Hello, sir," she greeted him, as she sat down. She focused on the Captain's brand new blue carpeting as she waited for him to speak.

The Captain wheeled around in his chair to face her. "Here's your FITREP, Miss Conner," he said dryly, handing it to her. "You can look it over. If you have any questions, you're free to ask."

Brenda took it from him and immediately saw an "*X*" next to the "*Promotable*" block, essentially, the lowest block on the ratings scale. Her face dropped, her spirit dropped. *Promotable.* There was *Must Promote* and *Early Promote*, but her *X* was next to the least desirable of the choices, *Promotable*. She had been ranked the lowest of the ensigns, the only ensign to have rated the promotable block. From the "*summary*" block underneath, she could see that all of the other ensigns onboard, including Julie, Brad, Neil, had made the higher blocks. She was that lone *promotable* ensign; she was that failure she thought she was.

"All set?" the Captain asked.

"Yes, sir," she answered, panicked inside. "I'll work hard to earn my SWO pin, sir," she started. "I would like to attend Nuclear Power School." Then after a pause, she asked, "What would happen if I didn't qualify? If I didn't get my SWO pin?"

"Nothing good. That's for sure," the Captain answered. And it was clear he was done with her.

"I'll sign it," she said. And he handed her a pen. She felt her evaluation was true and accurate because she had received one high mark, a 4 out of 5 for "*above standards*" in the preprinted "*teamwork*" block, for "*understands team goals, employs good teamwork techniques, reinforces others' efforts, meets personal commitments to team.*" As well, she noticed a few comments in the freehand "*comments on performance*" section about the repair of the gun and VLS, and that morale in her division was high. She recognized the crisp, concise, well-worded, and praise-packed writing in the freehand comments section as that of her department head.

But *promotable*, and being ranked last and alone. She felt ashamed of herself and of her performance. She didn't dare ask the

Captain any more questions or bring up further discussion.

"That's all, Miss Conner. Have a nice afternoon," the Captain said.

"Thank you, sir," she answered before closing the door behind her. The Captain and XO were spot on in their assessment of her, she believed.

Chapter 61: The lowest and the worst

Brenda rushed back to her stateroom, opened the door, and felt her body collide with the floor. There was no question anymore that she had failed at everything for which she had worked. And she might never get off this ship. If the Captain's assessment of her resulted in nonattainment of surface warfare qualification, she could expect an extra year onboard.

She felt rational one moment, and irrational the next. She got up off the floor, walked to WEPS' stateroom, and knocked on his door. When he answered, she said, "I saw my FITREP, sir. Why not tell me, why not warn me? Why blindside me like that?"

"It's a good ensign FITREP," he answered, softly. "I wrote strong comments; you were ranked right in there with the pack. I've got my notes right here."

His stateroom was dark, as always, except for the illumination of his desk light.

"I was ranked the lowest and worst of the ensigns. I'm the only ensign in the promotable block."

"What? I'm sorry, I didn't know anything about that," he answered. "The Captain and XO made the final rankings." Brenda felt dizzy. "Ensign FITREPs don't matter," he tried to console her. "They have no bearing on anything, on career. Don't worry about it," he was shaking his head. "Nothing to worry about," he repeated.

"Okay, sir," she said, and left his stateroom for her own.

*

Somehow, she had reentered her stateroom and had lain down on the floor, but she couldn't remember having done so. She decided that she was going to leave the ship for the day. She put her ballcap on and walked out of her stateroom. But the command career counselor, NC1 (navy counselor, first class) Nolan, stopped her in the passageway. "I know, ma'am, that you've taken an interest in helping Seaman Chapman. I'm sorry to tell you that she didn't pass the journalism rating exam. She'll remain a deck seaman, for a while longer at least."

Brenda remained in front of her door. "Thank you, NC1, for letting me know." He nodded, and then left the passageway. Then, she reentered her stateroom. *"Goddamn it!"* she screamed! *"This fucking place!"*

Chapter 62: We're nothing alike ... The pain of self-discovery

Inside her stateroom, Brenda felt the full impact of her isolation and fear. She leaned back against her stateroom cabinets, focusing on the clanging sound of the deck hands chipping paint, banging their tools incessantly against the metal hull. She wondered if Seaman Chapman was among them.

In retrospect, she felt beyond angry with herself for not trying harder to convince the seaman to "strike" for a rating that would realistically be within her grasp, and which accepted a higher percentage of applicants. The journalism rating was a relatively small, highly competitive community. A few months ago, Brenda had spoken to NC1 about Seaman Chapman. In his role as the command career counselor, Brenda wanted him to encourage Chapman to strike for a rating similar to journalism, but with more openings. "She's bright," Brenda had said to NC1, "but I fear she doesn't have a strong enough academic background for the journalism rating. She hasn't been to enlisted "A" school, and there's no opportunity for her to get OJT (on the job training) onboard in journalism."

"Striking for journalism is a bit like reaching for the stars," NC1 had agreed. "As a deck seaman, her best bet would be to try for boatswains mate. That's where most deck seaman end up."

"She doesn't want boatswains mate," Brenda had answered.

Brenda kneeled down on her stateroom floor and clasped her hands over her head, wishing she had tried harder to persuade Seaman Chapman to strike for a different rating. She felt on the verge of breaking down, and giving in to the hatred, confusion, desperation, and despair she had felt since the first day she had checked onboard, or in truth, almost since she had started engineering and ROTC.

There was a knock at her door. She didn't answer, as she could tell it was the XO. Lieutenant Commander Gates had moved, temporarily, back into the stateroom across the passageway, bumped down from her own stateroom by an embarked dignitary. Now, Brenda could hear her cold-blooded rants all day and night, as if they were taking place in her own stateroom. Each target officer warranted a distinct tone and rhythm. Brenda had developed the ability to recognize the variations in screams lashed at each officer. The sound of failed leadership, Brenda thought, as she massaged her eyes.

"*I hate this! I hate it here!*" she kept repeating to herself, under her breath. She eased herself up off the stateroom floor. She wanted to be alone with her anger, alone to wish that she wasn't there.

"GUNNO, it's the XO!" she heard. "Meet me in my stateroom in a minute."

"Yes, ma'am," she answered, and then she washed her face and tidied her hair.

She entered the XO's temporary stateroom and sat down. "I hear you're upset over your FITREP, GUNNO," HAG began. "You have nothing to worry about. You're a very bright ensign. You remind me of myself when I was your age. You do just fine onboard; you're going to be just fine," she said.

"Yes, ma'am, thank you," Brenda said, stoically. And she got up to leave. But she wanted to tell Lieutenant Commander Gates that she was nothing like her, that there was much they didn't have in common. She wasn't going to pretend to be a naval officer. She was going to get out as soon as her legal commitment ended. She cared about the crew and her division. She wasn't going to spend her career sacrificing the safety of others for her own selfishness. She was going to search out her talent and what in life resonated with her. She wasn't going to try to survive as someone else, or simply as a persona, because such a way about life led to misery and repression and couldn't be sustained without a tragic injury to the self. She wasn't going to remain onboard ships, or in the Navy, where she couldn't be herself.

She wanted to ask Lieutenant Commander Gates why she had stayed in the Navy when she wasn't very good at it, and didn't seem to like it. She saw the XO as miserable and bothered. She never wanted to shoot the guns; she was a terrible shiphandler. Why stay in the Navy, and strive to captain a warship, if she wasn't interested in the core of what the service did – drive warships through the ocean and shoot guns and missiles from them? Why stay in a place where one's presence wasn't a positive contribution?

Some said Lieutenant Commander Gates stayed in because her father had been a Navy captain, and her older sister was a career naval officer. And that aspect of adhering to family history, on the surface, may have been a driving factor, but Brenda saw it mostly as a symptom that Lieutenant Commander Gates hadn't individuated from her family; and for that reason, she remained out of touch with the self, never trying to search and discover who *she* was. Lieutenant Commander Gates was living a persona, a mask, unrepresentative of her inner self, intended only to show an image of a naval officer and commander. Her emphasis on development of *ego*, focusing mainly on her presentation to those outside of her, instead of on development of *self* (concentrating on an inner-directed search) had kept her from awareness of her true center, or innermost center; she was cut off from self. Her lack of understanding and acknowledgement of the self resulted in the repression of a whole range of emotional material, and this unrecognized, unaccepted emotional energy found expression in countless forms of rageful outbursts and cruelty toward others, which she seemed unable to control.

Her daily actions were governed by internal unresolved issues (insecurity, repressed emotions, antisocial behavior from mental illness, and fear), as well as her innate character. Her intellect and skill level for military and technical aspects couldn't sustain the naval persona that she had worked for years to construct. Since Lieutenant Commander Gates had no knowledge of who she was, and lacked the courage to be honest about who she was, she banged her head against the wall trying, but failing, to fulfill the persona of a naval officer.

A few onboard said that Lieutenant Commander Gates was driven by a hatred for men, or that she was trying to act like a man. But Brenda believed those assessments were mischaracterizations. She acted with equal barbarism towards men and women, and her actions did not indicate that she was trying to "act like a man."

In consideration of the Navy, the service had failed, as it had failed with many other male commanders throughout history, who had gained status for political expediency.

During the last few months, Brenda had thought almost daily of a character from a short story by an Argentine writer, and of the reference material she had used to compose her paper on the character's process of self-discovery and search for wholeness. At the time, she had made fun of the story and of the character's search "to become conscious of himself." The man, left tired and empty from an outer-directed, technology-driven, task-oriented, and utilitarian life, had embarked on a journey "to reconnect with the stirrings in his soul," and use those stirrings as a guide. He was drawn to visit an ancient circular area – *el círculo*, or comparatively, in Jungian terms, *the mandala*, near his village. She remembered a quote from a source she had used in her paper, *"It is the characteristic of the introverted intuitive personality that the inner image constitutes the most convincing aspect of the totality of life experience. This inner image, the symbol, carries for the intuitive introvert more than for any other personality type the essential meaning of existence."*[9]

The character's upbringing, education, and family life had centered on fitting in with mainstream society, with his inherited religion, and on adapting pragmatically to the world. He had been taught to believe that feeling was a sign of weakness, and stoicism (as the term is defined in the general sense) a sign of strength. But the character no longer wanted to live cut off from *self*; so he searched the unconscious regions of his personality through dreams and through spending time in isolation and reading. As the character allowed himself to feel more, both emotionally and physically, he experienced more of what it was like to live in his body; he sat quietly each day, allowing free play of the unconscious regions of his mind, surfacing areas of his personality that had once been purely unconscious. From the unconscious, he learned of, and brought to light (to consciousness), those previously unexplored aspects of his personality. He had sought an awareness of the totality of the human psyche in an effort to integrate the conscious and unconscious regions of his personality.

During his visits to *el círculo*, he explored the symbolism of the collective unconscious. He began to feel more connected to the world; and as he became more aware of his mind and body, he emerged a more compassionate person. With a new sense of compassion, awareness, and honesty, he embarked on a more creative life, which in turn, fed his inner self and provided a medium for self-expression. He had discovered his unique voice. Through creativity, and newly discovered expression, the character found his possibilities limitless. He found the liberation of his creative forces rewarding.

The character learned that he had kept himself from wholeness, from the birth and growth of himself as an independent individual, from consciousness of himself. By the conclusion of the story, the character had reevaluated his values and relationships based on the

---

[9] Jung, C.G. *Psyche and Symbol*. p. xxv.

new reality of his own emerging self-knowledge and individuality. It had taken profound reflection to search out what was truly individual within him. But going forward, he carried a new human awareness, which had given him a sense that he had gained a mature personality. He had left behind an infantile personality and was progressing toward an individuated self that was free from the parental archetype. His search had laid the foundation for a new acceptance and awareness of himself, his relationships, and his circumstances.

Onboard the ship, Brenda had been forced to face herself and who she was, and she had learned that fully experiencing the pain of self-discovery was the only way that she could move forward with her life – openness with herself, fearless honesty, and humility were essential. She had realized, recently, that much of her conduct in the past that now made her cringe and that she regretted, had stemmed mostly from being cut off from herself, in a nearly complete lack of awareness of self and of body and of physicality.

If Brenda had learned anything from literature, and from her time onboard, it was that being an adult, in the true or authentic way she now envisioned, entailed honesty with self and with others, even when honesty seemed difficult, or not an option. Honesty seemed the most humane way to live in the world, as it allowed one to make informed decisions, instead of subjecting oneself to a painful life mediated by denial, secrets, lies, and suppressed truths. The inability of Lieutenant Commander Gates to be honest with herself caused an entire warship to suffer, affecting everyone around her, driving all of them – the officers and crew – to their own forms of disaster and mental illness.

Brenda realized, that she had, like Lieutenant Commander Gates, gone about the world *unindividuated*, unthinkingly replicating her earliest influences, and gliding the surface without self-reflection. None of her choices had been based on self-knowledge, or on an independent personality free from the parental material she had internalized. Her choices had been, rather, symptoms. Her search was forcing her to face issues, regarding herself and her family, that she would have rather denied or ignored. Since her earliest years, she had learned from experience that honest (and sometimes contrary) expressions – and especially those that did not replicate her parents' views, attitudes, and way of being – would result in her parents seeing her as difficult, as an annoyance to them. Consequently, a fear of rejection and an impulse to please had taken root. So much so that, in time, Brenda had gone about the world unknowingly conducting herself out of that fear; and her way of being had created frustration for her because it did not stem from authenticity. She had spent tremendous energy getting people to believe in, and to buy into, her persona.

Brenda kneeled down on her stateroom floor; she leaned forward, and finally, slept.

She awoke to Chief Dering's knock. After he knocked on her door, he walked right in. "I heard you were upset."

"What can I do for you, Chief?" she asked, sighing because no one would leave her alone.

The chief shifted his stance. He rested his right elbow against Julie's closet and supported his head by the palm of his hand. He jutted his opposite hip out to one side, bouncing slightly, as he tightened his grip on his coffee mug. It was all so familiar. He adjusted his tinted glasses. "You're a good division officer."

She looked at his tinted glasses, mustache, macho-posture, and exaggerated macho hand positioning, as he held his black-stained coffee mug. "Thank you, Chief," she said. She knew that he had come to her stateroom, partially, out of genuine concern for her, and partially, out of obligation as a chief petty officer (CPO) to aid and support his division officer. "Chief Walden and I have told you this before," he continued. "We run the division. You don't have to worry about that. The job of a junior officer is to earn qualifications. That's what you're onboard for," he pointed out. "So, my advice would be to get your SWO pin and get off this ship; you do that, you'll survive, you'll be okay."

Brenda looked up at him. "I've learned to listen to the chiefs," she said. "Thank you, Chief Dering, you don't have to stay any longer."

"You know where I'll be if you need anything," he said.

"I do, Chief, thank you," she answered.

"Keep your head high, and you'll be fine," he advised as he left.

She stared blankly at her stateroom door, which the chief had just closed. She didn't know if there was anything else she could do onboard to help herself, the ship, or anyone else. She had failed Seaman Chapman, and as long as she continued to stand watch, she would fail her colleagues and shipmates, as well. She couldn't stay; she couldn't leave.

She was clear now about the source of her trouble. She had rejected all that wasn't pragmatic and strictly intellectual. A person who had worked to integrate the ego and the self, the conscious and the unconscious, would have chosen a path to nourish the spirit. She had presented herself to the Navy as an engineer, and the Navy had accepted her based on her credentials. It wasn't that something bad was happening *to* her; everything that was happening was based on her own choices, ones that had been made while having been cut off from much of herself.

She had shaped her sense of self externally, and not internally...and she no longer wanted to rely on external direction and validation; she wanted to rely on her own resources, from within. If only she could have helped Seaman Chapman, she regretted.

Her heartfelt, determined intentions of serving in the military had turned into a painful diary of daily survival.

Chapter 63: Essential tremor ... Every waking moment ... The will that got her there can get her out

Brenda left a note for Brad in his stateroom, which read, *"Took car, had to leave. Brenda."*

As she exited the ship, a welcoming sunshine awaited her that afternoon. While she walked down the brow, she heard the 1MC announcement, *"There are personnel working aloft. Do not rotate, radiate, or energize any electrical or electronic equipment while personnel are working aloft,"* followed by, *"Liberty call, liberty call. Liberty commences for sections one, three, and four to expire onboard at 0600."*

Brenda meandered through the cars parked in the pier lot. She found her Japanese Toyota Corona but swore when she reached for the door handle, realizing that she had walked to the wrong side of the car. She walked back around to the right side, the driver's side. She opened the driver's side door, tossed her backpack inside, and crashed into the seat. She threw off her ballcap, as she despised wearing a hat while driving or doing anything that required concentration. She felt completely drained, and she dreaded the end of the next twelve hours when she would have to return to the ship.

Across the pier lot she noticed CSO getting into his car. She knew that recently, while driving through one of the many mountain tunnels on the Yokosuka highway (Route 16), on his way to the ship at three a.m., he had considered ramming his car straight into one of the tunnel walls. Thoughts of suicide, of release, had consumed him. He had confided to Rob that he feared he must have been insane in those moments. On that early morning, he had wanted anything but to come to the ship.

He hadn't wanted SWO, and his family hadn't wanted Japan. When CSO had attempted to transfer out of SWO and into meteorology and oceanography (METOC), the Captain had chastised him, "I guess your lateral transfer application means that you don't want to be a SWO. I don't need officers onboard who don't want to be SWOs. Don't ever step foot on my bridge again." And CSO's daily life onboard had further deteriorated from there.

To complicate matters, the SWO detailer had neglected to inform CSO that *Curtis Wilbur* would be shifting its homeport from

San Diego to Japan, when he had initially accepted orders.

Brenda started her drive back to the house. She liked her house, but she was never able to sleep during the nights she spent at home – she agonized over returning to the ship the next morning. She had bought an alarm clock at the Navy Exchange (NEX), wired for Japanese electricity (100 V, 50 Hz), but she hadn't once needed it. SHE COULD NOT SLEEP. If she got two to three hours of sleep at night, while home, she was lucky.

She drove on autopilot, scarcely aware of her actions. She normally indulged herself in the experience of reentering Japan, as an end-of-day reward, something good to which she could look forward. But on this evening her interest in Japan had waned and none of the excitement of living in an exotic country mattered. She continued driving because she knew a couch and a warm comforter awaited her. She had decided that she would have to rely on immediate safe havens, short term lifesavers. She would go from one to the next until she could get out of the Navy. Tonight, she just wanted to get home to her couch.

She normally approached the narrow driveway at the side of her Japanese house with caution; she usually pulled the side mirror in, drove slowly, and stressed over every inch. But she pulled the car right in, not caring that only scant inches separated the side of the car from the house on the left and a concrete retaining wall on the right. She stopped the car, remained seated, and stared up at the massive house. *She lived in a dream house! What was the matter with her? Who didn't dream of living in such a house? At her age! Just out of college!*

Brenda edged out of the car into waist high grass. She struggled to open the tall wrought iron gate against thorny weeds and bushes. She thought of her Japanese neighbors, and felt ashamed of the overgrown yard. But she, Brad, and Matt had no spare time; they were always at sea or on duty. When any one of them came home, it usually was out of pure exhaustion.

She opened the front door to bitter cold air. The housing counselor's warning – that their house would be cold – was correct. She grabbed her winter coat, which hung by the door, and went to the kitchen to fetch matches for the kerosene heater. She pulled the heater away from the *shoji*, the thin rice paper sliding door that separated the tatami room from the western style rooms. After lighting the heater she crashed on the couch and focused on the warm glow.

On the cardboard box in front of the couch, which doubled as a coffee table and storage unit, Matt had left a note. *"Brenda, Gone underway to Vladivostok. Might find a Russian wife! Russian girls can't wait to marry American GIs. Ha, ha, Matt."* She shook her head; he constantly yanked her chain.

Brad hurried in the door. He was wearing jeans, a polo shirt, and boat shoes without socks. Over his left shoulder he carried a backpack; his right hand held a plastic bag from the NEX video store. She figured they had rented every video in the store, even the Tagalog (Philippine) language ones. "I left the ship right after I saw your note in my stateroom," he said.

"What about OPS and the XO?"

"I don't care about OPS and the XO. Are you okay?" Brad kneeled next to the couch and handed her a can of Japanese coffee. She considered canned coffee, available everywhere in vending machines, to be one of the best products in Japan.

"Thank you," she said, laying across the couch.

"You'll get qual'd; we all will," he assured her. "Then you'll go on to nuclear power school."

"I hope I can survive these next three years in the Navy," she answered.

"I hate the Navy more than you do," Brad said. "I hated the Academy, all four years of it. I hate SWO. I've put in for an oiler out of Earle, New Jersey next tour, where hopefully, I won't have to hear, *'COMMO, get the fuck out of my stateroom!'* from the XO. I was almost scared of what I might do after she threw me out again today."

"She sucks; she makes it worse. I couldn't take it anymore today," Brenda answered. But she knew that SWOs were supposed to be able to withstand the treatment and derive pride from surviving it, and even find humor in it. The peer pressure to take it, to buy into it, to think it was normal, and believe that there was something wrong with you if you didn't react well to it ...it was sick thinking.

"That woman hates me," Brad said.

He bent down to open the "ice box" door, built into the kitchen floor, where their soda was refrigerated by the cool ground. "I thought we'd throw a frozen dinner in the microwave and watch this movie," he said, "but you have to get off the couch."

Brenda sat up slowly. She knew he was right. Last Saturday, she had spent the entire day on the couch, and Brad had warned her that her depression was getting scary. On most days when they had time off together, they traveled around Japan, going to Tokyo, the mountains, and visiting temples, some overnights. They had climbed Mt. Fuji, reaching the summit at over 12,300 feet. In the South Pacific, they had enjoyed sunsets and beaches on tropical isles. But no matter what they did and where they were, they always talked about the ship and HAG; it was a primary conversation; it was what they had in common.

She wasn't sure what was in store regarding her relationship with Brad. They were limited by the circumstances of living and working onboard a forward deployed warship, homeported in Japan; most weeks (and weekends) they were underway. Regardless, she felt grateful for Brad's companionship in the evenings and while exploring Japan and Asia. Together they helped each other through their time onboard. Brad was this gentle guy, and she would have found it difficult to explain the world of the ship to someone outside of the Navy (and SWO).

She noticed, as Brad stirred the microwave dinner, that his hand tremor had significantly worsened. Essential Tremor, he called it. She could barely read the last note he had written to her. "Your hand tremor is worsening," she said.

"I know," he answered. "My naval experience is a make-work waste of time, getting screamed at, changing a few insignificant words in messages."

"I can picture you driving the oiler around the ocean all day, honing your bridge skills, conducting UNREPs. Don't get seduced into staying in, or going into the reserves, since life onboard the oiler will probably be tolerable with a mostly civilian crew," she warned.

"An oiler out of Earle, New Jersey, the SWO detailer was shocked at my request," he said. "But he also was open to it and said it should be no problem."

"It cost nearly a half million tax dollars to put you through the Naval Academy," she answered, as she walked toward the kitchen. "I bet he begged you to use your Academy knowledge and Aegis weapons system training, and tried to talk you into selecting another cruiser or destroyer."

"He's all too happy to slate me for the oiler, something no one else wants."

"Chief Dering gave me advice," she said, feeling herself gradually coming back to life. "I'm going to dedicate every waking moment from now on to qualifying. I'm going to park myself at every watchstation and make sure my efforts are visible to the

Captain."

She felt she had enough energy remaining. And she realized, that crying and laying around her stateroom floor and this couch weren't going to get her off the ship. The same will that had landed her onboard, and in the Navy, with an engineering degree, could get her off the ship. "I hope we go on that unscheduled deployment coming up," she said to Brad. "I hope we'll be underway for the next six months, continually. Then I'll get qualified."

Chapter 64: A little South Korean hazing

During the ship's port visit in Busan, South Korea, the officers of the *Curtis Wilbur* were invited to a formal dinner at the Korean naval base. On a cool night, Brenda had accompanied her fellow officers to the Korean officers club, where they dined in traditional style in a sala reserved for VIPs. At a long table, just above floor level, the Americans sat opposite the Koreans, with members of both groups dressed in the service dress blue uniform.

Brenda was sitting next to Julie. On the other side of Julie was a Korean junior officer – another ensign like them – who attempted to instruct them in how to use Korean chopsticks, which were stainless steel and a different length and shape than Japanese chopsticks. Brenda found that the stainless steel chopsticks felt heavy in her hand. After she and Julie struggled with them, the three of them laughed, and the Korean JO retrieved a fork for them. As Brenda looked around the table, she saw most of the Americans struggling, and many had switched to forks. But despite their awkwardness, she and Julie still made an effort to eat their meals with the metal chopsticks.

Towards the end of the night, a senior Korean officer stopped the conversation at the table to make an announcement. It was time to introduce the American officers to a Korean military tradition, one in which a waiter poured a drink – some extremely strong Korean alcohol drink – into a tumbler, and the individual had to swirl it into a whirlpool before drinking the content of the glass in one try. They started around the table, on the American side. Everyone participated, one officer at a time. After each officer drank, everyone laughed and cheered. Brenda was put off by it. She found it no different than American military hazing games, which she neither valued nor participated in. She always found herself on the outside when it came to group activities, especially hazing for camaraderie. And in reality, this was nothing more than a form of Korean hazing for macho camaraderie.

When Julie's turn came, the room silenced. One of the Korean officers announced it would be a first for a woman to participate in the tradition. The Americans from *Curtis Wilbur* remained silent because they all knew that Julie had never taken a drink before in her life. "Don't do it if you don't want to," Brenda whispered to her. "You don't have to do it. I'm not going to," she had said. But Julie swirled the glass and drank the liquid. She took the first drink of her life, the strongest alcohol one could probably find, possibly anywhere. Everyone cheered and laughed, except for Brenda.

After Julie, she was next. Everyone in the room cheered her. WEPS and others were saying, "C'mon, you have to do it! Be diplomatic, they're hosting us."

"No, thank you," she said. And the volume of the room roared louder with everyone trying to get her to take the drink as she was supposed to.

"Please move on to the next person," she simply said, trying not to be rude or insulting. And eventually they did. Later that night, some of the participants in the drinking ritual were sick, without any immediate or effective relief.

But Brenda had enjoyed talking to the Korean junior officers. She wondered if women served in the South Korean Navy. But she never asked, deciding to leave the topic alone.

It was in Korea that Brenda had volunteered for her first COMREL (community relations) mission. COMREL projects were organized by the Navy League (an American civilian organization in place to support the U.S. seagoing services) in various ports, in an effort to bolster relations between the U.S. Navy and the countries and local communities frequented by its warships. For many officers and sailors, COMREL projects were a main activity inport. In Busan, Brenda took a bus trip, with officers and crewmembers, to paint a local orphanage. During the few hours they were at the orphanage, they were so rushed to paint the entire inside (with white paint provided from the ship) that Brenda wasn't sure how much they had "helped" – they had to slap the paint on the walls as fast as they could. At the end however, many PR pictures were taken showing *Curtis Wilbur* sailors standing next to orphaned Korean children, and an article praising the event later appeared in a Navy newspaper.

COMREL projects were a means of demonstrating to foreign countries that the U.S. Navy really was a peaceful force out "doing good in the world."

Brenda had one free day on her own in Korea. On that day, she had gone shopping in the city, but got hopelessly lost in the outskirts of town. By herself, she panicked for five hours while she couldn't identify a restaurant in which to eat, a sign she could discern, or a way back to the ship. She rode in a taxi for an hour trying to draw pictures of warships, attempting to indicate to the taxi driver that he should take her back to the naval base. It was the only time in her travels that she had found no way to effectively communicate. At the time, she wondered if the driver wasn't able to conceive that a woman would be asking to get to the military base. He had taken her to a few different industrial ports before finally taking her to the naval base. Fifteen minutes before liberty expired that night, she frantically ran back aboard the ship.

Chapter 65: Second deployment ... Throw out the lifeline

The port visit to South Korea was the start of Brenda's second southeast Asian deployment. Following the Christmas holiday stand-down, the ship was given one month notice that they would leave for an unscheduled "public relations" deployment. Although they were scheduled to meet up with the USS *Independence* (CV-62) battle group at various times, the *Curtis Wilbur* was slated to "steam" from port to port, by herself, as part of the Navy's *forward presence* mission. They were scheduled to enjoy such ports as Guam, Hong Kong, Darwin and Townsend, Australia, Thailand, Malaysia, and Singapore.

When the ship pulled out of Yokosuka, Brenda vowed never to sleep and to qualify as a surface warfare officer. As soon as the ship got underway, she kept her promise to herself: She slept but little and she stood watch constantly. When she wasn't scheduled for her normal bridge watch, she stood extra watches under instruction in the combat information center. She threw herself into studying every aspect of Aegis combat systems, nearly all day and night. She read manual after manual. She spent slow watches with the warrant officer, Bill, and with the limited duty officer (LDO), Jason Arnett, asking them question after question. She spent time at the plot table, and asked the operation specialists (OS) to challenge her on the MO Board.

Two months into the deployment, she had exhausted herself. But her presence in CIC had been so continual and persistent that on one quiet night at sea the Captain had approached her. "I'm very impressed by what I'm seeing, Miss Conner," he said. "You've dedicated yourself to the study of surface warfare."

"Yes, sir, thank you," she answered him. But afterwards, even though she had gotten what she had wanted – she had "been noticed" by the Captain – she felt she had betrayed herself and had misrepresented herself to the Command...which sent her further into depression. But at the same time, it was then that she began to hope again that she might actually qualify. If she could keep this pace and her morale up, she might just be able to call the SWO nuclear detailer for orders off the ship.

Since the ship was mostly steaming by itself, Brenda's stress level had decreased, as there was little opportunity for DIVTACS and all of the real-time evolutions on the bridge that she still wished to avoid. DIVTACS – formation steaming in close company with other ships – was the evolution dreaded most by junior officers. During DIVTACS, ships "steamed" as if they were marching in drill and ceremony, maneuvering uniformly, turning, wheeling, changing courses and speeds together as they made way through the ocean. The maneuvers required fast and accurate MO Board calculations. DIVTACS were a naval necessity, but very dangerous due to the threat of collision. Brenda wanted no part in them.

The unscheduled deployment had created hardship for most, especially for those with families. She now understood why her orders to the *Curtis Wilbur* had included the designation, "unusually arduous sea duty." The ship had just returned from one deployment, only to leave for another six months later, with many two and three week underways in between. And to make matters worse, HAG had restricted the department heads to the ship for the duration of the deployment. Now, in most ports, the department heads weren't allowed to leave the ship at all. The XO still threatened to fire the operations officer on most days, and his actual firing had become inevitable.

The only saving grace was that a new assistant operations officer (AOPS) had recently arrived to the ship – a female lieutenant, just below department head level, who had experience in Aegis combat systems from working her way up the normal SWO career pipeline. From the first day she checked onboard, it was apparent that she thoroughly understood Aegis combat systems. And she was a knowledgeable and able shiphandler on the bridge.

But no matter how many port visits were ahead for the *Curtis Wilbur*, the officers and crew remained disgruntled and morale was low. Even during the pre-deployment stand-down, the XO continued to restrict leave in the cruelest and most vindictive ways. When a petty officer in Neil's division requested emergency leave during the stand-down to visit a terminally ill family member in Hawaii – someone especially important to him – she denied his leave. Neil appealed to HAG, as the petty officer wasn't asking to travel far. Then Neil's chief appealed personally to HAG, but she wouldn't let STG2 Castillo, a well-respected sonar tech, go. Neil's chief later said to him, angrily, "I will never go in there again," referring to the XO's stateroom. "It's a suicide mission," the chief added.

By Christmas, HAG seemed to have decided that she *loathed* Neil, and so she had made him a target. Neil and Danielle married over the holiday stand-down, but not without Neil receiving two Letters of Caution from the Captain over the issue of his wedding leave chit. By mid-fall, Neil's chit had been sitting in the XO's inbox for six months. The last time he went to her stateroom to ask about his wedding leave chit, she answered, "You listen here, Neil," and she poked her index finger into his chest, "there are 283 people aboard this ship, and you aren't getting special consideration. I haven't made the holiday watchbill yet. I'll sign your chit when I'm goddamn good and ready. Now, get the fuck out of my stateroom. I don't want to see you or the weapons officer in here. I don't give a goddamn about you or your personal problems."

The situation spiraled when the Captain of USS *Blue Ridge* (LCC-19), the Seventh Fleet command ship, came by the navigation office to ask Danielle (his navigator) how her wedding plans were going. "All set for the wedding?" he had asked. And she had answered, "Neil doesn't have a signed leave chit, sir." When a few weeks later, the Captain of *Blue Ridge* ran into Neil and Danielle at the officers club, and learned that the chit still wasn't signed, he called Commander Brier, Captain of *Curtis Wilbur*, who was an O-5, junior in rank. Commander Brier assured Captain Rohrer of *Blue Ridge*, an O-6, that he would sign the chit. The Captain of *Blue Ridge* also emailed the DESRON commodore (the ship's immediate superior in command), stating, "*My navigator is getting married. I want her to relieve stress before going to Singapore and Hong Kong. Fiancé on Curtis Wilbur can't get wedding leave chit signed for last six months. Can you look into it?*"

The next morning, Commander Brier called Neil into his stateroom and handed him a copy of the email Captain Rohrer sent to the DESRON commodore. Once Neil read the email, the Captain handed him a Letter of Caution (addressed to Neil and signed by Commander Brier), which stated, "*You are not to take problems outside the lifelines.*" Twelve hours later, Neil received a signed leave chit.

Emotions were running high, and Danielle informed the Captain of *Blue Ridge* of the Letter of Caution Neil received. The captain of *Blue Ridge* (Captain Rohrer) called Commander Brier (captain of *Curtis Wilbur*) about Neil's Letter of Caution. Commander Brier was then dressed down by his own boss, the DESRON commodore.

When Neil returned to the ship from San Diego, after getting married, another Letter of Caution for *"going outside the lifelines"* awaited him, from Commander Brier. Brenda remembered shaking her head, and telling Neil, "that's the rigmarole a SWO has to go through to get married."

"That's why I've put in for a transfer to EDO," Neil had answered, referring to the engineering duty officer community, "and why I won't be able to write my letter of resignation fast enough."

While Brenda was waiting outside of the XO's stateroom one morning to route a message, she heard HAG flame spraying CSO. *"I know it was you who went above our Captain's head and informed the DESRON commodore!"* she screamed, out of the blue. Even though that wasn't the case, Brenda guessed CSO didn't see the point in trying to convince her otherwise. But having endured months of pettiness, he finally pushed back, angrily yelling, "This is all your bullshit!" She backed up slightly, a momentary flicker of fear in her eyes. And the conversation was over.

Chapter 66: The chaplain's last prayer

At the halfway mark in the deployment, the DESRON commodore had sent a chaplain – the DESRON chaplain – to ride the ship for two weeks. Everyone hoped the chaplain was experiencing, firsthand, what morale was like onboard. Both officer and enlisted were seen talking to him, and word around the ship was that he was being inundated with stories about the XO. Brenda knew that WEPS had sat down and spoken honestly with the chaplain, as had CSO.

One night in CIC, she had cornered the chaplain. For two hours, she told him of every story about the XO that she could think of. In response, he had nodded complacently, but she wasn't sure of his takeaway. After all of her effort, she had received nothing but pat answers from him that seemed more annoying than comforting. "Are you going to report all of this, in detail, to the DESRON commodore?" she had asked, more than once, trying to get a direct answer from him. "Everyone is depending on you to do that," she had emphasized. But his responses had remained noncommittal. He had given her the same manner of artificial smile she had often experienced with priests and ministers, a response he seemed to have mastered…a smile that feigns support yet masks ones true thoughts.

Toward the end of their conversation, she had said, "Thank you for your prayer the other night." He nodded and smiled, but it was in that "fakey" way she couldn't read. On most nights, just before taps, the chaplain recited a prayer over the 1MC. But the other night, he had offered a prayer to the effect "that the Lord watch over the officers and crew of *Curtis Wilbur*, who were facing trying times, who struggled in spirit. May the Lord lift them from their darkness." Rich Windmiller later told the JOs that when the chaplain climbed down the ladders from the bridge (where he had used the 1MC) the XO was waiting for him. The XO pulled the chaplain aside, enraged. She ordered the chaplain to remain clear of the 1MC, and admonished him, "Don't you ever say another prayer on this ship again!"

"I hope you report what you've seen and heard to the Commodore, sir," she emphasized before their conversation had finished. Although, even if the chaplain did make a full report, she doubted even the Commodore would make waves about Lieutenant Commander Gates.

Chapter 67: Don't make fun of me ... Thank you for your service

In Pattaya, Thailand, Brenda and Julie shared a hotel room out in town, not because of cost, but to be safe. Neither wanted to be a lone woman in the port area (comprised mostly of dirt streets) where the majority of the establishments seemed to be brothels and go-go bars.

In town, they found a beautiful hotel room with an inviting pool for the equivalent of twenty dollars. While on liberty, they planned to visit some of the nearby temples and historic sites they had missed on their first visit. Thailand and its ancient culture seemed fascinating. In a brochure, she had read that Thailand was the only southeast Asian country that had never been colonized by a European nation.

All in all, however, she and Julie shared a limited relationship. They approached life onboard differently, according to their interests and talents. Although Julie was an able watchstander and technically gifted, she didn't take as much of an interest in the welfare of her seamen, in terms of their professional growth and personal advancement – enlisted such as Seaman Chapman. Brenda had once suggested to Seaman Chapman that she talk to Ensign Wettlaufer (Julie) about her career plans, but the seaman had answered that she was apprehensive about approaching her division officer directly. And when Seaman Chapman failed to pass the journalism rating exam, Julie hadn't seemed all that concerned, or interested, while Brenda had feared the potential for a suicide attempt.

On one afternoon, in their stateroom, Brenda had asked Julie about Jon the navigator. "Jon jokes about me sometimes, doesn't he?"

Julie grew uncomfortable. "Yes, sometimes," she admitted.

"And you laugh?" Brenda asked her, "or giggle in response to what he says?"

"Yes," she answered, looking down.

"Please stop," Brenda said to her, and added, "I try to defend you whenever I can. We're all struggling onboard, in different ways."

Julie had nodded and said that she was sorry. But Brenda told her that there was no need to apologize. She understood that at times her lack of ability for shipboard life annoyed Julie, and she empathized with those feelings. She hoped that Julie would stop going along with Jon, and especially refrain from laughing or giggling with him when he talked about her. But that was Julie's decision.

The other day, Brenda grew more uneasy regarding her relationship with Julie. Her highly visible efforts at dedicating herself to qualifying had worked. She was selected by the Captain, over Julie and Brad, to receive an OOD *"murder"* board, i.e., a practice oral board. During the next week, Brenda's official oral board to qualify OOD underway was scheduled to follow. OOD underway was "the big one," the major qualification leading to a SWO board. It was also the watchstation that carried the most responsibility and required the most skill onboard.

Brenda felt self-conscious to have been slated for an OOD murder board before Julie. It seemed obvious that Julie (or Brad) should have received their OOD boards before her. Brenda had been surprised by the show of congratulations she had received from her colleagues. Brad told her not to feel self-conscious, because she had demonstrated incredible effort and she had deserved a board. But Brenda had answered him that her efforts were merely an exhibition, a farce for the Captain so she could qualify SWO and move on to nuclear power school. Brad had answered, "What do you think all of us are doing?"

She wanted to believe that Brad was right, that she was no less suited to watchstanding and seamanship than an average JO. But recently, she had been faced with another episode that brought her back to reality, when she had tried to show herself in engineering – as an engineer.

While they were underway, she approached the warrant officer in engineering, the main propulsion assistant (MPA), about standing some EOOW watches with him under instruction. Qualifying EOOW wasn't a requirement for SWO qualification, but there were some line items in the SWO PQS book involving the propulsion system that she needed to get signed off. She had felt apprehensive about discussing the engineering line items in her book with MPA. She feared revealing her lack of conceptual understanding of engineering systems. She was supposed to have been this sharp engineer, with a B.S. in mechanical engineering, who was headed to nuclear power school. Discussing a gas turbine propulsion plant should have been second nature. With her background, she should have been able to walk into the engineering spaces and speak with him conceptually about the plant nearly on his level, based on her education and even without having actual experience in such a plant.

After several four-hour watches in CCS (central control station), MPA still hadn't signed off any of her engineering PQS line items. She had sat with him, watch after watch, with her PQS book open, going over each line item involving the propulsion system, one by one. She had expected him to take her book and start signing. But he never offered to sign any of her engineering line items. And out of self-consciousness, she never had the courage to ask him directly: Okay, we discussed this, can you sign it off? At one point, he had indicated that she should speak with CHENG and that he could possibly sign the items off for her.

In contrast, Julie's SWO PQS qualification book was filled with MPA's signatures. Julie had gone down to engineering a few mornings to talk to him about the systems and he had signed off her entire engineering section.

*

While on a four-hour shore patrol shift with Bill, the warrant officer, Brenda was faced with her ambivalence toward her military service when two American tourists stopped them outside of a Thai shopping mall to "thank them for their service." She and Bill had been wandering the streets of Pattaya, walking and taking busses, patrolling the establishments frequented by sailors. As soon as the couple said hello, they started into what Brenda – in her tired, hot, and irritable malaise – had perceived as clichéd chatter about how "the troops were our heroes." The wife had looked at her and Bill and told them that, "they were heroes and their service was greatly appreciated." Bill was a good sport and smiled through it, but the temperature was over one hundred degrees and Brenda's eyes felt painful from no sleep in over twenty-four hours, having stood the midwatch the night before; she felt hindered in her ability to play along and react with the enthusiasm she knew was expected of her in her role as a service member in uniform. And the couple's praise "for their service" had surfaced her bitter confusion over the Captain, HAG, the low morale onboard *Curtis Wilbur*, and this multi-hundred-million-dollar-port-hopping-public-relations
deployment they were on, that used untold amounts of fuel and resources. Raised too were her feelings of self-consciousness and insecurity about her own performance and contribution as a service

member. And she could not help but be aware that her anxiety regarding her very participation in the military was growing. The interaction with the couple was too short and vague to allow her to fully understand the motivation behind what they had said to her and Bill. And she didn't have enough time, nor would it have been appropriate, to begin to tell them of her personal and professional challenges in the military, and to explain why she felt uncomfortable accepting their tributes – tributes which were generalized statements that certainly applied to some military members, but not to her.

Finally, a "10-baht bus" (a taxi service comprised of a pickup truck with two benches on the inside edges of the truck bed) arrived and they were able to escape the couple politely. While riding through town, as she and Bill passed go-go bars and hotels, she thought about how she had tried to thank the couple for their words and compliments, wanting still to represent the Navy as professionally as possible while dressed in Navy whites with officer shoulder boards. At a stoplight, she got a view inside one vintage hotel, where just inside the patio area she noticed a system of pulleys and belts and faux palm-frond fans, which provided both relief from the heat and the feel of an earlier time. She had felt bound by her military commitment to show the couple everything she thought they expected to see of military personnel, in spite of her mixed feelings.

"Those who love the military so much were never in it," she commented to Bill, "or they aren't in it any longer but have allowed their memories to evolve into something positive over time. While in, they probably couldn't stand it and couldn't wait to get out; but then they develop an exaggerated sense of service pride later in life," she finished, feeling adrenaline and anger welling inside her, as they bounced along, riding in the truck bed of the 10-baht bus.

Bill laughed, but then made an attempt to bring her out of her seriousness, her annoyance…"I can show you all the ropes in Thailand," he teased.

"I bet you could," she smiled, and couldn't help laughing, "but, I've signed up for an MWR tour into Bangkok tomorrow, instead."

The truck bounced unmercifully along its way. As the hard bench seats magnified the unforgiving nature of the dirt road, she sat in silence, searching for a meaning to military service that was deeper than repeated slogans and long-existing clichés. She resented when acclamations of "thanks and heroes" seemed reactionary and not thought-out, becoming, nothing more than mindless repetitions of cheapened conceptions of military service, pandering that lifted the speaker into the feeling that they had contributed or done something to "support the troops." She had come to believe that reciting such slogans and clichés – if done so perfunctorily and compulsorily, even if well-meaning – reflected the inundation of propaganda from the first Gulf War that had the result of building support for continued similar wars and hawkish foreign policies. These phrases had the indirect effect of quashing honest conversation and critical thinking regarding the recent wars, leaving Americans afraid to examine and criticize the wars and missions to which the military was sent, for fear of not "supporting the troops." All while countless service members continued to be sent overseas to fight for questionable causes in an era where nationalistic accolades could help clear the consciences of civilians.

Every service member joined for individual reasons. While parting from the couple, she remembered the wife saying something about her nephew who was deployed overseas, how he was making a sacrifice, that he was brave like they were. Brenda wished that she could have told the couple not to thank her, because she had volunteered for the Navy for all the wrong reasons. She hadn't known or understood herself very well; she hadn't individuated from her parents; she hadn't thought beyond the surface of her surroundings and of what she had been taught. She had "toed the line" all of her life, always doing as she had been told, appeasing others, performing for them, and it had resulted in her being assigned – of all things – as a gunnery officer. If she could only have told the couple of her reality aboard ship: She was participating in an overseas deployment and had little understanding of the overall purpose, mission, and far-reaching consequences of it, and she was misplaced within the Navy in her current position.

As she actively questioned the beliefs she had trusted her entire life, she appreciated more and more that there were no easy answers. It was the most destabilizing feeling she had ever known. She thought of those parades she had attended where there was enormous group pressure from the crowd to honor the United States by cheering – blindly with militaristic style patriotism – for any military personnel as they passed by. She had confused an anti-military and anti-war stance with anti-Americanism, equating patriotism with militarism. She had thought that she was entering into a noble and worthwhile cause in the Navy, and that a "stable and ordered" world was one in which the United States dominated.

But she had started to view the Navy in a more realistic, unadorned light, more as a fighting organization funded by the taxpayers of the United States with duty and accountability to them, and less in the hallowed, religious sense and mindset that equated the Navy to America or to the spirit of America. The religious symbolism of the Navy that had heightened since the first Gulf War was a mythos, she now believed, created by those in power – who held to a specific world view on foreign policy – to coax average people to go to war to kill and die for their power and profit. And the mythos had the added effect of stemming criticism. Those in power told average people they were deploying and fighting for God and country. It was a lesson she had derived recently from the Gulf War, when she had begun to wonder how fighting there equaled the protection of freedom for Americans in any way.

Always faithful. First to fight, she thought of the common Marine recruitment poster, which carried, at once, an ethereal and lionized message. The poster showed two Marines donned in full dress uniform, engaged in the exactness and discipline of drill and ceremony, their image superimposed partly against the raising of the American flag on the Iwo Jima battlefield, and partly against a military cemetery. Below one poster, she remembered a plaque that read, *"The call to serve is at once invisible and always present, for those who choose to answer the call for their country, for their fellow man, for themselves. It is the most powerful force on earth. For pride, for country. God, country, corps."*

She no longer believed that the military was very often a healthy way for a young person to start his or her life.

But, she was still affected by the account of a World War II veteran, who she had met in the grocery store. He was collecting money for wounded veterans. When she approached the older man, wearing his VFW members cap, to drop a few dollars in his collection jar, she told him of her ROTC scholarship. He told her of his service in Italy during the war, when his unit's young lieutenant commanding officer ordered his enlisted men to remain onboard their patrol boat while he jumped off the boat and swam over to some unexploded ordnance. Rather than his enlisted crew be killed, the young officer saved the lives of his men, perishing in the subsequent explosion. The elderly man in the grocery store had wanted to tell someone about the young officer and how he died, and she had been moved by his story.

Despite her growing inner conflict over her role in Navy,

and the Navy's role in the world, she still was moved by the veteran's account, and she wondered if maybe there were times, such as during WWII, when the reasons for war were more clear. Where was the line between supporting individual troops, and supporting the wars in which those troops were fighting?

Brenda had been drawn in by the enduring challenge to serve in the military...sent from the past and preserved for the future. She thought again of the Marine poster, which provided a lasting reminder to future generations that those before had forged a path of military greatness. It taught the next generation that they, too, could serve with honor and take part in the same great legacies of the past, if they had the courage to serve, as those before them had served.

Chapter 68: When can we leave? ... Lessons learned

In Townsville, Australia, Brenda enjoyed an overnight stay on Magnetic Island, a beautiful barrier reef island. She had gone to a tourism office in town, and signed up for a short boat ride out to the island to get away from the ship and to be alone. When she walked onboard the ferry, it was crowded with her shipmates who all shared her same desire.

When she returned to the ship the next morning, she barely stepped off the brow and onto the quarterdeck of the *Curtis Wilbur* when WEPS approached her, as if he had been waiting. He was all keyed up. "Your career and my career are over," he stated frantically, as he rushed her off to the side. And she couldn't help saying, with a smile, "Great, when can we leave."

"The ammo count's off," he said. He was angry and confused and agitated, and she began to feed off of him, taking on his nervousness.

"I'll stay onboard and look into it until it's resolved, sir. I'll recount it myself," she tried to reassure him. "We can send out a correction message with the right numbers, or expend some ammo next underway to level the numbers." She knew that WEPS was aware of the remedies she had suggested, but the XO, with her cruel ways, was on his back every second. A few days before, HAG had officially fired OPS, the operations officer who had replaced Lieutenant Commander Quinton (Julie's original boss). OPS was flown off the ship – some said – in one of the helos that had landed while underway. Others said that he had quickly departed the ship after pulling into Townsville; that he was going to fly from Sydney back to Japan to the DESRON. No one who knew the facts talked about it. It was as if the "new OPS" had never existed. Courtney, the new assistant OPS, who had only been onboard a few weeks, became the acting operations officer.

WEPS and Neil had another crisis in play. The XO was furious over the "lessons learned" message they had drafted following a recent antisubmarine exercise with the Australians. "It was a straightforward, scripted exercise," Neil had told Brenda. "There was no free play or serious sub hunting, but there were areas for improvement and I wrote about them." Brenda knew from Neil's previous attempts at routing his lessons learned messages that the

Navy preferred to downplay (or exclude) any defeats or deficiencies, rather than expose areas to improve upon. In multinational exercises, the "right" language included the U.S. Navy as victorious in all aspects, as a result of superior technology. Any language in lessons learned messages that indicated otherwise had career-ending potential. SWO culture dictated that suppression of failures in exercises and going along "for the good of the Navy" was one's duty. It was why the community didn't attract progressives and free thinkers, but instead, mostly "yes men." Reform-minded officers, thinkers, or those who refused to go along, were often forced out through the promotion system. Brenda didn't understand; it seemed officers who thought and who questioned were the ones who were truly loyal to the Navy.

Brenda remembered Neil placing his hands on his hips and shaking his head, while stating, "It's especially difficult because the XO doesn't grasp the exercises, so she's primarily concerned with the write-up, showing the ship in just the right light to the rest of the fleet."

"FITREP bullets for the Captain and XO," she had answered.

On a larger scale, lessons learned messages had high-level consequences. Results were spun for many reasons: the interests of combat/weapons systems developers and industrialists, lobbyists in congress, and the desire of Navy brass to fund a particular combat/weapons system. The drafting of lessons learned messages brought serious tension to ships, and their crafting was extremely (and intentionally) convoluted – a SWO art.

*

The first day underway from Townsville, Australia, on the way to Darwin, Australia, Brenda was scheduled for her OOD murder board. She had been fortunate during the last few days underway, before pulling into Townsville, that an Australian SWO-equivalent lieutenant – a specialist in navigation – had come onboard to serve as their pilot through the Great Barrier Reef. The USS *Curtis Wilbur* was to be the first ship of her class to pass through the reef. Navigating through the reef was tedious, and sometimes it appeared as though the coral and small islands were but a few feet from the side of the destroyer, a precarious but breathtaking sight. The Australian pilot remained on the bridge 24/7 without much break. Before Brenda's murder board, she had a chance to study the intricacies of navigation by observing and asking questions of the lieutenant.

Chapter 69: Memorization is murder

During her OOD murder board, Brenda felt history repeating itself. She was reminded of a Thermodynamics II exam she had taken during her senior year of college. Prior to the exam, she had memorized pages and pages of formulas and verbiage; she had spent days, locked in her dorm room, mechanically working problems, without giving much thought to the meaning or application of the solutions. While sitting for the thermo exam in the large college lecture hall in the engineering building, she had suddenly experienced a disconnect, followed by panic. She couldn't recall, by rote, one of the components in the line drawing for a gas turbine engine. Simple understanding would have prevented the need for memorization, but she wasn't able to employ conceptual understanding. Because she couldn't remember that one component, she nearly failed the entire exam.

Even though she had understood that her memorization approach had let her down, she didn't act on that or consider changing her major. In fact, during her senior year of engineering, she had convinced herself that she had taken to her mechanical engineering classes, and even that she liked them. After all, she had gotten through two years of introductory engineering courses – four semesters of Advanced Calculus (Calculus I, II, Multivariable, and Differential Equations), Physics I and II, Vector Analysis, etc. – and a year of advanced junior year engineering courses, such as Fluid Mechanics I and II, Statics and Dynamics I and II, Materials Science, Mechanics of Materials, and Heat Transfer.

But her experience during the thermo exam – her memory glitch and subsequent panic – had lodged itself in her mind. It wasn't until recently that she understood the meaning behind what had happened: She had mistaken memorization and passing exams by rote, for learning. She wished that she could have understood that fundamental concept at the time, as that understanding might have changed the course of her life.

Her OOD murder board had gone fairly well. It was informal. CSO, WEPS, AOPS, Jon the navigator, Neil (who had recently qualified OOD), and MPA (who sat in for CHENG), had all sat at one end of the wardroom table, while she sat by herself at the opposite end, fielding questions. During the board, she had the feeling that she was doing well. She couldn't completely tell, as each board member maintained a blank expression throughout. When she had finished answering a particular question, there was no acknowledgement from the board members (whether through gesture or facial expression) if she had answered correctly, somewhat correctly, or in error – just blank looks. But she had a lot of material memorized, and she was able to recall it.

CSO and WEPS had teamed up, asking her to solve a few MOBoard problems: avoidance, intercept, CPA (closest point of approach), formation steaming with own ship as the guide, and formation steaming with a different ship as the guide. The problems ranged from warm-up scenarios:

Time, 0800, Curtis Wilbur on course 320, speed 12 knots. Contact bearing 310, 12,000 yards. Contact course 120T, 15 knots. OOD orders you to change course when contact at 11,000 yards. Determine course to avoid contact by 4,000 yards...

to more difficult formation steaming problems, involving DIVTACs:

Curtis Wilbur on course 000, speed 15 knots. Distance to guide 5,000 yards, guide bears 090. USS Destroyer 5,000 yards ahead of guide. USS Destroyer ordered to take station 5,000 yards off guide's starboard beam, formation speed, 15 knots. Curtis Wilbur to occupy USS Destroyer's previous station, use 25 knots. Solve for course and time to station for both ships, CPA to USS Destroyer, CPA of both ships to guide.

As during her Thermo II exam, she went about solving the problems according to steps she had memorized and practiced repeatedly for each type of problem. MPA asked basic questions regarding various engineering casualties (malfunctions) and how they affected the OOD's actions on the bridge – scenarios such as high turbine inlet temperature, low lube oil pressure, and cooling system failure. He asked her to explain battle override.

Later, she met with each board member individually and received positive feedback. Each one had recommended her for an official OOD board. She couldn't believe it. And she still couldn't believe that Todd, Jon, Rob, and Neil – the ship's primary OODs – had supported her in receiving a board.

Chapter 70: To cross the equator

Boom! Boom! Boom! Boom!
Boom! Boom! Boom! Boom!

"Awake all ye slimy pollywogs!"

Boom! Boom! Boom! Boom!
Boom! Boom! Boom! Boom!

"Awake all ye slimy pollywogs!"

In her rack, on a Sunday morning, Brenda drifted in and out of sleep to drum beating and repetitious chanting of "**Awake all ye slimy pollywogs, Awake all ye slimy pollywogs**," outside her stateroom door. Exhausted from the 0000-0400 midwatch, she tuned out most of the noise until she heard, *"Know all ye by these Presents: and to all pollywogs, mermaids, sea serpents, whales, porpoises, sharks, dolphins, eels, skates, crabs, lobsters and other living denizens of the sea, that you are to report to the fantail of USS Curtis Wilbur for Shellback initiation,"* announced over the 1MC.

Boom! Boom! Boom! Boom!
Boom! Boom! Boom! Boom!

"Awake all ye slimy pollywogs!"

Brenda angrily swung her stateroom door open. "Brad, that *is* you beating the drum! And Julie! It's Sunday and a holiday routine. I intend to sleep," she told them. Brad and Julie were dressed in pirate garb – ripped up khakis and felt pirate hats. Brad wore an orange yarn beard, with chains around his waist. The arms and legs of his shirt and pants were sheared like cut rags. Brad and Julie were "trusty and honorable shellbacks," and had already gone through the "official" ceremony of crossing the equator and entering the "Kingdom of Neptune" during midshipman cruise. Although Brenda had crossed the equator during her first deployment, she was still a "slimy pollywog," "scum of the earth," because she hadn't yet been initiated through the "crossing the line ceremony," appearing before King Neptune's court.

Neither Brad nor Julie offered sympathy for her lack of sleep and they stayed in character. Brenda, dressed in sweats and a Navy sweatshirt, felt annoyed by another hazing activity. As former Naval Academy students, Brad and Julie seemed to have found the event great laughs. Naval Academy life was regimented according to class, drill, sports, and meals, and then there were group cultural activities to "let off steam." It was the first morning that she had had a chance to get some sleep and she had no interest in participating.

But as she thought more about it, she had a change of heart, because Petty Officer Marcello had told her that the gunners mates had planned "some revenge" from "the little people," as he joked – which meant – the GMs had some activities planned for her during the ceremony.

She knew that whatever they had planned would essentially be harmless. It was another hazing event, but at least, the political correctness of the '90s had resulted in such ceremonies being tempered. The Navy had cracked down on crossing-the-line ceremonies, as sailors had been killed in the past when events had gotten out of hand. Stories of beatings and torture were not uncommon. She knew personally of one story in which a seaman was made to climb a one hundred-foot antenna pole on an aircraft carrier, only to fall to his death. The occurrence was then covered up by the Navy.

"Wog, ye has to change into ye dirty slimy wog clothes. I'll be beatin' this drum until I see ye coming out to the fantail," Brad chanted, adding an occasional pirate's "arggg."

Brenda rolled her eyes and closed her door, resolving to go along. She put on a bathing suit, then a pair of older khaki pants turned inside out, followed by an older t-shirt that she knew would be written on. She knew that she was destined to be drenched in eggs, whipped cream, mustard, ketchup, and all other manner of gross concoctions.

Brad beat his drum louder while her stateroom door was closed. "Ye be not gettin' away, ye slimy wog!" he kept chanting. "The gunners mates be waitin' fer ye," he said. "Get ready for the wog gauntlet, lest we be feedin' the fish with ye."

The next thing she knew, she was standing on the ship's fantail behind the wogs of A-gang (auxiliary division). Their shirts were labeled with marker, *"Pretty Boy Wog, Chubby Wog,*

Deliverance/Redneck Wog." The gunners mates had greeted her, and had labeled her, *"GUNNO Wog."*

"You're a late-coming late-bloomer wog, GUNNO Wog. You got here late," Petty Officer Brooks said, before they all started cracking eggs over her head.

"No! Stop! No!" she was screaming, her hands over her face, but she had no defense. Then, a shellback with a mustard filled squirt gun fired at her nonstop. She begged him to stop pulling the trigger, but then another shellback came at her with a ketchup bottle.

She curled into the fetal position on the deck, drenched in a running mass of ketchup and mustard (two condiments that in real life she already disliked), as they continued to attack her. All she could do was be a good sport, resign, and bear it. "Oh my God," she screamed repeatedly, in dread of whatever was coming next.

Then, King Neptune (Greg, the combat systems warrant officer) addressed all wogs in line for the gauntlet, waiting to appear before King Neptune's court. "Now hear this all ye scummy slimy pollywogs," he announced, while she picked herself up from the deck. The gunners mates were drenching her hair with water and green goo. "You must crawl on your slimy bellies down these here fifteen-foot pads while pushing an egg with your nose. Don't worry. The pad you'll crawl on will be frictionless. We've prepared a special formula for sliding wogs through the gauntlet. We will now commence with accompanying music!" With the announcement, a group dressed as the Village People karaokied to "In the Navy." Brenda closed her eyes and did everything they asked her to do, until, at the end of the slimy pad, she was deemed by the court of King Neptune and Davey Jones as an "official shellback."

"All ye shellbacks and pollywogs gather round the fantail for the official indoctrination and to receive ye official certificates!" King Neptune announced, once all of the wogs had gone through. The shellbacks gathered on one side of King Neptune, and the wogs gathered on the other side, regardless of rank. (In this case, shellback vs. pollywog determined rank.) The ceremony commenced, and with hair and clothes drenched from head to toe with unknown concoctions, Brenda appeared before the podium, when her name, "Honorary Shellback Ensign Conner" was announced. She had earned rights as an official shellback:

"IMPERIUM NEPTUNI REGIS, Know All Ye by These Presents: and to all pollywogs, mermaids, sea serpents, whales, porpoises, sharks, dolphins, eels, skates, crabs, lobsters and other living denizens of

the sea. *Greetings: Know ye that in Latitude 00000 and Longitude 105° 49.9'E near to the Natuna Sea of Indonesia there approached within Our Royal Domain the USS Curtis Wilbur (DDG 54) at the equator. Be It Known: That the said Ship with Officers and Crew thereof, has been examined and passed on by Ourselves and Our Royal Staff. ALSO BE IT KNOWN: By all ye who go down to the sea as well as ye lowly Landlubbers who may be honored by the presence of **ENS BRENDA CONNER** WHO HAS BEEN FOUND QUALIFIED TO BE NUMBERED AS ONE OF OUR HONORED SHELLBACKS AND HAS BEEN DULY INITIATED INTO THE Solemn Mysteries of the Ancient Order of Shellbacks.* BE IT FURTHER KNOWN: *That by virtue of the power invested in me I do hereby command all my subjects to show this illustrious Shellback due honor and respect.* DISOBEY THIS ORDER UNDER PENALTY OF OUR ROYAL DISPLEASURE. *Signed Davey Jones, His Majesty's Scribe and King Neptunus Rex, Ruler of the Raging Main.*"

Chapter 71: Another milestone ... Ensign Conner has the deck

At an official OOD board, Brenda sat before the Captain and all of the department heads – with the additional presence of the navigator. The XO was absent for the board. The OOD board followed the same arrangement as the murder board, with Brenda seated by herself at the far end of the wardroom table while the Captain and department heads asked her questions as they maintained expressionless faces. She had walked into the wardroom thinking that she had no choice but to try her best. And if she faced humiliation, then she would have to accept it.

At the end of the board, as the Captain walked out of the wardroom, he had complimented her, saying that she had done well. But then, before he closed the door, he had added, "I'm surprised." Immediately afterwards, other JOs asked her how her board had gone and she was unsure how to answer them. A few hours later, CSO, as the senior watch officer, knocked on her stateroom door and congratulated her on passing. She was relieved beyond belief, and encouraged. She received her OOD letter, signed by the Captain, which read:

From: Commanding Officer, USS CURTIS WILBUR (DDG 54)
To: ENS Brenda A. Conner, USN
Subj: QUALIFICATION AS OFFICER OF THE DECK   (UNDERWAY)
Ref: (a) NAVEDTRA 43101, series, PQS for OOD (UNDERWAY)
       (b) U.S. Navy Regulations, 1990
       (c) CURTISWILBURINST 3121.1E
       (d) OPNAVINST 3120.32 (Series)

1. Having completed the requirements of reference (a) and passed the requisite qualification onboard, you are hereby qualified as an Officer of the Deck (Underway) onboard CURTIS WILBUR (DDG 54).
2. This important qualification is earned only through experience, study, aptitude, and the application of the principles of Seamanship. You are to be congratulated for having achieved it.
3. You are directed to review and remain thoroughly familiar with your duties as an Officer of the Deck as outlined in references (b) through (d). You are reminded that during the period of your watch, you serve as my direct representative, charged with the safety of the CURTIS WILBUR and her crew.
4. A copy of this qualification will be made part of your official record.

T. M. Brier

***

On the bridge, Brenda looked out to open ocean. She had just taken her first OOD watch from Rob. After over a year of standing JOOD and conning officer, she had nevertheless been in disbelief when – following a review of the details of the watch – Rob, a senior OOD, had turned to her and asked, "Ready?" She still could not believe that the enormous responsibility now lay solely on her.

"*Attention in the pilothouse,*" Rob announced, "*this is Lieutenant Trenton. Ensign Conner has the deck.*"

Then she announced, "*This is Ensign Conner. I have the deck,*" and her first OOD watch became official, legally. She watched the quartermaster of the watch (QMOW), who maintained the deck log (a legal record) under the instruction of the OOD, log the change in OOD.

In that moment, she had remembered her first bridge watch with Rob – which seemed like forever ago – when she had just checked onboard the ship in Sydney, Australia and had immediately been assigned to conn the ship out of the harbor.

Her second southeast Asian deployment was nearing its end. Since she had passed her OOD underway board, she assumed the Captain would schedule her SWO board as soon as the ship returned to Yokosuka. Since the SWO nuclear detailer had instructed her, "Call me as soon as you get your OOD letter," she couldn't wait to get into port, when the phone lines would be hooked up, so she could get orders and free herself.

But she knew that she was accomplishing nothing more than "ticket punching." Was there any real ability behind her on-paper accomplishments? she constantly asked herself.

Before the ship pulled into port in Shimoda, Japan, she was scheduled to stand two watches as OOD underway. It was then a half day's transit back to their homeport of Yokosuka. She only hoped her watches would fall during calm seas and in areas of no traffic. She wasn't sure that she was ready to be "*the* person" up on the bridge, prepared to take action during a crisis.

Brenda stood on the bridge, trying not to let one detail slip by her. She constantly scanned the horizon for contacts with her binoculars and checked the radar. She was hyper-vigilant about confirming the radar picture with CIC. QM1 Westgear, the lead quartermaster, was her quartermaster of the watch (QMOW). His presence gave her comfort. She trusted him and worked with him to ensure the ship's navigation chart and deck log remained accurate.

She was fortunate that her first OOD watch had occurred during tranquil seas, with clear blue skies, with no events or evolutions scheduled. The ship was "steaming" through open ocean, completely alone, no contacts in sight or on radar, and she was sure that scheduling her first watch during such an uneventful time was no accident on the part of the Captain and CSO.

Four hours during a quiet afternoon came and went, with no fanfare, before she turned the watch over to Neil, the oncoming OOD.

Chapter 72: An end in sight

Afternoon had turned to evening. Brenda remained on the bridge after turning the OOD watch over to Neil. With the opportunity to leave the ship on her horizon, she wanted to seek advice from those onboard whom she trusted, her peers who were more experienced, regarding whether or not she should leave (i.e., "request orders to detach"). As much as she wanted to leave, she also felt guilty for detaching two months shy of her original tour length. She didn't want to be selfish.

After officers call and quarters that morning, she had asked Bill, the warrant officer, for a few minutes of his time. "I was thinking of calling the SWO(N) detailer," she said to him. "But leaving when others can't...is it right?" she asked.

"I may not be one of the big gods, the W-3 or W-4," he answered, jokingly referring to higher warrant officer ranks, "but I can tell you that in the Navy, you work with good people, you do your job to the best of your ability, and then you move on to work with more good people, in or out of the Navy. Your job is to qualify and go where the Navy sends you next, in this case to nuclear power school. In life, I've learned that no one should ever get the idea that they're irreplaceable. Call the nuke detailer," he said, "you've earned it; you've done the time."

"Thank you, Bill. I guess a new crowd's coming aboard anyway," she answered, thinking of the new strike officer who had replaced Pete, and Kirsten, the new ASWO, Neil's soon-to-be relief. And there were more new people coming – a new supply officer and someone to replace Julie.

*

On the darkened bridge, Brenda observed Neil at the chart table, working under the red table lantern. She had no illusions that she should be standing OOD watches. She wasn't sure what would come out of nuclear power school, besides a year of intense shore duty schooling. But once she left the *Curtis Wilbur*, she intended never to put herself in charge of the bridge of a warship, ever again, for everyone's sake.

It was a slow evening and the stars were becoming visible. At sea, away from the lights of civilization, the brightness of the stars was overwhelming. On many nights, the Milky Way was clearly visible.

"I was thinking of calling the SWO(N) detailer," she said to Neil.

"Absolutely," he answered in his confident way. "Do it."

"I've been accepted to EDO pending my SWO qualification," he said, referring to the engineering duty officer community. "After my EDO tour, I'll submit my letter of resignation." Neil had qualified OOD underway awhile back, but the Captain was holding back on his SWO board – most likely in retaliation for the circumstances surrounding his wedding leave chit. "Personally, this has been a great tour, because I met Danielle. But professionally, I've received two letters of caution. I'll miss many of the people," he said. "But when I walk off this ship in a few weeks, I won't look back."

***

Upon arrival in Shimoda, Japan, many family members of *Curtis Wilbur* sailors were on the pier, ready to welcome the ship "home" from deployment. Shimoda was only a two to three-hour train ride from Yokosuka. The Black Ships Festival, held annually in Shimoda to commemorate the arrival of Commodore Matthew Perry during the 1850s, was the last stop on the ship's public relations deployment.

When the shore power and phone lines were connected in Shimoda, Brenda went to the admin office to call the SWO(N) detailer. In many ways, she couldn't wait to report to him that she had received her OOD underway letter, and that her SWO board would be imminent. Reaching the detailer was quickly accomplished, and he informed her that spots were open in the first class to be held at the brand new nuclear power school in Goose Creek, South Carolina, as the Orlando school was closing. He would immediately cut her orders to detach from *Curtis Wilbur* in three months. She was to be in one of the first nuclear power classes to include women. She would join two other female SWOs in the class (one a graduate of MIT, the other from the Naval Academy). The other hundred or so students (all males) would be newly commissioned ensigns from the Naval Academy, who were all going subs (submarines). She, along with the two other female SWOs, would be assigned as section leaders, in charge of the recently commissioned ensigns.

The detailer related how well women were doing in the nuclear program, both officer and enlisted, and that enlisted women slated for nuclear aircraft carriers were entering the program in increasing numbers. He explained that after high school, the females often scored higher on the ASVAB and entrance exams. He had referred to the statistic as reflecting "a maturity factor." On the enlisted side, the student body of the next nuclear power class was going to be close to fifty percent female.

After her time aboard *Curtis Wilbur*, acting as section leader along with the other female SWOs sounded fine to Brenda. And by the time she arrived at the school, she would no longer be an ensign; she would be an O-2, lieutenant junior grade (j. g.). The first six months of nuclear power school were strictly academic, so she predicted that she would be able to lock herself in the classroom building, study, pass the exams, and do well. She had forty hours per week of class time to look forward to. Outside of that, she had 128 hours of study time available. She was willing to work, and she knew that working would keep her from having to go back to sea for another year. She would study all summer and winter, all day long, to ensure she passed the exams and remained ashore.

Brenda walked on air through Shimoda during the Black Ships Festival, as she remained hopeful that the Captain would grant her a SWO board, and she *would* be able to leave. Shimoda held a parade which included Japanese and American dignitaries and officials. The governor of the prefecture (province) and the U.S. ambassador to Japan were in attendance, along with many high-ranking Japanese and American military officials. Reenactments and traditional ceremonies were held throughout the city, celebrating international friendship between the U.S. and Japan. In the 1850s, Commodore Matthew Perry sailed into Shimoda, requesting that the Japanese open their ports to trade with the U.S. But Japanese leaders wished to maintain a policy of isolation. The next year, the commodore returned with nine warships – "black ships" – and U.S. trade with Japan opened from that point on.

The nuclear detailer had cut her orders immediately following their phone conversation. The orders from BUPERS (Bureau of Naval Personnel) arrived during the half day transit. After OCall, WEPS called her aside. "I have something exciting for you," he said as he handed her the orders. She grabbed her orders to detach from the ship, elated, not able to remember when she had felt more relieved.

Chapter 73: VLS misfire

On a two day underway following the post deployment stand-down, embarrassment to the Command had come by way of Chief Walden, and Brenda could not say that she was completely surprised. The Commander, U.S. 7th Fleet (C7F), a three star admiral, had come onboard to observe a VLS missile firing from *Curtis Wilbur* during a battle group exercise. To have an admiral, especially the Seventh Fleet admiral, aboard a destroyer such as the *Curtis Wilbur*, was both extremely rare and a privilege for the ship, a chance for the ship (in reality, the Captain) to shine. As in the last missile firing, all preparations had been set, all checklists had been routed and approved, and all safety and exercise briefings had been given in the wardroom.

Just prior to the firing, Brenda had stood in the back of CIC, by herself, shielded from the admiral by an entourage of assistants and aides. The admiral was standing behind the Captain, who was standing behind the TAO (WEPS). But just prior to launch, CIC became silent for a second. Standing in the back, barely able to hear, Brenda struggled to gain an idea of what was happening. "We had to abort," she heard Jason Arnett say to another watchstander, as he rushed around her. She was surprised, and a little panicked, but still unaware of the cause. She asked an OS (operations specialist) what was going on, and he answered, "The missile firing was aborted, ma'am, some minor checklist item on the VLS." Then she heard the admiral comment, "We'll delay the firing a day then," before he walked out of the space, followed by his entourage. But Brenda knew that the admiral and his staff wouldn't stick around aboard *Curtis Wilbur* for a firing on the next day. The event was an embarrassment for the Captain of *Curtis Wilbur*.

She ran from CIC to the VLS space, and asked, "What happened? What went wrong?" as she swung the door to the missile space open. She couldn't get a read on the GMMs (the gunners mates - missiles). She wasn't able to tell if they looked sullen, disappointed, torn up, embarrassed, regretful, ambivalent; their reactions appeared mixed. But then she saw Chief Walden standing in the back, next to the metal desk in the space, where Petty Officer Mimms usually worked at ammo admin tasks. "Just something that happened," he said. "We'll get it tomorrow."

"We'll get it tomorrow, ma'am," Petty Officer Marcello repeated. She looked at him but didn't answer him. She didn't want to inquire any further about what had happened in front of the guys. GMM2 Marcello picked up on her signal, and motioned for the more junior petty officers and seamen to follow him out the door. She was left with Chief Walden and her LPO (leading petty officer), Petty Officer Brooks.

"What happened? How could this happen?" she asked.

"It's one of those things, ma'am," Petty Officer Brooks answered. He pulled out a diagram and checklist, and pointed to the missed step. Then he left, and she was left alone with Chief Walden. "Glitches happen once in a while. It'll be right tomorrow," he assured her.

"I have no doubt, Chief," she answered him. But she wanted to tell him that this wasn't the way to do it, to purposely embarrass the Captain and XO, if that was in fact what happened. We were supposed to be better than them. It wasn't ethical, and it didn't set a good example for the younger guys.

For the next few weeks, she and Chief Walden didn't speak much, except to conduct business. She knew that she would never know whether "the glitch" was on purpose or not.

Brenda was left with mixed feelings regarding Chief Walden. Since her first day onboard, he had been the more supportive chief. She had become casually friendly with his wife and liked his children. His wife had invited her to their apartment on the top floor of the base housing towers to enjoy Filipino food with them. She had attended his daughter's christening party.

Onboard *Curtis Wilbur*, no one – neither the officers nor the crew – appeared bothered by the aborted firing, except for the Captain and XO. After talking to Chief Walden in the VLS immediately following the attempted missile firing, Brenda had gone straight to WEPS, CSO, and AOPS claiming responsibility, that the aborted firing was her fault, and to blame her, that it should reflect on her. But all three had assured her that it wasn't her fault. She couldn't help thinking...if only she had been more knowledgeable about the VLS, she might have prevented this from happening. The only angry sentiment that WEPS had expressed was, "And Chief Walden spent all that fucking time in the Captain's stateroom awhile back, complaining to the Captain during his chief eval appointment."

Following a successful firing on the next day – which went off without a hitch, and without the presence of the Seventh Fleet admiral – the daily shipboard routine continued. Julie and Brad both passed their OOD underway boards. Brenda learned just how well Julie had performed during her board when Rob knocked on their stateroom door to congratulate her. "I heard you passed with absolute flying colors," he exclaimed to Julie. Brenda immediately shook Julie's hand. "I couldn't be more unsurprised," she said to her.

Excited, Julie informed Rob that following her SWO board, she wanted to be "blood-pinned." In contrast, Brenda had warned her colleagues that if anyone restrained her and tried to blood pin her with a SWO pin, "they would end up on the cover of *Navy Times*." The "tradition" sounded gruesome and pointless to her, and she wanted no part in it. In actuality, the officers of the *Curtis Wilbur* were a fairly straight-laced and professional group, and most weren't from the Academy. She had difficulty picturing them conducting a blood pinning…on Julie no less.

Chapter 74: Hail and farewell ... Hang it on the wall

On a clear and warm evening, Brenda arrived at the officers club to attend Neil's Hail & Farewell party. She felt sorry to see her shipboard friend and mentor leave, a straight-up and honest naval officer who had rejoined the Navy after serving as an enlisted seaman. But of course, she was happy for him personally, since he would soon be out from under this oppressive command – which had targeted him along with the other most capable officers. As a professional colleague, he had listened to her and advised her on technical and leadership matters whenever she had come to him, at all times of the day and night, often several times in the same day. On one midwatch, when her self-worth had fallen to a particularly low level, he normalized her feelings, reminding her of a bigger picture: "I think that you're a very bright young woman who seems extraordinarily unhappy aboard a ship and in the military. Don't think that your feelings aren't normal because I've never felt so miserable and so unstable myself, to be honest. I've questioned everything." She felt relieved to hear positive regard from someone she trusted, and she had kept his words in mind through her darkest times.

When she entered the sala reserved for Neil's party, she found a subdued crowd. The officers appeared tired and uncomfortable, scarcely bothering to strike up conversation. Brenda scanned the room but didn't see Neil. When she walked over to Rob to ask of his whereabouts, he merely pointed outside to the patio. She approached Neil who was seated in a garden area. She knew this "party" was against his will. He had gone to the XO's stateroom to request that he not be given a party, but she had screamed, *"It's required for morale! All officers will have a Hail & Farewell party!"* She then stipulated that it had to take place at the officers club, also against Neil's will.

"Did you deliver the speech you had planned?" she asked him, as she leaned against a trellis.

"I was going to give this big speech describing my experiences onboard, mainly for the benefit of the Captain and XO, but I decided not to bother. It's a disgruntled group that already knows what's going on, and the Command's not going to change."

"Nothing would have come of it," Brenda agreed. "I'm sorry I wasn't there. I couldn't get off watch and switch duty in time."

Neil proceeded to show her the plaque the Captain had presented to him. During Neil's tenure as Bull Ensign, the Captain had obsessed over gifting flawless plaques – which had the ship's seal mounted on a wood signboard – to visiting dignitaries and officers detaching from the Command. But sometimes, an order of plaques was shipped with minor dings or cracks, often unnoticeable without a magnifying glass. In his stateroom, the Captain had a box of "defective" plaques. He used to make Neil order more and more plaques until he found ones that were "pristine" to give away. The extra plaques were billed to the wardroom mess, a process which in turn inflated the monthly mess bill for each individual officer tremendously.

"On stage at the Hail & Farewell," Neil explained, "the Captain congratulated me for *finally* earning my SWO pin on the previous day. He then turned to me and said, 'Here, this is especially for you.' And he handed me a plaque with a large crack across both the ship's seal and the wooden base."

Brenda continued looking at Neil but said nothing. "That was very personal," he went on to say, "because the Captain had, in the past, put great care into those plaques."

Later that evening, Brenda and Brad joined Neil at the Yakitori restaurant out in town. The three of them sat at the restaurant bar reminiscing, but in actuality commiserating about their time onboard. When Neil ordered another beer, the owner, a friend of his, said enthusiastically and innocently enough, "I'd like to have one of those plaques from the ships to hang in my bar." Neil laughed, shook his head, and said, "Well, this one's cracked, but you're welcome to have it." The owner beamed, extremely grateful to Neil for this piece of Navy Americana.

When the owner hung it high up on the wall, Brenda, Brad, and Neil sat staring at it. "I'm glad it's made him happy," Neil said as they left the bar. "I had that plaque for a total of two hours. It'll have new meaning here for everyone to enjoy."

***

The ship was out to sea for another five day – Monday through Friday – underway. For the past three weeks, the ship had been going out during the week, and pulling back into port for the weekends. During the underways, Brenda had started spending most of her time in engineering, standing EOOW (engineering officer of the watch) under instruction (U/I). It was a great way for her to gain some experience at the watchstation in preparation for nuclear power school. She would be expected to qualify EOOW at the nuclear prototype trainer, and again when she was eventually stationed onboard the aircraft carrier. The nuclear prototype trainer was a real nuclear power plant which she would encounter in the second six months of nuclear power school, and would prepare her – in theory – for her billet on the aircraft carrier. The engineering plant aboard a carrier differed entirely from that of the gas turbine powered *Curtis Wilbur*, but she could still gain an overall sense of the watch by standing EOOW U/I now.

CSO had offered to schedule her for EOOW (U/I) watches, and she had been more than willing to accept. Besides her desire to gain engineering plant experience, standing EOOW coincided with her wish to stand as few OOD underway watches as possible during the short time she had left onboard. Once she detached from the *Curtis Wilbur*, she knew that she would never find herself on the bridge of a warship again.

In actuality, CSO had created a split watch schedule for her. She stood EOOW (U/I), but in addition, she stood a few night bridge watches, when the ship was completely alone at sea.

At 0345 on a dark and quiet bridge, Brenda looked back at the bridge ladders, watching for Julie, who was scheduled to relieve her as OOD. Some good news had come Julie's way. She now wore a gold SWO pin above her left uniform pocket. She had performed so outstandingly at her SWO board (like at her OOD board) that the Captain stopped the board half way through and declared that, "Miss Wettlaufer deserved her pin, it was clear."

During Lieutenant Commander Gates' tenure as XO, she had found a reason to be absent for every SWO and OOD board, but she had attended Julie's – a first. Part way through Julie's board, the XO scribbled a note to CSO, which read, *"What should I ask?"*

CSO read the note and thought she was kidding, so he didn't respond. After all, he had later said, she was a lieutenant commander and the XO of a destroyer, senior to him. When the XO's turn came to ask a question, she asked, *"Which way do the screws turn?"* referring to the propellers. It was a very basic question and the only one she asked.

Immediately after the board, HAG called CSO to her stateroom and flame sprayed him, screaming and cursing him out for not answering her note and providing her with a few questions. Everyone up and down the passageways heard her screaming and ranting, and so word of the XO's performance at Julie's SWO board spread quickly around the ship. She ordered CSO to provide her with a list of SWO questions for future boards.

Chapter 75: Thrown off the bridge

It was a quiet night onboard. Brenda glanced into the porthole on the wardroom door. She saw that the room was empty and she entered. By this time of night, on the eve of the multinational exercises scheduled for the following day, she had a feeling that a special watchbill might be posted. She hoped that she wouldn't find her name on it, listed next to any exercise event, for any watchstation. Some new junior officers had checked onboard, and she hoped that CSO had given them priority for bridge time. This was her last underway onboard the ship. And she kept reminding herself that after this tour, she would never stand watch on the bridge of a warship ever again. If her name was listed on the watchbill, she wanted to find it next to aft steering or EOOW (U/I).

She approached the bulletin board and found that a new watchbill had been posted. Her eyes scanned it, searching out her name. She found it next to *"MOBoard operator,"* under the DIVTACS portion of the exercises. Her stomach dropped, and she cursed her luck. In her almost year and a half onboard, she had never been assigned to stand bridge watch during DIVTACS, and so far, they had been cancelled every time they had been scheduled. Until a few moments ago, she had convinced herself that she had made it – that she had made it through her shipboard tour without standing watch on the bridge during DIVTACS. She didn't want anything to happen during these last days underway to jeopardize her upcoming SWO board or her orders to detach from the ship.

While climbing up the ladder to officers country from CSMC (combat systems maintenance central), a few moments ago, she had been thinking that not all was bad onboard. She still savored the atmosphere of the ship at night, when it was dark and quiet and the engines droned and the nautical lanterns dimly lit the ship's passageways. Even when she had opened the door to the wardroom, nervous to look at the watchbill, she had felt somewhat free in the knowledge that this was her last underway.

Outside CSMC, Petty Officer Mimms had stopped her. "I would like you to perform my reenlistment ceremony, ma'am, if you would," he stated, seriously. "When we get back to Yoko, I'd like to have the ceremony in front of the giant Buddha in Kamakura, in service dress whites, with the division there and a few other guys."

Brenda was stunned and moved. "Yes, Petty Officer Mimms," she answered. "I would be honored."

"Yes, ma'am. Chief Walden and I will arrange it," he said, and then he walked past her. Brenda remained standing in the passageway, in disbelief. Petty Officer Mimms had done well for the division. He had worked dependably, researching above and beyond in his ammo admin duties. She constantly thanked him for the quality of his work and told him that she respected his opinions. They had developed a professional relationship after a difficult start. She had submitted him for a Navy and Marine Corps Achievement Medal (NAM) for his work and dedication. Since her time onboard was short, she made WEPS promise to follow through with Mimms' award. It was to be Petty Officer Mimms' first NAM.

A few minutes later, she saw Chief Walden in the passageway. "Did Mimms talk to you?" he asked, in his quiet way.

"Yes, he did, Chief," she answered.

"It's truly an honor," he said, "to be asked to reenlist someone."

"I know, Chief," she said. Normally, petty officers and seamen chose to be reenlisted by the ship's captain.

*

In the wardroom, Brenda stared at her name next to "*MOBoard operator*" on the special watchbill for the multinational DIVTACS exercise with the navies of Thailand, the Philippines, Malaysia, Singapore, and Australia. She decided that she had no choice but to talk to CSO about her doubts – about her ability to calculate MOBoard solutions in rapid real-time, sometimes with only a few hundred yards separating the *Curtis Wilbur* from the other 8,000-ton warships.

With shame and embarrassment nagging her, she knocked on CSO's stateroom door. When he opened it, she said, "I have to tell you something, sir. I shouldn't be in a position to be the one calculating MOBoard solutions during DIVTACS. I don't feel I can do it. I'm not proficient enough at MOBoards. I still struggle with the calculations even though I accepted the OOD letter."

"Have you been on the bridge during DIVTACS before?" he asked.

"No, sir, not for DIVTACS."

"It's a problem," he said, "that many times JOs aren't able to get much real life experience with DIVTACS. It's hard to coordinate getting that many ships together for DIVTAC exercises, especially out here in Japan. And it's difficult to coordinate DIVTACS so that JOs can get some real training with them. But they're necessary for tactical study."

"I don't understand MOBoards well enough, sir. I'm not fast enough," she repeated. "Please take me off the watchbill for this one."

"I have confidence you can do it," he answered. "I'll put Neil on the watchbill, and the two of you can act together as co-MOBoard operators. I have to make sure you get the training. It'll be a good way for you to get some experience at it."

"I'm not sure the Captain will like that setup, of Neil helping me."

"That's my concern," CSO said. "I'll talk to him and get it approved beforehand."

"Okay, sir," she answered. But it wasn't the answer she had wanted, and she had doubts that the Captain would find the arrangement acceptable. She feared CSO didn't understand how dire was her lack of MOBoard proficiency. She had gotten people to trust her who really shouldn't have trusted her. She had studied enough to pass her OOD board, and now, she had placed the ship's senior watch officer in the position of trusting her that she could in fact stand bridge watch and solve MOBoard problems with the requisite knowledge and skills of a qualified OOD.

That night Brenda didn't sleep. And usually onboard the ship she could sleep no matter what was happening. Before climbing into her rack, she practiced MOBoard problems. In addition, she spoke with Bill, CSO, and WEPS about how the exercises would most likely play out. She also talked to Neil about what to expect, and about who would do what at the MOBoard table.

She dreaded the upcoming DIVTACS all morning and during lunch. She wanted them over with, and she wondered what "over with" would mean in a few hours.

As Brenda climbed the ladders to the bridge to take the watch as *"co-MOBoard operator,"* she heard scratchy radio chatter and foreign accents from the other ships. The bridge was hectic and crowded, with Rob as OOD, and Courtney as JOOD. She carried her MOBoard paper and plotting tools as she approached the MOBoard table, nervous, not knowing what would happen. She just hoped that somehow, she could perform her part. The Captain was seated in his bridge chair, right next to the MOBoard table. The seas were choppy. Out the bridge windows, through faint haze, she could see destroyers and frigates from various nations.

The DIVTACS exercises started, when over the radio came:

"ALL UNITS IN ALPHA-FIFE-ALPHA, THIS IS ALPHA-FIFE-ALFA. EXECUTE TO FOLLOW, SCREEN JULIET - CALL SIGN ALPHA-FIFE-ALPHA, 0918-0204 CALL SIGN TANGO-TREE-WHISKEY, 1827-0204 CALL SIGN MIKE-NINER-JULIET, 2700-0204 CALL SIGN NOVEMBER-SIX-YANKEE, BREAK, BRAVO CORPEN 000, ALPHA SPEED ONE-FIFE, WHISKEY SPEED TWO-ZERO, OVER."

As the signal came over the radio, Courtney logged it, while struggling to understand the words and numbers uttered by the thick-accented radio talker. She answered, "THIS IS TANGO-TREE-WHISKEY, ROGER, OUT," while Neil and Brenda decoded the signal and checked it against the screen they had drawn out on the MOBoard paper. Brenda began solving for a course to station at the center of the ship's assigned sector, along with the time to arrive at that point, and the CPA (closet point of approach) to the guide at the center of the screen, taking into account the CPA, bearing, and ranges to the other ships. The calculations had to be done instantly, and as she used her plotting tools – the dividers, parallel rulers, and the rolling plotter – she knew that it was a basic type of problem to solve. But she couldn't do math in her head and certainly not at that speed.

The pressure was on for quick MOBoard solutions. Even before the tactical signal was completed over the radio, the Captain started yelling over her shoulder, continuously, *"Course and time to station now! Course and time to station now! Let's go!"* And it seemed like all the watchstanders were bent over the plot table, anxiously watching her, as she drew lines and solved the calculations on the MOBoard paper. Neil checked every step, while talking though the steps as she completed them. But really, she was too labored and she lacked proficiency, and the Captain was angry until she finally announced, "course and time to station…"

She felt overwhelmed, confused, and embarrassed because of her slow math speed, and she barely understood the calculations and the reasons behind them, feeling that studying and force of will and memorization were not going to bring her through this. She tried to sort out in her mind the many types of lines she would need to be drawing on the MOBoard sheet – speed of relative movement, relative motion line, plotting the e-r vector, plotting m1, m2, etc., extending the relative motion line to the outer ring for degrees true, paralleling the relative motion line to the center of the MOBoard, using the nomogram – but the spatial picture seemed jumbled in her head.

She thought of Todd, who while standing OOD, regularly calculated entire MOBoard solutions in his head.

She thought of SWOS and of how many students, including her, had failed the MOBoard exam and had had to take it over. And now she understood that the right thing, the honest thing, would have been to wash out of SWOS, to allow herself to fail. But at that time, she didn't think failure was an option, and she studied and pushed. And now she was onboard this warship, in this situation, performing Hamlet without the prince.

When, "ALL UNITS IN ALPHA-FIFE-ALPHA, THIS IS ALPHA-FIFE-ALFA, STANDBY, EXECUTE, OVER," came through the radio, and it was time for the conning officer to give course and speed orders to the helm, she almost wished to be relieved of her duties. But she stayed, still hoping she would somehow get through this, working with Neil. She had definitions and procedures running through her head, unsure if she could interpret them and apply them correctly. She thought about how, if she had failed SWOS, the instructors would have made her repeat SWOS until she passed, which wouldn't have changed the makeup of her brain in the way of improving her spatial understanding and math skills.

Time passed quickly, and it seemed the ship was on station in seconds. And then the next radio signal came in.

"ALL UNITS IN ALPHA-FIFE-ALPHA, THIS IS ALPHA-FIFE-ALFA. EXECUTE TO FOLLOW, FORM PORT NINER – MIKE-NINER-JULIET – NOVEMBER-SIX-YANKEE – TANGO-TREE-WHISKEY, STANDBY, EXECUTE, OVER."

At the same time, she heard Courtney on the red phone, saying, "THIS IS TANGO-TREE-WHISKEY, ROGER, OUT." And in her mind she was going through all of the MOBoard rules and calculations she had ever studied. At that moment she couldn't remember if FORM PORT NINER meant to form on a true bearing or on a relative bearing of 090 from the guide. She thought that FORM 090 meant that the ships would form on a true bearing of 090 from the guide, and that FORM PORT NINER meant that they would form on a relative bearing of 090 from the guide, but she couldn't remember if she had it right. She thought that it should have been obvious that for a relative bearing, direction would have to be given, and that in this case the word PORT wouldn't make sense for true bearing, but she didn't have the confidence and presence of mind to be sure. As she grabbed the plotting tools to begin the calculations

– uncertain as to how to proceed exactly – she asked Neil that question, if the ships would form on a true or relative bearing. And the Captain heard and looked down in disgust because they had just started the calculations…and he threw her off the bridge. "This is ridiculous, have Neil take over," he muttered. Just then she didn't know whether to feel relief at being fired and leaving the task to Neil, who was capable, or to feel sick and utterly revulsed by her incompetence and failure.

She left the bridge, walked back to her stateroom, entered it, and crashed onto the floor. Then she sat on the floor in silence, broken down. She had the most intensive and painful headache she had ever experienced. Eventually – possibly an hour or two hours later – she left her stateroom and walked down to the vending machines. She wanted soda, something. Rob happened to be there as well. DIVTACS and the exercises had ended by that point. He looked at her and said, "I can't believe you. You don't know how to do MOBoards. That's unacceptable for an OOD. It's shameful. It's not right. It's ridiculous. It's really wrong." She stared up at him with a blank face, understanding that every word he had uttered was true. And she was especially ashamed because it was Rob telling her this. "You're right, Rob," she answered. "I am ashamed. I'm sorry, I know."

She felt worse when he didn't stop there and pounded at her, repeating, "It was seriously wrong, unacceptable. CSO got reamed out by the Captain for it." And she knew she deserved every word that he had to say to her, and that she deserved to stand there and listen to him and to take her punishment. She was hunched over slightly, with her hands crossed against her stomach, trying to hold herself together, while being confronted with her incompetence, and with the chaos and risk she had inflicted on others. Her head flooded with thoughts of all manner of mistakes she had made that were so complex, and with such deep roots, that she had only just begun to decipher them. But she knew clearly that Rob saying those things to her delivered the worst possible shame and punishment.

She couldn't find words for a response. Partially doubled over, she looked at Rob. "I don't know what to say except that I'm sorry," she said. And he walked away.

Chapter 76: Recovering

According to *Curtis Wilbur* tradition, officers scheduled to detach, or leave the ship, conned into port one last time in celebration of their tour onboard. Brenda stood in front of a packed wardroom, among the Captain and her peers, waiting to begin the navigation brief, thinking that this celebratory conning-into-port tradition could not have fallen at a worse time for her. After her MOBoard disaster on the preceding afternoon, she felt ashamed to stand before her peers giving a navigation brief. When she began the briefing, she spoke into the paper, looking at it, rather than facing her superiors and peers. She wished that CSO had broken with tradition and had kept her off the watchbill.

After the brief, while climbing the ladders to the bridge, she tried to recover mentally from the MOBoard incident of the preceding day. She tried to show some character, knowing that she needed to take the watch as conning officer and interact with the watchstanders as if nothing had happened on the day before. She had no grand illusions about conning the ship for one last glorious time. In a pragmatic nuts and bolts way, she simply desired to stand her final underway watch professionally and competently.

To her surprise, comfort, and relief, she stood the conning watch well, with no issues. She had conned into Yokosuka many times before. When, *"Secure the special sea and anchor detail,"* was announced over the 1MC, the Captain gave her a nod. "Good, that went well," he commented.

She had spent the morning before the navigation brief trying to avoid everyone. She soon found out that it wasn't necessary to dodge her peers. "These things happen to all of us," Courtney told her in CIC, with compassion. "It takes a lot of experience and practice," Neil said to her when he asked her aside after quarters. "Remember, I was a quartermaster after I was a deck seaman, so I've been up on the bridge for years." Even Rob joked with her before OCall, nudging her while poking fun at SWO and life onboard. She didn't hear Rob's joke, but she laughed a sort of relief laugh that came out instead of tears...although she could barely look at him. It was difficult to face them. WEPS seemed unfazed by what had happened, and had made some abstract reference about the event that blamed the Captain. She didn't have anything to say about what had happened; she thought that the event had spoken for itself.

Rob later came to her stateroom and apologized for what he had said at the vending machines. "It's hard to perform under pressure at something you've never done before," he said.

"What you said was the truth, Rob," she told him. "There's no need to apologize."

She assumed her SWO board would be called off, and that she would remain onboard the ship for another six months, with either a letter of nonattainment of surface warfare qualification – which would end her chance at nuclear power school and banish her to some far off basement of some obscure naval command in the middle of Oklahoma or some similar place – or she would remain on the ship, continuing the training; she would be forced to qualify, and then accept another SWO billet on another ship.

On the evening after her MOBoard disaster, she had apologized to CSO in the combat systems office. But despite his disappointment, he told her, "Had I understood what you were trying to tell me, how serious it was, I wouldn't have put you in that position. I would have provided you with additional training in a less intense environment."

But she felt the responsibility for the disaster rested solely on her. She was an OOD qualified officer, and she had accepted a letter of qualification for OOD (underway). As she stood in the combat systems office, she wished that she could explain her psychology and background to CSO – the history of how she had lacked maturity and the awareness to embark on any inner search. And further, that she had gone along and fallen in line with what she had been taught and told, as if unconscious. She had stampeded through engineering and Navy schools with force of will, never having the wherewithal to reflect on the impact to herself and to others. She was obnoxious, acting out, bullheaded, and eager to show off her accomplishments. She had never been honest with herself about her difficulties in engineering, nor had she stood up to her father. She had shied away from such a pushback, unwilling to risk him not liking her and being annoyed by her. Security and living within the lines had been paramount values in her family. And the pressure to not individuate from family, to not rebel and to "be good," to sacrifice oneself to satisfy family and their expectations, to be loyal to family, was enormous and crushing. Onboard, she had placed all of her peers and everyone onboard the ship in the crosshairs of her psychology.

"I'm sorry for letting you down and the ship down and everyone, sir," she said to CSO. "Where do I stand? Where do I go from here?"

Chapter 77: Limbo ... Facing the board

Following her discussion with CSO, Brenda was in a state of limbo for the next week, not knowing whether or not she would be scheduled for a SWO board. CSO had provided her with a list of guides and manuals to study in preparation for her board. She studied those, and spent time as well with Bill the warrant officer, the ship's Aegis expert. One morning, she was startled but relieved to see the POD which showed her SWO board scheduled for later that afternoon.

Brenda's nuclear candidacy apparently had worked in her favor, and created pressure for the Captain to qualify her. She assumed the Captain had ultimately granted her a SWO board because he felt that he had to. The selection process for the nuclear community was considered grueling, and only the elite – those highly capable technical students – were selected. Since she was slated for nuclear power, and the nuclear community was short on personnel, how would the Captain be able to explain that such an "elite" nuclear candidate did not qualify SWO on his ship? But even putting her nuke status aside, the successful qualification of JOs was expected of SWO captains, and captains' SWO qualification rate was a significant factor in their officer FITREPs. Many articles had recently appeared in the *Navy Times* discussing the pressure on COs to qualify junior officers.

Brenda entered the wardroom and took a seat at the far end of the dining table, facing the ship's department heads, the Captain, and XO. As she remained seated – the room silent except for a few murmurs between department heads – Brenda thought about how she had marketed herself well in the past – a mechanical engineering degree, all the "right" activities in school, the ability to look a person in the eye and shake their hand. She had presented confidently.

For her however, nuclear candidacy was a hollow status, a result of her calculated and designed resume-building.

She wanted to declare to the SWO board, "Captain, XO, Department Heads, please excuse me from this board and from qualifying as a surface warfare officer, and I promise, I'll make my service count...I'll serve the Navy in another capacity." But she knew that such a declaration was but a secret fantasy; it reflected one aspect of her many conflicting feelings. Her motivations for surviving the board and successfully completing her SWO qual did not comprise a straight line...qualifying was a way off the bridge, off the ship, away from HAG. Avoidance of the repercussions of not qualifying was also a motivating factor to succeed. And in addition to these mixed motives – and even after such a long road toward self-discovery – she still had remnants of an entrenched inner voice, tilting backward, that insisted that failure was not acceptable. The result was that in one corner of her mind lurked a commitment to her obligations and responsibilities onboard: It was her job as a SWO JO to make every effort to qualify.

So as she looked at everyone, the board began, kicked off by CSO. They asked her questions, and she tried to answer them as best as she could. But for all of her studying, she found that she couldn't answer many of their questions. When she couldn't answer, or when she felt her answers were unsatisfactory, she promised to write the questions down and look the information up after the board. They gave her two MOBoard problems. She solved the first one, but she wasn't sure of her methodology and solution of the second. When they gave her a third, more complex problem, she gently pushed the MOBoard paper aside, and respectfully told the board that she would have to get back to them. During the board, she struggled with the reality that she did not want to qualify SWO or go to nuclear power school – anymore.

She wavered between her desire to be honest with the board and to pass the board. Sometimes, she wasn't able to dismiss the persistent thought that there was nothing worse in the Navy than being a failed SWO, the lowest of the lowest of failures. A few times, she looked blankly at WEPS and CSO, trying to conceal her sense of shock, as they asked her high-level Aegis questions, covering details that she hadn't before heard of about the capabilities and limitations of various combat sensors and communications systems that reached beyond her studies. It was common during SWO boards to ask about systems on other classes of ships, or about sensor and weapons systems onboard submarines and naval aircraft, such as the F-14. But this board remained focused on Aegis and the Arleigh Burke class guided missile destroyer (DDG).

She felt sure that Neil and Julie had known the answers to all of the board's detailed combat systems questions. But neither she, Julie, nor Neil had ever officially stood watch in CIC. As Brenda sat at her SWO board, she wanted to know, right then: How did Neil and Julie still manage to learn high-level operational details without having stood the watches? What was their secret? Aptitude and a personal interest, she assumed.

At a few points during the board, Brenda felt like breaking into tears, but she kept her composure. She was at least able to answer some of the questions. She attempted all of them.

She wondered how her performance compared to that of most junior officers. She tried to read the faces of the board members, but all of them kept poker faces throughout, as during her OOD board.

There was a pause before the Captain asked his final question. He was known for asking the same final question at each board: How do you tie a bowline knot? As she expected, the Captain threw a piece of rope at her across the table. "Miss Conner, tie a bowline for me," he said.

She silently used the memory aid Julie and Brad had taught her. Make a rabbit hole. The rabbit comes out, runs around the tree, and hops back into the rabbit hole. Having no experience at tying knots, she laid the rope down flat on the table and tied it.

"I've never seen anyone lay the rope flat on the table," the Captain commented, "but that's correct." She actually felt relieved because she had never tied a nautical knot before Julie and Brad had showed her "the rabbit hole memory aid" a few days ago.

The department heads gave her one last round of questions, and after an hour, the board concluded. The Captain was the first to leave the wardroom. As he placed his hand on the door knob, he turned and said, "At least you tied the bowline knot."

She left the wardroom after the board members, with no idea of her future.

Chapter 78: Broken ... Brenda's Hail & Farewell

A few days had passed and Brenda hadn't received word of her SWO board. She was afraid – and too ashamed – to ask anyone about it. One morning while she was in the wardroom, she overheard the Captain and XO as they walked in the passageway. "She has the capacity to memorize, but does she understand?" she heard the XO commenting to the Captain, as she followed him towards his stateroom. Brenda assumed the comment referred to her and to her recent SWO board. Hearing such a truth actually verbalized – a truth that she had heavily guarded as a private thought – made her feel exposed. She couldn't help thinking that she wasn't surprised that the XO would be the one to recognize her ability to survive by memorizing without understanding, possibly from personal experience.

Not having heard a decision for her SWO board had left her fearing that her qualification status was in limbo, if not actual jeopardy. But in an unrelated event, she received her automatic promotion to lieutenant junior grade (j. g.), O-2. After two years of service, the promotion was automatic, unless one had committed a crime or other serious offense. Her "promotion ceremony" consisted of going to admin to sign her letter of permanent appointment which was placed in her service record. Following her trip to admin, she went to the NEX uniform shop with Brad to buy silver O-2 bars. All in all, it was better to be a lieutenant (j. g.) than a lowly ensign.

During the walk to the NEX, Brad insisted that she had passed her SWO board. "You know all this stuff cold," he kept saying. She answered him that she wasn't so sure.

Her limbo status was further complicated by CSO's knee injury and subsequent stay in the hospital. Immediately following her SWO board, she researched her unanswered questions, including the MOboard problem, and provided a written report to CSO. But a few days later, CSO broke down mentally, under stress, in what was the most heart-wrenching event she had witnessed onboard, the result of debased and continual mental cruelty imposed by one human being onto another – in this case – by Lieutenant Commander Gates onto an officer subordinate to her. Worst of all, CSO's breakdown and the events leading up to it, had unfolded in a manner not unheard of in surface warfare officer culture – in SWOrrior culture or in SWOdom, as many called it, in irony. The normally most levelheaded, intelligent, and well-respected department head onboard had reached the brink, overcome and consumed by suicidal thoughts and psychosis. In a moment of insanity and all-out distress, CSO fell apart emotionally, crying uncontrollably in his stateroom, while pounding his knee against the metal cabinet beneath his stateroom sink dozens of times until he stopped, presumably, because his knee had broken and he could no longer pound it. Brad and Rob, who shared the stateroom next door, heard CSO speaking – mostly incoherently. But there was one statement they had heard repeatedly: He could not handle getting underway one more time under Lieutenant Commander Gates.

As Brad and Rob heard CSO breaking down, they tried to speak to him through his stateroom door, attempting to convince him to open it. "Then suddenly CSO's cries went silent," Brad later explained to her. CSO eventually opened his stateroom door, appearing calm and docile, and walked into the passageway like nothing had happened. He walked out of aft officers country, hobbling on his good leg while using the bulkhead as support. "How are you guys? I need to head up to CIC," he said to them. Brad ran to get the corpsman, as CSO's knee appeared to be broken or nearly so, while Rob stayed with CSO, who seemed intent on limping up to CIC. When Brad and the corpsman arrived in CIC, CSO collapsed on the floor, while crying. His leg was shattered at the knee, contorted in an unnatural position. A minute later, HAG arrived. And upon seeing such a horrifying sight, she broke into tears. She just stood in CIC crying uncontrollably before she stormed off. Brenda, as the OOD inport, listened to much of the event as it unfolded over the walkie-talkie. When the ambulance arrived, she stood in silence as CSO, for the most part unconscious, was carried down the brow in a stretcher. Medical staff bussed him to the hospital on base.

In the following weeks, CSO's situation grew worse, as the Captain appeared focused on revenge. Brenda wasn't the least surprised by what had happened to CSO – his breakdown from exhaustion, stress, and cruelty. The event was the result of SWO culture, that revered and traditional style of leadership that hailed from those "good ole days of iron men and wooden ships."

The Captain set out on a rampage against CSO. He was heard screaming that CSO was never to return to the ship, which meant that CSO Rooney would not be able to finish the last year of his tour. When Brenda personally heard the Captain ranting in his stateroom, she knew that further disaster was in store for CSO. If he didn't finish the last year of his tour onboard, he would have to remain in Japan for an additional two years since the Navy had already moved his family over from the States. From the hospital, CSO had asked to return to the ship, but the Captain had answered, "No." Following surgery and six months of limited duty at Afloat Training Group (ATG) Western Pacific, CSO was then transferred to Seventh Fleet staff.

When CSO came back onboard one last time – on crutches – to meet with the Captain to review his FITREP, he noticed that the Captain had documented a falsified midterm counseling date, and that the *"screening for next career milestone"* block was left blank, indicating that the Captain hadn't recommend him for XO. Among the three lieutenant commanders (O-4) onboard – HAG, CSO, and WEPS – the Captain had ranked HAG number one, awarding her the *"early promote"* recommendation, WEPS was ranked second, receiving a *"must promote"* rating, and CSO was ranked last, in the *"promotable"* block.

Immediately after CSO signed his FITREP, with a check next to the *"I intend to submit a statement"* block, the *Curtis Wilbur* officers were called into the wardroom. *"Assemble all officers in the wardroom,"* was announced over the 1MC.

Inside the wardroom, twenty or so officers stood around awkwardly wishing CSO well. Most didn't seem to know what to say. Brenda stood behind the crowd, refusing to participate in what she predicted would be a setup by the Captain to humiliate CSO. Her suspicions that the Captain would have something demeaning in store for CSO were confirmed the moment he began to speak. "Let's all say goodbye to our combat systems officer," the Captain started, as he picked up a green and orange Navy and Marine Corps Achievement Medal (NAM). He walked up to CSO and pinned the medal on his chest. The officers looked on with horror and disbelief. In SWO culture, for a department head and lieutenant commander, a Navy Achievement Medal (NAM) was a humiliating end-of-tour award.

Then, the Captain said, "Let's go gong him off the quarterdeck," and everyone followed in silence. Julie, on quarterdeck watch, hurried two makeshift side boys into place. The officers lined up in two rows. No one knew what to do or what to say. CSO walked through the line, shaking hands with the officers. Brenda stood off to the side, refusing to get in line. Everyone wished him farewell, in a forced situation. At the end of the line, CSO requested permission to go ashore from the Captain. When the Captain granted his request, stating, "Permission granted," CSO suddenly ripped the NAM off of his shirt and threw the medal into the water.

*

The next night, the officers of the *Curtis Wilbur* were forced to endure another Hail & Farewell party – Brenda's. The only positive she had derived from her scheduled Hail & Farewell was its possible significance: it seemed likely that she would be given a SWO pin and the opportunity to fulfill her orders to leave the ship. But a shred of doubt remained in her mind. Orders were often changed/revoked at the last moment…so even though the Command was giving her a party, she could not assume what it meant with regard to her SWO pin. She had witnessed the Command give Hail & Farewells, only to later cancel orders.

At the food court on the roof of the Yokosuka mall – the XO's choice of venue – Brenda tried her best to mingle and chat with the officers in attendance. But she was uncomfortable with the idea of a party – any party – being thrown for her. She disliked being the center of attention in a social situation. A few days before, while routing a routine message, she had tried to explain how she felt to the XO, but the XO had snapped, *"Everyone has a Hail and Farewell party, GUNNO! Got it?"*

She had to admit that the venue was a beautiful spot, overlooking the lighted city skyline. For the duration of the party, as at Neil's party, the officers sat around looking miserable, although everyone wished her well. When she finished walking around, she sat down at a table beside Courtney and SUPPO. "Thank you for coming," she said to them.

"We wouldn't have missed it," SUPPO said.

"Absolutely," Courtney agreed. They both smiled at her.

In her lap, Brenda held the framed photo of the *Curtis Wilbur* that was given to her at the start of the evening. In it, the ship stormed mightily through the seas. As she started to read the notes written by the officers who had signed the matting, she noted that her peers had written some nice words. *"It has been a pleasure serving with you. Thanks for keeping my thoughts positive,"* one officer wrote. Tara, also headed for nuclear power school, who had arrived onboard two months ago to replace Rob, wrote, "*In the short time I have gotten to know you, I have truly appreciated your help and friendship. Please don't ever change your open, honest, and down to earth style; it is a great asset. See you out there on the carrier.*" Susan, the supply officer, wrote, "*Brenda, I hope that you find success in all that you do. Stay grounded but keep your head up.*" And Courtney, the assistant operations officer and acting OPS, wrote, "*It has been a pleasure serving with you. Best of luck in nuke school. I hope that it is everything you expect it to be. Fair winds and following seas.*" At the close of the evening, the Captain presented her with a crack-free and intact plaque.

On the following afternoon, it came time for Petty Officer Mimms' reenlistment ceremony. She had her service dress whites newly pressed for the occasion, and made sure her brass and white leather shoes had been shined, as she knew uniform appearance was important to Petty Officer Mimms. Chief Walden had reserved the ship's MWR van, and his wife drove a few remaining petty officers in their personal minivan. On a stone walkway, in front of the over forty-foot tall, giant bronze Buddha statue, which dated from the thirteenth century, Brenda and Chief Walden performed the reenlistment ceremony. Brenda stood before Petty Officer Mimms; she asked him to raise his right hand, and he repeated the oath of enlistment after her: "*I, do solemnly swear that I will support and defend the Constitution of the United States against all enemies, foreign and domestic; that I will bear true faith and allegiance to the same; and that I will obey the orders of the President of the United States and the orders of the officers appointed over me, according to regulations and the Uniform Code of Military Justice. So help me God.*"

Afterwards, everyone who attended the ceremony congratulated Petty Officer Mimms. Brenda presented him with a certificate and a folded flag; and Chief Walden and a few petty officers took pictures of Brenda and Petty Officer Mimms shaking hands, and of Brenda and Petty Officer Mimms standing side by side, and of the entire group standing together. Outside of their circle, many Japanese visiting the site took pictures of their group. In the parking lot, next to the vans, Chief Walden's wife set up a small table with snacks and drinks. Brenda was glad as well to see Chief Walden's wife one more time before she was scheduled to leave *Curtis Wilbur*, assuming she would leave. She hoped Petty Officer Mimms would do well and continue to progress under whoever might replace her. All of these people who had been a significant part of her life for a short time, and who she would probably never see again...

Chapter 79: Unknown future ... Can parents understand?

Brenda surveyed the living room of her Japanese house. She had been given only one day to pack her household goods. Ship admin had informed her that a Japanese moving company, contracted by the Navy, was scheduled to arrive at her house on Saturday morning. Fortunately, her day off to pack had fallen on one of those rare, beautiful days when the sun was shining and the temperature outside felt perfect. She opened the windows and blinds throughout the house on both stories, letting the sun and breeze inside. She opened the sliding rice paper shoji doors and admired how the sun lit the tatami room. The house she shared with her roommates, Brad and Matt, was all hers for the day. Brad had duty, and Matt was out at sea somewhere in the northern Pacific Ocean.

But her enjoyment of this beautiful day off from the ship was hampered by the nagging question of her SWO board, and whether or not the Command would ultimately allow her to detach from the ship in accordance with her orders. She was constantly nauseous from nerves, wondering what was going to happen to her over the next two to three years – another year onboard *Curtis Wilbur*, nonattainment...or would she be sent on to nuclear power school? Her up-in-the-air status felt like some sort of command-sponsored torture. If she had failed her SWO board, why not just tell her? At this point, she just wanted to know one way or the other.

The fact that she had been ordered to pack her household goods meant nothing. Her goods could just as easily be unpacked. These sudden swings in one's life didn't just occur aboard *Curtis Wilbur*. No one in the Navy lived with any sense of control over their lives. Some personnel seemed to prefer to put their lives in the hands of the Navy. The Navy decided where they would live and work and how they would dress. She often remembered what her Naval Academy friend from midshipman cruise used to say: The Navy was like mom and dad.

At one point, she had asked WEPS if she should call the SWO nuclear detailer to let him know about the uncertainty of her qualification status.

"Absolutely not," WEPS advised her. "Assume you've passed

your board. In my view, you passed just fine," he told her.

As she looked around the house, she realized that most of the boxes from her original move to Japan hadn't even been unpacked. She stared over at a floor-to-ceiling stack of shopping bags, in what was supposed to be the dining room. Before leaving for Japan, and in her letters and emails, her mother had encouraged her to buy "nice things and knickknacks" in Japan and around Asia "to decorate her house someday." As Brenda stared at the shopping bags filled with knickknacks she purchased in Hong Kong, Singapore, Thailand, South Korea, Malaysia, and Japan, her head filled with nightmares of some future house in the suburbs, in which every square inch of wall, floor, and shelf spacing was covered with chotskies – exactly the way her mother's house was filled to the brim with this stuff. She decided to donate most of the "collectibles" to a thrift store not too far from the base that was dedicated to helping homeless animals.

She carried the shopping bags and boxes to the car, keeping a few paintings and water colors that she liked. She donated her box full of Tom Clancy novels, as she was no longer interested in spending her time reading idealized Cold War military/spy novels.

Afterwards, she decided to take a break to give her parents a call. On the phone, she updated them on HAG stories and lamented about how much she hated the ship. As she spoke with her parents, she became aware of how much she had changed. She found that in order to talk to her parents, she had to switch back to being the person she was; she had to devolve, in a sense. They would never understand the lessons she had learned about herself, the ways in which she planned to go forward with her life based on her recent self-discoveries. She felt that her relationship with her parents hadn't matured to the level that would permit her to discuss the deeply personal and subjective changes she had undergone.

But her parents clearly did understand the events that had taken place – the blatant cruelty of the Command – and the concrete reasons why she loathed life onboard the ship.

While talking to her parents, she found herself unable to drop her persona – the competent mechanical engineer and naval officer. She realized that her parents were going to walk away from the phone conversation with the following understanding: Navy life was miserable due to bad leadership and management, the job, watches, no sleep, the blatant tyranny and cruelty of HAG, and the Captain's cowardice and unwillingness to stand up to her. But they weren't privy to her role in the mix of dynamics – the way in which her personal history and psychology had collided with the Navy, her shipboard duties, and with HAG. They seemed to believe that she was perfectly suited to attend nuclear power school.

She wasn't sure if they would be able to comprehend the growth she had experienced in terms of individuation, discovery of the self, and acceptance that she was an introvert – inner directed and drawn to the subjective realm of intrapersonal life. Would they understand that she wanted to switch gears in her life to focus on the arts and humanities?

Over the course of the conversation, her mom repeated, several times, "You're a woman in engineering. These companies want women. You'll have no problem getting a job when you get out."

Conversational topics with her parents that previously had not fazed her she now found annoying. When she asked her mother how their cousin was coping with the loss of his wife from cancer, her mother gave a typical pragmatic answer, "Gary's searching for the insurance papers and going through the files since Betty was the one that handled the finances..."

The phone call was leaving Brenda feeling disconnected, as if there was an absence of any depth of emotional life in their family. And she further understood why she had started out in life with such a utilitarian bent.

About another set of cousins Brenda asked, "Are you so sure Lori and Jessica are truly happy in their office jobs, in the same office their mom worked in for decades?" Brenda asked.

But her mom didn't understand that question, and she sounded irritated as if she didn't want to hear it. She simply insisted that they were good jobs. Brenda just sighed. They may have been good jobs, but she wanted to know if Lori and Jessica found fulfillment in how they spent the majority of their days. "Maybe Jessica can get in at the post office if she doesn't like the office job," her mother then said.

Annoyed, Brenda leaned against the wall with the phone to her ear, silent. The conversation illuminated for her how she had been programmed to focus her decisions and thinking on the pragmatic side of life. While holding the phone, she thought of similar conversations. Her mother had kept her updated on a coworker who suffered from cancer. Though she knew her mother cared and felt for her friend, Brenda noted that her mother always focused her reports on the status of the woman's medical insurance and how much her meds were, rather than on the emotional well-being and feelings of her friend.

She remembered that she had had difficulty accepting physical changes that came with adolescence. She had put off wearing a bra because her mother, through years of unconscious signals, had made her feel "funny" about those changes, with the result that Brenda did not talk about them, nor desire to acknowledge them. She recalled many painfully embarrassing moments from those times, ones that haunted her still.

After she got off the phone with her parents, she stood within the quiet, Japanese house. She looked inside the tatami room, furnished with a black lacquered table with two Japanese sitting pillows on either side; she was going to miss that room. Starting life anew in a way her parents might not understand seemed difficult. But she decided that she was unwilling to go back to the way she was just to satisfy her parents. Embarking on a creative life would be different from what her parents would understand; she would be alone in pursuing that life, at least at the onset. And ultimately, even though her parents might not understand, they (especially her mother) would most likely come around and become supportive. But with or without support and understanding from family, she was going to explore her new path.

She thought again about what WEPS had told her. "Keep packing and prepare your household goods to be picked up as if you're leaving. Don't call the detailer and alert him to any issues. Just keep going." She took his advice and got back to work packing her things.

Chapter 80: Talk of war ... You shook me all night long

On Saturday afternoon, Brenda waited at the Nobi train station for WEPS to pick her up. Since the train station was only a half mile from her house, and she had been running early for a change, she had decided to walk to the station instead of taking the bus. It was a cool, overcast day requiring only a light jacket – perfect for a walk. She loved to walk, wherever she was and whenever she could. And she was feeling nostalgic that this particular walk to the train station might be her last before she left Yokosuka forever, or at least for many years to come. Before she detached from the ship, she had wanted to walk one final time past the convenience store in her neighborhood, the seamstress shop where she had asked the woman to make her two sitting cushions using some beautiful Japanese fabrics she had picked out, and the small candy shop where she could get one last green tea ice cream. The storekeepers always recognized her. She regretted that all she could say to them was *hai* and *domo*, words meant to approximate *yes* and *thank you*.

Being a few minutes early, she walked inside the train station to buy a can of hot coffee from a vending machine. She was going to miss all of the bright colors used in Japan on the signs, and the massive Kanji figures jutting out at consumers. She had come to admire the intricacy of the Kanji characters, and she had to admit to herself that some of the characters just looked crazy when they were blown up on some trendy advertisement, manically exploding out of the sign between exclamation marks and Japanimation figures. She was going to miss canned vending machine coffee. She was going to miss Japan. In her remaining time, she wanted to get one last fill of everything she had experienced there. She didn't know when she would return, if ever. Yes, she had liked Japan, if only she could have been there for any other reason besides for the SWO Navy.

She was meeting WEPS at the train station because she never could have explained the streets and narrow turns to pick her up at her house. When she spotted WEPS' car, she waved. On Friday, he had called her at home to invite her to a get-together at his house to celebrate her departure. At first, when the phone rang on her day off – when she was packing her household goods – she had panicked, afraid that it was WEPS calling to tell her that she needed to report back to the ship. But immediately after picking up the phone – to her relief – she heard WEPS state rather rapidly, "I'm not calling you to come back to the ship or because there's a problem." He had called to invite her to his house for pizza and snacks, a small "going away" party for her. Only JOs from the department would be there.

At the train station, she approached his car at the curb. She was feeling uplifted, excited that this get-together was yet another event that made her feel as if she might actually be able to leave the ship according to her orders. But WEPS wasn't smiling, or in the mood to say hello. "You're leaving just in time," he said, when she opened the door to get into his car. "We just got word that the ship might deploy to the Gulf next month."

Brenda sat down in the passenger seat (on the left side of the car) not knowing how to respond. "Deploying to the Gulf. Unbelievable," she said. She thought of the DESRON commodore, who had recently visited the ship to discuss the then remote possibility of deploying to the Gulf. He kept repeating: "This is what we train for. But of course, none of us want to go to war." But as Brenda listened to him, she could hear the excitement in his voice, as much as he had tried to subdue it. He kept vocalizing that "he didn't want to go to war," but it was obvious that part of him was eager for a chance to fulfill his years of training. A war would enable him to implement strategies he had studied, and to test the viability of exercises he had practiced over the last twenty-five years of his career, since graduating from the Naval Academy. She was reminded of the fundamental problem with the peacetime military: It was boring; a war was necessary to allow the hundreds of thousands of officers, sailors, and soldiers in the military to do their jobs. They needed something *real* to do. After years of relative "peacetime," there was a thirst for action. It was a common saying that those in the military were the last ones who wanted to go to war, *because they were the ones who had to fight*. But as she sat in the audience in the wardroom, feeling the spike of adrenaline and the mood of anticipation in the room, she wondered.

"We just got back from deployment. It'll probably get cancelled," she answered WEPS, as he pulled the car out of the station. She stared out the window at the sprawling suburbs of Yokosuka. Once ancient hamlets, these towns had grown into small cities. Evidence of long-past centuries were still visible in temples and gardens that abutted modern high-rises.

She remembered how her friend Kathleen from high school had pleaded with her not to join the military, *"because she might get killed for a reason that might not be good enough, or for no reason at all."* Their rides to and from high school, and living together in their student apartment in college, provided many opportunities to have conversations about the war and the military. Kathleen had never strayed from her position that the Gulf War was fought over cheap oil and corporate profiteering. But Brenda had gravitated toward the unconditional wave to support Desert Storm; she had no problem adopting the newly-emerged and popular nationalistic language, which encouraged believing in the troops and embracing their patriotic sacrifice, and referring to troops as "heroes." In this, she had also adhered to the widespread and political penchant against "upsetting" troops, veterans, and their families with raw press coverage of deaths, atrocities, and movements that were anti-war. Kathleen had argued that it was better to tell the truth, as truth was the only healer. Brenda had minimized Kathleen's views at the time by writing them off as belonging to a free-spirited but unrealistic nonconformist. Brenda argued that people fought and lost their lives for their country, so that others could protest. She wore a yellow ribbon and placed a "support our troops" bumper sticker on her car, even though she didn't quite understand the war…she knew it was about "liberating Kuwait," but she also thought it had something to do with protecting our access to oil…it didn't really matter. "We can't go back to the protests of Vietnam," she had argued with Kathleen. But Kathleen had countered that she supported the troops, by not sending them into senseless wars of choice, and by not blindly supporting wars.

But one day while on deployment in Singapore, Brenda finally came to admit to herself how she truly felt about these issues. On cable news, while sitting across the table from Pete and Neil at a restaurant, she had learned that in 1991, President Bush had banned the media from broadcasting images of caskets of war veterans sent home. "You didn't know about the censorship?" Pete had asked her. "Real press coverage is difficult in this political climate following the Gulf War," he said. "We're in an era where it's now unacceptable to criticize the military, the troops, or the wars we're involved in, for fear of being branded as unpatriotic, or unsupportive of the troops, of hurting morale when troops come home or are deployed."

"I guess the American press was compliant in the war by

cooperating with the military," she said. She realized that the press really hadn't done their job, in that they hadn't presented the casualties, the carnage, and the realities of the war, for both sides, as reporters had done during Vietnam. They hadn't really dug into and reported stories on wartime ops, the real violence and horrors of war, or the aftermath. They seemed satisfied just to report information sanitized by military censors, or simply relay information taken from official briefings. "As if raw, truthful, war coverage would somehow violate the 'troops as heroes' sentiment," she added as they ate. In talking to sailors and other officers, she had learned that most troops and veterans wanted the truth reported, in all of its raw forms.

When she returned home, she decided that she was going to remove the support our troops bumper sticker from her car. Not because she didn't support the troops, and their aftercare, but because that kind of "pro-war-culture" promotion made the climate acceptable for more wars – a climate in which the military consisted of heroes, no matter what it engaged in, right or wrong. She now felt that the "support our troops" philosophy was a subtle public brainwashing campaign, intended to make it difficult to criticize an organization made up of heroes. It also made it difficult to philosophically separate supporting the military versus supporting wars.

"The Captain didn't screen me for XO," WEPS interrupted her thoughts. "I'm not sure if you knew that."

"I'm sorry, sir," she answered, upset by the news, "because you deserved it. It's one injustice after another."

"It's no matter," he said, "really. I'm leaving SWO. I've been accepted into Foreign Affairs."

"Then, congratulations," she said. Although she knew that the Captain not screening him for XO was a major upset for WEPS – and insult. WEPS had been ranked the number one division officer on his first two ships. "Don't worry about the SWO Navy," she added. "The Navy's in good hands because HAG will get promoted early to commander. She'll make O-5 and O-6 and be given command of a destroyer and then of a cruiser. They'll make her the first female captain of both a destroyer and cruiser; she'll make history."

"She's already made history being one of the first female XOs of a warship," WEPS responded. "And the whole waterfront knows of her reputation and of our low morale. CSO told me that the orthopedic surgeon at the base hospital was well aware of the XO's reputation."

Brenda said nothing. Her solution was to rid herself of SWO and of the Navy and of leaders like HAG – male and female – once she finished her service obligation. She vowed to never again put herself in a position where she was legally obligated to remain in a job. She was determined to search out a positive work environment in her future.

That morning, the Japanese moving company had picked up her household goods. The two movers had a small truck, and they had packed her things with an extreme precision that was impressive. One of the men cut cardboard around each of her kitchen chairs. She swore his method of packing her kitchen chairs was an art. "You don't have to do that, they're really cheap chairs," she had told him. "For protection," he answered, and went about what he was doing with care and skill. She didn't interrupt the movers further.

On the same day as WEPS' get-together, the gunners mates had planned a late-night party for her at a bar in Yokosuka. At the bar, the gunners mates sang karaoke to her. Their theme song throughout the night was, *"You shook me all night long"* by AC/DC. She allowed them to buy her one drink. Petty Officer Brooks had advised her that some of the guys had planned to get her drunk so that they could convince her to get a tattoo. She had looked at him dryly and answered, "You know that I would never allow that to happen." But they still had a great time and lots of laughs.

At the end of the night, the division presented her with a card, signed, *"Best of luck at your new command - the 'B' team."* Comments on the card included, *"I can't believe you're deserting us, but good luck anyway." "Ride hard. Die free." "Good luck at your next command and stay cool."* Petty Officer Marcello wrote, *"What words of wisdom can I give someone who is two months younger? ...Be happy... Best wishes on your new assignment. Please keep in touch. P.S. Never let them see you sweat."* The always quiet, but hard working GMG1 Falk wrote, *"Best of luck in school and at your next command. You were a great DIVO!"* And Petty Officer Mimms wrote, *"Well, at least you won't forget any of us. Good luck!"* On the back of the card, Petty Officer Finn wrote, *"Bye, GunZ. Good luck at school. Bend your hat properly when you get there."*

Chapter 81: Orders to detach from USS *CURTIS WILBUR* DDG-54

UUUUUUUUUUUUUUUUUUUUUUUUUU
U UNCLASSIFIED U
UUUUUUUUUUUUUUUUUUUUUUUUUU

RATUZYUW RUCCBWF6240 0400005-UUUU--RUCOFAF.
ZNR UUUUU ZUI RUCOMCA5304 0401419
R 081339Z SEP 98 ZYB PSN 818655I33
FM COMNAVPERSCOM MILLINGTON TN
TO USS CURTIS WILBUR YOKOSUKA JP//JJJ//
RUCCBWF/BUPERS MILLINGTON TN//JJJ//
RUDIDFB/DFAS CENTER CLEVELAND OH//JJJ//
RUCOFAK/PERSUPP DET NAVSTA CHARLESTON SC//JJJ//
INFO PERSUPP DET YOKOSUKA JP//JJJ//
BT
UNCLAS //NO 1875//
MSGID/GENADMIN/CHNAVPERS//
SUBJ/BUPERS ORDER//
RMKS/
BUPERS ORDER: 1945 (02) 574-99-2226/1160 (PERS-248C)
PCS ORDERS FOR ENS BRENDA A. CONNER   USN
WHEN DIRECTED BY REPORTING SENIOR, DETACH IN SEP 98 EDD:
SEP 98
FROM USS CURTIS WILBUR YOKOSUKA JP UIC: 35687
PERMANENT DUTY STATION JP, YOKOSUKA
PERSONNEL ACCOUNTING SUPPORT: PERSUPPDET PAC UIC: 65463

PRESENT CO DIRECTED TO DETACH MEMBER NOT LATER THAN 30 SEP 1998

REPORT NOT LATER THAN 31 OCT 98 EDA: 31 OCT 98
TO NETC NNPTC UIC: 45217
PERMANENT DUTY STATION CHARLESTON SC
FOR DUTY ACC: 156
TYPE DUTY SEA/SHORE CODE SSC 6
PERSONNEL ACCOUNTING SUPPORT PERSUPP DET WPSTA CHARLESTON SC UIC: 65879

...

Brenda walked onboard the ship at six a.m., an hour before officers call and quarters, not knowing whether or not she would be able leave the ship that afternoon for good, i.e., if the Command would allow her to fulfill her orders to detach. According to her orders, the thirtieth of the month was to be her last day onboard. Her household goods were packed and in possession of the Navy, or at least they were in possession of the Japanese moving company; her stateroom was almost packed. She had a set of civilian clothes laid out on her rack, ready to be stuffed into her backpack where they would be more accessible than in her seabag. But if the Command did not award her a SWO pin, all of that had the potential to be reversed.

Without a surface warfare qualification – a SWO pin – her orders were subject to modification. Language on the second page of her orders read, "pending surface warfare qualification." She found it difficult to accept that the decision as to what direction her life would take in the next six months, year, or during her remaining time in the Navy – SWO qualification, non-qualification, or a full two year tour onboard with the goal of SWO qualification – would be made by Commander Tom Brier and Lieutenant Commander Heather Gates. Brenda's newly found self-awareness made it especially uncomfortable to be hanging by a swinging thread that they were in charge of.

She spent the morning saying goodbye to the gunners mates. She spoke to them individually in the division spaces prior to quarters, and as a division at quarters. But as she spoke with them, she was conscious of the fact that the inch or two above her left shirt pocket was bare: There was no SWO pin on her uniform. She wasn't sure how much they knew about her qualification status. She said her farewells to them under the assumption that she would never see them again. She thanked them for their dedicated work and support, and wished them happiness and the best for their futures – whether in or out of the Navy. At quarters, she passed out pamphlets outlining college programs for GIs, and ways that they could start right then with correspondence courses. As she stood before the gunners mates at quarters, she justified her suspense, thinking that many JOs received their SWO pins on their last day. In fact, the "last day SWO pin" had almost become the norm onboard *Curtis Wilbur*.

Conversations with her colleague officers over the course of the morning went more tentatively because they were aware of the uncertainty surrounding her qualification status. Some of her colleagues seemed unsure of what to say to her. Most asked, "So, have you heard anything?" followed by variations of, "You'll be fine. You'll be out of this hellhole," or, "You'll be out of here for good. I'll be out of here soon enough, too." In her final conversations with the officers, she felt the strongest sense of camaraderie with those who had suffered under HAG from the very beginning – from those first days of the Hong Kong port visit and the missile onload in Okinawa.

Since HAG had only been onboard the ship just over a year, she had more than six months left of her eighteen month XO tour. The newer junior officers had a long way to go under HAG's command. And unfortunately, the XO had targeted a new group of JOs. The extremely competent remained her primary targets. Others, she nitpicked subtly – here and there – with effects that seemed to accumulate and drive some to the edge of breakdown. She focused on the most trivial of mistakes, and then she never let her officers forget those small mistakes. Last month, while en route to a wardroom function for local Japanese dignitaries, Brenda noticed that Kirsten, Neil's replacement as antisubmarine warfare officer (ASWO), was wearing pearl earring studs with her khaki uniform. She tried to warn Kirsten about her earrings – the XO couldn't navigate a ship, but she loved to zero in on mistakes such as wearing the wrong earrings with a uniform. "Kirsten," Brenda stopped her in the passageway. "I would take those earrings off."

"These earrings are perfectly fine," she answered, "They're within the regs."

"No, Kirsten, they're not," Brenda tried to warn her. "Small, ball shaped pearl earrings are allowed only with formal uniforms, not with khakis. Only small gold balls are allowed for female officers with informal uniforms. I'm sorry, Kirsten, I'm just warning you that the XO's not going to like it."

"I know these pearls are fine," she insisted, and continued on to the reception.

At the wardroom reception, Brenda watched as HAG immediately focused on Kirsten's earrings. Before long, she took Kirsten aside, and seconds later, Kirsten was following the XO out the wardroom door. After a minute or so, Brenda followed. Outside of HAG's stateroom, she heard Lieutenant Commander Gates dressing down Kirsten in screams and shrieks laden with physical threats. Brenda lost count of how many times the XO sadistically berated Kirsten "for being a worthless junior officer." The XO had chosen to tear Kirsten down, rather than to instruct her, guide her, or lead her into finding her niche onboard, or encourage her to develop her potential. Kirsten's "initiation session" in HAG's stateroom seemed to have severely affected her. After that afternoon, Brenda noticed an obvious change in Kirsten, a sort of loss of confidence, a sense that she had become indifferent to her job onboard. After the earring episode, it appeared that HAG had decided for good that she disliked Kirsten, and that she would target her on a daily basis for the most minor of infractions.

Now that Brenda was finishing her first shipboard tour, and poised to leave, she started to notice that many of the new junior officers faced some of the same challenges that she had faced – suitability and shipboard aptitude. The billet assignment practices of the military didn't reflect most conventional civilian hiring practices. In the civilian world, if a new hiree didn't work out, the hiree could move on to something else, be let go, or be transferred to another department. But the military was rigid, and it held its recruits by legal contract. The SWO community swallowed up every college graduate they could find, and then tried to mold each one in the same likeness. Brenda could see that Derek, her possible replacement as gunnery officer, struggled with SWO and seamanship in the same way that she had. Derek appeared to be a bright college graduate; but like her, he was a young person thrown in as a manager and leader right out of college, in a field that didn't seem to suit him.

Chapter 82: SWO pin right or wrong ... Part of the club

1MC Shipwide Announcement: *"Assemble all officers in the wardroom."*

On edge, Brenda left her stateroom and filed into the wardroom with the other officers, wondering if her departure was the reason for the impromptu meeting. The Captain and XO had established a command atmosphere in which the officers were made to constantly guess what was in store for their futures, both short and long term. The status of her SWO qualification, and the question of whether or not she would be able to leave the ship that afternoon, had come down to the wire. She just wanted to know one way or the other if she was going to qualify. If she had to remain onboard for another six or seven months, she just wanted to be informed as much.

The officers stood awkwardly around the wardroom, not knowing what to say to each other. Most seemed to suspect that Brenda was about to receive her SWO pin. "The Captain's going to walk in any second with your SWO pin," one of the JOs said to her. As her other colleagues made similar comments, she shrugged nervously, answering, "I hope so, but I don't know." Courtney, the assistant OPS, and Josh, the disbursing officer (DISBO), had brought cameras with them so they could take photos of her receiving her SWO pin, for the ship's yearbook and to later mail to her. After about ten minutes of making the officers wait in the wardroom, standing around in nervous anticipation, the Captain walked through the door with a gold SWO pin clasped in one hand, and a certificate folder in the other. Then Brenda knew...she would be leaving. She remained standing at the front of the wardroom, next to the cappuccino maker.

Before the gathering of officers, the Captain approached her and pinned a gold SWO pin over her left shirt pocket. *She had done it.* Flashes went off as Courtney and Josh snapped photos. People were clapping. After having waited so long to know the outcome, Brenda felt a wave of powerful – even conflicting – emotions...surprise, ambivalence, shame, embarrassment, happiness, relief. And maybe she was a little proud, that she could wear the pin while on ships, and around naval bases, and at nuclear power school. The pin confirmed that she had done it; she'd been through it; she had served onboard a combat ship and had endured the hardship and at-sea training; and she was a qualified surface warfare officer now – *she had proven capabilities.* But just as suddenly, a feeling of shame came over her, as she wasn't sure she actually *did* have any proven shipboard capabilities. What did her SWO pin mean, really? Maybe, it simply meant that she had worked hard and that she had given it her best onboard. And now it was official that she would detach in accordance with her orders; she would move on to Naval Nuclear Power School (NNPS).

As she stood at the front of the wardroom, next to the Captain, the entire scene started to feel wrong and inauthentic. After clasping her pin on her khaki shirt, the Captain shook her hand and congratulated her – all smiles. But in response, she suddenly looked at him as if at a loss. She wanted to ask him: Was she accepting a credential that she didn't deserve and hadn't earned? As she shook his hand, she tried to smile as much as she could. She wondered what the photos taken by Courtney and Josh would reveal of her emotions and in the facial expressions shown by her and the Captain and the rest of the officers as she received her pin. But before she could think much more about those issues, the Captain presented her with a certificate and a letter of surface warfare officer qualification:

From: Commanding Officer, USS CURTIS WILBUR (DDG 54)
To: LTJG Brenda A. Conner, USN, 574-99-2226/1110

Subj: DESIGNATION AS SURFACE WARFARE OFFICER, (SWO)

Ref: (a) OPNAVINST 1412.2G
     (b) CURTISWILBURINST 3120.1A

1. Per references (a) and (b), you are hereby designated a Surface Warfare Officer. You may display the SWO insignia on all uniforms to distinguish your commitment to the command and the surface warfare community. This designation is the reward for your diligence and is an indication of the trust and faith the Commanding Officer has in you and your abilities.

2. Well done!

                                         T. M. BRIER

Copy to:
CHNAVPERS (PERS 412)
COMCARGRU FIVE
COMDESRON FIFTEEN

Out of protocol, she shook the Captain's hand once more as she held her SWO letter and certificate. She was now officially part of the club. She was a surface warfare officer (SWO), designator 1110. Tentatively, she walked down the line of officers to shake each one's hand. Behind them hung those portraits of ships of old that sailed and steamed into harm's way while bombs, cannons, and guns roared around them, with the seas stirred into a fierce frenzy. The officers smiled and shook her hand as they congratulated her; each offered her well wishes and good luck. She smiled back and thanked them, but she was uncomfortable, and unsure of their true thoughts. In some ways, she was embarrassed to receive this attention for accepting a SWO pin and certificate. She especially found herself unable to look Rob in the eye when she shook his hand.

Chapter 83: Parting ways ... An awkward goodbye ... A final salute

She had an idea of what the year ahead of her would be like. She imagined that at nuclear power school, she would be one of those students who, dressed in polyester shore duty khakis, would find herself sitting at a study carrel in the classroom building, logging over fifty hours of study time per week, in addition to the forty hours per week of classroom time. Material taught at the school – nuclear power, nuclear physics, mathematics – was classified, which meant that all studying had to be done on school grounds, inside the building. It was prohibited to carry any notes or books outside the building. She pictured herself living in some nondescript one bedroom apartment a few miles from base, maybe taking Friday nights off to rent a movie and grab some Chinese food.

After all that had happened, after the ways that the Captain had experienced her onboard, she wondered how he could have brought himself to smile, shake her hand, look proud, and congratulate her while awarding her a SWO pin. But nevertheless, he had enabled her to check off another milestone among the many on her list – mechanical engineering, ROTC, naval commission, SWOS, ship, SWO pin, nuclear power school, nuclear aircraft carrier. As she stood in the wardroom while the officers mingled and chatted for a few minutes, she thought about how she had never lived in or for the present. She had spent her life obsessing over good grades (with less regard for actual learning), appearing superior on paper with the right degrees and activities, and studying for the sake of milestones that were supposed to lead her to some kind of pragmatically perfect adult future.

A few days before, the yeomen (YNs) in the admin office had informed her that a Japanese car service would be scheduled to pick her up at the brow of the ship on the afternoon of her last day, as soon as that was known. The car service would drive her to Yokota Air Base – three hours away – where she would board a military transport flight back to the States.

After her SWO pin ceremony in the wardroom, which lasted about fifteen minutes, Brenda followed the officers out of the wardroom. She felt ambivalent, unsure of what her first shipboard tour had meant. What was the significance of the last year and a half of her life? There had been so many things happen to her, and she had learned so much about herself, that she decided that only time and distance would allow her to understand it fully, and the impact it had had on her.

The lead yeoman (YN1) stopped her in the passageway, "The car service will be here in forty-five minutes, ma'am," he advised her.

"Thank you, YN1," she answered. As she headed back to her stateroom to gather her seabag and backpack, she saw Brad walking with the crowd of officers. She and Brad had left matters of their relationship to the last minute. On the afternoon before, assuming she was leaving, Brad had come to her stateroom. He knocked on her door while she was still packing, going through drawers and cabinets, still finding odds and ends here and there. When she opened the door, he found her standing next to her green seabag, which was stuffed to the top; she was trying to stuff more into it, mostly books. "Come in," she said, knowing why he was there. "Here, let me help you clasp the top of your seabag," he offered.

She spoke first, and spared him from having to introduce the subject on both their minds. With the trauma and uncertainty of her qualification status, she had felt innerved, void of emotion, and drained. She wasn't completely sure she wanted to say what she was about to say. "I think we both enjoyed the time we spent together, traveling all over Japan on weekends and days off, and the Pacific rim during port visits. I know I did. I'm thankful," she said. Brad nodded and smiled. She added wistfully, "But I guess this is probably the end for both of us. And from here we'll go on separately."

Brad appeared relieved. And she knew right then that their relationship, or whatever it was, was over. "I'm really relieved," he answered, somewhat awkwardly. "Because I was thinking the same thing. But write and keep in touch," he said. "And if I find any of your things around the house, I'll send them to you at power school," he added. He gave her a big hug. Their relationship had ended as it had begun over a year ago – nice, tidy, in a way that seemed, under normal conditions, not possible. Their personal and professional struggles aboard ship, and especially, under the leadership of the XO, had exhausted them of any emotion or feeling they might have had for each other. Their relationship had centered around the ship, the Navy, and HAG. They had walked the streets of southeast Asia and Japan together – shopping and visiting gardens and temples – while talking nonstop about the ship and SWO and surviving the ship. They listened to each other, and because they were both living through the same circumstances onboard, they didn't have to explain themselves to another person who couldn't relate. They had understood each other's daily challenges onboard and had been there for each other.

Brad left her stateroom, giving her one last hug goodbye. "You did it. I knew you would," he said. Brad's words had reflected what he had written on the matting surrounding the framed photo of the *Curtis Wilbur* – signed by all the officers – that she had received at the Hail & Farewell, "*You made it - I knew you would! Stay focused at Nuke school and do well ... I know you've got plenty of motivation to do well!*"

*

While Brenda gathered up her bags to leave the ship forever, Julie entered their stateroom on crutches. "You're on crutches?" Brenda asked.

"I'm sorry I wasn't there for your ceremony. My ankle gave out this morning. I was forced to go to medical. Bill and Greg took me. That's why they weren't there."

"They're not going to allow you to stay on the ship on crutches," Brenda said.

"I know," Julie answered. "I'll probably be transferred TAD, limited duty for a short time until this can heal. The end of my tour's coming up in two months anyway," she said. "I've applied for EDO, like Neil, to get out of SWO. I think I'll be able to do my TAD at the pentagon until I hear from the EDO board. I'll be leaving the ship immediately, and won't be coming back."

The roommates wished each other good luck and expressed how nice it was to have known each other. They had lived together for what had seemed like forever; they had endured both operations officers, the Command, and HAG. "It's been a pleasure serving with you onboard *Curtis Wilbur*," Julie told her. They shook hands. "I think you're a brilliant officer," Brenda professed. "I'm not sure if we'll ever see each other again."

"Oh, I don't know. Maybe we will. The Navy's a small world and we'll both be on the East Coast. The only person I would hope to never see again once I get off the ship would be HAG," Julie said at the end of their goodbyes.

None of the goodbyes Brenda shared with people she had lived with and worked with under such intense, confined conditions onboard, felt adequate or seemed to offer her the right closure. It seemed there were no words, customs, or gestures that provided any sort of satisfying ending to her time onboard...and nothing she could do or say to ameliorate her knowledge that she would probably never see any of her colleagues, or others she had come to know on the ship, ever again.

In front of the women's head, HAG approached her carrying an object wrapped in a brown paper bag. "Brenda, I have something for you," she said.

"What's this, ma'am?" she asked. Brenda couldn't imagine...had the XO gotten her something after all they had been through together? Annoyed with that prospect, and not wanting to be in a position of having to show any thanks or receive an offering of atonement, her heart pounded for a moment, waiting.

"I'm returning your Tokyo guidebook, GUNNO," she answered. Recomposing her thoughts, Brenda managed to reply, "thank you, ma'am." She wondered if the circumstances surrounding her borrowing the guidebook somehow held a key to HAG's mental illness. Brenda had just assumed that HAG would never return the book, a gift her mother had given Brenda prior to leaving for Japan. HAG had borrowed it months ago during her father's visit to Yokosuka. During the visit, HAG had revealed to Neil – under inappropriate conditions – that she *hated* her father. Did there exist some dark secret concerning her father that justified her hatred, and that had exacerbated her mental illness and her sadistic personality?

After an awkward pause, she said, smirking and tilting her head with a look that seemed to size up Brenda, "We knew we were going to qualify you all along, GUNNO." And with that, they walked away in separate directions. Brenda, her heart beat slowing, hoped it was the last bizarre interaction she would ever have with the XO.

She thought it was no wonder that there were rumors of a SWO-wide safety and leadership stand-down. But she knew that the surface warfare community would continue in its present form for years, as it had long before her, with its mishaps and labyrinth of dysfunction, made possible by a long list of unavowed deficiencies: lack of training, lack of experience, poor seamanship, weak navigation, a tendency to drive exceptional officers out of the Navy, the officer as jack-of-all trades mentality, verbal abuse and public degradation, the existence of explosive screaming of profanity from superiors who rarely imparted constructive feedback, sleep deprivation, forcing division officers to use entire workdays to route messages for minor changes, the obstinate belief in Aegis technology as the path to superiority, bullying on the part of unrelenting department heads and senior SWOs, and its consequential "learning the game of avoiding their wrath" on the part of subordinates. An instructor at Surface Warfare Officer School once said to her class, "If you can survive all that, you can wear your SWO pin with pride!"

As she struggled to arrange and pick up her bags, she heard the 1MC announcement, *"Assemble all officers on the quarterdeck."* She knew that the announcement meant that the officers would assemble on the quarterdeck, and ceremoniously form two lines, with two side boys; she would walk through the lines of officers, shaking the hands of her soon-to-be former colleagues; she would exit the ship down the brow and meet up on the pier with the Japanese car service.

Had she fulfilled any of the ideals for which she had first joined the Navy? Many of her ideals had evolved or been dropped altogether. But her feelings about equality for women had not changed, and possibly had become even more clear to her. The doors had opened to women and there was no going back. Despite everything, she could feel excited that she had existed as part of a wave. Thousands of young surface warfare officers earned commissions and resigned each year, and many of them were now female.

It was only a few years since Tailhook and its aftermath. The scandal had forced the Navy into a penetrating soul search and played a significant role in not only opening the Navy to women, but making the Navy tolerable as a work environment in which sexual harassment was no longer the daily norm. But then, in a too-soon swing of the pendulum in the opposite direction, the Navy had chosen Lieutenant Commander Heather A. Gates as the new, highest example of female command and leadership, representing the future of the Navy. Sadly, it was no stretch to predict that she would go on to become the first woman to captain a destroyer, and the first woman to captain a cruiser, the most tactically advanced warships in the Navy. For all Brenda knew, she might have been on her way to become admiral.

Carrying her seabag over her shoulders, dressed in khakis, she made her way through officers country, down the ladderwell, and out the watertight door to the quarterdeck, one final time. On the quarterdeck, which was set up on the aft fantail, starboard side, the officers stood in two lines. WEPS was waiting for her at the beginning of the line. He presented her with an end-of-tour NAM, a suitable award to receive as an outgoing division officer.

DEPARTMENT OF THE NAVY
THIS IS TO CERTIFY THAT
THE SECRETARY OF THE NAVY HAS AWARDED THE

NAVY AND MARINE CORPS ACHIEVEMENT MEDAL

TO

LIEUTENANT JUNIOR GRADE BRENDA A. CONNER, UNITED STATES NAVY

FOR

PROFESSIONAL ACHIEVEMENT AS GUNNERY OFFICER, IN USS CURTIS WILBUR, WHILE DEPLOYED TO THE WESTERN PACIFIC OCEAN. LIEUTENANT JUNIOR GRADE CONNER PERFORMED HER DUTIES IN AN EXEMPLARY AND HIGHLY PROFESSIONAL MANNER. SHE PLANNED AND COORDINATED THE SUCCESSFUL EXECUTION OF OVER TWENTY GUN FIRING EXERCISES, TWO LIVE-FIRE MISSILE SHOOTS AND DOZENS OF SMALL ARMS DEMONSTRATIONS. IN ADDITION, HER SINCERE CONCERN FOR THE WELFARE OF HER SUBORDINATES LED TO AN UNPRECEDENTED LEVEL OF TEAMWORK AND DIVISIONAL MORALE. ENSIGN CONNER'S PROFESSIONALISM AND DEVOTION TO DUTY REFLECTED GREAT CREDIT UPON HERSELF AND WERE IN KEEPING WITH THE HIGHEST TRADITIONS OF THE UNITED STATES NAVAL SERVICE.

FOR THE SECRETARY OF THE NAVY
C.W. MOORE, JR.
REAR ADMIRAL, UNITED STATES NAVY
COMMANDER, CARRIER GROUP FIVE

All of the officers clapped. WEPS must have submitted the NAM for approval, despite her uncertain status with regard to her SWO pin and leaving. She sort of looked at him like, "How did you know to submit this?" And as if he read her face and thoughts, he motioned to her not to worry about it. She smiled as she walked down the lines of officers, shaking everyone's hand. Josh, the disbursing officer, carried her seabag and backpacks for her. When she looked back up at the ship, for one last time, she noticed Petty

Officer Mimms standing high up on the superstructure, watching her leave. She knew that he would have had to find a substitute for his CSMC watch in order to be there. She waved goodbye to him. On the aft deck, she noticed many of the gunners mates watching her leave, and she waved to them one last time. She had said her goodbyes that morning. She then turned, stepped down the brow, saluted the *Curtis Wilbur* ensign, and got into the car waiting for her on the pier, from the Japanese car service.

EPILOGUE: Final ride ... Final days ... The end of the Long Way Out

From the passenger seat of the car service limo, Brenda looked over at the driver as they drove off the pier. "I'm free," she said to him, smiling. "I'm really free." As she looked behind her, she could no longer see the massive concrete piers, which stretched along Yokosuka harbor for at least a mile, securing U.S. warships – cruisers, destroyers, frigates, an aircraft carrier, a command ship, and currently, a few visiting amphibious ships.

"I'm sorry, I don't speak English well," the driver managed, smiling and nodding.

As they passed through the base gates, Brenda experienced for the last time the contrast between the U.S. naval base and the Japanese city of Yokosuka. She wondered if she would ever return to Yokosuka or to Japan. She imagined that one day she probably would, years or decades later, when she was no longer in the Navy. For sure, she wouldn't return to Japan onboard a nuclear carrier, because only conventionally-powered (non-nuclear powered) aircraft carriers were homeported out of Yokosuka.

"I'm looking forward to one last drive through Japan," she commented to the driver – doubting if he understood that either – as she looked out her window, trying to take in all of the scenery – the lights, the signs, the colors, the bustle, the Kanji.

"How...about...music?" the driver asked, as they drove deeper into Japan. He was about her age.

"Hai, domo, arigato gozaimasu," she answered in broken Japanese, which she assumed was far from correct, but relayed her meaning. The driver smiled, and nodded again. "Very good," he said, and they both laughed.

Late in the afternoon, at the Yokota Air Base BOQ (bachelor officer quarters), Brenda rested on the hotel bed, in relief. She slept deep into evening, still dressed in the shore duty khakis she had changed into just before leaving the ship. When she woke up hours later, close to nine p.m., she changed into civilian clothes and walked over to the McDonalds on base – the only "restaurant" open at that time. She celebrated by ordering a hot fudge sundae. Before she went to bed for the night, she placed her shipboard black leather steel-toe shoes in the hotel room trash can. She was headed to shore duty...and she had made it through her time onboard.

***

Her military flight back to the States, operated by a contracted civilian commercial airline, lasted two days and included seven stops. When she boarded the plane at Yokota Air Base, she anticipated a nonstop flight to LAX, and then on to Boston. Each proceeding landing and takeoff, at the various U.S. military bases around Japan, came as a surprise. It seemed that no one – the passengers nor the flight attendants – was sure of the schedule and of where the plane would land next. When she asked one flight attendant about the schedule, she answered, "I don't know. It's always different. I do these flights all the time; eventually, we end up back in the States." The passengers were a mix of military, military families with children, lone spouses with children, and civilian contractors, all of whom had to deplane at each stop, wait in the passenger area, and reboard the plane. After the plane stopped at the forth U.S. airbase in Japan, they flew on to Anchorage, Alaska, followed by Seattle, Washington, before finally arriving at LAX. From Los Angeles, she flew commercial to the East Coast, with one stop in Chicago.

***

After thirty days of leave and visiting family and friends, Brenda started nuclear power school, in Goose Creek, South Carolina, where she began to live exactly as she had predicted before she had left the ship. She spent most of her time – outside of the required forty hours of classroom time – in the nuclear power school building, in the designated "quiet study" room across the hall from her classroom, studying late into night, sitting in a carrel buried in the far back corner of the room.

The school consisted of forty hours of required classroom time per week, during which students copied notes on nuclear physics verbatim from the chalkboard, as was the teaching style at the school. The lieutenant instructors were required to write down nearly every word they said on the chalkboard, and the students were required to copy every word off the chalkboard into notebooks. After the initial two weeks of the school, Brenda began logging fifty hours of study time per week, in addition to the forty hours of required classroom time. Two months into the school, she started logging upwards of seventy hours of study time per week, in addition to the forty hours of required classroom time, for the remainder of the six month school. She slept but little. She found her own capacity to memorize pages and pages and notebooks full of nuclear physics notes verbatim, incredible. She passed all of the weekly Friday morning exams, and she received two points over the minimum GPA required for graduation. At the end of six months, exhausted, she graduated from Naval Nuclear Power School and received her diploma – another milestone.

But even though she had to study nuclear physics for over fifty hours per week for six straight months, nuclear power school still felt like heaven compared to shipboard duty under Lieutenant Commander Gates. That realization, and memories from shipboard duty, kept her studying nuclear physics when she was exhausted on late nights. Her lieutenant advisor, a submariner, was extremely supportive of her efforts, and encouraged her throughout her time at the school. "I've never seen anyone scrape and claw their way through this school as you have," he told her after graduation, "you're a fighter."

While at the school, she rewarded herself on Friday nights by renting a movie and grabbing Chinese from a restaurant in the strip mall next door to her apartment complex. Over the course of the six month school, she was so pressed for time that her one bedroom apartment grew into a disorganized disaster area, to the point that it had become nearly impossible for her to walk across the floor. And it was a lonely time, getting up at four a.m. every morning and going to bed after midnight.

Not all students required as much study time as she did. Many naturally brilliant engineering students attended the school, understood the material as taught in class, and studied minimally.

There were two other females in her class – a class that comprised nearly one hundred, junior officers. The other two females were lieutenant (j. g.) surface warfare officers, as well. Females at the school were barred by law from serving onboard submarines after graduating from nuclear power school; they were required to serve aboard nuclear powered aircraft carriers. The male students in the class were recent Naval Academy graduates slated for submarines. Brenda, and the two other female SWOs, served as classroom section leaders over the male Naval Academy graduates.

***

After graduating from the initial six month Naval Nuclear Power School, she failed to graduate from the six month follow-on practical school, or prototype, where students operated a live nuclear reactor under instruction. At the prototype school, she passed all of the written exams, including the major six-hour long midterm exam, and the final watch board practical (evaluation while standing engineering officer of the watch (EOOW) in charge of the nuclear reactor). She was so accustomed to standing shipboard watches that she received the second highest grade in her class on the final watch board practical. She survived six months of twenty-four hour rotating shift work, working in the reactor spaces, and standing all of the engineering watches. Months earlier she had been given orders to report to the nuclear-powered aircraft carrier, USS *Enterprise* (CVN-65), upon successful completion of the school.

But she didn't pass the crucial final oral board exam, given by a panel of instructors – even after two tries. Both boards had been train wrecks, stopped in mid test. Up to the very end, she had tried to fulfill her Navy obligation as well as her desire to not fail. But by the end of the second attempt, it was with a spirit of resolution, and even relief, that she accepted that she would not be a nuclear officer (SWO N), a title she had realized would never be a suitable fit. She was informed that a third board attempt would not be provided. The head civilian nuke instructor, concerned for her mental state following this announcement, asked Brenda, "Are you going to be ok?" Knowing that the outcome was best for both herself and the Navy, she wanted to laugh and burst out, "I am fine!" The only down-side was that this put her in a kind of no-man's land, where her disposition for her future billet was uncertain.

She silently feared going to another shipboard SWO billet, where she would be expected to stand OOD watches and watches in CIC as a trained expert; she feared another onslaught of seasickness. Fortunately, the XO of the nuclear prototype school – a nuclear surface warfare officer (as opposed to a submariner) – had respected her hard work at the prototype school. He assisted her in negotiating with the SWO detailer, and she accepted a billet as assistant operations officer for an amphibious squadron – a joint Navy/Marine Corps unit.

The amphibious squadron commodore was a fair commander to work for, as was her immediate SWO department head supervisor, the operations officer. But she had difficulty overcoming the memories of her first ship. Exploring the personal dynamics that had led her to the Navy she found to be a continuing challenge, and her desire grew to break her unending cycle of working towards milestones that could not bring her real happiness. She knew that it would take leaving the Navy to finally be able to fully evolve in the directions she had discovered and now longed for. During one long underway on the amphibious ship, she felt herself exhausted and nearly on the brink of a breakdown. At sea, she sought help from the onboard chaplain. In port, she sought help from a psychologist at the naval hospital, and then from a private therapist in Virginia Beach. She would later interpret all of these events, as well as her efforts to heal, as being connected to her inner longing to individuate, while in an environment and on a path that were strongly antithetical to that process. A Navy psychiatrist at the hospital had called her issue, "situational depression." He assured her that she would later be fine once she was out from under the Navy, and that her depression was not "organic." Fortunately, by that time, her naval commitment was coming to a close.

Brenda learned a lifetime of lessons in the Navy. At the completion of her ROTC scholarship obligation, she resigned her commission and received an honorable discharge. When she submitted her letter of resignation to the amphibious squadron commodore, a person she thought of as a genuinely nice man, he said, "I know there's nothing I can say, Miss Conner, to change your mind about staying in the Navy, so I'll sign and submit your letter. But, we'll miss your service. Thank you."

At nuclear power school, and at the amphibious squadron (PHIBRON), she had tried to tell her superiors and colleagues about the leadership style of Lieutenant Commander Gates. But the stories were so outrageous that they seemed beyond belief to many of the listeners. In her letter of resignation from the Navy, she attached a ten page addendum – as was her right according to the instructions within the officer resignation procedures manual – detailing the many reprehensible acts of Lieutenant Commander Gates onboard *Curtis Wilbur*. No official ever contacted her regarding these allegations.

When her final day in the Navy arrived, she signed her discharge paperwork at the Norfolk Naval Station PSD (personnel support detachment), and received her DD-214. She drove out the gates of the Norfolk Naval Station one last time, by herself, with no fanfare. She stopped at a McDonalds a few blocks outside the gates and in the restroom she changed out of her naval uniform for the last time and into civilian clothes. She then drove north, back home to New England.

***

She left engineering and the Navy behind forever, and enrolled in graduate school to study Spanish literature. She dedicated her life to reading, writing, and researching literature and psychology. Literature aided her in continuing on her journey of self-discovery, and led her to a deeper awareness of the world around her and the ways she could interact with that world for the good. She remained committed to accepting and exploring the hard truths about herself as they were uncovered. She continued to study the collective works of Jung, and continued to engage in prolonged self-reflection which allowed her to further understand her personal dynamics, her family dynamics, and the relationships she had had with those onboard the *Curtis Wilbur*.

She gained an insight-oriented perspective, which for the first time, gave her a peace that stemmed from self-understanding and from the solid ground of the self, so she could move forward with her life in a way that felt authentic. Her new self-awareness brought with it an ever-expanding dedication to the humane movement, environmental issues, and building a culture of peace. A few years following her time in the Navy, she married a jazz musician and visual artist, and still resides in New England. After receiving her master's degree in Spanish literature, she dedicated herself to writing full time.

***

After serving as executive officer (XO) onboard USS *Curtis Wilbur* (DDG-54), Lieutenant Commander Gates was subsequently promoted to Commander (O-5), and Captain (O-6) – an extremely difficult rank to obtain in the Navy, reserved only for a top few. Captain Gates was given command of two cutting-edge warships, becoming the first woman to captain an Aegis destroyer, and the first woman to captain a cruiser. In 2010, she was relieved of her command for "cruelty and maltreatment" and "conduct unbecoming an officer" following an Admirals Mast.

AUTHOR'S NOTE – A primer on Jungian Psychology

Psychological journey as story

When I started my writing path, I began to reflect on the nature of the inward journey – the process of individuation – which had begun for me while in the Navy. It is one thing to intuitively know that you have started and are engaged with this process, which is a lifelong journey of self-discovery and self-acceptance; it is an entirely different matter to describe it in depth, in such a way that readers not only understand it, but can apply the very concepts to their own lives in a way that can lead to insight and change.

I had many questions to think about as I wrote. What does it mean to "get to know yourself," or to "find yourself"? Is this a universal process? Do we have to abandon everything our parents taught us in order to do this? Does the process always have to be brought on by crisis? Is it something I can engage in on my own or is it only accomplished in the context of therapy? At what age does one normally enter this process, if they ever do enter it? I first encountered these questions, and the beginnings of their answers, during the process that I went through twenty years ago, when I found myself on the brink of a personal and psychological disaster.

Writing the story has been a therapeutic experience for me, in that it helped me to further name and even more clearly identify the period of profound psychological change I had unwittingly begun while I was a young woman serving as an officer in the Navy. The internal, psychological process I had entered was that which Dr. Carl Jung refers to as *individuation*. This is a process that is usually brought on by a crisis, a disaster, an event that is so disturbing that one turns inward to find a solution, to find insight, to find new and deeper meaning, and hopefully, to realize personality growth that takes one in a different and healthier direction of healing and wholeness. My crisis became apparent, and approached its zenith, when a number of historic factors came together: I was faced with ineptitude in my chosen field, my unhappiness had mounted to a disturbing level, my self-doubt was unmanageable, and my efforts to make others see me in the way I hoped to be seen were coming undone. While early in my term of commitment to the Navy, I was no longer able to deny these inner conflicts that had threatened my ability to cope and maintain sanity. In the true Jungian understanding, I was in the midst of the crisis that served as a catalyst for entering the process of individuation. Engaging actively in that process put me on a path to understanding what had happened to me, what was happening to me in the moment, and how I could heal, grow, change, and move on to a higher level set of challenges to which I would be more suited. It was a time of "creative illness," a long hard path, often confusing, that required the honest facing of fears and insecurities, the experiencing of grief and sadness, the letting go of sacred beliefs, and the acceptance that the future would be uncertain. In every sense, I experienced the literal meaning of the Greek word krino (crisis), a turning point wherein one has to *decide*...in this case to decide to work towards greater authenticity through a process of honest self-reflection. As you read the book, you will share with Brenda, her (my) pain, conflict, and angst in going through the detailed process. It may even inspire some readers, that the journey is exciting, possible, and is even a natural one to be drawn to. Jung felt we all possess an inherited drive that moves us toward the process, which he saw as the central task of life.

Although the individuation process (the therapeutic or insight-oriented process of moving towards greater authenticity and wholeness) is different for each person, there are striking similarities for those who can identify being in, or having gone through it. My story illustrates the particular circumstances that I went through. Due to my particular set of events, it is not coincidental that I was in the Navy at the time that my psychological crisis began, but it is coincidental that one of the recent catastrophes in naval history was evolving on the very ship that I happened to be on. The latter added even more intensity to my situation and a greater sense of crisis and urgency than might have otherwise occurred. Persons "called upon" to enter into a psychological journey of this type could find themselves involved in any number of different crisis situations...a divorce, a death, an accident, a major life decision that goes badly, a natural disaster that forever changes one's life, an episode of depression, a disease, a change in direction. The possibilities for the backdrop stage on which such a journey might begin are limitless. The commonality is the crisis, the point of decision, the event or unfolding *something* that calls the person to gain insight and make appropriate changes in direction, or face symbolic destruction. But in all settings, the individuation process has as its aim, greater wholeness and authenticity; a *self* fully realized through the integration of hitherto repressed (unconscious) aspects of the personality.

In writing this psychological journey, my over-arching goal was to produce a work that would blend a woman's experience as a young naval officer, with all of the growing pains associated with honestly facing the self (as defined by Jung, below) during a time of crisis.

If the reader is patient through Brenda's reflections, the unfolding purpose of the main character's work – a literal quest to find her soul – will become apparent: a spiritual journey from persona-orientation to self-orientation. In other words, a psychological shift from being what she thinks society wants her to be, to that which she wants herself to be (an authentic person).

Jungian psychology; The principle of individuation is the essence of the human being

A few Jungian terms

This book chronicles a Jungian journey of self-exploration, the central plot being the main character's (my) inward journey, a young woman's quest to explore her past (feelings, choices, family life, roles she chose, etc.) as a means to discovering her authentic "self." In Jungian psychology, the *self* is defined as the totality of the *psyche*, which includes both the conscious and unconscious regions of our minds. This is in contrast to the *ego*, which consists of the conscious region of our minds only. The unconscious, a realm of the mind of which we are mostly unaware, is made up of all that is forgotten, repressed, perceived unknowingly, and of those thoughts and feelings yet undealt with or unknown to the conscious mind.[10] Often, the unconscious stores that which is painful or which we would rather deny. It includes our darkest being, the shadow, the part of the self that is too threatening to accept, a region that includes everything that we refuse to acknowledge about ourselves. For progress toward selfhood to be made, the shadow must be explored, accepted, and integrated…no easy task, and years of work. Without so doing, the shadow's presence is nonetheless felt in a wild variety of destructive symptoms, creating "great danger,"[11] as is illustrated

---

[10] As a point of correctness, the unconscious includes the "collective unconscious" as well as the "personal unconscious," as these terms are defined by Jung.

[11] Jung, C.G. *Memories, Dreams, Reflections*. p. 380.

in my experience and story. "Everyone carries a shadow," Jung wrote, "and the less it is embodied in the individual's conscious life, the blacker and denser it is."[12]

Ironically, it is following the searching out, acceptance of, and, finally, integration of the shadow that a distinct, authentic – and mentally healthier – self emerges. The natural striving of the creature, Jung taught, "goeth toward distinctiveness,"[13] and that is the essential nature of individual consciousness: to strive towards individuation and the distinctive, authentic self. As we all intuitively possess a natural inclination toward individuation, akin to an instinct, it then can become one's natural course to seek such a state. It follows that it can even become possible for the process to happen anywhere, anytime, over and through one's lifetime, and in the case of Brenda, outside the bounds of a classical therapist/client paradigm.

Jung thought that the breakdown of the *persona*, or mask, [see below] leads to confrontation with the shadow in a way that benefits integration and personal growth. This very process unfolds throughout my narrative, as Brenda moves away from a life that is the result of unconscious identification with her parents' influence, toward a life that has the gaining of insight as its objective, and finally toward the integration of aspects of herself that had been unconscious; all of which plants her firmly on a self-directed path that results in an entirely new sense of self. The narrative illustrates how engagement in the process of individuation can bring a new ability to cope with prior symptoms, and even in a diminishing of those symptoms.

I have found the unconscious to be all-knowing, and the exploration of this region of our minds rewarding, a path to freedom, empowering one to live in a way that is true to one's own self, based on an ever-growing self-knowledge. In the story of Brenda, her (my) unconscious actions and motivations slowly come to light, to the level of consciousness, and bring a new awareness and a radical change in emotional life. As *Long Way Out* illustrates, the path towards self-discovery is often painful and at first unwelcomed, but once begun, can be freeing and lifesaving.

Finding the "self" entails becoming aware of who we are, accepting all that we have discovered, and going about life in a way that is authentic, in harmony with our own nature. During the

---

[12] Jung, C.G. *Psychology and Religion*. p. 93.
[13] Jung, C.G. *Memories, Dreams, Reflections*. p. 380.

process of individuation, we seek to bring that which is unconscious to consciousness, to know ourselves fully, and to rise out of collective thought to become a distinct psychological individual. From birth we are pressured (or sometimes forced) to conform strictly to societal and familial beliefs, mores, influences, and expectations, with the result that most of us grow up without awareness of who we truly are, having sacrificed that which may have been truly and uniquely ourselves, for the relative safety and security of conformity. Without realizing it consciously, we often live in disharmony with our true selves, and build our lives according to others' concepts of who we should be. As is true of Brenda's situation, this scenario often leads to *repression* (the subjugation of authentic feelings, thoughts, desires), and subsequently to feelings of emptiness and disturbance which we don't understand. For we have gone into the world mistaking the conscious *ego* (the *persona*, or mask) for the *self*. The persona, or mask, might be defined as that which we construct for the benefit of satisfying others, for concealing our true natures, for playing a certain role in society, or for showing ourselves to others in the way we think we want to be seen. Trying to navigate life solely out of the perspective of the mask (the persona) is bound to be fraught with inner unnamable conflict, tension, and indecision, as conscious and unconscious forces exert their presence in opposing directions.

An insight-oriented path toward "selfhood" can help free us from the burden of living according to the expectations of others (e.g., society, family, and especially parents), and from placing our ultimate concern on how we are perceived by others. On such a path, the perception or judgement of others no longer exists for us as *the* marker of success in life. Selfhood can give us a sense of having "located a solid ground"[14] within ourselves to go forward with our lives in a way that feels inwardly sound and congruous. And not surprisingly, greater self-knowledge can lead us to an increased awareness and empathy toward those around us.

As a teenager and then young woman, I lived almost entirely unaware of who I was, living solely in accordance with my parents' expectations and values. I had mistaken the conscious ego for the self. In other words, I had unknowingly convinced myself and come to believe that I was someone other than who I actually was (i.e., other than what was authentic to my nature). This was my

---

[14] Dowrick, Stephanie. *Intimacy and Solitude*. p. 25.

unconscious reaction to satisfying the expectations of others around me, as a way to survive early life. One of the results was that I soon found myself locked into a lifestyle and career for which I was incompatible and ill-suited, which even had the potential to result in danger for myself as well as for others. But prior to that time I couldn't conceive of the concept of asking myself such questions as *Who am I? What is my authentic nature? Are my life choices compatible with who I truly am? Why is it I don't know what I want? What are my authentic feelings, separate from those of my parents?* My actions and efforts at self-expression were almost entirely driven by an unconscious process (which had left me in full identification with the persona). Unaware of self, it was impossible for me to express myself in any way that was not in accordance with what I had been taught as a child. And more importantly, I feared that any veering from familial values and expectations would result in repercussions, which – having little to no sense of self – I wasn't prepared to deal with at the time. It is in many ways a vicious psychological loop to be in.

Jung warned, "But, as always, every step forward along the path of individuation is achieved only at the cost of suffering."[15] The drive toward selfhood, which Jung felt is a natural direction in life, can take us on a painful, honest, terrible, wonderful, and hard-fought path which has as its result one's individuating into an authentic and whole person. In this process we face truths about our psychological past, our families, and ourselves. Shedding the layers of persona and stepping out into the world as our authentic selves can at first seem terrifying, especially if society, family, friends, and others around us expect us to continue to act and "be" in accordance with their concepts of who we are (or were) for their sake – even when those concepts are toxic to our inner wellbeing. Brenda's inner search reveals that living a life based on meeting the expectations of others, or based on pressures to live a conventional life with security, cannot be satisfying since they are not rooted in a person's authenticity.

Finally, we need to briefly define the Jungian personality types *introvert* and *extravert*, the understanding of which are vital to the story. Simply stated, the introvert is drawn to that which is internal, to an inner life, finding meaning in that which is subjective and symbolic. The extravert identifies foremost with that which is external to him/herself, to outward life and stimuli rather than inner

---

[15] Jung, C.G. *Psychology and Religion: West and East.* p. 272.

life and feelings. As I wrote in the narrative: "...inner-directed versus outer-directed; the introvert searches for meaning through an inner process rather than concentrating interest solely on objects and events external to oneself." *Long Way Out* pits Brenda against a real-life naval seascape in her search for her place in a military world that is often insensitive to the introvert soul-searcher.

What is asked of the reader

Readers that are consciously engaged in their own path of psychological development, (or those who want to be for the first time, or those who are in therapy and desire a cathartic experience), all might benefit from investing themselves in the story of Brenda. Whereas a commercial (up-market) novel might have its main character "do all the work for you," even becoming entertaining, a literary work – of which *Long Way Out* strives to be – asks the reader to do the work, through thoughtful study and reflection. Brenda reveals the human condition that we all share: drive and desire to be at peace with ourselves, to be whole, to be integrated, to individuate from parents and institutions, to become a distinct self, and to survive crisis and conflict and emerge on the other side as a new or renewed person. Readers can use the opportunity of this story to question themselves, to put themselves in the place of the main character, to join the character in seeking psychological answers for those actions and feelings that are of concern, and to reflect on Brenda's (and their own) emotional journey in-depth. I also hope to challenge readers' preconceived and existing notions about their own life journey, about self, and about family – summoning readers to ask themselves why they have made the life decisions they have made, and in some cases, why they might feel empty, restless, or unfulfilled.

In literature, it is not rare to find characters who learn lessons from their journeys. But often such characters do not engage overtly in psychological self-exploration – as Brenda does – that concludes with the naming and understanding of their history, motives, and actions, keys with the potential to lead to a higher level of self-understanding and self-acceptance. For some fellow-sufferers, Brenda can serve as a catalyst, introducing readers to these processes. It is a road that is not for the faint of heart.

AUTHOR'S NOTE – Naval History

Even as early as the time that I was honorably discharged from the Navy, I knew I had the makings of an interesting story, one I had actually lived and survived. It seemed of such great importance to me that I felt taking eight years to write *Long Way Out* was justified. Not only does the book explore the changing roles of women in military service from the inside, but it also brings to greater light the largely undocumented and far reaching tragedy – inspired by one female commander – that occurred from trying to change women's roles too quickly, without allowing for proper training and experience, and out of thoughtless political expediency.

Long Way Out examines the challenge of becoming an authentic woman in this, an era that still struggles with the modernization of women's roles. When I checked aboard USS *Curtis Wilbur* (DDG-54) as a young junior officer in March 1997, I began serving within the first wave of women to be stationed aboard combatant ships. At time of this writing, 1.8 million of the 22 million veterans living in the United States are women. Over 200,000 women are currently serving on active duty, comprising 14% of the total force.

But the debate over inclusion – and its devilish details – is ongoing, and the greatest concern in 2015 is *how do we reach integration in the military and what will it look like five years from now, ten, or more?* Will women be drafted? Will women be able to fill some 250,000 military positions that currently remain closed to them? How will integration on submarines unfold? What will the role be for women in mixed gender platoons? Will the Marine Corps integrate women into combat positions? What will integration look like in the Navy SEALs and Army Rangers? Will some hardliners within military leadership continue to argue that women do not belong in combat?...just to name a few of the questions that still perplex our military leaders.

The *San Diego Union Tribune*, Feb. 14, 2015, summed up the executive mandate to move toward gender equality, and also captured the difficulty of the "how and when" that accompanies that order: *In 2013, then-Defense Secretary Leon Panetta stunned many when he eliminated the last vestige of federal law or Pentagon policy restricting women from combat service. He gave the services three years to figure out how to integrate women into all combat roles without reducing combat readiness, [without] worsening sexual harassment rates and [without] breaking women's bodies by assignments for which they don't qualify.*

This transition toward gender equality has been fraught with disagreement, struggle, even hostility, but it has also been peppered with positive regard for progress being made. I have tried to capture the reality of the ongoing struggle in *Long Way Out*, as characters discuss roles of women, women in combat situations, men's feelings about women serving on submarines, even down to the nitty-gritty of how to handle restrooms, berthing, and security requirements. It is a fascinating and exciting discussion!

An undocumented history

Long Way Out has an intimate connection to one of the largest Navy scandals of recent years: the historic relieving of command of the first female commander of an Aegis warship in U.S. history for "cruelty and maltreatment" of her crew. This story was in all major headlines in 2010 and occupies a significant position in recent Navy history, particularly among its most notable scandals and disgraces. The woman who could have become one of the most historically important female officers in the U.S. Navy has – arguably – one of the most tragic histories associated with her naval service. The warships she commanded now occupy a legendary and unfortunate chapter of naval history, spotlighting twelve years of cruelty and maltreatment of the officers and crew who served on them. *Long Way Out* takes place during this commander's first tour as second in command, as Executive Officer (XO) of USS *Curtis Wilbur* from 1997-1999. Until now, this was a history confined to the memories of the nearly three hundred officers and crew onboard the *Curtis Wilbur* who lived it, or confined to the oral sea stories these men and women shared among family, friends, and colleagues. *Long Way Out* provides both a history of the first female Aegis warship commander that has not previously been told, and a testimonial on the relationships between the men and women aboard one of the first mixed gender combatant ships.

The Navy's 2010 scandal headlines

During the period that I was writing *Long Way Out* (having started in 2008) the woman who was the first female in U.S. history to serve as executive officer of an Aegis destroyer and then as first female to serve as captain of an Aegis destroyer and cruiser was finally – after twelve years of execrable leadership – tried by Admirals Mast and relieved of command in January 2010. The Naval Inspector General (IG) report cited "cruelty and maltreatment" as grounds for being stripped of command, a charge unprecedented in recent naval history. The historical event caught the attention of *Time Magazine's* national security correspondent, Pulitzer Prize winning journalist Mark Thompson. The story was then covered extensively throughout the press, gaining national and international headlines, making the disgraced female warship commander a public figure, widely discussed and debated. Countless blogs and web posts on the former commander have emerged throughout the internet. Although the press has reported on this history, and internet topics abound on the subject, formal detailed firsthand accounts remain absent from the historical record.

From the days of her first executive officer (XO) tour as second in command of USS *Curtis Wilbur* (DDG-54) in the late 1990s, it took eleven more years for the Navy to take administrative action against her, and to cease promoting her to ever-increasing command responsibilities. This is true despite the fact that as far back as 1997, officers were making reports to Navy command regarding her leadership style as being characterized by maltreatment and hostility. It had also been reported to naval leadership that officers and crew of the *Curtis Wilbur* were even endangered due to her glaring lack of shipboard knowledge and experience. Since this particular commander was female, and since her appointment as executive officer of an Aegis destroyer was the launching point of the Navy's effort to integrate women fully into shipboard combat positions, the Navy remained apparently unwilling to act against her. Regardless of reports made by *Curtis Wilbur* officers and crew – both male and female, including department heads of the level of lieutenant commander – she continued to rise to the distinction of becoming the first woman to captain an Aegis destroyer and an Aegis cruiser, the Navy's most cutting edge warships.

The 1990s, too rapid a change?

The early 1990s was both a transitional and exciting time for women in the U.S. Navy. Following the 1991 Tailhook scandal involving the sexual assault of over eighty women and seven men at a convention of Navy and Marine Corps aviators, the Navy was forced to update its policies regarding gender equality. In 1994, after congress repealed the law that excluded women from serving aboard surface combatant ships, USS *Curtis Wilbur* (DDG-54) made history as the first Arleigh Burke class Aegis destroyer to go to sea with women as part of her crew. Change and gender integration within the Navy proceeded rapidly through the '90s. But there was an unforeseen drawback to the rapidity: The Navy felt pressured to promote a woman to a command position aboard an Aegis warship, and they did so on the *Curtis Wilbur*. Since insufficient time had passed for female officers to gain tactical and operational experience aboard these ships, it was a premature move, albeit well intentioned. The results were disastrous...the Navy's mistake in promoting a woman to second in command of an Aegis warship too soon were paid for by the officers and enlisted men and women who served under her.

AUTHOR'S NOTE – War culture

In writing *Long Way Out,* I sought to challenge the philosophy that is behind the multiple wars we have entered into, as well as readers' thinking about these elective wars (wars out of which has emerged our ongoing "war culture"). Since the first Gulf War, public relations campaigns aimed at garnering support for our Middle East wars have created a mythos in which the military is exalted to a nearly religious status. A phenomenon in the form of a nationalistic language has emerged, and along with it, enormous social pressure to espouse, repeat, and to not challenge such phrases as *support our troops, the troops are our heroes, they defend our freedom, they fight so we don't have to, we have to fight them over there so we won't have to fight them here,* and *thank you for your service,* to name but a few. These phrases are in fact propagandistic and have had the effect of stifling honest conversation and critical thinking regarding our recent wars, fought by an all-volunteer force. This nationalistic language has as its goal keeping us mired in questionable (and even unnecessary) wars, by leaving us afraid to examine and criticize for fear of not "supporting the troops."

How can a war – fought exclusively by heroes and "supported troops" – be criticized, even constructively? If the military has risen as an institution to "sacred" status, deifying "duty" and "honor," how can our country's wars and actions – even when those actions are undeniably egregious – be questioned? In some ways it is a sign of hope that the self-serving and gratuitous *thank you for your service* has over time created some controversy among service members, although in countless daily conversations it is still the automatic response that is heard when someone states that he/she is or was in the military.

In the atmosphere of our current society, it seems that hard questions about our wars and our military are subtly discouraged as if they would threaten some newly emerged sense of inviolable nationalistic pride we have developed since the first Gulf War. *What is acceptable to say or discuss, publicly, when it comes to the military?* It is not at all clear in the present era. The press itself has been complicit in this restrictive and nationally zealous atmosphere, in filtering news so as not to challenge the prevailing pro-military milieu. Military and civilian casualties are not covered in any detail (and sometimes are not covered at all!) as they were in the Vietnam era. Such coverage is apparently considered too divisive, explicit, or revulsive, and is avoided in lieu of feel-good stories of American heroes, e.g., homecomings, troops aiding foreign citizens in various ways, "wounded warriors" that are starting over in civilian life, dogs adopted by troops in other countries, etc. This selective reporting on the part of the press started with President Bush's 1991 censorship ban on broadcasting images of caskets of war veterans sent home. There have now been decades of pressure to sanitize the larger truths and realities of war, which have been presumed as improper to fully present to the public and, as well, deemed as a violation of troops' sensibilities.

Americans have in large part been pressured to refrain from unflinchingly honest dialogue and debate regarding the ethical, moral, and philosophical issues raised by our wars. The result is nothing other than military members being kept in harm's way – for questionable causes. Comfortable at home, we can go on presuming that what our military is sent overseas to do is just, worthwhile, and beneficial to our country and our lasting freedom. Words such as "duty" and "honor," used perfunctorily and without thought, keep susceptible young people joining our all-volunteer military.

All truths – from the worst and most painful and revulsive, to what makes us feel good – honor military members and veterans; seeking and expressing the unvarnished truth in all its forms is what ultimately facilitates support of troops and country. *Long Way Out* makes an effort to illustrate the idea that honest reflection and dialogue about our nationalistic and military directions offer the best hope for our country's future and longevity.

Shipboard Titles

Command level

CO	Commanding Officer, Captain
XO	Executive Officer, second in command

Department Heads

CSO	Combat Systems Officer
WEPS	Weapons Officer
OPS	Operations Officer; spoken as "Ops" rather than "O-P-S"
CHENG	Chief Engineer
SUPPO	Supply Officer

Division Officers

Combat Systems/Weapons Department

FCO	Fire Control Officer (in charge of Aegis combat systems)
STRIKE	Strike Officer
ASWO	Antisubmarine Warfare Officer; spoken as "As-wo"
GUNNO	Gunnery Officer

Operations Department

AOPS	Assistant Operations Officer; spoken as "A-ops"
COMMO	Communications Officer
FIRST	First Lieutenant/Deck Officer

Administration

NAV	Navigator

General definitions for the purposes of this book

1MC – Ship's public address system.

5"/54 naval gun – 5-inch/54 caliber; anti-ship, anti-aircraft, and shore bombardment; large gun on ship's forecastle.

Aegis – Aegis Combat System (ACS); advanced technology, highly complex, integrated naval weapons and sensor system designed to defend the ship and destroy enemy targets; employs radar; detection to kill.

ASW – Antisubmarine Warfare.

BMOW – Boatswains Mate of the Watch; stands watch on the bridge; responsibilities include seamanship tasks, ceremonial functions, and passing the word (announcements).

CDO – Command Duty Officer; commanding officer's representative inport.

CIC – Combat Information Center; darkened space below decks with consoles and displays for processing information to operate, defend, and fight the ship, e.g., radar, sonar, combat systems, navigation.

CIWS – *(*pronounced *sea-whiz)* Close-in Weapons System; short range anti-missile and anti-aircraft gun weapon system; looks like R2D2 of *Star Wars.*

Conning officer – Gives engine, rudder, and line handling orders to control movement of the ship.

CPA – Closest point of approach; the closest distance between individual ships at sea.

CSMC – Combat systems maintenance central; a space and watchstation for centralized control of maintenance, repair, and operations related to combat/weapons systems.

DESRON – Destroyer Squadron; the DESRON commander is referred to as Commodore.

Division – Unit comprising a junior officer, a chief petty officer (normally), and enlisted technicians.

DIVO – Division Officer.

Ensign – Ship's American flag; also, lowest naval officer rank (O-1).

EOOW – Engineering Officer of the Watch; watchstander in engineering responsible for ship's propulsion and auxiliary systems.

Exercise – Naval training.

Fantail – Aft (rear) outside deck of ship.

Forecastle – (pronounced *fowk-sul*) Forward outside deck of ship.

FITREP – Officer fitness report; performance evaluation.

Inport – Refers to the status of the ship as being moored to the pier, as being "in port."

IVCS – Integrated Voice Communications System; a phone aboard Navy ships with a computerized ring tone.

JOOD – Junior Officer of the Deck.

LDO – Limited Duty Officer; prior enlisted officer who is a technical expert and serves as an officer in a specific field corresponding to his/her technical expertise; a bachelor's degree is not required.
Line officer – Officer eligible for command at sea.
LPO – Leading Petty Officer; senior petty officer in a division
Midshipman – Officer candidate in training while in college and ROTC or at the Naval Academy.
Midshipman cruise – Officer candidate training cruise aboard a Navy ship, usually during summer between junior and senior years of college.
MOOW – Messenger of the Watch; enlisted assistant to the POOW on the quarterdeck.
OOD – Officer of the Deck; the commanding officer's representative on the bridge (underway), or on the quarterdeck (inport).
QMOW – Quartermaster of the Watch; stands watch on the bridge; keeps ship's navigational charts.
Quals – Qualifications.
POD – Plan of the Day; ship's daily schedule.
POOW – Petty Officer of the Watch; enlisted assistant to the OOD on the quarterdeck.
ROTC – Reserve Officer Training Corps.
SIMA – Shore Intermediate Maintenance Activity.
Space – A room or compartment aboard ship.
SWO – Surface Warfare Officer; a line officer who has met prescribed qualifications while serving aboard a surface ship; also refers to the surface warfare officer community.
SWO pin – Insignia worn by qualified surface warfare officers.
SWOS – Surface Warfare Officers School.
TAO – Tactical Action Officer; commanding officer's representative in the combat information center (CIC); responsible for employment of weapons systems.
U/I – Under Instruction; an unqualified watchstander who stands watch under the guidance of a qualified watchstander for training.
Underway – Ship is not at anchor or moored to the pier.
UNREP – Underway replenishment; refueling and/or onloading supplies at sea.
Watchbill – A list of watches and personnel assigned to those watches.
VLS – Vertical Launching System; stores and launches missiles.

Enlisted Terminology, Enlisted Ratings (Occupational Specialty)

Boatswains Mate (BM) – Deck and boat seamanship tasks.
Fire Controlman (FC) – Aegis and weapons systems maintenance, repair, and operation.
Gunners Mate (GM) – Maintain, repair, and operate small arms, naval guns, and missile systems.
GMG – Gunners Mate (guns).
GMM – Gunners Mate (missiles).
Mess Specialist (MS) – Food service preparation.
Operations Specialist (OS) – Operations in CIC, such as radar, communications, and navigation.
Torpedomans Mate (TM) – Maintain torpedos and associated launching systems.
Quartermaster (QM) – Navigation.
Yeoman (YN) – Secretarial and clerical work.
Rate – Enlisted pay grade.

Navy Officer Ranks

O-1	Ensign, ENS
O-2	Lieutenant Junior Grade, LTJG
O-3	Lieutenant, LT
O-4	Lieutenant Commander, LCDR
O-5	Commander, CDR
O-6	Captain, CAPT
O-7	and above are Admiral ranks

Enlisted Paygrades

E-1	Seaman Recruit
E-2	Seaman Apprentice
E-3	Seaman
E-4	Petty Officer Third Class
E-5	Petty Officer Second Class
E-6	Petty Officer First Class
E-7	Chief Petty Officer
E-8	Senior Chief Petty Officer
E-9	Master Chief Petty Officer

Examples: Chief Gunners Mate (E-7), GMC
Quartermaster First Class (E-6), QM1
Gunners Mate (guns) Second Class (E-5), GMG2
Fire Controlman Third Class (E-4), FC3

Bibliographic reference

Psychology

Dowrick, Stephanie. *Intimacy and Solitude*. New York: W.W. Norton, 1991.
Jung, C.G. *The Basic Writings of C.G. Jung*. Princeton: Princeton University Press, 1990.
Jung, C.G. *The Collected Works of C.G. Jung*. New York: Pantheon Books, 1983.
Jung, C.G. *Man and His Symbols*. New York: Dell, 1981.
Jung, C.G. *Memories, Dreams, Reflections*. New York: Vintage Books, 1989.
Jung, C.G. *Modern Man in Search of a Soul*. New York: Harcourt, Brace, Jovanovich, 1933 (first published).
Jung, C.G. *On the Nature of the Psyche*. Princeton: Princeton University Press, 1973.
Jung, C.G. *Psyche and Symbol*. New York: Anchor Books, 1958.
Jung, C.G. *Psychology and Religion*. New Haven: Yale University Press, 1938.
Jung, C.G. *Psychology and Religion: West and East*. Princeton: Princeton University Press, 1969.
Jung, C.G. *The Undiscovered Self*. Boston: Little, Brown, and Company, 1958.
Rogers, Carl. *On Becoming a Person*. Boston: Houghton Mifflin Company, 1961.

Naval Science

Bearden, Bill. *The Bluejackets' Manual*. Annapolis: United States Naval Institute, 1990.
Stavridis, James. *Division Officer's Guide*. Annapolis: United States Naval Institute, 1995.
Mack, William, with Thomas Paulsen. *The Naval Officer's Guide*. Annapolis: United States Naval Institute, 1991.
Stavridis, James. *Watch Officer's Guide*. Annapolis: United States Naval Institute, 1992.

Other

Brontë, Charlotte. *Villette*. New York: Harper and Brothers, 1853.
Updike, John. *Self-Consciousness: Memoirs*. New York: Alfred A. Knopf, 1989.

Subjects include: self-discovery, journey of self-discovery, psychology memoir, psychology memoirs, women in the military, Navy, self-discovery books, women in the military books, military memoirs, military history, women military, military women, military history, military leadership, military memoir, military biographies and memoirs, true stories of military women

Printed in Great Britain
by Amazon